Saved by Grace through Faith
—— or Saved by Decree? ——

Saved by Grace through Faith
—— or **Saved by Decree?** ——

A Biblical and Theological Critique of Calvinist Soteriology

Geoffrey D. Robinson

WIPF & STOCK · Eugene, Oregon

SAVED BY GRACE THROUGH FAITH OR SAVED BY DECREE?
A Biblical and Theological Critique of Calvinist Soteriology

Wipf & Stock
An Imprint of Wipf and Stock Publishers
199 W. 8th Ave., Suite 3
Eugene, OR 97401

www.wipfandstock.com

PAPERBACK ISBN: 978-1-6667-3389-1
HARDCOVER ISBN: 978-1-6667-2888-0
EBOOK ISBN: 978-1-6667-2889-7

03/28/22

Yet no matter how convincing such disproofs might appear, no matter how contradictory and unreal much of the Darwinian framework might seem to anyone not committed to its defense, as philosophers of science like Thomas Kuhn and Paul Feyerabend have pointed out, it is impossible to falsify theories by reference to the facts or indeed by any rational or empirical argument. The history of science amply testifies to what Kuhn has termed the "priority of the paradigm" and provides many fascinating examples of the extraordinary lengths to which members of the scientific community will go to defend a theory just as long as it holds sufficient intrinsic appeal.

—Michael Denton, *Evolution: A Theory in Crisis*

Although the geocentric theory was not the only theory proposed to account for the movements of the heavenly bodies . . . by the late middle ages it had become a self-evident truth, the one and only sacred and unalterable picture of cosmological reality.

—Michael Denton, *Evolution: A Theory in Crisis*

His prescription to avoid faith's pitfalls was that people should exercise "critical judgment" in relation to their beliefs so that the faith held is reasonable.

—Barry L. Callen, concerning Clark H. Pinnock

Contents

Introduction

Calvinism, the understanding of Scripture that stresses God's sovereignty over all things, including an individual's salvation, is not as popular as it once was in decades past.[1] However, more recently there has been something of a resurgence, especially among younger people.[2] Nevertheless, even when the term is not used, often the concepts associated with Calvinism (known also as "the doctrines of grace") continue to play a significant role in the life of both individual believers and in the church. This is especially so amongst churches that trace a Reformed heritage, though by no means limited to such traditions.

My own spiritual pilgrimage began in a context where a weak but clearly present form of Calvinism existed. However, as I progressed in my understanding of the faith and in my own reading of the Bible, I gradually became increasingly aware of a certain discomfort between the Calvinism I heard preached and taught and my own understanding of Scripture. Was it really the case that God unilaterally decided who would be saved and who would not? Was God's grace really not resistible and, if so, how did my sinning fit in? Was it true that human nature was so depraved that a person was totally incapable of even responding to the gospel invitation apart from God's effectually causing him to respond? Was faith really a gift of God; if so then who was to be blamed when individuals refused to believe? And so on. These were the sorts of questions I struggled to come to terms with.[3]

It would be many years before I could precisely identify and articulate the source of my discomfort, but even at an early stage of my Christian life I realized that what I heard being taught and believed by godly Christians did not seem to correlate with my own reading of the Bible (especially the New Testament). The result was confusion. How

1. Calvinism usually refers to the doctrine of salvation (soteriology) within the Reformed tradition; accordingly, Reformed theology is broader than Calvinism and includes other distinct doctrines such as ecclesiology, bibliology, and eschatology.

2. They are sometimes known as "The Young, Restless, and Reformed" after Collin Hansen's book by the same title.

3. I suspect my own story has been replicated many times over. A well-known one concerns the theologian Clark Pinnock, who recounts his story in *The Grace of God*, 15–30. Another is Austin Fischer, in his book *Young, Restless, No Longer Reformed*, as is the New Testament scholar Scot McKnight, who offers the preface to Fischer's book.

could these preachers, teachers, authors, and friends possibly be mistaken? Even the possibility seemed inconceivable to me. Weren't they merely expressing what Calvin, Luther, and the other great Reformers of the Protestant Reformation had taught?

The focus of my confusion lay in the doctrine of salvation, formally known as soteriology. However, since this doctrine is intimately connected with other doctrines—in this case the doctrines of Humanity, Grace, God, Christ, the Spirit, and Providence, to name a few—it was not easy to understand the issues and how they related to one another and so bring the needed clarity. Eventually, however, after much reading and after eight years of theological education, clarity did come, confusion was greatly reduced and a peace concerning the truth about the meaning of salvation enjoyed.

This present study arises from the conviction that many sincere Christians are today as confused about this doctrine as I was. This confusion is held by both lay persons and by pastors.[4] My goal is to help us all see more clearly and more accurately what the Bible really teaches about this important doctrine. My hope is that uncertainty and confusion will be replaced by understanding, clarity, and a confidence in working out our salvation borne of insights that faithfully reflect God's word.

A word about terminology; I use the term Calvinism somewhat reluctantly and only because it concisely encapsulates the distinct set of beliefs associated with the name of the great sixteenth-century Reformer John Calvin. There really is no other term or phrase that can accurately and succinctly take its place. Furthermore, this is the term traditionally and historically used in this sort of context.[5] My reluctance stems from the perception that the term may be used here pejoratively. That is most certainly not my purpose. My purpose has to do only with descriptive efficiency. For the same reason, I have chosen to designate all soteriological views that contrast significantly with Calvinism by the term non-Calvinist.[6]

4. The confusion may be seen, for example, by preachers who make both a Calvinist and a non-Calvinist point concerning salvation in the same sermon! It is inconsistent, for example, to insist that a born-again believer simply cannot choose to forfeit his or her salvation (a Calvinistic belief) and at the same time stress that an unbeliever's experience of salvation depends entirely on the choice he or she makes in response to the gospel. The confusion is also evident when some Christians jokingly use the term "Calminian" to summarize their beliefs in this area.

5. There are in fact a variety of "Calvinisms." Felipe Diez, for example, lists no less than eight distinct versions of Calvinism in his blog post. More commonly, reference may be made to hyper-Calvinism, Orthodox Calvinism, or High Calvinism. The differences lie in some aspect of Calvinism's soteriology—for example, some Moderate Calvinists may hold to a universal atonement (so-called four-point Calvinists), whereas other Calvinists would limit the atonement to only those God has chosen to save (so-called five-point Calvinists). In this study, most of the time I shall be referring to the form of Calvinism that is most internally consistent to the entire system. Consistent Calvinism is sometimes labeled "hyper-Calvinism" by other Calvinists.

6. As just noted, while there are varieties of Calvinism, on the whole and generally speaking Calvinism is more tightly defined than non-Calvinistic views of salvation; the elements of Calvinistic soteriology cohere well. If one had to describe non-Calvinists by a single term that term would be Arminian, after the Dutch theologian Jacobus Arminius (1560–1609), who disputed several of the tenets of Calvinism in his day. Like Calvinism, there is no single non-Calvinist view, but rather a variety of perspectives each differing in one respect or another from the other. Examples would be Classical

My approach follows from the desire to bring clarity to the doctrine of salvation in order to remove confusion caused by those who espouse a view that is, I believe, fundamentally flawed. Consequently, I will use the Calvinist's view of salvation as a foil with which I can interact with the doctrine. This indirect approach will serve on the one hand to show where and why Calvinism fails and, on the other hand, to provide a more biblically faithful and coherent understanding of the doctrine, though the emphasis will necessarily fall upon the former given the focus of this study as stated in the title of the work.

There are several reasons for Calvinism's popularity and appeal both in the past and also today. First, Calvinism is a well-defined and internally consistent doctrinal system. All the elements that make up a Calvinistic soteriology "hang together" very tightly with no internal contradictions.[7] As we shall see, part of the reason for such internal coherence is the prominent role the Calvinistic understanding of predestination holds within the system. Of course, internal consistency need not necessarily mean the doctrine is true. Consistency is a necessary but not sufficient criterion of veracity. Nevertheless, the coherence of Calvinistic soteriology has a certain appeal that serves to reinforce the belief that the Calvinistic perspective must be true.

Another reason that helps explain Calvinism's appeal is its concern to uphold the glory of God. This is apparent in John Calvin's own writings and in the writings of many Calvinists to this day.[8] It is probably true to say that concern for God's honor and glory is a high motivation for the embracing of the Calvinist's "doctrines of grace." (Of course, this may also explain why some Calvinists not only hold fast to their Calvinist convictions, but also why they sometimes appear rather dogmatic in their defense of Calvinism).

Yet a third reason why Calvinism is so popular is due to the comfort to be had in believing that God fully "controls" the situation when one learns, for example, that one has cancer.[9] It is also comforting to believe that one's salvation can never be "lost" and that one's ultimate destiny is infallibly certain from the moment one believes the gospel. The comfort a Calvinistic view of God's sovereignty provides is clearly seen in Robert Peterson's book on election and free will. Under the heading "The Insecurity of Contemporary Life" Peterson appeals to a Calvinistic understanding of election (God chooses who will be saved) as functioning "to comfort the

---

Arminianism, Wesleyan Arminianism, or Traditional/Provisionalist non-Calvinism.

7. At least, from a Calvinist's perspective. However, as we shall see there are indeed "tensions" within Calvinism that are often resolved by appeal to "mystery."

8. An example from Calvin is his conviction that some people (the non-elect) are established in their depravity "that [God's] name may be glorified in their destruction." Calvin, *Institutes*, 3.24.14.

9. Within a Calvinistic system God retains full control only by ultimately causing the event in question—such is God's sovereignty. Few Calvinists, however, will directly acknowledge God's causing their cancer, preferring to use the softer term "control."

people of God and assure them that underneath all their meager efforts to live for him are God's everlasting arms to hold, protect, and caress them."[10]

Another reason for the appeal of Calvinism is the central role its most prominent theologian, John Calvin, played in the history of the Protestant church. The Reformation is rightly viewed by the evangelical Christian as the key event in church history that liberated the people of God from the ecclesiastical bondage and corruption of the Roman church in the sixteenth century and toward a Scripture-focused faith. Not surprisingly therefore Calvin and the doctrines of salvation associated with his name should come to be viewed as authentic (and orthodox) Christian belief. The fact that Calvin was the first theologian to systematically and comprehensively expound the Bible no doubt reinforces the close connection between the Reformation, Bible centered theology, and the distinctive doctrine of salvation taught by Calvin.[11] In short, part of Calvinism's appeal is tied to a great event in church history (the Reformation), and a great leader of that Reformation (John Calvin).[12]

A final reason that may explain Calvinism's current popularity concerns the perception that it provides a strong, robust, and substantial theology—in contrast to what is considered by many to be shallow, emotionally oriented church preaching and life. There is no doubt that many of the church's intellectual heavyweights, both in the past as well as the present, have espoused Calvinism. Most books on theology and related disciplines (apologetics, philosophy, ethics, and so on) have been written by Calvinists. The rise of "seeker sensitive" churches and the ubiquitous contemporary Christian worship music, often with shallow and highly repetitive lyrics, can lead to a longing for a church life with more substantial theological content. In short, Calvinism is a reaction to much that is perceived to be superficial in the church today.

Let me say a word about the approach taken in this study. Each chapter will begin with some introductory remarks intended to orient the reader with respect to the topic to be discussed. This will be followed by a clear presentation of the Calvinist's position consisting of quotes from Calvinist writers. I want to present the Calvinist position as fairly as possible and avoid any kind of misrepresentation. I will then identify a few of the most commonly cited biblical texts used by Calvinists to support their viewpoint. These texts will be carefully evaluated and analyzed to see whether the Calvinist interpretation is in fact the correct one. Biblical texts supporting a non-Calvinist understanding of the doctrine will also be given. Following the biblical examination, I will provide a theological critique of the doctrine under consideration. This is accomplished

10. Peterson, *Election and Free Will*, 10.

11. Not that Calvin was the first to stress divine predestination and sovereignty in salvation—this was also stressed by Augustine in the fifth century. My point, however, is that Calvin's name has been strongly associated with this view of salvation, an association reinforced by the formative period in church history in which he lived.

12. Calvin's teachings in this area also received legitimacy because of the great dependence Calvin (and Luther before him) had on Augustine's teachings. Arguably, Augustine (354–430) is the most influential Christian theologian in church history.

by a series of theological issues related to the doctrine at hand. For example, under the study of election I raise and discuss eight theological issues, and under the irresistibility of grace I raise and discuss eleven theological issues.

The study is structured around the so-called five points of Calvinism summarized by the acronym TULIP: *T*otal depravity, *U*nconditional election, *L*imited atonement, *I*rresistible grace, *P*erseverance of the saints.[13]

In the first chapter I seek to provide a historical perspective. It will be seen that the issues raised in the present study are not new. In fact, the debate between a Calvinist and non-Calvinist soteriology go back at least to Augustine's dispute with Pelagius in the fifth century AD.[14] This chapter will also serve to show that godly Christians on both sides have existed down the centuries right up to the present time. It also reminds us of the need to exercise humility and love whenever we find ourselves in debate with Christians with whom we disagree doctrinally. Unfortunately, the lack of such Christian virtues has sometimes marred the debates over this doctrine in the past.[15]

In the second chapter we examine the Calvinistic perspective on the human condition, i.e., the nature of human nature. We will see that Calvinism takes a very dim view of human nature subsequent to the fall of Adam and Eve into sin. Human nature is held to be totally depraved, which is understood to include a total inability to even respond to the gospel call to be saved. In this chapter both the doctrine of original sin as well as the doctrine of total depravity will be critiqued.

The third chapter examines the difficult doctrine of election. Here, it will be seen that Calvinism is quite insistent that God chooses who will be saved—and therefore also, either directly or indirectly, those who will *not* be saved. Here is where the concept of an eternal, all determining divine decree comes to the fore. In addition to examining the key biblical scriptures used to justify the Calvinist position, theological considerations around the ideas of election and predestination are discussed.

Chapter 4 considers the scope of Christ's atoning sacrifice and some implications of the Calvinist's view that the benefits of Christ's death (salvation) was intended only for the elect. Variations on this theme (four-point Calvinism, Amyraldism) are examined for their validity. Since Scripture closely ties the atonement to

---

13. These five aspects of Calvinistic soteriology were first explicitly stated at the Synod of Dort in 1619.

14. Of course, it is anachronistic to speak of a "Calvinist" soteriology before the time of John Calvin (1509–1564), but the concepts and issues involved predate Calvin. However, as indicated earlier, I am using the term "Calvinism" as a descriptor of a set of consistent beliefs having to do with the doctrine of salvation and which, in this sense, transcends any particular historical period.

15. In my experience I have found that it is often Calvinists who lead exemplary godly lives and who are the most enthusiastic students of God's word. Rarely, however, a Calvinist may misspeak, as in this example from the well-known and highly respected theologian J. I. Packer: "The difference between them [Reformed and Arminian theology] is not primarily one of emphasis, but of content. One proclaims a God who saves, the other speaks of a God who enables man to save himself. . . . One makes salvation dependent on the work of God, the other on a work of man." Packer, "Introductory Essay," 4. Of course, no responsible Christian of any stripe views his salvation as self-salvation or a work of man!

the love of God, then an atonement limited by God necessarily carries implications for the scope of God's love. The implication of a limited atonement for the task of evangelism is also examined.

In chapter 5 we will examine the Calvinist belief that God's grace, insofar as the application of salvation is concerned, is irresistible. Those whom God chooses to save cannot resist God's grace that inevitably leads to that person coming to salvation. Here, the concept of grace is discussed as well as the different ways God's grace finds expression in Scripture. Of crucial importance in this chapter is the reality and role of free will insofar as a person's response to the gospel call is concerned. Other crucial issues concern faith as a God-given gift and what that entails, as well as the idea that regeneration (new-birth) must precede faith.

Finally, in chapter 6, the view that those whom God calls to be saved will infallibly continue in the faith until the end—the perseverance of the saints—will be carefully assessed. Does the Bible support the notion that a believer may never "lose" his or her salvation? Crucial related issues will also be examined, including assurance of salvation, and the possibility and reality of apostasy. Finally, some pastoral implications of the doctrine will be discussed.

In the concluding chapter, several important problems associated both with Calvinism's methodology and content are identified and discussed.

As we examine these five aspects of salvation, we will inevitably be discussing other closely related doctrines. Examples would include the nature of faith, the nature of divine sovereignty, the basis for assurance, the relation between redemption accomplished (at the cross) and redemption applied (to the individual Christian). Several hermeneutical issues will also be noted as they often play a key role in interpreting any particular passage or text.[16]

Throughout this study it will be apparent that the concept of the decree of God is crucial to a Calvinistic soteriology. A divine decree refers to God's unilateral, unconditional decision or action. For example, God decreed to make a world. Having made a world, he decreed that its human inhabitants who willfully violated the Creator's moral precepts would suffer punishment. So, in principle, there is nothing problematic with the idea of divine decree. But I shall argue that, within consistent Calvinism, the decrees of God are comprehensive, fine grained, particular—ultimately responsible for everything that occurs within the created order. This includes an individual's salvation. It is this notion of decree that is shown to be very problematic for a doctrine of salvation that seeks to be biblically faithful.

---

16. Biblical hermeneutics is the science and art of biblical interpretation. It is a distinct field within Christian studies.

1

A Brief History of the Doctrine of Salvation

The history outlined below focuses on those aspects of salvation denoted by TULIP. There are other aspects of salvation that will not be included such as justification, sanctification, and adoption into the family of God. While undoubtedly Christians differ on their understanding of these aspects of salvation also, the differences are not pivotal in the same way as TULIP.

The Early Church[1]

The early church fathers tended to stress the role of human free will in decision-making in general, and in responding to the gospel call specifically. This emphasis was, at least in part, due to the prevailing philosophies and worldviews of the day that emphasized fatalism and absolute, impersonal determinism.[2] "For Origen, as for all the early fathers, freedom was vital as the antithesis of fate or necessity."[3]

Of course, the early church's theologians recognized the references to predestination in the Christian Scriptures, especially in Paul's writings, and understood predestination to salvation to be based on God's foreknowledge of how people would respond to the gospel call; those who responded favorably (by exercising faith and repenting of their sins) were predestined to salvation. Justin Martyr (d. AD 163) for example, held that "the people foreknown to believe in [Christ] were foreknown to pursue diligently the fear of the Lord."[4] However predestination was understood, there was the general conviction that it would not entail the overruling of human choice in the matter of salvation.

At this early stage of doctrinal development, the view that subsequently came to be known as synergism—the idea that God and man cooperate in the appropriation

---

1. The early church period is roughly the time between the apostles and the death of Augustine of Hippo in AD 430.

2. Stoicism would be an example. Burke writes concerning this worldview: "Fate also plays a key role and underlies the belief in the cyclical character of the natural order, in which each cycle is identical to all the others." Burke, "Stoics," 1055.

3. Bromiley, *Historical Theology*, 46.

4. Cited by Allison, *Historical Theology*, 454.

of God's gift of salvation—was naturally dominant. Clement of Alexandria (150–215) is a good example:

> And as the physician ministers health to those who co-operate with him in order to health, so also God ministers eternal salvation to those who co-operate for the attainment of knowledge and good conduct; and since what the commandments command are in our own power, along with the performance of them, the promise is accomplished.[5]

This state of affairs was radically changed around 410 when Pelagius, a British monk and Christian moralist who was distressed by the lax moral conditions prevailing at Rome in his day, took offense at a prayer of Augustine, Bishop of Hippo, in which the latter stated: "Give what thou commandest and command what thou wilt."[6] He believed Augustine's prayer would lead to a resignation to sin. If God's grace was such that only God could give what God commanded then this raised the question as to the role of man's responsibility for his behavior in moral affairs. For Pelagius moral responsibility implied moral ability. If Augustine was right, what room was there for human choices and moral responsibility?

Pelagius opposed the sentiment that a given moral responsibility is "too hard and difficult. We cannot do it. We are only human and hindered by the weakness of the flesh."[7] Such an outlook, argued Pelagius, implied God was unaware of the weaknesses of men in giving commands that men could not consistently fulfill. Also, God was not so unjust as to condemn a man for what he could not help.

With respect to the question of human freedom, Pelagius argued that three elements exist: (1) the possibility to make moral decisions (*posse* in Latin), (2) the will to make moral decisions (*velle*), and (3) the capacity to effect or realize the moral decision (*esse*).[8] The first (the possibility) may be ascribed to God and associated with man's creation by God, the other two elements (will and capacity) he attributed to the human agent. Consequently,

> man's praise lies in his willing and doing a good work; or rather this praise belongs both to man and to God who has granted the possibility of willing and working, and who by the help of his grace, ever assists this very possibility. That a man has this possibility of willing and effecting is due to God alone.[9]

In addition to ascribing to man significant capacity to do the moral good, Pelagius also denied the view concerning the origin of man's sinfulness, namely original

---

5. Clement of Alexandria, *Writings of Clement*, 441.

6. Augustine, *Confessions*, 10.29.298.

7. Bettenson, *Documents of the Christian Church*, 52.

8. Bettenson, *Documents of the Christian Church*, 52.

9. Bettenson, *Documents of the Christian Church*, 53.

sin.[10] "Everything good and everything evil in respect of which we are either worthy of praise or of blame, is done by us, *not born with us*."[11]

Finally, for our purposes here, Pelagius and his disciple Coelestius also taught the following: (1) that a person can be without sin if he chooses, and (2) that unbaptized infants have eternal life.[12] (3) God's grace is manifested (a) in providing a revelation of his will in the Bible and in (b) forgiving those who repent of their sin. (4) Predestination to salvation was based upon God's foreknowledge (prescience) of those who would respond favorably to God's grace of forgiveness and thereby be saved.

Through his writings and his interactions with Augustine, Pelagius raised key issues concerning the doctrine of salvation that reverberated down the centuries to this day. The origin and extent of sin, the origin of the soul, the relationship between grace and human moral freedom, the extent of a person's ability to do moral good, the nature of grace itself, the basis and nature of God's predestination, and ultimately the nature of divine sovereignty. Most fundamentally, is salvation monergistic (all of God in every respect) or synergistic (aspects uniquely of God and also aspects that require man's cooperation)?

Augustine strongly opposed Pelagius. Though, in his disputes with the Manichaean sect, Augustine had stressed the role of free will in being the source of evil, later in his disputes with Pelagius Augustine agreed the will was free—but only to do evil, to sin. The will was in fact in bondage to sin. Furthermore, it was in this state from birth.

While a few of the early church fathers had hinted at a connection between Adam and subsequent humanity's sin, it was Augustine who almost single-handedly synthesized and developed this notion which he called "original sin."[13] Augustine's strongly negative view of man's ability to not sin was strongly influenced by his conversion experience. In his book *The Confessions* Augustine describes his depravity and struggle with sexual sins. This experience convinced him that human nature is so depraved that an unregenerate person is "not able not to sin."[14] Furthermore, Augustine found justification for this understanding of sin in his view of original sin in Rom 5:12–21, where Paul connects Adam's disobedience with sin, death, and condemnation. The

10. Original sin is the doctrine that every person born subsequent to Adam and Eve is born with a sinful nature and with the associated (original) guilt before God due to Adam's sin. This doctrine relies heavily on Paul's teaching in Rom 5:12–21.

11. Bettenson, *Documents of the Christian Church*, 53, emphasis mine.

12. Bettenson, *Documents of the Christian Church*, 54.

13. See Toews, *Story of Original Sin*.

14. Allison, *Historical Theology*, 348. Ridderbos also notes that "in [Augustine's] own experience he had known the meaning of moral impotence. It seemed to him quite unreal to speak with the Pelagians of a free will and an uncorrupted nature." *Churches of Galatia*, 234. Similarly, Wand, *History of the Early Church*, 231, also notes the influence of Augustine's conversion experience upon his view of sin and grace: Augustine "relied upon his own experience of special grace, without which he was sure that he could never have recovered from his evil ways." Augustine is known for saying that before the fall Adam was able to not sin, Jesus Christ was not able to sin, fallen man is not able to not sin.

prevailing common practice of baptizing infants was appealed to as further evidence of the devastating effects of the fall on subsequent humanity.[15]

> Through his emphasis on the corporate solidarity between Adam and the rest of humanity, the tragic situation of original sin into which all people are born, the liability to condemnation for all unbaptized persons because of the guilt of Adam that they bear, and the inheritance of a corrupt nature that spells the inevitability of actual sins whenever unbelievers will to act, Augustine both defeated Pelagius and left a legacy of a robust theology of sin.[16]

Unlike Pelagius, who ascribed the universal sinfulness of humanity subsequent to Adam as being due to living in a fallen world and in following the example of Adam, Augustine attributed universal sinfulness to original sin.

Before leaving Augustine, it is necessary to briefly summarize other key aspects of his soteriology. Given the inherently sinful state in which every person enters the world, Augustine's teachings inevitably raised the question concerning how any person could be saved. Since total depravity entailed a total inability to do any morally or spiritually good including, of course, a turning to God in response to the call to repent and believe the gospel then salvation would depend exclusively on the grace of God. For Pelagius grace was conceived objectively in terms of God's undeserved actions for our good—such as revealing himself to mankind, sending his Son, providing a universal call to salvation. For Augustine, however, grace was understood as some kind of internal, subjective force that acted directly upon the will and was infused into the person.[17] This understanding of grace was necessitated by his view of original sin as entailing total depravity, which in turn entailed a total inability to do any good, especially the good of responding in repentance and faith to the gospel call. If anyone was to be saved it would be because God would choose to act supernaturally to provide grace that would free the person's will from its bondage to sin and enable the desired response of repentance and faith. "Unless this damage [to our moral nature due to sin] were overcome by the assistance of grace, no one would turn to holiness; nor would anyone enjoy the peace of righteousness unless the flaw were mended by the operation of grace."[18]

Furthermore, Augustine insisted that this grace is irresistible. If God chooses to apply grace then its actions upon the will cannot be thwarted or resisted. "Grace

---

15. Allison, *Historical Theology*, 232: "The practice of infant baptism for the remission of sins presupposes that infants arrive polluted by sin; since they have committed no actual sin, remission must be for the guilt attaching to a fault in their nature. Therefore, if babies die unbaptized they are damned."

16. Allison, *Historical Theology*, 349.

17. "Augustine understood grace as a divine power or fluid that is infused into us. For him grace is no longer an attitude on God's part, but rather the manner in which God acts in us." Gonzalez, *History of Christian Thought*, 2:49.

18. Augustine, *Retractions*, 104.

moves the will, but only through a 'soft-violence' that acts in such a way that the will agrees with it."[19]

Intrinsic to the strong monergism developed by Augustine are the issues of election, predestination, and perseverance.[20] The logic is clear; since no one is capable of responding to the gospel due to sin (both original and personal), then if anyone is to be saved such salvation must require and be due to the initiative of God. God chooses who will be saved unconditionally.[21] Since it is obvious that not everyone is saved, then God's election of individuals is selective. The basis of the choice made by God is a mystery. God is not subject to the charge of injustice because he is under no obligation to save anyone from the consequences of their sin (divine wrath and judgment)—they are merely getting what they deserve. Since God's choosing is accomplished "before the foundation of the world" then we may rightly term this sovereign electing act of God as predestination. God predestines those who will be saved. "The elect are pulled out of this 'mass of condemnation' which is humanity through a sovereign act of God, who has predestined them for salvation."[22] Finally, since God has determined a fixed number of the elect then their salvation is assured, and that requires that they persevere to the end of their lives. God grants a persevering grace that guarantees the elect continue in their faith.

Unsurprisingly, given the emphasis until Augustine by the church fathers upon the reality of human freedom as opposed to the deterministic tendencies of the gnostics and prevailing religious cults as noted earlier, and the relatively novel teaching concerning the irresistibility of grace and Augustine's strong predestinarian thrust, his views were not left unchallenged. As Henry Chadwick remarks: "Augustine's propositions provoked a quick reaction in several quarters."[23] Julian (380–455), bishop of Eclanum, in Italy, insisted Augustine was wrong to view sex negatively (as concupiscence)[24] and a contributing factor in the transmission of original sin.[25] As

---

19. Gonzalez, *History of Christian Thought*, 2:47.

20. Monergism is the belief that every aspect of salvation originates in, is accomplished and applied by, God alone. That Augustine was a pioneer in this respect is seen in the Calvinist Loraine Boettner when he remarked concerning the early church before Augustine's day: "The earlier church fathers placed chief emphasis on good works such as faith, repentance, almsgiving, prayers, submission to baptism, etc., as the basis of salvation. They of course taught that salvation was through Christ; yet they assumed that man had full power to accept or reject the gospel. . . . They taught a kind of synergism in which there was a cooperation between grace and free will." Boettner, "Reformed Doctrine of Predestination," 364, 432. This coheres with our earlier observation that the early church fathers emphasized the reality of human free will in the role of salvation; Boettner, like all Calvinists, denied the will an ability to freely choose "to accept or reject" the gospel.

21. There is nothing outside of God that conditions whom God chooses to save. If there were any condition, such as repentance and faith originating as a human response, then God's choice would be conditioned on such faith and salvation would not be viewed as all of God.

22. Gonzalez, *History of Christian Thought*, 2:48.

23. Chadwick, *Early Church*, 232.

24. The inclination and tendency to long for fleshly, often proscribed, appetites.

25. "The sex instinct is only wrong when used in a way outside the limits laid down by God, and

Chadwick comments, "Julian thought . . . Augustine had brought his Manachean ways of thinking into the church, was defaming the good handiwork of the Creator under the influence of a hagridden attitude to sex resulting from the adolescent follies described in the Confessions, and was denying St. Paul's clear teaching that God wills all men to be saved."[26]

John Cassian (360–435), a theologian in one of the monasteries in southern Gaul (France), was likewise distressed to hear of Augustine's strong predestinarian views, coupled with a grace that was irresistible. He was convinced these emphases in Augustine represented "a most disturbing innovation, quite out of line with 'orthodoxy' . . . that body of belief which is held undeviatingly by the universal church."[27] Wand concurs: Cassian "felt considerable difficulty in accepting Augustine's teaching, and . . . denied that divine grace was irresistible. He asserted that man's will always remains free."[28] Cassian's soteriology accepted Augustine's stress on the need for divine grace to assist the will; however, he also agreed with Pelagius that the nature of human freedom was such that the will could choose to either do good or evil, and not as Augustine asserted, that the will could only choose to do evil. This mediating view came to be known as semi-Pelagianism (though it could just as easily have been called semi-Augustinianism).

Despite these voices of dissent, Augustine's views generally prevailed in the church of his day. In AD 416 two African synods condemned the Pelagians. In AD 418 Emperor Honorius ordered Pelagius to be exiled. However, that same year a council met at Carthage in north Africa to condemn Pelagius's teachings in favor of Augustine's views of sin and salvation. Again, a few years later, despite the fact that nineteen bishops refused to sign the document of condemnation, Pelagius's views were formally anathematized by the Council of Ephesus in AD 431.[29]

Debate in the church continued beyond AD 432, however. Due to the influence of Cassian and others who took a softer, semi-Pelagian, line, the Synod of Arles condemned certain aspects of Augustine's theology in AD 473. The offending aspects included Augustine's denial of the need for the human will to cooperate with God's grace (synergism), and the destruction of free will.[30] The latter was viewed as weakened or warped, but not eliminated.[31]

Finally, in AD 529 another ecumenical council at Orange opposed the tendency toward semi-Pelagianism evident at Arles. This council was more Augustinian in

---

[Augustine] is quite wrong to confuse original sin with concupiscence." Chadwick, *Early Church*, 233.

26. Chadwick, *Early Church*, 233.

27. Chadwick, *Early Church*, 233.

28. Wand, *History of the Early Church*, 233.

29. Wand, *History of the Early Church*, 432.

30. Understood as a human capacity to choose either good or evil.

31. Allison, *Historical Theology*, 350.

flavor,[32] insisting that even beginning moves toward God followed from God's grace that enlightened the mind and enabled belief. Grace was prior to faith. (This kind of grace was later to be called prevenient grace.) However, the council also strongly condemned any notion of double predestination—the idea that God not only predetermines those whom he would save, but also predetermines those who would be lost.[33]

The Medieval Church[34]

The influence of Augustine's soteriology on subsequent church history cannot be exaggerated. Erickson sums up Augustine's impact on subsequent centuries thus: "In the fifth century Augustine developed a synthesis of Platonic philosophy and theology (*The City of God*) which in many ways dominated theology for more than eight hundred years."[35] Gonzales also notes the tremendous influence Augustine has had on the history of Christian theology: Augustine's "theology was to such an extent responsive to the needs of human existence as well as to the requirements of the human mind that for centuries, and even to this day, Augustine has been, after Paul, the most influential thinker in the history of Christian thought."[36] Noting the influence of Augustine's conversion experience on the subsequent history of the doctrine of salvation Gonzales likewise notes that "the overwhelming and dynamic experience set forth in the *Confessions* is being transformed into an entire system of grace—a process that was perhaps inevitable, but nonetheless unfortunate."[37]

As far as the doctrine of salvation is concerned Augustine's views were reinforced, consolidated, and solidified through the various councils noted above that were convened (often at Augustine's insistence) in response to the Pelagian controversy.[38] The significance of all this is that if Augustine's soteriology is mistaken and does not in fact

32. Though Gonzales comments, "The synod itself, while condemning Pelagianism . . . did not adopt more than a diluted form of Augustinianism." Gonzales, *History of Christian Thought*, 2:61.

33. "Both those who are saved and those who are lost are so predetermined." Geisler, "Augustine," 106. See also Allison, *Historical Theology*, 458: "On the doctrine of predestination it was reluctant to embrace Augustine's theology." Bromiley also notes Augustine's double predestination: "Augustine, in *The City of God* and the *Enchiridion*, teaches predestination to both salvation and perdition." *Historical Theology*, 167.

34. Approximately the time between Augustine's death in 430 and the beginning of the Reformation in 1517.

35. Erickson, *Christian Theology*, 60.

36. Gonzales, *History of Christian Thought*, 1:55.

37. Gonzales, *History of Christian Thought*, 2:63. Gonzales is here remarking upon the conclusions of the Council of Orange in 529 on the brink of the medieval period. The reference to Augustine's view of grace on subsequent church history as "unfortunate" is all the more significant since Gonzales himself is quite sympathetic to Augustinian theology.

38. There was also, to some extent, a softening of rigid Augustinianism during the medieval period associated with leaders such as Pope Gregory the Great (590–604), Peter Abelard (1079–1142), and John Duns Scotus (1266–1308)—all taking a more semi-Pelagian view of the effects of original sin; Adam's sin weakened human nature but did not fatally corrupt it.

accurately represent the biblical data then subsequent outworking of church history is likewise, at least to some extent, mistaken in its doctrine of salvation.

As was to be expected, though Augustine's views did not become immediately universally accepted, his views ultimately prevailed during most of the medieval period.[39] Anselm, Archbishop of Canterbury (1033–1109), understood sin in conformity with the notions of his day concerning the relationship between a lord and his serfs. To sin is to dishonor God and to fail to give God the honor due to him as protector and provider. Thomas Aquinas (1225–1274), a giant in medieval church history and a key theologian of Roman Catholic theology, viewed sin as a voluntary act by which people choose a perceived good in the created order rather than the ultimate good, God. For Aquinas then, sin is essentially idolatry. Neither God nor Satan can be held responsible for a person sinning. Aquinas distinguished between two types of sin. There is a form of sin in which a person deliberately chooses to turn his back on God as a willful and defiant act; such sins are termed "mortal" and deserve eternal punishment. Venial sins, on the other hand, occur when a person sins but does so without hostility toward God or a desire to permanently turn away from God. This distinction between mortal and venial sins was to play a significant role in subsequent church practices.[40]

Aquinas followed Augustine on the question of original sin. "Through origin from the first man, sin entered into the world. According to the Catholic faith, we are bound to hold that the first sin of the first man is transmitted to his descendants by way of origin."[41] In keeping with the traditional view of original sin from Augustine onward, Aquinas understood the sin of Adam to entail a loss of original righteousness, with an associated corruption of human nature. Consequently, men's sins flow from a "disordered" nature stemming all the way back to Adam. Aquinas argued that the "disorder which is in people born of Adam is voluntary, not by their will but the will of their first parent. By the process of generation, Adam moves all who originate from him, even as the soul's will moves all the members [of the body] to their actions."[42] In other words, just as a hand or foot does not move independently from the soul (the originating source), so a person's sins today flow from the original originating source, a corrupt nature inherited from Adam.

---

39. Those who opposed some parts of Augustinian soteriology became known as semi-Pelagians. Though, as Gonzales notes, "the so-called semi-Pelagians were in truth 'semi-Augustinians' who, while rejecting the doctrines of Pelagius and admiring and respecting Augustine, were not willing to follow the Bishop of Hippo to the last consequences of this theology." Gonzales, *History of Christian Thought*, 2:57.

40. Allison, *Historical Theology*, 352. I am indebted to Allison for much in this section on medieval soteriology.

41. Allison, *Historical Theology*, 351. Note the appeal to church tradition here, not to biblical exegesis or even appeal to a biblical passage.

42. Cited by Allison, *Historical Theology*, 352. The idea of a voluntary action on the part of a contemporary person that flows inevitably from the actions of a past event or person seems dubious to me.

The relationship between grace and the human will featured also in the medieval theology of conversion. Was the will completely in bondage to sin so that it played no constructive role in the reception of salvation as Augustine taught? Or was the human will free in some sense to choose to accept the gospel call to salvation? If it was free then to what extent, and in what way did it relate to God's grace in the gospel?

On the topic of predestination, the Gottschalk debate "shows plainly that the issues raised in the Pelagian controversy had not been satisfactorily settled."[43] Gottschalk (808–867), an astute student of Augustine, was a Saxon monk who soon after ordination preached in Italy. His very strong and uncompromising preaching of Augustinian monergism led to him being condemned in AD 848 and even eventually to his imprisonment in AD 849.

> His message included the theses (1) that God foreordained both to the kingdom and also to death those whom he willed, (2) that there is absolute certainty of salvation and perdition, (3) that God does not will the salvation of all, (4) that Christ did die only for the elect, and (5) that fallen man has freedom only for evil.[44]

The controversy created by Gottschalk's forthright preaching of Augustinianism was unfortunate and showed his detractors in a poor light, but also serves to show how aspects of Augustine's soteriology—unconditional election, double predestination, limited atonement, total depravity—were not universally accepted by the church. There were always those who felt Augustine went beyond the bounds of Scripture in these formulations.

Anselm sought to harmonize predestination and free will by positing that God ordains directly all good deeds (by his grace working in the elect) and he ordains evil deeds indirectly by permitting the evil to happen. Starting from the premise "that whatever God decrees to happen in the future shall necessarily happen," it is "in the sense that it is by permitting the [evil deed] that God is said to be the cause of evils which he does not actually cause."[45]

Aquinas related predestination to providence. Essentially, he argued that since salvation was beyond a rational creature's natural capabilities its only source must be from God. Such supernatural directing (special providence) he called predestination. Conversely, the predestination of the reprobate (the non-elect) occurs when God permits the punishment justly deserved. It is interesting that Aquinas uses the

---

43. Bromiley, *Historical Theology*, 169.

44. Bromiley, *Historical Theology*, 166. Bromiley inadvertently says, "Christ did not die only for the elect." But in his later elaboration makes it clear that Gottschalk taught limited atonement in keeping with his teacher Augustine. I have omitted the word "not" for clarity. The second point means that the elect can never perish and that the reprobate can never be saved.

45. Anselm, *The Compatibility of God's Foreknowledge, Predestination, and Grace with Human Freedom* 2.1, 2.2, cited by Allison, *Historical Theology*, 459.

language of permission to soften the harshness of positive predestination of the non-elect to eternal punishment.

Baptism played a prominent role in medieval views about regeneration and conversion. Generally, newly converted adults were baptized and infants of Christian parents within the church were also baptized. In both cases regeneration—the new (spiritual) birth—was associated with the rite. Baptism of infants was needed to remove the effects of original sin.[46]

Generally, Augustine's theology dominated the first centuries of Western theologians.[47] Augustine had made use of Neoplatonic thought in developing his theology and Neoplatonism was the dominant philosophy during most of the medieval period.[48] In the thirteenth century a more philosophical approach to theology took place under the influence of Aristotelian philosophy. The main impact of this new thought form was in the area of epistemology—how God could be known—rather than soteriology. The next major church period, the Reformation, however, saw a revival of the conflicts seen earlier between Augustine and Pelagius. It is to that tension we now turn.

The Reformation

The Protestant Reformation is formally dated to the time when the Augustinian monk and theologian Martin Luther (1483–1546) pinned his ninety-five theses listing complaints against the church of his day on the Wittenberg church door in Germany in 1517.[49] The primary issue for Luther was the sale of indulgences by the Roman church for the purpose of raising money for the rebuilding of St. Peter's Basilica in Rome.[50] As the flames of the Reformation spread throughout Europe other issues quickly came to prominence. Chief among these was the view that a person was justified (declared not guilty by God) only on the basis of faith in God—justification and salvation was not in any way aided or supplemented with good works. The recovery of this important doctrine together with other biblical ideas such as the priesthood of all believers, the

46. Infant baptism preceded Augustine and was generally viewed as the initiation rite into the church. Augustine later appealed to the rite to justify his view of original sin—baptism washed away the guilt of Adam's sin in the newborn.

47. The Eastern, Greek-speaking church was relatively uninfluenced by Augustine's teachings in contrast to the Western, Latin-speaking church.

48. Gonzales, *History of Christian Thought*, 2:244. The Greek philosopher Plato taught that Forms represent the ideal copies from which realities in the sense world are patterned.

49. There had been predecessors to Luther in the decades up to 1517. For example, the English scholastic philosopher John Wycliffe (1331–1384) anticipated the central role of the Bible in the Reformation by insisting that the Bible needed to be translated from the Latin to the vernacular so that all people could have access to the word of God.

50. An indulgence was a declaration by the church that a loved one's soul would spend less time in purgatory or even be released altogether to heaven.

unique authority of the Bible, and salvation as a gift of grace alone became the hall-mark of the Reformation and was accepted by all the Reformers.[51]

However, as a student of Augustine and holding to the prevailing Augustinian view of key aspects of salvation, Luther accepted the monergism of his day with respect to predestination, election, human depravity, and the perseverance of the saints in faith. Due to sin and the resulting total inability of man to do good, faith itself must be a gift from God: "It is up to God alone to give faith contrary to nature, and ability to believe contrary to reason."[52] In fact, the will is in bondage to sin, we can only do evil. Luther likens the human will to a horse ridden either by Christ or the devil: "If God rides it, it wills and goes where God wills. . . . If Satan rides it, it wills and goes where Satan wills; nor can it choose to run to either of the two riders or to seek him out, but the riders themselves contend for the possession and control of it."[53] God elects unconditionally those whom he wills to be saved.[54] There is such a thing as a general, outward call to salvation and an inward call which effectually saves the elect. The general call cannot be responded to in faith because of sin.[55] The close connection between salvation and the (unconditional, secret) electing work of God naturally tends to raise questions of uncertainty regarding the reality of one's own salvation. Luther countered this by en-couraging believers to assurance of salvation by continuing to trust God's word.[56] He taught that the elect would persevere in faith to the end.[57]

The great Genevan Reformer John Calvin (1509–1564), like Luther, imbibed deeply of Augustinian soteriology.[58] Calvin, like Augustine, held to the doctrine of original sin. The original righteousness of Adam prior to the fall was replaced by "those dire pests, blindness, impotence, vanity, impurity, and unrighteousness [which] involved his [Adam's] posterity also, and plunged them in the same wretchedness."[59] This resulted in the propagation of a corrupted human nature in all of Adam's poster-ity: "We are not corrupted by acquired wickedness, but by an innate corruption from the very womb."[60] Consequently, "before we behold the light of the sun we are in God's

51. Luther made a big distinction between grace and law, and gospel and law. Not all followed him in such a radical disjunction.

52. Cited by Gonzales, *History of Christian Thought*, 3:45.

53. Gordon Rupp and Watson, *Luther and Erasmus*, 140.

54. There is nothing outside of God himself that conditions his choice of whom to save. This is in contrast to the idea of conditional election which holds that salvation is conditioned on faith and that God elects those whom he foresees meets the condition, i.e., believes.

55. Allison, *Historical Theology*, 485.

56. Allison, *Historical Theology*, 550.

57. Allison, *Historical Theology*, 550.

58. Han notes that "Calvin frequently referred to and quoted Augustine in his writings. Augustine undoubtedly exerted an influence on Calvin's views and arguments." Han, "Investigation into Calvin's Use of Augustine," 1. According to Han, Calvin cites Augustine about 1214 times in Calvin's Institutes of the Christian Religion.

59. Calvin, *Institutes*, 2.1.5.

60. Calvin, *Institutes*, 2.1.5.

sight defiled and polluted."[61] The will is "enchained as the slave of sin, it cannot make a movement towards goodness, far less steadily pursue it."[62] The elect are those chosen by God unconditionally for salvation. In fact, the saved have been predestined for salvation and the reprobate have been destined for judgment:

> As the Lord by the efficacy of his calling accomplishes towards his elect the salvation to which he had by his eternal counsel destined them, so he has judgments against the reprobate, by which he executes his counsel concerning them. . . . The Supreme Disposer then makes way for his own predestination, when depriving those whom he has reprobated of the communication of his light, he leaves them in blindness.[63]

Thus, Calvin did not shy away from the notion of double predestination; both the saved and the lost were predestined for their respective ends. For Calvin, the predestination of the reprobate is for the glory of God: the reprobate "were raised up by the just but inscrutable judgment of God, to show forth his glory by their condemnation." And all this is the outworking of an unchangeable and eternal decree of God: "[God's] immutable decree had once for all doomed them to destruction."[64] Since the sinner cannot believe, then faith itself must be a gift given by God.[65]

Quite consistently, Calvin (citing Augustine) taught that God's grace acted continuously to prevent the believer from failing to persevere in the faith: "To meet the infirmity of the human will, and prevent it from failing, how weak soever it might be, divine grace was made to act on it inseparably and uninterruptedly."[66]

While Luther's view on the extent of the atonement was that the work of the cross was intended for the whole world, Calvin's position has been debated among scholars. However, there can be no doubt that subsequent Calvinism held to a limited atonement—Christ's death was only intended for the elect.[67]

In the years following Calvin's death in AD 1564, a certain hardening of Calvin's teachings toward a rigorously consistent position developed. This came to be known as Protestant Scholasticism. A pioneer of this more rigorous approach to Augustinian soteriology was the contemporary of Calvin, Peter Martyr Vermigli (1499–1562), who, under the influence of Aristotelian philosophy,

> introduced into Reformed theology a methodological approach that would have profound influence on the later development of that theology. Whereas Calvin started from the concrete revelation of God, and always retained an

61. Calvin, *Institutes*, 2.1.5.

62. Calvin, *Institutes*, 2.3.5.

63. Calvin, *Institutes*, 3.24.12.

64. Calvin, *Institutes*, 3.24.14.

65. Calvin, *Institutes*, 2.3.8.

66. Calvin, *Institutes*, 2.3.13.

67. Allison, *Historical Theology*, 404.

awesome sense of the mystery of God's will, later Reformed theology tended more and more to proceed from the divine decrees down to particulars in a deductive fashion.[68]

As during the Pelagian controversy, and for similar reasons, not all agreed with the determinism associated with Calvinism.[69] A famous dispute arose between the Dutch theologian Jacobus Arminius (1560–1609) and the Reformed soteriology of his day. Arminius was a pastor of a church in Amsterdam until AD 1603 and then a professor of theology at Leiden until his death. Arminius was very much a thinker in the Reformed tradition in which he had been educated and moved.[70] His teacher at Geneva had at one time been Calvin's son-in-law Theodore Beza.

Arminius's distinct teaching relative to certain key aspects of Reformed soteriology began soon after he began his teaching position at the University of Leiden in Holland. The occasion that prompted dispute involved the teachings of his colleague at Leiden Franciscus Gomarus (1563–1641) concerning the doctrine of predestination, specifically the supralapsarianism taught by Gomarus. Supralapsarianism is the view that God decreed not only who would be saved (the elect), but that God also decreed the fall of Adam and Eve and the entrance of sin into the world.[71] Arminius thought Gomarus's view of predestination too detached from a Christ-focused understanding and argued for a doctrine of predestination that was less rationalistic, more christocentric, and which served to edify God's people. But the distinctive aspect of Arminius's teaching on this subject was that predestination was not, as Gomarus and the other strict Calvinists taught, unconditional, simply following from God's decree to save some, but rather was conditional on the foreseen faith of those who would come to believe the gospel.

Gomarus and his followers sought to pressure Leiden University for the removal of all theologians that were of an Arminian persuasion. This in turn prompted a reaction by forty-six pastors who signed a Remonstrance in AD 1610 upholding Arminius's views. It is easiest to summarize the Arminian perspective by examining the five points of the Remonstrance:

Article #1: Addresses the issue of predestination. It affirms God's predestination but makes it apply to "those who . . . shall believe on [God's] son Jesus . . . and

---

68. Gonzales, *History of Christian Thought*, 3:268.

69. I am using the term Calvinism here to refer primarily to the theology of Protestant Scholasticism. Determinism is the belief that God determines all events and outcomes.

70. "By sixteenth century standards, Arminius and the Remonstrants would have been seen as Calvinists by both Catholics and Lutherans." Gonzales, *History of Christian Thought*, 3:286. The Remonstrants were those who sided with Arminius.

71. This view is in contrast to an alternative Calvinist notion called infralapsarianism, which holds that God decreed who the elect would be but only did so after the fall.

shall persevere in this faith."[72] God predestines those to salvation who believe the gospel.

Article #2: The atonement is not limited to the elect only, but rather the Savior "died for all men, and for every man . . . yet so that no one is partaker of this remission [of sins] except the believers."[73]

Article #3: With Calvinism, Arminius agreed that human depravity is total in the sense that the human will is so corrupted that, unaided by grace, no one would be saved.

Article #4: God does provide a grace that is prevenient—it goes before and enables the person to believe the gospel. However, unlike Calvinism, this grace is resistible. (Though not stated in this Article #4, Arminianism understands prevenient grace to be universal.)

Article #5: This article addressed the issue of the perseverance of the saints—that those once truly saved cannot fall away from the faith. Unlike Arminius himself who felt that it was indeed possible for a Christian to fall away from the faith, the fifth article did not reach a conclusion on this point and asserted that it "must be the subject of more exact inquiry in the Holy Scriptures before we can teach it with full confidence of our minds."[74]

Eventually, and after some political tussle involving the cities of Rotterdam, which was supportive of the Remonstrants, and Amsterdam, which opposed the Remonstrants,[75] and in response to the Remonstrance, a synod was called for at Dort in the Netherlands to consider the teaching of Arminianism generally and these articles specifically. It was from Dort that the acrostic TULIP emerged. The synod met from 1618 to 1619 and adopted the classic Calvinist position on these contentious aspects of the doctrine of salvation. Predestination is not based on God's foreknowledge of those who would respond to the gospel but rather is based unconditionally on God's sovereign choice. This choice would be put into effect through a grace that was irresistible, and which would inevitably result in faith being granted the elect person. Whereas the Arminians viewed grace as a necessary prerequisite to overcome the effects of human depravity (prevenient grace) and thus make it possible for a believer to choose to respond to the gospel, the synod viewed grace to be irresistible in order to ensure the salvation of the elect. The synod rejected the possibility of a believer falling away and insisted that such a person would persevere to the end. By God's design the atonement would be limited only to the elect; the death of Christ was not intended for everyone.

72. Bettenson, *Documents of the Christian Church*, 268.

73. Bettenson, *Documents of the Christian Church*, 268.

74. Bettenson, *Documents of the Christian Church*, 269.

75. Gonzales, *History of Christian Thought*, 3:283.

The synod members required the Remonstrant ministers at that time to refrain from preaching and conducting other ministerial duties. They agreed to this demand when ministering in state churches, but insisted on the right to continue teaching Arminianism among those churches that met and held to the teachings of the Remonstrants.

Post-Reformational Developments

The broad contours of evangelical soteriology as outlined so far have remained surprisingly constant down the centuries following the Reformation. That is because evangelical Christianity traces its heritage back to the Reformation and with the key stands made back then: sola Scriptura (the Bible alone as a source of divine authority), sola gratia (grace alone as the basis for salvation, not meritorious works), sola fide (by faith alone, not faith plus works). These essentials have not changed for all expressions of evangelical faith. In addition, the key aspects of the doctrine of salvation argued over first by Augustine and the Pelagians, and then by Arminius and scholastic Calvinism have remained surprisingly persistent—right up to the present day. These include predestination, election, the resistibility of grace, the extent of the atonement, and the perseverance of the saints. For this reason, I will only very briefly sketch the development of this doctrine in subsequent church history, slanting the focus toward the people and movements influenced by these aspects of salvation. We will see that, broadly speaking, the two positions, Calvinism and Arminianism, have largely crystallized into denominational movements holding to their respective theologies.

In England, the struggle over Christian expression in the land involved mainly the Protestant / Roman Catholic division, with the form of Protestantism being decidedly Calvinistic. In AD 1534 King Henry VIII proclaimed himself the head of the church in England (not the pope). This was done for personal and political reasons, not religious, and Henry himself remained somewhat sympathetic to Roman Catholicism. Subsequently civil war broke out in England as various monarchies tried to impose either their Catholicism or their (Calvinistic) Protestantism. It was from within this turbulent period of English church history that the Puritans were formed. These Christians were staunch Calvinists and were not happy with the compromise with Rome that the Church of England represented. They sought to "purify" the church. Most of the Puritans sought to work within the Anglican church to reform it. However, a small separatist movement was formed that chose to seek reform exclusively outside the established church. The Separatists, led by Robert Browne (1550–1633), were persecuted and many fled to Holland. Eventually, a small group of these Puritan Separatists (subsequently known as the Pilgrim Fathers) led by John Robinson (1576–1625) emigrated to the New World (America) crossing the Atlantic in the Mayflower in AD 1620. In this manner early American Christian expression was decidedly Calvinistic.

Beginning around the 1730s a revival, known as the First Great Awakening, occurred among the nominal Christians at that time. A key figure who played an instrumental role in the early stages of the revival was the Puritan pastor-theologian Jonathan Edwards (1703–1758), who ministered at a Congregational church in Northampton, Massachusetts. Edwards, in addition to furthering the revival through his preaching and writings, was a highly intellectual Calvinist and his impact on subsequent church history—especially in providing Calvinism with a strong philosophical and theological rationale—cannot be overestimated. Interestingly Edwards, like Augustine, had a dramatic conversion experience which he recounted in his work *Personal Narrative* (AD 1739). Sainsbury remarks concerning Edwards that he "had an experience which gave him a new awareness of God's absolute sovereignty, and on his own dependence on God."[76]

In addition to a strong sense of God's sovereignty Edwards also had a keen sense of human depravity and the bondage of the will. "Edwards produced his most important work at Stockbridge on the *Freedom of the Will* (AD 1754). In it he denies that man is free to choose. This viewpoint fitted with his Calvinistic doctrines of election, predestination and the fallenness of man in every respect."[77]

Another significant church figure associated with the First Awakening was the English Anglican priest and outstanding Calvinist outdoor evangelistic preacher George Whitfield (1714–1770). His outdoor preaching alienated him from the Church of England and later he became associated with a Calvinistic form of Methodism. In fact, he founded the English Calvinistic Methodist Connexion, later absorbed into Congregationalism. In addition to preaching in England, Scotland, and Wales, he also visited America (Georgia) on several occasions on evangelistic trips. "Whitfield centered his theology on the old English Puritan themes of original sin, justification by faith and regeneration."[78]

Contemporary with Whitfield and Edwards were the Wesley brothers, John (1703–1791) and Charles (1707–1788). Both were members of the Church of England and were heavily involved with the English Revival that occurred in the early 1740s. Charles Wesley is most famous for his many devotional hymns that he wrote—many of which endure to this day. John Wesley, however, had great organizational abilities and spearheaded what initially were called societies—groups of Christians touched by the revival and who tended to meet in one another's homes for methodical study of the Bible. Later these societies evolved into the Methodist Church.

Unlike Edwards and Whitfield, however, John Wesley strongly opposed the doctrine of unconditional election. Instead, he made election conditional on faith in

76. Sainsbury, "Jonathan Edwards," 438.

77. Sainsbury, "Jonathan Edwards," 438. Actually, Edwards didn't deny man's freedom outright, merely the freedom to choose either x or y (known as libertarian freedom). In fact, as we shall see later, Edwards developed another form of freedom that was compatible with Calvinism's determinism.

78. Sainsbury, "Jonathan Edwards," 441.

Christ. Similarly, the reprobate were such because of their refusal to trust Christ for salvation, not because of a supposed unconditional decree of God; "God proceeds according to the known rules of his justice and mercy, but never assigns his sovereignty as the cause why any man is punished with everlasting destruction."[79] Wesley agreed with Augustinians in the idea of original sin—thus all babies are born with a sinful devilish nature and subject to divine condemnation. On this basis Wesley justified infant baptism. The corrupted human nature that follows from Adam's sin (as well as the guilt of Adam), results inevitably in sinful human acts, and it is for these personal sins that one can be justly punished by God. So Wesley, along with the Calvinists, held to total depravity. To counter the total inability for any good that results from original sin, Wesley taught the idea of prevenient grace. This grace is provided to all men and removes the fatal disablement associated with original sin and thereby enabling the sinner to believe the gospel. Unlike the Calvinist's irresistible grace, prevenient grace can be resisted and so does not guarantee salvation—it merely removes any impediments to the sinner hearing and responding to the gospel call to be saved. Not surprisingly, Wesley denied the Calvinist view that it is impossible for one of the elect to fail to persevere to the end. Not only was it possible for a true believer to turn his back on God, but also to be reconciled if that person subsequently repents and exercises faith again.[80]

In the first half of the nineteenth century another revival broke out in America. This time, the Second Great Awakening was more directed toward the saving of the unconverted (as opposed to the convicting of those professing Christian faith). A key figure during this period was the Arminian Congregationalist minister Charles G. Finney (1792–1875). Finney is best known as an innovative revivalist, especially during the years 1825–1835 in the New York area.

Finney's anthropology was more Pelagian than typically Arminian. For example, Finney denied original sin, viewing it as unjust of God to hold subsequent humanity guilty for the sin of Adam. He also denied that human nature was fundamentally corrupted by the fall of Adam into sin. He viewed sin as only an external matter—a willful disobedience to God's moral law—not an inevitable consequence of an inherited corrupted human nature.

> Moral depravity is not then to be accounted for by ascribing it to a nature or constitution sinful in itself. To talk of a sinful nature, or sinful constitution, in the sense of physical sinfulness, is to ascribe sinfulness to the Creator, who is the author of nature. It is to overlook the essential nature of sin, and to make sin a physical virus, instead of a voluntary and responsible choice.[81]

---

79. Wesley, *Predestination Calmly Considered*, 220.

80. Allison, *Historical Theology*, 558.

81. Finney, *Moral Depravity*, para. 8.4.

Finney, while denying that all people would be saved (universal election), denied the Calvinistic view of unconditional election. Rather election was conditioned upon foreseen faith: "The elect were chosen to salvation, upon condition that God foresaw that he could secure their repentance, faith, and final perseverance."[82]

While Augustinians[83] separated regeneration (the new birth) from conversion (turning to God), arguing that the latter was only possible due to the former because of total human depravity, Finney denied such a separation, viewing both as two sides of the same coin. "The fact that a new heart is the thing done, demonstrates the activity of the subject [God]; and the word regeneration . . . asserts the Divine agency. The same is true of conversion, or the turning of the sinner to God. God is said to turn him, and he is said to turn himself. God draws him, and he follows."[84]

Finney held to what is known as the governmental theory of the atonement. In this understanding of the significance of Christ's death there was not penal substitution, but rather "the atonement is a governmental expedient to sustain law without the execution of its penalty on the sinner."[85] The concern is with the preservation of public order—the sustenance of law. It was public, not retributive justice that mattered—it would not be just for God to punish an innocent person for the crimes of another. In this understanding of the atonement God's intent in putting forth his Son was not limited to an elect few, but rather to all sinners; Finney held to a universal understanding of the extent of the atonement.

Not surprisingly Finney held to perseverance as conditional on faithful obedience to the end: "Perseverance in obedience to the end of life is also a condition of justification."[86] Apostasy is a real possibility even for the true Christian: "It must be naturally possible for all moral agents to sin at any time. Saints on earth and in heaven can by natural possibility apostatize and fall, and be lost."[87]

While the doctrines of sin and salvation developed, especially following the Renaissance and the rise of liberal Protestantism, as far as evangelical theology is concerned the broad contours of the debate between Calvinism and non-Calvinists had been set by the end of the Second Great Awakening noted above. Subsequent American church history has been a history of denominations that are essentially Calvinistic in outlook and those that are more Arminian. Among the former denominations may be listed the Presbyterian, Congregationalist, Lutheran, Episcopalian, and varieties of Reformed churches (Dutch—including the Christian Reformed Church, German, Baptist, and Charismatic). Among the latter would be the United Methodist Church, Wesleyan

---

82. Finney, *Election*, 4.4.

83. That is, those who followed Augustine's soteriology, including Lutherans and Calvinists and all of Reformed persuasion.

84. Finney, *Election*, 4.4.

85. Finney, "Atonement," line 19.

86. Finney, *Justification*, 3.

87. Finney, *Systematic Theology*, 841.

Church, the Free Methodist Church, Pentecostal churches, Holiness churches (Nazarene, Christian & Missionary Alliance, etc.), some Baptist churches (e.g., Free Will Baptist), Christian Churches and Churches of Christ, and the Salvation Army.

Having briefly sketched the historical background to the doctrine of salvation, with a focus on human depravity, election, the extent of the atonement, the role of grace in an individual's salvation, and the nature of Christian perseverance in the faith, we are now positioned to critically examine both biblically and theologically the Calvinist understanding of these aspects of salvation.

2

Total Depravity: Too Depraved to Respond to the Gospel?

A substantial portion of this chapter will necessarily be on the doctrine of original sin.[1] This is necessary because of the Calvinist's understanding of what is
entailed by this doctrine. If it were only the case that all are, in some sense, guilty
before God because of Adam's sin, then this topic could be noted and then passed
on. This is so because the Bible is clear, and all agree, that everyone without exception is guilty because of their own personal sins: *"For all have sinned and fall short of
the glory of God"* (Rom 3:23).[2] However, it is because of the Calvinist's understanding
of what original sin necessarily entails—a total depravity that manifests itself in a
total inability of the sinner to even respond to the gospel call—that requires that we
examine this doctrine in some detail.[3]

Since a significant portion of those professing Christian faith reject the notion
of original sin altogether, namely the Eastern Orthodox churches, as well as those
following Charles Finney, who played an influential role in the Second Great Awakening as noted in the previous chapter, we shall examine the doctrine specifically
in its own right before going on to then examine the Calvinist's inference that this
doctrine entails total inability. My approach will be to clearly express *what* the Calvinist believes concerning this doctrine and then go on to show *why* they hold these
beliefs, what scriptures are appealed to. I will also then critique the way Calvinists
understand these texts.

---

1. The effects of Adam's sin on his posterity.

2. All Bible references are from the New American Standard Bible, Lockman Foundation, 1995 ed.

3. Note that classical Arminians follow the Calvinists here in the understanding of the effects of
original sin on Adam's posterity.

The Calvinist Understanding of the Doctrine of Original Sin[4]

Here I shall focus on the writings of modern influential Calvinists and seek to let them speak for themselves as much as possible to ensure that the view presented is an accurate expression of their beliefs.

Wayne Grudem[5]

"Inherited Guilt: We are counted guilty because of Adam's sin. . . . When Adam sinned, God thought of all who would descend from Adam as sinners."[6]

"Inherited Corruption: We have a sinful nature because of Adam's sin. . . . Our nature includes a disposition to sin. . . . [We have an] inherent tendency to sin that attaches to our lives from the very beginning."[7]

Thomas Schreiner

"Human beings are born with a corrupt nature. . . . Human beings by nature are deserving of wrath, indicating they are all born with a nature that is sinful."[8]

Robert Peterson

"Original sin includes both original guilt and original pollution. Original guilt is the truth that because of Adam's sin we are all guilty. . . . Original pollution (or, as it is also called, original corruption) means that our lives and relationships are stained by sin."[9]

George J. Zemek

"The spiritual results of the fall were of the greatest magnitude—separation from God . . . the guilt of sin."[10] "The Bible connects man's actual sin to his sinful nature."[11] "The Bible connects man's actual sin and his sinning nature back to the first sin of Adam."[12]

---

4. Also known as "Inherited Sin, Original Pollution, Original Corruption."

5. All the references to Grudem are taken from his highly influential *Systematic Theology: An Introduction to Biblical Doctrine.*

6. Grudem, *Systematic Theology*, 494.

7. Grudem, *Systematic Theology*, 496.

8. Schreiner, "Prevenient Grace," 229.

9. Peterson, *Election and Free Will*, 127.

10. Zemek, *Biblical Theology*, 85.

11. Zemek, *Biblical Theology*, 86.

12. Zemek, *Biblical Theology*, 88.

R. C. Sproul

"Since the fall human nature has been corrupt. We are born with a sin nature."[13] "Original sin is the corruption visited on the progeny of our first parents as punishment for the original transgression."[14]

Michael Horton

"Adam and Eve had the freedom to choose immortal life, but in breaking covenant with God, they and their posterity became a race of rebels: born in corruption, guilt, and death. . . . It is the concrete act of covenant-breaking that marks the descent of humanity into guilt and corruption."[15]

John Calvin

"We are not corrupted by an acquired wickedness, but bring an innate corruption from the very womb. . . . Before we behold the light of the sun we are in God's sight defiled and polluted."[16] "Being thus perverted and corrupted in all parts of our nature, we are merely on account of such corruption, deservedly condemned by God."[17]

"I again ask how it is that the fall of Adam involves so many nations with their infant children in eternal death without remedy, unless that it so seemed meet to God? . . . The decree, I admit, is dreadful; and yet it is impossible to deny that God foreknew what the end of man was to be before he made him, and foreknew, because he had so ordained by his decree."[18]

An Examination of Key Biblical Texts Used by Calvinists

In examining the claims made by the above authors for original sin, three features appear most prominently: original guilt, corrupted human nature, and universal scope. Adam's sin, and the state of being considered guilty before God because of it, is attributed to his posterity. We are guilty because of Adam's sin. This judgment arises either directly (Augustine, Grudem) or indirectly because we sin due to our corrupt nature (Calvin). Generally, Calvinists seem to be reluctant to dwell on this aspect of original sin (guilt due to Adam)—possibly because it does not sit well with modern sensibilities. What is clearly presented however by all Calvinists is the supposed devastating

13. Sproul, *Reformed Theology*, 119.
14. Sproul, *Reformed Theology*, 121.
15. Horton, *For Calvinism*, 39.
16. Calvin, *Institutes*, 2.1.5.

17. Calvin, *Institutes*, 2.1.8. Here Calvin is stressing that man is guilty before God for the actions flowing from a corrupted nature—not directly because of Adam's sin as Augustine taught. See Lane, *Reader's Guide to Calvin's Institutes*, 66. Though, of course, corrupted human nature is a direct consequence of Adam's sin.

18. Calvin, *Institutes*, 3.23.7. Calvin here makes clear his belief that Adam's sin was decreed by God.

effect of Adam's sin on the human nature of all his descendants—inherited corruption. More will be said about this later when we examine the consequence of inherited corruption; here we will focus on the claim of inherited corruption itself. Suffice to say that this aspect of original sin means we all suffer a depravity that is fatal as far as relating to God is concerned. Humankind's proclivity is to do only sin. Finally, all Calvinists are agreed the effects of the fall are universal in scope—everyone, without exception, has been impacted negatively because of Adam's sin.

While undoubtedly this doctrine relies heavily upon Augustine's teachings on this subject and on subsequent church counsels and confessions, proponents of original sin also feel that the Bible itself justifies such a doctrine. We shall now go on to examine the key texts of Scripture commonly appealed to as a basis for these views.

Psalm 51:5

"Behold, I was brought forth in iniquity,
And in sin my mother conceived me."

Grudem is typical of the Calvinist understanding when he comments: "Even before he was born [David] had a sinful disposition: he affirms that at the moment of conception he had a sinful nature. . . . Here is a strong statement of the inherent tendency to sin that attaches to our lives from the very beginning."[19]

This psalm was written by King David after Nathan the prophet had confronted David concerning his adultery with Bathsheba and his arranging the murder of Bathsheba's husband (2 Sam 11). The enormity of his sin was heavy upon his heart. The immediate context makes clear, as Grudem points out, that David was expressing contrition over his own personal sin. In the preceding four verses there is no hint that David sees any source for his sin other than his own chosen actions. Furthermore, this psalm, like all the psalms, is poetic in genre. David is not writing a clinical systematic theology about the doctrine of sin—he is using powerful poetic imagery to describe the depths of his sinfulness. To isolate this verse and treat it as a systematic theologian would is to run the danger of misinterpretation through over-precision. In short, David here is using hyperbole, a common expedient in Hebrew poetry, to underscore the vile nature of his sin. "The main point is the comprehensive nature of the suppliant's own sin."[20] Jack Cottrell is surely correct when he remarks concerning this verse: "[David] is humbling himself before God in figurative language, in the same way that biblical writers sometimes refer to man as a worm (Ps 22:6; Job 17:14; 25:6; Isa 41:14). This is hyperbole, or exaggeration for emphasis."[21]

19. Grudem, *Systematic Theology*, 496.

20. Tate, *Psalms 51–100*, 20.

21. Cottrell, *Faith Once for All*, 181. Psalm 22:10 is similar: "Upon You I was cast from birth; you have been my God from my mother's womb." David's point, as the context indicates, is that his trust in God was complete. Obviously, David could not have known and trusted God when a baby.

Psalm 58:3

> *"The wicked are estranged from the womb; These who speak lies*
> *go astray from birth."*

Wright remarks: "The verses in Psalms 51 and 58 only confirm that this sin nature is original to our conception, it is not acquired, but manifests itself 'from the womb,' causing sinners to go astray as soon as they are born."[22] No attempt is made to justify the claim. However, it is obvious that this psalm, like Ps 51, is essentially poetic in nature. Those "estranged from the womb" are said to have venom like the venom of a cobra, and stop up their ears like a deaf cobra. Appeal to God is made to *"shatter their teeth in their mouth; Break out the fangs of the young lions, O Lord"* (v. 6). Appeal is made that the wicked *"flow away like water that runs off"* (v. 7), and that they be *"as a snail which melts away as it goes along"* (v. 8). Clearly this is the language of poetry. Usually, in poetic genre the author is using vivid imagery to make a point. In this case the concern of the psalmist is that the wicked get their full desert and that God be seen to be a God who judges wickedness (v. 11). This is not, as Calvinists argue, a statement of human anthropology concerning the precise moment a person begins to sin. The psalmist's point in v. 3 is that wickedness is so rampant and ubiquitous that it is *as though* the wicked sin the moment they are born. A moment's thought will show that the verse is meant to be understood poetically, not literally, since babies cannot speak! This is another use of hyperbole—exaggeration for effect.

Ephesians 2:1–3

> *"And you were dead in your trespasses and sins, in which you formerly walked*
> *according to the course of this world, according to the prince of the power of the*
> *air, of the spirit that is now working in the sons of disobedience. Among them we*
> *too all formerly lived in the lusts of our flesh, indulging the desires of the flesh and*
> *of the mind, and were by nature children of wrath, even as the rest."*

There are two aspects of these verses that make it especially appealing to the notion of original sin as entailing inherited corruption: being *dead* in trespasses and sins, and being *by nature* children of wrath. According to Horton, v. 1 proves "we come into the world 'dead in . . . trespasses and sins.'"[23] Schreiner and Ware commenting on the "dead" aspect of this verse state that "the deadness of fallen humanity indicates that we are devoid of life upon our entrance into the world. We have no inclination towards genuine righteousness or goodness."[24] Sproul understands to be dead in sin to mean

22. Wright, *No Place for Sovereignty*, 113.

23. Horton, *For Calvinism*, 41.

24. Schreiner, "Prevenient Grace," 230.

the unbeliever is "in a state of moral and spiritual bondage."[25] William Hendriksen, like most Calvinists, does not deny that unbelievers do good things, and so being dead in trespasses and sins need not preclude the doing of natural, civic, or even moral good things. But the key aspect of this deadness is the inability to do *spiritually* good things. "Such a good deed does not spring from the root of gratitude for the salvation merited by Jesus Christ. It is not a work of faith, therefore."[26] Of course this deadness is due to the corrupted nature allegedly inherited from Adam and results in a total inability to do any spiritual good.

Several observations are in order at this point. First, it is very easy to push the metaphor of death too far, after all a lifeless body cannot do anything at all, it is utterly unresponsive to any form of stimulation. However, like any metaphor, the key point of the author's intention in using the metaphor must be identified and applied—not every aspect of the metaphor need apply.

Second, while Calvinists understand this condition to be the direct result of a morally and spiritually corrupted nature inherited from Adam, nowhere in these verses does Paul make that connection—it is merely an inference that fits well the Calvinist's theory of original sin.

Third, it is necessary to ask what Paul meant when he used the metaphor of death in Eph 2:1. We know from other biblical passages that to be spiritually dead means to be cut off from relationship with the ultimate source of life, God himself. The basic concept is relational separation.[27] This is not the concept emphasized by the Calvinists referenced above who tend to understand deadness in ethical and spiritual inability terms. Is there a clue in the Ephesian passage as to what Paul meant by being dead in trespasses and sins? Yes. Just a few verses later Paul amplifies what the Ephesian believer's former (unregenerate) manner of life was like. It was characterized as being not in relationship to God. "*Therefore remember that formerly you, the Gentiles in the flesh, . . . were at that time separate from Christ, excluded from the commonwealth of Israel, and strangers to the covenants of promise, having no hope and without God in the world. But now in Christ Jesus you who formerly were far off have been brought near by the blood of Christ*" (Eph 2:11–13, emphases mine).

In short, to be dead in trespasses and sins means to be cut off from God due to one's sins. This is to be dead, not as a lifeless corpse, but rather dead as the Prodigal Son was in the parable Jesus taught: "*For this son of mine was dead and has come to life again; he was lost and has been found*" (Luke 15:24). The son was "dead" metaphorically

25. Sproul, *Reformed Theology*, 130.

26. Hendriksen, *Ephesians*, 112.

27. See, e.g., Gen 2:17, where God assures Adam that he would die the day he disobeyed God's command. But Adam did not die physically that day, he died immediately only in the sense that his relationship with God was seriously disrupted—he became separated from a good relationship with God. Most references to death in both testaments are to physical death, but where spiritual death is in view the idea of separation is prominent. E.g., in Rom 6:11, believers are to consider themselves dead to sin—i.e., not in relationship with sin. To die to the Mosaic law is to be joined to Christ (Rom 7:4).

speaking, not literally; he was not in relationship with his father, rather than utterly lifeless in the pig pen. The very fact that the prodigal "came to his senses" (v. 17) indicates that the nature of his "deadness" was not total moral inability. Apparently, it is quite possible for someone to be "dead" and yet recognize his true condition and seek to do something about it.

Since Paul nowhere here connects this state of affairs with Adam and his sin, the presumption has to be that unbelievers are dead in the sense that they are not reconciled to God because of their own personal sins. Contrary to Horton, Eph 2:1 does not prove that we come into the world "dead in . . . trespasses and sins," but rather merely that before being united to Christ by faith people are not in relationship to God. This lack of relationship, this "deadness" is clearly attributed to *their* trespasses and *their* sins—not Adam's. As Renault notes:

> Being "dead in trespasses" in this passage [Eph 2] means that we're in bondage to death and decay, living sinful lives separated from God. It doesn't mean that we can't choose to say yes to God's grace, just as being "dead to sin" doesn't mean we can't choose to sin (Rom 6:11).[28]

Furthermore, the metaphor of deadness must not be allowed to contradict other metaphors used in the Bible to describe the sinner outside of Christ. For example, the image of enslavement to sin is used by Jesus in John 8:34. Slaves are not dead. Another metaphor is that of sickness (Luke 5:31). Sick people are not dead people. Lostness is another metaphor used to describe the sinner (Luke 15); lost people are not dead people. Certainly, these metaphors speak of persons who are not in relationship with God, but each allows for the possibility that they may seek to have their condition changed for the good; the slave may strongly desire to be set free, the sick may well desire to be made whole, and the lost may want to be found. Similarly, the spiritually dead may seek to find life in relationship with One who offers them true life and sustenance (John 6:35).

What does Paul mean when he reminds his Ephesian readers that they were formerly "by nature children of wrath" (Eph 2:3)? Are Zemek and other Calvinists correct in seeing in this verse a corrupted human nature due to Adam's sin? Is it really the case that "the Bible connects man's actual sin *and his sinning nature* back to the first sin of Adam"?[29] The first thing to note is that, as remarked earlier, Paul nowhere in this passage, or in the immediate context, hints that the Ephesians' former condition was due in any way to Adam's actions or the consequences of Adam's sin. The omission is surprising because, had their former sinful condition been due to an inherited corrupt nature from Adam, it would have been very easy for Paul to refer to Adam as the cause of this state of affairs. Adamic corruption would have offered Paul a succinct explanation of their pre-Christian behavior.

28. Renault, *Reconsidering TULIP*, 20.
29. Zemek, *Biblical Theology*, 88, emphasis original.

A careful examination of Eph 2:1–3 shows that Paul attributes their former pre-Christian state of being "by nature children of wrath" as being due to choices and decisions they made and which resulted in a pattern of living that was contrary to God's will and which resulted in them being subject to the wrath of God. They chose to engage in sinful acts—they "walked" in trespasses and sins, they succumbed to the lusts of the flesh, they indulged the desires of the flesh and mind. The consequence of all these lifestyle choices corrupted their nature in the sense that they became habituated to sin and consequently subjected themselves to divine wrath.[30] (Verse 2 is difficult, but suggests that the Ephesians succumbed to satanic temptation and influence in choosing to act the way they did.)[31]

While Calvinists interpret the passage to mean that the Ephesians *inherited* a corrupt nature from Adam, the text itself suggests the Ephesians *developed* a corrupt nature because of their persistent sinful choices and habits.

Other Passages

There are surprisingly few passages that are appealed to by Calvinists to justify a concept of original sin. Surprising, that is, for a doctrine that is so foundational for an entire system of soteriology and which relies heavily on such a concept to justify the monergism characteristic of Calvinism.

Schreiner appeals to Col 2:13[32] and Titus 3:3. The former passage, like Eph 2:1, emphasizes the "deadness" of man outside of Christ—and speaks to the broken relationship of the unbeliever in relation to God. Schreiner comments, "The deadness of fallen humanity indicates that we are devoid of life upon our entrance into the world."[33] However, nothing in the verse or the immediate context links this broken relationship to Adam or subsequent generations through the inheriting of a corrupted human nature or that any person is born with this broken relationship. Such notions are read into the passage by Calvinists because it fits a preconceived theology. The time frame referenced by Paul is to their pre-Christian days, not their post-birth days. Babies are not, for example, *"enslaved to various lusts"* (Titus 3:3).

In his discussion concerning the enslaving nature of sin Schreiner cites Titus 3:3.[34] The near context of Schreiner's comments, however, make it clear that the catalog of sins listed in Titus 3:3 is viewed by Schreiner as the condition of unbelievers

30. The Revised Standard Version (1975) captures this sense well in translating v. 3 as *"following the desires of body and mind, and so were by nature children of wrath"* (emphasis mine).

31. They "had rebelled knowingly and voluntarily, against the loving authority of God and so had fallen under the dominion of Satan." Stott, *Message of Ephesians*, 75.

32. Col 2:13: *"When you were dead in your transgressions and the uncircumcision of your flesh, He made you alive together with Him, having forgiven us all our transgressions."*

33. Schreiner, "Prevenient Grace," 230.

34. Titus 3:3: *"For we also once were foolish ourselves, disobedient, deceived, enslaved to various lusts and pleasures, spending our life in malice and envy, hateful, hating one another."*

who "are all born with a nature that is sinful."[35] Once more, however, there is nothing in Titus 3:3 itself, which merely catalogs various sins characteristic of pre-conversion people, that locates the source of this condition and behaviors. It is merely eisegesis to read into the passage this condition as going back to one's birth.

There is one passage however that, superficially at least, would seem to lend strong support to the idea of original sin—Rom 5:12–21.

Romans 5:12–21

Therefore, just as through one man sin entered into the world, and death through sin, and so death spread to all men, because all sinned—for until the Law sin was in the world, but sin is not imputed when there is no law. Nevertheless death reigned from Adam until Moses, even over those who had not sinned in the likeness of the offense of Adam, who is a type of Him who was to come. But the free gift is not like the transgression. For if by the transgression of the one the many died, much more did the grace of God and the gift by the grace of the one Man, Jesus Christ, abound to the many. The gift is not like that which came through the one who sinned; for on the one hand the judgment arose from one transgression resulting in condemnation, but on the other hand the free gift arose from many transgressions resulting in justification. For if by the transgression of the one, death reigned through the one, much more those who receive the abundance of grace and of the gift of righteousness will reign in life through the One, Jesus Christ.

So then as through one transgression there resulted condemnation to all men, even so through one act of righteousness there resulted justification of life to all men. For as through the one man's disobedience the many were made sinners, even so through the obedience of the One the many will be made righteous. The Law came in so that the transgression would increase; but where sin increased, grace abounded all the more, so that, as sin reigned in death, even so grace would reign through righteousness to eternal life through Jesus Christ our Lord.

All the Calvinists referenced so far appeal to this passage as primary evidence for the doctrine of original sin—that humanity subsequent to Adam is held guilty by God for Adam's sin, and also inherit a fatally corrupted nature from Adam. Grudem, for example, appealing to Rom 5:19 asserts that "Adam, our first representative sinned— and God counted us guilty."[36] Schreiner says, "Paul teaches that all human beings are born with a corrupt nature inherited from Adam (Rom 5:12–19). . . . It is clear from the text that we are sinners because of Adam's sin. Through Adam's sin we . . . are constituted as sinners"[37] Similarly R. K. McGregor Wright asserts that "since the Fall

35. Schreiner, "Prevenient Grace," 230.

36. Grudem, *Systematic Theology*, 495.

37. Schreiner, "Prevenient Grace," 229. Little effort is made to justify this conclusion. The

of Adam and Eve, all are born spiritually dead in their sin nature." Appealing to Rom 5:12 he says, "The essential point is that death passed to all because of Adam's sin."[38] It is clear that Wright believes that all sinned "in Adam" even though the text does not say that. Generally speaking, little effort is expended by these authors to carefully consider the entire section—that the passage teaches original sin is presumed to be self-evident and clear.

Another way in which this passage may be understood is presented by Jack Cottrell, in his Romans commentary, who sees in this passage, not original sin, but what he calls "original grace." Cottrell begins by accepting the Calvinist assessment of the devastating effect of Adam's disobedience upon subsequent humanity. However, he notes that Paul's "purpose is not to emphasize what happened to the race as the result of Adam's sin, but to emphasize what has happened to it as the result of Christ's saving work."[39] Noting the stress in the passage upon the exceeding sufficiency of Christ's work relative to any negative effects of Adam's sin, Cottrell holds that "the whole point of the passage is that Christ's 'one act of righteousness' (5:18) has completely intercepted, nullified, canceled, and counteracted *whatever* was destined to be ours because of Adam."[40] Cottrell consequently concludes that the passage does not in fact teach a doctrine of original sin—there are no consequences to humanity following Adam's sin. Why? Because they have been intercepted and cancelled by Christ's saving work. "No child is actually conceived and born under the curse of Adam's sin. If anything, this passage teaches a doctrine of *original grace*; every child is born under the grace of God, born saved, 'born free' from all spiritual effects of Adam's sin."[41] Every child is born with a clean slate spiritually speaking. This does not lead to universalism, the belief that everyone is saved, because the Bible makes it clear that all stand under the judgment of God for their own personal sins.

While Cottrell's thesis is plausible and seeks to take seriously the superlative work of Christ over any consequences of Adam's sin as well as the symmetry between Adam and Christ,[42] it suffers from the same problems inherent with any notion of guilt imputed by God for Adam's sin in the first place, and also that human nature itself could be negatively impacted by inheriting a corrupt nature from another. These problems will be discussed later.

The following analysis of the passage I believe avoids these problems and fully addresses Paul's intent in the passage. But, before focusing on the passage itself, it

---

assumption seems to be that it is self-evident.

38. Wright, *No Place for Sovereignty*, 112.

39. Cottrell, *Romans*, 1:332.

40. Cottrell, *Romans*, 1:332, emphasis original.

41. Cottrell, *Romans*, 1:333, emphasis original.

42. All agree that the entirety of humanity is identified in some way with Adam, but Calvinists limit the scope of Christ's salvific work to only those who believe, and so introduce an asymmetry in Paul's comparison of Christ and Adam. Cottrell's model addresses this asymmetry head on.

is worthwhile asking why Paul introduces Adam at this point in his epistle. The answer is found in the immediately preceding verses—vv. 6–11.[43] Verses 12–21 serve as an amplification and development of a motif emerging in vv. 6–11. In vv. 6–11 Paul contrasts the powerful effect of Christ's ministry on behalf of the believer with the negative effects of sin on sinners:

- Christ died for the helpless ungodly (v. 6).

- Christ died even for sinners (v. 8).

- Believers can therefore have great confidence that through Christ the believer's beginning in the Christian life (justification) will continue on to final salvation ("saved from the wrath of God") (v. 9).

- Also, the believer can be confident that if reconciliation was effected even for sinners, then final salvation is assured (v. 10). Note the expression "much more then" used twice in these six verses (vv. 9, 10).

It is precisely this same thrust that Paul develops in the following passage, vv. 12–21. A notable difference, however, is the exchange of the term "sinner" used consistently throughout vv. 6–11, with the word "Adam" in vv. 12–21. While it is true of course that Paul refers to Adam the man and his specific acts, nevertheless what Adam stands for, represents, is a type of the class of human beings known as sinners.

So, the basic purpose of Rom 5:12–21 is to encourage believers to have confidence that the work begun in their lives through faith in Christ will most certainly find completion and final victory at the end. Christ's salvific work far supersedes any of the negative effects of sin introduced into the world by Adam, the very first sinner.

Through a careful reading of this passage the following points may be noted:

- Paul's focus is on comparing the person Christ with the person Adam. Certain consequences are associated with "Adam" and certain consequences are associated with "Christ."

- With "Adam" come death, sin (vv. 12, 17a, 21), judgment, and condemnation (vv. 16a, 18a).

- With "Christ" come grace (15, 20b, 21), justification (vv. 16b, 18b), righteousness (vv. 17b, 18b, 21b), eternal life (v. 21b).

- In this sense Adam is a type of Christ (v. 14c)—both stand for a class of humanity—lost humanity and redeemed humanity.[44]

43. C. E. B. Cranfield connects vv. 12–21 with the entire preceding verses, namely 5:1–11. Cranfield, "Interpretation of Romans 5:12," 324–25. Cranfield holds that "all sinned" (Rom 5:12b) refers to personal sin, but personal sin resulting from a corrupted human nature inherited from Adam.

44. Bob Utley of East Texas Baptist University, Bible commentary on Rom 5, commenting on the phrase "*who is a type of Him who was to come*" (Rom 5:14), notes that "this expresses in a very concrete way the Adam-Christ typology (cf. 1 Cor 15:21–22, 45–49; Phil 2:6–8). Both of them are seen as the first in a series, the origin of a race (cf. 1 Cor 15:45–49)."

- It is not Paul's interest, and nowhere is the attempt made, to explain *how* a person may be related to either Adam or Christ. This point is very important since all theories of original sin rely on an explanation of exactly how one comes to be related to "Adam" (usually through federal headship or seminal identity).[45] Since Paul does not state how one may be identified with either Adam or Christ then purported explanations are theories which are not found in the text itself.

- Positively, Paul appears to be using the names "Adam" and "Christ" as shorthand for two kinds of humanity. There is a humanity which has been untouched by the gospel of Christ, and which is outside of Christ—they are "Adam"; on the other hand, there is a humanity which may be identified with Christ—they are "Christ."[46]

- From other passages in Scripture, one knows that simply failing to be united to Christ by faith makes one subject to death, sin, judgment, and condemnation. And this state of affairs arises from personal sins—not Adam's sin. Personally sinning aligns oneself with the first sinner Adam, and puts one in the "Adam" class of humanity.

- From other passages in Scripture one knows that one comes into alignment with the "Christ" camp through repentance and faith in the gospel of Christ.

- The thrust of Paul's argument appears to be that just as all the negatives associated with personal sinning that began with Adam, so all the blessings that personal faith made possible began with Christ. Adam ushered in one form of humanity—those who sin personally; Christ ushered in another form of humanity—those who are of faith in God/Christ.

- The man Adam was the *occasion* of all other personal sins, not the source of personal sins. The man Jesus Christ was the *occasion* of all subsequent blessings for those who exercised personal faith. Adam was the pioneer or prototype of all who would sin personally; Christ was the pioneer or forerunner of all those who would be righteous through faith.

- Nowhere does the passage ground the basis of human sin, condemnation, etc., in Adam's personal sin. Augustine misread v. 12 to read "and so death spread to all men, because all sinned . . . in Adam." Tatha Wiley explains the origins of the idea that all sinned when Adam sinned:

> The anonymous fourth-century commentator on Paul, referred to as Ambrosiaster, derived original sin from his exegesis of Rom 5:12. His interpretation of this text was adopted by Augustine of Hippo and became a central

45. Federal headship is the view that God made Adam man's representative, so that whatever happened to Adam also happened to those Adam represented. Seminal identity is the view that the negative consequences of Adam's sin—guilt and corrupted nature is passed on through sexual intercourse—physical descent. Both models have been hotly debated in the history of the doctrine of sin.

46. F. F. Bruce suggests the same idea when he says, "In Paul's thought Christ replaces the first man as the archetype and representative of a new humanity." Bruce, *Romans*, 134.

component of the classical doctrine. In the modern NRSV [New Revised Standard Version], the Greek text of Rom 5:12 is correctly translated this way: *Therefore, just as sin came into the world through one man, and death came through sin, and so death spread to all because all have sinned.*[47] The Latin Vulgate translation Ambrosiaster used, however, rendered the latter part of the sentence [as] "in whom all sinned," not "because all sinned."[48]

- Is there a hint in the passage that Paul was thinking of personal sins with respect to the spread of sin and death in v. 12, so that the passage could be legitimately read as "and so death spread to all men, because all have sinned *personally*"? I believe there is. In vv. 13 and 14 Paul's point is that sin was universally present in the world even from the time of Adam (as demonstrated by the universality of death); this supports Paul's assertion in v. 12 that "death spread to all men." But how could sin, which is a violation of God's law, be present when the Mosaic law was given many hundreds of years after Adam? The implied answer is that all men violated the moral law that all human beings have because "God has made [it] evident to them" (Rom 1:19). How does one sin with respect to this moral law? By choosing to personally not honor God as God or to give thanks to this God (Rom 1:21). But this is a good definition of *personal sin*, not original sin. In fact, throughout the entire Epistle of Romans, Paul has consistently meant personal sins when he speaks of sin as, for example, when he says that "all have sinned and fallen short of the glory of God" (Rom 3:23).

If this understanding of Rom 5:12–21 is correct then we can see that, though Paul makes reference to Adam, and even specific acts of the man Adam, Paul does this not to show how everybody is guilty and under condemnation because Adam sinned, but rather to show how all personal sin, beginning with Adam's sin, can never challenge the efficacy of Christ's salvific work begun in the believer. In short, *"where [personal] sin increased, grace abounded all the more"* (Rom 5:20).

Essentially this understanding of Rom 5:12–21 is also the hermeneutic of David L. Smith in his work on the theology of sin.[49] He begins his analysis of the passage by noting the presence of several parallels between Christ and Adam, the first of which

---

47. The verb translated "have sinned" is ἥμαρτον (*hēmarton*), which is in the aorist tense. This tense usually denotes a completed action rather than an ongoing action. Some have argued that the fact that the verb used here by Paul is aorist in tense points back to the single completed action of Adam, i.e., Adam's sin. However, the way Paul uses the verb even within Romans suggests that it can refer to a present condition that is expressed as a past event. For example, Paul says in Rom 2:12, *"For all who have sinned* (ἥμαρτον, *ēmarton*) *without the Law will also perish without the Law, and all who have sinned* (ἥμαρτον (*hēmarton*) *under the Law will be judged by the Law."* Certainly, Paul does not think all sinning was confined to the past alone. The same logic holds in Rom 3:23, *"for all have sinned* (ἥμαρτον (*hēmarton*) *and fall short of the glory of God."* Paul again couches a present condition in terms of a past event.

48. Wiley, *Original Sin*, 51.

49. See Smith, *Willful Intent*.

occurs in v. 12. In this verse both sin and death are personified. He goes on to note the mistranslation of the end of v. 12 by Augustine, who could not read Greek and therefore relied on the extant Latin translation as noted earlier. Smith comments, "Augustine's whole doctrine of original sin and inherited guilt was founded upon this mistranslation."[50] He goes on to say,

> Adam is the prototype of every human being. Just as he sinned, so does each one of us. . . . Just as death came to Adam and Eve because they sinned, it comes to all human beings because each one has sinned. The text [v. 12] does *not* say that all have sinned collectively, nor does it say that all have sinned in Adam. Paul does note that because of Adam sin and death were able to enter the world, but death has spread to all humanity because each individual has sinned.[51]

Smith concludes his exegesis of the passage by saying,

> Although there is an obvious dissimilarity between Adam and Christ, there is a definite parallel between Adam-and-humanity and Christ-and-humanity. It is in this parallel structure that we see Adam as a "type" of Christ. As human beings identify with Adam in his sin, death is their lot. As they identify with Christ in his righteousness, they receive life. It comes down to solidarity with sin or solidarity with righteousness.[52]

Essentially the same view is expressed by Warren when he says: "Adam and Messiah serve as representative heads of their respective 'kinds of mankind.' Distrust identifies with Adam; trust identifies with Christ. . . . Identification with either primary representative establishes the state of the one who identifies with him."[53]

Finally, let us consider briefly the reasons why the influential British scholar Cranfield rejected the understanding of Rom 5:12 advocated here. Cranfield holds that the reference to "all have sinned" in Rom 5:12b does indeed refer to personal sins, and so (as explained above) rejects the idea of all sinning "in Adam." However, he believes that the reason all sin personally is indeed connected with Adam because everyone has inherited Adam's post-fall corrupted nature. This seems to be an unjustified and unnecessary inference.

Cranfield provides three reasons as to why the simple affirmation that all have sinned personally and quite independently of Adam's specific sin is incorrect. The first is "it reduces the scope of the analogy between Christ and Adam to such an

---

50. Smith, *Willful Intent*, 291.

51. Smith, *Willful Intent*, 291.

52. Smith, *Willful Intent*, 295.

53. Warren, *Salvation*, 92. Warren also rightfully notes, in his observation of the parallelism in v. 18, "Many theologians have not kept Christ and Adam sufficiently parallel. Unless potentiality enters the picture on both sides, it becomes most difficult to avoid the inference that all men are in fact eternally saved in Jesus Christ as they are eternally damned in Adam." Warren, *Salvation*, 27.

extent as to virtually empty it of real significance."[54] But, while rejecting any kind of formal, organic connection with Adam for the sins of post-Adamic persons, Adam's significance is retained in that he represents the first of a long line of sinners and, in that sense, there is a close connection between the man Adam and his posterity. Consequently, Paul's analogy between Christ and Adam is still a valid comparison between sin and death introduced into the world by Adam, and the blessings introduced into the world by Christ.

A second reason given by Cranfield is that to break a formal/organic connection with Adam is to fail "to do justice to the thought of vv. 18, 19."[55] However, as noted previously, the symmetry of these verses makes the justification and righteousness of all men as certain and assured as the connection of all men in Adam (either in the Augustinian sense or in the indirect sense that Cranfield holds). Since universal salvation is generally rejected as unbiblical, the universal sinning through organic connection to Adam must be rejected too. The idea of "identification with" or "alignment with" either Adam and his sin or Christ and his righteousness would suffice to "do justice to the thought of vv. 18, 19."

A third and final reason given by Cranfield is that to restrict the connection to Adam to one of identification rather than organic connection does not do justice to "that solidarity of men with Adam which is clearly expressed in 1 Cor 15:22."[56] This seems to be a case of begging the question since Cranfield clearly understands the Corinthian text in the light of the Rom 5 passage, but this is precisely the point at issue—how should these texts be understood? Furthermore, we again have the problem of scope in the Corinthian passage—if all die because of being "in Adam" then equally all are made alive because of being "in Christ." The problem is relieved however if the connection is not one of formal solidarity, but one of identification. Those who identify with Adam and his sin (by sinning themselves, personally) gain their desert, namely death. Those who identify with Christ (through repentance and faith) gain their desert, the grace of salvation.

Theological Issues Related to the Doctrine of Original Sin

In the discussion so far on original sin, I have argued that the doctrine, as employed by Calvinists and which forms a foundational element in their soteriology, has no biblical basis. No one is held accountable for another's sin, only their own personal

---

54. Cranfield, "Interpretation of Rom 5:12," 335.

55. Cranfield, "Interpretation of Rom 5:12," 335. Verses 18 and 19 state: *"So then as through one transgression there resulted condemnation to all men, even so through one act of righteousness there resulted justification of life to all men. For as through the one man's disobedience the many were made sinners, even so through the obedience of the One the many will be made righteous."*

56. Cranfield, "Interpretation of Rom 5:12," 335. First Cor 15:22 states: *"For as in Adam all die, so also in Christ all will be made alive."*

sin. I want now to raise several theologically and biblically oriented issues which support this claim.

a) Biblical Texts That Assign Guilt Only for Personal Sins Committed

Deuteronomy 5:8–9 states: *"You shall not make for yourself an idol, or any likeness of what is in heaven above or on the earth beneath or in the water under the earth. You shall not worship them or serve them; for I, the Lord your God, am a jealous God, visiting the iniquity of the fathers on the children, and on the third and the fourth generations of those who hate Me."*

As the children of Israel were about to enter the promised land, Moses restates the heart of the covenant law, the Decalogue, on the plains of Moab. This is a necessary reminder to the new generation that was formed after forty years of wilderness journeying. The commandment referred to in vv. 8 and 9 is the second law forbidding Israel to make idols. Of interest in these two verses is the explicit mention of children's welfare resulting from the parent's sin. The effect of the parent's sin is said, not to be passed on indefinitely to their offspring as the doctrine of original sin states, but to be limited to the immediate subsequent generations of children. Unfortunately, the sins of a parent usually do have negative consequences upon the next generation. A good example today would be the poverty inflicted upon children due to a parent's alcoholism. In the case of Israel in its covenant relationship with God, idolatrous parents would not be in a position to instruct their children in the importance of obeying the covenant stipulations, with all the negative consequences that entailed for a people whose existence as a community depended upon their relationship with God. As Peter Craigie well states:

> Anything that detracted from this essential relationship, the commitment of love, led to the jealousy of God. And such false forms of worshipping the Lord inevitably had consequences for future generations, for it meant that children and grandchildren would not be instructed properly concerning the covenant relationship which was essential to their life and well-being (see Deut 4:10). Thus, in the covenant community, no man was an island: his acts had repercussions for others and the breach of this commandment could affect his posterity for more than one generation.[57]

The expanded commentary by God concerning the prohibition on idolatry here in Deut 5 clearly undermines a notion of original sin since, in the terms of original sin, the sins of the parents have enduring effect on all subsequent generations and is not limited at all.

Also, in the Mosaic law we read that the assignment of culpability was to be limited to the guilty party—not another: *"Fathers shall not be put to death for their*

---

57. Craigie, *Deuteronomy*, 154.

sons, nor shall sons be put to death for their fathers; everyone shall be put to death for his own sin" (Deut 24:16). Interestingly, in 2 Kgs 14:6 this Deuteronomic precept was explicitly applied. When Amaziah became king of Judah he put to death those servants who had slain his father Joash. But he refused to put to death the sons of the slayers citing the Deut 24 law. (This law must have been well known for the same incident is repeated in 2 Chr 25:1–4.)

In Jer 31 the same principle is upheld as seen in that a proverb that blamed a previous generation for the misfortunes of the current generation will no longer apply during the postexilic period: *"In those days they will not say again, 'The fathers have eaten sour grapes, And the children's teeth are set on edge.' But everyone will die for his own iniquity; each man who eats the sour grapes, his teeth will be set on edge"* (Jer 31:29–30).

Ezekiel, prophesying in exile, recounts the same proverb—and again, the re-joinder is made by God that only the sinning person will be held accountable for his own sin. *"Then the word of the Lord came to me, saying, 'What do you mean by using this proverb concerning the land of Israel, saying, "The fathers eat the sour grapes, But the children's teeth are set on edge"? As I live, declares the Lord God, you are surely not going to use this proverb in Israel anymore. Behold, all souls are Mine; the soul of the father as well as the soul of the son is Mine. The soul who sins will die"'* (Ezek 18:1–4, emphasis mine).

It seems that the proverb had become so well entrenched in Israelite thinking that they were surprised that God would insist that justice called for only judgment to be applied to the sinner, not the innocent party. *"Yet you say, 'Why should the son not bear the punishment for the father's iniquity?' When the son has practiced justice and righteousness and has observed all My statutes and done them, he shall surely live. The person who sins will die. The son will not bear the punishment for the father's iniquity, nor will the father bear the punishment for the son's iniquity; the righteousness of the righteous will be upon himself, and the wickedness of the wicked will be upon himself"* (Ezek 18:19–20, emphasis mine).[58]

There is no reason to suppose that the moral principle clearly stated by God in these passages would be different when applied to a distant sinner (Adam) as the doctrine of original sin requires.

Virtually every biblical reference to sin locates the source, and accompany-ing consequence, in the person or persons so accused—not to anything derived or inherited from Adam. A good example is the familiar incident involving Cain and Abel found in Gen 4:1–16. The story begins with God accepting Abel's offering and rejecting Cain's offering. As a result, Cain became angry (v. 6). This anger finds expression in Cain murdering his brother (v. 8). When confronted by God and duly punished, Cain's response is instructive. Rather than blame his sin on a corrupted

58. In fact, the whole of ch. 18 stresses personal guilt for personal sins committed in contrast to the prevailing notion of inherited guilt for the sins committed by a previous generation.

nature inherited from his father, Adam, *"Cain said to the Lord, 'My punishment is too great to bear!'"* (v. 13). In other words, Cain agreed with God's judgment and recognized that he was being justly punished for his own sinful actions, and that by his own sinful choice he was found to be guilty. No appeal was made to his father's sin to justify his own behavior.

The same principle holds with respect to the sins of national Israel. In Lev 26:1–38 the covenant blessings and curses are clearly stated to the young nation soon after the covenant was established at Mt. Sinai. The Israelites could expect blessings from God if they obeyed the covenant stipulations. Divine punishment could be expected for disobedience and covenant disloyalty.

> But if you do not obey Me and do not carry out all these commandments, if, instead, you reject My statutes, and if your soul abhors My ordinances so as not to carry out all My commandments, and so break My covenant, I, in turn, will do this to you: I will appoint over you a sudden terror. If also after these things you do not obey Me, then I will punish you seven times more for your sins. And if by these things you are not turned to Me, but act with hostility against Me then I will act with hostility against you. (Lev 26:14–23)

Clearly national sin is seen to be due to the sinful decisions and choices of its citizens which they willfully choose to make. These stipulations would not make sense if their sinning was unavoidable due to a corrupted nature inherited from Adam. It would not be just for God to exact punishment for unavoidable behavior.

Another example is seen in Ezekiel 14:

> Then the word of the Lord came to me saying, "Son of man, if a country sins against Me by committing unfaithfulness, and I stretch out My hand against it, destroy its supply of bread, send famine against it and cut off from it both man and beast, even though these three men, Noah, Daniel and Job were in its midst, by their own righteousness they could only deliver themselves," declares the Lord God. "If I were to cause wild beasts to pass through the land and they depopulated it, and it became desolate so that no one would pass through it because of the beasts, though these three men were in its midst, as I live," declares the Lord God, "they could not deliver either their sons or their daughters. They alone would be delivered, but the country would be desolate." (Ezek 14:12–16)

Here again is the operating principle when it comes to punishment for sin: only the guilty party, those actually committing the sins, would be held accountable for their actions. Even the righteous (Noah, Daniel, Job) could not cancel the consequences of the personal sins of another.[59] Just as the righteousness of a Noah or Daniel could not "deliver either their sons or their daughters," so neither could appeal be made to the sins of another (Adam) to absolve responsibility for the people's own sins.

59. There is such a category of persons as "righteous." These are only *relatively* righteous, they are not righteous in an absolute sense—only God is righteous absolutely.

Sometimes, Adam's sin is used as an example or illustration—but, significantly, not a source—of Israel's sins, as in Hos 6:7: *"But like Adam they have transgressed the covenant; There they have dealt treacherously against Me."*

One of the clearest expressions concerning the source of sin is found in the book of James. In Jas 1:14–16 we read: *"But each one is tempted when he is carried away and enticed by his own lust. Then when lust has conceived, it gives birth to sin; and when sin is accomplished, it brings forth death. Do not be deceived, my beloved brethren."*

James makes clear that the source of sin resides in the human heart—"in his own lust." If James was aware of the notion of original sin as entailing guilt for Adam's sin and an inherited corrupted human nature it would be very strange for James to completely ignore such states when discussing the source of evil. Furthermore, such notions would strongly undermine his purpose—locating responsibility for personal sins clearly with the person and within the human heart, and not connected in any way with the sins of another. "The point of emphasis here is to fasten moral responsibility on the individual. . . . James's main purpose is to trace the genealogy of sin no further than to the person tempted by [lusts]."[60] Verse 16 is important too for our purposes here. James urges his readers to "not be deceived" into thinking God is the source of temptations that lead to sin—on the contrary, God, the Father of lights, is the source of only good. Just as his readers were not to blame God for their temptation to lust, even more so, they should not blame another (Adam) for their predicament. It is inconceivable that James would hold to the idea of original sin and fail to address the possible excuse his readers would have to blame Adam for their sinning. "The nub of the problem James addresses is that when his readers are caught in the throes of evil conditions it will not do to blame either God or others. . . . Individual accountability is at the root of the matter."[61]

James's teaching above was also taught by Jesus: *"And He was saying, 'That which proceeds out of the man, that is what defiles the man. For from within, out of the heart of men, proceed the evil thoughts, fornications, thefts, murders, adulteries'"* (Mark 7:20). The Bible consistently locates the source of sin as residing in the human heart, the person himself, and makes no attempt to go beyond this for a yet additional explanation beyond the person. It would comprise a major oversight, even a contradiction, if in fact, the ultimate source of evil lay in another (Adam).

b) Further Considerations of Romans 5:12–21

I have already noted that the Rom 5 passage is the most persuasive in support of some notion of original sin. It is appealed to by all who support such a doctrine. While a fairly detailed response has been given above, there are some additional aspects of the passage that warrant more thought.

60. Martin, *James*, 36.

61. Martin, *James*, 37.

A key consideration is the reason Paul wrote vv. 12–21. What was Paul seeking to do in these verses? Murray addresses this question head on and, after noting that Paul is still dealing with the grand theme of justification by faith, answers the question by asserting that the apostle in vv. 12–21 seeks to show that the principle of solidarity holds: "The apostle is now demonstrating that the divine method of justifying the ungodly proceeds from and is necessitated by the principles in terms of which God governs the human race. God governs men and relates himself to men in terms of solidaric relationship."[62]

Just as salvation is found in solidarity with Christ, so condemnation is found in solidarity with Adam. This approach is the opposite to the one I have adopted where I emphasize the individual's sin as the cause for condemnation. A problem with the solidaric perspective, typical of most Calvinistic approaches, is that whereas solidarity with Christ is gained on the basis of voluntary association (by faith), solidarity with Adam is completely involuntary. This raises the serious issue of God's justice (discussed below). Another problem with Murray's answer to the question of purpose is that it does not give due weight to the immediate context, vv. 1–11, where the apostle stresses not only justification but many other blessings to be found associated with the salvation Christ has brought. Paul's point is not solidarity with Christ but rather the blessings that union with Christ brings for believers.

Another answer to the question of why Paul wrote vv. 12–21 is given by the Arminian Jack Cottrell. "This passage is best understood as continuing the theme of assurance that began with 5:1."[63] From what has been said so far in his epistle Paul makes clear the power of the gospel to save all who would turn to Christ. This raises the question "How could what one man did at one time in history have such an absolute effect on mankind?"[64] In answering this question Paul appeals to the scope of Adam's act on his posterity.

> In order to show that this is not as far-fetched as we might at first think, Paul calls attention to the man whose one act has already been demonstrated to have a universal effect upon the human race, namely, Adam. Then he uses this by way of comparison and contrast to show that the "one righteous act" of the one man, Jesus, will surely be just as efficacious and universal as the "one sinful act" of the one man, Adam—and even "much more" (5:15, 17).[65]

Cottrell's approach has the advantage of seeking to take the immediate context into account. However, he, like Murray above, holds to the notion of solidarity. Unsaved humanity as a whole is viewed as being "in Adam" while saved humanity is viewed as

---

62. Murray, *Romans*, 179.

63. Cottrell, *Romans*, 1:530.

64. Cottrell, *Romans*, 1:530.

65. Cottrell, *Romans*, 1:530.

being "in Christ."[66] The problem with any notion of solidarity has been noted above in connection with Murray. Furthermore, Cottrell, can affirm universal inclusion of all "in Adam" and all being in Christ because of his view of original grace—that even before birth the universal effect of Christ's saving work has been applied to all and that consequently every person is born with a clean slate—Adam's sin has been dealt with universally. (Cottrell's approach would result in universalism, the idea that everyone is saved by "original grace," if he failed to emphasize that no one in fact remains in this state of original grace due to subsequent personal sinning following an age of account-ability.) While Cottrell's solution seeks to take seriously the universality of verses like vv. 15 and 17, there does seem to be a speculative element in his approach that makes one uncomfortable. Nowhere in Rom 5:12–21 does Paul explicitly address a concept of "original grace"; Cottrell infers it from the passage.

My own answer to the question of Paul's purpose in writing 5:12–21 would rely heavily on Paul's teaching in the immediately preceding verses (1–11) without losing sight of his broader message throughout the letter up to this point. In Rom 1, Paul establishes the guilt of the Gentiles for their sin. This is followed in ch. 2, where God's impartiality is stressed. Anyone, including the Jews, who sins will be subject to divine condemnation: *"For all who have sinned without the Law will also perish without the Law, and all who have sinned under the Law will be judged by the Law"* (2:12). Chapter 3 reinforces the universality of sin—all have in fact sinned. In this chapter Paul introduces his solution to universal sin—justification by grace through faith. Chapter 4 shows us that this principle of justifying faith was operative under the old covenant too—as illustrated in the case of Abraham. It is important to stress that in these four chapters, while a lot has been said about sin, there is not a hint that the cause of this sin is rooted in anything other than personal choices and attitudes; there is no hint of a theory of original sin to account for the sins of Jew and Gentile. Personal sin, and personal sin alone is stressed.

Romans 5 opens with a brief recounting of the blessings flowing from justifica-tion by faith—peace with God, hope of the glory of God, and future hope. Paul then shifts to the basis for such blessings—Jesus Christ and his work accomplished on behalf of the justified. There is a distinct focus on the person of Christ—Christ died for the ungodly (5:6), Christ died for sinners (v. 8), salvation secured through the life of Christ (v. 10), reconciliation with God is through Christ (v. 11). Now, in vv. 12–19, Paul continues and intensifies this focus on Christ by contrasting those who are identified with Christ (by faith) with those who are identified with Adam simply by being sinners. In other words, *Adam functions in this passage as a foil with which to amplify and glory in the work and blessings of Christ.* As in the preceding verses, Paul's focus is on Christ, but he amplifies Christ and the blessings he brought by contrasting the person Christ with the person Adam. Just as those who identify with Christ (Christians) receive the blessings of salvation, those who continue to

---

66. Cottrell holds to federal headship.

identify with the forerunner of sinners (Adam) receive condemnation, judgment and death. Christians are those who are aligned with the forerunner and founder of their salvation, Christ; Adam is the founder (the prototype) of those who remain in their unforgiven sins and who suffer the consequences.[67] Paul is using Adam as a shorthand for the whole human race outside of Christ.[68] Rather surprisingly, from a Calvinistic perspective, nowhere in this passage does Paul use the terms "in Adam" or "in Christ"—and nowhere is the *cause* of man's sins attributed to Adam. It serves Paul's polemic by condensing all of sinful humanity under the heading of the first sinner, Adam, since it is Paul's primary purpose to highlight the work and blessings of the second man (1 Cor 15:47), the man Christ Jesus.

c) Original Sin and the Justice of God

Another issue related to the doctrine of original sin concerns the justice of God. The Bible is very clear, God is a just and righteous God. One need look no further than God's dealings with the ancient kings of Israel. Where there was idolatry and injustice, God responded in righteous judgment. A good example is when Ahab, the king of the northern kingdom of Israel, acquired his neighbor Naboth's vineyard essentially by force and through violence, God's judgment comes to him through the prophet Elijah: *"Ahab said to Elijah, 'Have you found me, O my enemy?' And he answered, 'I have found you, because you have sold yourself to do evil in the sight of the Lord. Behold, I will bring evil upon you, and will utterly sweep you away, and will cut off from Ahab every male, both bond and free in Israel'"* (1 Kgs 21:20–21).

Throughout the Bible, the justice of God is clearly seen as an essential attribute—God is not partial in his dealings with men; he is perfectly fair (Lev 19:15; Deut 16:19; Matt 22:16; Acts 10:34; Rom 2:11, etc.). However, the doctrine of original sin calls into question the justice of God. Is it really the case that "when Adam sinned, God thought of all who would descend from Adam as sinners"?[69] To view those not yet born "as sinners" is a repudiation of the justice of God. We have already seen that there are several passages where the question of assigning blame for sin is to be restricted only to the person committing the sin. This is patently just. It would be patently unjust to hold that God himself is "above the (moral) law" in this respect.

The contrast between God's justice and the doctrine of original sin can be seen in this quote from Calvin: "The first man fell because the Lord deemed it meet that

---

67. "Each man by his own sin has identified himself with First Adam, thus joining 'the company of the condemned.' . . . By acting faith each man identifies himself with Second Adam, thus joining 'the company of the committed.'" Warren, *Salvation*, 178.

68. Wibbing makes essentially the same point: "Adam's act of disobedience has binding results for all; they stand there as sinners. . . . Adam here is a representative of 'man' used to illustrate the fact of man's being a 'sinner' because of his disobedience." Wibbing, "Determine, Appoint, Present," 1:472.

69. Grudem, *Systematic Theology*, 494.

he should."[70] Calvin, like most Calvinists today, insists that everything that happens flows from the decree of God—including the fall of Adam. Many non-Calvinists consequently conclude that God is effectively the author of sin. Calvin also insists that "God not only foresaw the fall of the first man, and in him the ruin of his posterity, but also *at his own pleasure arranged it*."[71] Now compare Calvin's view with that of the psalmist: "*The Lord is righteous in all His ways, and kind in all His deeds*" (Ps 145:17). The difference could not be plainer.

Grudem is aware of this objection and provides three responses. The first is to assert that "everyone who protests that this [imputing Adam's sin to his posterity] is unfair has also voluntarily committed many actual sins for which God holds us guilty."[72] However, this observation is irrelevant to the question of original sin—no one disputes the assignment of guilt for personal sins committed; it is the assignment of guilt for Adam's sin that is at issue. Second, anyone in Adam's place would have sinned as Adam did anyway. Again, this speculation is irrelevant—it does not address the actual alleged assignment of Adam's guilt to his posterity. Even Grudem acknowledges this argument is so weak as to "not help very much to lessen someone's sense of unfairness."[73] Third, and Grudem's "most persuasive answer" is "that if we think it is unfair for us to be represented by Adam, then we should also think it unfair for us to be represented by Christ and to have his righteousness imputed to us by God."[74] Grudem here begs the question, for he assumes that the imputation of Adam's guilt is precisely the same as the imputation of Christ's righteousness—but this assumption is exactly what is being questioned. The symmetry in Grudem's argument would be valid only if the application of an arbitrary solidarity held for both Adam and Christ. But while Calvinists like Grudem would admit that an arbitrary solidarity[75] exists in the case of Adam, they would deny that an arbitrary solidarity exists between believers and Christ. For anyone to have Adam as their representative[76] requires nothing on the part of any individual, but to have Christ as a believer's representative is conditional on a conscious decision to repent and believe the gospel, to exercise faith. Grudem's point would have validity only if there was unconditionality in both cases, Adam's and Christ. While there is an aspect of injustice for God to unconditionally impute Adam's

---

70. Calvin, *Institutes*, 3.23.8.

71. Calvin, *Institutes*, 3.23.7, emphasis mine.

72. Grudem, *Systematic Theology*, 495.

73. Grudem, *Systematic Theology*, 495.

74. Grudem, *Systematic Theology*, 495.

75. By arbitrary solidarity I mean that God was not forced to assign Adam's guilt to his posterity—this was something God chose to do for no obvious reason. Solidarity merely expresses the idea of unity between Adam and the whole of subsequent humanity.

76. Nowhere in the Bible are we explicitly told that Adam is our formal representative, though admittedly, it may be possible to argue that such is the case based on passages like Rom 5:12–21.

sin and associated guilt to men, there is nothing unjust about assigning Christ's righteousness to those who choose to align with Christ by faith.[77]

d) Original Sin and the Problem of Connection to Adam

Another problem relating to a concept of original sin concerns exactly how the guilt and corrupted nature allegedly passed on from Adam to his posterity is actually transmitted. Smith is quite right in noting that "scholars can agree that Adam's transgression has some bearing on the universality of sin. But there is very little agreement on exactly what the link is, or on how sin is communicated from one person to another."[78]

Traditionally there have been three basic possibilities: federal headship (also known as representative headship), realism, and seminal transmission.[79] The first, as mentioned earlier, entails understanding that Adam was formally designated to be humanity's representative. Horton, for example, says this about Calvin on this point: "Calvin refuses to become mired in the finer historical debates over the transmission of the soul from one generation to another, content to assert with Scripture that Adam stood as the covenantal representative for the human race."[80] A major problem with this view is that nowhere in Scripture is Adam so designated! It is merely an inference, usually drawn from the comparison between Christ and Adam in Rom 5:12–21. It is valid to draw inferences in constructing one's theology, however, the paucity of biblical data available to draw such an important inference is definitely troubling.[81] This sounds suspiciously like an inference generated to bolster a preexisting theology of original sin.

---

77. Erickson, *Christian Theology*, 635, explains federal headship thus: "Adam . . . was our representative. God ordained that Adam should act not only on his own behalf, but also on our behalf. The consequences of his actions have been passed on to his descendants as well. Adam was on probation for all of us as it were; and because Adam sinned, all of us are treated guilty and corrupted." The speculative nature of this theory is clear. Nowhere in the Bible is this construct taught.

78. Smith, *Willful Intent*, 358.

79. Federal headship is the more common understanding today and is linked most easily with the idea of imputation—God imputing, counting toward someone, the effects of Adam's sin (guilt and moral corruption). The difficulty of this question of methodology of assignment of Adam's sin is seen in that most of the Calvinist works consulted thus far in this study do not address the question—preferring merely to assume it. Zemek helpfully distinguishes three theories of connection: (1) the strictly realistic view (seminal headship), (2) the strictly representational view (federal headship), (3) the mediate imputation view. Zemek, *Biblical Theology*, 89.

80. Horton, *For Calvinism*, 40. Horton himself nowhere discusses the how question—how is Adam's sin assigned to his posterity.

81. Not every doctrine in Scripture needs to be explicitly stated; the doctrine of the Trinity is a good example. However, unlike the doctrine of the Trinity, which can be inferred from many passages in Scripture, the doctrine of federal headship as the mechanism of assignment for Adam's sin can only be appealed to from one passage (Rom 5). Surely, such a foundational doctrine as original sin would be expected to be either explicitly taught or, at the least, implicitly taught throughout the New Testament, but it is not; personal sin is, but not original sin.

The theory of *realism* seeks to explain why God holds every individual subsequent to Adam guilty and suffering the consequences of his disobedience. Here the role of human nature itself is important. In the words of David Smith: "The theory of Realism teaches that all human nature existed in Adam prior to his transgression. When he sinned, therefore, the common human nature that was in him fell too. Thus, Adam's act of disobedience was quite literally the disobedience of all humanity."[82] Millard Erickson holds to this view:

> We were present in germinal or seminal form in our ancestors; in a very real sense, we were there in Adam. His action was not merely that of one isolated individual, but of the entire human race. Although we were not there individually, we were nonetheless there. The human race sinned as a whole. Thus, there is nothing unfair or improper about our receiving a corrupted nature and guilt from Adam, for we are receiving the just results of our sin.[83]

This theory has several problems as an attempt to explain the connection between a contemporary person and Adam's sin. First, what exactly is meant when the claim is made that "all human nature existed in Adam"? How can all human nature exist in one person? Is the concept even coherent—does it make sense? Second, this theory suffers the same problems associated with the federal view; there is no supporting biblical data for the theory. It appears as though its proponents are implying that God set up this arrangement. But this seems like an arbitrary assignment made to fit a preexisting theory of original sin. Finally, such an arrangement like all theories that arbitrarily connect Adam's act to the contemporary person, were it true would violate the justice of God. Smith sums up this problem well:

> [Realism] makes God appear to be vindictive and arbitrary. If we who are sinful human beings would not punish anyone who committed a wrongful act but who was incapable of responsibility, God who is perfect in His character and justice would not condemn his creatures for an act they supposedly perpetrated before they were even born.[84]

---

82. Smith, *Willful Intent*, 360.

83. Erickson, *Christian Theology*, 635. The language here of being present in Adam effectively seems, in some sense, to literally locate the individual in Adam and his actions. Sometimes appeal is made to the similar concept of corporate solidarity as seen, e.g., in Heb 7:9–10. In this passage the author, in desiring to demonstrate the greatness of Christ, appeals to the incident when Abraham gave tithes to the mysterious figure Melchizedek. *"And, so to speak, through Abraham even Levi, who received tithes, paid tithes, for he was still in the loins of his father when Melchizedek met him."* In a similar way, some Calvinists argue that everyone was "in Adam" when he sinned, and from birth suffer the consequences of Adam's sin—guilt and corrupted nature. However, we are told explicitly that some die due to transgressions that were *"not . . . in the likeness of the offense of Adam"* (Rom 5:14). If all die because "in Adam" then there would be no way that anyone could avoid transgressing *"in the likeness of the offense of Adam."*

84. Smith, *Willful Intent*, 361. Smith himself rejects any sense of Adam's guilt being passed on from Adam onward. He does, however, hold that Adam's sin had an effect similar to a virus in human nature—providing a tendency to sin in all subsequent humanity.

The *biological transmission* view holds that the negative effects of Adam's sinning is passed on from generation to generation sexually, through physical intercourse.[85] Sin is considered to be passed on from Adam to his posterity biologically. Since no current person was literally present when Adam sinned some mechanism needs to connect a current person to a preexistent person "in Adam." That mechanism must be physical transmission through procreation. This view is not without its difficulties.

The advantage of this model is that it is at least intuitively reasonable and is something that can be fairly easily grasped.[86] A major problem with biological transmission, however, is that it fails to explain how *physical* descent can transmit *spiritual* and *moral* conditions such as guilt and moral corruption. The assumption here appears to be that spiritual and moral categories cohere with a person's genes. This is like saying I have a genetic disposition to lying. Not many would agree with this claim. While physical descent from Adam (and Eve) can be easily grasped, moral or spiritual qualities transmitted by natural descent seems quite problematic. Furthermore, were such moral and spiritual traits passed on from individual to individual then why would not humanity after Noah be viewed as having his righteousness passed on to them?[87]

The difficulties connected with this question of connection to Adam is reflected in Augustine's own views on the matter, particularly as it relates to the question of the soul's transmission. "Augustine was inclined to reject 'traducianism'—the doctrine that the soul is transmitted from parents to children—and to uphold 'creationism'—the doctrine that God directly creates a soul for each individual. On the other hand, the difficulties that creationism posed for an understanding of original sin led Augustine back to traducianism. On this point, he remained hesitant throughout his life."[88]

In sum, all the theories examined here as means of identifying the current person with Adam's sin do more than hint at theological expediency, appear to make God act arbitrarily, and violate the clear principle discussed earlier that only the actually sinning person is morally responsible for his own sin and cannot be held responsible for the sins of another. Furthermore, the variety of theories put forward by theologians down the years testify to the lack of biblical warrant explaining the alleged connection between Adam's sin and his posterity.

---

85. Related to this idea is the question of the origin of the soul. From whence does an individual's soul arise? The two basic options are (1) from parent to child seminally, or (2) a special new creation for each individual at conception. Biological transmission and realism are usually allied with the former, while federal representative aligns more often with the latter.

86. Heb 7:9, 10 may be an example of such a connection.

87. "Noah was a righteous man, blameless in his time; Noah walked with God." Gen 6:9.

88. Gonzalez, *History of Christian Thought*, 2:45.

e) The Influence of Augustine on This Doctrine

An appreciation for the historical setting in which a key theological idea is developed is crucial both to understanding the idea itself, but also in alerting the reader to the real possibility of theological distortion in a non-biblical direction due to the historical circumstances prevailing at the time. Anizor addresses this concern when he writes: "The historical context of the ideas of an individual or community is not merely dispensable background material to understanding those ideas: the evaluation of those ideas cannot proceed on the basis of the questionable assumption that thought is a socially disembodied process dealing with essentially timeless issues."[89] Assessing the validity of a particular doctrinal formulation, especially a relatively novel one as introduced into Christian theology by Augustine, cannot be accomplished apart from an appreciation for the prevailing historical milieu in which the doctrine is developed. "Like every other human action, theology is contextual; it is a decidedly human act that takes place within a particular historical, social, cultural, and ecclesial setting."[90]

As discussed in chapter 1, Augustine's influence upon classical Christian theology cannot be exaggerated. This is especially the case with respect to the doctrine of original sin. We have good reasons to be suspicious of the doctrine first, because it was largely developed by Augustine in his disputes with Pelagius.[91] Pelagius espoused the anthropology I am holding here—especially on the accountability of each person for their own sins and not because of any supposed connection to Adam and his sin.[92] Augustine reacted very strongly against this view. As is so often the case with public disputes the responder tends to exaggerate his position in order to clearly differentiate himself from his opponent and reinforce his own position. Only later, in the case of theological historical disputes sometimes centuries later, is the exaggerated swing recognized and a more balanced and nuanced—and biblically faithful—position reached.

Second, Augustine was greatly influenced in his understanding of God's grace and its workings by his own conversion experience which was sudden and dramatic.

89. Anizor, *Read Theology*, 28. On p. 77 of the same work, and in a discussion on the problem of proof-texting for doctrinal formulation, Anizor reinforces this point hermeneutically: "We can become blinded by, for example, the controversies of the past, so that we interpret passages from the Bible chiefly in light of those controversies rather than in light of their immediate [biblical literary] context."

90. Anizor, *Read Theology*, 29.

91. This can be seen, e.g., in the church historian Henry Chadwick's comment to the effect that, following the initial skirmishes between Pelagius and his detractors, "the theological discussion, however, was far from being concluded, and it was only at this stage that Augustine began to give a really full exposition of his theology of grace." Chadwick, *Early Church*, 231.

92. There were other aspects of Pelagius's views which I do not espouse—for example, that death is a natural part of human existence as opposed to a consequence of sinning, or that the souls of babies who die prematurely go to any sort of middle place—not heaven and not hell. I am only agreeing with Pelagius that there is no necessary and causal connection between Adam's sin and our own sinning today.

In particular, because of the personal context in which Augustine was saved, namely that of being a flagrant and utterly depraved sinner, he was convinced that God was responsible not only for providing for salvation in the sending of his Son, but also of effecting salvation in Augustine's own life. Thus, in theological terms, he became convinced that salvation was monergistic—all of God—and that the individual's role in appropriating salvation was effectively insignificant. Grace was sovereign and the human response itself a gift from God.[93] A theology of sin so highly influenced by personal experience ought to be viewed suspiciously.[94] It is what the Bible actually teaches that is decisive.

Third, as noted in chapter 1, Augustine based his understanding of the one key passage in the entire Bible that could be used to justify an appeal to some sort of original sin (Rom 5:12) on a faulty translation of the Greek into Latin. Since Augustine could not read New Testament Greek, he was dependent on this faulty translation which read "in whom all sinned" instead of the correct translation "because all sinned."[95] So, Augustine argued his position based on the mistaken understanding that the Bible taught that all sinned in Adam, whereas the text merely says that all sinned—period. To be consistent with the rest of Scripture, the assumption must be that all sinned personally.[96]

Finally, Augustine's influence on modern discussions of original sin stem largely from the incorporation of his view in ecumenical church councils of his day—especially the Council of Carthage in AD 418. This point is discussed further below. Suffice to note here is the role these councils played in subsequent Christian theology. Due to Augustine's influence as both a churchman and theologian coupled with the incorporation of his view of the relationship between Adam's sin and his posterity, Christian orthodoxy subsequent to these early church councils includes the notion of original sin. The validity of this position will be examined below.

Bearing all these factors in mind, therefore, the student of the Bible must be cautious in accepting unquestioningly Augustine's understanding of sin with respect to its

93. According to Chadwick, Julian of Eclanum, a contemporary of Augustine thought that "Augustine had brought his Manachee ways of thinking into the church [and] . . . was under the influence of a hagridden attitude to sex resulting from the adolescent follies described in The Confessions." Chadwick, *Early Church*, 231.

94. Gonzales, *History of Christian Thought*, 2:63, remarking upon the conclusions of the Council of Orange in 529 on the brink of the medieval period states that "the overwhelming and dynamic experience set forth in the Confessions is being transformed into an entire system of grace—a process that was perhaps inevitable, but nonetheless unfortunate."

95. "According to the doctrine that Augustine opposed to the Pelagians, the entire race fell in Adam (*the Latin version of Rom 5:12 said so* [my emphasis])." Chadwick, *Early Church*, 232. See also my earlier critique of Rom 5:12–21.

96. E.g., Rom 3:23. Interestingly, precisely the same Greek wording is used in this passage, πάντες γαρ ἥμαρτον (*pantes gar hēmarton*), "for all have sinned," as in Rom 5:12, ἐφ ᾧ πάντες ἥμαρτον (*eph ō pantes hēmarton*), "for all have sinned." There is no disputing the fact that Paul is addressing the issue of personal sin in Rom 3.

alleged connection to Adam's sin. This cautionary note is even more pertinent in that until Augustine, the church "was reluctant to attribute the guilt of Adam to humanity in general and to children in particular."[97] This last point, the novelty of Augustine's view of the effect of Adam's sin on his posterity, is worth underscoring. Prior to Augustine, the early church fathers, generally speaking, did not hold to a doctrine of original sin as this extended quote from the Reformed theologian Louis Berkhof indicates:

> [The anthropology of the early Greek Fathers had] a preponderant emphasis on doctrines which show a manifest affinity with the later teachings of Pelagius rather than with those of Augustine. In a measure, it may be said, they prepared the way for Pelagianism. . . . Their view of sin, particularly at first, was largely influenced by their opposition to Gnosticism with its emphasis on the physical necessity of evil and its denial of the freedom of the will. . . . Adam could sin and did sin, and thus came under the power of Satan, death and sinful corruption. This physical corruption was propagated in the human race, but is not itself sin and did not involve mankind in guilt. *There is no original sin in the strict sense of the word.* They do not deny the solidarity of the human race, but admit its physical connection with Adam. This connection, however, relates only to the corporeal and sensuous nature, which is propagated from father to son, and not to the higher and rational side of human nature, which is in every case a direct creation of God. It exerts no immediate effect on the will, but affects this only mediately through the intellect. *Sin always originates in the free choice of man,* and is the result of weakness and ignorance. Consequently, infants cannot be regarded as guilty, for they have inherited only a physical corruption.[98]

f) The Universality of Sin as Justification for a Doctrine of Original Sin

A powerful impetus toward the acceptance of original sin is found in the universality of sin both throughout history and throughout a given population at any time. For example, after noting the references to Gen 3 in Rom 5:12–21, Shuster remarks, "The rest of the OT, however, does not lack support for the idea of original sin, in the sense that it depicts all as sinful (hardly a likely outcome were there no predisposition to sin")[99] She then goes on to cite several OT passages underscoring the universality of sin (Eccl 7:20; 1 Kgs 8:46; Ps 130:3; Isa 53:6, etc.).

The universality of human sin is also a feature of the New Testament—notably in Rom 3:10–17. The sentiment is succinctly summarized by Paul in v. 23: *"All have sinned and fall short of the glory of God."*

97. Allison, *Historical Theology*, 345.

98. Berkhof, *History of Christian Doctrine*, 128, emphases mine.

99. Shuster, *Fall and Sin*, 172.

The paucity of biblical support for a doctrine of original sin is indirectly acknowledged by Shuster when, in a section of her book titled "The Biblical Basis of the Doctrine of Original Sin," she only appeals to Rom 5:12 and the universality of sin—and nothing else![100]

We shall return to this observation of the universality of sin later when considering the Calvinist's understanding of depravity. At this point, suffice to say that, absent any explicit, unambiguous supporting teaching to the contrary, there is absolutely no necessary connection between the universality of sin and Adam's sin.[101] Original sin is an inference associated with these texts on the universality of sin that fits well with Calvinist soteriology. It is an exercise in eisegesis. In short, appeal to the universality of sin says nothing concerning the origins of the sin. (Though, as noted earlier, the Bible does clearly locate the origin of sin in the human heart, and not in the sin of another [Jas 1:14, 15].) If Adam and Eve could sin while living in, literally, a paradise completely devoid of sin, and while experiencing God's intimate presence as witnessed by God's walking in the cool of the evening, and hearing God's voice directly, then the likelihood of subsequent generations sinning, subsequent to the curse upon creation, would seem to be virtually unavoidable.

g) The Council of Carthage in AD 418

In the early church, following the edict of Emperor Constantine in AD 312 and before the fall of Rome to the northern pagans, controversial church doctrines were often developed in the context of a complex dynamic involving regional church leaders, bishops, priests, popes, synods, and emperors! The latter often carried great influence and the emperor's favorable view would have been sought in order to influence the dispute one way or another.[102] Strong convictions and strong personalities also abounded.

"In the year 418–19, all canons formerly made in sixteen councils held at Carthage, [and] one at Milevis, [and] one at Hippo, that were approved of, were read, and received

---

100. After acknowledging it is not found explicitly anywhere in the Old Testament and after acknowledging her heavy dependence on the New Testament, Shuster says, "We consider Paul's particular appropriation of Genesis 3 in Romans 5:12 to be highly significant. . . . [This is] about as close as one could come to affirming original sin without actually using the term." Shuster, *Fall and Sin*, 172.

101. Some might counter that there is no explicit reference to the Trinity in the Bible and yet the doctrine is clearly present. In other words, a concept might be present even though there are no explicit references to it. This is quite true of course. However, with nearly every major theological construct (such as the Trinity or the divinity of Christ, or the personhood of the Holy Spirit) there is a wealth of clear, unambiguous biblical data supporting the concept. This is most definitely not the case with the idea of original sin. A straightforward reading of the New Testament would inevitably lead one to conclude that the Father is God, the Son is God, and the Holy Spirit is God; the same volume of supporting texts cannot be said concerning original sin. In fact, with respect to the latter, only personal sin would describe the many references to sin in the Bible.

102. A good account of this politico-religious dynamic can be seen in Chadwick's account of the Pelagian controversy in his *Early Church*, 227–35.

a new sanction from a great number of bishops, then met in synod at Carthage. This Collection is the Code of the African Church." So begins the introduction to a listing of 138 canons (theological statements/affirmations).[103] Most of these canons were generated earlier than AD 418, the earliest being AD 345, but they were solemnly reaffirmed at Carthage in AD 418 by the bishops then present. It was at this council specifically that Pelagius's views of sin and grace were declared to be anathema.

Interestingly, it is within the context of the need for infants to be baptized for the remission of sins, a point that Pelagius denied, that the condemnation for the denial of original sin occurs. I shall look more closely into the connection between a doctrine of original sin and infant baptism below, but for the moment I wish to point out that, while appeal to this council is made by Calvinists to reinforce the idea that original sin was upheld by the early church, the council also upheld beliefs as orthodox that many Christians today would find objectionable. These would include:

- The call to celibacy on the part of church leaders (Canon 3).

- That church leaders should abstain from sex with their wives (Canons 4, 25, and 70).

- The need for a bishop to be ordained by a minimum of three other bishops (Canon 13); obviously, a formal, hierarchical form of church government is presupposed.

- Any church leader who, upon being charged with a crime, refused to be judged by an ecclesiastical body choosing rather to be judged by a secular court, would automatically lose his office (Canon 15).

- Certain church officers were required to make a declaration of intent to be celibate or to marry. "Also, it seemed good that Readers when they come to years of puberty, should be compelled either to take wives or else to profess continence" (Canon 16).

- That the sons of clergy should not marry heretics (Canon 21).

- No church leader was to give any of their possessions away to non-Christians—even to their own relatives (Canon 22).

- Included with the canonical Scriptures were the apocryphal books of Tobit, Judith, Maccabees (Canon 24).

- No bishop or clergyman was to be ordained unless he had made all his family Christians: "None shall be ordained bishop, presbyters, or deacons before all the inmates of their houses shall have become Catholic Christians" (Canon 36).

- No feasts were to be had in any church (Canon 42).

- A sick person who is too ill to speak is to be baptized (Canon 45).

- Theatrical spectacles (shows) were not to be held on Sundays (Canon 61).

103. Knight, "New Advent Introductory Note to Nicene and Post-Nicene Fathers," line 1.

- Spouses who fail to remain separated from their partner and seek to marry another should do penance. The counsel also stipulated that "an imperial law be promulgated" to this effect (Canon 102).

- Slaves, freedmen, heretics, heathens, and Jews are not permitted to bring an accusation against a church official (Canon 128).

The point in noting all these canons is twofold: First, at this early stage in church history, we clearly see the establishment of what would later become known as Roman Catholicism. Many of these canons would be rejected at the Reformation, for example the call to celibacy on the part of church leaders and the inclusion of apocryphal books in the biblical canon. Second, many Protestant Christians would have no compulsion in rejecting outright most of the canons noted above. Those of Free Church persuasion would incline to reject infant baptism. This shows that, historically, not every doctrine or precept advocated by the Counsel of Carthage was necessarily accepted as binding by Christians of later generations. Therefore, to reject the counsel's proclamations on Pelagianism (Canons 108–16) need not, in principle, automatically imply genuine heresy. The ultimate arbiter of Christian truth is not the judgments of councils in church history, but the biblical teachings and evidences. Councils and their pronouncements are historical documents and the Council of Carthage is no exception. They reflect the historical circumstances of their day—witness the reference to slaves, the conflating of Jews with heathens, the celebration of church feasts, etc. Council pronouncements are not, unlike Scripture, infallible statements necessarily reflecting the mind of God.

h) Scripture and Tradition

The relationship between Scripture and Tradition is a complex one and functions subtly in the previous discussion concerning the Council of Carthage.[104] While Scripture is foundational, often in the history of the church ecclesiastical bodies have felt the need to support Scripture with contemporary formulations designed to make clear the teaching of Scripture. The motive for such moves is varied; to counter heresies, to formulate succinctly the teachings of Scripture on a particular topic or doctrine, to clarify the boundaries of acceptable beliefs that are presumed consistent with Scripture, and so on.

While virtually all truly Christian bodies recognize the supreme role given to Scripture with respect to what the church is required to believe and practice, a potential problem can arise when a Tradition can subtly become elevated to the status of Scripture in practice, even if not in theory. Here the Tradition inexorably moves from

---

104. By Tradition (with a capital T) I refer to the ecumenical councils, church councils, creeds, and confessions formulated over the past centuries of the Christian church.

a servant of Scripture to its master.[105] Now, the believer is required to accept, affirm, and adhere to not only Scripture, but also the Tradition. Within the Catholic tradition this process has been formalized in the church's Magisterium—that body of teaching officially recognized as embodying Christian truth. Within Lutheranism, the Formula of Concord serves the same purpose; within Calvinism the Westminster Confession of Faith serves as the supporting Tradition. Here the Tradition serves a dual purpose; first to purportedly support Scripture,[106] and second to provide a body of teaching that serves to identify that particular Christian body.

The problem outlined in the previous paragraph is not insignificant. When a Tradition or specific theological formulation is elevated to the status of Scripture, even when done with the conviction that the Tradition accurately reflects the teachings of Scripture, the danger is that Scripture is no longer allowed to speak for itself—God's word has now been qualified by man's formulations. What the Bible is understood to be saying must now be consistent with the associated Tradition. The invalidity of such a move arises from the fact that the Tradition is always, and cannot help but be, a historically bound statement. This in turn, it seems to me, must, at least potentially and to some extent, lead to historically induced distortions of the Tradition as an accurate guide to Scripture. This means that the Tradition should be listened to, its teachings carefully noted, but that these should never be fossilized and considered inviolable and unchangeable teachings. Worse, the Tradition should never be allowed to dictate what a doctrine in the Bible must be made to say in the light of that Tradition. The Tradition may be consistent with biblical teaching, but allowance must always be made that it may not be. In the latter case, Tradition must bow down to Scripture.

This interplay between Scripture and Tradition is discussed by the German Roman Catholic theologian Bruce Vawter in the introduction to Herbert Haag's book on original sin. Vawter writes in connection with his tradition (Roman Catholicism), but the principles discussed apply across the spectrum of ecclesiastical traditions. Vawter writes:

> The theology . . . of our recent past tended to take the formulations of ecclesiastical magisterium as its starting point when dealing with a given doctrine of faith. In their light it interpreted the biblical passages that were thought to be relevant. Methodologically, the procedure left much to be desired. The

105. Tradition is a valuable resource for the church; no doubt we would be much impoverished without the Nicene Creed (AD 325), which clarified the relationships within the godhead, or the Chalcedonian Definition of AD 451, which describes the relationship between Christ's human and divine natures. However, Anizor goes too far when he says, "While creeds have the authority of a herald, not a magistrate, they have real and binding authority. There is unlikely to be a biblical, historical, or experiential argument strong enough to cause us to reject *any clause* of the creeds." Anizor, *Read Theology*, 106, emphasis mine.

106. I say "purportedly" because unlike Scripture, no formulation of a Tradition is infallible. Furthermore, the accepted Tradition often reflects a particular *interpretation* of Scripture—an interpretation consistent with the founding beliefs of that particular ecclesiastical body. We may call this "biased interpretation" and may or may not cohere with what Scripture *actually* teaches.

formulations are, of course, valuable and necessary to theology, embodying as they do the church's periodic evaluations of its tradition under the guidance of the Spirit. . . . These conciliar decrees had certainly intended to say no more than the Bible says: they were attempts to formulate biblical faith *as the church then understood it*. [However] when, in their letter, they were converted into criteria of how the church must continue to understand biblical faith, the true direction of theology was reversed. The church was no longer permitted, by arriving at a deeper understanding of the biblical word, to distinguish in the formulations of the past between the perennially valid article of faith and the contemporary presuppositions that had been its vehicle. *Theology now began to determine the word instead of being determined by it.* Indeed, in this topsy-turvedom of priorities, the dogmatic theologian was encouraged to regard the biblical exegete as the troubler of his sureties rather than as the indispensable member of his resource personnel, and the biblical word, from being his inspiration and direction, became instead a source of bothersome "objections" to be solved.[107]

The alleged doctrine of original sin is a classic case of precisely this problem. Once the doctrine gained a foothold through the teachings of the highly esteemed Augustine as explained earlier in this chapter, it became a cardinal doctrine, not to be questioned and thus shielded from both evaluation and criticism. It is a classic case of the theology driving the text of Scripture.

One further point needs to be made concerning the relationship of a biblical theology and Christian tradition, specifically with respect to either the addition of a perspective not addressed in the tradition, or as in the current case, the rejection of a tradition believed to be found in Scripture by the tradition. The rejection of a traditional interpretation of an alleged biblical teaching need not automatically or necessarily make the rejection invalid. The traditional interpretation may be mistaken for the reasons given above. Anizor states the point well: "As we engage doctrine critically, we cannot sidestep the question of a theology's fidelity to the Christian tradition. [However] some sensitivity is required since, as Lints notes 'consensus among theologians ought not to be a criterion of adequacy in theology, nor ought the lack of consensus to be a criterion of inadequacy.' Along similar lines, theological novelty does not equate with error, nor does antiquity equal truthfulness."[108]

---

107. Haag, *Original Sin in Scripture?*, 13, emphasis mine.

108. Anizor, *Read Theology*, 119. His citation of Lints is from Lints, *Fabric of Theology*, 98.

i) Infant Baptism, the Virgin Birth, and the Immaculate Conception of Mary

Infant Baptism

While infant baptism was practiced in the early church before Augustine's day, Augustine appealed to this practice to support his belief in original sin. "[Augustine] was firmly convinced that baptism was indispensable for salvation. In his dispute with Pelagius he justified the baptism of infants, developing the link between baptism and original sin."[109] This connection between the need for infants to be baptized and original sin was reinforced by his conviction that the procreative act itself was tainted by "concupiscence"[110] Henry Chadwick explains:

> The transmission of hereditary sinfulness is bound up with the reproductive process. The general belief that virginity is a higher state than marriage proved for Augustine that the sexual impulse can never be free of some element of concupiscence. In any event the practice of infant baptism for the remission of sins presupposes that infants arrive polluted by sin; since they have committed no actual sin, remission must be for the guilt attaching to a fault in their nature. Therefore if babies die unbaptized they are damned, even though it will be a "very mild" form of damnation.[111]

This sentiment became codified in Canon 110 of the aforementioned Counsel of Carthage in AD 418:

> Likewise it seemed good that whosoever denies that infants newly from their mother's wombs should be baptized, or says that baptism is for remission of sins, but that they derive from Adam no original sin, which needs to be removed by the laver of regeneration, from whence the conclusion follows, that in them the form of baptism for the remission of sins, is to be understood as false and not true, let him be anathema. For no otherwise can be understood what the Apostle says, By one man sin has come into the world, and death through sin, and so death passed upon all men in that all have sinned, than the Catholic Church everywhere diffused has always understood it. For on account of this rule of faith (*regulam fidei*) even infants, who could have committed as yet no sin themselves, therefore are truly baptized for the remission

---

109. Burnish, "Baptism," 71.

110. "Concupiscence usually refers to sinful physical desire, especially sexual longing or lust. The term is derived from the Latin word *concupiscentia*, meaning 'a desire for worldly things.' In its widest sense, concupiscence is any yearning of the soul; in its specific sense, it means a desire of the lower appetite contrary to reason. The term has become especially important in discussions on the Christian concept of original sin, especially as developed by Augustine of Hippo." New World Encyclopedia contributors, "Concupiscence," *New World Encyclopedia.*

111. Chadwick, *Early Church*, 232.

of sins, in order that what in them is the result of generation may be cleansed by regeneration.[112]

What is of particular interest here is Augustine's logic. Babies, by definition, are born suffering the consequences of Adam's sin; they are to be viewed as sinful because of Adam. Since baptism is the church's ritual designed for "the remission of sins" it is quite consistent to insist on the baptism of infants to cleanse them from the effects of original sin. The counsel insisted that if anyone denied the need for infant baptism "let him be anathema."

Large segments of Christian expression today deny the need for infant baptism and, strictly speaking, if the early church's pronouncements on infant baptism is by definition to be viewed as representing historic orthodox Christianity, then these Christians (denying the need for, and legitimacy of, infant baptism) are heretics! No one today would seriously make such a claim. If the early church can be mistaken on its linkage between salvation and infant baptism, it can also be mistaken on its view of the underlying assumption driving this link, namely original sin.

The Virgin Birth

The virgin birth[113] of Jesus is recorded in Matt 1:18–25 and Luke 1:26–37. The Matthean passage states: *"An angel of the Lord appeared to him [Joseph] in a dream, saying, 'Joseph, son of David, do not be afraid to take Mary as your wife; for the Child who has been conceived in her is of the Holy Spirit.'"* The Lukan passage likewise states: *"The angel said to her, 'Do not be afraid, Mary; for you have found favor with God. And behold, you will conceive in your womb and bear a son, and you shall name Him Jesus. . . . The Holy Spirit will come upon you, and the power of the Most High will overshadow you; and for that reason the holy Child shall be called the Son of God.'"*

In addition to seeing a reference to the deity of Christ in this event, Calvinists believe that an additional rationale is to protect Jesus from any taint of original sin. Grudem is a good example:

> The virgin birth also makes possible Christ's true humanity without inherited sin. . . . All human beings have inherited legal guilt and a corrupt human nature from their first father, Adam. . . . But the fact that Jesus did not have a human father means that the line of descent from Adam is partially interrupted. . . . And this helps us to understand why the legal guilt and moral corruption that belongs to all other human beings did not belong to Christ.[114]

112. Knight, "New Advent Introductory Note to Nicene and Post-Nicene Fathers," Canon 110.

113. More accurately, the term should be virgin conception. There was nothing exceptional about the birth of Jesus, just his miraculous conception.

114. Grudem, *Systematic Theology*, 530. It is not clear why original sin should have been connected to Adam and not Eve. Both sinned, as have all subsequent humanity. Erickson notes that the idea that "the transmission of sin is related to the father . . . does not have any scriptural grounding." Erickson,

Two related observations need to be made concerning the biblical passages. The first is that neither Matthew nor Luke even hint at a connection between the virgin birth and original sin. This may be a logical inference if one holds to the idea of original sin, but the passages themselves provide no basis for justifying such a doctrine. Second, both Matthew and Luke explicitly relate the angelic pronouncements concerning the virgin birth to the person of Jesus and his mission of salvation—*"She will bear a Son; and you shall call His name Jesus, for He will save His people from their sins"* (Matt 1:21). *"And behold, you will conceive in your womb and bear a son, and you shall name Him Jesus. He will be great and will be called the Son of the Most High; and the Lord God will give Him the throne of His father David; and He will reign over the house of Jacob forever, and His kingdom will have no end"* (Luke 1:31–33).

In sum, the purpose of the two passages is to underscore Jesus's uniqueness as the One qualified to be the Savior of the world—Jesus is God in the flesh. "The only real significance of the virgin birth lies in its necessary relation to the deity of Jesus."[115] With respect to the concept of original sin as Cottrell aptly puts it: "There is no basis for this idea, however. Some (including myself) reject it because they can see no biblical evidence for a concept of original sin in the first place."[116]

The Immaculate Conception of Mary

The doctrine of the virgin birth has as its focus the sinlessness of Christ. The doctrine of the immaculate conception of Mary has as its focus Mary's sinlessness. As noted above in connection with infant baptism, the early church held the status of virginity to be highly regarded. This general notion was probably derived from Paul's teaching in 1 Cor 7:25–38 concerning the desirability of remaining single in order to be free to single-mindedly serve God. The exalted status of virginity was, no doubt, also reinforced by the accounts of the virgin birth of Jesus by Mary. As time went by, the position of Mary in (Roman) Catholic thinking became increasingly prominent. Under Augustine's influence and his emphasis on original sin, it would only be a matter of time before the Roman church would take the next logical step and explicitly "protect" Jesus from the stain of original sin by postulating that Mary herself was also born sinless.[117] As the *Catholic Encyclopedia* states: "In the Constitution *Ineffabilis Deus* of 8 December, 1854, Pius IX pronounced and defined that the Blessed Virgin Mary 'in the first instance of her conception, by a singular privilege and grace granted by God, in

---

Christian Theology, 756.

115. Cottrell, *Faith Once for All*, 253.

116. Cottrell, *Faith Once for All*, 252. Interestingly, Erickson argues that an incarnation could have taken place apart from a virgin birth; see Erickson, *Christian Theology*, 754–56.

117. The early church father Origen (184–253) seems to be the first to link the virginity of Mary to a notion of inherited sin. "Only Jesus my Lord was born without stain. He was not polluted in respect of his mother, for he entered a body which was not contaminated." Cited by McGrath, "Origen on Inherited Sin," 215.

view of the merits of Jesus Christ, the Saviour [sic] of the human race, was preserved exempt from all stain of original sin.'"[118] The Protestant church has rightly rejected such notions. But the logic holds—if original sin is a reality then Jesus's sinless status is indeed bolstered if Mary herself is viewed as sinless. This, it seems to me, is a classic case of one theological error (original sin) leading, almost inevitably, to subsequent theological error (Mary's immaculate conception).

j) Original Sin and the Reality of the Incarnation

The doctrine of the incarnation, God becoming man, is an extremely important one and reaches to the core of Christian faith. This doctrine entails the belief that Jesus in his being was both fully God and fully man.[119] Both poles of the doctrine must be held together. A death on a cross of one who was not fully God would not qualify to atone for the sins of the world; a death on a cross that was not the death of a true human being would not allow humanity to identify with that work and thus not enjoy the fruit of that death, subjective redemption. In addition to the works that Jesus did during his earthly ministry, we have additional references in the epistles that clearly underscore this doctrine. *"He who has seen Me has seen the Father"* (John 14:9), says Jesus to Philip. Paul exhorts the Philippian Christians to emulate the humility of Christ: *"Have this attitude in yourselves which was also in Christ Jesus, who, although He existed in the form of God, did not regard equality with God a thing to be grasped, but emptied Himself, taking the form of a bond-servant, and being made in the likeness of men . . . he humbled himself"* (Phil 2:5–7). Paul's point is that Jesus was indeed equal with God in his being, in his pre-temporal state as the Second Person of the Trinity. But Jesus was willing to "empty himself" of all the prerogatives that adhere to that status and was willing to humble himself and become a man.[120]

A key passage in which the author stresses the need for Christ to be fully human is Heb 2:14–18. The two portions of this text that clearly make this point is v. 14, *"Since the children share in flesh and blood, He Himself likewise also partook of the same,"* and v. 17, *"He had to be made like His brethren in all things."* The former was required in order to make his death on the cross a truly atoning sacrifice for flesh and blood children, and the latter was required in order to function as a merciful and faithful high priest. The author's point is that Jesus had to be exactly like those human beings he came to save—he had to take on our flesh and blood, and be like human beings in every way, including our human nature. Lane makes the point well: "Since

---

118. Holweck, "Immaculate Conception," line 1.

119. Of course, in a real sense we are dealing with mystery here, and yet Scripture requires such a formulation concerning the identity of Jesus of Nazareth.

120. "He existed in the divine 'condition' or 'rank' as the unique image and glory of God, but refused to utilize this favored position to exploit his privileges and assert himself in opposition to his Father." Martin, *Philippians*, 102.

'the children' share a common human nature (blood and flesh), it was necessary for the one who identified himself with them (v. 13b) to assume the same full humanity. This assertion grounds the bond of unity between Christ and his people in the reality of the incarnation. In the incarnation the transcendent Son accepted the mode of existence common to all humanity."[121]

Consistent Calvinism, with its view that human nature is intrinsically sinful because it has been corrupted as a consequence of Adam's sin, cannot affirm the simple statement that Jesus shared humanity's nature and was "like his brethren in all things." To say on the one hand that Jesus shared fully in the human condition and was identical to his brethren "in all things," and yet on the other hand, to deny that Jesus's human nature was like our nature is not to do justice to what the writer actually affirms. It is in fact a form of Docetism—the ancient heresy that said that Jesus only appeared (δοκεω [dokeō]: to seem/appear) to be fully human and have a human nature but that in reality he was only divine. We see this tendency worked out in Bekhof's discussion of Christ's humanity. After stating that "the term 'flesh' denotes human nature" he then goes on to affirm Christ's full humanity when he says, "The Bible clearly indicates that Jesus possessed the essential elements of human nature, that is a material body and a rational soul." But then he goes on to separate precisely what the Bible wishes to unite, namely the strong identification of Jesus's humanity with the humanity of those he came to save. He does this by insisting that Jesus could not sin "because of the essential bond between the human and divine natures."[122] But the Bible does not teach that Jesus could not sin, but rather it shows the glory of the fact that even though he was tempted in every respect like us, he in fact *did not* sin. In short, affirming Christ's divine nature must not be done in a docetic manner that threatens the reality of his human nature and thus the reality of the incarnation itself. Jesus's humanity was like ours "in all things," or "in every respect" (English Standard Version), or "in every way" (New International Version).

Since it is evident that Jesus could not identify with sinful human nature (because he was in fact sinless), Heb 2:14, 17 indirectly affirms that basic human nature is not sinful or corrupted in itself; there is nothing intrinsically corrupt about the human nature Jesus identified with. The sinful component of being human is not in a sinful human nature, but in the sinful choices and decisions people actually make and then execute.

---

121. Lane, *Hebrews 1–8*, 60. We have the same sentiment expressed by Paul: "*But when the fullness of the time came, God sent forth His Son, born of a woman, born under the Law, so that He might redeem those who were under the Law, that we might receive the adoption as sons*" (Gal 4:4, 5). The reference to being born under the law and born of a woman serve to cement the identification of Christ with those he came to redeem.

122. Berkhof, *Systematic Theology*, 318.

k) Why Do Babies Die?

I have argued against the sinfulness of infants and later I will argue that babies do not become "sinners" until an age of accountability, at which point they consciously break God's moral law, and effectively identify with Adam and his or her fellow sinners. Scripture is also clear between the link between sin and physical death (*"The sting of death is sin, and the power of sin is the law,"* 1 Cor 15:56).[123] These statements naturally raise the question: Why do babies die physically? Calvinists, as we have seen above, see here clear proof of the presence of original guilt and an inherited sin from Adam. In a system that denies original guilt and inherited Adamic sin, the death of infants remains to be answered.

The answer is found in the nature of the present creation. This creation is not functioning as God originally intended. Adam's sin had consequences for the creation. This is clear from Gen 3 where four consequences of Adam's disobedience are stated: (1) Satan is cursed (3:14), (2) Eve was to experience pain in childbirth (3:16), and (3) the ground is cursed and would yield to Adam its fruit only in toil and sweat (3:17–19), (4) mortality moved from being merely potential before Adam sinned to a reality that extended to Adam and his posterity following his sin as symbolized by Adam and Eve being cast out from the garden (God's intimate presence) and barred access to the tree of life (3:22–23). The precise way the third element is worked out in nature and natural forces is unclear, but Paul describes the present creation as: *"The whole creation groans and suffers the pains of childbirth together until now"* (Rom 8:22).

Believers, together with the rest of mankind, are not exempt from this condition (8:23). We currently live in a world that is subject to natural forces (hurricanes, volcanoes, viruses, bacteria, and so on) that threaten all human life quite irrespective of whether any one individual is unusually depraved, or relatively righteous. Babies are not immune from this state of affairs of course, which explains why babies too are subject to death even though they are not considered guilty of personal sins.[124] Morally accountable people die because of the intimate connection between sin and death, and all morally accountable persons have sinned. The way they die varies— perhaps through starvation, perhaps through disease, perhaps through a tornado or some other natural force. Infants on the other hand, die merely due to these latter forces to which they are inescapably connected.

Babies do, unfortunately, also die at the hands of sinners, depraved people who deliberately kill infants. This is yet another reason why infants die physically. However, interestingly, this is universally recognized as particularly unjust and heinous, not only because such deaths at the hands of wicked people are avoidable, but also

---

123. See also Rom 5:12, 14, 21; Jas 1:15.

124. Warren, reflecting on the relationship between sin and physical death, notes: "Death has come upon all men . . . because they themselves have all sinned, . . . and therefore share death with Adam, or because natural and social vehicles transmit death even to those who have not sinned, including children. . . . Death is penalty to the sinner, but simply pain to the sinless." Warren, *Salvation*, 89.

because such deaths cannot, in any sense, be viewed as deserved, since babies are morally and spiritually innocent.

Total Depravity

If the question of whether original sin is a reality or not was the key issue concerning sin's origin then, though Christians may differ about it, in some sense it would not be very consequential. This is so because all Christians agree that *"all have sinned and fall short of the glory of God"* (Rom 3:23)—everyone has sinned personally and suffer the consequences of condemnation, judgment, etc. The precise reason why everyone sins may be interesting, but hardly decisive with respect to salvation. Everyone, regardless of the origin of personal sin, actually sins and needs a Savior from the resulting devastating consequences (alienation, enslavement to sin, death).

Furthermore, all Christians agree that the nature of sinful depravity is such that no part of the person is unaffected by sin—the body, the spirit, the mind, the will. And this fact counts for the many exhortations in Scripture for even Christians to be alert, to be on guard, to put on the full armor of God lest we be tempted and fall prey to sin. Furthermore, total depravity does not mean that the unregenerate person is as evil as it is possible to be, a view sometimes called utter depravity.[125]

It is, however, the distinctive Calvinistic understanding of human depravity that flows from the fall and original sin that requires further study on the question of original sin and its effects, especially its effects with respect to man's ability to do good or even to respond to the gospel call to repent and believe the gospel. For the Calvinist, the most serious consequence of original sin is a total human depravity, understood to entail a total inability to even repent and believe the gospel.

The Calvinist Understanding of Total Depravity

As we have seen, Augustine was the first influential church father to systematically teach what is now known as original sin—that Adam's sin has left a devastating effect on his posterity. This effect includes both guilt and, more importantly for a doctrine of total depravity, a corrupted human nature. It was Augustine who famously taught that before the fall, Adam was able not to sin, but after the fall he (and subsequent humanity) was not able not to sin. This did not mean that man lost his (free) will entirely, merely "that whenever unbelievers use their free will, they always use it to choose evil instead of good."[126]

---

125. This statement is somewhat ambiguous, however. While most Calvinists would agree, many would also insist that due to human depravity no unregenerate person can do any good whatsoever. Even outwardly good actions (helping an elderly lady cross the road for example) is, in reality, to be judged as evil because it is not done with the right motive—to glorify God.

126. Allison, *Historical Theology*, 348.

Luther, who was an Augustinian monk, in his disputes with the Christian Renaissance humanist Erasmus, insisted on the bondage of the will subsequent to the fall: "If we believe that original sin has so ruined us that even in those who are led by the Spirit it causes a great deal of trouble by struggling against the good, it is clear that in a man devoid of the Spirit there is nothing left that can turn toward the good, but only toward evil."[127]

Calvin likewise insisted that because of original sin "our nature is not only utterly devoid of goodness, but so prolific in all kinds of evil, that it can never be idle."[128] Even for babies "their whole nature is, as it were, a seed-bed of sin, and therefore cannot but be odious and abominable to God."[129]

The Synod of Dort (AD 1618) was important because it was the first consistent statement against Arminius and the Remonstrants; it is where the acrostic TULIP emerged. It was thoroughly Augustinian in its doctrine of salvation. Under the chapter concerning man's corruption, we find in Article 3 concerning man's total inability: "All men are conceived in sin, and by nature children of wrath, incapable of saving good, prone to evil, dead in sin, and in bondage thereto, and without the regenerating grace of the Holy Spirit, they are neither able nor willing to return to God, to reform the depravity of their nature, or to dispose themselves to reformation."[130]

Modern Calvinists take a similarly dismal view concerning fallen human nature. John Piper, for example, speaks of man's depravity as total in four senses: (1) our rebellion against God is total; (2) in his rebellion everything man does is sin; (3) man's inability to submit to God and do good is total; (4) our rebellion is totally deserving of eternal punishment.[131] Similarly, Wright states, "The doctrine of total depravity states that fallen human nature is morally incapable of responding to the gospel without being caused to do so by divine intervention."[132] Schreiner and Ware express their sympathy with Luther's views on this issue: "We are convinced that Luther was correct in his understanding of sinful human inability to know, please, or seek after the true God. Prior to the provision of God's effectual drawing grace, the human will is in bondage to sin. . . . Apart from grace, sinful humans persist in their love affair with evil and their hatred of God's glorious truth. . . . Human beings do not have the ability or the desire to break the power of sin."[133] R. C. Sproul asserts that "the moral inability of fallen man is the core concept of total depravity or radical corruption." He then rightly goes on to show the crucial role this doctrine plays in the whole Calvinistic soteriology: "If one embraces this aspect of the *T* in TULIP, the

127. Rupp and Watson, *Luther and Erasmus*, 332.

128. Calvin, *Institutes*, 2.1.8.

129. Calvin, *Institutes*, 2.1.8.

130. Canons of Dort, "Third and Fourth Heads of Doctrine," art. 3.

131. Piper, *Five Points*, 18–22.

132. Wright, *No Place for Sovereignty*, 111.

133. Schreiner and Ware, *Still Sovereign*, 13.

rest of the acrostic follows by a resistless logic. One cannot embrace the T and reject any of the other four letters with any degree of consistency."[134]

Grudem concurs with the above assessments. Under the heading of Inherited Corruption, he makes the point that "we have a sinful nature because of Adam's sin." He then explains, "Our inherited corruption, our tendency to sin, which we received from Adam, means that as far as God is concerned we are not able to do anything that pleases him." Amplifying on this point he notes that "in our natures we totally lack spiritual good before God," and that "in our actions we are totally unable to do spiritual good before God."[135] Grudem here clearly connects total depravity with original sin and its alleged effects.

It is important to note that all Calvinists insist that, because of the radical inability to choose spiritually significant good (like repent and believe the gospel), God must first intervene to regenerate the human heart and enable one to believe.[136] Whereas a straightforward reading of the New Testament would seem to suggest that in order to be saved one must first repent and believe the gospel in order to be regenerated, Calvinism insists the order is reversed—one must first be born again (regenerated) and then believe. "Since the flesh makes no provision for the things of God, grace is required for us to be able to choose them. The unregenerate person must be regenerated *before* he has any desire for God. The spiritually dead must *first* be made alive . . . before they have any desire for God."[137] Wright concurs: "Since the Fall of Adam and Eve, all are born spiritually dead in their nature, and therefore require regeneration to a life they do not naturally possess."[138]

In short, Calvinism holds that total depravity:

a. Is due to a corrupted, sinful nature inherited from Adam

b. Causes everything that man does to be sinful and in fact man is in constant rebellion against God. This is true in an absolute sense with respect to anything spiritually significant. Any good that man does (feed the dog, love the children) is either only apparently so, but is in reality sinful due to wrong motives, or

---

134. Sproul, *Reformed Theology*, 128. Two caveats need to be made here. The first is that there are branches of non-Calvinism that do in fact embrace the Calvinist's notion of total depravity but without adhering to the other four letter of the acrostic—a good example would be Classical Arminianism. Second, by the same token, it follows from the point that Sproul makes here that if total depravity can be shown to be false, then the whole Calvinistic system falls with it.

135. Grudem, *Systematic Theology*, 496–97. Somewhat inconsistently, Grudem speaks of "a disposition to sin" and an "inherited tendency to sin" and "the sinful tendencies of our hearts." Such softening of the impact of original sin and an alleged inherited corrupted nature is not really consistent with the idea that "we are not able to do anything that pleases [God]."

136. Of course, within a Calvinistic framework, only the elect are the recipients of this divine action.

137. Sproul, *Reformed Theology*, 136, emphases mine.

138. Wright, *No Place for Sovereignty*, 112.

if genuinely good is due only to God's "common grace" and is not spiritually significant.[139]

c. Prevents a person from responding to the gospel's call to repent and be saved.

d. Makes man totally incapable of rectifying this situation unless and until God decides to regenerate an individual first.

An Examination of Key Biblical Texts Used by Calvinists

The Old Testament nowhere connects human sin with the sin of Adam. Not surprisingly, therefore, the bulk of alleged biblical support for the notion of corrupted human nature inherited from Adam is found in the New Testament. We will examine briefly the common passages appealed to in order to justify total depravity. As we do so, however, we will see two mistakes commonly made by those arguing for the notion of total depravity. The first concerns the tendency to appeal to a verse or two here and there and use those verses to argue for a particular position. This way of constructing a doctrine is very common among Calvinists,[140] and especially among systematic theologians whose task is to construct a doctrine from the Bible. The major problem with this approach is that the verses appealed to are often divorced from their literary and historical context and made to fit the preconceived idea of what the doctrine must be. It is, of course, valid to appeal to scriptural texts to make a point, but great care needs to be made in ensuring the text is truly applicable. Failure to do this results in eisegesis, not exegesis.[141]

The second mistake is to universalize a verse. So, for example, a verse or passage may be a prophetic announcement against the idolatry and wickedness of ancient Israel, but is applied to the modern unbelieving individual today with no thought or justification for making that direct application. The problem here is that the verse may only be addressed to, and relevant for, a particular people at a particular time and ought not be extended to unbelievers (or Christians) today without some sort of justification. This is a surprisingly common procedure and can easily lead to a distorted construction of doctrine. The same mistake can be made in the area of application: "Here we can move too quickly in universalizing a specific action or

139. Common grace is a mainly Calvinistic concept used to explain how the unregenerate appear to do good despite being totally depraved—it refers to the grace God gives to all people to enable society to function.

140. It must be admitted that this hermeneutical error is not limited to Calvinists, it is a danger for all those who begin with a doctrine (like total depravity or original sin or free will) and then seek to find verses that seem to support the doctrine.

141. Eisegesis occurs when the interpreter or reader inserts a meaning to the text that is not really there; the goal of all Bible students ought to be exegesis—to extract from the text its true meaning, what the biblical author intended to say.

instruction, assuming that one ancient Israelite experienced can and should be experienced by all contemporary Christians."[142]

a) Indictments against Specific Groups of People

There are a series of passages appealed to by Calvinists that describe individuals or a group of people who exhibit remarkable depravity. This is then understood to be descriptions of all unregenerate persons.[143]

Genesis 6:5

"Then the Lord saw that the wickedness of man was great on the earth, and that every intent of the thoughts of his heart was only evil continually."

Derek Kidner is a good example of the tendency to universalize this passage: "A more emphatic statement of the wickedness of the human heart is hardly conceivable. . . . The New Testament is the true exponent of the passage, finding 'no good thing' in our fallen nature."[144] Erickson provides a more careful assessment when he correctly notes that "in the Old Testament, we do not usually find general statements about all men at all times, but about all men who were living at the time being written about."[145] Nevertheless, despite his cautionary note, he himself goes on to universalize human depravity based on this verse when he states that "the image of *the scheming heart* is found as early as the account of the flood; God observes of *sinful man* . . ."[146] He explicitly connects this state with a doctrine of total depravity.

Granted that, generally speaking, human depravity at the time before the flood was very extensive, there is no justification for extrapolating this state of affairs to an absolute, timeless, state of affairs somehow inherent in the human condition. The fact that at that time at least one man (Noah) was found to be "righteous," "blameless," and found to be walking with God (Gen 6:9) underscores this point. Furthermore, nowhere does the text itself make a connection between the sinful state of pre-flood people and a universal "total depravity" that all persons from Adam on possess and which they have inherited from Adam. It is simply reading into the text such a notion from a precommitment to original sin and its supposed effects.

---

142. Schultz, *Out of Context*, 19.

143. I am indebted to Bible teacher Steve Gregg for some of the ideas developed in what follows. See Narrow Path Ministries, https://www.thenarrowpath.com/topical_lectures.php.

144. Kidner, *Genesis*, 85. Kidner is citing C. Vriesen here.

145. Erickson, *Christian Theology*, 622.

146. Erickson, *Christian Theology*, 626, emphasis mine.

Isaiah 64:6

> *"For all of us have become like one who is unclean, And all our righteous deeds*
> *are like a filthy garment; And all of us wither like a leaf, And our iniquities, like*
> *the wind, take us away."*

Grudem comments concerning this verse: "Though from a human standpoint people might be able to do much good, Isaiah affirms that 'all our righteous deeds are like a polluted garment.'"[147] Calvinists seem to oscillate between holding, on the one hand, that no one can do anything of any good at all—all apparent good is merely that, *apparent*—and, on the other hand, believing that nothing of any *spiritual* good (believe, repent, seek God, etc.) can be done by the totally depraved sinner. Grudem's comment above seems to suggest he believes the sinner can do no good of any kind; what appears from a human standpoint as good is, in reality, like a filthy garment.[148]

While Calvinists generally apply this verse to all people at all times, in its context this verse appears in a passage where the prophet laments the fact that Yahweh's covenant people Judah have rebelled against their God. The prophet contrasts Judah's present sinful condition with God's willingness to act *"in behalf of the one who waits for Him"* (64:4) and God's willingness to *"meet him who rejoices in doing righteousness"* and *"Who remembers You in Your ways"* (64:5). The prophet's affirmation of such spiritual goods is inconsistent in a theological context of total depravity where any sort of genuine good is impossible. Yes, Judah collectively has sinned and the prophet, using poetic language, describes her sin in vivid terms and appeals to Judah's God to exercise grace to his covenant people: *"Do not be angry beyond measure, O Lord, Nor remember iniquity forever; Behold, look now, all of us are Your people"* (64:9). Far from being a universal statement about all of humanity for all time, in its context Isa 64:6 applies to the sins of a specific people in unique (covenantal) relationship with God at a specific point in the nation's history. No doubt God had many in Judah at the time that "did not bow the knee to Baal."

Jeremiah 13:23

> *"Can the Ethiopian change his skin or the leopard his spots? Then you also can*
> *do good who are accustomed to doing evil."*

"Left to themselves, those dead in trespasses and sins have no spiritual ability to reform themselves, or to repent, or to believe savingly." As part of his justification for this assertion Wright goes on to say, "Jeremiah 13:23 is the well-known comparison

---

147. Grudem, *Systematic Theology*, 497.

148. Grudem cites Isa 64:6 in a passage headed "In Our Actions We Are Totally Unable to Do Spiritual Good before God"—underscoring the ambiguity mentioned above.

of sinners, who are unable to change themselves, with leopards who cannot get rid of their spots."[149]

Here again is an example of citing a verse without any attempt to appreciate its literary context, and to universalize the application to all "sinners." The former error, not surprisingly, leads to the latter error. In its context, this verse appears as part of a series of verses written in Hebrew poetry. The interpreter, ever sensitive to the literary genre of the material he is handling, will make allowance for typical features of poetry—exaggeration for effect (hyperbole), vivid metaphors, generalizations, a general lack of precision in language. It is a mistake then to appeal to this verse as though it were a rigorous statement suitable for contribution toward a systematic theology of human nature—as Wright and most Calvinists are wont to do.

This verse comprises a rhetorical question concerning ancient Israel's ability to start to exercise covenant loyalty after many years (decades and even centuries) of covenant unfaithfulness on the part of Judah. Its persistent sinning as a nation makes it ripe for divine judgment: "'This is your lot, the portion measured to you from Me,' declares the Lord, 'Because you have forgotten Me and trusted in falsehood'" (Jer 13:25).

It is in this historical context that Jeremiah sarcastically asks, "Can a leopard change its spots?" After years of willful covenant disloyalty and national idolatry, the expected answer, of course, is no. So, we have here not a precise theological "data point" or proof text that can be pigeonholed into the systematic theologian's doctrine of total depravity, but an expression of skepticism on the part of God through his prophet directed to a disobedient nation shortly before experiencing national exile in Babylon.

Finally, it is noteworthy that the reason for the Israelites' inability to change (repent or reform) is they have become "accustomed to doing evil." Presumably there was a time when they were not in this habit, but now they have become used to practicing evil. Again, there is no hint of some unavoidable, inescapable evil condition of the heart present from birth that accounts for their present actions.

Jeremiah 17:9

> *"The heart is more deceitful than all else And is desperately sick;*
> *Who can understand it?"*

Like the above analysis, this verse appears in a poetic section of Jeremiah. Like Jer 13:23 above, the broader context is historical judgment on Judah for their idolatry (17:2). However, from v. 5 to the end of the chapter the focus shifts to Jeremiah himself.[150] While the passage under consideration (v. 9) is understood as comprehensive

---

149. Wright, *No Place for Sovereignty*, 115.

150. See Thompson, *Jeremiah*, 419. The comparison and contrast between the cursed man who fails to trust in Yahweh and the blessed man who is blessed because he trusts in Yahweh is reminiscent of Ps 1 where the wicked and the righteous are contrasted.

and without exception, its literary context prevents such a view. Verses 7 and 8 speak of the blessings that accrue to the man who trusts in Yahweh (Jeremiah himself?), and v. 10 speaks of God searching the heart in order to *"give to each man according to his ways, according to the results of his deeds."* If the condition spoken in v. 9 was unqualifiedly and always the case, there would be no reason for God to search the heart—he would know its content already.

So, what is v. 9 affirming? Just as words gain there meaning from the context in which they are located, so with this verse. Some turn away from God (v. 5b), some trust in God (v. 7). It would appear as though, while there is a mysterious aspect to the human heart and its proclivities that would allow it to be either faithful to God or unfaithful—God knows and sees the true state of the heart because he searches the heart in order to *"give to each man according to his ways, according to the results of his deeds"* (v. 10). Verse 9 then functions to alert the reader that the heart's condition is always tempted to stray, to do wrong, to betray God and trust in worthless things and that there is always an element of uncertainty—*"who can understand it?"* Most in Jeremiah's day failed the test, both at the personal and national level, but some (the righteous remnant) did not; God searches and God knows. If v. 9 were understood in a Calvinistic sense as justifying a total depravity that made trusting God apart from regeneration impossible, there would be no category of the righteous who do in fact choose to trust God; there would be nothing for God to search for—he would know that everyone, without exception, were totally depraved.[151]

Romans 1:18

> *"For the wrath of God is revealed from heaven against all ungodliness and unrighteousness of men who suppress the truth in unrighteousness."*

Verse 18 to the end of the chapter comprises an indictment by God against "all ungodliness . . . of men who suppress the truth." In his discussion of justification, Murray, after citing Rom 1:8, concludes, "This is our situation and it is our relation to God."[152] Likewise, Sproul speaks of God directing "his wrath to mankind because of their repression of natural revelation."[153] As these citations illustrate, it is common to assume that Paul is here speaking of the whole of unregenerate humanity. However, in its historical context, Paul is referring to pagans living in first century Rome. Such society was characterized by overt idolatry (1:20–23) and gross immorality (1:24–27). The form of immorality specifically identified is homosexuality. Of course, it is true that where such sinfulness exists the wrath of God is revealed, but it is reading

---

151. Of course, there is nothing in the text itself that even hints at such regenerating work of God. It would have to be read in.

152. Murray, *Redemption Accomplished and Applied*, 117.

153. Sproul, *Reformed Theology*, 15.

into the text to see this applying to all men at all times. The universalizing tendency of many commentators is unjustified from the text itself. Not all people "suppress the truth in unrighteousness"—Cornelius in Acts 10, for example, is described as a Gentile God-fearer. Those "noble Bereans" of Acts 17 *received the word with great eagerness, examining the Scriptures daily to see whether*" the things taught by Paul were indeed so. As a result of their research *"many of them believed, along with a number of prominent Greek women and men"* (Acts 17:12).

Romans 1:18 describes God's justified response to rampant sin prevalent in much of pagan society in his day, but it is reading too much into the text to universalize it to all people at all times everywhere—especially if used to justify a doctrine of total depravity as entailing total inability to respond to the gospel. The verses following v. 18 indicate that this degree of depravity was not something inherited from birth since *"they* became *futile in their speculations"* (v. 21), God *"gave them over"* to their chosen degree of depravity (vv. 24, 26, 28), *"they did not see fit to acknowledge God* any longer" (v. 28, emphases mine).

Paul's point in these verses is to show that Gentiles have sinned; in the next chapter he will show that the Jews also have sinned, and in ch. 3 he will underscore the point: *"for all have sinned and fall short of the glory of God"* (3:23). No one disputes that everyone has sinned and so stand in need of salvation, but Rom 1:18 indicates that this state of affairs has been reached by a conscious suppression of truth, not because of a supposed defect in human nature inherited from Adam. It is a mistake to confuse inability to save oneself with an inability to respond to a gospel which Paul has just indicated *"is the power of God for salvation for everyone who believes"* (1:16).

Romans 3:9–12

> *"What then? Are we better than they? Not at all; for we have already charged that both Jews and Greeks are all under sin; as it is written, 'There is none righteous, not even one; there is none who understands, there is none who seeks for God; all have turned aside, together they have become useless; there is none who does good, there is not even one.'"*

This passage is a favorite for Calvinists because superficially it seems to bolster the idea that man is a helpless, rebellious sinner—after all, no one, not even one, seeks after God; they have become useless. Wright states that "Romans 3:9–18 is a chain of quotations from the Old Testament intended to show what God thinks of sinners in general. 'There is no one who does good, not even one.'"[154] The highly influential Calvinist pastor John Piper concurs:

> The totality of our rebellion is seen in Romans 3:9–11 and 18. "We have already charged that all, both Jews and Greeks, are under sin, as it is written:

154. Wright, *No Place for Sovereignty*, 115.

'None is righteous, no, not one; no one understands; no one seeks for God.
. . . There is no fear of God before their eyes.'" Any seeking of God that honors
God is a gift of God. It is not owing to our native goodness. It is an illustration
of God mercifully overcoming our native resistance to God.[155]

As always, it is important when seeking to understand this passage to not lose
sight of Paul's purpose in writing these verses. His series of citations from the Psalms
and Isaiah is to underscore one simple fact that has concerned him in Rom 1–3,
namely the universality of sin: "both Jews and Greeks are all under sin" (3:9), and
"all have sinned and fall short of the glory of God" (3:23). More specifically in this
chapter, Paul is focusing on the Christian Jew's claim in the church at Rome to be
better than the Gentiles in the church. Why should the Jews think this? Because they
were privileged to have access to divine special revelation: *Then what advantage has
the Jew? Or what is the benefit of circumcision? Great in every respect. First of all, that
they were entrusted with the oracles of God"* (3:1–2). Despite this privilege, however,
the Jewish Christians were not in a superior position relative to their Gentile brethren: *"What then? Are we better than they? Not at all; for we have already charged that
both Jews and Greeks are all under sin"* (3:9). What counts for Paul is not access to
divine revelation (the law), but obedience to the law and, on this score the Jews, like
their Gentile brethren, fail miserably.

To underscore this point, that the Jews (as well as the Gentiles) have sinned, Paul
cites from the OT revelation to show that even the Old Testament itself clearly shows
the Jews to have failed to keep the law. It is worth stressing at this point that this is
Paul's *only* purpose in citing these verses from the Old Testament—he is not seeking
to elaborate on a theory of total depravity, total inability to respond to God, etc. "No
matter what privileges the Jews may have enjoyed in relation to their unique role as
the people through whom the Messiah would come, in reference to sin and judgment
and their standing before God, they have no advantage whatsoever."[156]

In underscoring his point, Paul selectivity cites a series of verses from the Psalms
(primarily), especially Ps 14:1–3. Also cited is Isa 59:7–8. Paul deliberately chooses
these Old Testament texts because they serve his purpose in that they clearly show the
Jews to have sinned despite being recipients of Yahweh's privileges as the old covenant
people of God. While the language suggests comprehensive depravity, it is evident that
Paul is using these texts in a hyperbolic fashion—exaggerating to make a point. Did absolutely no Jews "seek after God," had every Jew under the old covenant failed to "seek
after God"? The answer is no. God always had a righteous remnant who had sought
after God and who had "not bowed the knee to Baal" (1 Kgs 19;18; Rom 11:4). Even Ps
14:5 itself speaks of God being "with the righteous generation." The point is that Paul
appeals to these specific Old Testament texts because they serve his purpose—they

155. Piper, *Five Points*, 19.
156. Cottrell, *Romans*, 1:235.

clearly underscore the reality of universal sin. But to appeal to these texts to support a doctrine of total depravity inherited from Adam and entailing total inability to respond to God's call to repent and believe the gospel is to fail to appreciate how and why Paul appeals to these specific verses. In short, it is a mistake to build a doctrine of total depravity by appealing to verses used in a hyperbolic manner to make another point—that all have sinned. Comprehensive sinning is not the same as, and does not support, a doctrine of total depravity as understood by Calvinism.

Ephesians 4:17–19

> "So this I say, and affirm together with the Lord, that you walk no longer just as the Gentiles also walk, in the futility of their mind, being darkened in their understanding, excluded from the life of God because of the ignorance that is in them, because of the hardness of their heart; and they, having become callous, have given themselves over to sensuality for the practice of every kind of impurity with greediness."

Wright, cites these verses to back up the claim that "being fallen, the natural heart and mind is sinfully corrupt and unenlightened." He then goes on to elaborate: "Ephesians 4 contains one of the most negative evaluations of the unbelieving mind in the Bible. The mind of the Gentiles is empty, lifeless, ignorant and blind."[157] If these comments referred only to personal sins there would be little to object to; no one doubts that sinning has strongly negative consequences on the heart and mind. But most consistent Calvinists (like Wright) appeal to these and similar verses to support or bolster a doctrine of total depravity understood as total inability to respond to the gospel call and deriving from Adam's sin, that is, original sin.

Paul is describing pagan society and its characteristics in general and reminding the Christians at Ephesus to be sure to continue repudiating such behaviors and attitudes. Again, Paul speaks in general terms—not all pagans necessarily fit this description. Warren states the situation well: "Paul might not have classified Sergius Paulus with the majority Greek life style of his day (Acts 13:7, 12). We hesitate to consider bound for hell men like the proselytes and God-fearers . . . attached to Jewish synagogues. . . . Paul's *general* impression of Greek morality put such exceptions aside."[158] Furthermore, there is no warrant in this passage for a doctrine of total depravity originating at birth. Wright's comments above fail to make the connection; he merely *assumes* the passage contributes to such a doctrine. These pagans *became* callous to sin and *gave themselves over* to sensuality—presumably, there was a time when they were not callous and had not given themselves over to sin. Paul is describing a chosen state of depravity, not a condition from birth.

---

157. Wright, *No Place for Sovereignty*, 114.

158. Warren, *Salvation*, 108, emphasis mine.

b) Indictments against Corrupted Human Nature

There are a few scriptures that relate to the human condition, human nature, and which are understood by Calvinists to support a theory of total depravity. We shall examine below the most commonly appealed to passages to see whether they do in fact teach or support this doctrine.

Romans 7:18

> *"For I know that nothing good dwells in me, that is, in my flesh; for the willing is present in me, but the doing of the good is not."*

This verse is located in a passage in which Paul is describing his own personal experience (Rom 7:14–25). Whether Paul writes as a Christian or about his pre-conversion days is disputed. I believe Paul is describing his experience as a Christian; surely only a Christian could write, "For I joyfully concur with the law of God in the inner man" (v. 22). As indicated in the immediately preceding context (Rom 7:1–13), Paul is addressing the broader issue of the validity and role of the law in the light of the gospel.

"Nothing good dwells in me," is a principle operating in the apostle's life whereby "evil is present in me" (v. 21), also in his flesh he finds himself serving "the law of sin" (v. 25). It is this aspect of the human condition to which Calvinists appeal to show that human nature is so corrupted that no one is able to do anything of spiritual worth and especially not having an ability to even respond to God's call to repent and believe the gospel. Grudem, for example, appeals to this text (and other related texts) to assert that "Scripture is not denying that unbelievers can do good in human society *in some senses.* But it is denying that they can do any spiritual good or be good *in terms of a relationship with God.*"[159] (Calvinists tend to view responding to the gospel call as a meritorious good work contributing to one's salvation.)

In the passage, Paul is describing his struggle between what he would like to do in his inward self and what he often finds himself doing (vv. 15, 19), and he brings up this struggle in order to affirm the goodness of the law (v. 16). Yet, if this passage is speaking about Christian experience, then this is a struggle about sanctification—the Christian's desire and ability to live a holy life and says nothing about the ability or inability to respond to the gospel call since that has already taken place. If, on the other hand, this is a passage describing a person prior to their regeneration (new birth) as Grudem seems to view it, only then does Grudem's point become relevant. Sproul says:

> The struggle between the spirit and the flesh is the struggle of the regenerate person. The unregenerate, natural man has no such struggle. He is in bondage to sin, acting according to the flesh, living according to the flesh, and choosing according to the flesh. He chooses according to the inclination that

159. Grudem, *Systematic Theology,* 497, emphases original.

is dominant at the moment, and this inclination is never a desire to honor God out of a natural love for him. The desires of the unregenerate are wicked continuously. This is the bondage or spiritual death with which the doctrine of original sin is concerned.[160]

Both Grudem and Sproul merely state that this passage is relevant in supporting a doctrine of total depravity—*but neither provide any supporting evidence from the passage itself*. I presume it is taken as self-evident that a person declaring "nothing good dwells in me" cannot even respond to the gospel call and is totally unable to turn to God in repentance and faith, but in fact the latter does not necessarily follow from the former. Furthermore, *if* Paul were writing about his pre-conversion state then he affirms he does the things he hates (v. 15), he wills to do good (v. 18), the sin he commits is the very thing he does not want (v. 20), he wants to do good (v. 21), and he joyfully concurs with the law of God (v. 22). None of these desires are consistent with a person so totally depraved that they are unable to even respond to God's invitation to receive salvation!

The lack of good Paul speaks of concerns his "flesh," that is, his body, not his entire being. Even as a Christian Paul's body is unredeemed and so is a source of opposition to his inward desires. "Thus the statement 'nothing good lives in me' is qualified by being limited to the body."[161] Far from being a statement pertinent to the unregenerate and a corrupted *nature*, this verse describes the state of the regenerate in relation to the body's struggle to conform to the law's requirements.

Romans 8:6–8

> "For the mind set on the flesh is death, but the mind set on the Spirit is life and peace, because the mind set on the flesh is hostile toward God; for it does not subject itself to the law of God, for it is not even able to do so, and those who are in the flesh cannot please God."

Schreiner and Ware comment regarding v. 8, "Those in the flesh have an intense hatred of God burning within them, whether they are conscious of this or not. . . . Those in the flesh have no moral ability to keep the law perfectly or to glorify God. The power of sin is so great that they 'cannot please God' (Rom 8:8) and do his will."[162]

No Christian would dispute the claim that no one has the moral ability to keep the law perfectly. However, why would one extrapolate from inability to perfectly keep the law to assert that all unregenerate persons have "an intense hatred of God burning within them"? Certainly, the mind that is consistently set on the flesh is, by definition, not going to be open to God or the things of God and indeed cannot, while in this

---

160. Sproul, *Reformed Theology*, 134.

161. Cottrell, *Romans*, 1:449.

162. Schreiner, "Prevenient Grace," 232.

state, be subject to the law of God. In this sense it is true of course that such a condition (mind set on the flesh) represents a hostility to God and cannot please God. But to suggest that this necessarily entails a fixed condition until God unilaterally changes the heart so that they are enabled to believe the gospel is reading too much into the text. The passage is dealing with a fixed, ongoing stance of people who set their minds on the flesh—i.e., live for this world, the things of this world, and have no regard for God. But this need not mean this stance is utterly unchangeable and that such a person when presented with the gospel could not respond in faith.

Cottrell makes the point well. Concerning v. 8 he writes:

> As long as he exists according to the flesh, [a person] cannot submit to God's law in his heart (Gal 5:6; Heb 11:6). One simply cannot do both at the same time: he cannot set his mind on the flesh and submit to God's law simultaneously. Thus, as long as he is in the flesh he cannot please God with respect to his law. The key words are "as long as." A person cannot be pleasing to God in obedience to his law *as long as* his mind remains set on the flesh. But here is the crucial point: there is no indication whatsoever in this text that a sinner is unable to respond to the gospel, or unable through the power of the gospel to redirect the set of his mind from flesh to Spirit. The context shows that "cannot please God" refers only to an inability to be subject to the law, and does not imply an inability to respond to the gospel. The failure to make this distinction is the main error of Calvinist's interpretation of these verses. In other passages it is clear that sinners are able and expected to respond to the gospel in faith and repentance (John 3:16; Rom 1:17; Rev 22:17; Matt 23:37).[163]

1 Corinthians 2:14

> *"But a natural man does not accept the things of the Spirit of God, for they are foolishness to him; and he cannot understand them, because they are spiritually appraised."*

Wright notes that "the doctrine of total depravity states that fallen human nature is morally incapable of responding to the gospel without being caused to do so by divine intervention (1 Cor 2:12–15). Once the soul is sovereignly regenerated, it willingly responds in saving faith to God's command to repent and believe the gospel, but not before."[164] Note how Wright cites our verse to support a doctrine of total depravity. But is it really the case that Paul's observations concerning the "natural man" supports a doctrine of total inability to respond to the gospel?[165] To answer

---

163. Cottrell, *Romans*, 1:468.

164. Wright, *No Place for Sovereignty*, 111.

165. Anthony Hoekema, like many, presumes Paul is contrasting the unbeliever and the believer: "Paul refers here to man as he is by nature, to unregenerate man." Hoekema, *Saved by Grace*, 81.

this question, as always, we must look at the issue Paul is addressing in the broader context in which 1 Cor 2:14 sits.[166]

In the opening chapters of his letter to the Corinthians Paul is addressing two interrelated issues. The first concerns his reader's immaturity, and the second concerns his authority and his right to be listened to as an apostle. Their immaturity is manifested in two ways; first in their divisive spirit (1:10–17; 3:1–9), and second in their inability to receive the wisdom from God through Paul and the apostles, and consequently are prey to worldly wisdom (1:18—3:2). It is clear that Paul considers his readers to be carnal, immature Christians: *"And I, brethren, could not speak to you as to spiritual men, but as to men of flesh, as to infants in Christ"* (3:1). Paul, when he was with them previously, had given them milk and not solid food, and yet they were not able to receive even that level of apostolic teaching (3:2). It is important to note that throughout the entire epistle Paul is presuming his readers are Christians; Paul is not dealing with those outside the church. His focus is on the spiritual status of the church. It is weak, divisive, unable to appreciate the wisdom of God, but rather still *"walking like mere men"* (3:3). Paul contrasts two classes of Christians throughout these opening chapters: those who are carnal (fleshly)—the Corinthians as demonstrated by their party spirit—and the spiritual who were open to God's wisdom as communicated by his apostle (Paul): *"And when I came to you, brethren, . . . we . . . speak wisdom among those who are mature"* (2:1, 6). It is this historical and literary backdrop in which 2:14 appears.

Paul insists that he is in the "spiritual" class, and especially so since he came to them as an apostle with apostolic authority. His claim to authority did not rest on his speaking eloquently (2:4), but rather *"in demonstration of the Spirit and of power, so that your faith would not rest on the wisdom of men, but on the power of God"* (2:5). Paul is the bearer of God's wisdom (2:7–9), which he, *as an apostle*, is uniquely qualified to have insight into through the Spirit given to him (2:10–13). This is what qualifies him to consider himself as a mature Christian, and not subject to appraisal by others: *"But he who is spiritual appraises all things, yet he himself is appraised by no one"* (2:15). Paul stands in sharp contrast to those within the church who are carnal, fleshly, soulish and who do not accept the things of the Spirit of God (the wisdom which is from God) and cannot even know them because they are spiritually discerned and received (2:14). Paul's message concerning the wisdom of God and his being "stewards of the mysteries of God" (4:1) required a certain level of maturity, but the Corinthians were unable to appreciate Paul's apostolic qualifications or his message of divine wisdom because they were, to all intents and purposes, behaving and thinking just like the world, carnally, fleshly.

166. As is commonly done by Calvinists (and non-Calvinists too) Wright simply cites this verse in his statement concerning total depravity, and makes no attempt to understand why Paul says such a thing. Ignoring the literary context makes the danger of reading into the verse what one has already concluded must be there (eisegesis) very real. The goal of proper interpretation must be exegesis—explaining what the text itself is saying, taking into account the broader literary context.

From this reconstruction of the dynamics between Paul and the Corinthians, together with their carnal thinking and behavior contrasted with Paul's spiritual thinking, we see that the passage has nothing to do with unbelievers being unable to receive the gospel as Calvinists read the passage; this would simply be a non-sequitur. Rather, in 2:14 Paul is simply making the point that, as long as the immature Christians at Corinth insist on retaining their immature stance toward Paul and the mature wisdom and teaching he sought to give them, they were in effect no different from those outside the fold who also failed to appreciate the wisdom of the gospel.

Ephesians 2:1–3

> "And you were dead in your trespasses and sins, in which you formerly walked according to the course of this world, according to the prince of the power of the air, of the spirit that is now working in the sons of disobedience. Among them we too all formerly lived in the lusts of our flesh, indulging the desires of the flesh and of the mind, and were by nature children of wrath, even as the rest."

"Ephesians 2:3 . . . says we are by nature 'objects of wrath.' Human beings by nature are deserving of wrath, indicating that they are all born with a nature that is sinful. . . . The deadness of fallen humanity indicates that we are devoid of life upon our entrance into the world."[167] Sproul concurs:

> In our former condition we willingly fulfilled the lusts of the flesh and the mind, behaving like creatures who are (because of original sin) by nature children of wrath. When Paul says we are children of wrath "by nature," he plunges a stake in the heart of Pelagianism. . . . To be dead in sin is to be in a state of moral and spiritual bondage.[168]

This is a favorite passage for Calvinists since it appears to underscore the fatality of human depravity prior to conversion with respect to any capacity to turn to God. The idea of "deadness" and being "by nature" children of wrath is especially appealing in this regard. "The point of deadness is that we were incapable of any spiritual life with God. . . . In our deadness we were 'children of wrath.' That is, we were under God's wrath because of the corruption of our hearts that made us as good as dead before God."[169]

It is clear that most Calvinists understand deadness in terms of capacity—the inability because of corrupted human nature to turn in any way to God. Biblically, however, when the metaphor of death is used it is nearly always in connection with a lack of relationship with God. The key concept is *relationship*, not capacity. For example, Adam was assured that the day he ate the forbidden fruit would be the day

167. Schreiner, "Prevenient Grace," 230.
168. Sproul, *Reformed Theology*, 129.
169. Piper, *Five Points*, 22.

he died (Gen 2:17). Obviously, Adam did not die physically that day (in fact he lived physically for 930 years); however, that very day he was banished from the garden, making clear that the close, intimate relationship Adam enjoyed in the garden with God was now ended.

Paul, in this passage is reminding the Christians at Ephesus of their former lack of relationship with God due to their sinfulness. Speaking to the Gentiles in the church at Ephesus concerning their pre-Christian days, Paul's language is the language of lack of relationship: *"Remember that you were at that time* separate *from Christ, excluded from the commonwealth of Israel, and strangers to the covenants of promise, having no hope and* without God *in the world"* (v. 12). In this passage (ch. 3) Paul is underscoring the reality of God's grace toward the Gentiles in incorporating them into the one people of God (Jews and Gentiles). Again, in making this point, Paul uses the language of relationship: *"But now in Christ Jesus you who formerly were far off have been brought near by the blood of Christ. For He Himself is our peace, who made both groups into one and broke down the barrier of the dividing wall"* (Eph 2:13–14).

Like the previous two passages considered (Rom 8:6–8; 1 Cor 2:14), Paul in our passage here in Eph 2:1–3 is describing the Gentile's former manner of life, and certainly many pagans living in the first-century Roman empire could be expected to, and did, live depraved lives. But, as before, this says nothing about their ability to respond to the gospel when called upon to do so. The book of Acts is full of accounts of pagans who turned to Christ upon hearing the gospel proclaimed. An example would be the Philippian jailor in Acts 16:30–31 who sought salvation: *"Sirs, what must I do to be saved?"* They (Paul and Silas) said, *"Believe in the Lord Jesus, and you will be saved, you and your household."* It is simply reading too much into Eph 2:1–3 to assume the passage means that no one is capable of responding to the gospel invitation in order to be saved.

Just as in Rom 6:2, Paul in describing Christians as being dead to sin does not mean that the Christians at Rome were incapable of sinning, so here, to be dead in trespasses and sins does not mean that unbelievers are incapable of turning to Christ under the power of the gospel. Even in this letter (Ephesians), Paul cites an early Christian hymn that urges unbelievers, *"Awake sleeper, and arise from the dead, and Christ will shine on you"* (Eph 5:14).

While Calvinism views men as dead like Lazarus, whom Jesus called to life from the tomb (John 11), a better biblical example of the kind of death the Bible relates to sin and which is consistent with the emphasis on broken relationship as noted above is dead like the prodigal son. The father in this parable proclaims upon the return of his son[170] to restored relationship with his father: *"This son of mine was dead and has come to life again; he was lost and has been found"* (Luke 15:24).

---

170. Note that the son in the parable, even in the midst of his depravity, *"came to his senses"* concerning his lost condition and subsequently resolved to return to his father (Luke 15:17).

c) Passages That Speak about Enslavement to Sin

There are several passages in Scripture that picture the relationship of the unbeliever to sin as that of enslavement. We will now examine some of these texts to see whether this concept supports the notion of total depravity as entailing total inability to respond to the gospel call.

John 8:34

> *"Jesus answered them, 'Truly, truly, I say to you, everyone who commits sin is the slave of sin.'"*

The idea of enslavement carries with it the connotation of complete inability and lack of freedom to do other than what the demands of sin require. For this reason, such texts carry great weight with Calvinists. For example, this text is used by Schreiner and Ware to justify the statement: "The bondage of the will, then, is a slavery to our own desires. Unregenerate human beings are captivated by what they want to do!"[171] Amplifying the concept of enslavement to sin, the authors go on to say, "Unbelievers are enslaved to sin in the sense that all they want to do is sin. They are free to do what is good in the sense that they have opportunities to do so. They fail to avail themselves of these opportunities, however, because they do not desire to do what is good. The captivity of sin is so powerful that they always desire to sin."[172]

Without a doubt, Scripture teaches that there is an enslaving component to sin. In the context of John 8, Jesus is in dispute with those Jews who adamantly retained the belief that being a descendant of Abraham was sufficient to justify before God: *"They answered Him, 'We are Abraham's descendants and have never yet been enslaved to anyone; how is it that You say, 'You will become free?'"* (8:33). In refusing to budge from this stance they demonstrated their enslavement to a false belief—and, in the process, denied and resisted the One who alone could bring true freedom. Such commitment on the part of the Jews to their Jewishness for salvation in effect made them incapable of hearing the true word of God through Jesus (8:43).

The error the Calvinist makes is in supposing this situation is absolute, that there is no way open to the unbeliever to receive the truth from Jesus or his emissaries. But there is nothing intrinsic to the idea of enslavement that prevents a slave from desiring to be free. Historically, many slaves longed to be free! In the broader context of John's epistle, John's whole purpose in writing was to solicit those in bondage to sin to be set free through believing the gospel: *"These have been written so that you may believe that Jesus is the Christ, the Son of God; and that believing you may have life in His name"* (John 20:31). Biblically, it is quite consistent to be enslaved to sin and yet turn to the source of freedom. There is an inherent inability associated with

171. Schreiner, "Prevenient Grace," 230.
172. Schreiner, "Prevenient Grace," 231.

enslavement to sin, and that inability is an inability to save oneself—not an inability to turn to the one who freely offers salvation. The two must not be confused. Jesus's invitation is made to tired sinners enslaved by sin: *"Come to Me, all who are weary and heavy-laden, and I will give you rest"* (Matt 11:28).

John 8:44

> *"You are of your father the devil, and you want to do the desires of your father. He was a murderer from the beginning, and does not stand in the truth because there is no truth in him. Whenever he speaks a lie, he speaks from his own nature, for he is a liar and the father of lies."*

The appeal of this verse for Calvinists is that it is used to prove that all unbelievers have the devil as their father and only seek to do the devil's desire. Wright is typical: "In John 8:44 the phrase 'of your father the devil' is a reference to the Hebraic concept of the father 'begetting' offspring, and therein communicating his own nature to them."[173]

The context in which this verse appears is one in which Jesus is in conflict with those who resist him and his message (John 8:31–59). The passage begins with the assurance by Jesus that if the Jews hearing him would remain in his teaching they would find true freedom (8:31), and ends with these same Jews seeking to kill Jesus by stoning (8:59). By their words and actions the Jews are seen to become progressively more hostile to Jesus and his message. Their desire to hold tenaciously to their Jewish traditions and to kill Jesus matches perfectly with the devil's desire to deceive, lie, and murder.

Two observations may be made here. The first is the historical fact that not all Jews who were not Christians reacted to Jesus's message in this hostile manner. For example, we are told that many of the Jews who followed Jesus to the region where John the Baptist ministered "believed in Him there" (John 10:42). Whatever the connection is to the devil, it obviously does not mean, contrary to Calvinists, that a Jew (or a Samaritan) could not come to believe upon Jesus. Being "of your father the devil" does not entail unavoidable and continuous bondage and enslavement to Satan so that all unbelievers can do is sin. According to the gospels, many unbelievers chose to believe upon Jesus. In fact, this is stated to be the specific purpose John wrote his gospel (John 20:31).

The second observation concerns the nature of the connection with the devil exhibited by the hostile Jews who were opposing Jesus in John 8. When Jesus accuses those Jews of being "of your father the devil" he is speaking metaphorically—the devil does not literally have children. Wright, along with most Calvinists, understands the connection with the devil to be one of like (identical?) nature. But the devil's nature

173. Wright, *No Place for Sovereignty*, 114.

is different than human nature. The devil is not a being made in the image of God, which is the case even for the most sinful person. No, the connection with the devil is not one of like nature, but of loyalty. Those Jews were aligning themselves with the devil's will rather than with God's will for them. In fact, John's gospel is structured to highlight this battle of wills—most Pharisees for example are clearly seen to oppose Jesus and in so doing effectively align themselves with Satan's will. Others submit to Christ's lordship, align themselves with God's will and come to salvation.[174]

The issue of alignment or loyalty is seen clearly in an incident following Jesus's teaching concerning himself. Some *"withdrew and were not walking with him anymore"* (John 6:66). By contrast, in response to Jesus's question to his disciples concerning their loyalty to him (v. 67), Peter affirms the disciple's commitment to Jesus since they have come to believe in him (v. 68–69). Jesus's response is very telling here: *"Jesus answered them, 'Did I Myself not choose you, the twelve, and yet one of you is a devil?' Now He meant Judas the son of Simon Iscariot, for he, one of the twelve, was going to betray Him"* (v. 70–71). Judas's choosing to betray Jesus aligned perfectly with Satan's purposes and desire. The disciples display loyalty to God and his will for them while Judas chose to align himself against God and with the devil's desire. The basic dynamic is not the nature of human nature (contra Wright) but rather loyalty and alignment.[175]

All four gospels bear eloquent testimony that God desires people to change alignments and loyalty from effectively aligning with Satan's will and purposes to aligning with God's redemptive purposes for them. Far from a rigid and inescapable enslavement to the devil, Jesus came to call people to align with him and his message of hope and salvation. Many chose to switch alignment and loyalty when urged to do so.

Romans 6:16–18

> *"Do you not know that when you present yourselves to someone as slaves for obedience, you are slaves of the one whom you obey, either of sin resulting in death, or of obedience resulting in righteousness? But thanks be to God that though you were slaves of sin, you became obedient from the heart to that form of teaching to which you were committed, and having been freed from sin, you became slaves of righteousness."*

174. See John 7:40–52 for a good example of the way John structures his gospel to highlight the response of various individuals and groups to the claims of Christ. Sometimes the struggle for alignment and loyalty is seen explicitly. For example, following Jesus's temple teaching in John 7 we read that some were seeking to seize Jesus (v. 30), and others were believing upon him (v. 31).

175. The issue of alignment appears even more starkly in Mark 8. Following Jesus's teaching for the first time that *"the Son of Man must suffer many things and be rejected"* (v. 31), Peter took Jesus aside and began to rebuke him. In so doing Peter was, without realizing it, aligning himself with Satan's purposes for it was the Father's purpose that Jesus should suffer: *"He rebuked Peter and said, 'Get behind Me, Satan; for you are not setting your mind on God's interests, but man's'"* (Mark 8:33).

Schreiner and Ware, commenting on this passage, remark, "Paul says in Romans 6:15–23 that unbelievers are 'slaves of sin.' Slaves to sin cannot do what is right, nor do they want to do what is right. Being a slave to sin involves a willing captivity to its power."[176] The assumption seems to be that once enslaved a sinner is in a vice grip, a locked system that makes escape impossible unless and until God intervenes to enable a person to believe; "slaves to sin cannot do what is right." But is this really the case?

There are several indicators in the text that suggest Calvinists push the metaphor of slavery too far. First, the apostle speaks of those who *present themselves* to either sin and death or obedience to the gospel and righteousness. This suggests that, in the apostle's mind, there are two equally valid options or choices—enslavement or liberty. He is thankful that the Christians at Rome chose to "become obedient from the heart" (v. 17) to the gospel. This is not the language of total inability to respond to the gospel call, or of a fixed condition which the sinner is unable to change when presented with the gospel.

Second, just as being a slave of righteousness does not mean that it is impossible for a Christian to sin, so being a salve of sin does not mean that it is impossible for a non-Christian to become *obedient from the heart* to Paul's message (v. 17).

Finally, as before, the way Paul uses the metaphor of slavery here is that of chosen loyalty or alignment. The Calvinist John Murray captures this idea well: "The apostle shows in this verse [v. 16] that there are only two alignments in the ethico-religious realm and that the criterion of our alignment is that to which we render obedience."[177] Each alignment reflects a chosen enslavement, either to sin or to righteousness according to Paul in these verses. Again, there is nothing in the concept of slavery per se that necessarily requires, or even implies, a rigid fixity due to a total inability to respond to God's grace in whatever form that may take.

Titus 3:3

> "For we also once were foolish ourselves, disobedient, deceived, enslaved to various lusts and pleasures, spending our life in malice and envy, hateful, hating one another."

Schreiner and Ware cite this verse, together with Eph 2:3, to conclude that "the bondage of the will, then, is a slavery to our own desires." They also claim that "it is fair to conclude that people who are enslaved by their own desires are under the dominion and tyranny of sin. . . . To describe this pursuit of their own desires as slavery because they have no desire, inclination, or aspiration to do good is appropriate."[178] The picture is clear, the unregenerate person is locked into a slavery to sin with no

---

176. Schreiner and Ware, *Still Sovereign*, 13.

177. Murray, *Romans*, 231.

178. Schreiner, "Prevenient Grace," 230.

inclination or capacity for good, and therefore totally unable to do a "good" like respond to the gospel call.

As we have noted before, this verse, however, describes the state of people before they became Christians *in general terms.* It is characteristic of pagans living in the first century in the Roman Empire. As a generality, it was characteristic of the life of most pagans at that time. The Calvinist tendency to dehistoricize the text and make it apply universally to all people at all times is unwarranted; Paul was writing to his disciple Titus to provide guidance as to how Titus should shepherd the church in Crete sometime during the second half of the first century. Guthrie retains a sensitivity to the historical context when he notes concerning Titus 3:3, "The contrast between paganism and Christianity (3:3–7): (i) Characteristics of paganism (3:3). The apostle first describes the characteristics of paganism. The Christian's past life is described as blind slavery to passions, which manifested itself in many vices."[179]

As noted previously in our discussion of John 8:34, there is indeed truth in the idea that sin entails being "enslaved to various lusts" *for those who choose to remain in such a condition.* However, there is nothing intrinsic to the idea of enslavement per se that prevents such a person from wanting to be released form his or her slavery to sin. The New Testament provides many examples of pagans who were glad to have the opportunity to respond to the gospel. The Jews at Berea in the Roman province of Macedonia (northern Greece today), who were certainly not Christians and were unregenerate are described by Luke in Acts 17:11 as being *"more noble-minded than those in Thessalonica."* The following verse (17:12) records how *"many of them believed, along with a number of prominent Greek women and men."* Another example concerns Paul's ministry in Ephesus during his third missionary journey, following the overpowering of the seven sons of Sceva we read:

> *This became known to all, both Jews and Greeks, who lived in Ephesus; and fear fell upon them all and the name of the Lord Jesus was being magnified. Many also of those who had believed kept coming, confessing and disclosing their practices. And many of those who practiced magic brought their books together and began burning them in the sight of everyone; and they counted up the price of them and found it fifty thousand pieces of silver. So the word of the Lord was growing mightily and prevailing.* (Acts 19:17–20)

In conclusion, other passages appealed to by Calvinists could be cited and analyzed, some of which have been discussed above. But in every case three observations can be made, similar to the observations made in the preceding analysis. The first is the tendency to merely proof text—isolate the text and use it as part of an argument without any further consideration, the assumption, presumably, being that the meaning of the verse or text is self-evident. However, it is poor hermeneutics to appeal to a text in isolation to support one's preconceived notions as to what the text must be

179. Guthrie, *Introduction,* 631.

saying.[180] Ignoring the literary context in which the verse sits easily lends itself to eisegesis—reading into the text what the author never meant to communicate. It also, of course, runs the danger of ignoring or missing altogether what the author did intend to communicate because the flow of his argument is ignored.

A second problem with the way Calvinists appeal to, and use, biblical texts, and related to the first point, is the tendency to dehistoricize the text—to ignore the historical context of the passage. In the case of Jer 13 above, God, through his prophet Jeremiah, is addressing *"this wicked people, who refuse to listen to My words, who walk in the stubbornness of their hearts and have gone after other gods to serve them and to bow down to them"* (v. 10). Jeremiah 13:23 forms part of an indictment against wicked Judah, which had persistently failed to maintain covenant loyalty for centuries, and which forced God to conclude that, like a leopard's spots, Judah would not change now. This verse does not necessarily apply to all people at all times.

Finally, none of the passages cited by Calvinists in support of a doctrine of total depravity that entails total inability actually says that! Again, Jer 13:23 says nothing about anyone being unable to respond to the grace of God either in Old Testament times or now. The problem is not a universal inability to respond to God's overtures, whether to appeals of the prophets or appeals of the gospel, because of a totally depraved nature, but rather the *unwillingness* of individuals to listen to God.

We conclude that the Calvinist's theory of total depravity expressed as a total inability to respond to the gracious call of God is unfounded and unbiblical. On the other hand, there are many passages which indicate that God expects man to respond to God's call and appeals and to obey his commands.

Theological Issues Related to Total Depravity

The Calvinist doctrines of original sin and total depravity generate several questions of a theological nature and of the Bible's testimony concerning this aspect of sin. We shall examine some of them below.

a) Some Passages That Deny Depravity as Total Inability

In the passages cited below there is a consistent assumption that those addressed are not only called to obey God or respond in some other manner to God's overtures, but are in fact able to do so, expected to do so, and will be rewarded or punished accordingly.

---

180. In all fairness, this problem of ignoring both the literary and historical context is one that both Calvinists and non-Calvinists are prone to. But in my readings, Calvinists seem to do this in a remarkably consistent manner when it comes to justifying the five points of Calvinism.

Deuteronomy 30:11–14

> *"For this commandment which I command you today is not too difficult for you,*
> *nor is it out of reach. It is not in heaven, that you should say, 'Who will go up to*
> *heaven for us to get it for us and make us hear it, that we may observe it?' Nor is*
> *it beyond the sea, that you should say, 'Who will cross the sea for us to get it for*
> *us and make us hear it, that we may observe it?' But the word is very near you,*
> *in your mouth and in your heart, that you may observe it."*

This passage appears in the context of an appeal by Moses to the children of Israel as they are about to enter the promised land to be careful to obey the covenant stipulations given at Sinai. Great blessing from God can be expected (in keeping with the covenant blessings of Deut 28:1–14), but only *"if you obey the Lord your God to keep His commandments and His statutes which are written in this book of the law, if you turn to the Lord your God with all your heart and soul"* (Deut 30:10). Moses then goes on to assure the Israelites that these commandments and statutes are easily accessible to them; God has given it to the Jews at Mt. Sinai through Moses—unlike the peoples of foreign nations who were not so privileged and would indeed have to travel far and wide to gain access to this special revelation. The important thing to note for our purposes here is that Moses insists that the ability to obey these commandments *"is not too difficult"* for them. How could this be if, as the Calvinist understanding of total depravity is true? It would be impossible for the Israelites to obey because they would have been totally unable due to their depravity.

Furthermore, the proximity of the commandments (the word of v. 14), should make it easy for them to "observe it" (v. 14). God expected the Israelites to observe the covenant stipulations given at Mt. Sinai. Again, one must ask how this expectation could be present given a total inability to do anything of spiritual good as Calvinism insists? Craigie is surely right when he states that "the commandment did not impress on the people conditions that were totally impossible to fulfil."[181]

Deuteronomy 30:19

> *"I call heaven and earth to witness against you today, that I have set before you*
> *life and death, the blessing and the curse. So* choose life *in order that you may*
> *live."* (emphasis mine)

Like the preceding text above, this option presented to the people of Israel on the plains of Moab to "choose life" is not even a remote possibility if the people suffered a total depravity that made them totally unable to respond in this manner. Assuming God, through Moses, is addressing the people with integrity and not engaging in some

---

181. Craigie, *Deuteronomy*, 364.

form of mockery or deception, then the call to the people to choose life and blessing rather than death and curse belies the Calvinist notion of total depravity.

Amos 5:4

> *"For thus says the Lord to the house of Israel, 'Seek Me that you may live.'"*

In this chapter God, through Amos the prophet, is urging the northern kingdom of Israel to repent and turn from their wicked ways in order to avert the disaster that is looming from the north in the form of Assyrian invasion. There are several instances in this chapter alone that show God calling upon Israel to seek after God, do the right thing in order to avert imminent disaster—divine judgment at the hands of a foreign invader. Israel is urged to embrace several moral and spiritual imperatives:

> *"Seek the Lord that you may live, Or He will break forth like a fire, O house of Joseph"* (v. 6). *"Seek good and not evil, that you may live; And thus may the Lord God of hosts be with you"* (v. 14). *"Hate evil, love good, and establish justice in the gate!"* (v. 15). *"But let justice roll down like waters And righteousness like an ever-flowing stream"* (v. 24).

Again, the question must be asked: How could God call upon a people to do that which is in fact impossible given a Calvinist view of total depravity? Such imperatives would simply be incoherent. A totally depraved Israelite would be incapable of seeking God, or seeking good, or hating evil, or loving good, or establishing justice! The fact that, generally speaking, Israel failed to heed these imperatives does not deny the validity of the call. If Israel had chosen to seek God, they would have enjoyed the covenant blessings and lived. God does not offer false hope to Israel![182]

Amos 4:6

> *"'But I gave you also cleanness of teeth in all your cities, and lack of bread in all your places, yet you have not returned to Me,' declares the Lord."*

In this verse we are told that God sent famine to Israel in order to motivate the people to repent of their wicked ways and turn to God. God laments that despite his efforts to call the people to repentance, they failed to respond as he desired—they did not return to the God of Israel. God acted similarly and with the same motive by withholding rain (vv. 7–8), and again the people failed to turn to God. Again, God acted through crop failure and infestations in order to urge the people to look to God for deliverance—but with the same response: *"Yet you have not returned to Me, declares the Lord"* (v. 9). God sent a plague in their midst and brought defeat

---

182. The call to seek God is not restricted to the book of Amos. The following scriptures also note Israel's quest to seek after God: Job 5:8; Ps 69:6; Prov 8:17; Isa 51:1; Jer 29:13; Hos 5:15; Mal 3:1.

in battle: *"'Yet you have not returned to Me,' declares the Lord"* (v. 10). God allowed foreign invaders to inflict hurt upon the Israelite cities and again the response is the same: *"'Yet you have not returned to Me,' declares the Lord"* (v. 11).

The lesson is clear, God sought by a variety of means to get Israel to repent and seek him for relief and deliverance. But why would God have such expectations given a Calvinistic view of depravity? Didn't God know that they would be totally unable to repent, to seek after God? Rather, God expected the people to repent—and they were judged because, even though they could have repented they chose not to. The Israelites behavior was indeed perverse, but there is no notion of Calvinistic depravity here; the Israelites failed to repent, not because they *could* not, but because they *would* not; they chose to ignore God's pleas through his prophet, and rather, chose to continue living in a manner that violated their covenant obligations.

Isaiah 65:1–2

> *"I permitted Myself to be sought by those who did not ask for Me; I permitted Myself to be found by those who did not seek Me. I said, 'Here am I, here am I,' to a nation which did not call on My name. I have spread out My hands all day long to a rebellious people, who walk in the way which is not good, following their own thoughts."*

It seems best to understand this chapter as distinct from the immediately preceding chapter. In ch. 64 we see a prayer entailing confession of sin (Isa 64:6), a recognition of God's sovereignty (v. 8), a calling upon God to forgive (v. 9). Isaiah 65 seems to apply to a rebelling nation—a nation that engages in gross idolatry (vv. 3–4).

In these two verses (65:1–2), there is irony at play here. Historically, v. 1, cited by Paul in Rom 10:20, applies to the Gentile nations where God would permit himself to be found by those seeking him whereas Israel, God's covenant people, refused God's appeals. God is portrayed as strongly desiring to be sought and found but the people of Israel were not looking or interested in seeking God. Despite God's spreading out his hand "all day long" in a gesture of welcome, the people chose rather to follow their own ways. For our purposes, the important aspect of this dynamic between God and his ancient people is the fact that God is portrayed as earnestly desiring to be found, to be called upon, to be sought by the people—all spiritual goods which, according to the Calvinist notion of total depravity a "rebellious people" (v. 2a) could not do. Why would God seek to be found by a people intrinsically incapable of looking for him? No, the passage only makes sense on the assumption that the people were expected to respond positively to God's loving overtures, and could have had they been willing. As the rest of the chapter indicates, the nation will suffer the consequences of their willful rejection of Yahweh.

Matthew 3:1–2

> "Now in those days John the Baptist came, preaching in the wilderness of Judea, saying, 'Repent, for the kingdom of heaven is at hand.'"

Mark 1:14–15

> "Now after John had been taken into custody, Jesus came into Galilee, preaching the gospel of God, and saying, 'The time is fulfilled, and the kingdom of God is at hand; repent and believe in the gospel.'"

Both John the Baptist and Jesus began their public ministries in the same way—preaching that all the hearers should repent and believe the gospel. Such a call made indiscriminately would make no sense if the hearers were in fact unable to do so because of a total inability to respond. If, as Calvinism holds, every unregenerate person is a God-hater, completely unwilling and unable to do anything good including responding to God's overtures and commands, then calling people to do what they in fact cannot do (for whatever reason) is a farcical waste of time, and worse, somewhat deceptive.[183]

Mark 6:5–6

> "And He could do no miracle there except that He laid His hands on a few sick people and healed them. And He wondered at their unbelief."

This response on the part of Jesus to those in his home town Nazareth, is quite unexpected assuming Jesus knew all about total depravity. Renault expresses the situation well:

> It is quite curious to note that Christ "marveled" because of their unbelief. It actually surprised and amazed him. This is different than what one would expect if the doctrine of Total Depravity were true. If it were true that fallen man is completely unable to believe without God giving him a unique grace to believe, then Christ would not have been surprised at all or amazed at their unbelief. He would have expected them not to believe until He Himself had decided that they should believe.[184]

---

183. Calvinists counter that God determines the means whereby the elect become saved, and he uses the indiscriminate preaching of the gospel as the means of calling the elect to salvation. This notion will be examined in some detail in the next chapter on unconditional election. Taken at face value, and there is no hint whatsoever in the passages (or their contexts) that the passages are not to be taken to mean what they plainly state, the points noted above seem quite valid.

184. Renault, *Reconsidering TULIP*, 11.

The fact that Jesus expressed surprise at the unbelief of his fellow citizens is a clear indication that Jesus did not hold to total depravity.

John 4:41–42

> *"Many more believed because of His word; and they were saying to the woman, 'It is no longer because of what you said that we believe, for we have heard for ourselves and know that this One is indeed the Savior of the world.'"*

John wrote his gospel specifically to enable those who were exposed to his gospel "to believe that Jesus is the Christ" (John 20:31). This coheres well with the confidence the New Testament generally expresses in the power of the gospel to save (Rom 1:16). The antidote to human sin according to the New Testament is not to be first regenerated by the Holy Spirit and then believe, but rather to hear the gospel and be challenged to respond to God's gracious overtures. God's desire is that all would respond positively to the gospel (1 Tim 2:4).

Before the gospels came to be written, Jesus appealed to his teaching and miracles as reasons to believe in him and his message. John 4:41–42 above is illustrative of such a procedure. The common people from Samaria heard both the Samaritan woman's testimony concerning Jesus, and Jesus's own message and were as a result convinced of Jesus's true identity. They heard, they believed—it's as simple as that! We read of a similar occurrence when Jesus revisited Cana in Galilee. There, a certain royal official who, upon hearing that Jesus was in the area, sought Jesus out and implored him to heal his son. This is hardly what one would expect of a God-hater and someone utterly blind to spiritual realities and totally incapable of any morally or spiritually significant good! The result? When he discovered that his son was miraculously cured "he believed and his whole household" (v. 53).[185]

Luke 10:30–37

> *"Jesus replied and said, 'A man was going down from Jerusalem to Jericho, and fell among robbers, and they stripped him and beat him, and went away leaving him half dead. And by chance a priest was going down on that road, and when he saw him, he passed by on the other side. Likewise a Levite also, when he came to the place and saw him, passed by on the other side. But a Samaritan, who was on a journey, came upon him; and when he saw him, he felt compassion, and came to him and bandaged up his wounds, pouring oil and wine on them; and he put him on his own beast, and brought him to an inn and took care of him.*

185. John 10:40–42 is another good example of ordinary people responding as Jesus desired and in response to his miracles: *"And He went away again beyond the Jordan to the place where John was first baptizing, and He was staying there. Many came to Him and were saying, 'While John performed no sign, yet everything John said about this man was true.' Many believed in Him there."*

> *On the next day he took out two denarii and gave them to the innkeeper and said, "Take care of him; and whatever more you spend, when I return I will repay you." Which of these three do you think proved to be a neighbor to the man who fell into the robbers' hands?' And he said, 'The one who showed mercy toward him.' Then Jesus said to him, 'Go and do the same.'"*

The context is important here. Jesus gives this parable in response to a lawyer's question concerning who was the neighbor that Jesus required him to love.

> *"And a lawyer stood up and put Him to the test, saying, 'Teacher, what shall I do to inherit eternal life?' And He said to him, 'What is written in the Law? How does it read to you?' And he answered, 'You shall love the Lord your God with all your heart, and with all your soul, and with all your strength, and with all your mind; and your neighbor as yourself.' And He said to him, 'You have answered correctly; do this and you will live.' But wishing to justify himself, he said to Jesus, 'And who is my neighbor?'"* (Luke 10:25–29)

Even though the lawyer's motives may not have been upright, the basic truth of Jesus gracious reply still stands—the law of God requires love of neighbor. The point of the parable, is that the neighbor we are to love is anyone in need. But the significant feature for our purposes is that Jesus deliberately took a despised non-Jew (an unregenerate Samaritan) as the focus of his teaching concerning neighborly love. Again, the parable would be meaningless if the Samaritan's heart in the parable was so depraved that he was totally incapable of doing anything spiritually good. Loving a neighbor is both a spiritual good—it fulfills a fundamental aspect of God's law (love of neighbor)—and a moral good.

Luke 15:17–20

> *"But when he came to his senses, he said, 'How many of my father's hired men have more than enough bread, but I am dying here with hunger! I will get up and go to my father, and will say to him, "Father, I have sinned against heaven, and in your sight; I am no longer worthy to be called your son; make me as one of your hired men."' So he got up and came to his father."*

The parable of the prodigal son is well known, again illustrating God's love for lost sinners. For our purposes, I want to focus on the son's circumstances that caused him to "come to his senses," repent and return to his father after squandering all his inheritance. Even though a parable, the elements in the parable must ring true for this genre to be an effective teaching tool used by Jesus. What caused the prodigal to repent and return to his father? The answer is his dire circumstances and his memory of his father's love. Nothing about first being regenerated and then repenting here! The prodigal did a good (repent) because he realized his situation was not good and he was humble enough to repent and return back home. The whole point of the parable is to illustrate what God requires of all people—a willingness to acknowledge the futility of their lives apart from relating to a loving heavenly Father, repent and come to God. Significantly, the father's response in the parable is telling: *"The father said to his slaves, 'Quickly bring out the best robe and put it on him, and put a ring on his hand and sandals on his feet; and bring the fattened calf, kill it, and let us eat and celebrate; for this son of mine was dead and has come to life again; he was lost and has been found'"* (vv. 22–24). The "dead" son has now been restored to life through being reunited with his father. The parable is indeed a beautiful picture story of God's love for all those who find themselves spiritually dead and lost due to their sin and who "come to their senses," choose to repent and come to God.

Acts 10:1–2

> *"Now there was a man at Caesarea named Cornelius, a centurion of what was called the Italian cohort, a devout man and one who feared God with all his household, and gave many alms to the Jewish people and prayed to God continually."*

Cornelius was a God-fearer—one who affiliated himself with the Jewish synagogue and who sought to align himself religiously with the God of Israel.[186] But the whole point of the passage is to underscore his inclusion into the New Testament people of God through regeneration; in other words he was not regenerated when the description of him is given in Acts 10:1–2. But how could, according to Calvinism, such an unregenerate man do so many good things—be devout, fear God, give alms, pray? Such behavior is impossible for unregenerate persons according to Calvinism.[187]

Acts 16:30–34

> *"After he brought them out, he said, 'Sirs, what must I do to be saved?' They said, 'Believe in the Lord Jesus, and you will be saved, you and your household.' And they spoke the word of the Lord to him together with all who were in his house. And he took them that very hour of the night and washed their wounds, and immediately he was baptized, he and all his household. And he brought them into his house and set food before them, and rejoiced greatly, having believed in God with his whole household."*

In this case, the Philippian jailer was not a God-fearer and in fact there is no indication that he was religiously anything but a pagan. Yet, in response to the dangers posed to him by the earthquake that threatened to allow all the prisoners in his charge to

---

186. Perkin, "God-fearer," 888.

187. Calvinists deal with this problem by insisting all Old Testament saints and New Testament God-fearers were in fact regenerated. I shall consider this issue later, but note that here in the case of Cornelius we are told explicitly that Cornelius was a devout man *before* receiving the Holy Spirit.

escape, and having heard Paul and Silas singing hymns, he seeks salvation, is told what to do (believe in the Lord Jesus), responds positively to the gospel call and is converted. Again, we must ask, if total depravity were true, how could the jailer seek a good (search out for salvation) and then respond as God would have him respond? There is nothing in the text whatsoever to suggest that God's Spirit was somehow working secretly to cause him to be regenerated before believing.

Acts 17:11

> "Now these were more noble-minded than those in Thessalonica, for they re-ceived the word with great eagerness, examining the Scriptures daily."

Paul and Silas had just fled Thessalonica because of the hostility of the Jews there, and had arrived at Berea where, as was Paul's custom, they proclaimed the gospel to the Jews in the synagogue (v. 10). In sharp contrast with the Jews in Thessalonica, we are told that the Berean Jews received Paul's message eagerly. Significantly, Luke comments that this openness to the gospel was because these Jews *"were more noble-minded than those in Thessalonica."* Here we are told specifically that the reason for the Jew's positive reception of the gospel (a spiritual good) followed a characteristic in the people them-selves—their relative noble-mindedness.[188] Furthermore, as a consequence of their research into Paul's claims based on their study of the Old Testament Scriptures, we are told that *"therefore many of them believed, along with a number of prominent Greek women and men"* (v. 12). This incident hardly fits well a notion of human depravity so extensive as to result in a total inability to do anything of spiritual value at all.

b) Ought Implies Can

If an authority were to command me to fly from one town to the next, and then punish me for failing to do so when I protest that I am not equipped to fly like a bird, an independent observer would find the whole incident quite ludicrous and indeed laughable. And yet this sort of scenario is effectively what is postulated when, for example, the command to repent and believe the gospel (Mark 3:2) is openly proclaimed to a people completely unable to respond to this command because of their total depravity. Similarly, with respect to the command given by Paul to the Philippian jailor to *"believe on the Lord Jesus"* in order to be saved (Acts 16:31)—it would be incoherent for Paul to say this if he knew the man would not be able to follow though because of a total depravity that entailed a total inability to respond in the prescribed manner. In other words when the Scriptures urge a spiritual or moral imperative (ought) the operating assumption is always that the individual(s)

---

188. The relevant word is εὐγενης (*eugenēs*), from which the word *eugenics* comes, meaning "good/superior race" in ethical discussions.

involved can in fact comply if they wish to do so. As the German philosopher Immanuel Kant stated, "Ought implies can."[189]

Calvinist's struggle with this moral precept because they effectively deny the saying; for them ought need not imply can. Addressing this specific issue, Wright says,

> God . . . may have many reasons for commanding sinners to do what they cannot do. One reason would be to reveal the seriousness of slavery to sin. That is, he may command righteousness in order to show sinners their spiritual incompetence (Rom 7:14–24). Another reason might be that by convicting the people of their sinful inability to be good, he might thereby induce them to seek God's mercy (Rom 7:22—8:4). Or perhaps he wishes to cause them to act in a way that will bring them into judgment (Jer 50:24).[190]

Wright suggests three possible reasons as to why God would command unbelievers to do what he knows they cannot do. The first is to show the seriousness of slavery to sin. As noted previously, however, enslavement to sin carries with it the idea of a total inability to save oneself, not an inability to turn to a Savior from sin. Calvinists consistently fail to maintain this important distinction and thereby extend the metaphor of enslavement beyond the scriptural warrant. In any case, it would hardly be necessary to show a person that he is a consistent sinner by telling him or her to do the impossible! This could lead to frustration or anger, not necessarily insight into their spiritual or moral condition.

The second reason given, to induce sinners to seek God's mercy, doesn't really make sense within a Calvinistic soteriology since sinners are simply not free to "seek God's mercy" under any circumstances because of their total depravity.

The third reason, that through a sinner's inability to do as commanded by God he is thereby brought into judgment, while superficially seems plausible, in fact has problems too. The assumption made is that the judgment is justified because they fail to do what is commanded. But this is the very question in dispute—would God judge someone for failing to do what they are in fact unable to do? This third reason only holds if the formula "ought implies can" is valid.[191]

Wright provides a fourth rationale for why God would command unbelievers to do what he knows they cannot do: "God may have reasons that he does not (and is not obliged to) tell us. Although he tells us a great deal about his plans and purposes,

---

189. See Kahn, *Kant, Ought Implies Can*.

190. Wright, *No Place for Sovereignty*, 162.

191. The quote from Jer 50:24 refers to Babylon's judgment by God because of its brutal assault of Jerusalem. But even though God used the Babylonian aggression for his own purposes (as an instrument of punishment upon Judah for its sins), Babylon could justifiably be held accountable for its actions because it could have done otherwise. Again, the moral principle "ought implies can" holds here—Babylon ought not to have exercised political aggression because it could have refrained from such actions. In short, the citation does not support Wright's third contention.

God owes human beings no explanation of his actions."[192] This, of course, is nothing more than the common Calvinistic appeal to mystery to justify what appears, at least on the surface, to be incoherent.[193]

The linkage between a call to resist sinning and an ability to do so is made explicit in Gen 4:4–7 concerning the incident of Cain murdering his brother Abel. Because Cain's sacrifice was not acceptable to God and Abel's was, Cain became angry and it showed in his facial expression: *"And the Lord had regard for Abel and for his offering; but for Cain and for his offering He had no regard. So Cain became very angry and his countenance fell."* God of course, observes this reaction on the part of Cain: *"Then the Lord said to Cain, 'Why are you angry? And why has your countenance fallen?'"* God then seeks to encourage Cain to *"do well"*—probably by being careful to offer better sacrifices—with the assurance that his *"countenance [will be] lifted up"* (NASB; or that he will be *accepted*, NIV and ESV): *"If you do well, will not your countenance be lifted up?"* Failure to follow through on God's exhortation to Cain to *"do well"* will leave him vulnerable to sin: *"And if you do not do well, sin is crouching at the door."* Sin here is pictured as an alien force that is seeking for opportunities to attack and harm Cain: *"and its desire is for you."* In these series of questions on the part of God there is warning about sin, personified as a crouching being or animal, and sin's malevolent intent, as well as an exhortation to resist sin: *"but you must master it."* Cain ought to master sin because failure to do so would leave him open to sin's destructive power. The narrative would not make sense if God told Cain what he ought to do knowing all along that Cain could not do it. Exhorting Cain to master sin, at face value, clearly indicates this was something that was within Cain's power to do and so avoid the harm that sinning does. Here is a clear case where "ought implies can."[194]

In fact, every exhortation, every command, every warning in the Bible is predicated on the assumption that "ought implies can." Even Calvinism's appeal to believe that the human condition is such that no one is able to repent and believe the gospel until first regenerated by God itself relies on the assumption that ought implies can; one ought to believe the Calvinist account because one can understand the claim and can see that it is in the Bible.

c) A Brief Review of the Bible's Assessment of Man

Certainly, the Bible's overall emphasis and tone is on man's sinfulness. This is hardly surprising since the Bible is God's word addressing man's need for salvation from the

192. Wright, *No Place for Sovereignty*, 163.

193. This is not to deny that there are some truths in the Bible that may justifiably be termed a mystery—the exact way Jesus's human and divine natures cohere, the exact nature of God (as Trinitarian), etc. But these are relatively few. Calvinism on the other hand, quite often appeals to mystery or paradox to explain an aspect of its theology.

194. This passage is not easy to interpret, but the difficulties do not invalidate the basic point being made here. See Wenham, *Genesis 1–15*, 102–6.

consequences of his sin and God's redemptive purposes to deal with this spiritual need. In other words, to appreciate God's provision of salvation both the extent of man's need (all have sinned, Rom 3:23), and its reality need to be underscored. God sent his son to be the savior of the world (1 John 4:14), and so the Bible makes very clear man's need of salvation by highlighting his predicament—his sinfulness and the resulting alienation from God.

Calvinism tends to focus almost exclusively upon man's sinfulness, and it is but one small step to understand man after the fall as being virtually exclusively defined by his sin. This may be seen, for example, in Augustine's "mass of perdition."[195] Calvin likewise took a very dim view of man after the fall. Unregenerate mankind is "a very miserable creature . . . [that] can beget nothing but the materials of death . . . [human nature has] no part in which it is not perverted and corrupted . . . all the thoughts which proceed from [the human mind] are derided as foolish, frivolous, perverse, and insane."[196] Modern Calvinists take a similar view: Zemek speaks of "the ethically grotesque picture of the race in its post-fallen estate"[197] John Piper likewise says, "Our sinful corruption is so deep and so strong as to make us slaves of sin and morally unable to overcome our own rebellion and blindness."[198]

However, according to the Bible the sinfulness of man is not the only characteristic of man as he now exists before God. In order to get a more balanced understanding of who human beings are in the eyes of God I shall examine the biblical data under the rubric of several theological categories.

1) Man, Even in His Sinful State, Is an Image Bearer of God

Genesis 1:26–27

"Then God said, 'Let Us make man in Our image, according to Our likeness; and let them rule over the fish of the sea and over the birds of the sky and over the cattle and over all the earth, and over every creeping thing that creeps on the earth.' God created man in His own image, in the image of God He created him; male and female He created them."

James 3:8–10

"But no one can tame the tongue; it is a restless evil and full of deadly poison. With it we bless our Lord and Father, and with it we curse men, who have been made in the likeness of God; from the same mouth come both blessing and cursing. My brethren, these things ought not to be this way."

195. "Augustine here develops the idea that all of humanity constitute a single mass of sin." McGrath, "Origen on Inherited Sin," 218.
196. Calvin, *Institutes*, 2.3.1.
197. Zemek, *Biblical Theology*, 3.
198. Piper, *Five Points*, 15.

As is well known, man was uniquely created in the image and likeness of God. This status establishes that man stands in unique relationship to God and the rest of creation. There is an intrinsic dignity to man given to him by his creator. Most importantly, this status is not removed after Adam's sin as the reference to Jas 3:9 indicates. Genesis 9:6 grounds the justification of capital punishment for murder in that murder entails a gross violation of the image of God. In a difficult passage, Paul explains that a man ought not to worship in the congregation with his head covered *"since he is the image and glory of God"* (1 Cor 11:7)—the context indicates Paul is thinking of man as created by God. Scripture's insistence that all people, both men and women, retain the unique quality of reflecting in some way God himself, provides a basis for viewing all people as endowed with a dignity and even honor that even sin cannot remove.[199]

2) Man Is Granted Authority to Rule over God's World

Psalm 8:4–6

"What is man that You take thought of him, and the son of man that You care for him?

Yet You have made him a little lower than God, and You crown him with glory and majesty!

You make him to rule over the works of Your hands; You have put all things under his feet."

Closely related to man being created in, and continuing to bear, the image of God is the authority delegated by God to rule over God's creation on God's behalf. Psalm 8 above reflects the so-called cultural mandate in Gen 1:28 for man to "subdue" and "rule over" the created order. While sin has made fulfilling this mandate difficult and manifests itself in the abuse of this call to stewardship, the divine call for man to exercise this delegated rulership has never been rescinded, and reflects the high view God has of man as his special creation. According to the psalmist, man is only "a little lower than the angels" and "crowned with glory and majesty"! While it is true that only Jesus meets this high calling perfectly (Heb 2:5–9), the principle of delegated authority to rule on God's behalf has not been abrogated and reflects a high view of man which Adam's sin did not nullify.

3) The Incarnation Underscores Man's Significance

John 1:14

"And the Word became flesh, and dwelt among us."

---

199. "Man is unique in every aspect of his existence; for not some part of man or some faculty of man, but man as such, man in his integrity, is the image of God. The biblical concept is not that the image is *in* man, but that the man *is* the image of God." Shepherd, "Image of God," 1:1018.

Galatians 4:4

"But when the fullness of the time came, God sent forth His Son,
born of a woman."

The fact that God chose to become man in the person of Jesus of Nazareth directly indicates the importance to God of his human creation. God did not choose to take the form of a lion or an elephant, rather the incarnation—God becoming man— clearly reflects the esteem God places on the human race. The same high value placed by God upon the human race is seen in Jesus's befriending Christians: *"For both He who sanctifies and those who are sanctified are all from one Father; for which reason He is not ashamed to call them brethren"* (Heb 2:11). While it is true that the immediate subjects of the verse are believers, the principle of identification holds. In that sense, this passage in Hebrews is an instance (applying to believers) of the broader category of incarnation. In the incarnation God identified with humanity and took on the form of a man.

The principle of identification comes across strongly in the immediately following verses in the Heb 2 passage: *"Therefore, since the children share in flesh and blood, He Himself likewise also partook of the same, that through death He might render powerless him who had the power of death, that is, the devil"* (Heb 2:14). Again, while it serves the purpose of the writer of the book of Hebrews to focus the identification of Christ with God's redeemed people, the basis is seen in the universal principle that since humans are characterized by flesh and blood, *"He Himself likewise also partook of the same."* It is not only Christians but also everyone that possesses "flesh and blood," and the necessity of the incarnation to effect God's redemptive purposes underscores God's redemptive concerns for all people. In short, all these passages which connect the reality of the incarnation to God's human creation highlights the importance, dignity, and intrinsic value God places on all human beings.

4) The Universal Fatherhood of God

God is Father of people in two ways; first by creation and second by redemption. A good example of the Bible's witness to the former is seen in Acts 17:26–28:

> *He made from one man every nation of mankind to live on all the face of the*
> *earth, having determined their appointed times and the boundaries of their hab-*
> *itation, that they would seek God, if perhaps they might grope for Him and find*
> *Him, though He is not far from each one of us; for in Him we live and move and*
> *exist, as even some of your own poets have said, "For we also are His children."*
> *Being then the children of God . . .*

Paul, at Athens, seeks a point of contact with the Athenians in order to proclaim the gospel to them. Despite their being idol-worshipping pagans, Paul recognizes an entryway, a point of commonality in a shared humanity and appeals to their sense that the true God *"is not far from each one of us,"* and that everyone in fact lives in close proximity to this God (*"in Him we live and move and exist"*), and that therefore in this sense all persons can be justly called the children of God. Certainly, these Athenians were far from knowing God through redemption, but significantly for our purposes, Paul is quite comfortable acknowledging a common humanity that unites all persons equally before the Creator God. This God, through Paul, would be willing to be known as everyone's Father by creation, and thereby indirectly testifying to the high view God has of his human creation. As F. F. Bruce remarks: "We are, then, the offspring of God, says Paul, not in any pantheistic sense but in the sense of the biblical doctrine of man, as beings created by God in his own image."[200]

5) The Concept of Relative Righteousness

As we have seen, the picture portrayed by Calvinism of man after the fall is a very dark one—no unregenerate person can do anything of genuine good, that counts as good in any morally or spiritually significant sense before God. Grudem is typical when he remarks that "in our actions we are totally unable to do spiritual good before God." Even though they may appear to be good, in actuality all actions are in fact morally worthless: "Though from a human standpoint people might be able to do much good, Isaiah affirms that *'all our righteous deeds are like a polluted garment'* (Isa 64:6)."[201] In the final analysis, no human action is authentically good—all good deeds are filthy rags. But is this the final word Scripture has to say on human actions?

First, let us briefly examine the context in which Isa 64:6 occurs. Isaiah, in the passage cited, is recalling God's historical actions on behalf of Israel. He recalls God's mighty acts of deliverance "in the days of old, of Moses" (Isa 63:11), especially the exodus and the parting of the waters (v. 12). Isaiah is aware that God's people have strayed grievously and longs for the day when God would again act decisively to bring salvation to his people (*"Oh, that You would rend the heavens and come down, That the mountains might quake at Your presence"* [Isa 64:1]). He recalls God's coming down at Mt. Sinai when *"You did awesome things which we did not expect, You came down, the mountains quaked at Your presence"* (Isa 64:3). He recalls the old days when God would graciously act on behalf of *"the one who waits for Him"* (v. 4b). He longs for the days when *"You meet him who rejoices in doing righteousness, who remembers You in Your ways"* (v. 5a). Then, in sharp contrast to those days, present Israel has continued the sin that also characterized the nation from its earlier days: *"Behold, You were angry, for we sinned, we continued in them a long time; And shall we be saved? For all of us have become like one who is unclean"* (vv. 5b, 6a). Then

---

200. Bruce, *Acts*, 340.
201. Grudem, *Systematic Theology*, 497.

follows v. 6b: *"And all our righteous deeds are like a filthy garment; And all of us wither like a leaf, and our iniquities, like the wind, take us away."*

Two points may be noted from this analysis of Isa 64. The first is that Isaiah is making a statement about ancient Israel's sinful behavior—a state that is all the more offensive in that Israel alone of all peoples was in covenant relationship with God. Rather than choosing to maintain covenant loyalty and follow her God, Israel chose to adopt sinful practices—idolatry, and injustices. While systematic theologians like Grudem tend to view a text like Isa 64:6 as a clinical, systematic-theological statement contributing to a doctrine of biblical anthropology,[202] in fact the statement concerning Israel's behavior is a historically rooted one and need not necessarily be seen as a universal, historically independent statement about human nature and all human behavior. Isaiah is describing, in general terms, what was true for a particular people at a particular time. It is a generally true description of Israel in Isaiah's day, but not necessarily true even of all Israel in an absolute sense; even Elijah forgot that God had seven thousand who had not bowed the knee to Baal in his day (1 Kgs 19:18).

The second point concerns the acknowledgment by Isaiah that there was a time in Israel's history when Israelites waited for God (i.e., expressed trust and confidence in Yahweh), and rejoiced in doing righteousness, and who remembered God's ways! (The latter sentiment occurring in the verse immediately before the reference to filthy garments.) Of course, no Israelite then, or anybody now (including Christians), exhibits perfect righteousness—only God has that characteristic; but a relative righteousness is a reality.[203] This is a righteousness of those who seek after God, who are desirous of following God and God's commandments, who are concerned about injustices, and who reject idolatry. Cottrell, addressing the issue of relative righteousness well, says:

> Despite the lack of absolute righteousness, the Bible often speaks of "the righteous," and not simply in the sense of their having received the gift of Christ's righteousness through faith. On the contrary, they are called righteous because in a relative sense, they are righteous. They have a measure of piety and good works, of trust in and dependence upon God, that makes it proper for them to be called righteous—in comparison with the wicked. While such incomplete and relative righteousness is not sufficient to establish any kind of legal or moral claim upon God's blessings, nevertheless God is pleased with such righteousness and chooses to bless those who possess it.[204]

202. Of course, isolating the verse and ignoring its context lends plausibility to the Calvinist interpretation.

203. It is true that Christians in a sense own perfect righteousness, but it is one that is imputed to them by Christ (1 Cor 1:30).

204. Cottrell, *What the Bible Says about God the Redeemer*, 202. Calvinists are aware of the righteous in contrast with the wicked, of course, but assert that those righteous are only so because they have been regenerated. We shall examine this contention later. Suffice to say now that no passages in the Old Testament links *regeneration* to righteousness for any individuals; it is an assertion required by Calvinism to sustain its view of total depravity. Furthermore, the relative righteous are often compared

6) Man Is Worthy of Redemption

Man's value to God is further established in that man was worth redeeming. In fact, even the term redemption means a return to rightful owner. All mankind belongs to God by way of creation and God has taken very costly steps to bring back to himself those who are lost. Such actions taken by God through Christ, *"who gave Himself for us to redeem us"* (Titus 2:14), is motivated by God's great love for his human creation and expresses the tremendous value placed by God upon every single person. As Paul notes: *"God demonstrates His own love toward us, in that while we were yet sinners, Christ died for us"* (Rom 5:8). From God's perspective, even sinful man is of such worth and value as to motivate him to act sacrificially on our behalf.

d) Paul's Evangelistic Technique—Persuasion, Reasoning, Etc.

Paul, in his evangelistic efforts sought to persuade his audience of the truth of the gospel. For example, at Corinth Paul *"was reasoning in the synagogue every Sabbath and trying to persuade Jews and Greeks"* (Acts 18:4). For those Jews who visited Paul while the latter was under house arrest in Rome we read that when *"they had set a day for Paul, they came to him at his lodging in large numbers; and he was explaining to them by solemnly testifying about the kingdom of God and trying to persuade them concerning Jesus, from both the Law of Moses and from the Prophets, from morning until evening"* (Acts 28:23).

Likewise, Paul sought to reason with his hearers:

Acts 17:17: *"So he was reasoning in the synagogue with the Jews and the God-fearing Gentiles, and in the market place every day with those who happened to be present."*

Acts 18:4: *"And he was reasoning in the synagogue every Sabbath and trying to persuade Jews and Greeks."*

Acts 19:8: *"And he entered the synagogue and continued speaking out boldly for three months, reasoning and persuading them about the kingdom of God."*

Paul also did not hesitate to argue for the gospel before his hearers. For example, in Acts 9:29 we are told that *"he was talking and arguing with the Hellenistic Jews; but they were attempting to put him to death."*

Some at Corinth had questioned Paul's apostolic authority and gospel and so Paul has to use the language of evangelistic preaching to appeal to the Corinthians to be reconciled to God: *"Therefore, we are ambassadors for Christ, as though God were making an appeal through us; we beg you on behalf of Christ, be reconciled to God"* (2 Cor 5:20). Paul viewed himself as an ambassador for Christ and, as Kruse

---

with the wicked in a general sense—they both coexist in a community.

notes, "the God who reconciled the world to himself through the death of his Son, now actually appeals to the world, through his ambassadors, to be reconciled to him."[205] There can be little doubt that Paul, in his evangelistic ministry in fulfillment of his call to be an apostle to the Gentiles, would appeal to his hearers to respond to the gospel he proclaimed.

This is another example of "ought implying can." The people ought to believe the gospel proclaimed by God's ambassadors, and the expectation is that they could and should. Calvinists deny this. "Invitations to come to Christ, to repent and believe, are found throughout the Word of God and are the essence of the appeal of evangelism. Arminians seem to think that God's invitations presuppose the ability to respond in the right way. The Bible expressly denies this ability."[206] However, such a denial is not only counterintuitive but also incoherent. Why, one must ask, would Paul or any other ambassador for Christ appeal to, argue for, reason with, his hearers if he believed they were totally incapable of responding? This would be like appealing to a man to fly—it simply would not make sense. John Lennox indirectly addresses this scenario when he says: "Causal determinism cannot even be meaningfully affirmed, since if it were true then the affirmation itself would be determined. . . . The affirmation is therefore irrational. Furthermore, it is common for determinists to try to convince non-determinists to convert to determinism. But that assumes that the non-determinists are free to convert, and therefore their non-determinism is not determined in the first place."[207]

Calvinists typically respond by arguing that other scriptures show man's depravity is such that he cannot respond, and also that these efforts to communicate the gospel are merely the means God uses to call the elect to himself. The difficulty with such reasoning, however, is that there is absolutely no hint in the passages cited above that this is the case. The reader is expected to take the invitations to respond to the gospel at face value and it is unjustified to negate these expectations by imposing a Calvinistic interpretive grid on these passages.[208]

e) The Nature of Human Nature

One sometimes hears it said by Calvinists that one is not a sinner because one sins, but one sins because one is a sinner. The thought is that sinning flows inevitably from one's corrupted human nature. Human nature after the fall of Adam can only sin because the fall corrupted human nature.

205. Kruse, *2 Corinthians*, 128.

206. Wright, *No Place for Sovereignty*, 163.

207. Lennox, *Determined to Believe?*, 49.

208. John Stott, a Calvinist himself, takes Acts 17:17, e.g., at face value when he says that Paul "sought by the proclamation of the gospel to prevail on them [the Athenians] to turn from their idols to the living God." *Message of Acts*, 280.

The first point to note is that the Bible nowhere speaks of a "sinful nature" or "corrupted human nature."[209] However, even if the term is not used in the Bible perhaps the concept is present. But what exactly does it mean to have a corrupted or distorted or broken human nature? This is not a trivial question because, as noted above, Calvinists insist that all human decisions and choices flow inevitably from our natures—corrupted natures lead to sinful behavior.

If "human nature" is definitionally fixed and synonymous with "human being" then it would not make sense to speak of corrupted human nature. Human nature then is synonymous with what it means to be human; human nature is different from, say, dog nature because humans are different from dogs. A human nature is what humans as human beings are irrespective of their choices, decisions, behaviors, etc.[210] Furthermore, human beings are God's creation and, unless God creates sin, are intrinsically good—expressing the very likeness of God himself (Gen 1:26, 27). Following the creation of Adam and Eve God declared that all he had made was "very good" (Gen 1:31). To be made human is to be made good and in the image of God.

Of course, Calvinists argue that after the fall of Adam into sin all subsequent humanity suffered a changed (corrupted) nature. But if to speak of human nature is to speak of human beings then no change in such a being can take place since such a change would entail a change from a human being into some other sort of being.

Related to the above is the problem of confusing person with nature.[211] Renault asks the question, "What is a person?" and answers, "We might say that it is a unique manifestation of a nature. . . . There is only one human nature (or humanity) expressed uniquely in six billion different human persons."[212] He then raises the issue of choices and their source: "Do people choose to do things or do natures choose to do things?"[213] The answer, when posed in this manner, is clear—it is people that make choices. There is an intimate and personal dimension to persons that is lacking in the notion of nature. If, as Calvinists hold, all of a person's choices flow inevitably from his nature then, since it is God's nature to create, redeem, forgive and so on, God would have to create, redeem, forgive—God would have *had* to create the world, he would not have had a choice in the matter. Since, as all agree, God was not under compulsion to create despite his nature as a Creator, then his choice to actually create was a decision that flowed from his person, not his nature.

209. On two occasions the NIV mistranslates the Greek word σαρξ (flesh) as "sinful nature." The NIV is a translation that sometimes paraphrases, and in so doing occasionally betrays the biases of the translators. See Renault, *Reconsidering TULIP*, 21.

210. I am indebted to the Orthodox scholar Renault for this line of reasoning. Renault makes the point I am making here under his heading "Ontological Problems." Renault, *Reconsidering TULIP*, 3–4.

211. Another topic discussed in Renault, *Reconsidering TULIP*, 5.

212. Renault, *Reconsidering TULIP*, 5.

213. Renault, *Reconsidering TULIP*, 5.

The reality of the incarnation where Christ took on a fully human nature—yet was without sin shows that sin is not intrinsic to human nature. To be human in other words does not require that a person sins—that was true for Adam and also true for those born after Adam sinned. Adam as a human being was not under compulsion to sin; people today, as human beings, are not under compulsion to sin. Just as Adam chose to exercise his God-given freedom in a manner contrary to God's will, so today all persons may choose to exercise their God-given freedom in a manner contrary to God's will (known either through conscience or natural law (Rom 2:14, 15), or through special revelation, the Bible). The ability to make moral choices is not a function of human nature, but is integral to being human. In other words, choice-making is not determined by a human nature but by a human being.

Sinning certainly impacts one's subsequent choices and patterns of living. Through force of habit sin becomes "second nature." Our true nature as human beings, our humanity, remains the same, but our capacities to make choices and decisions that are consistent with God's will (either through the Bible or through conscience) becomes diminished. The wrath of God is directed toward those persons who continually choose to "suppress the truth in unrighteousness" (Rom 1:18). The distinction I am making between sin on the one hand, and the person as a human being on the other may be seen in the Apostle Paul's struggle with sin in his life.

Throughout Rom 7:14–25 we see Paul struggling between his desire to do right and his inability to always follow through on the good that he wants to do.[214] The point of interest for us in this passage is the way Paul consistently differentiates between himself and sin's negative influence upon him. The following excerpts underscore this point:

> "So now, no longer am I the one doing it, but sin which dwells in me (v. 17). For the good that I want, I do not do, but I practice the very evil that I do not want (v. 19). But if I am doing the very thing I do not want, I am no longer the one doing it, but sin which dwells in me (v. 20). For I joyfully concur with the law of God in the inner man, but I see a different law in the members of my body, waging war against the law of my mind and making me a prisoner of the law of sin which is in my members" (vv. 22, 23).

Sin here is pictured as an alien force "dwelling in his members"—but separate from his true desires. Sin is one thing, he as a human being is another. The two are different and separate. Paul could will one thing, but recognize the presence of another alien principle in his body. Admittedly, the conflict is almost certainly heightened because

---

214. Scholars debate whether Paul here is describing his pre-conversion experience (as many Calvinists hold), or whether he is describing a struggle characteristic of the earnest believer seeking to live a holy life. However taken, this passage must not be understood to imply the Christian does not struggle in the manner described by Paul. As Warren states: "Romans 7 does not mean pre-Christian experience particularly if pre-Christian experience exempts the Christian life from this struggle." Warren, *Salvation*, 24.

Paul speaks as a Christian whose spirit has been renewed in Christ, but the same principle holds even for the unregenerate—for those who *do not have the Law* [and yet] *do instinctively the things of the Law, these, not having the Law, are a law to themselves, in that they show the work of the Law written in their hearts, their conscience bearing witness and their thoughts alternately accusing or else defending them*" (Rom 2:14, 15). The unregenerate do not have the presence of God's Spirit to help them with this struggle, but nevertheless as human beings created in the image of God, they still retain something of the same struggle; they too can know on the one hand how they ought to behave and yet find sin easily at hand to derail them. The principle in both cases holds: sin is to be differentiated from the person himself.

Virgil Warren's remarks on this topic rings true both to the biblical witness and to human experience:

> Everyone agrees that man is depraved, but the reason for this depravity does not necessarily reside in the nature that a person receives by birth. "Depraved" describes the way people act. Why they act this way goes beyond scripture at this point. . . . The powerful pull of sin comes from amoral bodily drives plus previous experience that produces "habitual" ways of behaving; if that pull has resulted from previous action, it may be reversed by personal influence instead of supernatural miracle on the structures of human nature. There is no adequate reason for supposing that the structural givens in Adam before his sin differed after he sinned or differed from those in a Spirit led Christian. Adam sinned; non-Christians sin; Christians sin: there is no need for natural explanations for any one of these more than for the other. We are satisfied to say that unfallen, fallen, and saved man have the same fundamental nature. Such a view, of course, allows for pull of bodily drives and the drag of previous sin on present resolve.[215]

If the nature of human nature outlined above is valid and accurately reflects a scriptural anthropology, then actions and choices made are not determined by one's nature as Calvinism teaches, but rather they are the freely chosen actions of persons. Certainly, sin has a "pulling" effect but a pulling effect is not determinism. One cannot be blamed or praised for actions which are determined by one's "nature"—but one can most certainly be blamed or praised for freely chosen actions that a person makes. "The relation between your nature and your will is not causation but influence. That is, your nature may influence your choices but it does not cause your choices. . . . The faculty of the will has this marvelous ability to originate moral choices, free from all internal or external necessity."[216]

215. Warren, *Salvation*, 24.
216. Morrell, *Does Man Inherit a Sinful Nature?*, 21.

f) An Age of Accountability

Calvinists deny the reality of an age of accountability, an age a child reaches at which point the child can be morally accountable for its behavior.[217] The reason is easy to see—all children are born in a state of guilt and moral corruption due to original sin; there is no time when a child reaches a state of moral accountability as though, in some sense, they are morally innocent prior to this age. The Calvinist theologian Wayne Grudem is a good example: "Even before birth children have a guilty standing before God and a sinful nature that not only gives them a tendency to sin but also causes God to view them as 'sinners.'"[218] Conversely, if there is such a thing as an age of accountability this would tend to undermine the doctrine of original sin since at least one class of people (babies) would not be viewed as morally guilty before God.[219]

Since the scriptures appealed to by Calvinists to justify a notion of original sin have been previously discussed I will concentrate here on biblical justification for the idea of an age of accountability for sin.[220]

217. "An indefinite time in the development of the person when he not only realizes the differences between right and wrong, but can understand the consequences of his behavior and can be held responsible for his actions in a practical sense." Warren, *Salvation*, 520.

218. Grudem, *Systematic Theology*, 499. Most Calvinists are reluctant to conclude from the doctrine of original sin that babies that die will suffer the damning effects of Adam's sin. Grudem himself seems to hold that believer's babies will be regenerated and thus qualified to enter heaven. With respect to the babies of unbelievers, "we simply must leave the matter in the hands of God and trust him to be both just and merciful." Grudem, *Systematic Theology*, 501. Whether such a perspective can be consistently held with a doctrine of original guilt and corrupted human nature I leave to the reader to ponder. Calvin himself believed no non-elect baby would be permitted to die prior to reaching an age at which they "procure" their own destruction due to their own impiety, wickedness and rebellion. Since no one knows who the elect are, this is an argument which is possible neither to demonstrate or refute and may thus be justly viewed as a mere expedient to fit his system. See Swan, "Calvin on the Death of Non-elect Infants," para. 1.

219. The Restorationist theologian Jack Cottrell has helpfully shown the elements necessary for a child to be accountable to God for their sin: "For there to be sin, four things are necessary: (1) the existence of law; (2) the existence of a Creator-God as the source of the law; (3) created free-will beings who are responsible for keeping the law; and (4) a knowledge of and understanding of that law on the part of these beings. Once a child understands the essence of this combination of things, he or she is accountable to God and under condemnation." Cottrell, *Faith Once for All*, 192.

220. It "is not that young children never do anything wrong as measured by God's law, but simply that they are not accountable to God for such wrongdoing. Thus we do not say a child reaches 'the age of sin,' but rather 'the age of *accountability*' for sin." Cottrell, *Faith Once for All*, 191.

Deuteronomy 1:39

"Moreover, your little ones who you said would become a prey, and your sons, who this day have no knowledge of good or evil, shall enter there, and I will give it to them and they shall possess it."

At Kadesh-barnea following the report of the spies, the people of Israel displayed remarkable unbelief and lack of trust in Yahweh who had led them by cloud and fire. As punishment God judged that generation and declared that none would enter the promised land. But the next generation of "little ones" and "children" who "have no knowledge of good or evil" would indeed enter the promised land. It seems that at some unspecified age children do gain an awareness of right and wrong and that prior to that age children cannot be considered morally accountable before God. Contra Grudem, God does not view infants as sinners.

Romans 4:15b

"Where there is no law, there also is no violation."

Romans 7:8b

"Apart from the Law sin is dead."

The close connection between law and sin is brought out throughout Scripture, especially in the book of Romans, and especially in these two verses. The Apostle Paul notes that *"I would not have come to know sin except through the Law"* (Rom 7:7). An awareness of God's law (either Mosaic or moral) which is subsequently deliberately violated brings condemnation and judgment. Since in fact we live in a moral universe and people generally know that to lie is wrong, to steal is wrong, then in what sense can Rom 4:15b and 7:8b apply? Is there any time when a person can be with "no law" (and hence "no violation") or be "apart from law"? The answer is yes—when a baby does not appreciate the law as a divine command. That is, "before he comes to understand the significance of living in a world subject to the laws of the Creator."[221] Before this age the baby/infant is not held accountable to God for violating a moral or spiritual law. The infant is not viewed as in any sense guilty before God. If this is the case, then no one is in fact born guilty due to Adam's sin.

Romans 7:9

"I was once alive apart from the Law; but when the commandment came, sin became alive and I died."

This verse is referring to Paul's personal experience of his awareness of the (Mosaic) law's requirements. In this case the law's requirement to refrain from coveting. The point is that even though the commandment was always there, it "came" one day for Paul—he recognized it as a divine command that, if violated, made him subject

221. Cottrell, *Faith Once for All*, 192.

to penalty. He realized he was a sinner when "sin became alive." The implication is that before this time—probably as a young child—he viewed himself as not guilty, even "alive." It was only when the day came when he understood the true significance of the law as an expression of God's will, and that breaking the law brought condemnation that he "died." We may say therefore that "the beginning of the age of accountability is the death of innocence, the time when a child becomes dead in his sins and subject to the penalty attached thereto."[222]

Isaiah 7:16

"For before the boy will know enough to refuse evil and choose good, the land whose two kings you dread will be forsaken."

This verse is perhaps the best example of the reality of the concept of an age of accountability. The context is set in the time of Ahaz, king of Judah. Jerusalem was under threat from an alliance of Syria and the northern kingdom of Israel. The prophet Isaiah assures the king that the imminent military threat would not hold and that God would bring deliverance. To confirm this supernatural event Isaiah asks Ahaz to ask God for a sign. Ahaz, pleading a false piety, declines. So, Isaiah assures Ahaz that God himself will give a sign: *"A virgin will be with child and bear a son, and she will call His name Immanuel"* (7:14). This sign will find fulfillment soon, before the boy is able to exercise moral discrimination (7:16). Within three years the capital city of Syria, Damascus, was destroyed and most of Samaria's villages plundered.[223]

As previously, it would appear that this Scripture testifies to the reality of the concept of an age of accountability, prior to which an infant is incapable of being held morally accountable for its decisions and actions. The fact that there is a measure of imprecision regarding the precise age or moment at which this age is reached is irrelevant for our purposes. The mere existence of such an age is enough to establish that no guilt attaches to infants prior to this age being reached and that therefore a doctrine of original sin which, by definition applies to infants, cannot be sustained.

g) Whence Universal Sin?

"For all have sinned and fall short of the glory of God" (Rom 3:23). The Bible is clear and unequivocal that everyone without exception has sinned; there is no such thing as a sinless person (except Jesus Christ of course). Even Christians sin (1 John 1:8). This truth has served to strongly bolster the idea that all sin because all are born with a corrupted human nature that makes sin inevitable and unavoidable. A good example

---

222. Cottrell, *Faith Once for All*, 192. The precise age at which accountability can be ascertained will vary from child to child, and Cottrell's remarks in this respect are noteworthy: "Discerning when a child reaches this point requires a careful and prayerful monitoring of his spiritual development." Cottrell, *Faith Once for All*, 192.

223. Oswalt, *Book of Isaiah*, 1:214.

of the way the empirical observation that all sin, even from a young age, is tied to a doctrine of original sin may be seen in the following quote from George Zemek:

> As the history of humanity abundantly proves, all mankind without exception turns aside to its own way. We are sinners in grain; every mother's son learns to be naughty without book. . . . Deny original sin and the state of our world becomes harder to construe than if you embrace the tenet. The evil principle lurks beneath the surface, seated in the heart.[224]

However potent empirical observation may be in supporting the notion of original sin, empirical observation is not an argument from the Bible. It must be the Bible's testimony that is decisive for an alleged doctrine of original sin. The question remains, however, why is it that sin is universal? Is there indeed something in the human condition from birth that makes sinning unavoidable?

Generally speaking, while the Bible is clear that all have sinned, both in its didactic portions as well as its narratives, nowhere is the attempt made to explain the origin of such sinning. Romans 5, as previously outlined, merely states that sin, and its corollary death, began with Adam. Everyone since Adam has sinned. The Bible is content to merely state the fact or describe the reality in its stories. The assumption seems to be that people simply choose to sin—to violate God's will in thought, word, and deed. This omission concerning the root cause of sin is somewhat surprising if the explanation lies simply in a corrupted nature inherited from Adam that makes sinning inevitable.

Another observation to be made is this: Jesus Christ was fully human and yet did not sin (Heb 4:15). In fact the very same author that insists that Jesus did not sin, emphasizes the reality and need for Jesus to be truly human in order that we too can identify with him and his work on the cross: "*Therefore, since the children share in flesh and blood, He Himself likewise also partook of the same, that through death He might render powerless him who had the power of death, that is, the devil*" (Heb 2:14). In fact, the entire passage in Heb 2:9–18 stresses Jesus's solidarity with man so that Jesus "*might taste death for everyone*" (2:9). The simple logic of vv. 14, 15 is expressed by Lane in his commentary thus:

A. Since the children

  B. shared a common human nature

A' he too likewise

  B' shared the same humanity[225]

---

224. Zemek, *Biblical Theology*, 87. Zemek here cites E. K. Simpson in his NICNT commentary on Ephesians. It is interesting that Simpson uses the word "learns" rather than "is naturally naughty."

225. Lane, *Hebrews 1–8*, 53. Significantly, Lane interprets the Greek idiom "flesh and blood" as "human nature" and justifies this interpretation because the term "flesh and blood" is an established Jewish term for man.

Lane clarifies, speaking of "the solidarity between the Son of God and the sons who are being led by God to their heritage. . . . The Son who consecrates human beings to God and the children who are being consecrated have one origin" (53). And, "since 'the children' share a common human nature, it was necessary for the one who identified himself with them (v. 13b) to assume the same full humanity" (60). Furthermore, the reality of Jesus's temptations also forms a part of his solidarity with man: *"For since He Himself was tempted in that which He has suffered, He is able to come to the aid of those who are tempted"* (Heb 2:18).[226]

The point of the above considerations is that they clearly indicate that there is nothing intrinsic to being human that makes sin inevitable. Sin is grounded in choices people make, not in a corrupted human nature inherited from another (Adam) from birth. If Jesus, who in his identification with humanity, did not sin then sinning is not intrinsic to human nature. Whatever reasons may be given for universal sinning, it need not be grounded in merely the outworking of a corrupt human nature. Cottrell agrees when he notes, speaking of the source of moral evil (sin) itself: "The source of evil is ethical, not metaphysical. It is not due to some inherent weakness in the creation; it is due rather to the freely-willed decisions of moral beings."[227] This conclusion is reinforced by the fact that Adam sinned by choosing to disobey God's command—even when he lived in a world that was "very good" and before sin entered the world. Note that sinning was a very real possibility given that God decided to create beings with the capacity to demonstrate their love for God voluntarily; there was no guarantee that such human agents would consistently choose to honor God in this way.[228]

Several factors may be mentioned that, when taken together, could explain sin's universal scope. First is the choice to abuse a good thing and thus turn it into a sin. Normal bodily appetites are a good example—eating is good and necessary, however taken to excess introduces the sin of gluttony. "Evil enters when the good things of God's creation are used for the wrong ends or are made ends in themselves, as when one's appetites become his god" (Phil 3:19).[229] Similarly with sex—a good gift from God. However, when abused this good gift manifests itself in a variety of sins including adultery and fornication. "People have bodily drives that are neither good nor bad in themselves, but they become the occasion for sin. Although there are acceptable ways of fulfilling these needs, there are also irresponsible and selfish ways of fulfilling them."[230]

---

226. Some argue that Jesus could not succumb to temptation because he was prevented from doing so by his divine nature. However, such an impossibility would invalidate the precise point being made by the author of Hebrews here in Heb 2:9–18. In this respect Jesus's uniqueness is seen not in that he could not sin, but rather in that he did not sin.

227. Cottrell, *What the Bible Says about God the Creator*, 145.

228. "Sin was not part of the original purpose of creation, but free will was. Thus this purpose involved a universe in which sin was a possibility, but not necessarily a reality." Cottrell, *What the Bible Says about God the Creator*, 181.

229. Cottrell, *What the Bible Says about God the Creator*, 145.

230. Warren, *Salvation*, 45.

The relation between God's law (moral or Mosaic), sin, and grace is a complicated one as anyone who has studied Rom 7 can testify. Throughout this chapter (Rom 7) Paul personifies sin and views it as an enemy. Paul's broader point in this chapter is to show that grace does not nullify law. While no one is saved by law keeping, but rather on the basis of God's grace, this does not mean the law of God is irrelevant or bad. The problem of sin is not the law but in the person sinning. I will examine in some detail one verse in Rom 7 that brings together several key concepts: *"For while we were in the flesh, the sinful passions, which were aroused by the Law, were at work in the members of our body to bear fruit for death"* (Rom 7:5).

In this verse (and in the chapter) the word flesh (σαρξ, *sarx*) refers to the body: "*Sarx* in this context is not some generalized sinful nature but is rather the physical body, especially viewed as sin-weakened and unredeemed and thus a source of evil desires and 'sinful passions.'"[231] The reference in v. 5 to "the members of our body" confirms this understanding of *sarx*.[232] Paul, reflecting on his pre-Christian experience, sees the body as a key avenue for sin giving rise to "sinful passions." Cottrell remarks:

> Thus to be "in the flesh" means to be governed by our bodily desires in such a way that they are the center of our lives and are promiscuously indulged without regard for moral boundaries. . . . Instead of controlling our bodies, our bodies controlled us. . . . Thus to be "controlled by the flesh" means to allow sinful passions to have free reign in the members of our bodies. Such sinful passions include those that are directly associated with our body, such as sexual lust, gluttony, and slothfulness.[233]

These sinful passions are *"aroused by the law."* Probably in the sense that simply knowing that something is against the law makes the action more attractive. Is there any sense in which the repeated practice of sinning in this manner (through the body) affects the spirit, the heart? The answer would appear to be yes. Jesus, in his disputes with the Pharisees who were preeminently concerned with externals, countered and insisted that *"out of the heart come evil thoughts, murders, adulteries, fornications, thefts, false witness, slanders"* (Matt 15:19).[234] Combining Paul and Jesus's teaching it would appear that sin initially gains entrance into a person's life through the body, but then through consistent and repeated indulgence, becomes a part of that person in his or her totality. Such a mechanism would make a significant contribution to the universality of sin since everyone has a body and everyone has knowledge of God's moral law (Rom 2:14, 15).

---

231. Cottrell, *Romans*, 1:427.

232. Even for the believer our bodies, unlike our spirits, are not yet redeemed.

233. Cottrell, *Romans*, 1:427.

234. James concurs: *"But each one is tempted when he is carried away and enticed by his own lust"* (Jas 1:14).

External temptation is another reason why sin appears universally. Even Adam and Eve in the garden of Eden, where God was present (Gen 3:8), were subject to satanic temptation (Gen 3:1–7). Scripture is clear that Satan prowls the earth like a roaring lion (1 Pet 5:8).[235] He is described as a liar and the father of lies (John 8:44). Unfortunately, like Adam, many succumb to this sinning influence.

A hostile environment aggravates the possibility of sinning due to temptations. While no mention is made concerning Adam's nature following his sin, his environment was adversely affected by his choice to sin through disobedience: *"Cursed is the ground because of you; In toil you will eat of it all the days of your life"* (Gen 3:17). The result is that *"the whole creation groans and suffers the pains of childbirth until now"* (Rom 8:22). The natural order is not functioning as God originally intended. This fact increases the possibility of persons sinning. For example, a building supplier might be tempted to charge exorbitant prices to needy people following the devastation of a hurricane. Or a doctor may exploit the needs of ill patients following a pandemic. Structural sins that manifest themselves in unjust laws can thrive in such an environment. Human culture itself is of course not immune to the problem of sin. As the Apostle John wrote: *"All that is in the world, the lust of the flesh and the lust of the eyes and the boastful pride of life, is not from the Father, but is from the world"* (1 John 2:16).

Given all the factors noted above[236] it is hardly surprising that sin manifests itself as a universal phenomenon—everyone has indeed sinned and come short of the glory of God.

h) Why Would God Have to Harden Totally Depraved Hearts?

If original sin is true, and total depravity (Calvinistically understood) is true then why does God harden unbelieving hearts? Are not their hearts already hardened, calloused against God from birth? Recall that Calvin believed that human nature "is not only utterly devoid of goodness, but so prolific in all kinds of evil, that it can never be idle."[237] God hardened Pharaoh's heart (Exod 7:3; 9:12; 10:1, 20). Certainly, this was a form of judicial hardening in response to Pharaoh hardening his own heart first. But the question remains—why would God even need to harden Pharaoh's heart? There was no way, according to Calvinism, that Pharaoh could ever have anything but a hardened heart toward God.

We find a similar action on the part of God toward rebellious Judah. In Isaiah's call to the prophetic office he was told to *"render the hearts of this people insensitive,*

---

235. While this Scripture strictly is directed toward Christians, there is no reason to suppose Satan's malevolent intents are not directed to all of God's human creation.

236. Warren identifies eight factors, including ignorance, sinful examples, social pressures, social reinforcement. Warren, *Salvation*, 44.

237. Calvin, *Institutes*, 2.1.8.

their ears dull, and their eyes dim" (Isa 6:10).[238] But, according to Calvinism, these people's hearts, ears, and eyes could never be anything but insensitive, dull, and dim—there was nothing more God need do.

Similarly, we may ask how, on Calvinistic assumptions, Satan could blind an unbeliever's eyes? Paul, reflecting upon his ministry among the Corinthians, describes unbelievers as those *"in whose case the god of this world has blinded the minds of the unbelieving so that they might not see the light of the gospel of the glory of Christ"* (2 Cor 4:4). A consistently applied Calvinism would find no need for Satan to do anything since all people are born in a spiritually blinded state unable to see gospel truth or even to respond to the gospel call. Similarly, Paul explains the rejection of God's word by Jews in Moses's time and in his own time as due to their minds being hardened and likened to a veil over their hearts (1 Cor 3:14, 15). But wouldn't Paul have known that all people were born in a state of hardened hearts and so there simply would not have been any need for their hearts to be further hardened?

We may also ask what sense it makes for Paul to assert that God gave anyone over to a depraved mind. According to Rom 1:28, *"And just as they did not see fit to acknowledge God any longer, God gave them over to a depraved mind, to do those things which are not proper."* God "gave them over" to depraved minds. And yet, according to Calvinism, all people are born with depraved minds; God would not need to do anything to make anyone depraved.

Also, why would God have to send upon unbelievers a "deluding influence" in order to ensure they believe what is false? *"For this reason God will send upon them a deluding influence so that they will believe what is false"* (2 Thess 2:11). Once more, on Calvinistic terms, God's efforts are redundant because everyone is born deluded and already only able to believe what is false.

Conclusion

We have seen how a doctrine of original sin, which undergirds the Calvinist's notion of total depravity, was unknown to the early church and was introduced by Augustine in his disputes with Pelagius. In fact the early church fathers, for the first three hundred and fifty years of the church, tended to emphasize the reality of human free will and the ability to freely choose to do either right or wrong.[239] Often, this was done to counter the philosophy of Manichaeism, which had strongly deterministic overtones.

---

238. The NIV translation is even more forceful: *"Make the heart of this people calloused; make their ears dull and close their eyes."*

239. Rather remarkably, Calvin himself thought all the early church fathers were mistaken in this respect: "The Greek Fathers, above others, and especially Chrysostom, have exceeded due bounds in extolling the powers of the human will, yet all ancient theologians, with the exception of Augustine, are so confused, vacillating, and contradictory on this subject, that no certainty can be obtained from their writings." Calvin, *Institutes*, 2.2.4.

Furthermore, the Old Testament says surprisingly little about Adam, mentioning his name just two times from Gen 5 onward.[240] And neither the Old Testament nor the New Testament says anything about all people being born inheriting a corrupted nature from Adam or being imputed with guilt from birth because of Adam's sin. Romans 5:12–21 is the only New Testament passage that may be inferred to even suggest the possibility of a direct connection between Adam's sin and the subsequent human condition in terms of corrupted human nature and guilt. But this passage and the way Paul uses the name Adam and the name Christ in these verses shows that Paul is not thinking in terms of inheritance or imputation from Adam or Christ, but rather in terms of classification; there are two classes of men—those who, through sinning, are in the Adam camp, and those who, through faith, are in the Christ camp. In short, Adam was the occasion for sin's entrance into the world, not the cause of all subsequent human sins. As Paul says: *"Through one man sin entered into the world, and death through sin, and so death spread to all men, because all sinned [personally]"* (Rom 5:12).

Given Calvinism's very bleak view of human nature and of man generally, it is no wonder that, when coupled with a strong notion of the supposed negative impact of Adam's sin on his posterity, human depravity is viewed as total, i.e., there is no good in man whatsoever. Augustine, for example, viewed all of humanity outside of Christ as a "mass of perdition," subject to eternal damnation upon birth. The Bible, however, gives a more balanced view of man, even sinful man. Man is created in the image of God and never loses this unique characteristic. Man, through his choice to sin and rebel against God, subjects himself to the wrath of God, and suffers depravity in himself. Yet, man as man is still always *a little lower than the angels, crowned with glory and honor"* (Ps 8:5 NIV). God's becoming man in order to redeem man underscores the inherent worth of man. Above all, man's sinfulness does not remove either his ability or responsibility to *"repent and believe the gospel"* (Mark 1:14).

240. Anizor, in his discussion under the heading "Is It Biblical? Principles for Assessing Doctrine," draws attention to the need for attentiveness to the whole canon when formulating a doctrine. He speaks of a principle called biblical convergence. "This principle requires that theologians allow the broadest and most diverse portions of Scripture, rather than one solitary verse, to bear on the theological issue in view. The convergence or agreement of the varied biblical witness regarding a particular proposal serves to strengthen that proposal." Anizor, *Read Theology*, 86. Judged by this criterion, the biblical support for a doctrine of original sin cannot be sustained.

3

Unconditional Election: Does God Choose Who Will Be Saved?

As mentioned in the introduction, Calvinism is a strongly coherent system of thought; all its elements fit very well together. So, the logic of God, and God alone, choosing who will be saved follows from the notion of total depravity.[1] If man is so depraved that he will not, indeed cannot, even respond to the gospel call to repent and believe the gospel, then if anyone is to be saved it must be because God has selected those who will in fact come to salvation. The rest are either chosen by God for damnation, or just left to suffer the consequences of their sins. The former, known as double predestination, was Calvin's preference while the latter is preferred by many Calvinists today.

As in the previous chapter, I shall attempt to present the Calvinist's position as fairly as possible; it is important that I don't set up a straw man and interact with a nonexistent doctrine. I will then go on to examine some of the key biblical passages appealed to by Calvinists to justify their view of unconditional election to see whether the interpretation applied to the text is in fact correct.

I shall then go on to examine some theological issues raised by a view of election that is not conditioned by anything outside of God himself. I will begin this section by examining some biblical passages which appear to assume election to be conditional on faith, repentance, and humility (minimally). This will be followed by a discussion of distinctly theological issues which will include topics such as the meaning of election and predestination and the view of divine sovereignty which undergirds these concepts. I will also discuss several problems unavoidably connected with a view of election that is unconditional. These will include God's relationship to sin, difficulties associated with a comprehensive divine determinism, problems with the idea of an overarching, comprehensive decree that governs all things, including the fall of Adam into sin. Finally, a discussion of "double predestination" is unavoidable, as is the relationship between God's decretive will and his preceptive will.

---

1. Cottrell makes the same point: Calvinists argue that "there is a total inability to come to the decision to put one's trust in Christ [due to total depravity]. This point is truly the keystone in the Calvinistic system. This is what makes unconditional election logically and doctrinally necessary." Cottrell, "Conditional Election," 68.

The Calvinist's Understanding of God's Election

John Calvin

"Of the great body of mankind some should be predestined to salvation, and others to destruction."[2]

"By predestination we mean the eternal decree of God, by which he determined with himself whatever he wished to happen with regard to every man. All are not created on equal terms, but some are preordained to eternal life, others to eternal damnation."[3]

"God by his secret counsel chooses whom he will while he rejects others. . . . God not only offers salvation, but so assigns it, that the certainty of the result remains not dubious or suspended."[4]

"I admit that by the will of God all the sons of Adam fell into that state of wretchedness in which they are now involved . . . [due to] the mere pleasure of the divine will, the cause of which is hidden in himself."[5]

"I say with Augustine, that the Lord has created those who . . . were to go to destruction, and he did so because he so willed."[6]

"God not only foresaw the fall of the first man [Adam], and in him the ruin of his posterity, but also at his own pleasure arranged it."[7]

Wayne Grudem

"Election is an act of God before creation in which he chooses some people to be saved . . . only because of his sovereign good pleasure."[8]

"The reason for election is simply God's sovereign choice . . . God chose us simply because he decided to bestow his love upon us."[9]

Robert A. Peterson

"Calvinists hold that God in his sovereignty and grace chooses people for salvation without taking their responses into account; God chooses for reasons within himself."[10]

2. Calvin, *Institutes*, 3.21.1.

3. Calvin, *Institutes*, 3.21.5.

4. Calvin, *Institutes*, 3.21.7.

5. Calvin, *Institutes*, 3.23.4.

6. Calvin, *Institutes*, 3.23.5.

7. Calvin, *Institutes*, 3.23.8.

8. Grudem, *Systematic Theology*, 670.

9. Grudem, *Systematic Theology*, 679.

10. Peterson, *Election and Free Will*, 2.

Bruce Ware

"God elected some to be saved according to the good pleasure of his will without respect for their individual qualities, characters, actions, or choices. His election, then, was unconditional as it pertains to particulars of the elect persons themselves while it is also clearly conditioned and dependent on God's own good pleasure and will."[11]

John Piper

"Election refers to God's choosing whom to save. It is unconditional in that there is no condition man must meet before God chooses to save him."[12]

A. W. Pink

"It is God Himself who makes the difference between the elect and the non-elect."[13]

"The cause of His choice then lies within Himself and not in the objects of His choice. He chose the ones He did, simply because he chose to choose them."[14]

Michael Horton

"The church of Christ was conceived by the triune God before the world was ever created. Out of the mass of our condemned race, a bride was chosen by the Father for his Son."[15]

"It is impossible to read the Bible without recognizing God's freedom to choose some and not others—and the fact that he does in fact exercise that right."[16]

The Westminster Confession of Faith

"All those whom God hath predestinated unto life, and those only, He is pleased, in His appointed and accepted time, effectually to call. . . . This effectual call is of God's free and special grace alone, not from anything at all foreseen in man, who is altogether passive therein."[17]

R. K. McGregor Wright

"From eternity, God willed, decided, planned, intended and chose to save some sinners. We do not know what his reasons were for not deciding to save

---

11. Ware, "Divine Election," 3.
12. Piper, *Five Points*, 53.
13. Pink, *Sovereignty of God*, 46.
14. Pink, *Sovereignty of God*, 55.
15. Horton, *For Calvinism*, 53.
16. Horton, *For Calvinism*, 54.
17. *Westminster Confession of Faith*, 10:1, 2.

all sinners. . . . To elect is to choose, and election is therefore God's choice of who will be saved."[18]

R. C. Sproul

"From all eternity God decided to save some members of the human race and to let the rest of the human race perish. God made a choice—he chose some individuals to be saved . . . and he chose others to pass over."[19]

Donald J. Westblade

"The apostle Paul affirms without hesitation that God elects individuals in the world to become heirs of his promises in Christ. . . . His theology requires this view of election, for he believes God is and must be acknowledged as the source and spring of all that is and occurs in creation."[20]

An Examination of Key Biblical Texts Used by Calvinists

From the quotes given above we may note the following aspects of election: first, it is unconditional, that is, there is absolutely nothing either good or bad in the person that conditions or influences God's choice of who will be saved and who will be lost. Second, the Calvinist's position involves the granting of salvation to individuals, not groups or classes of people. Third, election is entirely a prerogative of God and a manifestation of God's sovereignty. It is God as the Sovereign that has both the authority and power to decide and effect who will and (therefore) who won't be saved. Fourth, such a view of election follows inexorably from the Calvinist notion of human depravity as total and therefore making the sinner utterly unable to do anything of spiritual good, for example, believe the gospel. Finally, the decision by God as to who would be chosen for salvation and who would not be the recipients of such blessing was made by God from all eternity, i.e., before any specific individuals actually existed.[21] This last point is quite important in that it underscores the unconditionality of election—obviously, if God had a fixed number who would believe and hence be saved even before they were born, i.e., in eternity past, then those coming to salvation within time could only be those whom God had predetermined would comprise part of his elect, and was in no way conditioned by anything in the individuals themselves.

A further point is worth noting briefly before we go on to examine the key biblical texts appealed to by Calvinists to justify this view of election. The view of election outlined here is a subcategory of the Calvinists broader view of providence. Through his providence, the Calvinist believes, God governs the world to ensure everything in

18. Wright, *No Place for Sovereignty*, 119.

19. Sproul, *Reformed Theology*, 141.

20. Westblade, "Divine Election," 87.

21. For the reprobate—those determined by God to not receive salvation—the fact that the decision was made in eternity pasts has led to the phrase "doomed from the womb."

it unfolds exactly as he determines—the salvation of individuals is one aspect of this controlling providential activity.[22]

Acts 13:48

> "When the Gentiles heard this, they began rejoicing and glorifying the word of the Lord; and as many as had been appointed to eternal life believed."

The backdrop to this incident is as follows: Paul and his travelling companion Barnabas had left Syrian Antioch on their first missionary journey. On the way, they stopped at Pisidian Antioch in the Roman Province of Asia Minor (modern-day southeastern Turkey). Initially their reception at the Jewish synagogue there was positive, but when the two returned the following sabbath some of the local Jews resisted Paul and his teachings. Following Paul's citation of Isa 49:6 to the effect that God's mission would now turn from a priority to the Jews to the Gentiles, the Jews reacted by instigating persecution against Paul and Barnabas, while the Gentiles reacted quite differently and many embraced the gospel message, exercised faith and gained eternal life (Acts 13:44–48).

Calvinists of course view Luke's observation in v. 48 as proof that God has a predetermined number (the elect) designated for salvation. Wright is typical: "This indicates that Luke considered evangelism the provision of a predestined opportunity for the elect to come to faith."[23] Others concur. Pink, for example, makes the following observations: "Believing is the consequence and not the cause of God's decree, . . . a limited number only are 'ordained to eternal life,' . . . 'as many as,' not one less—who are thus ordained to eternal life will most certainly believe."[24] Piper comments: "Notice it does not say that as many as believed were chosen to be ordained to eternal life. It says that those who were ordained to eternal life (that is, those whom God elected) believed. God's election preceded faith and made it possible. This is the decisive reason some believed while others did not."[25] Grudem believes that "it is significant that Luke mentions the fact of election almost in passing. It is as if this were a normal occurrence when the gospel was preached. How many believed? 'As many as were ordained to eternal life believed.'"[26]

---

22. Paul Helm remarks that "all predestination is providential, and all exercises of providence are predestinarian." Later he favorably cites the Westminster Shorter Catechism's answer to the question "What are God's works of providence? God's works of providence are, his most holy, wise, and powerful preserving and governing all his creatures, *and all their actions*." Helm, *Providence*, 20, emphasis mine.

23. Wright, *No Place for Sovereignty*, 122.

24. Pink, *Sovereignty of God*, 48.

25. Piper, *Five Points*, 54.

26. Grudem, *Systematic Theology*, 671.

While superficially, this observation on the part of Luke seems to support a Calvinist understanding of election, closer examination would suggest a more nuanced conclusion. First of all, v. 34b should not be isolated from the broader context—and this context makes clear that the reason that some Jews were not recipients of eternal life is not because they were excluded from an eternal decree to elect them but rather because *they* repudiated Paul's preaching and *judged themselves unworthy* of eternal life (Acts 13:46). Conversely, it is not insignificant that immediately preceding Luke's comment we are told that, in response to the gospel proclamation the Gentiles rejoiced and glorified the word they heard. The Jews did not gain eternal life; the Gentiles did. Contra Piper, it would seem that Luke wishes to make clear that the reason some did not gain eternal life and that some did gain eternal life is intimately tied to their own attitude and response to the gospel. In fact, the entire passage, Acts 13:44–52, stresses conditionality; the Jews resisted Paul's message and consequently judged themselves unworthy of eternal life (13:44–46), the Gentiles rejoice and glorify (i.e., fully accept) the word of the gospel and obtain eternal life (13:48, 49), the Jews persecuted Paul and Barnabas and consequently are effectively subject to God's judgment (13:50–52). In short, however Acts 13:48b is understood it must not be made to nullify the contextual observations just made concerning the passage.[27]

Pursuing the above line of reasoning a little further, Luke's intent in expressing Gentile gaining of eternal life the way he did can be seen to fit a pattern that runs throughout the book of Acts. In sharp contrast to the Calvinist's simplistic appeal to a few words in one verse and their ignoring of both the immediate literary context as well as the broader theological context, an examination of Luke's theological goal in recounting the spread of the gospel sheds light on the intended meaning of Acts 13:48b. Theologically, Luke has structured his message of gospel advance in a distinct pattern. This pattern takes the form of (1) divine initiative (usually in bringing the gospel to a community), (2) response on the part of the hearers (positive or negative), (3) a following divine response according to human receptivity or rejection of the gospel. Often, the stated divine response is exaggerated, i.e., God makes his response abundantly and unambiguously clear.

The pattern is seen, for example, in Peter's sermon on the day of Pentecost in Acts 2: (1) Peter proclaims the gospel focusing on the resurrection of Jesus (the divine initiative) (vv. 14–36); (2) the hearers respond favorably (vv. 37–41a); (3) unambiguous divine blessing ensues with many being added to the church with clear evidence of a mighty work of God, including the working of "many wonders and signs" through the apostles (2:43). Tellingly, Luke concludes his account of gospel receptivity and expansion with a beautifully balanced expression of divine-human interaction in the saving of many: "And the Lord was adding to their number day by day those who were being saved" (2:47).

27. "Whatever be the precise nuance of the words, there is no suggestion that they received eternal life independently of their own act of conscious faith." Marshall, *Acts*, 231.

Similarly concerning Philip's preaching in Samaria (Acts 8:4–24): (1) God's initiative is seen once more in the gospel being proclaimed in the city by Philip (v. 5); (2) the positive human response on the part of the crowd (vv. 6–8; 12); (3) unambiguous divine blessing in response to belief (vv. 7–8, 13b).

A final example is seen with the incident involving Cornelius in Acts 10: (1) Peter proclaims the gospel to Cornelius (10:35–43); (2) Cornelius's favorable receptivity is not explicitly recorded but the preceding verses make it clear that Cornelius was already disposed to believing the gospel once he heard it;[28] (3) unambiguous divine blessing in the clear provision of the Holy Spirit to Cornelius and those present (10:44–47).

Not every evangelistic activity in Acts fits this pattern precisely; sometimes one or more elements are implied and not explicitly described. But generally speaking, whenever an evangelist brings the gospel to a region this pattern is operative: the gospel is brought and proclaimed, a human response on the part of an individual or group is recorded, and the resulting divine activity is either explicitly or implicitly stated. As noted above, often the divine response is clear and unambiguous—it is God who is at work either for blessing (salvation) or judgment. My point is that Acts 13:48b may be a rhetorical device whereby Luke is emphasizing divine blessing following a positive response on the part of the Gentiles to Paul's gospel proclamation. This would fit well Luke's theological pattern throughout the book of Acts.

The key word in Acts 13:48 is the Greek word τεταγμενοι (tetagmenoi),[29] which the NASB, ESV, and NIV translate as "appointed to." The root idea is that of assignment, appointment, placement. Significantly, this word in this form appears nowhere else in the New Testament. The appropriate meaning, from the range of possible meanings, must therefore be determined from the context. While the word "appoint" is certainly a possible translation of the word, the fluidity of meaning is seen in that, for example, the Bauer *Greek-English Lexicon of the New Testament* understands the word in its passive form to be best translated as "belong to, be classed among those possessing."[30] Packer seems to adopt this understanding when he says, "τασσō denotes God's appointment of . . . individual persons to attain eternal life through believing the gospel (Acts 13:48)."[31] That is, those who believe the gospel are classed among those appointed by God to receive eternal life. This translation seems a good one in

---

28. Cornelius is described as "*a devout man and one who feared God with all his household, and gave many alms to the Jewish people and prayed to God continually*" (Acts 10:2).

29. The word is a passive participle in the nominative case, masculine, plural, often translated as "they, having been appointed."

30. Bauer, *Greek-English Lexicon*, 806. The fluidity of meaning is again seen in the Friberg Lexicon where a possible meaning of the key clause is "as many as had become *disposed* toward eternal life [believed]." Friberg, *Analytical Lexicon*, 375.

31. Packer, "τασσω (tassō): arrange, appoint," 476 (τασσω is the root of τεταγμενοι, and may be translated as "I appoint'; τεταγμενοι is the passive form of this verb).

that it attributes a reasonable meaning to the key word τεταγμένοι, while also fitting well with Luke's theology throughout Acts.[32]

Acts 16:14

> "A woman named Lydia, from the city of Thyatira, a seller of purple fabrics, a worshiper of God, was listening; and the Lord opened her heart to respond to the things spoken by Paul."

This verse is sometimes appealed to by Calvinists to indicate the work of God on the elect with respect to the reception of the gospel. Wright is typical: "When Lydia 'attended unto' (King James Version) the gospel, Luke ascribes this to the prior fact that God had 'opened her heart' (16:14). This type of language is inexplicable if we assume that God waits for sinners to provide a condition before he can act in mercy."[33] Again, we see the characteristic tendency for Calvinists to isolate a single verse, ignore its context, and then to universalize the incident to apply to all people. The text actually describes the actions of God upon a specific person (Lydia), and there is no hint within the text or its immediate context that this description should apply normatively at all times for all unbelievers.

It is significant that Wright ignores the clear statement recorded by Luke to the effect that Lydia was "a worshiper of God." By so doing, he treats Lydia as an unbelieving sinner, part of the non-elect. John Stott acknowledges the remark by Luke concerning Lydia's being a worshipper of God but ignores the crucial significance of this fact, and seems to view her as an unbeliever who came to faith in God upon hearing the gospel; Lydia was "believing and behaving like a Jew without having become one."[34] F. F. Bruce is nearer the mark when he says Lydia "had possibly learned to worship the true God in her native Thyatira; there was probably a Jewish community there."[35]

The significance of Luke describing Lydia unqualifiedly as a worshipper of God, was that she was already a believer! True, she had not believed in Jesus prior to Paul's speaking, but she was in right relationship with the God of Israel. In short, she was

---

32. Before leaving the question of word meaning, it is worth noting that while the verb form is passive participle, the agent acting upon the subject is somewhat dependent on context. It is usually understood that the agent doing the appointing is God (a divine passive), but whereas the English language has two voices, active and passive, Greek has a third voice called the middle voice. In the passive middle voice, generally speaking, the agent is not necessarily acted upon by someone or something else, but rather acts upon himself. William McDonald raises this possibility for τεταγμένοι when he says: "The voice of the perfect participle is . . . ambiguous; *tetagmenoi* is best construed *in this context* to be middle voice. The disputed sentence (Acts 13:48) would look like this when the setting is fully honored and a divine passive is not read into it: 'When the Gentiles heard this, they gloried in the Lord's Word, *and as many as were putting themselves in a position for eternal life believed.*'" McDonald, "Biblical Doctrine of Election," 227, emphasis original.

33. Wright, *No Place for Sovereignty*, 123.

34. Stott, *Message of Acts*, 263.

35. Bruce, *Acts*, 311.

what Paul describes in Rom 9:27 as a remnant of Israel, those under the old covenant who were aligned with the God of Israel. In short, Lydia was already justified, already in right relationship with God, fully believing in Israel's God and desiring to follow this God. So what Luke records, in saying that the Lord opened her heart, was God's work, through his Spirit, in helping Lydia see that God was now revealing himself in a fuller and deeper way in sending his Son, and that God's redemptive purposes for the world had now moved away from the nation of Israel to Jesus, the Son of God. This was not, as Calvinists believe, God acting unilaterally to bring a sinner to himself, but rather God acting graciously to show Lydia that his focus for salvation was no longer through God's dealings with Israel, but would from now on be focused on the true Israel, Jesus of Nazareth. Because she was already a woman of genuine faith, she readily acknowledged God's new salvific work centering on Jesus.

Acts 18:9–10

> *"And the Lord said to Paul in the night by a vision, 'Do not be afraid any longer, but go on speaking and do not be silent; for I am with you, and no man will attack you in order to harm you, for I have many people in this city.'"*

This verse records Paul's eighteen month stay in Corinth during his second missionary journey. As was often the case, Paul's preaching was opposed by the Jews in the city. However, not all who heard the gospel opposed Paul at Corinth for we are told in the immediately preceding verse that *"many of the Corinthians when they heard were believing and being baptized"* (Acts 18:8). In the light of this verse (v. 8) concerning many coming to faith in Christ upon hearing the gospel, it is surprising to read Wright comment: "In 18:10 God promises Paul that he will be safe in Corinth even though there are no Christians there because 'I have many people in this city.' This seems to refer to the as-yet-unregenerate elect he had there to whom Paul was about to announce the good news."[36] Grudem likewise sees in this text a reference to an elect who would believe in response to Paul's preaching: "When Paul was told that God had many elect people in Corinth, he stayed a long time and preached, in order that those elect might be saved."[37] Both Wright and Grudem seem to interpret the clear statement "I have many people in this city" as "I *will have* many people . . ." It would seem that Calvinist's commitment to the idea that gospel proclamation is the means for the elect to come to salvation requires that any Christians at Corinth must be

36. Wright, *No Place for Sovereignty*, 122.

37. Grudem, *Systematic Theology*, 675. Rather inconsistently, Grudem, *Systematic Theology*, 670, immediately goes on to say, "Paul is quite clear about the fact that unless people preach the gospel others will not be saved." Taken at face value, this seems to suggest that he believes in conditional election after all! Of course, this affirmation cannot be taken straightforwardly because he has already defined election as "an act of God before creation in which he chooses some people to be saved . . . only because of his sovereign good pleasure." Typically, Calvinists seek to retain consistency by asserting that God ordains both the means (evangelism) and the end (salvation) in bringing his elect to faith.

due to Paul's preaching there. However, since Luke records no conversions in Corinth prior to v. 10 the reference to "many people in this city" (v. 8), cannot be taken at face value but must refer to what God will do through Paul. But the passage is clear—these Corinthians referred to in v. 8 believed and were baptized. It is these actual, living Christians that comprised the "many people" of v. 10b.

Even if we were not told in the immediate context exactly how God already had "many people in this city," there is no reason, from the text itself, to suppose that the many people God had were a preordained fixed number whom he had unconditionally chosen to be saved. It is simply reading into the text too much to reach this conclusion. In fact, the preceding verses strongly suggest that Paul's efforts to evangelize among the Jews in Corinth was at least partially successful—many Jews in fact responded favorably to Paul's efforts.

2 Thessalonians 2:13

> "But we ought always to give thanks to God for you, brothers beloved by the Lord, because God chose you as the firstfruits to be saved, through sanctification by the Spirit and belief in the truth."[38] (ESV)

Calvinists see in this verse God's determining hand of election because God chose the Thessalonian Christians to be saved. "Paul was obligated to give thanks to God for the Christians at Thessalonica because he knew that their salvation was ultimately due to God's choice of them."[39] Peterson comments: "God chose to save the Thessalonians, bringing his grace to bear on their lives when the Holy Spirit set them apart for salvation so that they believed the gospel."[40] Wright concurs: "God chose them from the beginning (of time) to be saved. . . . Election is of individuals to salvation. . . . The choice is God's, not ours."[41] Several writers stress that God ordains not only the end (salvation), but also the means (through sanctification and belief in the truth).

As before we shall attempt to determine the author's intent in writing this, taking due account of both the literary and theological contexts. First of all, it is important to note that Paul's gratitude to God recounted in this verse (2:13) continues the note of thanks to God expressed at the beginning of his letter to them:[42] *"We ought always to give thanks to God for you, brethren, as is only fitting, because your faith*

---

38. Some variants read ἀπαρχην (*aparchēn*) ("firstfruits," NIV, ESV, NRSV), others read the text as ἀπ ἀρχης (*ap archēs*), ("from the beginning," NASB, RSV, NKJV). "The evidence is slightly stronger for ἀπαρχην than for ἀπ ἀρχης" according to Bruce, *1 & 2 Thessalonians*, 190.

39. Grudem, *Systematic Theology*, 674.

40. Peterson, *Election and Free Will*, 95.

41. Wright, *No Place for Sovereignty*, 124.

42. "The subject of Antichrist has been dealt with and the recipient's uncertainty about the Day of the Lord has been cleared up; now the note of thanksgiving is resumed." Bruce, *1 & 2 Thessalonians*, 190.

is greatly enlarged, and the love of each one of you toward one another grows ever greater; therefore, we ourselves speak proudly of you among the churches of God for your perseverance and faith in the midst of all your persecutions and afflictions which you endure" (2 Thess 1:3–4). In the intervening verses up to 2:13, Paul is providing teaching concerning those in the church who mistakenly believed that the Day of the Lord had already come (2:2) and who were causing trouble within the church (1:6). Paul gives several reasons why he is grateful to God, and interestingly, many of these reasons have to do with the Thessalonians' attitude toward God and service for God as opposed to what God had done for them. They were a people of faith (1:3, 4, 11; 2:13), their faith and love for one another were increasing (1:3), despite their persecutions, they persevered in faith (1:4). For all this, God will count them worthy of the kingdom of God (1:5). It is also the case of course, that Paul seeks his reader's good by praying that God would encourage them to continue in the faith by his grace (1:11; 2:16). With all this in mind it is strange that nowhere does Paul attribute the Thessalonians' faith, love, or perseverance to God. Rather, it is the Thessalonians' themselves who have these characteristics. Unlike the trouble-makers who "do not obey the gospel of our Lord Jesus" (1:8), these readers will participate exultantly at the return of Christ *"for our testimony to you was believed"* (1:10). In short, the language used to describe the Christians at Thessalonica is of their positive response to the gospel and their enjoyment of resulting blessings—especially the blessings of salvation (2:13) and participation in the glory of Christ (2:14).

Given this contextual background to 2:13, it would seem most consistent to understand Paul to be saying in 2:13b that he is grateful to God because God chose them to enjoy the blessing of salvation because of their ongoing sanctification by the Spirit and because of their ongoing faith in the truth of the gospel. In other words, it would be quite incongruous for Paul to suddenly attribute their salvation to God alone apart from the receptivity and faith stance of the Christians themselves and because they were a people chosen specifically for salvation from a state of lostness from before eternity. It was their openness to the gospel proclaimed by Paul that allowed God to provide salvation. This thrust is consistent not only with this letter, but indeed with the general tenor of the whole of the New Testament.[43] Because they were a people of faith Paul could pray for their access to divine power and grace to enable them to do what they themselves wanted to do: *"To this end also we pray for you always, that our God will count you worthy of your calling, and fulfill every desire for goodness and the work of faith with power"* (1:11).

---

43. Marshall states concerning the word *elect* or *chosen*: "The term is used throughout the New Testament for Christians, for those who belong to the community consisting of people otherwise called the saints, the brothers, the people of God, etc. They are the group of people whom God has chosen; they have responded to his call and actually belong to the group." Marshall, "Universal Grace," 65. In this case Paul is writing to the "brothers and sisters" in Thessalonica (2 Thess 1:3).

2 Timothy 1:9

> "[God] has saved us and called us with a holy calling, not according to our works,
> but according to His own purpose and grace which was granted us in Christ Jesus
> from all eternity."

Grudem remarks that "once again God's sovereign purpose is seen as the ultimate reason for our salvation, and Paul connects this with the fact that God gave us grace in Christ Jesus ages ago . . . when he chose us without reference to any foreseen merit or worthiness on our part."[44] Likewise, Peterson connects God's sovereign purpose as the ground of God's choosing who would be saved: "God's power and our salvation go together in the apostle's mind. . . . We are saved entirely because of God's 'own purpose and grace' (v. 9). Here is a summary of the Bible's teaching on the ultimate cause of the salvation of all who are saved—it is because of God's purpose and grace."[45] Similarly, Pink asserts that "it is impossible to state the case more clearly, or strongly, than it is stated here. Our salvation is not 'according to our works'; that is to say, it is not due to anything in us . . . it is the result of God's own 'purpose and grace' . . . given to us in Christ Jesus before the world began."[46]

Calvinists here draw essentially three points from this verse: (1) anyone's salvation is in accord with God's purpose, (2) it is not related to anything about the person, (3) it was decided before the world was created. Let us consider each aspect. First, anyone's salvation is strictly in accord with God's purpose, by which Calvinists mean God's decision to save some (the elect) and to either choose to not save the non-elect, the reprobate (Calvin, Sproul),[47] or allow the non-elect to suffer the consequences of their sin, damnation (Grudem, Augustine). But is this what the Bible really teaches concerning God's salvific purpose? Many portions of Scripture make it clear that God desires everyone to be saved, not just a select few (Ezek 18:23; Matt 23:37; John 3:16; 1 Tim 2:4; 2 Pet 3:9, etc.).[48] An example would be 1 Tim 2:4, which says God *"desires all men to be saved and to come to the knowledge of the truth."* Furthermore, the basic message of the New Testament is that salvation is intrinsically bound with faith "in Christ" and with the subsequent union "with Christ." This

44. Grudem, *Systematic Theology*, 678. Grudem makes clear in the immediately following section of his book that he views the exercise of faith as "merit."

45. Peterson, *Election and Free Will*, 96.

46. Pink, *Sovereignty of God*, 53.

47. For example, Sproul comments regarding Rom 9:21, "If only some people are predestined to be saved, then it logically must follow that other people are not. The doctrine of predestination to salvation is called the doctrine of election, and the doctrine of predestination to damnation is called the doctrine of reprobation. . . . If we don't say that God predestines all things, we don't have a God at all. If He is not totally sovereign, He is only a 'big man' like Zeus or Baal." Sproul, "Doctrine of Reprobation," para. 1.

48. Of course, Calvinists have their own understanding of the passages, but I will assume that the straightforward way of reading these texts holds. We will examine these passages and the way Calvinists handle them later.

christocentric connection between faith in Christ and salvation is seen, for example, in Jesus's parable of the Good Shepherd: *"I am the door; if anyone enters through Me, he will be saved, and will go in and out and find pasture"* (John 10:9). Again, Jesus links salvation (here in the metaphor of light) and faithful discipleship in John 8:12: *"Then Jesus again spoke to them, saying, 'I am the Light of the world; he who follows Me will not walk in the darkness, but will have the Light of life.'"* John explains the purpose of his writing his gospel in strongly christocentric terms, again linking faith "in Christ" with salvation: *"But these have been written so that you may believe that Jesus is the Christ, the Son of God; and that believing you may have life in His name"* (John 20:31). Bearing in mind these and many other similar scriptures, we can see that what God has purposed in 2 Tim 1:9 is not the saving of some (an elect) for salvation, but rather the saving of any and all who are "in Christ" through responding in faith to the gospel call. In other words, in v. 9 Paul is reminding Timothy and the fellow believers ("us" believers) that God's purpose in salvation is accomplished on the basis of faith, not works, and is found "in Christ" alone. God's purpose is that those who are "in Christ" would experience salvation.

The second point—that salvation "is not due to anything in us" (A. W. Pink)—is not what the text actually says. Second Tim 1:9 says "not according to our works,"[49] that is, not due to good works that would be used to merit or earn or entitle one to salvation; the sinner is saved by grace, not works. But to say that no one can merit salvation is not to say that salvation is unconditional. The Bible makes it clear that repentance and faith are conditions for receiving the gift of salvation. The first recorded words of Jesus (Mark 1:15) are: *"The time is fulfilled, and the kingdom of God is at hand; repent and believe in the gospel."* It is simply reading too much into 2 Tim 1:9 to say that nothing whatsoever is required of anyone before they can experience salvation.

The third point, that "God planned our salvation before creation," as Peterson suggests, is related to the first point concerning God's redemptive purposes for the world. It is not specific individuals who were selected for salvation before the world was made, but rather God's intent before creation that those who would be saved would be so only through Christ—salvation in Christ is what God purposed before the worlds were made. As McDonald rightly notes: "The apostle Paul cited a choice God made 'before the creation of the world' (Eph 1:4). God preplanned to grant grace, not abstractly, but 'in Christ' to the church. He decided to do this 'before the beginning of time' (2 Tim 1:9)."[50] Furthermore, as we shall explore more fully later, there are scriptures that make it clear that the basis for God *predestinating* any individual to salvation is in God foreseeing that they would meet the conditions for being "in Christ," namely their faith.

---

49. The Greek is οὐ κατα τα ἐργα ἡμων (*ou kata ta erga hēmarton)mōn*)—literally "not according to the works of ours." Only the NIV translates the phrase "not because of anything we have done." The NASB, ESV, and KJV all reflect more accurately the Greek.

50. McDonald, "Biblical Doctrine of Election," 208.

John 10:26

> *"But you do not believe because you are not of My sheep."*

John Piper observes that Jesus "does not say, 'You are not among my sheep because you do not believe.' Who the sheep are is something God decides before we believe. It is the basis and enablement of our belief. . . . We believe because we are God's chosen sheep, not vice versa."[51] Wright makes the same point: "If Jesus were an Arminian, he would have said 'You are not of my sheep because you do not believe.' Throughout John's Gospel, Christ's sheep are the elect whom he has chosen out of the world."[52]

William Hendriksen, a staunch Calvinist, in his commentary on John's gospel writes: "The factor of divine predestination is more basic than that of human responsibility; more basic in this sense, that those who listen to Christ's voice and follow him, do so *because* they were *given and drawn*; and those who are not able to listen to him and to follow him remain in this state of inability *because* it has not pleased God to rescue them."[53] Leon Morris also stresses the predestinarian language in this verse: "The predestinarian strain in this Gospel comes out in the reason given for their failure: 'ye are not of my sheep.'"[54] The New Testament scholar Donald Carson makes similar points: "That they are not Jesus' sheep does not excuse them; it indicts them. But the predestinarian note ensures that even their massive unbelief is not surprising: it is to be expected and falls under the umbrella of God's sovereignty."[55]

As most scholars have noted, John's gospel is characterized by a strong emphasis on both God's sovereignty and human responsibility. Running throughout this gospel is the interaction between these two factors. This dynamic is underscored by the duality that is also a characteristic of the gospel. There are several dualities—light and darkness, law and grace, truth and lies. A key duality is that between those who accept Christ and those who reject him. The gospel is an overtly evangelistic one; John tells us that he wrote the gospel specifically that *"you may believe that Jesus is the Christ, the Son of God; and that believing you may have life in His name"* (John 20:31). All this is to set the passage we are studying in its broader context within the gospel of John.

The immediate context is vv. 32–39. Here Jesus is in dispute with "the Jews," a term that appears three times in these verses. They represent those who reject Jesus and his teaching. The key issue concerns Jesus's identity—who is this Jesus? Jesus answers this question in two ways: (1) by appeal to his miracles as evidence that he is who he claims to be—one with the Father (vv. 25, 37, 38), (2) by assuring them that those who have not rejected him, i.e., his sheep, do in fact recognize his true identity and enjoy the blessings such acceptance brings—eternal life, divine protection

---

51. Piper, *Five Points*, 54.

52. Wright, *No Place for Sovereignty*, 122.

53. Hendriksen, *John*, 122, emphases original.

54. Morris, *John*, 520.

55. Carson, *John*, 393.

(vv. 27–29). In other words, in v. 26 when Jesus says to his opponents, *"You do not believe because you are not of My sheep,"* he is providing an explanation of their rejection of him in characteristic dual form—those who believe upon Jesus are counted as his sheep, and those who do not believe thereby demonstrate they are "not of my sheep." The "because" in the verse is explanatory, not causal. The Jews indeed had an inability to believe in Jesus, but it was not an inability caused by God through an alleged eternal decree of reprobation or because "it has not pleased God to rescue them" (Hendriksen), but because of their own hardness of heart. Both the immediate and broader contexts show that the reason they did not believe was because of a self-generated hardness of heart and persistent rejection of Jesus and his claims.

It is probably significant that John immediately follows this encounter between Jesus and the hostile Jews in the temple in Jerusalem (v. 22) with the acceptance of Jesus by the common people "beyond the Jordan," where, John records, *"many believed in Him there"* (v. 42) and so became Jesus's sheep. Ultimately, belief or unbelief determines the status before God. In this respect, Jesus could indeed have just as easily said, "You are not of my sheep because you do not believe."

John 6:37

> *"All that the Father gives Me will come to Me, and the one who comes to Me I will certainly not cast out."*

John 6:39

> *"This is the will of Him who sent Me, that of all that He has given Me I lose nothing, but raise it up on the last day."*

John 10:29

> *"My Father, who has given them to Me, is greater than all; and no one is able to snatch them out of the Father's hand."*

In John's gospel alone are we told that the Father gives some people to Jesus. This is often taken to mean that God's elect are unconditionally caused to "come to" Jesus—i.e., believe upon him. Those so given are assured of final joyful resurrection, and divine protection. Peterson is typical: "The Father's giving people to Jesus is a picture of election. It is critical to understand that the Father's giving people to the Son precedes their believing in him for salvation."[56] Robert Yarbrough concurs: "Jesus indicates that those who respond to his call somehow do so at the Father's bidding."[57]

It is true, of course, that Jesus viewed a certain class of people as receptive to his message and person because "given" to Jesus by the Father. The question is: Who comprise this class of people? As we have seen, Calvinists answer unequivocally that those given are the elect, those sinners whom God has decreed will be saved by coming to Jesus. Are there any texts within John's gospel itself that might provide a clue as to whom John had in mind when he wrote these words? There are.

All agree that coming to Jesus is essentially synonymous with believing in him. The first clue to understanding whom Jesus is referring to when speaking of those whom the Father has given to him is seen in the previous chapter, in John 5:46, where again Jesus is in dispute with "the Jews" (5:18) concerning their rejection of him. Tellingly, Jesus asserts that *"if you believed Moses, you would believe Me, for he wrote about Me. But if you do not believe his writings, how will you believe My words?"* (John 5:46). Jesus clearly grounds their unbelief in him in their unbelief of Moses.[58] Conversely, had the Jews really understood and accepted Moses, they would have believed Jesus. Now, there were Jews in the old covenant who did indeed "believe Moses." These would have been those referred to by Paul as the remnant of true believers in God in Old Testament times, for example the seven thousand who did not bow the knee to Baal in the days of Elijah (1 Kgs 19:18; Rom 11:4). In other words, Jesus is implying that these OT saints *"would believe Me"* had they seen Jesus. And we have already noted that to believe in Jesus is to *"come to Me"* (John 6:37). And, in the context of John 6:37, those who *"come to Me"* are precisely those whom *"the Father gives Me."* In short, all that the Father gives to Jesus are those Old Testament saints living in Jesus's day who already belong to God, believe in God, and who now are given to Jesus, the fuller revelation of God. Good examples would be Joseph and Mary, Zacharias and Elizabeth, Simeon.[59]

John 8:47 echoes the same sentiment: *"He who is of God hears the words of God; for this reason you do not hear them, because you are not of God."* The ones in Jesus's audience who would be "of God" are precisely those who believe in God to

---

56. Peterson, *Election and Free Will*, 61. Often Calvinists will acknowledge the strong emphasis in John's gospel upon human responsibility (as well as divine sovereignty). Unfortunately, as we shall see later, their view of sovereignty causes them to see a "mystery" in how the two concepts cohere. Peterson, *Election and Free Will*, 62, confesses, "I do not fully understand how God can be absolutely sovereign and sinners fully responsible, but I am convinced that the Bible teaches that both concepts are true."

57. Yarbrough, "Divine Election," 58. Note the uncertainty again—"somehow."

58. It may be that, as Carson suggests, rather than any specific texts referring to Jesus in Moses's writings, "this verse is referring to a certain way of reading the books of Moses." Carson, *John*, 266. That way would be a Christ-focused way—in the spirit of Luke 24:27 where Jesus in a post-resurrection appearance to the two disciples on the road to Emmaus *"explained to them the things concerning Himself in all the Scriptures."*

59. See especially Luke 2:25–32 concerning the description and longing of Simeon.

the extent possible under the old covenant revelation prior to Jesus's coming. Now that the Father has sent the Son and spoken through the Son, these old covenant saints would readily accept the fuller revelation God is now providing in his Son and consequently readily hear the words of God as proclaimed through Jesus. Again, we have the same dynamic: these old covenant saints are the ones given to Jesus in response to Jesus's preaching and proclamation.

In an important verse, John 6:45 teaches the same idea: *"It is written in the prophets, 'And they shall all be taught of God.' Everyone who has heard and learned from the Father, comes to Me."* Jesus is echoing Isa 54:13, *"All your sons will be taught of the Lord."* Within the context of Jesus's public ministry, those Jews who would have "learned from the Father" are those who believed the God of the Old Testament and learnt his character and purposes from that revelation. Now, with the inauguration of a new covenant centering upon Jesus it is precisely those who have already *"heard and learned from the Father"* prior to encountering Jesus who readily come to Jesus and are in this sense given to Jesus by the Father.

Finally, Jesus in his high priestly prayer in John 17 makes reference to the same phenomenon: *"I have manifested Your name to the men whom You gave Me out of the world;* they were Yours and You gave them to Me, *and they have kept Your word"* (John 17:6). Twice in this passage Jesus refers to "all whom You [God the Father] have given Him [Jesus]" (17:2, 9). The reference in this case is to the disciples in the Upper Room—soon to be apostles. Again, we see the same pattern previously noted in connection with those who are given to Jesus by the Father—they are precisely those who were already God's, they already belonged to the Father, they already believed in the God and Father of the Lord Jesus Christ (Rom 15:6; Eph 1:3). So, when the next step in God's plan of redemption, the sending of his Son, took place, these disciples were already primed to hear Jesus's words, receive Jesus himself, and thus be given to Jesus by the Father.

John 15:16

> *"You did not choose Me but I chose you, and appointed you that you would go and bear fruit, and that your fruit would remain, so that whatever you ask of the Father in My name He may give to you."*

Citing this text, Horton remarks that "God's own love, mercy, and freedom determined that we would belong to him in his Son."[60] While some generalize this verse to all believers, as Horton does here, in fact these words were specifically spoken to Jesus's

---

60. Horton, *For Calvinism*, 58. Likewise, Hendriksen says, "All believers are chosen out of the world (v. 19) to bear fruit (vv. 2, 4, 5, 8). Though this is an act which takes place in time, it has its basis in election 'before the foundation of the world.'" Hendriksen, *John*, 308. Though Hendriksen links John 15:16 to election to salvation, in fact Jesus is reminding his disciples in v. 16 that he has chosen them for service (not salvation)—to bear fruit in their ministry.

disciples during the Last Supper. He was preparing them for his imminent departure, and laying out the groundwork of his expectations for the soon-to-be apostles. This context makes clear therefore that Jesus's electing was a choosing for service, not salvation. These were the men Jesus had chosen to continue his work of gospel proclamation throughout the world, and who would subsequently become the foundation of the church (Eph 2:20). So, this was a call to serve in that important role and bear fruit in that service, it was not a call to salvation; their own spiritual relationship would, like all other believers, require their ongoing faith and repentance.

Any connection between Jesus's choosing of his disciples and unconditional election to salvation is also seen to be unfounded because earlier in his ministry Jesus reminds the twelve: *"Did I Myself not choose you, the twelve, and yet one of you is a devil?"* (John 6:70). Judas Iscariot was just as chosen as the other eleven, but he chose to reject the high call of service for the sake of the gospel. Yet Calvinists insist that those whom God elects or choose will inevitably achieve the salvation to which God elected them.

Romans 8:28–30

> *"And we know that God causes all things to work together for good to those who love God, to those who are called according to His purpose. For those whom He foreknew, He also predestined to become conformed to the image of His Son, so that He would be the firstborn among many brethren; and these whom He predestined, He also called; and these whom He called, He also justified; and these whom He justified, He also glorified."*

This is an important passage universally appealed to by Calvinists to justify unconditional election.[61] The following quotes illustrate the point.

Piper views this passage as "perhaps the most important text of all in relation to the teaching of unconditional election."[62] Peterson also sees a clear reference to unconditional election in these verses when answering the question Why did Paul use the term elect in this passage as opposed to believers or brothers? The answer is "to designate them as people whom God has chosen for salvation. . . . The people whom God predestined for salvation will not fail to be justified."[63] Sproul helpfully explains the Calvinist logic entailed in these verses when he says that "Reformed theology understands the golden chain to mean that God predestines some people to receive a divine call that others do not receive. Only the predestined, or the elect, receive this call, and only those who receive this call are justified. A process of selection is clearly involved here."[64] Stressing the divine purpose, Dunn notes that "believers rest in the

---

61. Verses 29 and 30 are sometimes called "the Golden Chain" of salvation.

62. Piper, *Five Points*, 58.

63. Peterson, *Election and Free Will*, 92.

64. Sproul, *Reformed Theology*, 145.

assurance that their part in the people of God is not accidental or random, but part of a divine purpose whose outworking was already envisaged from the beginning."[65] Murray sums up Rom 8:28 by stating that "determinate efficacy characterizes the call because it is given in accordance with eternal purpose."[66]

Several key aspects of these verses deserve comment. The first concerns the phrase *"all things work together for good."* How is this so? How, exactly, does God work all things for the good of the believer? The preceding verses set the context for this verse: despite all appearances to the contrary, Paul teaches his readers God has not abandoned them and that, ultimately, God is at work for their good. Calvinists tend to understand this in terms of the outworking of an overarching, comprehensive plan of God for the life of the believer. Murray, for example, speaks of an "all-embracing plan of God."[67] In contrast to the idea of the outworking of some detailed blueprint of a plan, the working of God for good may be the result of a more dynamic working of God whereby, in his wisdom, God is able to use all circumstances for the ultimate good, in a general sense, of the believer.[68] Furthermore, this ultimate sense may only be fully realized in the eschaton and not temporally.[69] There is nothing in v. 28 per se that requires the working of God to be the outworking of an overarching determinate plan.

A second point worth noting concerns the purpose of God mentioned in v. 28. The immediate purpose of God for the believers in Rome was that they would be encouraged to persevere in faith despite the temptations of the flesh (v. 12), and despite the sufferings they were experiencing (v. 18), to persevere in hope of final and complete adoption as sons and the redemption of the body (v. 23), and to assure them that reliance on the Spirit of God demonstrates the reality of their status as true children of God (v. 16). It may be that Paul is thinking of God's broad purposes for the believer because the conjunction "because" or "for" (Greek ὅτι, *hoti*) that immediately follows v. 28 suggests a purpose that is general—conformance to the image of Christ, however that is worked out in the life of the believer. Taking vv. 29 and 30 as providing a further comprehensive description of God's purposes, we see that God's purposes entail the believer's participation in the redemptive purposes of God. In particular, God has predestined *believers* (not unbelievers) to be conformed to the image of God's Son.

65. Dunn, *Romans 1–8*, 482.

66. Murray, *Romans*, 315.

67. Murray, *Romans*, 314.

68. A good example would be the evil intent of Joseph's brothers being used for ultimate good in the saving of many lives in Egypt (Gen 50:20).

69. Some incline to see the good in time, e.g., "helping forward the maturing of the believer (cf. 5:4) and the mortification of the deeds of the body (8:13)." Dunn, *Romans 1–8*, 494. I am more inclined to see the good eschatologically—in the final analysis, at the end of time, God's present workings will end in the great good of the believer's vindication and full realization of his current hopes and expectations. Such a perspective can accommodate the situation in which a believer suffers a harm that results in death; it is difficult to see such a situation as working for good to the believer temporally. The preceding context contains eschatological references, viz., vv. 11, 23.

A third point concerns the phrase *"those whom He foreknew"* (v. 29a). In fact, most of the discussion in these verses focuses on this phrase.[70] Calvinists understand the phrase as meaning "those whom God fore-loved." Murray is typical: foreknowledge "is used in a sense practically synonymous with 'love,' to set regard upon, to know with peculiar interest, delight, affection, and action."[71] This understanding of foreknowledge in v. 29 supports the idea of unconditional election. As Peterson says: "Calvinists . . . usually hold that God's foreknowledge in Romans 8:28 . . . means his choosing of people for salvation."[72] Non-Calvinists on the other hand, prefer to interpret the word foreknowledge in the more straightforward sense of "know beforehand," prescience. The sense would then support the idea of conditional election. As Cottrell says: "God predestined to heaven those whom he foreknew would meet the required conditions."[73]

Calvinists argue that to know beforehand (foreknowledge) a *person* necessarily implies that knowing *about* that person is excluded. "Paul does not say here [v. 29] that God knows certain facts, such as whether people would believe the gospel or not. Rather, Paul says that God foreknows certain people."[74] But, how does one know a person apart from knowing things about them? Yes, God foreknows certain people, but it is quite natural to ask what exactly it is about those people he foreknows. It seems that intrinsic to knowing a person is to know certain things (facts) about them. So, to foreknow certain persons in v. 29 is to know certain facts about them in advance. In this case, the relevant facts would be whether those foreknown would be persons of faith.

Furthermore, the Calvinist understanding of foreknow as, in effect, meaning those whom God has chosen for salvation makes v. 29 say, "Those whom He chose beforehand, He also predestined . . ."—which may be shortened to: "Those whom He predestined, He also predestined." The redundancy is obvious.

A point of exegesis may also be noted. The tendency by many commentators to ignore v. 28 in addressing v. 29 is problematic. As previously mentioned, the conjunction ὅτι (*hoti*, because, for) clearly indicates that what Paul says in v. 29 follows directly from what he has just said in v. 28. This is a helpful observation because it helps to identify the people "foreknown." Paul was writing to Christians in the church at Rome whom he identifies as *"those who love God."* In other words, those whom God foreknows in v. 29 are already believers whom God knew would be *believers* in the church at Rome before the foundation of the world[75]—contra Calvinists who view

---

70. Murray comments, "Few questions have provoked more difference of interpretation than that concerned with the meaning of God's foreknowledge as referred to here." Murray, *Romans*, 315.

71. Murray, *Romans*, 317.

72. Peterson, *Election and Free Will*, 109. According to Harrison and Hagner, *Romans*, 142, foreknowledge here "refers to God's choice, his electing decision."

73. Cottrell, *Romans*, 1:504.

74. Peterson, *Election and Free Will*, 111.

75. Eph 1:4.

those foreknown as *unbelievers* who have been chosen or selected for salvation before creation. Cottrell makes the same point:

> God foreknew those who would love him. He foreknew that at some point in their lives they would come to love him and would continue to love him to the end. See the parallel in 1 Cor 8:3, "But if anyone loves God, he is known by him." This is exactly the same idea as Rom 8:29a, the former referring to knowledge and the latter to foreknowledge.[76]

A fourth and final point concerning Rom 8:29–30 is the precise nature of the predestinating work of God. The emphasis in these verses falls on the divine initiative and actions. This is consistent with Paul's purpose in encouraging the believers in Rome to persevere in sufferings (Rom 8:17, 18), to continue in the faith despite inwardly groaning (v. 23) by looking to the sovereign God who works all things for ultimate good. Each of the five elements in "the golden chain" of salvation listed in v. 30 are designed to provide certainty of their salvation—beginning with the predestinating of believers and ending with the believer's ultimate consummation of their salvation in glorification. (The fact that some intermediate steps are omitted, such as regeneration and sanctification, is of no consequence to Paul's purpose here.)

A key question is whether God predestines both the end (glorification) and the means (calling, justification, etc.). Calvinists answer this question in the affirmative; God unconditionally predestines his elect, efficaciously calls them, gives the faith and repentance required to believe the gospel by an irresistible grace, ensures their perseverance, and guarantees ultimate glorification. All this, from a Calvinistic perspective, applies to those and only those, whom God chooses to be saved. In this system all five elements listed in v. 30 are of a whole.[77] Non-Calvinists agree that God predestines "those who love God" (v. 28), and whom he foresees continue to love him, to ultimate glorification. But they deny that "those who love God" are caused by God to do so as part of an unconditional calling and election. Those who love God, i.e., Christians, have freely chosen to respond to the call of the gospel and thus become recipients of the assurances of v. 30. In other words, God predestines the end (glorification for believers), but not the means (faith, repentance, perseverance). In short, God "predestines all believers to heaven, but he does not predestine anyone to become a believer. Salvation is conditional and individuals must meet those conditions. . . . Therefore, predestination itself is conditional; God predestines to heaven those whom he foreknew would meet the required conditions."[78]

---

76. Cottrell, *Romans*, 1:505.

77. "Here is a summary of the meaning of the five verbs, starting with the last: God glorifies his own when he brings them to see Christ's glory and be changed by it. He justifies them by crediting Christ's righteousness to them and declaring them righteous. He calls them by causing the gospel to reach their ears and to take root in their hearts. He predestines them by selecting them beforehand for salvation." Peterson, *Election and Free Will*, 109.

78. Cottrell, *Romans*, 1:504.

Ephesians 1:4, 5, 11

> *"He chose us in Him before the foundation of the world, that we would be holy and blameless before Him. In love He predestined us to adoption as sons through Jesus Christ to Himself, according to the kind intention of His will. . . . In Him also we have obtained an inheritance, having been predestined according to His purpose who works all things after the counsel of His will."*

Understandably, Calvinists see in these verses, especially v. 11, clear references to the doctrine of unconditional election. Twice in these verses the word *predestined* (προορίζω, *proorizō*; predestine, foreordain, predetermine) occurs, and Paul speaks of his Ephesian readers as having been *chosen* in v. 4. Furthermore, this predestinating work is seen as consistent with God working out everything according to his will. "He determined to make us (who did not yet exist) his own children through the redeeming work of Christ (which had not yet taken place)."[79] Bruce Ware concurs: "At its heart, the doctrine of unconditional election assures the believer that salvation, from beginning to end, is *all* of God. From God's electing in eternity past of those whom he would save, of those whom he would make holy and blameless (Eph. 1:4)."[80] "In Ephesians Paul talks about certain people whom God chose . . . to talk about God choosing a group of people means that he chose specific individuals who constituted that group."[81]

Several observations about this passage in Ephesians can be made. First, as we have seen from the above quotes, Calvinists assume that Paul is discussing the transition of the Ephesians from a pre-Christian unsaved state to a state of being saved. So, the Ephesians have been chosen for salvation (vv. 4, 11), they have been predestined to be saved (vv. 5, 11). But I would argue that it is believers that are in mind exclusively here in this passage; the following series of statements, with the personal pronouns "us" or "we," underscores that Paul is addressing those who are already believers:

"he chose us" believers . . . (v. 4)

"he predestined us" believers . . . (v. 5)

"he made known to us" believers . . . (v. 9)

"we [believers] *have obtained an inheritance"* . . . (v. 11)

"to the end that we [believers]*"* . . . (v. 12)

What is the significance of this? It is this: while Calvinists assume the choosing and predestinating of God is directed toward making unbelievers Christians, Paul in actuality is stressing the blessings of salvation that people who are already Christians may enjoy. In short, it is not that unbelievers would be saved, but that those already saved would enjoy the fruits of that salvation. Ephesians 1:3 virtually states this explicitly:

---

79. Stott, *Message of Ephesians*, 36.

80. Ware, "Divine Election," 5, emphasis original.

81. Grudem, *Systematic Theology*, 677.

"Blessed be the God and Father of our Lord Jesus Christ, who has blessed us with every spiritual blessing in the heavenly places in Christ." It is believers whom God has chosen to be holy and blameless (v. 4), to be adopted as sons (v. 5), to enjoy the redemption and forgiveness of sins (v. 7). It is believers who are privileged to know the mystery of God's will (v. 9), to live for the praise of his glory (v. 12), who are sealed with the Holy Spirit (v. 13), and who are in consequence assured an inheritance (v. 14). God has not chosen individuals to be saved (unconditionally), but God has chosen believers—those who are already saved—to experience all that their salvation entails and provides access to. Cottrell makes the same point succinctly when he says that "rather than certain God-selected unbelievers being predestined to become believers, all foreknown believers are predestined to enjoy the benefits of salvation."[82]

The above analysis is also precisely consistent with the prayer of thanksgiving for the Ephesians and their faith (vv. 15, 16) that immediately follows the passage we have been considering: *"I pray that the eyes of your heart may be enlightened, so that you will know what is the hope of His calling, what are the riches of the glory of His inheritance in the saints, and what is the surpassing greatness of His power toward us who believe"* (Eph 1:18–19).

Another subtle distinction needs to be made that will help clarify Paul's point in these eleven verses (Eph 1:1–11). Calvinists hold that the predestination of unbelievers to be unconditionally chosen for salvation finds its grounds, its basis, in the pre-temporal decrees of God—hence the unconditional nature of election. God decided before the foundation of the world who would be saved and who would either be bypassed or positively selected for damnation. But Paul consistently links God's choosing and predestinating to Christ; it is being found "in Christ" that results in the blessings of salvation. Five times the phrase "in Christ" appears (in the NASB); three times "in him"; once "through Jesus Christ" (v. 5); and once "in the one" (v. 6). This raises the question of course as to how one becomes "in Christ." The rest of the Bible's answer is clear: though faith. It is faith in Christ that leads to union with Christ and hence to all the blessings that flow from that union as Paul is concerned to show in these verses. Thus, a believer is predestined (to the blessings of salvation) by faith, and a believer is chosen through the exercise of faith—not by an eternal mysterious decree.[83]

Finally, and related to the above point, Calvinists approach these verses with the understanding that God has predestined unbelievers *to be in Christ*, but the text does not say that. Paul says that God chose us *in Christ*, not that God chose us *to be* in Christ. The difference is significant. Nowhere in these verses (or anywhere else in Scripture) does God (unconditionally) select an unbeliever to be in Christ, but

---

82. Cottrell, *Faith Once for All*, 392.

83. Calvinists counter that while it is true that the blessings of salvation flow from union with Christ and union with Christ is established through faith, it is God who gives the faith. As will be shown later, such a notion has no biblical warrant and is an artificial expedient to maintain the consistency of a monergistic system.

he does select believers to enjoy all the blessings of salvation as a consequence of being in Christ. Thus, for example, Paul teaches that God chose us believers to be holy and blameless in his sight as a consequence of our union with Christ (v. 4). The blessing of believers to the fruits of salvation is fully consistent with the intent, plan and purposes of God (v. 11).

James 1:18

> "In the exercise of His will He brought us forth by the word of truth, so that we would be a kind of first fruits among His creatures."

Calvinists sometimes appeal to the first clause ("In the exercise of his will") to justify a form of unconditional election accomplished sovereignly by God. Thus, Moo commenting on this verse remarks, "This new birth is motivated by the sovereign determination of God, whose will, unlike the creation he made, is unvarying."[84] We agree that James here is emphasizing God's work of giving life, in contrast to the death that results from humans succumbing to temptations (1:14, 15), but the text does not indicate any conditions or lack of conditions involved with God providing this life. It is reading too much into the verse to suggest that God gives (spiritual) life unconditionally and as the outworking of a sovereign plan for some specific individuals. In fact, the reference to God acting to provide life "by the word of truth" suggests that it was in response to this word (gospel) of truth on the part of those James is writing to (i.e., believers) that God chose to provide life. This is reinforced when, just three verses later James urges his readers to "in humility receive the word implanted, which is able to save your souls" (Jas 1:21). Salvation here, as in the whole of the Bible, is conditional upon humble acceptance of the word of truth.

There are more texts appealed to by Calvinists to justify their view that God unconditionally chooses some to be saved (the elect) while bypassing others, but I believe those considered here so far provide serious grounds for doubting this understanding of election. Before leaving the alleged textual support for unconditional election, we must examine in some detail a passage appealed to by virtually all Calvinists in a discussion of election, namely Rom 9–11.

Romans 9:10–16

> "And not only this, but there was Rebekah also, when she had conceived twins by one man, our father Isaac; for though the twins were not yet born and had not done anything good or bad, so that God's purpose according to His choice would stand, not because of works but because of Him who calls, it was said to her, 'The older will serve the younger.' Just as it is written, 'Jacob I loved, but Esau I hated.'

84. Moo, James, 77.

What shall we say then? There is no injustice with God, is there? May it never be! For He says to Moses, 'I will have mercy on whom I have mercy, and I will have compassion on whom I have compassion.' So then it does not depend on the man who wills or the man who runs, but on God who has mercy."

This passage touches on several important aspects of election—its unconditionality, God's sovereignty in selection, the justice of God. Bruce Ware views this passage as "one of the clearest and strongest assertions of the unconditional nature of God's election."[85] Here, Ware means unconditional election by God to the salvation of certain sinners. Likewise, Thomas Schreiner observes that "Calvinists typically appeal to Romans 9 to support their theology of divine election. In particular, they assert that Romans 9 teaches that God unconditionally elects individuals to be saved."[86] It is important to keep in mind that the Calvinist interpretation of Rom 9 is in terms of God electing or choosing certain individuals to be saved, and that their salvation is not conditioned on anything in the person, for example their faith or repentance or humility.[87]

Calvinists view Rom 9 as Paul's response to the question he implicitly raises in Rom 9:1–5—i.e., why are not "my people" (v. 3), the Jews, saved? The answer given to this question, based on their reading of Rom 9–11, is that God determines unconditionally who will and who won't be saved—as demonstrated in the history of Israel. As Ware explains, "Paul's deepest concern for Israel was that so many Jews were not saved. His argument asserts, though, that God has not failed in his promise to save Israel (Rom 9:6) because God has saved some Jews throughout Israel's history . . . the election spoken of here is God's election of some in Israel to salvation."[88] God chose Jacob and rejected Esau; he rejected Pharaoh (v. 17). God decides whom he will have mercy and compassion upon (v. 15). And all this is so that *"God's purpose in election might stand"* (v. 11), that is, "God wishes to establish his rightful place and authority as God by being the one who . . . elects one but not the other."[89] Furthermore, so it is argued, the question raised in v. 14 concerning the fairness of God in selecting one over another confirms the unconditionality of God's prerogatives because superficially, such unconditionality seems unjust. As Ware points out: "[God's] election of Jacob specifically disregarded anything about either person [Jacob or Esau] and was based only and completely in the hidden purpose and will of God. Therefore, the question, Is there injustice with God?, makes sense!"[90]

85. Ware, "Divine Election," 9.

86. Schreiner, "Individual Election," 89. Wright makes the same point: "Romans 9 is the most famous chapter on election in the New Testament." Wright, *No Place for Sovereignty*, 123.

87. "By 'unconditionally' [Calvinists] mean that God, in eternity past, freely chooses specific individuals whom he will save (Eph 1:4) and that his choice is not based on their foreseen faith or effort (Rom 9:16)." Schreiner, "Individual Election," 89.

88. Ware, "Divine Election," 9.

89. Ware, "Divine Election," 10.

90. Ware, "Divine Election," 10.

What shall we say in response? We can agree with the Calvinist that unconditionality is definitely present in God's dealings with the individuals mentioned. It is clear in the passage before us that there is nothing in the persons themselves that causes God to choose one over the other. As noted earlier, the Calvinist answer to the question implicitly raised by Paul concerning the spiritual lostness of his fellow countrymen (Rom 9:2–5) is that God sovereignly and unconditionally exercises his right to choose who will be saved and who will not be saved. However, in v. 6 Paul explicitly answers his question: *"It is not as though the word of God has failed. For they are not all Israel who are descended from Israel; nor are they all children because they are Abraham's descendants."* In other words, the reason why the Jews, generally speaking, fail to enjoy salvation is because of their wrong assumption that God was somehow obligated to save them simply because they were descended from Abraham. But *"it is not the children of the flesh who are children of God, but the children of the promise are regarded as descendants"* (v. 8). God's word of promise of *salvation* never applied to physical Israel, but rather only to spiritual Israel—only to those who exercised Abraham-like faith.[91] This point is further developed by Paul in chs. 10 and 11.

But then, having made this point Paul goes on in Rom 9:9–29 to stress God's unconditional electing authority. Why does Paul do this? The Calvinist answers in terms of Paul proving the point that God decides who will and won't be saved and that such discrimination is entirely "in the hidden purpose and will of God."[92] The problem with this answer is twofold; first it fails to connect with the reason given by Paul himself (in v. 6 and ch. 10) in terms of failure of the *Jews themselves*, and second it ignores the broader context of the preceding chapters in Rom 1–8.

Romans 9–11, while legitimately viewed as a distinct section within the letter, nevertheless arises from and has definite thematic connections with the preceding chapters.[93] In fact "we wouldn't know *why* Paul wrote these three chapters without referring back to 1–8."[94] In these preceding chapters Paul clearly establishes that salvation is not based on law keeping (Rom 3:20, 28; 7:4–6) nor on ethnicity, simply being a Jew (Rom 2:17–29; 3:1, 9). A person, Jew or Gentile, is justified by faith, not by works of law (3:28), and as far as salvation is concerned such a person is not under law, but under grace (6:14). Indeed, in the final analysis, the distinction between Jew and Gentile is irrelevant as far as salvation is concerned, what matters is to have Abraham-like faith (Rom 4), to believe upon Christ for salvation. Now it is precisely these teachings that raises acutely the question with which Rom 9–11 deals. "Why did God focus his loving attention upon the Jews, and shower so many privileges upon them, if in the final analysis salvation is by grace, not law? . . . Has [God] gone

91. We might paraphrase Paul's statement *"not all who are descended from Israel are Israel"* as "not all who are physically Israelites are true, spiritual, Israelites."

92. Ware, "Divine Election," 11.

93. See Cottrell, *Romans*, 2:35.

94. Cottrell, *Romans*, 2:35, emphasis original.

back on his promises to the Jews?"[95] We are now better positioned to understand why Paul addresses the question of God's faithfulness in Rom 9–11, and specifically with the response in 9:6 that God's word has not failed. The Jew's assumption that being a chosen people automatically implied their salvation is mistaken—even in the Old Testament salvation always required faith, and apart from faith there is no salvation. Much of Rom 10 and 11 emphasizes this need for faith to be exercised (9:30–33; 10:3, 4, 9–10, 12–13, 21; 11:14, 20, 22, 23).

Granted all of the above contextual considerations, it is still legitimate to ask, why the emphasis on unconditional election by Paul in the bulk of ch. 9? How does God's sovereign choice of individuals and the nation of Israel relate to the question of the Jews salvation? The key to understanding this theme of unconditional election is to appreciate that Paul in Rom 9:6–29 is not talking about election to *salvation* at all, but rather God's election to *service*. The call of Abraham, Sarah, Isaac, Jacob was a call to further God's redemptive purposes for the world—this was a call to service, not necessarily salvation. This distinction is absolutely crucial for a proper understanding of the nature of the unconditional election Paul speaks about in Rom 9:7–24. Israel was chosen to be a light to the Gentiles and to bring forth Messiah. These are roles of service and do not have any necessary connection with the salvation of any particular Israelite. As Cottrell says:

> Being chosen as the people from whom the Christ would come carried with it some of the highest privileges known to man (Rom 9:4–5), but salvation was not necessarily among them. Whether an Israelite was saved or not did not depend simply on his membership in the chosen people. The nation could serve its purpose of preparing for the Christ even if the majority of individuals belonging to it were lost.[96]

The main point Paul seeks to establish in 9:6–13 therefore is to show the Jews in the church at Rome that God has the sovereign right to define the terms of his relationship with Israel—he can choose to call unconditionally those who will play a key role in the unfolding plan of redemption. He can choose Jacob over Esau, he can even choose to involve Pharaoh if he so wishes. In this respect, God is not unfair at all (9:14). Furthermore, in the exercise of God's right to select unconditionally those who will, or will not, play a role in the redemptive plan of God for the world, he also has the right to distinguish between this call of God to service, from a call to salvation. Romans 9:6–29 focuses on the former—God's sovereignty in electing unconditionally those who will serve his redemptive purposes, while 9:30—11:32 lays out clearly the conditionality associated with a Jew or Gentile's personal salvation, the main condition being faith in God. Again, Cottrell summarizes the teachings in these chapters well in terms of the outworking of God's sovereignty:

95. Cottrell, *Romans*, 2:36.
96. Cottrell, *What the Bible Says about God the Ruler*, 333.

God's sovereignty is exercised in his unconditional election of individuals and groups, Israel in particular, to roles of service in the working out of his redemptive plan. His sovereignty is also seen in the way he chooses to distinguish service from salvation, which allows him to choose and use Israel without guaranteeing the salvation of all individual Jews in the same package. Another expression of his sovereignty is his right to establish the system of salvation according to a way of his own choosing, in a way independent of works, namely, by grace. Those who accept this way to salvation become part of "the elect."[97]

It is the Calvinist's insistence on seeing every reference to selection in Rom 9 as selection of some for salvation and others for rejection of salvation by God that causes them to understand Rom 9 in terms of God's unconditional election of some to salvation. It overlooks Paul's answer in v. 6 as to why not all Israel are saved; in the outworking of God's redemptive plan for the world there is a crucial distinction between those "descended from Israel," national, ethnic Jews, and true Israelites who have the faith of Abraham and are consequently able to enjoy the salvation Christ came to bring. God can, and did, work unconditionally to choose whom among the former (national Israel) he would select for a role of service. However, for the personal salvation of any Jew the required condition of faith and repentance needs to be met.

Romans 11:5–7

> *"In the same way then, there has also come to be at the present time a remnant according to God's gracious choice. But if it is by grace, it is no longer on the basis of works, otherwise grace is no longer grace. What then? What Israel is seeking, it has not obtained, but those who were chosen obtained it, and the rest were hardened."*

This is another passage in Romans that Calvinists often appeal to in order to justify the view of unconditional election to salvation. Paul's point in v. 5 here is to show that God is faithful, he has not completely rejected the Jews, but rather, just as in Elijah's day there are now a relatively small number of Jews who are saved; these are the remnant (cf. 9:27). The reason Calvinists appeal to these verses is because of the phrase *"a remnant according to God's gracious choice."* As Ware observes: "One of the most striking phrases in Romans 11:5–7 is Paul's reference in v. 5 to the remnant as those 'chosen by grace.'"[98] Ware goes on to say,

> Here it is not salvation but election which grace gives. That is, the very choosing of the remnant to be a believing minority among the vast majority of those hardened is itself the gift specified that is granted by grace. Gracious election, in short, is unconditional election. . . . In other words, were it not

97. Cottrell, *Romans*, 1:43.

98. Ware, "Divine Election," 11.

for God's gracious choosing of the remnant, they, too, would be counted among the majority who did not find salvation at this time, the majority who have been hardened.[99]

It seems clear that "grace" in v. 5 functions for Ware as a synonym for "God." So, the phrase "chosen by grace" could equally have been stated by Paul as "chosen by God." But grace is not simply another term for God. Grace is a characteristic, a disposition, within God that prompts him to seek to grant sinners unmerited favor. This desire of God finds expression in response to the sinner's faith (but not his meritorious works): *"For by grace you have been saved through faith, . . . not as a result of works, so that no one may boast"* (Eph 2:8–9). Grace is almost always connected to Christ, and contrasted with meritorious works. So, for example, sinners are justified as a result of God's desire to save: *"being justified as a gift by His grace through the redemption which is in Christ Jesus"* (Rom 3:24). The fulfillment of God's promises of salvation follows and is based upon God's grace. His desire to grant blessings is in response to faith, not meritorious works: *"For this reason it* [the promise] *is by faith, in order that it may be in accordance with grace . . . to those who are of the faith of Abraham"* (Rom 4:16). So, for Paul, here in Rom 11:5 to speak of a remnant "chosen by grace" means that this remnant (believing Jews) enjoy their salvation as a result of, and on the basis of, God's desire to save all who exercise faith in Christ. Grace is contrasted, not with faith, but with meritorious works as 11:6 states: *"And if by grace, then it cannot be based on works; if it were, grace would no longer be grace."* In other words, God's desire to save (grace) finds expression in those who receive the gift of salvation when the divine requirement has been met, namely faith. No faith, then no grace, and therefore no salvation, justification, or redemption.[100]

The way the phrase "chosen by grace" functions in our text (v. 5) is shorthand for those who have obtained a righteousness by faith (Rom 9:30), those who have made the good confession "Jesus is Lord" and believed in their heart that God raised Jesus from the dead (Rom 10:9), and have called on the name of the Lord (Rom 10:13). In other words, "to say that the remnant has come into existence according to an election of grace means that God chooses to save those Jews (and Gentiles, 9:30) who themselves choose his way of grace rather than the futile way of law."[101] Given this grace/faith context, it is clear that "those who were chosen" (v. 7b) are those previously described as a believing "remnant"—these believers have obtained the righteousness/salvation that Israel sought but failed to attain. Why? Because the former exercised faith and the latter did not.

---

99. Ware, "Divine Election," 12.

100. Typically, Calvinists agree that faith is a condition for the reception of salvation, but they then need to insist that faith itself is a gift given unilaterally by God to those whom he has chosen for salvation. This error will be addressed later.

101. Cottrell, *Romans*, 1:215.

Some Texts That Clearly Show Election to Salvation to Be Conditional upon Certain Personal Qualities

Calvinism, as we have seen, holds that election to salvation is unconditional; an individual is chosen by God apart from anything in the person himself or herself. God's choice is inscrutable, the result of a decree established in eternity past before anyone was born. The Bible, however, seems to link salvation, not in some preexisting divine decree, but rather as a divine response to human choices that flow from certain personal characteristics that some people possess and others do not. The following texts indicate that God calls for certain requirements and seeks for certain attitudes in those who hear the gospel if they are to be saved and thereby counted among God's elect. These passages, among many others not addressed here, show that election to salvation is clearly conditional. The primary conditions are faith, repentance, and humility; when these are lacking, the God-required means of appropriating salvation is lacking.

a) Faith and Salvation

"But we should always give thanks to God for you, brethren beloved by the Lord, because God has chosen you from the beginning for salvation through sanctification by the Spirit and faith in the truth" (2 Thess 2:13). This is a very helpful verse for our present study since it underscores the idea that God's choice of the Thessalonian Christians for salvation followed their "faith in the truth." The sequence seems to be: belief in the gospel which allows the sanctifying work of the Holy Spirit to take place in their lives, and the result is described as having been chosen by God.[102]

"You, [Timothy] however, continue in the things you have learned and become convinced of, knowing from whom you have learned them, and that from childhood you have known the sacred writings which are able to give you the wisdom that leads to salvation through faith which is in Christ Jesus" (2 Tim 3:14–15). Again, Paul connects salvation with faith. This time Paul cites the Scriptures (the Old Testament) as the medium used by God to bring a person to salvation through their faith. It is Scripture, not a predetermined decree, that God uses to save.

"By faith Noah, being warned by God about things not yet seen, in reverence prepared an ark for the salvation of his household, by which he condemned the world, and became an heir of the righteousness which is according to faith" (Heb 11:7). In this great chapter on faith (Heb 11), the writes illustrates the crucial role faith plays in receiving salvation. In this one verse Noah's faith is mentioned three times. The phrase "according to faith," here in the NASB, is more helpfully translated as "in keeping with faith" in the NIV; that is, Noah's imputed righteousness was consistent with his exercising faith.

---

102. Of course, Calvinists would place the emphasis on God's initial choosing of the Thessalonians (arbitrarily and unconditionally chosen from the mass of humanity in the region at the time), and the giving of the Spirit and the giving of faith would function as the means whereby God's predetermined choice would be executed. Again, I will discuss later the mistaken notion that faith is a God-given gift.

Like Abraham, Noah's faith was accounted to him for righteousness. In this manner Noah was justified by faith. Faith plays such an important role in the salvation of a person because, as the writer has already said, *"without faith it is impossible to please Him, for he who comes to God must believe that He is and that He is a rewarder of those who seek Him"* (11:6). Faith on the part of the seeker of God plays a crucial role in, and indeed is an absolute requirement for, salvation.

"Though you have not seen Him, you love Him, and . . . believe in Him, . . . obtaining as the outcome of your faith the salvation of your souls" (1 Pet 1:9). Peter could not state more plainly that it is his reader's faith that leads directly to their salvation. In all these scriptures, it is most natural to read the references to faith as a human capacity, a human response to the grace of God—it is not something that is "behind the scenes" given by God such that the ultimate source of the person's faith is God himself as Calvinism postulates. The sequence is clear: first faith and then salvation follows as a direct consequence.

Closely allied with the word *faith* is the word *believe* and its cognates. There are several texts that correlate a person's belief with their salvation. In other words, salvation follows from, and is conditional upon, belief. It is not a secret decree of God that selects who will or who will not gain salvation, with belief playing an almost incidental, mechanical role in those chosen by God for salvation.

"Now the parable is this: the seed is the word of God. Those beside the road are those who have heard; then the devil comes and takes away the word from their heart, so that they will not believe and be saved" (Luke 8:11, 12). In this parable of the Sower belief, or rather the lack of it, plays a key role throughout the parable. Again, the close connection between a person's response to the preached Word and his, or her, salvific status is clearly illustrated. Whenever unbelief is present—whether due to succumbing to satanic temptation (v. 12), or due to merely a superficial response (v. 13), or due to worldly concerns (v. 14)—there is no salvation. The parable would make no sense if in fact, salvation was merely the end result of a prior, secret decree, and faith was something God either gave or withheld. Rather, the parable teaches that a genuine, rather than spurious, faith is the required response on the part of the hearers to the sown seed, the word of God (v. 11).

"They said, 'Believe in the Lord Jesus, and you will be saved, you and your household'" (Acts 16:31). When the Philippian jailor asked Paul and Silas "what must I do to be saved?" the answer is given that they were to believe upon the Lord Jesus. Again, the need for faith to be exercised is clearly seen as playing a crucial role in the person's salvation. As has been consistently shown so far, faith is a condition of salvation.

"If you confess with your mouth Jesus as Lord, and believe in your heart that God raised Him from the dead, you will be saved" (Rom 10:9). The structure of conditionality is clearly seen here: "if . . . then." Here, salvation is conditional on verbal confession of Jesus as Lord and sincere belief in the resurrection of Christ. The former reflects the genuineness of belief, and the latter comprises the grounds of salvation. Once more,

salvation is tied to the person's response to the gospel, not in some independent, impersonal decree that determines from eternity past who will or won't be saved.

"In Him, you also, after listening to the message of truth, the gospel of your salvation—having also believed, you were sealed in Him with the Holy Spirit of promise" (Eph 1:13).

To be "stamped" with the Holy Spirit is a mark of authentic salvation and follows belief. The Ephesian Christians' election, their inclusion in Christ, followed their hearing the gospel and then believing that gospel.[103]

"As a result of this many of His disciples withdrew and were not walking with Him anymore. So Jesus said to the twelve, 'You do not want to go away also, do you?' Simon Peter answered Him, 'Lord, to whom shall we go? You have words of eternal life. We have believed and have come to know that You are the Holy One of God.' Jesus answered them, 'Did I Myself not choose you, the twelve, and yet one of you is a devil?'" (John 6:66–70). Salvation is obviously connected with a true knowledge of God, and once more, we see a connection between believing and knowing God. Scripture consistently wishes us to understand that salvation is intimately connected to, and follows from, belief in Christ himself. The reference to Jesus's choosing Judas among the twelve shows that even when Jesus chooses someone (in this case, not for salvation, but for a task of service), there is no guarantee that the chosen person will himself infallibly continue to choose to cooperate with the purposes of God.

b) Repentance and Salvation

"'For I have no pleasure in the death of anyone who dies,' declares the Lord God. 'Therefore, repent and live'" (Ezek 18:32). This call to repent follows a persistent appeal to ancient Israel to *"turn away from all your transgressions"* (v. 30). The covenant curses (Deut 28) clearly indicated that persistent sin, especially the sin of idolatry, would invoke the covenant curses and inevitable result in death. Conversely, God, through the prophet Ezekiel pleads with his fellow Israelites to repent and live. Clearly, the choice as to whether the people will live depends on whether they will heed God's call through the prophet and meet the condition—repentance.

"Repent, for the kingdom of heaven is at hand" (Matt 3:2). The first recorded words of John the Baptist are for the people of his day to prepare for Messiah's arrival by repenting of their sins. Repentance is a prerequisite for entrance into the kingdom of God. Likewise, Jesus began his public ministry with precisely the same words (Matt 4:17); obviously repentance is an important condition to be met if acceptance by God was to be enjoyed. The appeal would not make sense if it was God

---

103. Romans 10:13–14 also clearly links salvation with hearing the gospel and responding with belief: *"Whoever will call on the name of the Lord will be saved. How then will they call on Him in whom they have not believed? How will they believe in Him whom they have not heard? And how will they hear without a preacher?"*

alone who unilaterally and unconditionally decided who would enter the kingdom. Those not selected by God to be saved could not repent, and those selected by God to be saved could not fail to repent! In either case the call, the appeal, would be a waste of breath at best and a charade at worst.

"*They went out and preached that men should repent*" (Mark 6:12). The command given to Jesus's twelve disciples to exercise Christ's healing authority on their mission entailed calling the common people to repent. Again, divine blessing is conditional on repentance. Failure to repent on the part of any individual merely manifested a heart set against God, and under such conditions salvation would be impossible.

c) Humility and Salvation

"*With the kind You show Yourself kind; with the blameless You show Yourself blameless; with the pure You show Yourself pure, and with the crooked You show Yourself astute. For You save an afflicted people, but haughty eyes You abase*" (Ps 18:25–27). The writers of the psalms, expressing as they do the heartfelt meditations and cries of the heart, often demonstrate dependence on God for deliverance and in so doing show their own humility and lack of pride in their own abilities or power.[104] In our verse here, in addition to humility, virtues which are pleasing to God include (covenant) faithfulness, (relative) blamelessness and moral purity. One is reminded of Noah. When God saved Noah and his family the text seems to indicate that it was because "*Noah was a righteous man, blameless in his time*" (Gen 6:9) that God acted to save him and his family from destruction. Noah demonstrated himself to be a man of faith, and humility is the handmaid of faith. These personal qualities, while certainly not meriting salvation, are equally certainly conditions to be met if salvation is to be received at the hand of God as a gift.

"*But to this one I will look, to him who is humble and contrite of spirit, and who trembles at My word*" (Isa 66:2). Unlike Israel of old which, generally speaking, displayed remarkable arrogance toward the Lord and his servants the prophets,[105] only those displaying a spirit of humility are looked upon with favor by God. Absent entirely in these accounts of those to whom God is favorably disposed is the idea of the outworking of a secret preordained plan or decree being worked out in a mechanical fashion in the psalmist, the prophet, or the godly person.

"*And His mercy is upon generation after generation toward those who fear Him. He has done mighty deeds with His arm; He has scattered those who were proud in the thoughts of their heart. He has brought down rulers from their thrones, and has exalted those who were humble*" (Luke 1:50–52). Mary in her song of praise for having been chosen to bear Israel's Messiah recognizes that God's mercy extends to those who fear him, and that, conversely, the proud are rejected. She gratefully understands that God

---

104. E.g., Pss 10:17; 25:9; 34:1; 37:11; 69:32; 76:9.

105. E.g., Jer 43:2; Ps 73:1–3; Mal 3:13.

has been *"mindful of the humble state of his servant"* (1:48). Mary, like Noah, exhibited the conditions necessary to further God's redemptive purposes for the world. While it is true that the Bible rarely describes the personal qualities of those who are justified and receive the salvation of God, the general characteristics noted so far make it abundantly clear that such people have open hearts toward God (faith), are willing to change their lives to bring them into line with God's will (repentance), and recognize their sinfulness and turn to God for help (humility).

"But the tax collector, standing some distance away, was even unwilling to lift up his eyes to heaven, but was beating his breast, saying, 'God, be merciful to me, the sinner!' I tell you, this man went to his house justified rather than the other; for everyone who exalts himself will be humbled, but he who humbles himself will be exalted" (Luke 18:13–14). In this parable, designed to teach the Pharisees that their arrogance, their confidence in their own supposed righteousness (18:9), prevented them from even recognizing the Messiah in their midst, Jesus focuses upon a key condition to receive salvation—humility. Notice it is those "who humble themselves" who are justified and exalted, not those who allegedly are caused to be humbled by God so that an unconditional election decreed before the foundation of the world could be enacted.

In all the scriptures examined above, we have consistently seen that those who are to enjoy God's salvific favor do so only because they have met the God-ordained conditions; they are people of faith who are willing to repent of their sinful ways, and whose character is marked by humility.[106] Since the coming of Messiah, God's elect people are those who are in union with Christ, those "in Christ," to use a characteristically Pauline phrase. To be in Christ, however, from the human side, requires the conditions noted above to be present. Anyone lacking faith, repentance, or humility will not be found "in Christ" and, consequently, will not be counted among God's elect.

Before leaving this question of God-specified conditions that need to be met in order to receive the gift of salvation, I wish to address briefly the notion that these conditions are somehow meritorious and can be viewed as earning salvation. This is a common Calvinistic accusation. A good example is Wayne Grudem: "Election based on something good in us (our faith) would be the beginning of salvation by merit."[107] But this view confuses the meeting of God-stipulated *conditions* (faith, repentance, humility) required to *appropriate* salvation, with good works that can be appealed to in order to *merit* salvation. It is quite misleading to confuse the two. Grudem considers grace to be operative only if God supplies everything—salvation, faith, humility, repentance. Any human response is viewed as a challenge to grace:

> What ultimately makes the difference between those who believe and those
> who do not? If our answer is that it is *ultimately* based on something God does
> (namely, his sovereign election of those who would be saved), then we see that

---

106. Several other texts could be cited that explicitly connect humility with salvation including 1 Pet 5:5–6; 2 Chr 12:7; Ps 25:9.

107. Grudem, *Systematic Theology*, 678.

salvation at its most foundational level is based on *grace alone*. On the other hand, if we answer that the ultimate difference between those who are saved and those who are not is because of *something in man* (that is, a tendency or disposition to believe or not), then salvation ultimately depends on a combination of grace plus human ability.[108]

But Scripture never contrasts grace and "human ability." Rather, it contrasts grace with *works* that are intended to *merit* or earn salvation. As shown above in our discussion of the role of faith, repentance, and humility, these human capacities or responses are commanded by God to be exercised, and are quite consistent with God's grace in providing salvation for man. Ephesians 2:8–9 summarizes the situation nicely: *"For by grace you have been saved through faith; and that not of yourselves, it is the gift of God; not as a result of works, so that no one may boast."* Salvation is *based* on grace and *appropriated* by faith. What is a *"gift of God"* and *"not as a result of works"*? It is simply "salvation by grace through faith." Faith is never contrasted with (meritorious) works as Grudem thinks, but to the contrary is a God-specified requirement or condition for the reception of the salvation God wishes to bestow. Grace is contrasted with (meritorious) works, but never with faith. Faith and grace go hand on hand; grace and meritorious works are antithetical.

Theological Issues Related to the Doctrine of Election

So far in this chapter we have focused on biblical texts to seek to understand and evaluate the Calvinist understanding of election and how it compares with the Bible's own portrait—at least with respect to one distinctive aspect of the doctrine, its conditionality or unconditionality. This question is important, indeed it is at the heart of the difference between a Calvinistic and non-Calvinistic understanding of election.[109] Nevertheless, for a truly well-rounded, biblical understanding of the doctrines of election and predestination it is fruitful to examine the Bible's teaching on election and predestination. This we will now do, and then we will examine several other doctrines that relate in one way or another to this doctrine.

a) The Meaning of Election and Predestination

Election and predestination both refer to the same reality—God choosing for certain purposes. The latter stresses the fact that sometimes God chooses before the event, and even before creation.[110]

108. Grudem, *Systematic Theology*, 678, emphases original.

109. Cottrell states that "the distinctive element in Calvinistic election is its unconditional nature. . . . The essence of the Calvinistic doctrine . . . is that election is unconditional." Cottrell, "Conditional Election," 57, 60.

110. Cottrell, "Conditional Election," 51. Since Cottrell provides an excellent overview of the

The Election of Jesus

All agree that Jesus was chosen by the Father to be the agent of salvation. He was qualified for this supremely important task because he was fully God and fully man. In a sense, all other expressions of election or being chosen are subordinate to Christ's election. Isaiah 42:1 refers to God's chosen one: *"Behold, My Servant, whom I uphold; My chosen one in whom My soul delights."* In Matt 12:17, 18, Matthew applies this Isaianic text to Jesus. Similarly, the heavenly voice at the transfiguration of Jesus affirms: *"This is My Son, My Chosen One; listen to Him!"* (Luke 9:35).

The Election of Israel—Corporate and for Service

God chose Israel, to play a key role in his redemptive purposes for the world. The primary reason God chose Israel was to be the people through whom the Christ was to come. As Israel was about to complete its wilderness wanderings, Moses reminds the people that they were to be a separated people, distinct from those whose land they were about to possess: *"For you are a people holy to the Lord your God. For you are a holy people to the Lord your God; the Lord your God has chosen you to be a people for His own possession out of all the peoples who are on the face of the earth"* (Deut 7:6). Deuteronomy 14:2 makes the same point; Israel was a specially chosen people: *"The Lord has chosen you to be a people for His own possession out of all the peoples who are on the face of the earth."*[111]

Three points are especially noteworthy in connection with God having chosen old covenant Israel. The first is that God elected to work with a group or nation and that God's redemptive purposes for the world would be worked out through the nation. This is *corporate election.* The Mosaic law, the lynchpin of Israel's relationship with God, was given to the nation (Exod 20:2), it was with the nation that God was entering into covenant relationship and to thus mark the nation as unique among all other nations.

A second noteworthy point with respect to the election of Israel was that its election was *an election of service*, not salvation.

> Being chosen as the people from whom the Christ would come carried with it some of the highest privileges known to man (Rom 9:4, 5), but salvation was not necessarily among them. Whether an Israelite was saved or not did not depend simply on his membership in the chosen people. The nation could

---

doctrine in his chapter titled "Election" in *Grace Unlimited*, I shall track his thoughts fairly closely here in what follows.

111. Other texts that underscore God's choosing Israel are 1 Chr 16:13; Ps 33:12; 105:6; Amos 3:2; Acts 13:17, 23. The last passage is particularly clear in connecting God's choosing Israel as a nation under the old covenant (v. 17) with the purpose of God bringing forth the Savior Jesus (v. 23).

serve its purpose of preparing for the Christ even if the majority of individuals belonging to it were lost.[112]

The importance of this point cannot be overstated. It is the fundamental error Calvinists make in appealing to Rom 9 as a basis for the doctrine of an unconditional election of individuals to salvation. For Rom 9 recounts God's unconditional right to choose whomsoever he will *for service*, not salvation. Israel was chosen to serve God's redemptive purposes for the world. It is true, as Calvinists often stress, that in Rom 9:1–3 Paul is expressing his anguish for the salvation of his countrymen in the light that most had rejected the gospel.[113] The next move Calvinists make is to understand the rest of Rom 9 in the light of these introductory verses to the chapter. That is, the entire chapter is dealing with the salvation of Israel and God is underscoring his sovereignty to exercise unconditional election of individuals by appealing to the way he has already chosen some Jews in the nation's past for salvation. As Bruce Ware states it:

> The context [Rom 9:1–3] establishes that Paul's deepest concern for Israel was that so many Jews were not saved. His argument asserts that, . . . God has saved some Jews throughout Israel's history. . . . In light of this context . . . the election spoken of here is God's election of some [individuals] in Israel to salvation.[114]

But this understanding of what Paul is doing in Rom 9:6–24 is mistaken; there is indeed a stress on divine sovereignty expressed through an unconditional election—however, as previously pointed out, it is not an election to salvation, but to service. The answer given by Paul to the question why his countrymen have not been saved is given in v. 6: *"But it is not as though the word of God has failed. For they are not all Israel who are descended from Israel."* Here, Paul is distinguishing between an ethnic Israel and a true or spiritual Israel. In other words, God has set up the scheme of salvation, not on the basis of ethnicity, as the Jews of his day expected, but rather on the basis of faith (Rom 4). And Rom 9:7–24 outlines God's sovereign right to unconditionally set up the parameters of salvation as he so chooses. This is demonstrated, so Paul shows, in God's dealings with both individuals (Rebekah, Isaac, Pharaoh), and nations (Jacob/Israel and Esau/Edom) in the outworking of redemptive history.[115] In each case, however, it was an election to further God's redemptive purposes, an election to service in other words.

112. Cottrell, "Conditional Election," 53.

113. Rom 9:1–3: *"I am telling the truth in Christ, I am not lying, my conscience testifies with me in the Holy Spirit, that I have great sorrow and unceasing grief in my heart. For I could wish that I myself were accursed, separated from Christ for the sake of my brethren, my kinsmen according to the flesh."*

114. Ware, "Divine Election," 9.

115. That the reference to Jacob and Esau is a reference to the nations of Israel and Edom, respectively, is easily shown since it was never true that the older (Esau) ever served "the younger" (Jacob) in their personal histories. But it was the case that the nation Edom served the nation Israel (2 Sam 8:14). Also, it was common to name the nations by the progenitor—e.g., Ps 14:7 (Jacob/Israel) and

Finally, once God's purpose in calling Israel into existence in the first place was satisfied, i.e., to bring forth Messiah, then national Israel's theological significance terminated. Its task fulfilled, God would now continue his plan of redemption for the world through Jesus and thence the church. The old covenant would no longer be valid as an enduring special covenant. God would now work through a new covenant inaugurated with the coming of Messiah. This is the precise point made in Heb 8:13: *"When He said, 'A new covenant,' He has made the first obsolete. But whatever is becoming obsolete and growing old is ready to disappear."* As Cottrell notes: "Since Israel was chosen specifically to prepare the way for Messiah's appearance, her purpose was accomplished and her destiny fulfilled in the incarnation, death, and resurrection of Jesus Christ."[116]

The Election of the Church—Corporate and for Service

God's redemptive purposes, begun in the Old Testament, find fruition in a chosen body of believers in Messiah called the church. In the opening verses of Eph 1 Paul makes reference to "us" believers in Ephesus: *"Just as He chose us in Him before the foundation of the world, that we would be holy and blameless before Him. In love He predestined us to adoption as sons"* (Eph 1:4, 5a). Robert Shank notes that "the thesis that the election [of the church] is corporate as Paul understood it and viewed it in the Ephesian doxology, is supported by the whole context of the epistle."[117] Illustrating the point he cites Eph 2:12, with its overtones of Israel's corporate election. The believers in the church at Ephesus were formerly *"excluded from the commonwealth of Israel, and strangers to the covenants of promise."* God's purpose in Christ was to break down all barriers to Jew and Gentile fellowship and so *"in Himself He might make the two into one new man, thus establishing peace, and might reconcile them both in one body to God through the cross"* (Eph 2:15, 16). Peter speaks of his readers collectively as being *"a chosen race, a royal priesthood, a holy nation, a people for God's own possession, . . . for you once were not a people, but now you are the people of God"* (1 Pet 2:9, 10). The echo of Israel as the corporate entity chosen by God is unmistakable (Exod 19:6). It is also probable that local churches are referenced by the Apostle John in 2 John 1 and 13 which he describes as "chosen."[118]

Just as for corporate Israel, God's election of the church was for a task of service—to be the agent of proclamation of the Good News of hope extended to all through faith in Christ. Peter insists his readers are a chosen people intended by God to *"proclaim the excellencies of Him who has called you out of darkness into His marvelous light"* (1 Pet 2:9). The church is to be salt and light in the world (Matt 5:13, 14). The church

---

Obad 1:6 (Esau/Edom).

116. Cottrell, "Conditional Election," 53.

117. Shank, *Elect in the Son*, 45.

118. *"The elder to the chosen lady. . . . The children of your chosen sister greet you."*

is to model God's love for the world, as well as reflect God's holiness. It is through the church's mutual love for its members and unity within the church that the world would perceive the truth concerning the mission of Jesus in bringing salvation (John 17:20–23). So, we see that while Israel was chosen for a role of preparation (for Messiah), the church is chosen for the role of proclamation (of the gospel).

The Election of Individuals—to Service

God not only chooses to work out his redemptive purposes corporately, but also through certain individuals who are called to play a key role in those purposes. Under the old covenant God called the patriarchs Abraham, Isaac, and Jacob to be the founders of the nation. Once the nation was formed (in Egypt initially), God called Moses to lead the people out of Egyptian enslavement. Joshua was chosen to lead the nation into the promised land. God called judges and kings to govern in his name. God could even call an Egyptian pharaoh to a role in the drama of redemption (Exod 7:1–4; Rom 9:17).

Similarly, with respect to the church, God called individuals to play key roles of service in the implementation of God's plan of redemption. For example, God called the twelve disciples (Matt 3:14–19), whom Jesus later called to be apostles (sent ones, Matt 28:19, 20), he called Paul to be a missionary to the Gentiles (Acts 9:15). God sent John the Baptist to prepare the way of the Lord (Matt 3:1–3). God called Mary to be the bearer of the Christ child (Luke 1:30, 31).

As before when considering corporate election to service for Israel and the church, so here with individuals chosen for service, there is no necessary salvific significance attached to these callings. The call to service was a privilege, not a call to personal salvation. Any one individual may or may not have been in right relationship with God. In either case, God's redemptive purposes would be worked out. Two examples suffice to establish this point. The first concerns the incidence when Moses came down from Mt. Sinai after receiving the tablets with the ten commandments and saw the people behaving frivolously and worshipping a golden calf. In response to this God declared to Moses, *"Now then let Me alone, that My anger may burn against them and that I may destroy them; and I will make of you a great nation"* (Exod 32:10). What is remarkable about this statement on the part of God is God's willingness to change his plans as to whom he would use to accomplish the task of preparation for Messiah. If Moses had not interceded for the people of Israel, the nation would no longer have been known as the children of Israel (i.e., descendants of Jacob), but rather the children of Moses![119] If there was salvific significance attached to the calling of Israel, how could God have threatened to destroy them? This incident illustrates the utilitarian nature of Israel's corporate election; it was an election to service, not national salvation. The second

---

119. As Cole states, these people were "the fulfillment of God's promises to Abraham and to Jacob, but the people would now bear the tribal name 'sons of Moses,' not 'sons of Israel.'" Cole, *Exodus*, 217.

example concerns the disciples Jesus chose: *"'Did I Myself not choose you, the twelve, and yet one of you is a devil?' Now He meant Judas the son of Simon Iscariot, for he, one of the twelve, was going to betray Him"* (John 6:70–71). The calling of the twelve was a calling to service; any individual's personal salvation was conditional upon faith. Where faith was present there could be both salvation and service, where faith was lacking, as in the case of Judas, his calling was a merely utilitarian service.

The Election of Individuals to Salvation

Nearly all Christian traditions would affirm what has been said so far concerning election. However, when we come to the question of the election of individuals, as opposed to groups, being elected for salvation as opposed to service, we see significant divergence.

Of course, as we have previously noted, Calvinists uniformly believe that God elects certain individuals to salvation. This choosing is unconditional, that is, it is not conditioned upon anything in the person herself. Recall that due to a total inability to do anything that is spiritually significant (e.g., exercise faith, genuinely repent, seek after God, etc.), a condition inherited from Adam, if anyone is in fact saved it must be because God unilaterally and unconditionally chose them.[120] The doctrine of total depravity leads inexorably to unconditional election for the Calvinist. The basis for such election is found in the eternal decree of God, hidden in the mind of God, secret and inscrutable to us and established before the world was made. "Scripture clearly proves this much, that God by his eternal and immutable counsel determined once for all those whom it was his pleasure one day to admit to salvation, and those whom, on the other hand, it was his pleasure to doom to destruction."[121] Those whom God has elected for salvation cannot but be saved; similarly, those not so elected (the reprobate) will never come to salvation.

> God, by his secret counsel, chooses whom he will while he rejects others, his
> gratuitous election has only been partially explained until we come to the case
> of single individuals, to whom God not only offers salvation, but so assigns it,
> that the certainty of the result remains not dubious, or suspended.[122]

While the Calvinist's understanding of election is simple and straightforward, the same cannot be said for non-Calvinists. It seems to me that most non-Calvinists would tend toward an understanding that is corporate, and either deny that God elects individuals for salvation or includes individual election within the corporate.

---

120. Piper, in his discussion of total depravity, asserts the following: "Our rebellion against God is total. . . . In his total rebellion everything man does is sin. . . . Man's inability to submit to God and do good is total." Piper, *Five Points*, 18–21.

121. Calvin, *Institutes* 3, 21, 7.

122. Calvin, *Institutes* 3, 21, 7.

Clark Pinnock is an example of the former: "Election is a corporate category and not oriented to the choice of individuals for salvation. . . . Election then [is] speaking of a class of people rather than specific individuals."[123] Shank is an example of the latter: "Obviously, the corporate body of the elect is comprised of individuals. But the election is primarily corporate and only secondarily particular."[124]

When considering the election of individuals to salvation, several issues are worth noting. The first is that election is a consequence of union with Christ. This is clear in Paul's characteristic phrase "in Christ." The clearest expression of this is found in Eph 1. The phrase "in Christ," or its cognates, appear eight times in the ten verses from Eph 1:3–13. Believers have been chosen "in Him" before the foundation of the world (v. 4);[125] predestination to adoption is "through Jesus Christ" (v. 5); redemption is "in Him" (v. 7); God's intent to unite Jew and Gentile (the mystery) is accomplished "in Him" (v. 9); the believer's inheritance is "in Him" (v. 11). Predestination entails conformance with the image of Christ (Rom 8:29). In all these ways, Scripture makes clear that election to salvation entails union and identification with Christ.

Secondly, and closely related to the first point above, is that the language of salvific election in the New Testament is the election of *believers* to the *blessings of salvation*. This is in stark contrast with Calvinism which holds that God chooses *unbelievers* to become *believers*.[126] Again, Eph 1 is a good place to see this. The first thing to note about this passage is that Paul is writing to believers, not unbelievers (Eph 1:1). It is believers who have been united with Christ and as a consequence enjoy "every spiritual blessing" (v. 3). God chose "us" (Ephesian believers) before the foundation of the world in order to enjoy a life of holiness (v. 4); believers have been predestined to the blessing of adoption as sons (v. 5), and redemption (v. 7); God's predestinating purpose is that "we" (Ephesian believers) should obtain a spiritual inheritance (v. 11). The Ephesian believers, having heard and believed the gospel, enjoy security in Christ through the Holy Spirit (v. 13). The elect are also predestined to the blessing of conformance to the image of Christ (Rom 8:29).[127]

---

123. Pinnock, "From Augustine to Arminius," 20.

124. Shank, *Elect in the Son*, 45.

125. It is important to note that it is the believer's being in Christ that is emphasized, not, as Calvinism effectively holds, that sinners are placed into Christ. "This is the import of Eph 1:4, which says that '*He chose us in Him*'—in Christ—'*before the foundation of the world.*' The elect are chosen *in* Christ, that is, because they are in Christ; they are not chosen *into* Christ, that is, in order that they may be in Christ. They are in Christ before the foundation of the world not in reality but in the foreknowledge of God." Cottrell, "Conditional Election," 61.

126. "The Calvinist says 'God unconditionally selects certain *sinners* and predestines them to become *believers*.' This is contrary to the teaching of Scripture, however, which instead says in effect, that God selects all *believers* and predestines them to become his *children* in glory" Cottrell, "Conditional Election," 61, emphases original.

127. Rom 8:29: "*For those whom He foreknew, He also predestined to become conformed to the image of His Son, so that He would be the firstborn among many brethren.*" Calvinists take the phrase "those whom He foreknew" not in the sense of simple prescience or precognition, but as referring to those

We may note that the election of individuals to salvation is a *conditional* election. Only those who meet the condition are elected. As noted earlier, a primary and basic condition is to be found in Christ. But one becomes united to Christ through faith, and repentance. So, for any individual to be chosen for salvation they must meet the necessary, God stipulated, conditions, namely they must believe upon Christ and acknowledge and repent of their sins. Galatians 3:26, for example, makes this clear: *"For you are all sons of God through faith in Christ Jesus."* Salvation is by grace through faith (Eph 2:8).[128] The first recorded words of Matthew are a call to repentance in preparation for the presence of the kingdom of heaven (Matt 3:2). Jesus began his public ministry with a call for his hearers to *"repent and believe in the gospel"* (Mark 1:15). To be chosen by God for salvation necessarily entails that the prerequisite conditions of repentance and faith be met.[129]

We have seen that it is indeed true that God elects specific individuals for the accomplishing of his redemptive purposes, but does God elect specific individuals for salvation per se? What has been said so far (election is "in Christ," entails believers experiencing the blessings of salvation, and is conditional) could apply to only a corporate view of election. One becomes part of the elect through faith and subsequent union with Christ and all the blessings that flow from that union. While all this is true, many non-Calvinists are reluctant to accept the stronger notion that God specifically elects certain individuals for salvation. "The reason why they are so determined to reject individual election is that they believe it to be inseparable from the Calvinistic doctrine of election."[130] However, as Cottrell indicates, the key aspect of Calvinistic election is its unconditionality, not its particularity. "The watershed is not between particular and general, but between conditional and unconditional election. The Calvinistic error is avoided by affirming *conditional* election."[131] If God elects certain individuals to salvation then, and this is the critical question, on what basis is such election made? We have already seen how Calvinists answer

___

unbelievers chosen by God to be saved. For example, John Murray says the phrase "means 'whom he set regard upon' or 'whom he knew from eternity with distinguishing affection and delight' and is virtually equivalent to 'whom he foreloved.'" Murray, *Romans*, 317. The problem with this interpretation of the phrase is that it is superfluous or even tautologous, effectively meaning "those whom he predestined he also predestined to be . . ." Most non-Calvinists view the phrase in its most straightforward way, as God knowing beforehand; the object of God's foreknowledge being then inferred from the rest of Scripture, namely, faith. Those whom God foresaw would believe he predestined to be conformed to the image of Christ. The "those" in v. 29 are "those who love God" in v. 28. Precisely the same idea is expressed in 1 Cor 8:3: *"But if anyone loves God, he is known by Him."* The former (Rom 8:29a) refers to God's foreknowledge, while the latter (1 Cor 8:3) refers to God's knowledge. See Cottrell, *Romans*, 1:505.

128. Likewise, 2 Thess 2:13 says, *"But we should always give thanks to God for you, brethren beloved by the Lord, because God has chosen you . . . for salvation through . . . faith in the truth."* Here again we see the close connection of individual election to salvation and faith.

129. Cottrell, "Conditional Election," 61, makes baptism also a necessary prerequisite for salvation.

130. Cottrell, "Conditional Election," 60.

131. Cottrell, "Conditional Election," 61.

this question, namely on the basis of God's eternal decree to save unconditionally certain unbelievers to become believers. The non-Calvinist rejects this explanation as unfounded in Scripture. Instead, the non-Calvinist grounds God's election of individuals to salvation on the basis of his foreknowing their meeting the necessary conditions—repentance and faith.[132]

Two scriptures in particular link individual election to foreknown faith. Romans 8:29 says, *"For those whom He foreknew, He also predestined to become conformed to the image of His Son."*[133] Here the foreseen faith of believers is explicitly linked to God's predestinating work. "In light of the biblical teaching concerning God's eternity and foreknowledge, and the relationship between foreknowledge and predestination, it should be evident that predestination must be of individuals."[134] The immediate context of v. 29 shows that "those whom he foreknew" are those who love God (v. 28)—and one loves God by exercising faith.

The second text is found in 1 Peter. Writing to *"those who reside as aliens, scattered throughout Pontus,"* Peter begins his letter by reminding his readers that they *"are chosen according to the foreknowledge of God the Father . . . to obey Jesus Christ and be sprinkled with His blood"* (1 Pet 1:1–2). The immediately following verses indicate what it is about the scattered believers that God foreknows. In the following seven verses (1 Pet 1:3–9), Peter makes reference to the faith of these exiled elect—it is the believer's faith that is fully known to God and, through God's foreknowing capacity, has always been known to God. Their faith enables them to experience God's protecting power (v. 5), their current suffering provides an opportunity to demonstrate the genuineness of their faith (v. 7), despite not having seen Christ they nevertheless believe in him (v. 8), in fact their faith will result in the full and final salvation of their souls (v. 9).

In conclusion of our study on the predestination of individuals to salvation Cottrell well sums up the case: "The biblical doctrine of election, then, definitely includes conditional election of individuals to salvation. Through his foreknowledge God sees who will believe upon Jesus Christ as Savior and Lord . . . then even before the creation of the world he predestines these believers to share the glory of the risen Christ."[135]

---

132. The early church, loosely before Augustine, adopted this view: "The early church generally associated divine predestination with God's foreknowledge of what people would be or do. . . . It was believed that predestination is based on divine foreknowledge." Allison, *Historical Theology*, 454.

133. Cottrell takes *"become conformed to the image of His Son"* eschatologically, i.e., as referring to the fact that one day "our resurrection bodies will be like that of Christ (Phil 3:21; 1 Cor 15:29; 2 Cor 3:18). Thus, we as believers are chosen to become God's glorified children (Rom 8:30) with Christ being the 'first-born among many brethren' [Rom 8:29b] because he was 'the first-born from the dead' (Col 1:18; Rev 1:5)." Cottrell, *Faith Once for All*, 392.

134. Cottrell, "Conditional Election," 60.

135. Cottrell, "Conditional Election," 62. An alternative understanding of Rom 8:29 is provided by the Christian apologist Leighton Flowers. He paraphrases Rom 8:29 as: "For those God formerly knew intimately, He previously determined them to be conformed to the image of His Son." He then goes on to explain: "The individual saints of old, with whom God had a personal relationship, were

b) The Nature of Divine Sovereignty

The Calvinist's View of Sovereignty

The Calvinist doctrine of election and predestination rests heavily on, and is in fact an outcome of, the view of divine sovereignty held.[136] The latter in turn depends upon the notion of an eternal decree that governs all things. The Westminster Confession of Faith expresses well the classic Calvinist position:

> God from all eternity, did, by the most wise and holy counsel of His own will, freely, and unchangeably ordain whatsoever comes to pass. . . . By the decree of God, for the manifestation of His glory, some men and angels are predestinated unto everlasting life; and some foreordained to everlasting death.[137]

While some Calvinists demur concerning the last clause of the above quote (a position known as double predestination), preferring instead to believe that God does not foreordain anyone to death, but merely bypasses the sinner to suffer the inevitable consequences of his sin, namely death, all Calvinists hold to the concept of an all-determining decree, and that such a decree is intrinsic to what it means for God to be sovereign in his universe. As the influential theologian Wayne Grudem explains: "The decrees of God *are the eternal plans of God, before the creation of the world, to bring about everything that happens*."[138] Note the phrase "everything that happens"—God's sovereignty is an executive activity that accounts for every single thing that happens in the universe at any given moment. Klooster, writing in the *Evangelical Dictionary of Theology*, states that "God's 'decree' is a theological term for the comprehensive plan for the world and its history which God sovereignly established in eternity."[139] Sproul concurs: "Predestination refers to God's sovereign plan for human beings, decreed by him in eternity."[140]

While the specific language of a comprehensive, all-determining divine decree is not as popular today among most Calvinists as it once was, the concept is definitely

---

predestined by Him to be conformed to the image of Christ. That is, God predetermined to bring their salvation to completion by the sacrifice of Christ on their behalf" Flowers, "Romans 8:28–30," 52/1:09. This provides a third alternative understanding of those foreknown and predestined in Rom 8:29: (1) Calvinism—God predestined those individuals whom he foreloved, (2) Classical Arminianism: God foresaw those whom he could see would believe the gospel, (3) God predestined those (OT saints) in the past who loved God (v. 28), to now be conformed to Christ (Flowers). The main problem I see with this last interpretation is that it does not fit well the immediate context—which speaks, not of past Old Testament saints, but of present (contemporary with Paul) believers.

136. The closely related doctrine of providence in turn expresses how God exercises his sovereignty in his dealings with the created order.

137. *Westminster Confession of Faith*, 3:1, 3. This affirmation is included in Grudem, *Systematic Theology*, 1181.

138. Grudem, *Systematic Theology*, 332, emphases original.

139. Klooster, "Decrees of God," 302.

140. Sproul, *Reformed Theology*, 141.

present and functions as a foundational belief within Calvinism. In his book on the sovereignty of God, A. W. Pink states that "the sovereignty of the God of Scripture is absolute, irresistible, infinite. . . . He is sovereign in the exercise of His power. His power is exercised as He wills, when He wills, where He wills."[141] When it comes to the actions of people, "we read the Scriptures in vain if we fail to discover that the actions of men, evil men as well as good, are governed by the Lord God."[142] The comprehensive and detailed scope of the exercise of God's sovereignty is emphasized: "No revolving of a world, no shining of a star, no storm, no actions of men, . . . nothing in all the vast universe can come to pass otherwise than God has eternally purposed [it]."[143]

With respect to salvation and "the election of grace" we are told that "from eternity, God willed, decided, planned, intended, and chose to save some sinners."[144] And that "God's decree of election is a sovereign decree. It is fully efficacious. All that is necessary for the elect to be saved is brought to pass sovereignly by God."[145] In fact, if God's sovereign will, expressed by his eternal decree, fails to occur then God is said to be taking a risk. This is a central concept in modern Calvinistic thought.

> We take no risk if we knowingly set in motion events which will turn out exactly as we want them to do. In the case of divine providence the events in question are all those which, in the history of the entire universe, are to become actual. We shall assume that if at least one of these events could be caused to turn out in a way other than the way that God believes that it will, then God is taking a risk.[146]

In short, the Calvinist notion of sovereignty is comprehensive, *ultimately* causing every single event in the entire history of the universe. It is also particular, specific, detailed, fine-grained.[147] With respect to salvation, it is God who elects those whom he chooses to save, and *ultimately*, it is God who decides who will not be saved. The term sovereign grace or sovereign election is used to describe God's so choosing. I have used the term "ultimately" above to acknowledge the fact that many Calvinists hold that God does not necessarily *directly* cause a particular event, but that he can

---

141. Pink, *Sovereignty of God*, 22.

142. Pink, *Sovereignty of God*, 41.

143. Pink, *Sovereignty of God*, 43.

144. Wright, *No Place for Sovereignty*, 119.

145. Sproul, *Reformed Theology*, 171. Efficacious simply means certain, effective, assured.

146. Helm, *Providence*, 40. Note that Helm here formulates no risk in terms of what God knows, but readily acknowledges that the same principle holds with respect to what God ordains: "If God takes a risk, however, where this is understood in terms of knowledge, then it would follow logically that he also takes a risk in terms of what he ordains. For what he ordains must be similarly risky." Helm, *Providence*, 40.

147. The "providence of God is a particular providence, extending to the individual actions of particular people. . . . The providence of God is fine grained; it extends to the occurrence of individual actions and to each aspect of each action." Helm, *Providence*, 104.

use secondary means. In either case, of course, God is required to be responsible if his sovereignty is to be maintained.

A Better Understanding of Sovereignty: Relative Independence

There are several problems with Calvinism's view of divine sovereignty. Not surprisingly, these most often, though not exclusively, have to do with how God relates to his human creation. Several of these problems will be discussed below. At this point, however, I would like to suggest a better, because more biblically faithful, alternative way of understanding God's sovereign rule.

The essence of sovereignty is not, as Calvinism posits, ultimate causation of every conceivable event or action. Rather, sovereignty has to do with authority. A king is sovereign if he exercises complete authority over his realm, and if he has complete power or ability to exercise that authority in a manner he sees fit. Perhaps the following illustration will help to make the point: Suppose I say to my eight-year-old son when he comes through the front door after school, "John, I want you to go to your room and play with your toys until I tell you to come out." John senses an obligation to obey because he perceives a legitimate authority at work. Now, that John in fact goes to his room is a consequence of the sovereign authority I have by being his father. In this entire sequence, from my "command" to go to his room, to his eventual exit from the room, my sovereignty has not been relinquished for one moment. But, and this is the point, what John decides to do in his room is not a consequence of my commanding him or causing him—he decides what form the play time in his room will take. And my sovereignty is not impugned or challenged one bit. Sovereignty resides in authority, not causation. Calvinism fails to appreciate this, thinking that God can only be truly sovereign if every fine-grained, particular thing that happens is ultimately caused by God.

Sometimes the word "control" is used to describe God's sovereign activity. God controls everything, we are told. There is nothing wrong with this term,[148] but unfortunately its use is ambiguous and, when used by Calvinists in a discussion of divine sovereignty, misleading. The way a Calvinist typically uses the term is as a synonym for "cause"—when God is ultimately causing everything he is said to be "in control." When God is not ultimately causing everything, he is "out of control." An example of this misleading use of the term "control" is Bruce Ware when he tells us on the one hand that "everything that occurs happens in agreement with the will and purpose of God," but then goes on to say that God "has absolute *control* over all that happens . . . that God exerts ultimate *control* over all evil [and that it] is the same God who *controls* both good and evil. . . . [And that] if God *controls* all that happens, it goes without

---

148. In the illustration above, I as John's father could legitimately be said to be in full control of everything—nothing in that dynamic resulted in me being out of control.

saying that he *controls* who is saved and who is not."[149] Obviously Ware, as a Calvinist theologian, is using the term "control" as a synonym for "causes," however the former sounds reasonable and is not likely to raise eyebrows, whereas to assert that God "causes" both good and evil because he decreed the events could raise uncomfortable questions about God's involvement with evil and sin. It is not a helpful term and its use to mask or soften the idea of ultimate causation of everything by God should be abandoned by Calvinists in my opinion.

The parable above of John and his room is a more accurate description of God's sovereignty. It is an understanding of sovereignty that I call *relative independence*.[150] In his dealings with creation God honors the relative independence he has granted his creation. This is seen as early as the first chapter in Genesis. In v. 11, for example, we see God authorizing the land to produce vegetation with *"plants yielding seed, and fruit trees on the earth bearing fruit after their kind with seed in them."* Could God have produced plants and trees directly by causing such vegetation to appear? Yes, of course. But he did not so choose. Instead, God granted a relative (not absolute) independence to his creation whereby the ability to reproduce naturally was built into their design—they were seed-bearing plants.

What was true for the plants was also true for the first human pair. God granted them a freedom to roam the garden wherever they wished. They were only barred from one tree—with a warning of death should they abuse their God-given relative independence. *"The Lord God commanded the man, saying, 'From any tree of the garden you may eat freely; but from the tree of the knowledge of good and evil you shall not eat, for in the day that you eat from it you will surely die'"* (Gen 2:16–17). They were free to eat from any tree—this is how God rules. He grants man a relative independence to decide, to act, to choose. Lennox, locating the genuineness of human (libertarian) freedom to man as created in the image of God, makes essentially the same point: "The remarkable thing about the creation of human minds in the image of God is that he has chosen to cede to them, to some extent at least, a real capacity to act independently of his direct control. In other words, human freedom is real."[151] Fischer concurs: "Although God has every right to issue only commands, he often issues invitations. God is always sovereign, but that means he—and not we—gets to decide what shape that sovereignty takes. And apparently, God's sovereignty makes room for human freedom so that God and humans can have a personal, not merely causal, relationship."[152]

---

149. Ware, "Divine Election," 22, 23, emphasis mine.

150. It is only a relative, not absolute, independence. Only God is absolutely independent. God has indeed granted a measure of independence within the created order, but man is still very limited in what he can do. Even a king's life-breath is in God's hands (Dan 5:23).

151. Lennox, *Determined to Believe?*, 55.

152. Fischer, *Young, Restless, No Longer Reformed*, 67. The kind of freedom God has granted his human creation is a bounded, not limitless, freedom. In the parable about John, I set the bounds—go to your room and come out when I say—but within those bounds John is granted authentic freedom

God also delegates his authority, his sovereign rule, to Adam: *"Then the Lord God took the man and put him into the garden of Eden to cultivate it and keep it"* (Gen 2:15). There is no hint that God is micromanaging Adam in how Adam fulfills this divine mandate. And this freedom, this relative independence from God and its implied delegated authority is seen throughout the pages of Scripture. God commands Noah to construct an ark according to certain broad specifications, but exactly where and how Noah was to acquire the wood, assemble the parts, collect the animals—all was left up to Noah and his family to figure out. God called Abram to play a key role in the drama of redemption: *"Now the Lord said to Abram, 'Go forth from your country, and from your relatives and from your father's house, to the land which I will show you"* (Gen 12:1). Abram obeyed the call, but was granted the independence to decide for himself who he would take with him, what possessions he took, even the precise date on which he left for Harran. The call of Moses to lead the people out of Egypt is another good example of the way God exercises his sovereignty in the execution of a key aspect of redemptive history. God calls Moses to lead the Israelites out of bondage in Egypt, and Moses has the audacity to argue with God by raising a series of objections as to why he was not qualified to be God's choice: *"But Moses said to God, 'Who am I that I should go to Pharaoh and that I should bring the sons of Israel out of Egypt?'"* (Exod 3:11); *"Moses said to God, 'Behold, I am going to the sons of Israel, and I will say to them, 'The God of your fathers has sent me to you.' Now they may say to me, 'What is His name?' What shall I say to them?'"* (Exod 3:13); *"Then Moses said, 'What if they will not believe me or listen to what I say? For they may say, 'The Lord has not appeared to you.'"* (Exod 4:1); *"Then Moses said to the Lord, 'Please, Lord, I have never been eloquent, neither recently nor in time past, nor since You have spoken to Your servant; for I am slow of speech and slow of tongue'"* (Exod 4:10). Finally, the Lord had had enough: *"Then the anger of the Lord burned against Moses"* (Exod 4:14). There simply is no room within Calvinism's view of fine-grained sovereignty to explain why it would be the case that "the anger of the Lord's burned against Moses." With the relative independence God has granted his human creation God lays out the broad requirements but leaves the details and the response up to man.

c) God and Sin

Within the Calvinistic view of sovereignty as both comprehensive and particular it is very difficult to absolve God from causing sin. The attempt to distance God from sin through some intermediary mechanism does not cancel the fact that ultimately a given sin, say King David's adulterous affair with Bathsheba, or his subsequent murder of Bathsheba's husband, Uriah, only takes place because it was determined by God that it should happen. Recall that God's sovereign decree is such that it encompasses

---

to act as he wills. Nothing in this dynamic challenges my sovereignty.

"everything that happens" according to Grudem. It is the comprehensiveness of the decree that creates the problem for Calvinism.

There is an intrinsic contradiction entailed in the assertion, on the one hand, that God decrees everything without exception that happens, and yet on the other hand, that God is not responsible for my sinning. Some are content to live with the contradiction and simply overlook or ignore the contradiction. The Westminster Confession is an example: "God, from all eternity, did . . . ordain whatsoever comes to pass . . . yet so, as thereby neither is God the author of sin."[153] No attempt is made to explain this contradictory state of affairs, rather appeal is often made to mystery, or paradox. Speaking about the lost, those not chosen for salvation (i.e., the reprobate), the confession is pleased to make reference to "the unsearchable counsel of his own will"[154] and the "doctrine of this high *mystery* of predestination."[155] In his discussion of predestination, Calvin appeals to mystery: It "is not right that man should with impunity pry into things which the Lord has been *pleased to conceal* within himself and scan that sublime eternal wisdom which it is his pleasure that we *should not apprehend*."[156] Commenting on Calvin's perspective, George Bryson states that "what Calvin is admitting is that he does not have a clue, and no clues are available to explain why some are going to be saved and others lost. . . . To even ask such a question was to Calvin the height of arrogance."[157] The appeal to mystery in the doctrine of election is necessitated by Calvinism's insistence that election is unconditional. Unfortunately, appeal to mystery, paradox, secret counsels, and concealment can function as nothing more than a mask to cover bad theology. To merely claim that the Bible teaches a doctrine of unconditional election and that it is a mystery as to how God chooses the elect is fraught with danger—the danger of asserting a non-biblical claim which can then supposedly gain plausibility by appeal to "mystery." In a discussion of appeals to mystery and paradox, Helm rightly notes that "during the history of Christianity there is scarcely a limit to the nonsense that has been believed because it is allegedly biblical in character."[158]

As mentioned earlier, some Calvinists appeal to secondary causes to distance God from the sin he ordains shall occur. Grudem is an example: "Though God ordained that it would come about, both in general terms and in specific details, yet God is removed from actually doing evil, and his bringing it about through 'secondary causes' does not impugn his holiness or render him blameworthy."[159] Those secondary and supposedly blameworthy agents that God "uses" may be human beings, angels, or

153. *Westminster Confession of Faith*, 3.1.

154. *Westminster Confession of Faith*, 3.7.

155. *Westminster Confession of Faith*, 3.8, emphasis mine.

156. Calvin, *Institutes*, 3.21.1, emphases mine.

157. Bryson, *Five Points*, 43.

158. Helm, *Providence*, 66.

159. Grudem, *Systematic Theology*, 328.

demons. But the language of "uses" is itself problematic. A little later, Grudem favorably cites Calvin to the effect that "thieves and murderers and other evildoers are the instruments of divine providence, and the Lord himself *uses* these to carry out the judgments that he has determined with himself."[160] Like the word "control" discussed earlier, Calvinism's appeal to God merely "using" evil people is disingenuous. It suggests that people (or wicked agents generally) have a will that acts independently from God—which God merely uses to accomplish his purpose. But Calvinism's view of providence and sovereignty is comprehensive and fine-grained, causally determining *every* event in the universe, and leaves no room for any independently acting will. Even the motives and desires of men are not removed from God's sovereign decree. Absolutely everything that happens, "both in general terms and in specific details," is ordained by God and only happens because decreed that it would—including the sin in the world. As the Classical Arminian theologian Roger Olson states it:

> The ultimate question Calvinists *must answer* is "Who is the ultimate author of sin, evil and hell?" They commonly want to say "humanity" or "Satan and humanity." However, what I am arguing is that their doctrine of God's sovereignty and especially providence excludes that as the correct answer when you pay attention to the word "ultimate." In that system of theology, combining and keeping together *providence* and *predestination* there is no escape from saying that *God is the ultimate author of sin and evil and hell.*[161]

A major advantage of the "relative independence" view of divine sovereignty discussed above is that it provides a biblical way to distance God from evil and sin—these are caused, not by God through an all-determining decree, but by human agents who choose to abuse their God-given freedom to make morally significant, genuine choices and decisions for good or ill.

d) The Problem with Divine Determinism

The view of divine sovereignty held by Calvinists is known as divine determinism. It is called such because it is God who determines everything that happens.[162] There are other forms of determinism, for example naturalistic determinism (sometimes known as mechanistic determinism). In this view "matter or nature is all that exists,

---

160. Grudem, *Systematic Theology*, 328, citing Calvin, *Institutes* 1.16.5, emphases mine. This is a similar to arguing that Hitler was not responsible for the holocaust because he personally never fired a bullet or flipped the switch in a gas chamber.

161. Olsen, "Conversations," para. 18.

162. With respect to the issue of free will and men's choices, there are three basic positions: (a) determinism, the belief that all of man's actions and choices are the result of antecedent or prior factors or causes; (b) indeterminism, the idea that there are absolutely no causes for man's actions, and (c) self-determinism, the belief that "man determines his own behavior freely, and that no causal antecedents can sufficiently account for his actions." Geisler, "Freedom, Free Will and Determinism," 428.

and it is completely controlled by natural laws. . . . These [laws of nature] are the sole causative agents in the universe."[163] In principle, if one knew the position and velocity of every particle in the universe at any given moment then, knowing all the governing laws of nature, one could calculate the exact state of the universe at any time in the future.[164] Psychological determinism seeks to explain all human behavior by appeal to antecedent causes that cause the person to act the way he or she does. Such antecedent causes may be hereditary, genetic, social, or environmental. Perhaps the most famous proponent of this form of determinism is the psychologist and social philosopher B. F. Skinner (1904–1990). The term behaviorism is often associated with his name. He boldly asserted that "the autonomous agent to which behavior has traditionally been attributed is replaced by the environment."[165]

Many people, and Christians especially, have looked rather unfavorably to such forms of determinism as an explanation for human actions and choices. The primary reason is not hard to discern: the sense of moral accountability for one's actions is undermined. The Calvinist Albert Mohler captures the sentiment well when he says:

> This link between moral choice and moral responsibility is virtually instinctive to humans. As a matter of fact, it is basic to our understanding of what it means to be human. We hold each other responsible for actions and choices. But if all of our choices are illusory—and everything is merely the "inevitable consequence" of something beyond our control, moral responsibility is an exercise in delusion.[166]

Such notions of determinism smack too close to fatalism to be comfortable. It is encapsulated by the saying "whatever will be, will be." If all one's actions and behaviors are determined by one's environment or "something beyond our control" then indeed any sense of moral responsibility would seem to be nothing but wishful thinking. The thief could claim that he was not responsible since he was brought up under very hard circumstances and learned to steal to survive; the rapist could blame his hormones for his behavior; the bully could absolve himself of responsibility by claiming he learned his behavior from a delinquent father, and so on.

Now, the point in bringing up determinism generally, is that it helps to highlight the problem with divine or theistic determinism, for all the problems associated with naturalistic or psychological determinism, especially the issue of moral accountability, apply equally to divine determinism.[167] Cottrell explains the problem well:

163. Cottrell, *What the Bible Says about God the Ruler*, 54.

164. Such a claim was first formulated by the French mathematician LaPlace in the nineteenth century.

165. Skinner, *Beyond Freedom*, 184.

166. Mohler, "So . . . Why Did I Write This?," para. 4. Of course, as I will shortly argue, it is quite inconsistent for the Calvinist Mohler to argue in this manner.

167. The fact that, unlike, e.g., naturalistic determinism or fate, divine determinism entails a personal agency (God) does not change the overall principle that a person's choices, behavior, decisions,

[Theistic determinism is the view] that the eternal Sovereign absolutely and directly ordains or causes everything that happens, including the thoughts and actions of human beings. This means that God is the primary causative agent of everything that happens in the universe. . . . As with any determinism, this calls into question the reality of human free will along with its corollary, moral responsibility.[168]

An all-determining God, in the final analysis, "could never have any more glory from men than he could receive from the operations of the laws of nature." Furthermore, "Although such a view of man accords well with much psychological and sociological presupposition in modern secular research, we feel compelled to set it aside as a final principle because it leads necessarily to manipulation, to irresponsibility, and to God as the ultimate author of sin."[169] In a realm where everything that happens flows inexorably from an antecedent cause, in this case God, then the reality of human responsibility for actions taken by a person is effectively undermined and removed. This is necessarily so because the human agent in the final analysis could do no other than he in fact does. In fact, to praise someone for doing what he was determined by God to do, or to blame someone for doing what they could not avoid doing becomes not only unjustified but ultimately meaningless.

Furthermore, if divine determinism were true, then God's character as a loving and gracious being is seriously called into question. The reason for this is clear: if everything that happens flows from the divine will expressed in a comprehensive decree that governs the world, then this would of necessity include all the evils and sins in the world. While no Calvinist would accept this conclusion, it seems to me to be inescapable. The Arminian scholar Roger Olsen summarizes the issue well: "Generally speaking, with few exceptions, Calvinists affirm God's perfect goodness and love, but their belief in meticulous providence and absolute, all-determining sovereignty (determinism) undermines what they say."[170] Olsen goes on to say, "The Calvinist account of God's sovereignty . . . inevitably makes God the author of sin, evil, and innocent suffering . . . and thereby impugns the integrity of God's character as good and loving."[171]

Another fundamental problem with any form of determinism, including divine determinism, where everything that happens is the consequence of an antecedent cause, whether natural, psychological, or divine, is that one is left with a massive "is." Perhaps this principle is best explained by way of illustration. Suppose John lied, then I could attribute his lying to God's determining that he lie. Now suppose, under the identical circumstances, John does not lie then I could attribute his non-lying to God's determining he not lie. Suppose John only told a half-truth, then I would have to attribute

---

actions are all due to causes outside of him or her.

168. Cottrell, *What the Bible Says about God the Ruler*, 67.

169. Warren, *Salvation*, 468, 469.

170. Olsen, *Against Calvinism*, 83.

171. Olsen, *Against Calvinism*, 84.

that half-truth to God's determining that John only tell a half-truth. Suppose John kept silent, that too would be attributed to God's all-determining powers. In fact, if John did not lie, but I thought that he did lie, then my viewpoint itself would likewise be determined by God. *Whatever* John did would have to be attributed to God's determining actions upon John, and *whatever* my own assessment of John's actions would also be determined by God. Under such circumstances, there is no way to judge an action right or wrong—it just is. To be able to judge an action one would need an independent, non-determined, stance from which a judgment could be made. But this is precisely what is lacking in a comprehensively determined environment.

Not only would ethical evaluations, as in the above illustration, be impossible, but so also would judgments of any kind: truth or falsity, justice or injustice, arguments valid or invalid, correct or incorrect, beauty or ugliness, right or wrong, even logical and illogical—all are rendered ultimately meaningless in an all-determining environment. Furthermore, in an all-divinely-determined environment there is no such thing as "ought." "For 'ought' means 'could have and should have done otherwise.' But this is impossible according to determinism."[172] There is simply no independent framework from which to evaluate the validity of a moral claim or action. This is true for any kind of determinism, including divine determinism. Hart expresses the problem thus: "To assert that every finite contingency is solely and unambiguously the effect of a single will working all things . . . is to assert nothing but that the world is what it is, for any meaningful distinction between the will of God and the simple totality of cosmic eventuality has collapsed."[173] Philosophers capture the idea in this succinct expression: "no ought from is." In other words, one cannot say what "ought" to be the case, when all one has is an all-determining "is."

While, as we have seen, God's sovereignty understood as divine determinism would allow for the idea of an unconditional election of individuals to salvation, the cost is exceedingly high; a world that is ultimately meaningless and irrational, populated by people who cannot be held morally responsible for their actions, and governed by a God who decrees not only goods but also every imaginable horror, evil, and sin.

e) The Problem with a Comprehensive, Eternal, Predestinating Decree

Related to the discussion above concerning divine determinism is a problem associated with the idea of a secret, comprehensive decree that expresses God's decretive will for the universe. The concept of God's decree is most often referred to by Calvinists in connection with God's predestining who will and who won't be saved. So, for example, as was noted at the beginning of this chapter when discussing the Calvinist's understanding of election, Calvin makes reference to God's "eternal decree": "By

172. Geisler, "Freedom, Free Will and Determinism," 428.

173. Hart, *Doors of the Sea*, 29; cited by Lennox, *Determined to Believe?*, 59.

predestination we mean the eternal decree of God, by which he determined with himself whatever he wished to happen with regard to every man."[174] And again: "Creatures are so governed by the secret counsel of God, that nothing happens but what he knowingly and willingly decreed."[175] A. W. Pink likewise speaks of God's decree: "Believing is the consequence and not the cause of God's decree."[176] Klooster defines the decrees of God as "the comprehensive plan for the world and its history which God sovereignly established in eternity."[177] As noted earlier, Grudem defines the decrees of God as "the eternal plans of God, before the creation of the world, to bring about everything that happens."[178]

Earlier, I noted the difficulty an all-encompassing decree creates for Calvinists in reconciling God and the presence of sin in the world. Here, I draw attention to another difficulty generated by such a concept. The difficulty is this: if God's decree in eternity past resulted inevitably and most certainly in an elect set of believers who would enter heaven at the end of time, then what significance does the middle part, within time, play, if any? For an elect people to infallibly and unconditionally be in existence and enjoy salvation at the end of time, and this because before time God decreed that this would be the case, does it really matter what steps took place between these two events?

Robert Shank discusses this very issue with respect to the significance of Christ's coming and death:

> Important questions arise concerning the instrumentality of Christ in election, the first of which is Was it necessary? Was the temporal career of Jesus essential to the realization of election, or was it actually extrinsic to the election? Was it the sole means, or at least *a* means, on which the election could be predicated, or was it optional? Was the redemptive career of Jesus in time actually decisive, or instead merely symbolic—only a temporal exhibit, the design of which was to reflect and delineate the dimension of an election (and reprobation) already accomplished by fiat of God in the counsels of eternity?[179]

174. Calvin, *Institutes*, 3.21.5.

175. Calvin, *Institutes*, 1.16.3.

176. Pink, *Sovereignty of God*, 48.

177. Klooster, "Decrees of God," 302. I prefer the singular, *decree*, since it is a comprehensive term and covers everything that happens; all subsequent decrees are contained in the overarching, all-encompassing decree.

178. Grudem, *Systematic Theology*, 332. Grudem helpfully shows the relationship between God's decree(s) and providence: "This doctrine [of the decrees of God] is similar to the doctrine of providence, but here we are thinking about God's decisions before the world was created, rather than his providential actions in time. His providential actions are the *outworking of the eternal decrees* that he made long ago." Grudem, *Systematic Theology*, 332, emphasis mine.

179. Shank, *Elect in the Son*, 32. Interestingly, Shank goes on immediately to note that as a consequence of certain features of Calvin's writings on election some have construed Calvin's "role of Christ in election as being merely to reflect what God already had accomplished in eternity by His decree. Thus Christ's 'redemptive' career—the incarnation, His death and resurrection, His ascension and

Thinking specifically about the death of Christ, Shank goes on to say: "But again, was it necessary? Even granting the necessity, or at least the expediency, of the incarnation and the life and ministry of Jesus among men, was his death actually necessary?"[180] Though Shank does not go on to develop this line of thinking (other than to show from the scriptures that, from his perspective, Christ's coming was indeed truly significant), it seems that, given Calvinism's belief in an eternal decree that predestines some men for salvation from eternity past and infallibly finds fulfillment in an eternity in the future, the answer to the questions raised by Shank must be no, ultimately it does not matter what happens in between. The beginning is certain (because decreed by God), and the end is certain (because decreed by God), what decisive significance can possibly be attached to anything in between? The sketch below outlines the problem:

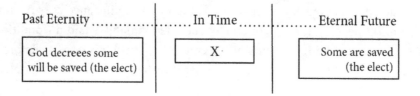

Past Eternity .... In Time .... Eternal Future

| God decreees some will be saved (the elect) | X | Some are saved (the elect) |

The left-hand box is certain, the right-hand box is certain, so what difference will the content of the center box make? What difference could it possibly make? This is not a trivial question. It makes the incarnation of Christ, his death, resurrection, and ascension, in the final analysis, all superfluous and arbitrary. The reality of X is not denied, just that it does not condition the outcome. If Christ did not come, or die, would that bring the eternal decree of God to elect some people to naught? Wouldn't that make the fulfillment of God's decree conditional upon something in time? How would such a state of affairs cohere with "the eternal decree of God, by which he determined with himself whatever he wished to happen with regard to every man."[181] It is the absolute certainty of the decree with respect to its fulfillment that makes whatsoever happens in time between the decree and its realization superfluous or arbitrary.

The concept of divine decrees itself is valid. For example, God's decree to create a world, his decree to punish sin, his decree to establish a new heavens and a new earth one day. These are all unilateral decisions made by God as he relates to his creation and would be unconditionally fulfilled with nothing to possibly prevent these decisions from being fulfilled. And it is precisely the unconditional nature of the alleged decree of God to predestine some to salvation that likewise ensures that nothing

---

intercession—are seen as incidental and symbolic divine pageantry rather than authentic saving acts. Election becomes predicated on God's decree in eternity *in abstractio* from all occurrences in time in the experience of Jesus." Shank, *Elect in the Son*, 32.

180. Shank, *Elect in the Son*, 33.

181. Calvin, *Institutes*, 3.21.5.

will or could prevent the decree from being realized—and hence makes anything between the establishment of the decree in eternity past and its future fulfillment ultimately irrelevant to the realization of the decree.

Calvinists typically assert that God ordains not only the end (a fixed number of the elect), but also the means to that end, say the death of Christ. The difficulty with that claim is that it makes the end conditional upon the means. But the distinguishing feature of an eternal decree is that its fulfillment is unconditioned in any way—the end is assured by virtue of the decree itself and not by anything interposed between the decree and its fulfillment. Furthermore, even if we allow that God decrees the means as well as the end, it makes the means arbitrary because *whatever* means were used by God to effect the end, the end decreed would still be infallibly assured. Nothing interposed between the decree and its fulfillment would or could alter the final outcome—because what is decreed *is* the outcome. Though most Calvinists would deny it, within the Calvinist system of salvation, *ultimately* salvation is by decree. Notions of grace, faith, repentance, atonement, incarnation, resurrection, while interesting, are in the final analysis irrelevant to who is saved or not. In short, for Calvinism salvation is ultimately by eternal decree and, in effect, not by grace through faith since the latter is redundant to final realization of the decree.

f) Does God's Decree Include the Fall?

This question is behind a long-standing debate among Calvinists concerning the relationship between God's eternal decrees and the fall of Adam into sin. It is known as the supralapsarian/infralapsarian debate, and extends back to the Pelagius and Augustine controversy in the fifth century.[182] Supralapsarians affirmed that God chose who would be saved (the elect) and who would not be saved (the reprobate) *before* the fall of Adam; infralapsarians placed the decree to elect *after* the fall. If the supralapsarians were correct, then this had implications for the fall of Adam itself: "The main difference [between supralapsarianism and infralapsarianism] was whether Adam's fall was included in God's eternal decree; supralapsarians held that it was, but infralapsarians acknowledged only God's foreknowledge of sin."[183]

During the Reformation period, and especially in the period after Calvin known as Protestant Scholasticism, debate intensified concerning the logical order of the decrees of God. Supralapsarians believed the decrees were ordered as follows:[184]

1. God's decree to glorify himself through the election of some [to salvation] and the reprobation of others [to damnation]

2. The decree to create those elected and reprobated

182. Klooster, "Supralapsarianism," 1059.

183. Klooster, "Supralapsarianism," 1059.

184. Klooster, "Supralapsarianism," 1060.

3. The decree to permit the fall

4. The decree to provide salvation for the elect through Jesus Christ

On the other hand, the infralapsarians held the order to be:

1. God's decree to glorify himself through the creation of the human race

2. The decree to permit the fall

3. The decree to elect some of the fallen race to salvation and to pass by the others

4. The decree to provide salvation for the elect through Jesus Christ

Calvin held to supralapsarianism: "God not only foresaw the fall of the first man, and in him the ruin of his posterity; but also at his own pleasure arranged it. . . . The first man fell because the Lord deemed it meet that he should."[185] Calvin does not flinch:

> I again ask how it is that the fall of Adam involves so many nations with their infant children in eternal death without remedy, unless it so seemed meet to God? . . . The decree, I admit, is dreadful; and yet it is impossible to deny that God foreknew what the end of man was to be before he made him, and foreknew, because he had so ordained by his decree.[186]

The classic Calvinistic theologian Loraine Boettner was infralapsarian on this issue: "Supralapsarianism goes to as great an extreme on the one side as does universalism on the other. Only the infralapsarian scheme is self-consistent or consistent with other facts."[187] Likewise R. C. Sproul strongly opposed supralapsarianism, opting instead for infralapsarianism.[188] Other Calvinists shy away from being dogmatic on the topic. Grudem, for example, rightly asserts that "there is very little direct biblical data" for either position.[189] Louis Berkhof on the other hand believes both are true and have biblical support.[190] Schnucker summarizes the position among Reformed councils: "Generally, most Reformed assemblies have refused to make either infra- or supralapsarianism normative, although the tendency has been to favor the former without condemning the latter."[191]

---

185. Calvin, *Institutes*, 3.23.7.

186. Calvin, *Institutes*, 3.23.7.

187. Boettner, "Reformed Doctrine of Predestination," 131/432. Note, however, it seems as though Boettner was not consistent in this matter. Later in the same work he remarks: "Even the fall of Adam, and through him the fall of the race, was not by chance or accident, but was so ordained in the secret councils of God" (239).

188. Sproul, *Chosen by God*, 142.

189. Grudem, *Systematic Theology*, 679.

190. Berkhof, *Systematic Theology*, 124.

191. Schnucker, "Infralapsarianism," 560.

Several observations can be made concerning this Calvinism in-house debate. The first concerns the preoccupation of the Reformed churches with the decrees of God. Reformed theology at heart is decretal theology. While the concept of divine decrees is legitimate, it is the Calvinistic tradition distinctively that tends to emphasis these decrees. This is hardly surprising, given the heavy emphasis within this tradition on the divine initiative in all things, but does suggest the possibility of a potential distortion in its theology given the relative paucity of explicit concern with decretal theology among virtually all other Christian traditions.

Second, Grudem is quite right—there is no biblical support for this topic. While Scripture does teach that God effected certain decrees, the decree to create the world for example, nowhere does Scripture show any concern with listing these decrees or indicating a logical order. Again, the sequence of decrees involved with the supra/infra debate flows naturally from Calvinism's distinctive soteriological monergism. From a non-Calvinistic perspective, most of the decrees listed above, for example the supposed decree to create a humanity with two classes in mind (the elect and the reprobate) is completely without direct biblical support and is only a theological construct consistent with Calvinism itself.

Given that Calvinists insist that "creatures are so governed by the secret counsel of God, that nothing happens but what he knowingly and willingly decreed,"[192] it seems that the supralapsarian position is the most consistent position to hold. However, this sequence suffers the rather strange *need* of God for Adam to sin in order to fit the view. Despite the language of permission used, in fact the fall of Adam is absolutely *required* in this case. And despite strong claims to the contrary by Calvinists, the supralapsarian position comes very close to, if not actually making, God the author of sin. Furthermore, the sin of Adam becomes merely the mechanism whereby God aims to glorify himself—through the damnation of perhaps most of mankind. The whole thought process here is contrary to what Scripture actually teaches concerning God's love for all people and God's willingness to express that love by sending his Son so that "none should perish, but [rather] have eternal life" if they but believe (John 3:16).

The infralapsarian position seems more compassionate, relieving God of necessitating the fall of Adam, but is of course quite inconsistent with the strong comprehensive determinism foundational to Calvinism's soteriology. Its inconsistency is seen in that God is considered to "react" to the fall of Adam, as though Adam's disobedience was not included within God's sovereign will but just "happened." Olsen makes the same point when he says that "if only in light of the fall does God work out his plan of redemption, then . . . redemption is a kind of 'Plan B' in God's mind."[193] Boettner commenting in

---

192. Calvin, *Institutes*, 3.21.5.

193. Olsen, *Against Calvinism*, 57. Calvin himself insisted that "God not only foresaw the fall of the first man, and in him the ruin of his posterity; but also at his own pleasure arranged it." *Institutes*, 3.23.7.

favor of the infralapsarian sequence says: "The infralapsarian scheme naturally commends itself to our ideas of justice and mercy; and it is at least free from the Arminian objection that God simply creates some men in order to damn them."[194]

Interestingly, Olsen, noting that both the infra- and supralapsarian sequences view God as being glorified through the creation of humans,[195] suggests that, as a consequence, in some sense God may be dependent upon the world: "[This] is because some in both camps emphasize that the entire program of creation and redemption (including reprobation and hell) is said to be 'for God's glory.' Does God need the world to glorify himself? Or is creation rather the result of the overflowing trinitarian love of God?"[196]

In most listings of the sequence of the decrees, reference is made to permitting the fall. The language of permission sounds strange if, as Sproul, for example, asserts, God's control (read causation) of the universe extends to the movement of every single molecule: "If there is one single molecule in this universe running around loose, totally free of God's sovereignty, then we have no guarantee that a single promise of God's will ever be fulfilled."[197] As we have seen repeatedly, for the Calvinist, if God's sovereignty is not of the totally comprehensive, particular, fine-grained, and absolute sort then God's sovereignty is threatened—ultimately, God must be the cause of everything that happens in the universe. Calvin himself was quite consistent and clear in rejecting the notion of permission. In a discussion on "the distinction between will and permission" he would "not hesitate . . . to confess with Augustine that the will of God is necessity, and that everything is necessary which he has willed."[198] Within such a view of divine sovereignty, to speak of God "permitting" anything, as though the one granted such permission could possibly do otherwise, not only makes no sense, it is disingenuous and merely indirectly indicates the Calvinist's unease with being fully consistent. It also once again raises acutely the question of whether such a God is indeed the author of sin.[199]

Finally, and connected with the previous paragraph, is the common appeal to mystery or ignorance or paradox to justify what appears to be a contradiction. These appeals are made for several aspects of Calvinism and not merely with the topic at hand. With respect to supralapsarianism the contradiction is this: God decrees that Adam sin, yet God is not to be blamed for the sin. Calvin, for example, states:

194. Boettner, "Reformed Doctrine of Predestination," 118.

195. Either humanity as such (infralapsarianism) or the two classes of humans, the elect and the reprobate (supralapsarianism).

196. Olsen, *Against Calvinism*, 57.

197. Sproul, *Chosen by God*, 27.

198. Calvin, *Institutes*, 3.23.8.

199. Olsen, *Against Calvinism*, 57–60, has an extended discussion on this aspect of the infra/supra debate and, after discussing the views of John Frame and John Piper concludes that "I agree with the Calvinists who say the typical Calvinist view of sovereignty requires confession of God as author of sin and evil."

"The first man fell because the Lord deemed it meet that he should; why he deemed it meet, *we know not.* . . . Man therefore falls, divine providence so ordaining, but he falls by his own fault."[200] Grudem likewise calls this topic a mystery: "In the last analysis it seems wiser to say that Scripture does not give us enough data to probe into this *mystery.*"[201] Berkhof, commenting on the topic, considers both sides as considering "the same *mystery* from different points of view," and that "in connection with the study of this *profound* subject we feel our understanding is limited, and realize that we grasp only fragments of the truth."[202] George Zemek, in his appendix on the divine decrees, says this: "The greatest *mystery* of this sovereign plan has to do with the origin of evil, especially the entrance of sin into God's sinless creation."[203] While undoubtedly there are some aspects of Christian theology that legitimately can be called mystery—for example the precise nature of the Godhead as Trinitarian or the relationship between Christ's human and divine natures—it is important to appreciate that these "mysteries" are well founded with unambiguous biblical evidences. This, unfortunately, is not the case with the infra/supralapsarian scheme as witnessed by the variety of viewpoints noted above. In this case, appeal to mystery merely masks unjustified theological constructs called for by a very questionable (Calvinistic) soteriology. Boettner, for example, is surely right: "The supralapsarian system seems to pass beyond mystery and into contradiction."[204]

g) Double Predestination?

From within a Calvinistic perspective, Sproul is surely correct when he says: "Given that the Bible teaches both election and particularism, we cannot avoid the subject of double predestination. The question then is not *if* predestination is double, but *how* it is double."[205]

Double predestination, a term mainly relevant to those committed to Calvinism, is the term used by theologians to describe the nature of God's predestinating work of electing some for salvation and damning the rest. There are two main ways this choosing of God is considered to work. The first, held by consistent Calvinists and mainly found in earlier (post-Reformation) Calvinistic writers, views God as positively choosing those whom he unconditionally elects for salvation and positively choosing those whom he selects for hell. Merely for convenience I will call this form of predestination "symmetric predestination." In the other form of this doctrine, God positively chooses unconditionally the elect for salvation and the rest he leaves in their

---

200. Calvin, *Institutes*, 3.23.8, emphasis mine.

201. Grudem, *Systematic Theology*, 679, emphasis mine.

202. Berkhof, *Systematic Theology*, 124, emphasis mine.

203. Zemek, *Biblical Theology*, 267, emphasis mine.

204. Boettner, "Reformed Doctrine of Predestination," 118.

205. Sproul, *Reformed Theology*, 158, emphasis original.

sin to take the consequences of unforgiven sin, hell. Again, for convenience, I will call this "asymmetric predestination."[206]

John Calvin is a good example of symmetric predestination:

> By predestination we mean the eternal decree of God, by which he determined with himself whatever he wished to happen with regard to every man. All are not created on equal terms, but some are preordained to eternal life, others to eternal damnation; and, accordingly, as each has been created for one or the other of these ends, we say that he has been predestined to life or to death.[207]

The Westminster Confession of 1646 likewise strongly affirms symmetric predestination: "By the decree of God, for the manifestation of his glory, some men and angels are predestinated unto everlasting life; and others foreordained to everlasting death."[208] In more recent times Wright is an example of a proponent of symmetric predestination: "God cannot logically choose some for salvation without at the same time choosing to reject others, even though they are no more sinful. This, of course, is the doctrine of reprobation taught today by all consistent Calvinists."[209] For Lorraine Boettner, "the doctrine of absolute Predestination logically holds that some are foreordained to death as surely as others are foreordained to life. . . . We believe that from all eternity God has intended to leave some of Adam's posterity in their sins, and that the decisive factor in the life of each is to be found only in God's will."[210]

Much more common among contemporary Calvinists is asymmetric predestination. For such thinkers, symmetric predestination jeopardizes God's goodness. Sproul is typical: "Reprobation is the flip side of election, the dark side of the matter that raises many concerns. It is the doctrine of reprobation that has prompted the label of 'horrible decree.' It is one thing to speak of God's gracious predestination to election, but quite another to speak of God's decreeing from all eternity that certain unfortunate people are destined for damnation."[211] Grudem too expresses the same reservations about symmetric predestination:

> In many ways the doctrine of reprobation is the most difficult of all the teachings of Scripture for us to think about and to accept, because it deals with such horrible and eternal consequences for human beings made in the image of

---

206. The technical term used to describe those who are not part of the elect is "reprobate." And the technical term used to describe symmetric predestination is "preterition."

207. Calvin, *Institutes*, 3.21.5. Several other passages could be cited, as for example this one in 3.21.7: "God by his eternal and immutable counsel determined once for all those whom it was his pleasure one day to admit to salvation and those whom, on the other hand, it was his pleasure to doom to destruction."

208. *Westminster Confession of Faith*, 3.3.

209. Wright, *No Place for Sovereignty*, 21. Notice his use of the term "consistent" here; in this respect I agree with him fully.

210. Boettner, "Reformed Doctrine of Predestination," 96.

211. Sproul, *Reformed Theology*, 157.

God. The love that God gives us for our fellow human beings and the love that he commands us to have toward our neighbor cause us to recoil against this doctrine, and it is right that we feel such dread in contemplating it.[212]

Grudem helpfully summarizes the asymmetric predestination position when he says that "reprobation is the sovereign decision of God before creation to pass over some persons, in sorrow deciding not to save them, and to punish them for their sins, and thereby to manifest his justice."[213] While God positively decides who will be saved, he only passes over the rest (the reprobate) who are consequently punished for their sins. Horton echoes the same logic: "God only has to leave us to our own devices in the case of reprobation, but it requires the greatest works of the triune God to save the elect."[214] Bruce Ware argues similarly: "In brief, reprobation is *conditional*, i.e., based on what sinners have done and deserve, whereas election is *unconditional*, i.e., based on the unmerited grace and favor of God despite what sinners have done and deserve. . . . None of what has been argued above militates against the fact that God has ordained both evil and good, both sin and obedience, both reprobation and election."[215]

Before critiquing the Calvinist's notion of symmetric predestination and asymmetric predestination, I want to briefly examine a few scriptures appealed to by Calvinists to justify the idea of God predestinating the reprobate.

Proverbs 16:4

> "*The Lord has made everything for its own purpose, Even the wicked for the day of evil.*"

Berkhof in his *Systematic Theology* cites this verse to justify the all-comprehensiveness of God's sovereign decree: "The decree includes whatsoever comes to pass in the world . . . whether it be good or evil" and includes the wicked acts of men.[216] Superficially, it is easy to see why appeal is made to Prov 16:4 for does it not say that God's purpose includes the wicked for a day of evil? However, as always, context and genre must be brought to bear to truly understand this (and any other) verse. The first thing to notice is that the saying is a proverb which, by definition, expresses a *general* truth. And what is the general truth being expressed in this verse (and the preceding verses)? It is that, despite what may appear on the surface, *ultimately* it is God who rules. In this case, God's rulership (purpose) includes the punishment of evildoers in the end. "The general

212. Grudem, *Systematic Theology*, 685. For this reason, Grudem feels that "double predestination is not a helpful term because it gives the impression that both election and reprobation are carried out in the same way by God and have no essential differences between them, which is certainly not true." Grudem, *Systematic Theology*, 670.

213. Grudem, *Systematic Theology*, 685.

214. Horton, *For Calvinism*, 58.

215. Ware, "Divine Election," 54, emphasis original.

216. Berkhof, *Systematic Theology*, 105.

meaning is that there are ultimately no loose ends in God's world: everything will be put to some use and matched with its proper fate. It does not mean that God is the author of evil: James 1:13, 17)."[217] A good historical example of this proverb is the punishment of Babylon for their iniquity (Jer 25:12) after the king of Babylon's wickedness has been used by God to punish disobedient Judah (Jer 25:7–9).

Isaiah 45:7

> *"The One forming light and creating darkness, causing well-being and creating calamity; I am the Lord who does all these."*

Grudem comments on this verse, "Isaiah 45:7, which speaks of God 'creating evil,' does not say that God himself *does* evil, but should be understood to mean that God ordained that evil would come about through the willing choices of his creature."[218] However the evil comes about, according to Grudem, God ordains the evil; it must therefore happen because God wills it to happen.

The Hebrew word that Grudem translates as *evil* has, like all words, a range of meanings.[219] The Hebrew Lexicon of Brown et al., for example, cites evil, distress, misery, injury, calamity, adversity.[220] In its context this verse underscores God's sovereignty to confirm his ability to call the Persian King Cyrus (Isa 45:1–4) to effect God's purpose for ancient exilic Israel, that they be granted permission to return to Jerusalem. The phrase *causing well-being and creating calamity* is typically assumed by Calvinistic scholars to express God's all-determining decretal will whereby all that happens in the universe is an outworking of God's ordaining before the creation of the world—in Grudem's words, "God ordained that it [the evil] would come about, both in general terms *and in specific details*."[221] Yet there is nothing in the verse itself that would indicate that such divine actions are the result or consequence of some preordained, detailed plan. The text merely says that God does these things—how or why he does it is not specified. Is there any portion of Scripture that might indicate why God might choose to act in such a way as to bring "calamity"? Yes. The covenant blessings and curses that comprise a very important part of the Mosaic covenant (Lev 26, Deut 28) clearly indicate that God will bring blessings ("*causing well-being*") for covenant loyalty by Israel, and God will bring disaster in the form of judgments ("*creating calamity*") for covenant disloyalty. Far from the outworking of an unconditional overarching decree that ordains all that unfolds in history, Isa 45:7 is a reminder of what God can do, and has done, in response to human actions

---

217. Kidner, *Proverbs*, 118.

218. Grudem, *Systematic Theology*, 328, emphasis original.

219. The NASB translates the word as *calamity*, the NIV as *disaster*, the KJV as *evil*.

220. Brown, Driver, Briggs, *Lexicon of the Old Testament*, 948.

221. Grudem, *Systematic Theology*, 328, emphasis mine.

and choices. This is simply the kind of God he is; he reacts negatively to human sin whether that sin be the idolatry of ancient Israel, or the wickedness of people who suppress the truth in unrighteousness (Rom 1:18).

Romans 9:18

> *"So then He has mercy on whom He desires, and He hardens whom He desires."*

Earlier in this chapter when discussing the significance of Rom 9:10–16, we concluded that yes, God does choose unconditionally—but his choosing is not for salvation but for service. God has the right to choose which individuals to call and use in the service of his redemptive purposes for the world. Furthermore, Paul's argument concerning God's right to choose how salvation would be applied to the Jews (by grace, not ethnicity [vv. 6–8]), and who will play key roles in his redemptive purposes (Isaac, Jacob, Pharaoh [vv. 7–17]), extends all the way down to v. 18. Consequently, this verse is to be understood within a context of election to service, not salvation. Calvinists are quite right to see God exercise his sovereign right to choose, but they are mistaken in seeing the choosing in terms of God's selecting some individuals for *salvation* and selecting (either directly or indirectly) some individuals for perdition.[222]

A word about the words *mercy* and *hardens*. These words are usually, especially by Calvinists, understood in salvific terms. God has saving mercy on some (the elect) and he hardens others (the reprobate) so that they cannot believe or are left in their unbelief. However, as always, the meaning assigned words is governed by the context,[223] and as we have seen, the context here has to do with God's choosing some for a task of service and rejecting others for that task. "'Having mercy' in this context refers not to saving mercy but to the favor of being chosen by God to play some role in the working out of his redemptive purposes (see v. 15). Whether one is conscious of being chosen and used is irrelevant; even whether one is saved or not is irrelevant (see Isa 45:4–5 concerning Cyrus)."[224] Similarly with the hardening: because God wanted to use Pharaoh in a negative way, to impede Israel's exodus from Egypt, God hardened his heart for that specific purpose (v. 17). The hardening of v. 18 expresses God's providential working at a crucial point in redemptive history, as well as God's judgment on an individual's persistent rebellious unbelief. In short, this verse (Rom 9:18) cannot be used to support the Calvinist's contention regarding God's unconditional choosing of the elect for salvation, and the reprobate for damnation.

---

222. Thus, e.g., Murray is mistaken when he says, "The whole argument of the apostle in this section in refutation of the objection that there is unrighteousness in God (vs. 14) is conducted on the premise that *salvation* is not constrained by the dictates of justice, that it proceeds entirely from the exercise of sovereign mercy." Murray, *Romans*, pt. 2, 29, emphasis mine.

223. "As readers we do not determine the meaning of biblical words; rather, we try to discover what the biblical writer meant when he used a particular word." Duvall and Hays, *Grasping God's Word*, 163.

224. Cottrell, *Romans*, 2:102.

Romans 9:21

> *"Or does not the potter have a right over the clay, to make from the same lump*
> *one vessel for honorable use and another for common use?"*

Calvinists tend to see Rom 9:7–29 as a whole, as Paul sustaining his explanation for the implied question behind Rom 9:1–5, namely, why aren't the Jews being saved in (supposed) fulfillment of Old Testament promises? The Calvinist answer is that God has the right whom to save and whom to not save. Romans 9:21 summarizes that contention. Michael Horton is typical of this perspective: In "Romans 9, God is said to be free to choose and to reject, to save and to harden, 'to make out of the same lump one vessel for honorable use and another for dishonorable use (Rom 9:21).'"[225]

A key to understanding Rom 9:21 is Rom 9:6: *"But it is not as though the word of God has failed. For they are not all Israel who are descended from Israel."* Fundamental to Paul's concern for his lost ethnic brethren (fellow Jews) is the idea of two Israels—physical Israel (those descended from Israel/Jacob) and spiritual or true Israel. In vv. 7–18 the focus has been on God's dealings with physical Israel, his calling the nation to a work of service in the redemptive outworking of God's salvific purposes for the world. But now in vv. 19–29 the focus shifts to true Israel, those within physical Israel (the one lump of v. 21) who will actually enjoy salvation and be "for honorable use" for God (v. 21), and also be "vessels of mercy" (v. 23). This latter group have always been a remnant within physical Israel (v. 27–29).

As Cottrell notes, "A major part of this section [vv. 19–29] is the fact that the calling and saving of spiritual Israel was all along a part of the very purpose for the existence of ethnic Israel. In other words, it has always been God's sovereign purpose to distinguish between the two Israels."[226] Bearing this in mind, we can paraphrase and expand the meaning of Rom 9:21 as: "Does not God have a right over the nation of Israel, to make from within the one nation one group that would enjoy salvation and another group that would function as the vehicle of God's redemptive purposes?" The *fact* of the two groups is established in vv. 19–29, but the *basis* upon which God distinguishes between the two is discussed in 9:30—10:21. The fact of the two groups lies in God's unconditional intent to call a saved people from within the ethnic nation; the basis of the saved people's existence is conditional upon an exercise of faith in God. It is clear from the above analysis that Rom 9:21 does not support the idea that God determines whoever will be personally saved or lost.

---

225. Horton, *For Calvinism*, 57. Cottrell makes the same point when he says that Calvinists "find this doctrine [unconditional election] especially in vv. 19–23, which they see as simply repeating the point of vv. 7–18." Cottrell, *Romans*, 2:108.

226. Cottrell, *Romans*, 2:107.

1 Peter 2:7–8

> *"This precious value, then, is for you who believe; but for those who disbelieve,*
> *'The stone which the builders rejected, this became the very corner stone,' and,*
> *'a stone of stumbling and a rock of offense'; for they stumble because they are*
> *disobedient to the word, and to this doom they were also appointed."*

Grudem, in typical Calvinistic fashion, commenting on the last clause, says: "Amazing as it may seem, even the stumbling and disobedience of unbelievers have been destined by God."[227] John Piper likewise makes it clear that he understands v. 8 to mean that God (pre)destined the unbelievers to not obey the word.[228]

In order to understand Peter's teaching here, it is necessary to capture the flow of thought in the larger context. In the passage (1 Pet 2:4–10) Peter identifies two groups of people. On the one hand are the Christians he is writing to and *"who believe"* and, on the other hand, *"those who disbelieve"* (v. 7). Here, as throughout the New Testament, belief in Christ and in God's word is crucial in demarking the two classes of people. These two groups hold two very different attitudes to Christ. For believers Christ is *"a living stone"* (v. 4) who is *"precious in the sight of God"* (v. 4) and recognize Christ as *"a precious cornerstone"* (v. 6). For unbelievers, however, Christ is *"a stone of stumbling and a rock of offense"* (v. 8a). The attitude toward Christ is markedly different for the two groups. The believers are *"coming to Him as to a living stone"* (v. 4) and glory in Christ's preciousness (vv. 4, 6, 7); in strong contrast, unbelievers reject Christ (vv. 4, 7). As a consequence of the two sharply differing attitudes and approaches to Christ, God's cornerstone, the two groups experience two sharply contrasting outcomes. Believers are being built up as a spiritual house, offer spiritual sacrifices to God (v. 5), and are not ultimately disappointed (v. 6b). Unbelievers, because of their disobedience to the word (gospel) by contrast, stumble over Christ who, for them, has become "a stone of stumbling and a rock of offense" (v. 8a).

By way of preliminary observation, we may note that even though the Greek does not explicitly make the causal connection between the disobedience of the unbelievers and their stumbling in v. 8 ("they stumble *because* they are disobedient") most translators recognize the implied connection and accordingly include it in their translation of v. 8.[229] Furthermore, the word doom in the NASB translation of v. 8 above is not in the Greek.[230] Unfortunately, the grammatical construction of the phrase "to this they were also appointed" does not resolve the question as to what the disbelievers were appointed.

227. Grudem, *1 Peter*, 106.

228. Piper, "Destined to Disobey," 5/13. Piper uses the ESV for v. 8, which says: "They stumble because they disobey the word, as they were destined to do."

229. This would include the NASB, ESV, NIV, NLT, Christian Standard Bible.

230. A woodenly literal translation v. 8b of the Greek ὁι προσκοπτουσιν τω λογω ἀπειθουντες εἰς ὁ και ἐτεθησαν (*hoi proskoptousin tō logō apeithountes eis ho kai, etethēsan*) would be close to this: "Who stumble at the word disobeying to which indeed they were appointed."

Because of the textual ambiguity of 1 Peter 2:8, grammatically the passage may be construed either as supporting, or as not supporting, the doctrine of positive reprobation. The matter hinges on the reference assumed for the phrase "to which they were appointed." Was the appointing to disobedience, or to both stumbling and disobedience, or to stumbling as the consequence of disobedience? All three assumptions have their advocates, and all are admissible grammatically.[231]

One way to resolve the issue is to examine elsewhere within Peter's letter whether he hints at God having appointed or destined the unbelief itself. This is easy to answer: nowhere within the letter is such divine action stated.[232] On the other hand, are there indications within the rest of the letter that God *reacts* negatively against unbelief and evil? The answer to this is also clear; there are at least four other passages where God is said to *react* negatively toward unbelievers. In 1 Pet 3:12 God is said to set his face *"against those who do evil."* In 4:5, Peter reminds his readers that the sinful practices of the Gentiles will be held accountable to God on the day of judgment. In 4:18, it is implied that severe judgment awaits *"the godless man and the sinner."* Finally, in 5:5, Peter tells his readers that believers are to clothe themselves with humility because *"God is opposed to the proud."* So, we may conclude, on the basis of Peter's teaching in other parts of his letter, that the stumbling referred to in v. 8 is a consequence of the unbeliever's disobedience toward Christ and the gospel. In short, *"for those who disbelieve . . . the very cornerstone* [Christ, has become] *. . . a stone of stumbling"* (vv. 7, 8).

Finally, the broader biblical witness likewise testifies against God's being responsible for the soteriological status of the reprobate. Just one scripture will make the point: 1 Tim 2:4: God *"desires all men to be saved and to come to the knowledge of the truth."* As Shank comments:

> [The fact the] immediate context militates against any assumption of support from 1 Peter 2:8 for the doctrine of unconditional reprobation is augmented by an evidence that must be regarded as finally decisive: such a doctrine radically contradicts the many explicit, categorical affirmations of Scripture of God's desire and provision for the salvation of all men. The great body of "universal" passages dictates the rejection of all interpretations (and translations) of 1 Peter 2:8 which, though grammatically allowable, are inadmissible in the light of the context of the whole body of the Holy Scriptures. Any assumption that the appointing was to *disobedience* or to *disobedience and stumbling* is in radical contradiction of 1 Timothy 4:10 and its many cognates.[233]

---

231. Shank, *Elect in the Son*, 188.

232. In fact, nowhere within any of Peter's two letters (other than, allegedly, 1 Pet 2:8b) is there any indication that God is responsible for the unbelief or disobedience or stumbling of the ungodly.

233. Shank, *Elect in the Son*, 189, emphasis original.

Joel Green captures the essence of the passage well when he says that "faith and unfaith are matters of human volition, but the consequences of faith and unfaith have been preset."[234]

Jude 4

> "For certain persons have crept in unnoticed, those who were long beforehand marked out for this condemnation, ungodly persons who turn the grace of our God into licentiousness and deny our only Master and Lord, Jesus Christ."

Grudem appeals to this verse to justify a doctrine of reprobation: "It is something that we would not want to believe, and would not believe, unless Scripture clearly taught it."[235] Likewise Berkhof appeals to Jude 4 to justify his contention that "reprobation is so clearly taught in Scripture as the opposite of election that we cannot regard it as something purely negative," as something only resulting from man's sin.[236]

Since Jude makes reference in this verse to "this condemnation," but has not yet spoken of any judgment or condemnation,[237] the reference must be to condemnations to be described in the following verses. The verb translated as "marked out" in the NASB has as its root form προγράφω (prographō)—literally, "written before." The NIV translates the word as "written about." Jude's point is that the condemnation of the ungodly men who were posing a threat to the church(es) to whom Jude was writing was foretold or prophesied. S. L. Bloomfield, cited by Robert Shank, summarizes the point clearly: "The expression [marked out beforehand for this condemnation] does not imply any predestination of the persons, but merely imports that they were long since foretold, and thereby designated, as persons who should suffer."[238] Baukham concurs: "Just such people, Jude claims, were long ago described in prophecy, which also predicted their condemnation by God."[239]

Is there justification in Jude's letter that would reinforce this understanding of v. 4, i.e., the understanding that it is not certain individuals unconditionally elected for damnation as Calvinists hold, but rather a specific type of persons—ungodly persons—to whom God reacts in condemnation as was foretold in previous times? Yes, there is. In the immediately following three verses Jude gives three examples of ungodliness incurring divine judgment: the people of Israel in the wilderness were destroyed for their unbelief (v. 5); angels who strayed from their assigned abodes God

---

234. Green, *1 Peter*, 58.

235. Grudem, *Systematic Theology*, 685.

236. Berkhof, *Systematic Theology*, 116.

237. The Greek word κριμα (*krima*), commonly translated as *judgment*, is used here in v. 4.

238. Shank, *Elect in the Son*, 191.

239. Baukham, *Jude*, 41.

has kept in darkness (v. 6); the inhabitants of Sodom and Gomorrah who indulged in immorality God punished with fire (v. 7).

Especially significant is the midrash from Enoch in vv. 14–15:[240] *"It was also about these men that Enoch, in the seventh generation from Adam, prophesied, saying, 'Behold, the Lord came with many thousands of His holy ones, to execute judgment upon all, and to convict all the ungodly of all their ungodly deeds which they have done in an ungodly way, and of all the harsh things which ungodly sinners have spoken against Him.'"*

This is probably a reference to the judgment to be meted out against the ungodly when Christ returns at the end of the age. "The message of Jude's whole midrash [is] that those who indulge in ungodly conduct, as the false teachers do, are those on whom judgment will fall."[241] The notion of any form of predestinarian language or thought is quite absent from this letter. Jude is simply concerned for the fidelity of his reader's faith (v. 3) and that they be warned about, and be on guard against, ungodly teachers who would bring true Christians into spiritual harm. Such, says Jude, will one day receive a just condemnation, and in any case were anticipated by earlier spokesmen for God.

By way of reminder, we are considering the doctrine of double predestination, the belief that God predestines some (the elect) to salvation and the rest (the reprobate) to hell. We noted at the beginning of this study that there are two forms in which this double predestination is said to occur. The first, the stronger version, I have called symmetric predestination because there is a fundamental symmetry between God's positively choosing those whom he saves and those whom he likewise chooses to damn. The weaker form I have labeled asymmetric predestination because, while God positively chooses those whom he saves, he merely bypasses the rest in their sins; the latter group are then considered to be justly condemned for their sins. We then considered six key scriptures often appealed to by Calvinists to justify the idea of reprobation, and have shown how, when due consideration is given to the literary and historical contexts in which these verses sit, there is no basis for reaching the Calvinist's conclusions; there is no such thing as reprobation in any form. I want now to go on to critique the entire notion of symmetric predestination.

Proponents of symmetric predestination are at least consistent with the Calvinistic view of particular sovereignty and "the eternal decree of God, by which he determined with himself whatever he wished to happen with regard to every man."[242] Wright, commenting on the ninth-century monk Gottschalk's view on this topic, says, "God cannot logically choose some for salvation without at the same time choosing to reject others. . . . This, of course, is the doctrine of reprobation

---

240. A midrash is an interpretation of an ancient Jewish text; usually in an Old Testament book, but occasionally, as here, an apocryphal book.

241. Baukham, *Jude*, 100.

242. Calvin, *Institutes*, 3.21.5.

taught today by all *consistent* Calvinists."[243] However, such consistency comes at a price—"the dark side of the matter that raises many concerns."[244] Sproul observes that "it is one thing to speak of God's gracious predestination to election, but quite another to speak of God's decreeing from all eternity that certain unfortunate people are destined for damnation."[245]

Calvin himself acknowledged the idea of symmetric predestination as "dreadful,"[246] and Grudem feels that the doctrine of reprobation "deals with such horrible and eternal consequences for human beings made in the image of God" that it causes us "to recoil against this doctrine, and that it is right that we feel such dread in contemplating it. It is something that we would not want to believe . . . [and] causes us to tremble in horror as we think of it."[247] But why would such a doctrine, if truly biblical, cause us to react in this way? How can such a sentiment be maintained in the light of such scriptures as Ps 119:24: *"Your testimonies also are my delight; they are my counselors."* Similarly, Ps 119:47–48: *"I shall delight in Your commandments, which I love. And I shall lift up my hands to Your commandments, which I love."* Surely, the revelation of God is something that should cause us great delight and joy—not dread and horror!

More seriously, what sort of God is the God who determines the eternal destinies of his human creation by means of symmetric predestination? Recall that according to symmetric predestination God actively had in mind men and women who would never, and indeed could never, find salvation because they were predestined by God before the foundation of the world to be consigned to hell. Furthermore, such a predestination is supposedly for the glory of God.[248] How, exactly, is God glorified in unconditionally consigning people to hell? Nowhere in Scripture is God said to be glorified for acting unilaterally and unconditionally in such an evil manner.[249] On the contrary, God is glorified when his goodness, wisdom, kindness, and so on is recognized and appreciated. Psalm 86:9–13 illustrates the point:

243. Wright, *No Place for Sovereignty*, 21–22, emphasis mine.

244. Sproul, *Reformed Theology*, 157.

245. Sproul, *Reformed Theology*, 157. Sproul himself considers the doctrine of symmetric predestination sub-Calvinism.

246. Calvin, *Institutes*, 3.23.7.

247. Grudem, *Systematic Theology*, 685. Grudem himself is a proponent of asymmetric predestination, not symmetric predestination. Grudem, like all Calvinists, holds to the doctrine of reprobation because he believes Scripture teaches it.

248. Grudem, *Systematic Theology*, 687, 686. As the Westminster Confession states: "By the decree of God *for the manifestation of his glory*, some men and angels are predestinated unto everlasting life; and others foreordained to everlasting death." *Westminster Confession of Faith*, 3.3.

249. It is important to maintain the distinction between, on the one hand, God reacting in judgment to evil people who deserve their judgment and, on the other hand, God unilaterally and unconditionally bringing evil upon certain individuals. The former is quite consistent with both the biblical testimony and moral sense, while the latter is neither.

All nations whom You have made shall come and worship before You, O Lord, And they shall glorify Your name. For You are great and do wondrous deeds; You alone are God. Teach me Your way, O Lord; I will walk in Your truth; Unite my heart to fear Your name. I will give thanks to You, O Lord my God, with all my heart, And will glorify Your name forever. For Your lovingkindness toward me is great, And You have delivered my soul from the depths of Sheol.

Once again, with a doctrine of symmetric predestination, it is difficult to see how God cannot be charged with being the author of evil and sin, given that it is evil and sinful to positively seek the harm of any individual. Grudem is quite right when he says that "the love that God gives us for our fellow human beings and the love that he commands us to have towards our neighbor cause us to recoil against this doctrine."[250] Can it really be the case that what God expects us to do (love our neighbor) he himself is not bound by? We are to love our neighbor, but God can damn them! In sum, while the doctrine of symmetric predestination is quite consistent with Calvinism's view of divine sovereignty it is quite inconsistent with God's attributes of love, justice, righteousness, and goodness clearly revealed on virtually every page of Scripture.

If symmetric predestination is consistent with Calvinism's "eternal plans of God, before the creation of the world, to bring about everything that happens," as Grudem states, then asymmetric predestination, the reprobate being those whom God merely bypasses, is quite inconsistent with this view of the outworking of the predestinarian decrees. The question of consistency is not insignificant to my mind. It is incoherent to say on the one hand x is all black and then also x is all white, in other words, to say God decrees everything to the minutest extent and also that men are accountable for their own sin—as though the latter were somehow independent of God's decree. Within Calvinistic thought, nothing, absolutely nothing, acts or wills independently of what God has decreed and determined will be the case. And so "Calvinists who accept unconditional election and at the same time propose to reject unconditional reprobation are radically inconsistent."[251] Consistency may not be a sufficient condition for a successful argument, but it is most certainly a necessary condition for a coherent argument.[252]

Crucial to the asymmetric predestination view is the idea of permission, God permitting men to suffer the consequences of their own sin and so, in a sense, reprobate themselves. The appeal of this notion of reprobation to modern Calvinists is quite apparent; it just seems too harsh to believe that God positively chooses some to be predestined for hell.[253] It sounds much more reasonable to say God just lets people

---

250. Grudem, *Systematic Theology*, 685.

251. Shank, *Elect in the Son*, 192.

252. Sometimes the inconsistency is explicitly formulated by Calvinists. Thus, e.g., Calvin speaking of Adam's sin says this: "Man therefore falls, divine providence so ordaining, but he falls by his own fault." Calvin, *Institutes*, 3.23.8.

253. "The problem for Calvinism is how to relieve God of responsibility for sin and rejection and

take the consequences for their own sin which is, of course, condemnation. Calvin roundly rejects this attempt to get God off the hook. Some "recur to the distinction between will and permission, the object being to prove that the wicked perish only by way of permission, but not by the will of God. . . . Nor indeed is there any probability in the thing itself—viz., that man brought death upon himself, merely by the permission, and not by the ordination of God; as if God had not determined what he wished the condition of the chief of his creatures to be."[254] Calvin is right, within a Calvinistic worldview there is no independent will of man operating apart from God's ordaining, determining, and decreeing. There is nothing to "permit" as though man's actions and choices were independent of God's determination. Intrinsic to the notion of permission with respect to symmetric predestination is the idea that God determines some things (who would comprise the elect), and the rest God merely "bypasses" to suffer the consequences of their own choices and actions. In this scenario "reprobation is conditional, i.e., based on what sinners have done and deserve, whereas [Calvinistic] election is unconditional, i.e., based on the unmerited grace and favor of God despite what sinners have done and deserve."[255] But note that "what sinners have done and deserve" is itself ordained by God: "God has ordained both evil and good, both sin and obedience, both reprobation and election."[256] Despite protestations from Calvinists, this way of thinking is simply incoherent, because actually contradictory. Roger Olson, in his thorough discussion of reprobation and in his assessment of Lorain Boettner's view, echoes my own sentiment above:

> Like all Calvinists I am aware of, Boettner claims that the reprobate *deserve* their punishment (eternal suffering in hell) because they "voluntarily chose to sin." Ultimately, he leaves this apparent contradiction in the realm of mystery: "Predestination [including reprobation] and free agency are the twin pillars of a great temple, and they meet above the clouds where the human gaze cannot penetrate." It seems, however, that this mystery is a blatant contradiction.[257]

A final point concerning the asymmetric predestination version of predestination concerns its logical status. The notion that God merely bypasses the nonelect and permits them to suffer the consequences of their own sins does not really achieve what the Calvinist hopes it will, namely distance God from direct responsibility for assigning the reprobate to their fate. This is because, within a given pool of

still retain the thesis of monothetism." Shank, *Elect in the Son*, 140. Monothetism is the belief in a single will (God's will) that determines everything.

254. Calvin, *Institutes*, 3.23.8. Sproul appeals to another work of Calvin in which Calvin seems to defend an asymmetric predestination view of reprobation as Sproul himself does. Sproul, *Reformed Theology*, 158. Calvin was not always consistent in his views.

255. Ware, "Divine Election," 54.

256. Ware, "Divine Election," 54. This is also why appeal to the justice of God in merely treating the reprobate as they deserve is meaningless.

257. Olson, *Against Calvinism*, 105, emphasis mine.

humanity, whoever is designated by God to be chosen for salvation is also thereby effectively identified and designated by God to be the non-elect (the reprobate). To determine who the elect will be is to determine who the non-elect will be. George Bryson expresses this logical situation in this way: "Even though most Calvinists will say that the unelect are damned because they deserved to be, the *logical implication* of Calvinism says otherwise. Since the unelect were not elected to be saved, they were never meant to be regenerated, to believe, to be saved, or to be anything other than totally depraved."[258]

h) Two Wills of God?

Within Calvinism there exists a tension concerning God's will. This is because, on the one hand, there are clear expressions of God desiring/willing one thing but determining/decreeing another. This raises the requirement that God have two apparently contradictory wills. Thus, Calvinists speak of God's moral will and his sovereign will, or God's permissive will and his efficient will, or God's revealed will and his secret will, or God's preceptive will and his decretive will. Providentially speaking God's revealed, prescriptive will is that "you shall not murder" (Exod 20:13); however, God's secret, decretive will is manifested every time a murder occurs. This is so because "we find out what God has decreed when events actually happen."[259] Within a context of election, God wills/desires that all men be saved and come to a knowledge of the truth (1 Tim 2:4), and yet God by decree wills only to save some (the elect). The former is God's open, revealed, moral will, while the latter is the manifestation of God's secret, decretive will.

Typically, Calvinists exegete verses such as 1 Tim 2:4 (*"[God] desires all men to be saved and to come to the knowledge of the truth"*) in such a way as to ensure God's alleged unconditional election is protected. So, the reference to "all men" in the verse is limited to "all *sorts* of persons."[260] Similarly, 2 Pet 3:9 (*"The Lord is not slow about His promise, as some count slowness, but is patient toward you, not wishing for any to perish but for all to come to repentance"*) is taken to refer to only "professing Christians."[261]

Scripture does indeed indicate several nuances attached to the concept of the will of God. The distinction between God's preceptive will expressed in laws and commandments and God's will whereby he unilaterally acts to effect his purposes, his decretive will, is quite valid. An example of the former would be the ten commandments, and an example of the latter would be God's will to create a universe and world. It is probably helpful, as Sproul does, to distinguish between God's preceptive will expressed in terms of laws or commandments and God's general desire that something be done—what

258. Bryson, *Five Points*, 39, emphasis mine.
259. Grudem, *Systematic Theology*, 213.
260. Piper, "Two Wills in God?," 108, emphasis mine.
261. Piper, "Two Wills in God?," 108.

Sproul calls God's will of disposition (e.g., Phil 4:18; 1 Thess 2:4; Heb 11:5; 2:15).[262] I would add that God may be said to have a "permissive will" whereby he allows his human creation to exercise a will independent of God's own will. For reasons which will soon become apparent, few Calvinists would agree with the latter.[263]

However, there are two problems with the Calvinist view on this question of the will(s) of God that reflects a distortion of a truly biblical view of how and when God exercises his will. The first is this: no matter how qualified or nuanced the will of God is parsed by Calvinists, in the final analysis, if they are to be consistent, it is always and only God's secret, decretive, sovereign will that is operative. This may be seen, for example, in Grudem's basic definition of God's will: "God's will is that attribute of God whereby he approves and determines to bring about *every action* necessary for the existence and activity of himself and all creation."[264] He appeals to Eph 1:11 (*"we have obtained an inheritance, having been predestined according to His purpose who works all things after the counsel of His will"*) for justification, stressing the "all things" in the verse and explaining that it refers to "*everything* that exists or everything in creation."[265] God's sovereign will in other words is comprehensive and determines everything; God "continually brings about *everything* in the universe according to the counsel of his will."[266] Within a Calvinistic system, God's decretive will trumps all other aspects of God's will—it is overarching and comprehensive. Thus, the claim that, for example, Grudem makes concerning 1 Tim 2:4 and 2 Pet 3:9, that it is "best to understand these references as speaking of God's revealed [i.e., preceptive] will,

262. Sproul, *Reformed Theology*, 169.

263. Neither Grudem, Sproul, nor Piper in their discussions of the will(s) of God make any mention of God's permissive will. By contrast, Cottrell, says that "the concept of the will of God has three main connotations, roughly corresponding to the ideas of purpose, desire, and permission." Cottrell, *What the Bible Says about God the Ruler*, 299. Such inability to acknowledge God's permissive will which would allow God to permit his will to be obeyed or not, causes Grudem, e.g., to attribute the will of God referenced in Jas 4:15 (*"You ought to say, 'If the Lord wills, we will live and also do this or that.'"*) as God's secret, decretive will rather than God's permissive will. Grudem, *Systematic Theology*, 214. The juxtaposition of, on the one hand, what one "ought" to do and, on the other hand, God's comprehensive decretive will seems strange.

264. Grudem, *Systematic Theology*, 211, emphasis mine.

265. Grudem, *Systematic Theology*, 211, emphasis mine.

266. Grudem, *Systematic Theology*, 212, emphasis mine. Calvinists assume the phrase "*all things according to the counsel of his will*" as referring to God's sovereign, decretive will which is worked out universally ('all things'). The context of Eph 1 must however determine what Paul was thinking of here concerning God's will. As Cottrell points out, "The term 'all things' is not necessarily absolute and must be understood within the limitations imposed by the context." Cottrell, *What the Bible Says about God the Ruler*, 307. The broad message of Ephesians concerns "*the mystery of [God's] will*" (1:9). What is that mystery? It is the uniting of Jew and Gentile in one body (2:11–16; 3:6, 11; 5:31–32). In 1:12–14 Paul distinguishes the "we" Jews from the "you" Gentiles, and it is both parties who have obtained an inheritance (1:11) and comprises a fulfillment of God's purposes. "Thus, we see that the 'all things' in Ephesians 1:11 does not have a universal reference; God's purposive or decretive will does not include all things that happen in the whole scope of nature and history. It does include the establishment of the church, however, as the body which unites Jews and Gentiles under one head, Jesus Christ." Cottrell, *What the Bible Says about God the Ruler*, 308.

his commands for mankind to obey and his declaration to us of what is pleasing in his sight," is, in the final analysis, empty, incoherent even—because it is always God's decretive will that determines who is saved, who comes to a knowledge of the truth, and who repents. Salvation is by decree within a Calvinistic system. The diagram on the left below illustrates the problem for the Calvinist; God's decretive will "swallows up" all other supposed expressions of God's will.[267]

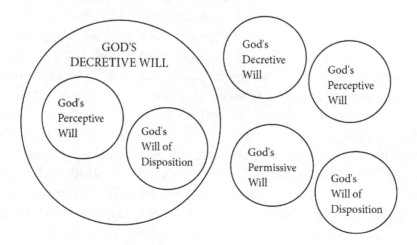

The diagram on the right reflects more accurately the biblical expressions of God's will(s). As usual, it is the Calvinist's insistence that everything is ultimately determined by God that effectively makes the expressions of God's will(s) other than his decretive will vacuous. The biblical model (the right-hand diagram) allows for genuine human relative independence and so allows for both the reality of God's preceptive will to be obeyed or not obeyed, for God to permit his human creation to obey or not obey, for God to express his wish and it to be followed or not. Each expression of God's will is both real and properly bounded—by God himself.[268]

It is the priority and all-encompassing nature of God's decretive will that creates the second problem for the Calvinist. A major tension arises when God's preceptive

267. The various wills of God may be summarized as: Decretive will is the overarching, all-encompassing will of God whereby he sovereignly determines whatever he determines; Prescriptive will is the will of God as revealed preeminently in his law; Will of Disposition is that which pleases, delights God. See Sproul, *Reformed Theology*, 169; permissive will is that which God permits to happen, especially regarding the choices and decisions of men.

268. In this model, the decretive will of God "differs from the determinist's view, however, in that the Scriptural concept of God's decretive will does not include everything that happens. This is in accord with the relative independence as God has granted it to both natural processes and his free moral creatures." Cottrell, *What the Bible Says about God the Ruler*, 304. See the excellent discussion of the will(s) of God in Cottrell, *What the Bible Says about God the Ruler*, 299–317. He helpfully explains all events as occurring (1) according to God's desire and God's decision, (2) according to God's desire and man's decision, (3) according to man's decision and God's permission. Cottrell, *What the Bible Says about God the Ruler*, 300.

will—you shall not murder—conflicts with God's secret, decretive will, the latter manifesting itself whenever someone is murdered.[269] The problem results in a contradiction within God, for it is God who expresses his will through laws and commands, and it is the same God who determines that those very precepts are violated on at least some occasions. Therefore, when Grudem rightly describes God's preceptive will as God's "commands for mankind to obey and his declaration to us of what is pleasing in his sight"[270] and yet God's preceptive will is trumped by his decretive will the conclusion must be that what God commands man to obey is contradicted by God's decision to have someone disobey that command. And so we have the rather strange situation in which God's decree contradicts his commands. Similarly, any disposition of God that is pleasing to him is contradicted when that disposition/desire is not followed because of God's decretive will, and once again we have the rather strange situation in which God's decree contradicts that which is pleasing to him!

These contradictions in the will of God are typically explained by Calvinists by appeal to mystery. After stating that "there is danger in speaking about evil events as happening according to [the decretive] will of God" and that "however we may understand the secret workings of God's hidden will, we must never understand it to imply that we are freed from responsibility for evil," Grudem goes on to conclude that "how this can be so may remain *a mystery* for us."[271] With Ezek 18:32 in mind (*"For I have no pleasure in the death of anyone who dies, declares the Lord God. Therefore, repent and live"*), Sproul says, "We know that God is not full of glee when a wicked person dies, yet he still wills that death *in some sense.*"[272] Piper confesses that "we are faced with the inescapable biblical fact that *in some sense* God does not delight in the death of the wicked (Ezek. 18), and *in some sense* he does (Deut. 28:63; 2 Sam. 2:25)."[273] Calvinists must struggle to harmonize two contradictory notions—God's desire for certain things and yet those very things being cancelled by his overarching decree.

Conclusion

We have seen how the Calvinist's understanding of election as God choosing sinners for salvation, apart from anything in the sinner himself, is not supported by Scripture. The texts appealed to are often taken out of context and forced to be

269. Recall Grudem's statement: "We find out what God has decreed when events actually happen." Grudem, *Systematic Theology*, 213.

270. Grudem, *Systematic Theology*, 214.

271. Grudem, *Systematic Theology*, 215, 216, emphasis mine.

272. Sproul, *Reformed Theology*, 170, emphasis mine.

273. Piper, "Two Wills in God?," 118, emphasis mine. He is referring to God's decretive will since he has no category of God permitting others to exercise a will contrary to God's will. This is made clear when he goes on to say, "Behind this complex relationship of two wills in God is the foundational biblical premise that God is indeed sovereign in a way that makes him ruler of *all actions.*" Piper, "Two Wills in God?," 119.

interpreted in a manner consistent with the doctrine of an unconditional election. We have also seen how a person's faith or lack thereof, willingness to repent, willingness to exercise humility—all are irrelevant as preconditions needed to enter the kingdom of God. The Bible, however, clearly indicates that to be accounted as part of the elect requires certain conditions to be met first. Furthermore, the language of predestination is usually associated with the blessings of salvation that God has predestined for those who believe upon the Lord Jesus Christ. Rather than predestinating unbelievers to become believers, predestination refers to the blessings of salvation that are predestined to believers.

The fundamental problem with Calvinism's soteriology flows from Calvinism's understanding of God's sovereignty as all-determining and comprehensive, thus requiring salvation to be understood entirely in monergistic terms. Salvation is all of God, not in the sense that God sets up the requirements for a person to be saved and sets up the basis for salvation (in the cross of Christ), but in the sense that God determines who will and who will not be saved—God has his elect, who will inevitably and unavoidably be saved. The rest of mankind is determined by God to be damned (consistent Calvinism) or left to suffer the consequences of their sins (inconsistent Calvinism). Since it is God who determines "everything that happens" by an overarching decree that foreordains everything, then ultimately salvation is by decree; those whom God has decreed to be saved will indeed inevitably, unavoidably, and most assuredly be saved. In such a scenario, the elements between God's decision and the final manifestation of that decision are ultimately irrelevant; they are merely means to a preordained end. God could just as easily have chosen different means to the same end. Within a Calvinistic framework of salvation all that really matters is God's decision to save some (the elect) and the actual salvation of the elect; all the elements between these two could have been different without altering the realization of God's decision to elect some to salvation. This includes the incarnation, the cross, the resurrection, the need for faith, repentance, humility. None of these elements can be allowed to provide conditions for the salvation of God's elect.

We have seen that Calvinism's soteriology is made to seem plausible because, when discussing God's sovereignty, power, glory then God's unilateral actions and workings are (consistently) stressed. However, when it comes to discussing evil, sin, depravity and non-election then Calvinists often speak as though people are responsible for that state of affairs. This fundamental inconsistency—that God exercises a sovereignty that is comprehensive and determinative of "everything that happens" and yet people can act independently of God when it comes to sinning and rejecting the gospel—should be recognized as the massive inconsistency that it is and calls into serious question the plausibility of Calvinistic soteriology.

Within a consistent Calvinistic framework of salvation, everything, literally everything, is of God, and all flows from God's decretal will. Ultimately, all other expressions of God's will (preceptive, disposition) are subsumed under God's decretive will. This is not a biblical portrayal of God's dealings with his human creation. In the latter case God interacts, pleads, exhorts, expresses his preceptive will with the understanding that his commands may not (and often are not) obeyed. Within a biblical framework, election to salvation is conditional upon faith, repentance, and humility.

4

Limited Atonement: Did Christ Die for Only a Few?[1]

Logically, that God would send Christ to be an atoning sacrifice only for the elect would be consistent with the TULIP system of salvation. The distinctive feature of Calvinism is that God has chosen a certain number of people to save. God has decreed within himself to save only a relatively few. Due to total depravity, as we have seen, no one is able to seek after God or even respond to the gospel call to repent and believe the gospel. As a consequence, if anyone is to believe it must be because God has determined that they would. Since salvation is intimately bound with the work of Christ on the cross, then to view Christ's death as being intended for anyone and everyone indiscriminately within such a system would not make sense.[2] Shank, commenting on John Murray's view of the atonement, makes this point well: "His definition of the atonement is dictated by the necessities of his doctrine of election—Calvin's doctrine of the unconditional election and reprobation of particular men effected by determinant decree before creation. Such an assumption requires a limited atonement."[3]

Not every aspect of the atonement is disputed in this discussion. For example, the theory of the atonement that views Christ's death as an atoning sacrifice in which Christ bore the penalty for a person's sins is assumed.[4] The sacrifice has propitiatory value, that is, it includes the effect of averting the wrath of God from the sinner. No one disputes the key elements in the work of the cross as such: suffering, an act of obedience to the Father's will, the abandonment of the Son by the Father, and the pain involved (both physical, but especially, spiritual). Furthermore, there is little dispute concerning the fruits of the atonement for those who benefit from it—reconciliation, redemption, forgiveness of sins.

---

1. The treatment of the subject here is by no means exhaustive—it is both beyond my ability and my need for the purposes of this chapter to delve into every aspect of this issue. A very thorough biblical, theological, and historical examination of this topic has been done by the non-Calvinist preacher and historian David Allen in an eight-hundred-plus-page book titled *The Extent of the Atonement: A Historical and Critical Review*.

2. As we shall see later, a certain assumption is made by Calvinists that make this statement true.

3. Shank, *Elect in the Son*, 72.

4. There are other theories, e.g., the governmental theory or moral influence, but the penal, substitutionary theory is probably the most common and the one assumed in this study. Grudem has a helpful summary of the most common alternatives. See Grudem, *Systematic Theology*, 581.

Some Calvinists view the term *limited* in this third point of TULIP as conveying a too negative impression and prefer the term *particular* atonement or definite atonement.[5] But, however one describes the view, most Calvinists limit the divine intent of the atonement to a restricted number—the elect.

This raises the question: What, exactly, is the root issue at stake here? The basic issue concerns the purpose of the atonement. Contrary to Grudem, who wishes to bypass this question and instead focus on what was actually happening at the cross, it is indeed necessary to concern ourselves with God's purpose in sending Christ specifically on a mission that entailed suffering and dying on a Roman cross.[6] The Dutch Reformed theologian Louis Berkhof states the key question precisely: "Did the Father in sending Christ . . . to make atonement for sin, do this with the design or for the purpose of saving only the elect or all men? That is the question, and that is the only question."[7] In short, the key question that we will focus on in this chapter concerns the intent, (and hence) extent, and application of the atonement.

The Calvinists' Understanding of the Extent of the Atonement

Most consistent Calvinists argue that God's intent in sending his Son as an atoning sacrifice was specifically in order to secure the salvation of a restricted number of people, that is, the atonement was limited to the elect only, and was not intended for the benefit of everyone.[8] In God's mind, only the elect were in view when Christ offered himself as an atoning sacrifice.

Wayne Grudem

"Particular redemption . . . holds that Christ died for particular people (specifically, those who would be saved and whom he came to redeem), that he . . . had them individually in mind in his atoning work. . . . It seems to me that the Reformed position of 'particular redemption' is most consistent with the overall teaching of Scripture."[9]

5. Sproul, *Reformed Theology*, 163, e.g., prefers the term "Purposeful Atonement."

6. Grudem believes the question of purpose "is just another form of the larger dispute between Calvinists and Arminians." Grudem, *Systematic Theology*, 601.

7. Berkhof, *Systematic Theology*, 394. Of course, there are other ramifications associated with this key question which are explored in the theological part of this chapter. Recall that whenever Calvinists refer to the elect they refer to a select group of sinners chosen by God to enjoy salvation. These sinners are chosen apart from anything in the person themselves—i.e., they are unconditionally chosen.

8. As previously noted, not all Calvinists would agree with this restriction to the divine intent, but for the most part this statement is true.

9. Grudem, *Systematic Theology*, 596, 600. Since Grudem holds to unconditional election, when he says "those who would be saved" he means those (and only those) whom God would choose to save from the mass of humanity.

SAVED BY GRACE THROUGH FAITH OR SAVED BY DECREE?

John Piper

"In the cross, God had in view the actual, effective redemption of his children . . . And we affirm that when Christ died particularly for his bride, he . . . really purchased and infallibly secured for them all that is necessary to get them saved."[10]

R. K. McGregor Wright

"Limited atonement [is] a view found in all the Reformed confessions and catechisms. . . . For the Calvinist, the death of Christ actually secured and accomplished the certain salvation of the elect."[11]

Michael Horton

"For whom did Christ die? . . . Calvinists believe that [the atonement] is limited (or definite) in its extent."[12] "Christ died for all the sins of the elect . . . the specific intention of Christ as he went to the cross was to save his elect."[13]

John Murray

"The question is: on whose behalf did Christ offer himself a sacrifice? . . . The doctrine of 'limited atonement' which we maintain is the doctrine which limits the atonement to those who are heirs of eternal life, the elect."[14]

Arthur Pink

"For whom did Christ die? . . . We answer, Christ died for 'God's elect.'[15] . . . The limited design in the Atonement follows, necessarily, from the eternal choice of the Father of certain ones unto salvation.[16] . . . Before the foundation of the world the Father predestinated a people to be conformed to the image of His Son, and the death and resurrection of the Lord Jesus was in order to the carrying out of the Divine purpose. The very nature of the Atonement evidences that, in its application to sinners, it was *limited* in the *purpose* of God."[17]

R. C. Sproul

"The efficacy of [the] atonement does not apply to the whole world, nor does its ultimate design. The atonement's ultimate purpose is found in the ultimate purpose or will of God. This purpose or design does not include the whole human race."[18]

10. Piper, *Five Points*, 40.
11. Wright, *No Place for Sovereignty*, 148.
12. Horton, *For Calvinism*, 80.
13. Horton, *For Calvinism*, 92.
14. Murray, *Redemption Accomplished and Applied*, 62, 64.
15. Pink, *Sovereignty of God*, 56.
16. Pink, *Sovereignty of God*, 57.
17. Pink, *Sovereignty of God*, 58, emphasis original.
18. Sproul, *Reformed Theology*, 177.

J. I. Packer

"The atonement thus appears as an effective propitiatory transaction that actually redeemed . . . those particular persons for whom Jesus on the cross became God's appointed substitute."[19]

An Examination of Key Biblical Texts Used to Justify a Limited Atonement

While it is probably true to say that the major thrust for a limitation of the divine intent in the application of the atoning work of Christ is connected logically to the Calvinist's notion of election, appeal is often made to certain scriptures that seem to support a limited atonement. It is to those passages we now turn.

Scriptures which speak of Christ dying for a specific, limited group:

John 10:11, Etc.

"I am the good shepherd. The good shepherd lays down his life for the sheep."[20]

John 15:13, 14

"Greater love has no one than this, that someone lay down his life for his friends. *You are* my friends *if you do what I command you."*

Acts 20:28

"Be on guard for yourselves and for all the flock, among which the Holy Spirit has made you overseers, to shepherd the church of God which He purchased with His own blood."

Ephesians 5:25

"Husbands, love your wives, just as Christ also loved the church *and gave himself up for her."*

Romans 8:33, 34

"Who will bring a charge against God's elect? God is the one who justifies; who is the one who condemns? Christ Jesus is He who died, yes, rather who was raised, who is at the right hand of God, who also intercedes for us."

19. Packer, "Love of God," 288.

20. Unless otherwise indicated the emphasis in the following citations are mine.

Ephesians 1:7, 8

"In him we have redemption through his blood, the forgiveness of our trespasses, according to the riches of his grace, which he lavished upon us, in all wisdom and insight."

There is no doubt that these passages, and others that could be appealed to, speak of Christ dying for a particular group—that is not in dispute.[21] The gospel writers and the apostles glory in the fact that they have experienced the salvation God intended for them to enjoy through the sacrifice of his Son. However, this fact does not necessarily preclude Christ having died for others who are currently outside the fold. To say that Christ died for the elect, his church, his sheep, his friends, does not necessarily or logically require us to conclude that current believers are the *only* ones for whom Christ died. To the contrary, as we shall see later, there are many scriptures that indicate the intended scope of Christ's death was universal. As Miethe puts it, "To say to any [particular] audience, 'Christ died for us!' does not [logically] imply 'for us and no one else.'"[22]

In fact, such argumentation is an example of the negative inference fallacy, which states that "it does not necessarily follow that if a proposition is true, a negative inference from that proposition is also true."[23] This is a logical error commonly made by Calvinists. In other words, if the proposition *Christ died for his sheep* is true, it does not follow that the negative inference, *Christ did not die for anyone else*, is also true. Logically, it is quite possible that Christ died for his sheep and for others too.

It is important to not lose sight of the fact that in all these passages the people being addressed are either incipient Christians (the gospels) or actual Christians (the epistles). The writer's focus is only upon those who have trusted Christ for salvation.[24] The corollary, of course, is that it is not the writer's intention to say anything about non-Christians, this class of people is simply not in the writer's mind. Consequently, to read these texts as saying something about non-Christians is inserting a notion into the text that is not there. "Hence, this amounts to an argument from silence. One cannot argue

---

21. Piper, e.g., speaks of "The Precious Logic of Romans 8:32" (*"He who did not spare his own Son but delivered Him over for us all, how will He not also with Him freely give us all things"*) and asks, "Who are the 'us' in this verse?" His answer is found in the preceding verses which speak of believers. Piper duly concludes that it is for these people alone that the atonement applies—it is limited to these people only. Of course, it is true, as Piper points out, that only believers enjoy the benefits of the atonement, but, as we shall see, that is different from saying that the intent of the atonement was limited to the elect only. Piper, *Five Points*, 50.

22. Miethe, "Universal Power of the Atonement," 73.

23. Carson, *Exegetical Fallacies*, 115.

24. As Allen observes, "In fact, all of these references in Scripture [to Christ dying for his sheep/church/friends] . . . do not speak of the elect as an abstract class in the sense of all those predestined for eternal life but refer only to the believing elect, those who are in union with Christ by virtue of faith." Allen, *Extent of the Atonement*, 21.

in positive support of a point when what is being argued is simply not in the grammar, language, or structure of the text."[25]

The fallacy of viewing these passages as directed only toward a limited number (the elect) and excluding all others may be illustrated by noting Paul's affirmation in Gal 2:20, where he says: *"I have been crucified with Christ. . . . And the life which I now live in the flesh I live by faith in the Son of God, who loved me and gave himself up for me."* On a Calvinist reading, one would have to conclude that Christ died only for Paul—no one else is stated as being the beneficiary of Christ's atoning sacrifice. But, of course, the rest of the New Testament clearly shows that Christ died for others besides Paul!

John 17:9

> *"I ask on their behalf; I do not ask on behalf of the world, but of those whom You have given Me; for they are Yours."*

Some Calvinists appeal to this text to justify a limited view of salvation (and hence a limited view of the atonement). Clowney, for example, says: "[Jesus] prays for them, not the world; he came to save them, and to lose none of them."[26] Citing John 17:6–12, Sproul argues that "the Father gave Christ a limited number of people. They are the ones for whom Christ prays. They are also the ones for whom Christ died. Jesus does not pray for the whole world. He says that directly and clearly. He prays specifically for the ones given to him, the elect."[27] Berkhof, after asserting that "the sacrificial work of Christ and his intercessory work are simply two different aspects of his atoning work, and therefore the scope of one cannot be wider than that of the other," goes on to ask, "Why should [Christ] limit his intercessory prayer, if he actually paid the price for all?"[28]

In response we may note that the criticisms mentioned above apply here too; the limited scope of those being addressed says nothing about the extent of the atonement beyond the limited number in view in the passage. As always, context is crucial for a proper understanding of a passage. Here, in the upper room, Jesus in his high priestly prayer is addressing his disciples, those men who would comprise the crucial work in redemptive history, who would subsequently become the foundation upon which the church would be built (Eph 2:20). Jesus is praying for them specifically because it is they alone and uniquely who would soon face this daunting task of furthering God's mission to the world. It is in this light, with Jesus's imminent removal from their midst, that Jesus differentiates the disciples from the rest of the world. The disciples had a unique task to accomplish soon, so naturally Jesus's focus

---

25. Allen, *Extent of the Atonement*, 21.

26. Clowney, *Preaching and the Sovereignty of God*, 331. See also Grudem, *Systematic Theology*, 595.

27. Sproul, *Reformed Theology*, 175.

28. Berkhof, *Systematic Theology*, 395.

is on them and their needs. To then extrapolate Jesus's prayer for the disciples, soon to be apostles, to all "the elect," as Calvinists do, is an unwarranted assumption and is in fact nothing other than eisegesis.[29]

In fact, later in his prayer, Jesus explicitly extends the scope of those for whom he prays to include all "those also who believe in Me through their word" (17:20). On at least one occasion, in a different historical context, Jesus did in fact pray for "the world" (unbelievers), when during his crucifixion Jesus prayed, "Father, forgive them; for they do not know what they are doing" (Luke 23:34). Followers of Christ are urged to pray for all people (1 Tim 2:1). If Berkhof is right in supposing there to be a connection between Christ's prayers (and by extension the prayers of his followers) and the atonement, then we see that in broader contexts, the atonement can have universal significance.

John 6:37–39

> "All that the Father gives Me will come to Me, and the one who comes to Me I will certainly not cast out. For I have come down from heaven, not to do My own will, but the will of Him who sent Me. This is the will of Him who sent Me, that of all that He has given Me I lose nothing, but raise it up on the last day."

Sometimes appeal is made to the fact that Jesus here refers to a select few—those given to Jesus by the Father—who would be resurrected on the last day. Wright, for example, cites these verses to show that "this group was known to God from eternity, and the sacrifice was designed for them, and for them alone."[30] Similarly, Packer appeals to these verses to support the claim that "this [prevenient] grace is given according to a pretemporal divine plan, whereby its present recipients were chosen as sinners to be saved."[31] The close connection between the Calvinist understanding of election, as God unilaterally choosing those sinners whom he would save, and their doctrine of limited atonement is seen in the appeal to these verses where the former is assumed and so justifies the latter.

Both the Calvinist and non-Calvinist agree that not all are actually saved, both agree that these verses speak of a certain number of people. The key question, however, is whether the Calvinist is correct in seeing those who are given to Jesus by the Father as a limited number chosen before the foundation of the world by the father to be saved, or whether those given by the Father are a potentially limitless number. In short, are those for whom Christ died limited to a select few chosen by God, or are they a select few because only a (relatively) few choose to believe in Christ and his saving work?

29. Eisegesis is the interpretive act whereby a meaning is unwarrantedly inserted *into* a text; the proper goal of the reader of a particular text is to extract the meaning *out* of the text (exegesis).

30. Wright, *No Place for Sovereignty*, 152. See also Grudem, *Systematic Theology*, 595.

31. Packer, "Love of God," 283.

Once more, the context helps us here. The motif of belief figures prominently in John's gospel, and this passage (John 6:22–59) is certainly no exception.[32] Jesus had just miraculously fed about five thousand people (John 6:1–15). He made it clear to the crowds that the feeding was intended as a sign (v. 14) indicating that he himself was the bread of God who had come down from heaven in order to give life to the world (v. 33). It is important to keep in mind that throughout this dialogue, Jesus was interacting with "the crowd"[33] who sought him out, and with "the Jews" in the synagogue in Capernaum (v. 59). As Jesus addressed the crowd, we see that the blessings he came to bring could apply potentially to anyone in the crowd:

> v. 35: *"Jesus said to them, 'I am the bread of life; he who comes to Me will not hunger, and he who believes in Me will never thirst.'"*

> v. 37: "All *that the Father gives me will come to me, and* whoever *comes to me I will never cast out"* (ESV).

> v. 40: *"For this is the will of My Father, that* everyone *who beholds the Son and believes in Him will have eternal life, and I Myself will raise him up on the last day."*

> v. 45: "*It is written in the Prophets, 'And they shall* all *be taught of God.'* Everyone *who has heard and learned from the Father comes to me."*

> v. 47: *Truly, truly, I say to you,* whoever *believes has eternal life* (ESV).

> v. 51: "*I am the living bread that came down out of heaven. If* anyone *eats of this bread, he will live forever. And the bread also which I will give for the life of the world* is my flesh."

> v. 54: *"Whoever feeds on my flesh and drinks my blood has eternal life, and I will raise him up on the last day"* (ESV).

> v. 56: *"Whoever feeds on my flesh and drinks my blood abides in me, and I in him"* (ESV).

> vv. 57, 58: *"Whoever feeds on me, he also will live because of me. . . . Whoever feeds on this bread will live forever"* (ESV).

The point is clear: Jesus considered the fruit of his atoning sacrifice as applying potentially to anyone and everyone, and actually to whoever responded in faith to him.

Among those in the crowd were potentially some whom the Father had already given to Jesus (vv. 37, 39). Who were these? Calvinists answer in terms of a predetermined and limited number whom God had predestined for salvation, the elect.

---

32. In fact John tells us that he wrote his gospel specifically "that you may believe that Jesus is the Christ, the Son of God, and that by believing you may have life in his name" (John 20:31).

33. The term *crowd* occurs in vv. 2, 5, 22, 24; *the people* in vv. 5, 10, 14; *the Jews* in vv. 41, 52 (NASB).

We know that whoever they are, they must be people who have exercised faith and believed upon Jesus. (John 6:40: *For this is the will of my Father, that everyone who behold the Son and believes in Him will have eternal life, and I Myself will raise him up on the last day.*) Verse 45 is crucial in understanding the class of those who are given by the Father to Jesus and who come to Jesus: "*Everyone who has heard and learned from the Father comes to me.*" Further insight concerning the status of these people is given in the first part of the verse where we are told concerning such people: "*It is written in the Prophets, 'And they shall all be taught of God.'*" The reference is probably to Isa 54:13: "*All your sons will be taught of the Lord, And the well-being of your sons will be great.*"[34] It is quite probable that those whom the Father gave to Jesus and who subsequently came to Jesus are those who are familiar with the words of the Old Testament prophets and are now in fact the subject of the prophetic prediction. These people, like the Old Testament saints, already believed in the Father and, now that God's redemptive plan had moved on and now focused on the Son, readily believed in Jesus. This understanding is reinforced in John 17, Jesus's high priestly prayer. In this prayer Jesus remarks concerning the disciples in the Upper Room: "*I have manifested your name to the men whom you gave me out of the world. They were Yours, and you gave them to me, and they have kept your word*" (John 17:6). These men were steeped in God's Old Testament word and loved the God revealed there.[35] In this sense they already belonged to God—"*They were Yours.*"

From the foregoing, those given to Jesus by the Father were not apparently arbitrarily chosen sinners given by God to Jesus, but rather those who already believed in God from their submission to God's Old Testament revealed word and who recognized that God was now doing a new thing redemptively in the coming of Jesus and readily believed upon Jesus, God's Son, when called to do so. We see precisely the same dynamic in the previous chapter, where Jesus confronts a potentially hostile Jewish crowd following his healing of a paralytic man by the pool of Bethesda on the Sabbath (John 5). Once again, the issue concerned Jesus's identity as Israel's Messiah. Jesus told the crowd that if they believed their Old Testament, and especially the Pentateuch (the writings of Moses), they would readily believe his messianic claims: "*For if you believed Moses, you would believe Me, for he wrote about Me. But if you do not believe his writings, how will you believe My words?*" (John 5:46, 47). An Old Testament saint who believed Moses's writings would perceive that Moses spoke of spiritual realities beyond the merely physical and, in that sense, anticipated God's anointed and

34. Carson helpfully points out that "the passage is here applied typologically: in the New Testament the messianic community and the dawning of the saving reign of God are the typological fulfilments of the restoration of Jerusalem after the Babylonian exile." Carson, *John*, 293.

35. Their writings reflect this—e.g., Peter, Matthew, John. This may also at least partly explain why they were so ready to forsake all when Jesus called them to follow him (Matt 4:18–22). While these men were in the world, a world generally characterized as in darkness and spiritually blind especially in John's gospel, there is no need to suppose that these people who belonged to God were themselves in darkness or spiritually blind prior their being given by the Father to Jesus.

recognized him when he appeared. Such people already were God's people and would be given to Jesus when Jesus was manifested in their midst.

Scriptures That Indicate the Intent of the Atonement Was Universal

a) Christ Died for Sinners

Some passages clearly indicate that Christ came and died for all sinners—not for only an elect people chosen by God unconditionally:

> Luke 5:32
>
> *"I have not come to call the righteous but sinners to repentance."*

> Romans 5:6, 8
>
> *"For while we were still helpless, at the right time Christ died for the ungodly. . . . But God demonstrates His own love toward us, in that while we were yet sinners, Christ died for us."*

> 1 Timothy 1:15
>
> *"It is a trustworthy statement, deserving full acceptance, that Christ Jesus came into the world to save sinners, among whom I am foremost of all."*

Every instance in the New Testament where reference is made to sinners, they are characterized as (a) those living immorally or contrary to the (Mosaic) law (Matt 9:11; 11:19; Mark 2:16; Luke 5:30; 7:34); (b) those hostile to Jesus (Matt 26:45; Mark 14:41; Luke 24:7; Heb 12:3); (c) those who fail to worship God and do his will (John 9:31); (d) those for whom Christ died (Rom 5:8); (5) those who are separated from Christ (Heb 7:26). So, when Scripture indicates that Christ died for "sinners" this must be understood as Christ dying for all people because all people without exception, prior to being regenerated by God's Spirit, are classified as sinners (Rom 3:23). Furthermore, the universal call to sinners to repentance mirrors the universal extent of the atonement: *"I have not come to call the righteous but sinners to repentance"* (Luke 5:32). In short, the scope of those defined to be sinners is precisely the scope of those for whom he came to atone.

Paul's describing himself as the foremost of sinners (1 Tim 1:15) does not invalidate what has been said above. "Christ Jesus came into the world to save sinners epitomizes the cardinal fact of Christian truth. It points to the heart of the gospel. . . . Paul never got away from the fact that Christian salvation was intended for sinners, and the more he increased his grasp of the magnitude of God's grace, the more he deepened the consciousness of his own naturally sinful state."[36]

---

36. Guthrie, *Pastoral Epistles*, 75.

b) Christ Died for Apostates

There are at least three passages which explicitly connect Christ's death, not only to sinners, but even to those who were formerly Christians but who subsequently apostatized. In a context where Paul is dealing with amoral issues (food offered to idols),[37] the apostle warns Christians who understand that there is no intrinsic value in avoiding food offered to idols, to be aware of the Christian brother whose conscience calls him to forbid eating such food for fear he may be dishonoring God. Failure to love the weaker brother in this manner could result in him imitating the stronger brother's actions and so violate his own conscience—with disastrous results: *"For if someone sees you, who have knowledge, dining in an idol's temple, will not his conscience, if he is weak, be strengthened to eat things sacrificed to idols? For through your knowledge he who is weak is ruined, the brother for whose sake Christ died"* (1 Cor 8:10, 11).[38] The point is that Christ's death applied to even this "ruined" former brother, thus indicating that Christ's death could not have been limited only to the elect, i.e., those chosen by God who infallibly are saved and who thereby infallibly persevere to the end.

Peter, in his letter, addresses the problem of false teachers who were bringing heretical teachings to the churches, to whom he wrote: *"But false prophets also arose among the people, just as there will be false teachers among you, who will secretly introduce destructive heresies, even denying the Master who bought them, bringing swift destruction upon themselves"* (2 Pet 2:1).[39] These false teachers were evidently at one time viewed as authentic Christians who benefited from the death of Christ; the term *bought* speaks of the cross.[40] Baukham comments: "2 Peter does not deny that the false teachers are Christians, but sees them as apostate Christians who have disowned their Master."[41] Later in the passage Peter speaks of these as having forsaken the right way (v. 15), and having formerly known the way of righteousness (v. 21). So, Christ's death applied to some who formerly were counted among the elect but who then chose to forsake the faith and become apostate. There is no hint, in this text or within the broader context (2 Pet 2:1–22), that Christ's death was not intended for and beneficially received by these false teachers. Once more, such a class of persons, those who denied the Master that bought them, could not be classified as among the elect Calvinistically understood, since such elect could never suffer "swift destruction."

---

37. 1 Cor 8:1–13.

38. Fee, *First Corinthians*, 387, is probably correct in seeing this destruction as actual, not merely hypothetical: "A Christian life is at stake. . . . In saying that the brother 'is destroyed' Paul most likely is referring to eternal loss, not simply some internal 'falling apart' because one is behaving contrary to the 'dictates of conscience.' The latter idea is altogether too modern; and elsewhere in Paul this word invariably refers to eternal ruin."

39. "*Bought* emphasizes both the seriousness of man's plight and the costliness of man's rescue." Green, *2 Peter and Jude*, 106, emphasis original.

40. "Jesus is the Master of his Christian slaves because he has bought them (at the cost of his death, it is implied—the only allusion to the cross in 2 Peter.)" Baukham, *Jude*, 240.

41. Baukham, *Jude*, 240.

A key purpose of the writer of the book of Hebrews was to warn Jewish Christians of the dangers of apostatizing, forsaking their Christian faith and reverting back to Judaism. Hebrews 10:29 is typical: *"How much severer punishment do you think he will deserve who has trampled under foot the Son of God, and has regarded as unclean the blood of the covenant by which he was sanctified, and has insulted the Spirit of grace?"* The blood of the covenant is a reference to Christ's atoning sacrifice (1 Cor 11:23–26). So, here the writer envisions the distinct possibility of a Christian who was formerly sanctified through Christ's death being subject to punishment for apostatizing.[42] The point once more is that the atonement is viewed as applying to someone who once was among the elect, but who then forsook the faith thus demonstrating that Christ's atoning sacrifice applied to those other than the elect alone.

c) Christ Died for the World

In addition to the John 6:37–39 passage noted above, there are many other scriptures that speak of Christ's death as intended by God for the whole world, for everyone without exception.

John 1:29

"The next day he [John the Baptist] saw Jesus coming toward him and said, 'Behold, the Lamb of God, who takes away the sin of the world!'"

John 3:16

"For God so loved the world that He gave His only begotten Son."

John 3:17

"For God did not send the Son into the world to judge the world, but that the world might be saved through Him."

2 Corinthians 5:19

"God was in Christ reconciling the world to Himself, not counting their trespasses against them."

1 John 2:2

"He Himself is the propitiation for our sins; and not for ours only, but also for those of the whole world."

How do Calvinists interpret these clear references to "the world"? They do not deny the references to "the world"—the Greek word is unambiguously stated. Instead, Calvinists reinterpret the term to fit within the Calvinist system. Thus, for example

---

42. F. F. Bruce, comments: "That outright apostasy is intended here is plain from the language of verse 29." Bruce, *Hebrews*, 259.

Carson comments with respect to John 3:17, "[Jesus] came into a lost world . . . in order to save some." The text seems to state that Jesus came into the world with the intent or desire that the world (that is, everyone, all peoples) would be saved—that was the purpose of Jesus's mission and God's sending of his Son. But Carson subtly shifts the meaning to say that God's intent was only "to save some."[43] How can "the world" become "some"? The logic behind the restriction is that since not everyone is in fact saved, then it was obviously not God's intent to save everyone. There is a mistaken assumption operating here which will be discussed later.

Grant Osborne commenting on the phrase "the world" in John's gospel notes that the influential puritan theologian John Owen interpreted the world in John to refer not to the reprobate, but to the elect—"a view that makes no sense of the meaning 'world' in John."[44] In a footnote he also notes this to have been Augustine's view, and adds: "This is a convenient approach, for all passages that connote universal atonement [then] automatically refer to the elect—a good example of a system dictating the interpretation of a text."[45]

Carl Trueman struggles to find a positive teaching in the 1 John 2:2 passage, claiming the passage to be obscure, and asserts that "the meaning of 1 John 2:2 is difficult to discern."[46] He suggests there may be elements of common grace in the passage.[47] Nevertheless, consistent with the hermeneutical point made above by Osborne, Trueman insists on interpreting the passage in a manner consistent with definite atonement: "It seems better to interpret [1 John 2:2] in the light of clearer passages and teachings of Scripture, such as the particularity of the Levitical priesthood . . . than to suggest positive meanings that seem to stand in tension with these."[48] First John 2:2 appears to be quite straightforward; John is explicitly stating that Christ died "for the sins of the whole world" and, as if to reinforce the point, insists the atoning sacrifice was made in addition to those believers he is addressing. There is nothing obscure or difficult to discern here.

d) Christ Died for All

If a key phrase denoting the universal extent of the atonement is "the world," then another term commonly found in the New Testament is "all." Such passages indicate Christ's death was for the benefit of all, for everyone without exception.

43. Carson, *John*, 207.

44. Osborne, "General Atonement View," 111.

45. Osborne, "General Atonement View," 111. In fairness this hermeneutical temptation—to interpret a text exclusively in the light of one's system—applies just as readily to non-Calvinists too.

46. Trueman, "Definite Atonement View," 39.

47. Common grace is a Calvinistic category of grace that refers to the goods God bestows on everyone—like sunshine and rain (Matt 5:45).

48. Trueman, "Definite Atonement View," 39.

Isaiah 53:6

"All of us *like sheep have gone astray, each of us has turned to his own way; but* the Lord has caused the iniquity of us all *to fall on Him.*"

1 Timothy 2:4–6

"*[God]* desires all men *to be saved and to come to the knowledge of the truth. For there is one God, and one mediator also between God and men, the man Christ Jesus, who gave Himself as a ransom* for all."

1 Timothy 4:10

"*For it is for this we labor and strive, because we have fixed our hope on the living God, who is the Savior of* all men, *especially of believers.*"

Hebrews 2:9

"*But we do see Him who was made for a little while lower than the angels, namely, Jesus, because of the suffering of death crowned with glory and honor, so that by the grace of God He might taste death* for everyone."

Hebrews 9:12

"*Not through the blood of goats and calves, but through His own blood, He entered the holy place once* for all, *having obtained eternal redemption.*"

Again, we may ask, how do Calvinists understand these references to all, everyone, all people? John Murray, the former professor of systematic theology at Westminster Seminary, has written extensively on the subject of the atonement in his influential book *Redemption Accomplished and Applied*. He devotes a chapter to the question of the extent of the atonement. The first point he makes in this chapter is that appeal to terms like all, everyone, and so on do not necessarily justify the conclusion that Christ's atonement was universal in its intent because "From beginning to end the Bible uses expressions that are universal in form but cannot be interpreted as meaning all men distributively and inclusively."[49] An example he gives is 1 Cor 6:12 ("*All things are lawful for me, but not all things are profitable. All things are lawful for me, but I will not be mastered by anything.*") Here, Murray rightfully argues that even though the language Paul uses is comprehensive, he cannot actually mean literally "all things." It was not lawful for Paul to oppose God's moral law, for example.[50]

This seems a fair observation. But how are we then to determine the extent or scope of the "all" in a given passage? The answer can only be from the context. What

---

49. Murray, *Redemption Accomplished and Applied*, 59.

50. Interestingly, sometimes the opposite can occur whereby a restricted form can have universal significance as, e.g., Rom 3:19, "*Now we know that whatever the Law says, it speaks to those who are under the Law, so that* every mouth *may be closed and* all the world *may become accountable to God.*"

is the point the biblical writer is seeking to make?[51] Furthermore, some comprehensive terms like "the world" seem far more universal in their scope and less amenable to a restricted meaning.

With respect to the passages noted above, in Isa 53:6 the "us" who have gone astray entails Isaiah's fellow countrymen, the whole people of Judah, most of whom were idolaters. And yet, according to the last part of v. 6, God's unique Servant bore the iniquity of these people comprehensively.[52] In 1 Tim 2:6, the "all" for whom Christ gave himself as a ransom is qualified by the term "all men"—a comprehensive term used to distinguish the whole of humanity as distinct from God. Later in the same epistle to Timothy, Paul states explicitly that Christ is *the Savior of all men* which also includes the category of believers (1 Tim 4:10). On a Calvinistic reading which restricts the intent of the atonement to the elect, Paul would effectively be saying, "Christ is the Savior of all believers, and especially believers"—clearly a nonsensical understanding of the verse.

The Heb 2:9 passage connects with and follows the quote from Ps 8:4–6 (LXX [the Septuagint]). In this passage the psalmist clearly speaks about man collectively, i.e., humanity, and expresses the wonder of the exalted status of man in the light of God's presence. The writer to the Hebrews in Heb 2:9 applies this exalted status to Jesus, though only after his having endured suffering. The tasting of death "for everyone" connects with the humanity of Ps 8 as Heb 2:9a indicates. Furthermore, there would appear to be an element of solidarity between the "man" of Ps 8 and Jesus himself. Jesus, in his redemptive ministry, identifies with "man" and sacrifices himself for "man." William Lane in his commentary on Hebrews makes this point when he says that Jesus "took upon himself *humanity's* full estate in order that by means of his own redemptive accomplishment he might bring the vision of the psalmist to its realization." A little later he remarks that Jesus's "coronation and investiture . . . provide assurance that the power of sin and death has been nullified and that *humanity* will yet be led to the full realization of their intended glory."[53]

In short, we must insist that the Bible be allowed to speak for itself without a preconceived theological system determining what the passage must mean. With respect to the aforementioned scriptures, references to the world, all/everyone, and so on must be allowed to carry their full weight and not be reinterpreted to mean a restricted number. Dave Hunt makes the same point: "The command and invitation

---

51. Unfortunately, even this is not always as simple as it seems because the perceived point being made by the biblical author is sometimes influenced, perhaps even determined, by the theological framework one presumes must be operating. Hermeneutics is both science and art, not science only.

52. *"All of us like sheep have gone astray, each of us has turned to his own way; but the Lord has caused the iniquity of us all to fall on Him."*

53. Lane, *Hebrews 1–8*, 50, emphases mine.

are given to all, not just to a select group. The words 'wicked' and 'unrighteous' and 'all' clearly mean what they say and cannot be turned into 'elect.'"[54]

Theological Issues Related to Limiting the Extent of the Atonement

Limiting the intent of the atonement in the redemptive purposes of God to only the elect raises not only biblical exegetical problems as discussed above but also serious theological problems. I shall begin by discussing the basic misconception Calvinism has regarding this aspect of salvation. Then I shall show why a limited atonement calls into question the extent of God's love. I will go on to show how Calvinists reduce the scope of universals (whole world, all, whoever, anyone, etc.) to a restricted number, the elect.

We must also address a common Calvinist claim, namely, that the atonement actually saves and does not just make salvation possible. I shall explore why it is that Christ's death that is universal in intent does not lead to the idea of a double payment for sins—at the cross and for the sinner in hell. Before concluding the chapter, I shall examine the validity or consistency of those who claim to be only "four-point" Calvinists as well as the attempt to find a middle ground through Amyraldism, and finally the rationale for evangelism within a Calvinistic soteriology.

a) The Basic Problem: The Failure to Distinguish between the Accomplishing of Redemption and Its Application

Calvinism does not separate the accomplishing of redemption at the cross from its application to the individual Christian. For Calvinism, the two go together, they are inextricably bound. This may be seen clearly, for example, in John Murray's book titled *Redemption Accomplished and Applied*: "The doctrine of 'limited atonement' which we maintain is the doctrine which limits the atonement to those who are heirs of eternal life, to the elect. That limitation *ensures* its efficacy and conserves its essential character as *efficient and effective* redemption."[55] Note the unity: "efficient *and* effective."[56]

---

54. Hunt, *What Love Is This?*, 250.

55. Murray, *Redemption Accomplished and Applied*, 64, emphases mine. Perhaps the following construction helps to make the distinction clear: Calvinism: (Accomplished and Applied); Non-Calvinism: (Accomplished) and (Applied).

56. Interestingly, the systematic theologian Louis Berkhof addresses this distinction explicitly when he says: "In defining the contents of Soteriology, it is better to say that it deals with the *application of the work of redemption* than to say that it treats of the *appropriation of salvation*. . . . Pope objects to the use of the former term, since in using it 'we are in danger of the predestinarian error which assumes that the finished work of Christ is applied to the individual according to the fixed purpose of an election of grace.'" But, Berkhof goes on to say, "This is the very reason why a Calvinist prefers to use that term." Berkhof, *Systematic Theology*, 415, emphases original.

Horton likewise connects the work of the cross inextricably to the actual salvation of the elect: "The 'once for all' accomplishment of Christ in his saving work at the cross leaves *nothing for sinners to complete by their own actions*, whether their decision or effort."[57] Here, again, the atonement is unconditionally applied to the elect only. Sproul also sees a unity between the atonement at the cross and its application: "[Salvation] is designed and ordained by the Father, accomplished by the Son, and applied by the Holy Spirit. All three persons of the Trinity are in eternal agreement on the plan of redemption *and its execution*."[58] The inability to separate Christ's atoning work from its effective application to the elect is also seen in this quote from Sproul: "The atonement's ultimate purpose is found in the ultimate purpose or will of God. This purpose or design does not include the entire human race. If it did, the entire human race would surely be redeemed."[59] For Sproul there is a watertight connection between the work of the cross and its effective application to the elect alone, an effective denial of the concept of appropriation.

A final example of the Calvinist's inviolable linking of the death of Christ to the elect alone such that the death of Christ would inevitably and unconditionally be applied to the elect is seen in Wright when he asks "whether an omnipotent God could be expected to fail to any degree in achieving what he intended in his Son's sacrifice?"[60] The answer is obvious—no. God has his elect, God intends to save them, the cross is the means to effect that salvation. The linkage is watertight: an election, the cross, the saved.

As has been hinted at already in these author's understanding, the logic is clearly driven by the concept of unconditional election. It is the Calvinist's notion of election that drives its understanding of the relationship between the atonement of the cross and its application to the individual. The work of the cross was intended for, designed for, planned for, purposed for, the elect and only the elect. Why? Because the cross is the means God has chosen to save the elect. The cross has no meaning, no bearing, no application in any sense to the reprobate. Given Calvinism's notion of election as unconditional, preplanned before the ages, and applicable to only a predetermined few, then the atonement must likewise bear the same characteristics.

Of course, if unconditional election is shown to be unbiblical, the product of an exaggerated notion of human sin entailing total inability, then the inviolable linkage between the cross and the individual could in principle be broken. There would be room for conditionality—the conditionality of faith. To see how this works I think it is helpful to distinguish between an objective and a subjective salvation. Objectively,

---

57. Horton, *For Calvinism*, 93, emphasis mine. Horton's use of the word "effort" is strange—no evangelical Christian of any stripe believes any "effort" on their part completes Christ's work on the cross.

58. Sproul, *Reformed Theology*, 163, emphasis mine.

59. Sproul, *Reformed Theology*, 177.

60. Wright, *No Place for Sovereignty*, 151.

salvation was achieved at the cross for all peoples—this was a transaction between the Father and the Son. No specific persons are in view with this aspect of salvation, rather the whole world was in view here. It entailed a transaction between the Father and the Son—the Son would give up his life as an atoning sacrifice designed to appease the wrath of God against sin. Thus, Paul speaks of *"the redemption which is in Christ Jesus; whom God displayed publicly as a propitiation in His blood through faith"* (Rom 3:24, 25). Likewise, Paul teaches that *"God was in Christ reconciling the world to Himself, not counting their trespasses against them"* (2 Cor 5:19). When Jesus exclaimed on the cross *"it is finished"* (John 19:30), he was referring to his atoning sacrifice as a completed work in terms of objective efficacy. Robert Shank makes the same point: "While the atonement is *for* man, it is essentially Godward rather than manward. Its authenticity and value in no way depend on the response of any man, but depend instead on its satisfaction of God and the demands of His righteousness."[61]

The other aspect of salvation is the subjective appropriation, by faith, of the objective work of the cross. Objective salvation was directed toward the benefit of the world (1 John 4:14).[62] This is the universal aspect of the atonement. But this is not all that can be said concerning God's intent in sending his Son as an atoning sacrifice, for the cross is a means to an end, it is not an end in itself. Rather, God's ultimate goal is the *"bringing of many sons to glory"* (Heb 2:10), and that through Christ *"all the families of the earth will be blessed"* (Gen 12:3). Obviously, not all people are saved—why not? Calvinists answer that it was never God's intent to save everyone and thus God limits the work of the cross to the elect only. Non-Calvinists answer that, while objectively, the cross had a universal intent, that intent was not fulfilled due to lack of subjective appropriation of the fruit of the atonement (salvation) by faith. Both parties acknowledge the lack of universal salvation, but whereas Calvinism locates the reason in God's decree to save only some, non-Calvinists locate the reason in unbelief and rejection of the work of the cross. It is this crucial distinction between objective and subjective salvation that makes the succinct description of the atonement as genuinely sufficient for all but efficient only for the elect a helpful and valid one.[63]

There is an Old Testament analogue of the point being made here. In the story of the exodus of the children of Israel out of Egyptian bondage, the Israelites were required to kill a lamb and sprinkle its blood on the doorposts of the house (Exod 12:7). And when the angel passed by and saw the blood, then *"no plague will befall you to destroy you"* (v. 13).[64] But note a crucial distinction; the shed blood of the lamb

---

61. Shank, *Elect in the Son*, 71, emphasis original.

62. *"We have seen and testify that the Father has sent the Son to be the Savior of the world."*

63. While many Calvinists affirm this summary statement concerning the extent of the atonement, they belie its surface meaning by limiting the "sufficient for all" to all the elect wherever they may be—not to all people everywhere. See Shank's discussion of this point in his *Elect in the Son*, 79–81.

64. Of course, this incident is a classic instance of the *"copy and shadow of the heavenly things"* of which the writer to the Hebrews spoke (Heb 8:5). In this case, the shed blood of the lamb is a type of which Christ's death is the anti-type.

in itself did not guarantee protection, it had to be applied to the doorposts. Failure to apply the blood would not deliver the Israelite family; deliverance would only be experienced when, by faith, the family took the next step and actually applied the blood to the post. Likewise, the shed blood of Christ, in itself, as an objective reality, saves no one; the work of the cross has to be appropriated, *received* (John 1:12; 4:45; Acts 2:41; 1 Cor 15:1; Col 2:6).

This important distinction between objective provision and subjective appropriation is well explained by the New Testament scholar Millard Erickson. He writes:

> Those who hold to limited atonement assume that if Christ died for someone that person will in actuality be saved. By extension they reason that if Christ in fact died for all persons, all would come to salvation; hence the concept of universal atonement is viewed as leading to the universal-salvation trap. The basic assumption here, however, ignores the fact that our inheriting eternal life involves two separate factors: an objective factor (Christ's provision of salvation) and a subjective factor (our acceptance of that salvation). In the view of those who hold to unlimited atonement, there is the possibility that someone for whom salvation is available may fail to accept it. In the view of those who hold to limited atonement, however, there is no such possibility. Although John Murray wrote of Redemption—Accomplished and Applied, in actuality he and others of his doctrinal persuasion *collapse the latter part, the application, into the accomplishment.* This leads in turn to the conception that God regenerates the elect person who then and therefore believes.[65]

By failing to make the crucial distinction between objective and subjective salvation and choosing to lump the two together under a decree of God to save only a certain number, Calvinism creates several problems. These include the exegetical gymnastics required to remove any truly universal component to the cross. So, for example, in John 3:14–15, where Jesus says concerning his death on the cross, *"As Moses lifted up the serpent in the wilderness, even so must the Son of Man be lifted up; so that whoever believes will in Him have eternal life,"* this must be understood to say that only the few chosen by God will in him have eternal life. Similarly, v. 16 (*"For God so loved the world, that He gave His only begotten Son, that whoever believes in Him shall not perish, but have eternal life"*) must be restated to mean that only the few chosen by God shall not perish.[66] Other problems, including the extent of God's love, will be examined below.

65. Erickson, *Christian Theology*, 835, emphasis mine.
66. Failure to recognize this important distinction between objective and subjective atonement has caused some non-Calvinists to reject the penal substitution theory of the atonement believing that "if Christ actually accomplished the salvation of sinners at the cross . . . then all for whom Christ died are actually saved." Horton, *For Calvinism*, 91. This concern about universalism is misplaced however when a clear distinction between a universal objective atonement only makes provision for salvation, and that an individual's salvation is conditional upon subjectively appropriating the work of the cross.

208

b) "God's Particular Selecting Love towards His Elect"?[67]

The extent of the atonement is intimately connected with the extent of God's love for mankind. Several scriptures connect God's love to the sending of his Son for a work of atonement:

> 1 John 4:9: *By this the love of God was manifested in us, that God has sent His only begotten Son into the world so that we might live through Him.*

> 1 John 4:10: *In this is love, not that we loved God, but that He loved us and sent His Son to be the propitiation for our sins.*

> Ephesians 5:2: *"Walk in love, just as Christ also loved you and gave Himself up for us, an offering and a sacrifice to God as a fragrant aroma."*

> John 3:16: *"For God so loved the world, that He gave His only begotten Son, that whoever believes in Him shall not perish, but have eternal life."*

> Romans 5:6–8: *"For while we were still helpless, at the right time Christ died for the ungodly. For one will hardly die for a righteous man; though perhaps for the good man someone would dare even to die. But God demonstrates His own love toward us, in that while we were yet sinners, Christ died for us."*

While some, or even most, of the verses relating God's love to the death of Christ are described as "for us," that is, the believers in the church to whom the letter was addressed, as noted earlier such references need not entail that it is *only* for the church that God's love was directed. So, in John 3:16 God's love is for "the world," and in the Romans passage "Christ died for the ungodly," including those who eventually became believers in the church at Rome.

So, the question remains—does God love everyone without exception and thus was impelled to send his Son "to be the Savior of the world" (John 4:42; 1 John 4:14)? Or, did God love only his elect, a predetermined number, limited in scope and so sent his Son to die for them only?[68] Does God love everyone equally, or does he love some more than others or in a different way than others? Or does he love some but hate others?[69] In particular, does God love everyone in the sense that he desires the salvation (the highest good) of everyone, or is his love restricted to only a few whom he loves in terms of salvation—and bypasses the rest? Most Calvinists feel uncomfortable flatly denying that God loves everyone. A. W. Pink, however, is

---

67. Carson, *Love of God*, 18.

68. Carson expresses the choice well: the non-Calvinist "holds that the Atonement is general, i.e., sufficient for all, available to all, on condition of faith; the Calvinist holds that the Atonement is definite, i.e., intended by God to be effective for the elect." Carson, *Love of God*, 74.

69. See below concerning Jacob and Esau.

a consistent Calvinist and does not hesitate to insist that "God's love is restricted to members of his own family."[70]

Before addressing the above questions, a point of clarification is needed. To say that God loves everyone does not mean to assert (or even imply) that God *accepts* everyone. Love is unconditional; acceptance is conditional upon repentance and faith. God can love even those who are opposed to him—as demonstrated by, for example, Christ's prayer for those who were crucifying him: *"Father, forgive them; for they do not know what they are doing"* (Luke 23:34). Or, the instance where we are told Jesus loved the rich young ruler even while the latter chose not to enter into a meaningful relationship with Jesus: *"Looking at him, Jesus felt a love for him and said to him, 'One thing you lack: go and sell all you possess and give to the poor, and you will have treasure in heaven; and come, follow Me.' But at these words he was saddened, and he went away grieving, for he was one who owned much property"* (Mark 10:21, 22). Every parent understands this distinction for they have had to apply it in their relationships with their own children: *"My son, do not reject the discipline of the Lord Or loathe His reproof, For whom the Lord loves He reproves, Even as a father corrects the son in whom he delights"* (Prov 3:11, 12). The point of noting this distinction is that failing to do so might lead one to conclude that God does not love everyone equally because not all are accepted by him and to thereby confuse particular acceptance (reconciliation, justification, union) with particular atonement.

Love is used in the Bible to denote God's love for men and the kind of love God desires that men express to one another and is an attitude that seeks the highest good in the object of one's love.[71] God seeks our highest good, and so sends his Son to redeem mankind. The Greek word agape (ἀγαπη, *agapē*) is the word used for this kind of love (as opposed to friendship love or physical love). It is ἀγαπη that is used in 1 John 4:10: *"In this is love, not that we loved God, but that He loved us and sent His Son to be the propitiation for our sins."*

It may come as a surprise to some that God's love is a difficult doctrine as the title of Donald A. Carson's book on the subject suggests: The Difficult Doctrine of the Love of God.[72] Carson notes five ways the Bible speaks of God's love. The first, we may say, is intra-Trinitarian, the mutual love within the godhead. The second is God's love

---

70. Pink, "Does God Love Everyone?," para. 4.

71. "ἀγαπη . . . seeks the highest good in the one loved, even though one may be undeserving." Hoehner, "Love," 657.

72. Despite the Bible's clear testimony concerning God's love for all mankind beginning with the call of Abraham through whom God would bring the Savior of the world (Gen 12:3; 1 John 4:14), and despite the fact that the Bible even defines God as love (1 John 4:8, 16), Calvinism hesitates to robustly and clearly affirm God's saving love for his human creation. This reluctance may be seen in the Westminster Confession's omission of any reference to the love of God in answer to the question in the Shorter Catechism "What is God?"—even though reference is made to God's wisdom, power, holiness, justice, goodness, and truth. Another example of Calvinism's downplaying God's love is found in Calvin's *Institutes*. Despite referencing over two thousand texts in his Scripture index, the two references that explicitly define God as love (1 John 4:8, 16) are omitted.

directed to all that he has made, his providential love that causes the sun to shine and the rain to fall on all. The third is God's love for the world or, as Carson puts it, "God's salvific stance towards his fallen world." The fourth is "God's particular, effective, selecting love towards his elect." And the fifth is a conditionality in God's love—God's people enjoy God's love only conditional on obedience.

What shall we say by way of response? The first two are obviously not problematic. The third, God's salvific love directed toward all people is also not problematic because clearly biblical—Carson cites John 3:16 and 1 John 2:2 as examples of God's universal love. Carson even goes so far as to explicitly reject the typical Calvinistic understanding of the world as referring only to the elect: "God's love for the world cannot be collapsed into his love for the elect."[73] We shall ignore the inconsistency in Carson using the term salvific here since, within a Calvinistic framework, whatever God desires, in this case that all should be saved, he accomplishes—God's sovereignty is such that there is no sense in which what God desires does not come to pass.

The fourth sense of God's love as a "selecting love towards his elect" is problematic. First, if God loves only some, the elect, and manifests this love in their salvation how much content can one really put into the third aspect of God's love—his universal salvific will? Surely, an all-powerful and all-loving God who "takes no pleasure in the death of the wicked, but rather that they turn from their ways and live"[74] could just as easily choose to save these too, to include them among the elect. What prevents an all-sovereign God from electing *all* who are the objects of his love? Why does God's universal salvific stance toward fallen humanity, Carson's third point, not find expression in a universal election (Calvinism), or potential universalism (non-Calvinism)?

Second, to justify this fourth sense of God's love as electing love, Carson quotes from Deuteronomy where Moses reminds the people of Israel as they are about to enter the promised land that it was *"because the Lord loved you and kept the oath which He swore to your forefathers, the Lord brought you out by a mighty hand and redeemed you from the house of slavery, from the hand of Pharaoh king of Egypt"* (Deut 7:8). As always, context determines the meaning of a word or phrase or even a passage (as here). The primary context in this case, when speaking of God's election of Israel, is the Pentateuch. The first thing to note is that God is dealing with the *nation*, not any one specific individual. The love here is God's love for the nation. Furthermore, the election of Israel was not an election to salvation but to *service*.[75] God selected Israel to be the vehicle whereby *"all the families of the earth will be blessed"* (Gen 12:3). Bearing all this in mind, we see that passages like Deut 4:37; 7:8; 10:14, 15 which speak of God's love for Israel is speaking of God's covenant faithfulness—God is committed to this particular people to work out his plan of redemption for the benefit of the whole world. This is not the same as God's love

73. Carson, *Love of God*, 17.
74. Carson, *Love of God*, 18.
75. See the discussion of Rom 9:10–16 in my chapter dealing with unconditional election (ch. 3).

directed to individuals for their personal salvation. The former was indeed selective (God only entered into covenant relationship with one nation), but the latter is not. Carson ignores these important distinctions and so conceives of God's love *in every case* as selective and an electing to salvation.

To further demonstrate God's love as discriminating and as "peculiarly direct- ed towards the elect," Carson also quotes Mal 1:2, 3a, *"I have loved Jacob; but I have hated Esau"* (Mal 1:2, 3a). It is somewhat surprising that Carson, a highly respected biblical scholar, would appeal to this verse to justify the notion that God would seek the highest good for Jacob (by the exercise of an electing love) and not seek Esau's highest good (but rather hating him). There is indeed discrimination going on here, but it has nothing to do with God's love, God's seeking the highest good of all individuals. First, historically, there is not the slightest hint that God hated Esau the man. Genesis 36:6–8 indicates that, following the death of Isaac their father, and upon his return from Paddan-aram, Jacob remained in the land of Canaan whereas Esau took his family and lived in Edom because *"their property had become too great for them to live together, and the land where they sojourned could not sustain them because of their livestock."* Jacob and Esau seemed to have separated quite amicably. Also, when Jacob encountered Esau when Jacob was on his way to Canaan after hav- ing served his father-in-law Laban for fourteen years in Paddan-aram, their meeting was on friendly terms. Genesis 33:10: Jacob said to Esau, *"If now I have found favor in your sight, then take my present from my hand, for I see your face as one sees the face of God, and you have received me favorably."* Certainly, there was no enmity be- tween the two brothers, and if Jacob did not hate Esau, there is no reason to suppose that God would do so either.

The context of the Malachi passage clearly shows the prophet referring not to individuals, but to nations. Below is the literary context of the passage:

> *The oracle of the word of the Lord to Israel through Malachi. "I have loved you," says the Lord. But you say, "How have You loved us?" "Was not Esau Jacob's brother?" declares the Lord. "Yet I have loved Jacob; but I have hated Esau, and I have made his mountains a desolation and appointed his inheritance for the jackals of the wilderness." Though Edom says, "We have been beaten down, but we will return and build up the ruins"; thus says the Lord of hosts, "They may build, but I will tear down; and men will call them the wicked territory, and the people toward whom the Lord is indignant forever." Your eyes will see this and you will say, "The Lord be magnified beyond the border of Israel!"* (Mal 1:1–5)

It is clear that God is dealing with Edom the nation, not Esau the individual who, by this time had been dead for several hundred years! The Bible frequently expresses a nation by the name of its progenitor (Jer 49:10; Obad 1:6, 8). Thus, the nation of Israel is often referred to as Jacob and Edom is often referred to as Esau as in the Malachi passage. Here, in Malachi, God is judging Edom for its arrogance.[76] Two nations are described, not the individuals themselves. In effect God's "loving" Jacob and "hating" Esau is a strong way of saying I have accepted and chosen to work out my redemptive purposes through Israel, and I have rejected Edom from serving this role.[77] God's love for Jacob here is an expression of God's covenant faithfulness and commitment to Israel—a commitment unique to Israel. In short, appeal to Mal 3:2–3 says nothing about God's salvific love for any individuals at a personal level.

The only reason Carson, and Calvinists generally, find any limitations or restrictions on the number of people who are the object of God's love is due to their tying their notion of an unconditional election to a necessarily equally limited atonement. And if the atonement is limited to the elect alone, then so must God's love be restricted also because, as noted earlier, God's love and the work of the cross are intimately bound. But this methodology, this hermeneutic, is a classic case of a systematic determining the meaning of a text rather than deriving a systematic from the text itself. Instead, if God's love extends to everyone in the world (John 3:16), and even to the ungodly (Rom 5:6) and sinners (Rom 5:8), then the extent of the atonement (objectively) must likewise be universal. This is really an appeal to logical consistency. The question of consistency is brought out rather pointedly by Erickson: "There seems to be a contradiction between the scriptural indications of God's love for the world, for all persons, and the belief that Christ did not die for all of them."[78] In short, as David Hunt states: "God repeatedly declares that He is gracious and merciful to all. And so it is with God's love, from which His grace and mercy flow—without partiality it reaches out to all mankind."[79]

Some Calvinists, wishing to retain some notion of universality in connection with God's love, deny any salvific component to this love, but rather speak of God's universal love in terms of God's common goodness—he causes the sun to shine and the rain to fall on all. Packer, for example says this concerning God's love for mankind:

> So it appears, first, that God loves all in some ways (everyone whom he creates, sinners though they are, receives many undeserved good gifts in daily providence), and, second, that he loves some in all ways (that is, in addition to the gifts of daily providence, he brings them to faith, to new life, and to glory according to his predestinating purpose. This is the clear witness of the entire Bible.[80]

76. The book of Obadiah in its entirety is an expansion of this theme.

77. Both Israel and Edom were judged by God, but God chose to continue to work out his redemptive purposes for the world through Israel as witnessed by God's enabling the nation to rebuild the temple in Jerusalem following the Babylonian captivity. God did not work through Edom in this way at all.

78. Erickson, *Christian Theology*, 832.

79. Hunt, *What Love Is This?*, 257.

80. Packer, "Love of God," 285.

But it is fair to ask, concerning God's love directed toward the all: What kind of love is this? Providential love is the provision of rain, shelter, food. But what use is this when man's greatest need is completely bypassed—his need of salvation? Apparently, for Packer, and many other Calvinists, such divine love for the whole of mankind is nonexistent. Is this alleged stance on the part of God toward his human creation in general consistent with, for example, 1 John 3:17, *"But whoever has the world's goods, and sees his brother in need and closes his heart against him, how does the love of God abide in him?"* Can it really be the case that God fails to do what John expects every Christian to do? Or, more pointedly, Jas 2:15, 16, *"If a brother or sister is without clothing and in need of daily food, and one of you says to them, 'Go in peace, be warmed and be filled,' and yet you do not give them what is necessary for their body, what use is that?"* In God's case, for God to give merely trinkets (relatively speaking) without providing an atonement that could meet everyone's greatest need, salvation, is a sort of cruel joke. Likewise, the whole point of the Parable of the Good Samaritan (Luke 10:30–37) is to show that love takes action to meet the needs of *anyone* needing help. Calvinism's selective, particular love is uncomfortably close to the actions of the priest and Levite who walked past the half dead man lying in the road.

c) Further Discussion on "All / Everyone / Whosoever / the World"

Some Calvinists object to applying any universal significance to the atonement because, since it is obvious that not all are actually saved, and if God's intent was a universal atonement, then obviously "in the case of some [the reprobate] his will is 'frustrated' by obstinate unbelief" and "frustration . . . of the divine will is impossible."[81] Here we have two factors at play—Calvinism's notion of absolute sovereignty whereby whatever God wills must necessarily always come to pass, and the conflating of the atonement itself with its application. Since both these elements have been discussed previously, and shown to be mistaken, I need not elaborate further.

Some deny the universal scope of the atonement by making references to all men refer to all Christians. For example, Geoffrey B. Wilson, commenting on Jesus's tasting death *"for everyone"* (Heb 2:9), says, "Christ did taste death for every son to be brought to glory and for all the children whom God has given him."[82] While it is true that the author of Hebrews speaks of the blessings of Christ's coming upon believers, clear universal statements must not be forced into a restricted meaning, especially when the immediate context of Heb 2:9 is a quote from Ps 8, where in v. 4 the question is asked, *"What is man that You take thought of him, And the son of man that You care for him?"* and is clearly universal in scope. By contrast, F. F. Bruce, commenting on Heb 2:9, following the author's train of thought, rightly notes that "as for the clause 'that . . . he should taste death for every man,' it does indeed

81. Hendriksen, *1 & 2 Timothy and Titus*, 153.
82. Wilson, *Hebrews*, 33.

express purpose . . . the purpose of the whole sequence of preceding events, the humiliation, passion and glory combined. Because the Son of Man suffered, because His suffering has been crowned by His exaltation, therefore His death avails for all."[83]

More commonly, an approach taken by Calvinists seeking to justify a limitation of the scope of the atonement is to interpret all as referring not to all without exception, but rather to all without distinction; Christ didn't die for every person but rather he died for all kinds of people. Take for example, 1 Tim 2:4–6: "*[God] desires all men to be saved and to come to the knowledge of the truth. For there is one God, and one mediator also between God and men, the man Christ Jesus, who gave Himself as a ransom for all.*" Commenting on this text, John Piper says, "It is possible that careful exegesis of 1 Timothy 2:4 would lead us to believe that 'God's willing all persons to be saved' does not refer to every individual person in the world, but rather to *all sorts of persons*"[84] As is typical, he notes the reference to kings and all who are in high positions in v. 2 in order to place a restriction upon the "all." Grudem likewise suggests that "a possible meaning is that God is the Savior of all sorts of people—that is, of people who believe."[85] Berkhof suggests that 1 Tim 2:4–6 refers "to the revealed will of God that both Jew and Gentile should be saved."[86]

As before, the attempt to limit the scope of the atonement in texts like 1 Tim 2:4–6 looks suspiciously like a response to the need to make the atonement limited to the elect only, which, within a Calvinistic soteriology, consists of a limited number of people God predestines for salvation. Commenting on this interpretive strategy we agree with Samuel Fisk's observation concerning a sermon by Charles Spurgeon: "[Spurgeon] derides those who would turn 'have all men to be saved' into 'some men' or into 'who will *not* have all men to be saved.'"[87] After acknowledging that the word all need not on every occasion refer to all without exception, Howard Marshall asks with respect to texts which speak to a universal atonement: "Is there any reason to suppose that any such restrictions are implicit in our texts? There is really nothing in the immediate context of any of the texts to suggest a limited set of people is intended."[88]

David Hunt, dealing with the Calvinist's move to restrict universal terms to the elect only, demonstrates how this works out with respect to the word whosoever:

> The word "whosoever" is found 183 times in 163 verses in the Bible, beginning with "whosoever slayeth Cain" (Genesis 4:15) and ending with "whosoever will, let him take of the water of life freely" (Revelation 22:17). "Whosoever"

83 Bruce, *Hebrews*, 39.

84. Piper, "Two Wills in God?," 108, emphasis mine.

85. Grudem, *Systematic Theology*, 599n38.

86. Berkhof, *Systematic Theology*, 396.

87. Fisk, *Divine Sovereignty*, 68.

88. Marshall, "Universal Grace," 61. Marshall has an excellent extended discussion on the 1 Tim 2:4–6 passage, and concludes, "We can find no good grounds for understanding 'all' in these texts in any other way than as 'all without exception.'" Marshall, "Universal Grace," 63.

clearly means everyone without exception. It is found in warnings ("whosoever eateth leavened bread" —Exodus 12:15) and in promises of reward ("whosoever smiteth the Jebusites first shall be chief" —1 Chronicles 11:6). Among the scores of other examples are "whosoever heareth, his ears shall tingle" (Jeremiah 19:3), and "whosoever shall call on the name of the Lord shall be delivered" (Joel 2:32). Not once in its 183 occurrences in the Bible could the word "whosoever" mean anything except "whosoever"! But wherever salvation is offered to whosoever will believe and accept Christ, the Calvinist changes the same Hebrew or Greek word to mean the "elect." He must in order to hold on to his Calvinism.[89]

A final strategy in dealing with passages which speak of a universal atonement is to simply ignore difficult texts. Again, for example, with respect to the works cited in this book so far, neither Horton, Murray, Sproul, Wright, nor Piper make any reference at all to 1 Tim 2:6![90]

d) Does the Cross Actually Save or Just Make Salvation Possible?

A common complaint of Calvinists against non-Calvinists is that Christ's death did not actually effect salvation for anyone but merely made salvation possible. Sproul poses the question this way: "Is Christ a real Savior or merely a 'potential' Savior? . . . Was [God's] divine plan to make redemption possible or to make it certain?"[91] John Murray makes the same point when he asks, "What does redemption mean? It does not mean redeemability, that we are placed in a redeemable position. It means that Christ purchased and procured redemption."[92] Likewise, Horton insists that the Calvinist view of limited atonement "maintains that Christ's death actually saves. Scripture nowhere teaches that Christ came into the world to make salvation possible, much less that it becomes actual because of faith in Christ."[93]

Two concerns are often expressed with the idea of a non-particular atonement. The first is universalism, the idea that everyone will be saved. "If it is unlimited in an absolute sense, then an atonement has been made for every person's sins. . . . It seems to follow from the idea of unlimited atonement that salvation is universal."[94] Since, of course, no one in this debate holds to universal salvation, the atonement, so the argument goes, must be a Calvinistic limited atonement. But what we have here is another form of the problem discussed earlier concerning Calvinism's failure to distinguish

89. Hunt, *What Love Is This?*, 259.

90. Piper even has a section heading titled "A Ransom For Many" yet fails to include or comment about 1 Tim 2:6: *"who gave Himself as a ransom for all."* Piper, *Five Points*, 48.

91. Sproul, *Reformed Theology*, 164, 168.

92. Murray, *Redemption Accomplished and Applied*, 63.

93. Horton, *For Calvinism*, 92.

94. Sproul, *Reformed Theology*, 164.

between an objective atonement that entailed a transaction between the Father and the Son, and a subjective appropriation of that atonement. The former is universal, the latter is limited to those who exercise faith. It is precisely the lumping together of the objective and subjective components of the atonement that artificially creates this supposed dilemma. That not everyone is actually saved despite the work of the cross is not because Christ's death was not intended for everyone, but rather because not everyone chooses to appropriate the fruit of the cross by exercising faith. So, the Calvinist's criticism is technically correct—the cross only makes salvation possible. But that is not a stripe against universal atonement, it is merely to say that God requires faith to appropriate the work of the cross. So, the cross makes salvation possible for anyone and everyone, but actual only for the person of faith. The Bible is clear: no faith, no salvation. In short, the work of the cross only becomes effective in an individual's life when appropriated by faith. The cross, technically, actually saves no one. "While the atonement is for man, it is essentially Godward rather than manward. Its authenticity and value in no way depend on the response of any man, but depend on its satisfaction of God and the demands of his righteousness."[95] Could no one have chosen to appropriate the work of the cross? Technically, yes, but this dynamic is intrinsic to the personal, relational interaction between man and God.[96] The scope of the atonement is succinctly described by Shank as "efficacious for all men potentially, for no man unconditionally, and for the Israel of God efficiently."[97]

The second concern among Calvinists is that if faith is a condition for receiving the benefits of the atonement then faith itself in some sense becomes a meritorious work. According to Sproul, "In this view [universal atonement] faith is not only a condition for redemption, but also one of the very *grounds* of redemption. If the atonement is not efficacious apart from faith, then faith must be necessary for the satisfaction of divine justice. Here faith becomes a *work* with a vengeance because its presence or absence in a sinner determines the efficacy of Christ's work of satisfaction for this person."[98] Horton concurs: "In this view, then, faith not only receives this reconciliation but accomplishes it, and faith becomes a saving work."[99] However, the Bible never views faith as a meritorious work that in any way contributes to the salvation of any individual; throughout the Bible, salvation is always and exclusively by grace which, by definition, excludes meritorious works (Eph 2:8, 9). Romans 3:23–25 explicitly indicates the relationship and sequence for the appropriation of the gift of salvation: "*For all have sinned and fall short of the glory of God, being justified as a gift by His grace through the redemption which is in Christ Jesus; whom God displayed*

---

95. Shank, *Elect in the Son*, 71.

96. "Definite atonement depersonalizes salvation. It does not retain the personal character of salvation. . . . Love, choice, and power are replaced by mechanical procedures." Warren, *Salvation*, 155.

97. Shank, *Elect in the Son*, 86.

98. Sproul, *Reformed Theology*, 165, emphasis mine.

99. Horton, *For Calvinism*, 96.

publicly as a propitiation in His blood through faith." Note the following: (i) the need (redemption) because all have sinned, (ii) justification (a fruit of the cross) is a gift motivated by God's grace, (iii) made possible by the blood of Christ, and (iv) this grace gift is appropriated by faith. Faith is never ever viewed as a meritorious work, rather it is consistently seen as the condition whereby God may impute his righteousness to the repenting and believing sinner, beginning with Abraham. As Rom 4:2, 3 makes clear: *"If Abraham was justified by works, he has something to boast about, but not before God. For what does the Scripture say? 'Abraham believed God, and it was credited to him as righteousness.'"*

Why do Calvinists view faith as a work that contributes in some way to one's salvation? The clue is found in Sproul's implied claim that the atonement has to be efficacious apart from faith, else faith becomes a meritorious work; as he states, "If the atonement is not efficacious apart from faith" then faith must be a contributing work. Again, only the failure to distinguish between the objective and subjective aspects of the atonement raises this specter. Objectively, the atonement is universally efficacious in satisfying the righteous demands of a holy God that sin be punished; subjectively, however, the atonement is not efficacious in the life of any individual apart from the *condition* of faith being met. This condition is a divinely required condition as many scriptures testify. (An example would be John 3:14, 15, *"And as Moses lifted up the serpent in the wilderness, even so must the Son of Man be lifted up, so that whoever* believes will *in him have eternal life."*) Any genuinely human entailment in the appropriating of salvation compromises Calvinism's monergism—all must be of God, including the redemptive application of the atonement as John Murray's book title makes clear: *Redemption Accomplished* and *Applied*. In this system the application of redemption must be all, and only, of God; there is no room for any form of genuine conditionality here. The biblical testimony however from Gen 2:16, 17 (the warning given to Adam to not eat of the fruit of the tree of the knowledge of good and evil) to Rev 22:14 (only those who have washed their robes may eat of the tree of life) is that the salvation of any individual is conditional upon faith. So, while the cross could save every single person potentially, whether the work of the cross is actually applied to any individual depends upon their faith. This is simply the way God, in his sovereign purposes, has set things up.

e) The Question of Double Payment for Sins

Jesus's death on the cross provided a payment for sins. Sometimes the Bible portrays the payment in terms of a ransom made (Mark 10:45; 1 Tim 2:6). The payment was required by God the Father and provided by God the Son. Only the death of the sinless Son of God would qualify as a sufficient payment for sins, this is why the animal sacrifices of the Old Testament are no longer required. His death was also vicarious, a death on behalf of sinners (Isa 53:4–5; 2 Cor 5:21; Gal 2:20). Jesus suffered the agonies of the cross as a propitiation—an atoning sacrifice designed to avert the wrath of a holy God against sin (Rom 3:25; Heb 2:17; 1 John 2:2; 4:10).

All this raises the question of whether it is just for Christ to give himself up "for all" and yet God demanding those who are non-elect to pay for their own sins in hell. This is an especially acute problem for those who advocate for an unlimited atonement. The puritan theologian John Owen addresses this issue in three related forms: (1) "If the full debt of all be paid to the utmost extent of the obligation, how comes to pass that so many are shut up in prison to eternity, never freed from their debt?" (2) "If the Lord, as a just creditor, ought to cancel all obligations . . . against such as have their debts so paid, whence is it that his wrath smokes against some to all eternity?" (3) "Is it probable that God calls any to a second payment and requires satisfaction of them for whom, by his own acknowledgement, Christ hath made that which is full and sufficient?"[100] For the Calvinist, only one of two possible answers can hold: (a) Christ's death did not cover all the sins of everyone, and so some sins are "left over" to be paid by the sinner himself, or (b) Christ fully paid the sins of only some (the elect). Since Scripture gives no grounds for the former, the latter must be true.[101]

The problem here is yet another manifestation of the initial basic problem previously discussed—the lumping together of the objective accomplishment of a universal atonement that is directed toward the just requirements of the Father, and the limited, restricted subjective appropriation of the benefits of the atonement (forgiveness of sin, reconciliation, etc.). By insisting on seeing these two aspects of the atonement as an indissoluble unit, proponents of limited atonement are forced to think in quantitative terms—those for whom Christ's death was intended are those, and only those, who actually have their sins forgiven.[102] If, as the Bible clearly does, we separate the event of the cross from its application in anyone's life, with the latter being conditional on faith, then it is quite reasonable to speak of a universal atonement that is objective and potentially universal in scope, and a particular application of the fruits of the cross to only those who meet the condition. Under these circumstances, it is only those who do not wish to receive the forgiveness the cross makes possible who must then pay the penalty for their sins themselves.

Related to this discussion is a rather fundamental point about the nature of salvation itself. The heart of salvation is not the cross, it is relationship, relationship with God. The cross is a means to that end, it is not an end in itself. Donald Lake puts it this way: "What condemns a man is not sins. Why? Because Christ's redemptive and

---

100. Cited by Sproul, *Reformed Theology*, 166.

101. Grudem, e.g., notes that "an important point that is not generally answered by advocates of the general redemption view is that people who are eternally condemned to hell suffer the penalty for all of their own sins, and therefore their penalty could not have been fully taken by Christ." Grudem, *Systematic Theology*, 507.

102. Berkhof is an example when he says, "It should be pointed out that there is an *inseparable connection* between the purchase and the actual bestowal of salvation." Berkhof, *Systematic Theology*, 395, emphasis mine.

atoning work is complete and satisfying. . . . The atonement is indeed a universal fact: the issue of every man's salvation turns not upon his sins, but rather upon his relationship to the Son."[103] And the key aspect of relationship with God is faith in Jesus Christ: *"For God did not send the Son into the world to judge the world, but that the world might be saved through Him. He who believes in Him is not judged; he who does not believe has been judged already, because he has not believed in the name of the only begotten Son of God"* (John 1:17–18). Belief in the Son is the criterion God has chosen for the appropriation of the fruit of the cross and hence salvation.[104] Again, no one need be excluded from the work of the cross (universal), but only those who exercise faith receive the benefits of the cross and hence actually enjoy salvation (particular). The offer of salvation is made to whosoever as a gift, made possible through the death of Christ—but the gift must be received, and the Bible clearly teaches that the God-ordained means of actually receiving the gift is faith.

f) Four-Point Calvinism?

The scriptural testimony seems so clear on general atonement that many Calvinists feel hard-pressed to deny it. Consequently, such believers are known as four-point-ers—holding to TUIP, but denying *L*, limited atonement. Millard Erickson is such a scholar. After carefully weighing all the arguments for and against both universal atonement and limited atonement he concludes "that the hypothesis of universal atonement is able to account for a larger segment of the biblical witness with less distortion than is the hypothesis of limited atonement."[105]

Bruce Ware is another Calvinist scholar who rejects a limited atonement. After summarizing the traditional Calvinist position on the extent of the atonement, he remarks: "I do not hold this view myself; I am a four-point Calvinist. . . . I am not convinced that this traditional Calvinist understanding is what the Bible teaches."[106] Other recent four-point Calvinists include the apologist Norman Geisler (1932–2019), theologian Donald G Bloesch (1928–2010), first president of Dallas Theological Seminary Lewis Sperry Chafer (1851–1952), and the Anglican John Stott (1921–1989).

I wish here to focus on just one aspect of this claim—the *consistency* of holding to *T, U, I,* and *P* while rejecting *L*. Recall that Calvinists believe that because of total depravity (*T*) no one is able to even respond positively to the call of the gospel and that, therefore, if anyone is to actually experience salvation it must be because God unconditionally

103. Lake, "He Died For All," 47.

104. Strictly speaking, in addition to the atoning sacrifice of the cross two other factors must be worked out before any individual experiences salvation itself: the first is the vindication of the cross by the resurrection of Christ (Rom 4:25), and personal appropriation of the benefits of the cross (forgiveness of sins, reconciliation, etc.) through the exercise of faith (Eph 2:8, 9).

105. Erickson, *Christian Theology*, 835.

106. Ware, "Calvinism and Arminianism," 5.

elected that individual (*U*); and also, that elect persons are brought to salvation irresistibly through the regenerating work of the Holy Spirit (*I*) and subsequently assured that he or she will persevere to the end (*P*). Is it really *consistent*, under these conditions, to hold that, despite all this monergistic work of God, from a four-pointer's perspective Christ's death was intended for everyone, and was universal in its purpose and scope, that Christ's sacrifice was for the benefit of the whole world?[107]

Some five-point Calvinists indirectly point out the inconsistency associated with four-point Calvinism by stressing the fact that all five points cohere together and are mutually dependent. Wayne Grudem is an example: "A balanced . . . perspective would seem to be to say that this teaching of particular redemption seems to us to be true, that it *gives logical consistency* to our theological system."[108] Millard Erickson, himself a four-pointer as noted earlier, admits that, after briefly reviewing the historical development of the doctrine of limited atonement, "These historical considerations suggest that being a consistent Calvinist requires holding to particular or limited atonement."[109] Piper, reflecting on the *I* of irresistible grace states, "You begin to see how closely this doctrine of [limited] atonement is connected with the previous one, irresistible grace."[110] John Murray concedes that "it is frequently objected that this doctrine [limited atonement] is inconsistent with the full and free offer of Christ in the gospel."[111] The logically consistent position is well summarized here: "If the Father has elected some sinners to eternal life and if the Holy Spirit applies the saving work of Christ only to the elect, then Christ, in harmony with the purpose of the Father and the Spirit, died on the cross for the elect alone."[112] Likewise, Dave Hunt is surely correct when he remarks that "while some who call themselves Calvinists reject Limited Atonement, it is irrational to do so while accepting the other four points. A leading Calvinist author writes: 'It is in this truth of limited atonement that the doctrine of sovereign election . . . comes into focus.' In other words, the whole Calvinistic system collapses if Limited Atonement is not biblical."[113]

But where, exactly, lies the inconsistency in four-point Calvinism? It lies in the indissoluble connection between the unconditional choosing of an elect few to be saved while at the same time holding to an atonement that is universal in scope.

107. Historically, not all Calvinists understood the universal aspect of the atonement in the same way. As David Allen explains: "Not all Calvinists who rejected limited atonement were lockstep in their explication of unlimited atonement. Some were English Hypothetical Universalists, some Amyraldian, some Baxterian, and some eclectic. The one common denominator is their belief in an unlimited atonement understood to mean that Christ died as a substitute for the sins of all people." Allen, *Extent of the Atonement*, xvii. The same variety of opinions would, no doubt, be true today.

108. Grudem, *Systematic Theology*, 603, emphasis mine.

109. Erickson, *Christian Theology*, 829.

110. Piper, *Five Points*, 38.

111. Murray, *Redemption Accomplished and Applied*, 65.

112. Godfrey, "Atonement," 57.

113. Hunt, *What Love Is This?*, 298.

There is an intrinsic contradiction between believing in a restrictive, limited number chosen by God for salvation while at the same time believing that the atonement, the basis upon which the elect become saved, is universal. All five points of Calvinistic soteriology cohere together and it would do violence to deny any one element while holding to the others.[114] In particular, within a Calvinistic soteriology, given a limited number of the elect chosen by God for salvation, and given that Christ's death did not merely make salvation possible but actually efficacious, then it is quite inconsistent to argue, as four-point Calvinism must, that Christ's atonement was universal, for all men. In short, as Lake states it: "The issue of the atonement cannot be separated from the larger framework of the issue of election."[115] Yet this is precisely what four-point Calvinism does.

g) Amyraldism

Amyraldism takes its name from the French theologian Moise Amyraut (1596–1664). Amyraut developed his distinctive theology as a reaction to what he perceived to be an excessive emphasis on predestination and election in Reformed theology with its restrictive view of the intent of the atonement.[116] He believed that such an emphasis compromised the chief theme of biblical theology which was on the faith that justifies. Amyraut, while agreeing with the basic Reformed covenantal perspective on the duality of a covenant of works that held before the fall, and a covenant of grace subsequent to the fall, modified the latter in a distinctive way. "In Amyraldianism the covenant of grace was further divided into two parts: a conditional covenant of universal grace, and an unconditional covenant of particular grace."[117] In this way Amyraut sought a mediating position between the strict particularism of Calvinism and the universal thrust of Arminianism.[118] The resulting theology as far as predestination was concerned came to be known as hypothetical universal predestination.

Amyraut's theology had direct consequences for the question of the extent of the atonement. This may be summarized as "Christ bore the sins of every person without exception, but since God knew that no one would embrace Christ apart from the gift of faith, he elected some to receive the benefits of Christ's work."[119]

---

114. It would probably be fair to say that a significant cause of the appeal of Calvinism to many as a doctrine of salvation is its coherence—all the elements dovetail together and are interdependent in a comprehensive and systematic manner.

115. Lake, "He died for All," 45.

116. Much of this discussion is adapted from Demarest, "Amyraldianism," 41. The terms Amyraldianism and Amyraldism are synonymous.

117. Demarest, "Amyraldianism," 41.

118. It is probably true to say that Arminianism, as discussed in the chapter on the history of the doctrine of salvation, is the major non-Calvinistic view even today. It is characterized by its stress on the universal bone-fide offer of the gospel to "all, everyone, the world."

119. Horton, *For Calvinism*, 92.

Amyraut's theory hinged on an important distinction. While all persons possess "the natural faculties (i.e., intellect and will) by which to respond to God's universal offer of grace, he in fact suffers from a moral inability due to the corrupting effects of sin upon the mind."[120] Thus, according to Amyraldism, the universal aspect of the gospel and its reception is purely hypothetical, whereas the particular application by God through the granting of faith to the elect is real. As Demarest puts it: "Amyraldianism thus involves a purely ideal universalism together with a real particularism."[121] With respect to the atonement specifically, this meant that on the one hand, Christ died for everyone, there was a universal intent in the atonement, but that on the other hand, in fact and in reality only the particular elect would obtain the benefit of Christ's death (salvation). In this manner Amyraut "viewed his theology as a corrective to much of seventeenth century Calvinism, which denied the universal, conditional will of God in its preoccupation with the unconditional decree. And he disputed with Arminianism, which failed to see that a person's salvation was effectively grounded in the absolute purpose of God conceived on the basis of his own sovereign pleasure."[122]

In assessing this theology, we may applaud the attempt to take seriously the many universal statements found in Scripture as noted earlier—and all within a generally Calvinistic framework. However, in the attempt to reconcile both the universal and the particular, Amyraldism must be judged to have failed. Why? Because, in reality, the particular overrules the universal. Once the notion of a depravity understood Calvinistically as entailing total inability is accepted, it logically follows that the witness of the universal texts must be cancelled in favor of an all-determining decree that stipulates that only a few shall be saved, and the work of the cross applied by God unconditionally to the elect alone. The hypothetical universalism is truly just that, hypothetical—and correspondingly redundant and vacuous of any salvific significance. It is no wonder that it is mostly Calvinists who are open to this theological model for it leaves fully intact Calvinism's particular atonement which, in both intent and application is limited to the elect preordained before the foundation of the world, while appearing to give weight to the many scriptures testifying to a general atonement. Once more, monergism reigns supreme.

h) The Problem of a Justification for Evangelism

No Calvinist can consistently say to anyone indiscriminately, "God loves you and sent his Son to die on the cross for the forgiveness of your sins." Why? Because this statement would only be true and applicable to the elect alone. Of course, the problem is that no one knows who the elect are.[123] What does it mean to evangelize, to proclaim

120. Demarest, "Amyraldianism," 41.

121. Demarest, "Amyraldianism," 41.

122. Demarest, "Amyraldianism," 42.

123. As we shall see later when discussing the issue of Christian assurance, within a consistently

the gospel, within a salvific context in which it is known that Jesus's death could only apply to a select unknown few chosen by God before the creation?

Grudem, after citing 2 Tim 2:10 (*"For this reason I endure all things for the sake of those who are chosen, so that they also may obtain the salvation which is in Christ Jesus and with it eternal glory"*), obviously understands the elect here to be those sinners chosen by God before the foundation of the world and who, at some point in time, would be saved. He says that Paul "knows that God has chosen some people to be saved, and he sees this as an encouragement to preach the gospel, even if it means enduring great suffering."[124] But the context indicates that the elect are the Christians who are *contemporaries* of Timothy, for Paul immediately goes on to speak of the glories awaiting Christians like himself. Furthermore, the salvation Paul is thinking about is future glorification—*"we will also live with him . . . we will also reign with him"* (vv. 11, 12). So, while Grudem understand v. 10 as applying evangelistically to contemporary unbelievers, the context indicates Paul's willingness to suffer for the benefit of Christians and their future hope of consummated salvation. If this analysis is correct, then Grudem's explanation for Paul's motivation to evangelize, namely that God has chosen some people to be saved, misses the point; Paul is not saying that he is motivated to evangelize for the sake of unknown (to him, but known to God) elect, but that he is willing to endure all things for the sake of his fellow Christians (v. 11).

Grudem's rationale for evangelizing is fairly typical among Calvinists, namely that God has chosen some to be saved even if we don't know who they are and so evangelism should take place so that the elect may be granted by God the faith needed to be saved. In this situation, however, evangelism is less a *proclamation* of good news, and more an *opportunity* for the elect to be identified. Evangelism here devolves down to the occasion when the elect become manifest. In this scenario, there is no component of evangelism that entails urging someone to carefully consider the call of the gospel and to consequently repent, rather, irrespective of how the gospel is communicated, the elect will infallibly believe and the non-elect will never believe.

Another rationale sometimes appealed to by Calvinists to justify evangelizing the lost is simply that God has commanded it (Matt 28:19; 2 Tim 4:2). But is this the best motivation? Isn't a better motivation one of concern for the lost as an expression of love for the lost? How does a cold "God tells us to evangelize" comport with Paul's agony and willingness to be accursed for the sake of his fellow Jews (Rom 9)? It is doubtful that Paul was motivated only by a strict obedience to a command of Christ; rather, he was acutely aware of the terrible consequences for those without Christ and, out of love for his fellow man, sought their highest good—which was to tell them about Christ and his saving work with the hope that they would repent and receive the salvation God, though Christ, graciously offers.

Calvinist framework, not even current Christians can be certain they are in fact among the elect.

124. Grudem, *Systematic Theology*, 674.

Calvinists typical respond to the requirement to evangelize by noting that God has not only foreordained the end (salvation of the elect and reprobation of the non-elect), but also the means to that end, namely gospel proclamation. It is true that God has ordained that the gospel be preached in order that individuals be given the opportunity to believe: *"So faith comes from hearing, and hearing by the word of Christ"* (Rom 10:17). But for the Calvinist those sinners chosen by God for salvation will inevitably and infallibly come to faith, and the reprobate will inevitably and unavoidably not come to faith. The whole process of evangelism and gospel proclamation has taken on a mechanical "press this switch and this must happen" flavor. In fact, Paul's following citation from Isa 65:2 in Rom 10:21, *"But as for Israel He says, 'All the day long I have stretched out MY hands to a disobedient and obstinate people,'"* really doesn't make sense within a Calvinistic framework. In an ultimate sense the concept of disobedience doesn't make sense. Why? Because the picture of God pleading with people to repent and believe the gospel suggests that it may be possible that anyone be able to oppose God's will and reject God's call. But for the Calvinist, in an ultimate sense, no one opposes God's will. There is no meaningful, personal dynamic between heaven and earth in gospel proclamation because what will be will be—the elect will infallibly and unavoidable be saved and the lost will likewise infallibly remain in that condition.

Furthermore, if Calvinists insist that God has ordained that the elect come to salvation through the evangelizing efforts of the church, this would seem to suggest that if the church or individual evangelists refrained from proclaiming the gospel then no one would be saved. But, of course, this is nonsense—by definition, the elect will be saved no matter what. Their salvation was decreed before the foundation of the world. To deny this and insist that God chooses to save the elect through gospel proclamation comes close to making the salvation of the elect conditional after all—conditional on the evangelizing efforts of the church.

Within a context of an atonement limited to only the elect, there is the question of sincerity in a universal proclamation of the gospel. The Calvinist William Hendriksen, commenting on the Great Commission (Matt 28:18–20), states that when Jesus commanded his disciples to "go" to all nations, the "time to make earnest preparations for the propagation of the gospel throughout the world had now arrived."[125] The motivation for such evangelism was that Christ "is worthy of the homage, faith, and obedience of all men."[126] This is a strange rationale. Jesus calls his disciples to make disciples of "all nations" and yet, according to Calvinism, this effort is pre-doomed to failure because, apparently, most people are unable to become disciples as witnessed by the majority who die in their sins. Their inability, in the final analysis, is not due to their choice to reject the gospel message, but rather because God has determined that they are not elect. Furthermore, for the majority of most groups of hearers, the gospel is not good news of hope and reconciliation, but merely the occasion whereby

125. Hendriksen, *Matthew*, 999.
126. Hendriksen, *Matthew*, 999.

their damnation by God becomes evident. How can a Calvinist make disciples of all nations under these circumstances? "Could it really be God's will for the gospel to be preached to those for whom Christ did not die, and for multitudes to be urged to believe from whom God withholds the necessary faith? Isn't this not only dishonest but cruel?"[127] Surely, God's call that the disciples, and by extension his church, proclaim a gospel of good news to all nations is because potentially all nations; may believe the gospel and find salvation. And if salvation may be potentially found by all it must be because the extent of Christ's death was universal—anyone without exception could be saved, conditioned on faith alone.

A strong sense of divine sovereignty, the bedrock of Calvinism, logically makes evangelism and its basis, the atonement, redundant and ultimately unnecessary. Famously, this sentiment was made explicit when the pioneer missionary to India, William Carey (1761–1834), approached the Calvinistic deacon board of his Baptist church to seek their backing for his proposal to engage in missions work in India. It is said that "at a meeting of Baptist leaders in the late 1700s, a newly ordained minister stood to argue for the value of overseas missions. He was abruptly interrupted by an older minister who said, 'Young man, sit down! You are an enthusiast. When God pleases to convert the heathen, he'll do it without consulting you or me.'"[128] Calvinists could agree that the deacon board were mistaken because they failed to recognize that God uses secondary means to bring the elect to himself. However, the weakness of this argument can be seen if the question is asked: Would the elect fail to come to salvation if Carey were not to go to India? The answer, from a consistent Calvinist perspective must be no. Why? Because the elect have been predestined for salvation before the foundation of the world and inevitably and unavoidably will be saved.

In the early decades of the twentieth century a controversy raged over what was then called "duty faith." Should consistent Calvinist preachers tell all their hearers that every person was duty bound to repent and believe the gospel? The problem lay in the doctrine of total depravity which, as held by Calvinists, states that no one is capable of doing anything good that is of any spiritual significance. Repenting and believing are spiritually significant goods. This dilemma vexed more than a few Calvinist preachers. Some simply denied the validity of calling anyone to duty faith. Some responded by denying the limited extent of the atonement. The famous English Baptist preacher Charles Spurgeon, who had a deep concern for the lost, was a four-point Calvinist and wrote: "I cannot imagine a more ready instrument in the hands of Satan for the ruin of souls than a minister who tells sinners that it is not their duty to repent of their sins or to believe in Christ, and who has the arrogance to call himself a gospel minister, while he teaches that God hates some men infinitely and unchangeably for no reason whatever but simply because he chooses to do so."[129]

---

127. Hunt, *What Love Is This?*, 260.

128. Galli and Olsen, *131 Christians*, 244.

129. Spurgeon, *New Park Street Pulpit*, 6:28–29; cited by Hunt, *What Love Is This?*, 299.

Spurgeon was quite inconsistent in rejecting the *L* of TULIP, but his concern accurately reflected the Bible's witness to God's universal love.

Finally, the issue of consistency needs to be addressed directly with respect to this matter of evangelism.[130] We may briefly note that Paul used various means to reach out to his unbelieving hearers. He reasoned with them (Acts 17:2; 18:19)—but what is the point of reasoning with someone predestined by God to a lost eternity? He viewed his ministry as being an ambassador for Christ through whom God would appeal to his unbelieving hearers to be reconciled to God, immediately appealing to the cross as a basis for such an appeal: *"Therefore, we are ambassadors for Christ, as though God were making an appeal through us; we beg you on behalf of Christ, be reconciled to God. He made Him who knew no sin to be sin on our behalf, so that we might become the righteousness of God in Him"* (2 Cor 5:20, 21). To reason, to beg, to appeal to an indiscriminate audience of unbelievers only makes sense if there was the real possibility that some would respond to the reasoning, to the begging, to the appealing—but is such a scenario consistent with a situation in which those who have been preordained to hell, apart from anything they do, will inevitably fail to listen? As Hunt notes: "If only those elected by God to salvation . . . believe . . . would it not be vain to attempt to persuade anyone to embrace the gospel? . . . Since there is nothing one can do to change one's eternal destiny . . . shouldn't one just let the inevitable take its course? Although many Calvinists would object to this view, inevitably, this is the practical conclusion to which this fatalistic dogma leads."[131]

The Calvinist preacher Spurgeon sometimes allowed his concern that the lost be saved to overrule the logic of the soteriological system he claimed to embrace. He said, "As it is my wish and your wish . . . so it is God's wish that all men should be saved . . . he is no less benevolent than we are."[132] But of course, such sentiments are not consistent with the Calvinism he held. This sort of inconsistency is heard virtually every Sunday by preachers who with their mind espouse Calvinism and yet, quite inconsistently, appeal to congregants to evangelize their unbelieving neighbors and friends. As Hunt remarks: "It is impossible to reconcile this statement [of Spurgeon's] with the doctrine of Limited Atonement, which Spurgeon at other times affirmed. It is irrational to say that God sincerely desires the salvation of all, yet sent His Son to die only for some."[133]

---

130. The question of logical consistency has been an underlying critique through most of this study, though not always brought out explicitly.

131. Hunt, *What Love Is This?*, 443.

132. Spurgeon, *Metropolitan Tabernacle Pulpit*, 26:49–52; cited by Hunt, *What Love Is This?*, 47.

133. Hunt, *What Love Is This?*, 47.

Conclusion

The Bible consistently speaks of an atonement made by Christ that was intended to benefit potentially the whole world, every single human being. That many do not enjoy the fruits of that atoning sacrifice Calvinism attributes to the decree of God that applies salvation to only a select few (the elect). Non-Calvinists on the other hand, explain the restricted number of people actually saved to their willful resistance and rejection of the work of Christ. The former is grounded in the inscrutable, secret will of God whereas the latter is grounded in the wickedness of men who "loved the darkness rather than the Light" (John 3:19). The biblical data is so pervasive that Calvinists have attempted, quite inconsistently, to ameliorate the many references to a universal atonement by appeal to only four of the five points of Calvinism (rejecting the *L*, Limited Atonement), or to a hypothetical universalism (Amyraldism). However, the Bible is clear—God loved the world and so sent his son as a propitiation for the whole world (John 3:16; Rom 3:25; 1 John 2:2).

Because of the close connection between the love of God and the atonement, to limit the latter is to limit the former. Consequently, Calvinists are often forced to speak of God's love in a qualified way—consistent Calvinists even stating that God does not love everyone. For example, Houck, a Reformed pastor, writes, quite consistently, "It cannot be that God loves everyone. Since God's love is sovereign and therefore always a saving love, only those who experience the salvation of the Lord can be the objects of His love.[134] However, such a limitation on the scope of God's love contradicts the many scriptures which clearly state that God loves the world (John 3:16), sinners (Rom 5:8), mankind (Titus 3:4). God is described as the God of love (2 Cor 13:11), and is defined as love (*"God is love,"* 1 John 4:8). From the beginning of God's plan of redemption, God's motivating love was that through Abraham's seed "all *the families of the earth will be blessed"* (Gen 12:3). In short, to limit God's love and hence Christ's atoning sacrifice to a few (the elect) is necessary in order to be consistent with Calvinism's doctrine of salvation, but is not consistent with the biblical witness of God's love for all.

The root cause for Calvinism's rejection of a universal atonement is the failure to distinguish between, on the one hand, an objective salvation that is universal in scope and relates to the sacrificial work of the cross directed toward appeasing the holy wrath of the Father against sin and, on the other hand, a subjective appropriation of that atoning sacrifice by faith on the part of the sinner. By lumping the two together, such that both the atonement itself and also its application in the life of a believer are a unit, Calvinism creates tensions regarding the doctrine of the atonement that Scripture itself knows nothing of, and which requires a doctrine that limits the atonement, even in its intent, to only the elect.

---

134. Houck, *God's Sovereignty in Salvation*, 10; cited by Hunt, *What Love Is This?*, 284.

Finally, a limited atonement doctrine has practical implications, especially in the motivation for evangelism. (It also has implications relating to Christian assurance of salvation, but that will be dealt with in the next chapter.) Since the salvation of the elect is grounded in the eternal decree of God and has been preordained, then the elect will most assuredly be saved—there can be no question about that. The salvation of the elect is unconditioned in anything in the elect persons themselves, but also not conditioned ultimately by anything outside of the will of God. This eviscerates the need to evangelize because, ultimately, whether that elect person is evangelized or not, his or her salvation is absolutely assured and can never be brought into question.

5

Irresistible Grace: Can God's Grace Not Be Rejected?

R. C. Sproul laments the fact that too many non-Calvinists (whom he pejoratively labels semi-Pelagians) find it hard to accept Calvinism and that even "conversion to Christ does not instantly cure us of our Pelagian tendencies." Apparently, this is due to the fact that "Pelagianism is reinforced on every side." Furthermore, "in the church we are widely exposed to Arminianism, which has had American evangelicalism in a stranglehold since the days of Charles Finney."[1] In his book *Reformed Theology*, Sproul recounts how John Gerstner was "startled" at learning that "regeneration comes before faith, not after it or as a result of it, presumably because Gerstner had, until that moment, been steeped in 'Semi-Pelagianism.'"[2]

There is something strange about this admission—it raises the obvious question: How is it that Bible-believing Christians, brothers and sisters in Christ, who love Christ and his Word, nevertheless have such strong "Pelagian tendencies" and struggle to see Reformed soteriology as precisely and accurately expressing biblical teaching? Could it be that the doctrines of Calvinism, and especially irresistible grace, are simply not to be found in a straightforward reading of the Bible? One has to be taught (indoctrinated?) Calvinism to "see" what the Bible *really* teaches concerning salvation, otherwise those pesky Pelagian tendencies get the Bible all wrong!

Like the previous elements in TULIP, the doctrine of irresistible Grace is logically required to retain the coherency of the entire system.[3] For God's sovereign will concerning the salvation of the elect to be assured the application of grace must be irresistible.[4] This close connection between election and irresistible grace may be seen, for example, in the following: "Those whom God chose before the creation of the

1. Sproul, *Reformed Theology*, 180.

2. Sproul, *Reformed Theology*, 179.

3. Of course, logical coherency is a necessary component of truth, but not sufficient in itself to validate the truth status of the system. The truthfulness of a doctrine depends on the degree to which it corresponds to reality—in this case, the reality of the biblical worldview.

4. Grace has a variety of nuanced meanings in the New Testament epistles, all related to the idea of undeserved favor, usually on the part of God toward his human creation. Here I shall be referring to saving grace, the undeserved favor, goodwill, or help God provides for the potential salvation of all people. See Bauer, *Greek-English Lexicon*, 877.

world, he also calls [effectually] in due time by his Spirit."[5] In other words, unconditional election requires an irresistible grace.

Furthermore, due to total depravity no one could possibly do a good such as believe the gospel apart from God causing them to be born again first—this makes the salvation of the elect both possible and certain. "If the doctrine of total depravity . . . is true there can be no salvation without the reality of irresistible grace."[6] Total depravity requires an irresistible grace. Here, as elsewhere monergism resigns supreme. Irresistible grace is a requirement of the system. In the words of Bruce Ware, the Calvinist doctrines of election, calling, and irresistible grace "are mutually dependent and mutually entailing."[7] It is the task of this chapter to carefully examine Calvinism's claim concerning the functioning of grace in salvation and see whether the Bible supports a doctrine of irresistible grace or not.

One final point is worth noting before proceeding with our study of this doctrine. It is probably fair to say that this particular doctrine is the most complex studied so far. Several interdependent doctrines and motifs intersect with this doctrine. For example, how exactly does the Holy Spirit relate to an unbeliever in the process of regeneration? What is the nature of faith? Human free will, its reality and nature, is also involved with this study. So too is the relationship between sovereignty, grace, faith, regeneration, and the logical sequence between faith and regeneration. How are we to understand those scriptures that speak of persons resisting God's grace (Acts 7:51)? And the reason why one person believes the gospel and another does not. All these questions and issues will need to be explored as we proceed.

The Calvinist's Understanding of Irresistible Grace

John Piper

"Irresistible grace refers to the sovereign work of God to overcome the rebellion of our heart and bring us to faith in Christ so that we can be saved." Furthermore, "The doctrine of irresistible grace means that God is sovereign and can conquer all resistance when he wills." In other words, "It means that the Holy Spirit, whenever he chooses, can overcome all resistance and make his influence irresistible."[8]

---

5. Horton, *For Calvinism*, 102. The effectual call is that call of God upon the elect sinner, usually through the proclamation of the gospel, whereby he or she is infallibly acted upon by God's Spirit such that they inevitably and unavoidably turn to God in faith. This is also a manifestation of irresistible grace. It is contrasted with the general call made to all through either creation or the gospel but which the non-elect inevitably reject.

6. Piper, *Five Points*, 27.

7. Ware, "Effectual Calling," 208.

8. Piper, *Five Points*, 26.

Michael Horton

"The Spirit melts the hard hearts of his elect and causes what was once an offense to become marvelously sweet and delightful."[9]

Wayne Grudem

Refers to the fact that "God effectively calls people and also gives them regeneration, and both actions guarantee that we will respond in saving faith."[10]

R. C. Sproul

Monergistic regeneration "describes an action by which God the Holy Spirit works on a human being without this person's assistance or cooperation. . . . To quicken a person who is spiritually dead is something only God can do. . . . In regeneration the soul of man is utterly passive until it has been made alive."[11]

R. K. McGegor Wright

"[God's] saving power cannot . . . be set aside by the creature, for saving grace is finally irresistible. . . . God regenerates each elect person so that he or she invariably responds willingly to the gospel. . . . The natural resistance of the fallen nature is invariably overcome."[12] Wright explains further: "When the gospel is heard by one of the elect, the Holy Spirit takes that word and applies it savingly to the heart, ensuring the begetting of eternal life within that soul."[13]

Bruce Ware

Effectual calling and irresistible grace are "the work of God's Spirit, through the word of the gospel, by which he opens the blind eyes and enlivens the hardened hearts of those dead in sin. . . . The Spirit supernaturally liberates the human heart from sin's clutches to turn from sin and joyfully accept God's gracious provision of salvation in Christ. . . . [This is] the doctrine of God's effectual calling of sinners to saving faith, by the word of the gospel and through the provision of irresistible grace."[14]

Westminster Confession of Faith

"All those whom God hath predestined unto life, and only those, he is pleased, in his appointed and accepted time, effectually to call, by his Word and Spirit, out of that state of sin and death, in which they are by nature, to grace and

9. Horton, *For Calvinism*, 101.
10. Grudem, *Systematic Theology*, 700.
11. Sproul, *Reformed Theology*, 184.
12. Wright, *No Place for Sovereignty*, 131.
13. Wright, *No Place for Sovereignty*, 132.
14. Ware, "Effectual Calling," 204. Ware here combines effectual calling and irresistible grace into a unity which he calls ECG: the effectual call and irresistible grace "are two aspects of one reality." Ware, "Effectual Calling," 204.

salvation, by Jesus Christ; enlightening their minds spiritually and savingly to understand the things of God, taking away their heart of stone, and giving unto them a heart of flesh; renewing their wills, and, by his almighty power, determining them to that which is good, and effectually drawing them to Jesus Christ, yet so, as they come most freely, being made willing by his grace."[15]

A. W. Pink

"Here then is the first thing, in time, which God does in His own elect. He lays hold of those who are spiritually dead and quickens them into newness of life. . . . By His irresistible power He transforms a sinner into a saint."[16]

From this sample of Calvinist writers, we see that irresistible grace entails:

- The Calvinist understanding of total depravity as meaning a total inability to respond to the gospel.

- A determination by God to unilaterally and unconditionally save a relative few, the elect.

- To effect this salvation through a regenerating operation of the Holy Spirit upon the individual which cannot be resisted, and which

- Enables the elect person to turn to Christ in faith—i.e., to believe the gospel, and thus

- Regeneration precedes faith.

An Examination of Key Biblical Texts Used to Justify Irresistible Grace

Ware helpfully reminds us that both Calvinists and non-Calvinists share much concerning the doctrine of salvation, including that salvation is by grace through faith, justification is by faith. Furthermore, there is much similarity of understanding concerning adoption, union with Christ, sanctification, and the glorification of true believers.[17] However, a key area of difference lies in the question concerning the calling of God to faith and repentance and the role of grace in the call-faith-repentance-regeneration nexus. Some of the most common texts used by Calvinists to defend their view of an effectual call that works through an irresistible grace are examined below. As in previous chapters we will examine these texts to see if they do in fact support the idea of an irresistible work of God's Spirit upon the elect.

15. *Westminster Confession of Faith*, 10.1.

16. Pink, *Sovereignty of God*, 79, 80.

17. Ware, "Effectual Calling," 205.

Ezekiel 36:26–27

> "*Moreover, I will give you a new heart and put a new spirit within you; and I will remove the heart of stone from your flesh and give you a heart of flesh. I will put My Spirit within you and cause you to walk in My statutes, and you will be careful to observe My ordinances.*"

Grudem, commenting on this verse, says, "[The] sovereign work of God in regeneration was also predicted in the prophecy of Ezekiel."[18] Likewise, Michael Horton cites this text to justify the claim that "the Spirit . . . [liberates] the will not only to assent to the truth but to trust in Christ. Regeneration or effectual calling is something that happens to those who do not have the moral capacity to convert themselves, yet it not only happens to them; it happens within them, winning their consent."[19] Wright also appeals to Ezek 36 "to show that God will certainly (irresistibly) fulfill [the] promise" of God's future regeneration of the elect in Israel.[20]

In its context, these verses form part of a series of promises God made to Israel in exile in Babylon. These included restoration to the land (vv. 24, 28), fertility of land (vv. 29, 30, 34), and the promise of the Spirit, as in our verses. Certainly, this passage (vv. 26, 27) refers to the Old Testament witness to a future work of God's Spirit in a new covenant (Jer 31). The same sentiment was expressed by Moses: "*Moreover the Lord your God will circumcise your heart and the heart of your descendants, to love the Lord your God with all your heart and with all your soul, so that you may live*" (Deut 30:6), and by Jeremiah: "'*But this is the covenant which I will make with the house of Israel after those days,' declares the Lord, 'I will put My law within them and on their heart I will write it; and I will be their God, and they shall be My people*'" (Jer 31:33).

The realization of this spiritual reality that God would accomplish occurs in the age begun with the coming of Jesus. Its clearest expression is found in John 3 in the metaphor of new birth. In this passage, Jesus insists that a new birth is necessary for anyone to enter the kingdom of God (John 3:3). This new birth is later described by Jesus as being "born of the Spirit" (v. 8). This is what theologians refer to as regeneration. Not insignificantly, in this same passage Jesus teaches concerning another eschatological gift, namely that of eternal life: "*As Moses lifted up the serpent in the wilderness, even so must the Son of Man be lifted up; so that whoever believes will in Him have eternal life. For God so loved the world, that He gave His only begotten Son, that whoever believes in Him shall not perish, but have eternal life*" (John 3:14–16).[21] What Jesus's teaching on regeneration shows is that it is conditional, not unilateral and

---

18. Grudem, *Systematic Theology*, 699.

19. Horton, *For Calvinism*, 110.

20. Wright, *No Place for Sovereignty*, 134.

21. It should come as no surprise that Jesus connects the Spirit's regenerating work with eternal life since the Spirit is the "*Spirit of life*" (Rom 8:2). In Gal 6:8, Paul connects the work of the Spirit specifically to eternal life: "*The one who sows to the Spirit will from the Spirit reap eternal life*" (Gal 6:8).

unconditional. What is the condition to be met in order to be born again and to receive eternal life? It is faith—it is only applicable to "whoever believes." Conditionality eliminates an unconditional application of the Spirit to anyone's life. Just as any Israelite who exercised faith by looking up to the bronze serpent would enjoy continued life (and not be killed by a serpent), so according to Jesus himself, anyone who exercises faith by looking up to him—especially his atoning work of the cross—would find eternal life. Certainly, whoever believed would be born again, be regenerated, be given a new heart that would motivate such a believer to obedience to the law of Christ (1 Cor 9:21; Gal 6:2). But certainty concerning the blessings of the Spirit following faith must not be confused with irresistibility toward the Spirit.[22]

In fact, even in the larger context of this promise made to ancient Israel, there is more than a hint of conditionality. Contrary to the desolation of Jerusalem that marked the beginning of the exile, God's plans included the blessings of the repopulation of the cities in Israel: "*I will increase their men like a flock*" (v. 37b). But, and this is an important qualifier, God would do this only in response to Israel's asking God to do this for them: "*This also I will let the house of Israel ask Me to do for them*" (v. 37a).

Another point worth mentioning is that the passage, even in its entire context (Ezek 36:22–37), says absolutely nothing about an irresistible work that God would do. Yes, he would do a marvelous work, that is most certainly assured (though conditionally as indicated above), but the passage nowhere hints that this would be done by God irresistibly as Calvinists claim. Such an understanding has to be read into the passage.

John 1:11–13

> "*He came to His own, and those who were His own did not receive Him. But as many as received Him, to them He gave the right to become children of God, even to those who believe in His name, who were born, not of blood nor of the will of the flesh nor of the will of man, but of God.*"

These verses, together with John 3:3–8 (Jesus interaction with Nicodemus and Jesus insistence that new birth is necessary to enter the kingdom of God), are often appealed to by Calvinists to reinforce the notion of an irresistibly applied grace in salvation. By rightly stressing that regeneration itself is a work of God alone, Calvinists bring in the assumption that *every* aspect of salvation is likewise a work of God alone. In other words, it supports the mistaken idea that salvation is entirely monergistic.

---

22. This confusion seems to be present when Wright says, "Deuteronomy 30:6 states as a promise of God that he will 'circumcise your hearts,' a reference to God's future regeneration of the elect in Israel. Later prophets (as in Ezek 36) show that God will certainly (irresistibly) fulfil that promise." Wright, *No Place for Sovereignty*, 134. However, certainty and irresistibility are two quite different things.

The subject of this verse concerns those authorized to consider themselves as children of God. Just as children enter the world through physical birth, so there is a spiritual analogue. There is an important difference, though, that John stresses here: whereas physical birth takes place within a strictly physical framework, spiritual birth does not entail physical categories of any sort. Carson helpfully explains: "Being born into the family of God is quite different from being born into a human family. 'Natural descent' . . . avails nothing. . . . Spiritual birth is not the product of sexual desire, 'the will of the flesh,' . . . [nor] the result of a husband's will. . . . New birth is, finally, nothing other than an act of God."[23]

Like the Ezekiel passage discussed above, the stress here is on God's role in regeneration—new birth, like new heart, is not something a person can provide or experience through self-effort. No one disputes this, and so it is somewhat strange to see Calvinists seemingly suggest that non-Calvinists may in fact deny this. Horton, for example, commenting on Jesus's interaction with Nicodemus in John 3, says, "Jesus is not telling Nicodemus how he can bring about his new birth, but how the Spirit accomplishes it."[24] Similarly, Piper says, "The birth that brings one into the family of God is not possible by the will of man."[25]

Why this stress by Calvinists on that which all Christians agree can only be accomplished by the work of God's Spirit? Because, by emphasizing the divine action in regeneration, the assumption is made that the *appropriation* of the Spirit's grace is also entirely a work of God. As Hunt points out: "John 1:13 is cited by Calvinists as proof that man can have no part whatsoever in his salvation, not even in believing the gospel (hence the necessity of Irresistible Grace)."[26] As Piper says, "This new birth is the effect of irresistible grace, because it is an act of sovereign creation."[27] Grudem also stresses the completely passive role associated with regeneration: "In the work of regeneration we play no active role at all. It is instead totally a work of God. . . . [Regeneration is] a sovereign work of God."[28] In short, Calvinists see this emphasis on the work of God in regeneration as reinforcing the notion of monergism in the whole of experienced salvation—all is of God alone. If anyone is going to be born of God's Spirit, it is because of a grace that has been applied unilaterally, unconditionally, and irresistibly.

However, our passage clearly indicates that those who are regenerated are those who "*received him*" (Jesus), and such reception is equated with those who choose to "*believe in His name*" (v. 12). It is unjustified exegetically to lump together God's

23. Carson, *John*, 126. Likewise, John 3:6 stresses the difference between natural and spiritual birth: "*That which is born of the flesh is flesh, and that which is born of the Spirit is spirit.*"

24. Horton, *For Calvinism*, 103.

25. Piper, *Five Points*, 35. Wright similarly feels the need to stress the obvious: "One thing is made very clear in the Bible: regeneration is *not* brought about by 'the will of the flesh, nor of the will of man, but of God,' (John 1:13)." Wright, *No Place for Sovereignty*, 133, emphasis original.

26. Hunt, *What Love Is This?*, 444.

27. Piper, *Five Points*, 35.

28. Grudem, *Systematic Theology*, 699.

work in regeneration with the condition required to be born again in the first place—namely faith. "Is the new birth imposed upon a man by a sovereign God's irresistible grace? Certainly not. It comes by faith in Christ."[29] According to the Apostle Peter being born again is for those who have been obedient to revealed truth and by the reception of *the living and enduring word of God*—not by an irresistibly applied grace (1 Pet 1:22, 23).

John 6:44

> *"No one can come to Me unless the Father who sent Me draws him;*
> *and I will raise him up on the last day."*

There are four verses in John 6 that appear to uphold a strongly deterministic account of those who come to Jesus for salvation. These are John 6:37, 39, 44, 65.[30] These verses are appealed to by Calvinists to justify a doctrine of unconditional election and irresistible grace.

With respect to v. 44, the drawing to Jesus by the Father, Calvinists see here a drawing that is effectual because irresistible: "Here the emphasis is on the divine decree of predestination carried out in history. . . . The drawing of which these passages speak indicates a very powerful—we may even say, an irresistible—activity. To be sure, man resists, but his resistance is ineffective. It is in that sense that we speak of God's grace as being irresistible."[31] John Piper describes this drawing as "the sovereign work of grace" and later, when explaining why Judas betrayed Jesus states that he "was not 'drawn' by the Father. The decisive, irresistible gift of grace was not given."[32] In a rather remarkable admission, Wright says, "This enablement is not mere influencing of people in general, but the pulling or *dragging* of individuals to Jesus by God's power."[33] Most Calvinists prefer to use the softer sounding "draw," but in effect mean precisely the same thing—God irresistibly brings the elect to Christ.

Non-Calvinists also hold that God draws people to Christ. For example, the Arminian theologian Jack Cottrell says: "No one can come unless he is drawn, that is true."[34] Similarly, Reichenbach states, "It is true that Scripture emphasizes that the work of salvation comes through the auspices of God" and then goes on to quote v. 44 as an

29. Hunt, *What Love Is This?*, 446.

30. Verses 37 and 39 have already been considered in some detail in the chapter on unconditional election.

31. Hendriksen, *John*, 238.

32. Piper, *Five Points*, 27, 30.

33. Wright, *No Place for Sovereignty*, 134, emphasis mine. No doubt, Wright is choosing to apply one possible meaning of the Greek word ἕλκω (*elkō*), which, in an appropriate context, can mean "to drag."

34. Cottrell, *What the Bible Says about God the Ruler*, 204.

example.[35] The key issue here is not whether God draws to the Son, but *how* that drawing takes place, and *who* are drawn. Calvinists answer that God sovereignly, *irresistibly* draws the *elect* (and only the elect) to Jesus. Non-Calvinists, while acknowledging that God draws, denies that he does so in a manner that cannot be resisted. Furthermore, the drawing by the Father is universal—all men are drawn, not just an elect few.

In the broader context of John 6:22–65 there is a dynamic involving two issues; the first concerns Jesus's identity, and the second concerns the question of faith or belief. Jesus affirms his unique identity as Israel's Messiah through the sign of the feeding of the five thousand (John 6:1–14) with its concluding affirmation: *"This is truly the Prophet who is to come into the world"* (v. 14).[36] Jesus later elaborates on the theme of bread and feeding by insisting that his body and blood are to be consumed if anyone is to gain eternal life (vv. 50, 51). But intimately connected with this question concerning Jesus's true identity is the question of response on the part of the Jews. Specifically, are they going to respond in faith or insist on unbelief? Significantly, in these verses (vv. 22–65) the word believe occurs no less than eight times. The drawing of the Father to Jesus is associated with these two features of John 6 (Jesus's identity, and whether those who observe will believe). Who Jesus is, and what he does as a sign of his credentials are meant by John to provide ample opportunities for those who see the signs and hear Jesus's teachings to be drawn to Jesus for salvation. Note how, in the following verses, there is a close juxtaposition between, on the one hand, belief and sign and, on the other hand, belief and the person of Jesus. Verse 29, for example, says: *"This is the work of God, that you believe in Him whom He has sent."* Here are others: *"What then do You do for a sign, so that we may see, and believe You? What work do You perform?"* (v. 30); *"Jesus said to them, 'I am the bread of life; he who comes to Me will not hunger, and he who believes in Me will never thirst'"* (v. 35); *"But I said to you that you have seen Me, and yet do not believe"* (v. 36); *"For this is the will of My Father, that everyone who beholds the Son and believes in Him will have eternal life"* (v. 40); *"Truly, truly, I say to you, he who believes has eternal life. I am the bread of life"* (vv. 47, 48). It seems clear that through Jesus's miraculous activity (feeding of the five thousand), and the claims of Jesus concerning himself (as the bread of life), the Father, who sent the Son to be the Savior of the world (1 John 4:14), is providing ample opportunities for all the Jews to be drawn to Jesus.

Is there anywhere else in John's gospel where the evangelist connects vindicating sign concerning the identity of Jesus, and drawing? Yes, there are at least two connected passages. In John 3:14, 15, Jesus says: *"As Moses lifted up the serpent in the wilderness, even so must the Son of Man be lifted up; so that whoever believes will in Him have eternal life."* And in 12:32, Jesus declares: *"And I, if I am lifted up from the earth, will draw all men to Myself."* The lifting up Jesus speaks of in both

35. Reichenbach, "Freedom, Justice, and Moral Responsibility," 293.

36. This sign is one of seven signs that structure John's gospel. All are intended to indicate Jesus's true identity as Israel's promised Messiah.

these verses is, of course, the greatest sign—the crucifixion.[37] Jesus clearly states that his being lifted up serves as a means of drawing all to himself. Verse 32 cannot be taken in a literally wooden manner for that would lead to universalism, the belief that "all" men are in fact drawn to Christ and saved. What makes the distinction between those who are drawn and find salvation and those who are drawn yet fail to enjoy eternal life? Calvinists answer this question in terms of those (elect) who are irresistibly drawn and those who are not so drawn. The difficulty with such an understanding, however, is that there is no hint anywhere in these verses (or any of the verses studied so far) that such an irresistible grace is being unilaterally applied by God to a select few. Rather, what is clearly stated time and again is that belief, faith, or unbelief, hardness of heart accounts for the difference. The signs (miracles), the teachings, the coming of Christ himself—all are intended to draw all men to God—however, some respond positively and some reject God's overtures intended to draw them to Christ. Furthermore, such a perspective is perfectly consistent with the reason given by John himself as to why he wrote the gospel: *"But these [signs] have been written so that you may believe that Jesus is the Christ, the Son of God; and that believing you may have life in His name"* (John 20:31).

A final point needs to be made concerning these verses, including v. 44; the scope of this drawing is universal. All are drawn. Just as any one of those in the wilderness who were bitten could look up to the bronze serpent and live (Num 21:8), so it is *"that* everyone *who beholds the Son and believes in Him will have eternal life"* (John 6:40). There is no hint here (or anywhere else in the gospel) that the determining factor concerning who looks and lives or who believes and lives is determined by an irresistible and secret application of grace upon a select few.

John 6:65

> *"And He was saying, 'For this reason I have said to you, that no one can* > *come to Me unless it has been* granted him *from the Father.'"*

As we would expect, Calvinists see such granting as a supernatural, direct influence of the Holy Spirit upon the elect alone—it is an effectual granting. "It is impossible for anyone to come to Christ without the Father's giving him the grace to do so. Left to himself the sinner prefers his sin."[38] "No one would ever respond to the gospel call without some special action by God. . . . God has selected some to be saved, and that our response to the offer of salvation depends upon this prior decision and initiative

---

37. The cross is the supreme sign of God's love—that none would perish, and that all would find salvation (John 3:16). It is also, for the same reason, a sign of Christ's identity as Son of Man and Son of God, for if he were a mere man, the cross would not be particularly significant.

38. Morris, *John*, 387.

by God."[39] Carson speaks of "the need for the divine initiative which draws those whom the Father has given to the Son and enables them to believe."[40]

Taken in isolation, such conclusions may possibly be drawn—but no responsible exegesis of a verse ignores the literary context. In this case, the relevant context includes not only John 6, but the entire gospel of John. The verse (6:65) speaks of something having been given/granted (it is the same Greek word)[41] to the unbeliever that allows him to "come to" Jesus. As noted above in Carson's commentary on this verse, for Calvinism the thing given is the capacity to believe. The main difficulty with this interpretation is that it is unsupported anywhere else in the gospel or the New Testament. Precisely the same Greek construction (ἠ δεδομενον αὐτω, ē dedomenon autō, unless it has been given him) occurs in John 3:27, and the same thought is expressed in John 19:11.[42] In the former instance John the Baptist is quoting an aphorism with the thought that Jesus's status as Israel's promised Messiah has been granted by God—is authorized by God. This, in stark contrast with John the Baptist himself who insists he is not the Promised One (3:28). In John 19:11 Jesus reminds Pontius Pilate that the authority Pilate exercises has been given him by God. The key question in John 6:65 is "What, exactly, has been granted the sinner?" (Note here, in v. 65, something has been granted/given to the sinner; this is in contrast to the previous verses which speak of the sinner having been given to Jesus by the Father [6:37], or drawn to Jesus by the Father [6:44]).

The immediate context is helpful in providing a proper understanding of what Jesus meant in 6:65. Immediately following Jesus's teaching concerning the need to exercise faith and trust in him through the vivid metaphor of eating his flesh and drinking his blood (6:48–58), many of the disciples present in the synagogue in Capernaum took offense and grumbled (6:60). Jesus responds by reinforcing his unique status and by asking how they would respond in the presence of a greater vindication of his unique claims (beyond being the bread of life [v. 35, 51]), namely by witnessing his upcoming ascension: "What then if you see the Son of Man ascending to where He was before?" (v. 62). (He had already asserted that he was the bread "which came down out of heaven" [v. 58].) The next point Jesus makes before his disciples is important: "It is the Spirit who gives life; the flesh profits nothing; the words that I have spoken to you are spirit and are life" (v. 63). Insight and understanding is dependent upon the words of Jesus—a specific application of an enduring spiritual principle: "That which is born of the flesh is flesh, and that which is born of the Spirit

---

39. Erickson, *Christian Theology*, 925.

40. Carson, *John*, 302.

41. διδωμι (*didōmi*), to give/grant/bestow/impart—is strongly dependent on context. See Bauer, *Greek-English Lexicon*, 192.

42. John 3:27 says, "*John answered and said, 'A man can receive nothing unless it has been given him from heaven,'*" and John 19:11 says, "*Jesus answered, 'You would have no authority over Me, unless it had been given you from above.'*"

is spirit" (John 3:6). How one responds to the words of Jesus is crucial for "coming to Jesus." This is why Jesus immediately follows his teaching concerning his words with reference to unbelief—both generally among his supposed followers, and specifically the failure of Judas Iscariot to believe the words of Jesus: *"But there are some of you who do not* believe. *For Jesus knew from the beginning who they were who did not believe, and who it was that would betray Him"* (v. 64).

Having studied in some detail the immediate context of v. 65, we are now better positioned to understand what Jesus meant when he said that *"no one can come to Me unless it has been granted him from the Father."* Two aspects are pertinent here. The first is that no one comes to Jesus apart from divine provisions. Salvation is not possible apart from the provision of grace exemplified in the coming of Jesus and in his teaching (words of life). In this sense, everyone is totally dependent upon God's initiative, and not in human ability or capacity to discover or in any way merit salvation. It is in Jesus, whose ultimate origin is from heaven, who comes as bread of life and whose words are life. The second aspect follows from the reference to belief in both the immediate context of v. 65 and indeed throughout John's gospel, and indicates that what the Father grants is *the opportunity to respond to the presence of Jesus and his words.* Both aspects—inability to save oneself, and the call to believe upon Jesus and his teachings—appear throughout John's gospel.[43]

Contra Calvinism, there is no hint here, or anywhere in the gospel, that due to a supposed inability to believe because of total depravity, no one is able to exercise faith—indeed the gospel presumes such ability and holds one accountable for failing to respond appropriately to the claims and words of Jesus. And certainly there is no hint that one is granted an ability to believe or that one must irresistibly be brought to belief anywhere in John 6 or elsewhere in the Bible.

> Christ is saying that we cannot demand salvation—it must be given us from God. Salvation involves a new birth, and no man can regenerate himself into God's family; that privilege can only be given of God and only God has the power to effect it by his Holy Spirit. In all of this however, there is neither rational nor biblical basis for believing that God only grants this for a select group and withholds it from the rest of mankind. Or that he irresistibly forces it upon anyone.[44]

---

43. This is seen most clearly in Jesus disputes with the Pharisees and scribes, and in his claims to be uniquely qualified to save all who trust him for salvation. John 1:11, 12 echoes the same sentiment: *"He came to His own, and those who were His own did not receive Him. But as many as received Him, to them He gave the right to become children of God, even to those who believe in His name."*

44. Hunt, *What Love Is This?*, 435.

Acts 16:14

> *"A woman named Lydia, from the city of Thyatira, a seller of purple fabrics, a worshiper of God, was listening; and the Lord opened her heart to respond to the things spoken by Paul."*

This verse has already been dealt with in the chapter on election, so will only briefly be considered here. This verse is appealed to by Calvinists to justify a doctrine of a saving grace that is applied prior to belief. "First the Lord opened her heart, then she was able to give heed to Paul's preaching and to respond in faith."[45] Likewise, Piper connects Lydia's experience with irresistible grace: "Unless God opens our hearts, we will not hear the truth and beauty of Christ in the message of the gospel. This heart-opening is what we mean by irresistible grace." He then goes on to say the same thing in terms of regeneration: "We do not bring about the new birth by our faith. God brings about our faith by the new birth."[46] Similarly, Horton sees Lydia as an example of effectual calling and concludes that "God's sovereign grace guarantees the success of evangelism and missions."[47]

Significantly, none of the authors cited above mention that Lydia was already "*a worshipper of God*" when she encountered Paul at Philippi on the outward leg of his second missionary journey. In addition, she was almost certainly a proselyte, a person who aligns herself with the God of Israel and the Jewish religion. Luke describes her as a worshipper of God in an unqualified manner—something he would not do if she was a worshipper of a pagan god. It was a sabbath day and Paul was seeking the place of prayer just outside the city (v. 13).[48] Lydia was obviously a sincere worshipper of the God of the Jews, what we today would call an Old Testament saint, or what Paul calls the remnant (Rom 9:27; 11:5). Lydia's heart was already open to the things of God; she was a praying woman who worshipped the true God. However, her knowledge of God up to the time she encountered Paul was restricted to the Old Testament revelation. Now, through Paul's preaching she became aware of the momentous step forward in redemptive history associated with the incarnation and the love of God manifested at the cross. Through the help of God's Spirit she gladly, voluntarily, and easily became a follower of God now seen in the form of the man Jesus Christ. This is far from any notion of God acting upon an unbeliever in an irresistible manner to regenerate her and cause her to believe.

Romans 9:19

> *"You will say to me then, 'Why does He still find fault? For who resists His will?'"*

---

45. Grudem, *Systematic Theology*, 703.
46. Piper, *Five Points*, 34.
47. Horton, *For Calvinism*, 102.
48. See Marshall, *Acts*, 266, for more details concerning the Jewish background to v. 14.

Again, the verses associated with v. 19 in Rom 9 have been discussed in the chapter on election. I will focus on this verse here because it is appealed to specifically to justify a notion of irresistible grace. Murray, for example, rephrases the question thus: "How can God blame us when we are the victims of his irresistible decree?"[49] Horton includes this verse with its broader context (Rom 9:6–24) to speak of the connection between (unconditional) election and effectual calling: "Those whom God chose before the creation of the world, he also calls in due time by his Spirit. The connection between election and calling is well attested. . . . In effectual calling, the Spirit unites us here and now to the Christ who redeemed us in the past."[50] As noted at the beginning of this chapter, an unconditional election to salvation requires an irresistible grace that guarantees the elect be actually saved.

Verse 19 comprises part of a section dealing with election in Rom 9:6–24. The universal assumption by Calvinists is that the election Paul is speaking about here is God's unconditionally electing who will be saved and who will not be saved. But the election discussed by Paul is *not* an election to salvation, but rather an election to *service*. The question raised in v. 19 "is based on a flagrant misrepresentation of Paul's teaching."[51] God has the right to decide unconditionally, those who would comprise key players in the outworking of his redemptive plans for the world. As Cottrell explains: "The objector's misunderstanding was in assuming that this purposive [i.e., decretal] will of God applied to Israel's salvation status. . . . However, . . . this is not Paul's point. In these verses he is affirming God's right to sovereignly choose and use anyone, even sinners [like Pharaoh] to serve his covenant purposes."[52]

In vv. 20, 21, Paul likens God's right to call whomever he wishes to further his redemptive purposes to a potter who works his clay, and "just as a potter decides on the special privileges of a pot so special privileges like the election of a nation are decided by God alone, for he knows the best strategy."[53] And, just as in previous scripture analyses, the "concept of an eternal, comprehensive, efficacious, unconditional, irresistible decree is simply not a biblical teaching; it finds no support in Rom 9"[54]—including Rom 9:19.

Ephesians 2:8–9

> "For by grace you have been saved through faith; and that not of yourselves,
> it is the gift of God; not as a result of works, so that no one may boast."

49. Murray, *Romans*, pt. 2, 31. He goes on to say, "The answer is the appeal to the reverential silence which the majesty of God demands of us."

50. Horton, *For Calvinism*, 102.

51. Forster and Marston, *Strategy*, 80.

52. Cottrell, *Romans*, 2:112.

53. Forster and Marston, *Strategy*, 81.

54. Cottrell, *Romans*, 2:113.

Calvinists see the three elements mentioned, grace, salvation, faith, all as the gift of God. Hence faith is affirmed as a gift. Hendriksen, for example, says, "Faith, as well as everything else in salvation, is God's gift."[55] Though he does not believe this verse upholds the belief, John Stott nevertheless holds that "we must never think of salvation as a kind of transaction between God and us in which he contributes grace and we contribute faith. . . . Saving faith too is God's gracious gift."[56] Citing Eph 2:5–9, 10, Horton says: "Even faith belongs to the gift that is freely given to us by God's grace (vv. 5–9).[57] Wright connects Eph 2:8–10 with Eph 1:11: "Ephesians 1:11 says that God works out (operates, energizes) everything by the power of his own will. This then becomes the foundation for the strong statement concerning irresistible grace found later (2:8–10)."[58]

By way of response, we may note that the grammatical construction of v. 8 does not allow for faith to be the gift of God. Strictly speaking, the phrase translated by the NASB committee "and that not of yourselves" in the Greek is "and this [τουτο, *touto*] not of yourselves." The word τουτο is functioning as a demonstrative adjective and as such the "case, number, and gender agree with the word [it is] modifying."[59] Τουτο is a neuter demonstrative and relates to a word that precedes it which must also be neuter in gender. The Greek word for faith in v. 8 (πιστεως, *pisteōs*), however, is feminine. So, whatever τουτο is modifying, it cannot be faith. What "this" (τουτο) in v. 8 is referring to is the entire complex of salvation by grace through faith. Paul is teaching that salvation is based on the grace of God, not works. As Stott explains: "Some commentators have taken the word 'this' . . . to refer to faith (i.e., 'you were saved . . . through faith, and even this faith by which you were saved is God's gift). . . . [However], Paul is not directly affirming this here [in v. 8] because 'this' (τουτο) is neuter, whereas 'faith' is a feminine noun. We must therefore take 'this' as referring to the whole previous sentence: 'By God's grace you are people who have been saved through faith, and this whole event and experience is . . . God's free gift to you.'"[60]

The other thing worth noting in this verse (v. 8) is that being saved by grace is *through faith*. Faith is the mechanism, the means, whereby salvation by grace is appropriated. In sum, v. 8 is teaching that salvation is a gift of God (not earned or

55. Hendriksen, *Ephesians*, 122. The main support provided is that if the "it" in the verse referred only to salvation it would have made Paul, in saying "it is the gift of God," "guilty of needless repetition."

56. Stott, *Message of Ephesians*, 83.

57. Horton, *For Calvinism*, 104.

58. Wright, *No Place for Sovereignty*, 134.

59. Mounce, *Basics of Biblical Greek*, 105. Greek, unlike English, uses words whose function in a sentence is determined by its case (nominative, accusative dative, genitive), number (singular or plural), and gender (masculine, feminine, or neuter).

60. Stott, *Message of Ephesians*, 83. The vast majority of scholars recognize this construct, however, a few Calvinists such as Hendriksen quoted earlier still try to insist that faith is a gift of God from this verse by arguing that, while the rule concerning agreement of case, number, and gender is generally true there can be exceptions and this is one of them.

in any way merited), and is based upon God's unmerited favor and love (grace), and that these spiritual realities are appropriated and experienced through faith, not by passing a test of any kind, or through intellectual prowess or supposed moral excellence. This latter point is being stressed by Paul in Eph 2:9, *"not as a result of works, so that no one may boast."* Interestingly, none of the writers cited earlier in connection with the interpretation of this verse (v. 8) makes reference to the role of faith in this salvation by grace. So, for example, when Westblade says, "In order that the grace of God receive all the praise, Paul leaves no room for human boasting that our hope for the future may be found in anything that is true about ourselves (2:8–9). Salvation is a gift of God and depends wholly upon God's call (1:18; 2:8),"[61] he omits an important truth. This truth, according to Eph 2:8, is that the salvation Westblade speaks of is only enjoyed when an individual believes these truths concerning salvation offered as a gift of grace; faith must be exercised on the part of the individual. Westblade's statement should more accurately be stated as: "Salvation, *when appropriated by faith,* is a gift of God and depends wholly upon God's call (1:18; 2:8)."

1 Peter 1:23

> *"You have been born again not of seed which is perishable but imperishable, that is, through the living and enduring word of God."*

As we have seen, according to Calvinism an irresistible grace works to first of all regenerate an unbeliever who is then enabled to believe the gospel mediated through an effectual (infallibly effective) call. Commenting on this verse, and noting the role God's word plays in the new birth, Grudem says: "As the gospel call comes to us, God speaks through it to summon us to himself (effective calling) and to give us new spiritual life (regeneration) *so that we are enabled to respond in faith."*[62] Horton links this verse with God's creative act out of nothing in creation: "[The gospel] is an announcement that *creates faith* in the Redeemer who makes it. . . . The gospel itself—and the Spirit's effectual calling through the gospel—remain distinct from anything done by us. The gospel is God's life-giving word, creating a new world out of nothing."[63] James Packer, after citing 1 John 4:8 (God's love for the elect) and Eph 2:1, 4–5 (believers being made alive in Christ), says, "What Paul speaks of here is the work of grace that elsewhere he describes as God calling—that is, *actually bringing unbelievers to faith* by his Spirit so that they respond to the invitation given and trust Christ to save them. Other New Testament passages designate this same work of grace, whereby God makes us Christians, as new creation . . . and as regeneration or new birth (1 Peter 1:23)."[64]

---

61. Westblade, "Divine Election," 72.

62. Grudem, *Systematic Theology*, 700, emphasis mine. Wright likewise cites this verse as a "key verse on irresistible grace." Wright, *No Place for Sovereignty*, 134.

63. Horton, *For Calvinism*, 102, emphasis mine.

64. Packer, "Love of God," 283, emphasis mine.

Note that each of these three authors cite 1 Pet 1:23 to justify, or at least to contribute toward the justification of and the belief in, an effectual call associated with the gospel proclamation that infallibly leads to salvation for the elect by granting the unbeliever the capacity to believe. But what does v. 23 actually say? In the immediate context (v. 22) Peter exhorts his readers to *"fervently love one another from the heart"* because they *"have in obedience to the truth purified your souls for a sincere love of the brethren."* First Peter 1:22, 23 comprise a series of exhortations given by Peter in his letter. His Christian readers, as obedient children are to not be conformed to their former lusts (1:14) and, as those who address the Father who is an impartial judge, they must conduct themselves in fear (1:17), they are to put aside all malice and long for the pure milk of the word. These exhortations follow from the fact that "in Peter's calculus there can be no dichotomy between character and performance."[65] Both here and throughout the letter, Peter addresses his fellow believers as though they are expected to assume responsibility for their conduct, and it is *their faith* that is called upon to work out their salvation in these various ways. There is not a hint that Peter is thinking about God "enabling them to respond in faith" (Grudem), or "creating faith" (Horton), or "bringing unbelievers to faith" (Packer). Such notions must be brought to the text—a classic case of eisegesis. Peter is addressing how believers are to demonstrate the reality of their faith; he is not addressing how they came to faith. Certainly, regeneration is a work of God (1 Pet 1:3), but nowhere in this epistle, and certainly not in our text (v. 23), is there any hint that regeneration is something done unilaterally by God upon unbelievers such that they become believers.

In citing these texts the authors are lumping together an unbiblical concept—effectual calling leading to regeneration—with texts that emphasize the reality of regeneration itself. Certainly, this is a methodology that not only Calvinists are guilty of, but unfortunately it is not a handling of God's word with care and integrity taking due consideration of the immediate literary context.

Scriptures That Indicate God's Spirit and God's Will Can Be Resisted

Psalm 78:40–41

> *"How often they rebelled against him in the wilderness and grieved him in the desert! They tested God again and again and provoked the Holy One of Israel."* (ESV)

In this psalm, the psalmist recounts God's dealings with the children of Israel during their wilderness wanderings. He recalls how, despite God's gracious provisions for them (v. 24, *"He rained down manna upon them to eat And gave them food from heaven"*) they persisted to rebel against the God who had led them out of Egypt.

---

65. Green, *1 Peter*, 48. Of course, many more exhortations from Peter's letter could be mentioned.

Admittedly, when we are dealing with God's ancient people there is not an identical parallel to Christians because, while the former are in covenant relationship with God, the latter are both in covenant relationship with God and regenerated. Nevertheless, it is clear that God expected the people of Israel to *"put their confidence in God and not forget the works of God, but keep His commandments"* (v. 7), and yet they still rebelled and were *"a stubborn and rebellious generation, a generation that did not prepare its heart and whose spirit was not faithful to God"* (v. 8). Despite the privilege of experiencing God's miraculous powers, the wilderness generation still chose to resist, reject, and rebel against the God who delivered them from Egypt.

Hebrews 3:7–9

> *"Therefore, just as the Holy Spirit says, 'Today if you hear His voice, Do not harden your hearts as when they provoked Me, as in the day of trial in the wilderness, Where your fathers tried Me by testing Me, And saw my works for forty years.'"*

Here, the writer to the book of Hebrews, citing Ps 95:7–11, warns his readers to not harden their hearts against God as the generation in the wilderness had done. In fact, the entire Letter to the Hebrews was written to warn Jewish believers of the dangers of turning their back on God, and rejecting the grace shown them in Christ; hence the writer's twofold strategy of (a) warning them of the dangers of apostasy and (b) showing them the superiority of Christ over anyone or anything in the old covenant. The entire letter, in other words, was predicated on the assumption that rejecting God, God's Spirit, and God's will for them was a very real possibility. He would not have written to them concerning an irrelevant danger.

Acts 7:51

> *"You men who are stiff-necked and uncircumcised in heart and ears are always resisting the Holy Spirit; you are doing just as your fathers did."*

Stephen, one of those godly men called upon by the apostles to administer the distribution of food to needy widows in Jerusalem, accused those stoning him of resisting God's redemptive purposes for the peoples. He clearly sees the ministry of the Old Testament prophets as inspired by the Holy Spirit: *"Which one of the prophets did your fathers not persecute? They killed those who had previously announced the coming of the Righteous One, whose betrayers and murderers you have now become"* (v. 52). Just as the word of the Spirit of God mediated by the Old Testament prophets had been rejected, so now Stephen accuses his persecutors of acting in precisely the same manner. Both groups had resisted the Holy Spirit.

Ephesians 4:30

> *"Do not grieve the Holy Spirit of God, by whom you were sealed for the day of redemption."*

In a very real sense, every time a believer sins (and every believer sins [1 John 1:10]), he or she is resisting God's Spirit and rejecting God's will for him or her. In every case, the believer is grieving the Holy Spirit, and so Paul urges the Christians at Ephesus to stop grieving/resisting the Holy Spirit. The Spirit of God is grieved whenever his will is rejected; and this is done whenever a believer sins. Hence the exhortations to stop sinning: they are to lay aside falsehood (v. 25), to not give the devil an opportunity to tempt them through their anger (v. 27), to cease from stealing (v. 28), to allow themselves no unwholesome words (v. 29), to remove bitterness and anger (v. 31). "Since he is the 'holy Spirit,' he is always grieved by unholiness, and since he is the 'one Spirit' (2:18; 4:4), disunity will also cause him grief. . . . Because he is also the 'Spirit of truth,' through whom God has spoken, he is upset by all our misuse of speech."[66]

Scriptures Indicating Human Cooperation Is Required to Experience God's Grace

1 Corinthians 15:10

> *"But by the grace of God I am what I am, and His grace toward me did not prove vain; but I labored even more than all of them, yet not I, but the grace of God with me."*

Here we find Paul expressing perfect synergy as he cooperated with God's grace that enabled him to labor more than his fellow apostles. Twice in this short verse Paul makes reference to the grace of God; the first was Paul's awareness that his apostleship itself was by the grace of God, and the second, that the grace of God empowered him for service. And yet he also acknowledged that God's grace toward him was not in vain—was not wasted, to no avail. Paul was conscious that, even though called to be an apostle as "one untimely born" (v. 8) and "least of all the apostles" (v. 9), and that therefore his call to service was undeserved, purely an act of God's grace, yet he was responsible for stewarding that grace carefully. As Gordon Fee puts it: "Although God's gracious gift of apostleship was the result of divine initiative, hence all of grace, nonetheless it required Paul's response."[67] Paul's labor is both a response to grace and an effect of grace. In Paul's case his call to apostleship coincided with his call to follow Christ (Acts 9:10–19) and both callings were acts of God's grace and both required that Paul willingly choose to respond to that grace so that God's grace not be directed toward him in vain.

66. Stott, *Message of Ephesians*, 189.

67. Fee, *First Corinthians*, 735.

2 Corinthians 6:1

> *"And working together with Him, we also urge you not to receive the grace of God in vain."*

Philip Hughes is probably correct when he says: "For [the Corinthians] to receive the grace of God in vain meant that their practice did not measure up to their profession as Christians, that their lives were so inconsistent as to constitute a denial of the logical implications of the gospel, namely, and in particular, that Christ died for them so that they might no longer live to themselves but to His glory (5:15)."[68] Since the Holy Spirit is "the Spirit of grace" (Heb 10:29),[69] for the Corinthian Christians to live in such a sub-Christian manner that required Paul to view them as having potentially received the grace of God in vain, is, in effect, to reject the Spirit's desire that they live god-honoring lives. For the Corinthians to resist the grace of God is tantamount to them resisting the Holy Spirit. Paul is urging his readers to cooperate with the Spirit's desire that they reduce the gap between their profession and behavior.

2 Timothy 2:1

> *"You therefore, my son, be strong in the grace that is in Christ Jesus."*

Here is a positive exhortation given by Paul to his son in the faith. What follows in the subsequent verses are specific exhortations designed to flesh out what it means to be strong in the grace of Christ; entrust the gospel to faithful men (v. 2), be prepared to suffer hardship (v. 3), be dedicated and steadfast in persevering in the faith (vv. 4–7). Again, the inference is that Paul saw the possibility of Timothy failing to cooperate with the grace of God and so fail to follow through on these exhortations. Donald Guthrie captures Paul's intent here well: "The personal exhortation to Timothy contrasts with the general defection of the Asiatics, as the opening words 'You then' show. The emphasis falls on 'you.'"[70] The exhortation to be strong in the grace found in Christ would be redundant if the failure to be strong was an impossibility. Timothy was not to be like those in Asia who had turned away from Paul (1:15).

Hebrews 4:16

> *"Therefore let us draw near with confidence to the throne of grace, so that we may receive mercy and find grace to help in time of need."*

---

68. Hughes, *2 Corinthians*, 218.

69. Commenting on this verse (Heb 10:29), Robert Shank says, "That the designation 'Spirit of grace' appears in the context of Hebrews 10:19—12:29, the longest of the five hortatory sections of the Epistle to the Hebrews which treat the peril of apostasy with such profound urgency, strongly forbids any assumption of the irresistibility of grace." Shank, *Elect in the Son*, 133.

70. Guthrie, *Pastoral Epistles*, 149.

Having reminded his readers of the reality of Jesus as the believer's great high priest (4:14), and that this high priest has been tempted as we are and is thus able to sympathize with our weaknesses (v. 15), the writer exhorts his readers to persevere in their Christian confession and to draw near to the throne of grace to help them persevere. This would be done through prayer. Twice the writer urges his readers: "*let us* hold fast" (v. 14), and "*let us* draw near" (v. 16). "The high priestly ministry of Christ includes an invitation to follow him with boldness into the holy place."[71] Once again, these exhortations and invitations underscore the writer's desire that his readers choose to cooperate with God's grace and find the help they need and be enabled to hold fast their confession. God has made every provision in the giving of his Son as the agent of grace—but the Hebrew Christians are expected to assume their responsibility to avail themselves of the grace available to them. As Hunt remarks in a similar context: "Even God's grace requires faith and obedience. Many scriptures make it clear that while grace is unmerited, we must accept it and respond to it. . . . Clearly Paul is declaring that God's grace is not irresistible but must be wedded to human will and effort."[72]

These four scriptures all stress the need for believers to cooperate with God's Spirit and avail themselves of the grace extended to them by a loving God. Far from being irresistible these passages show that it is indeed quite possible to quench the Spirit (1 Thess 5:19), lie to the Spirit (Acts 5:3), and resist the Spirit (Acts 7:51). Now, it is quite possible that most, perhaps all, Calvinists would agree with these statements, but be quick to point out they are applicable to believers and that the doctrine of irresistible grace applies to God unilaterally working upon an *unbeliever* to efficaciously bring him or her to salvation. Now this is a most strange situation— God's grace being utterly irresistible when unbelievers are in view but very much resistible for believers! Supposedly, coming to faith is the result of an irresistible grace applied to the unbeliever, but continuing and growing in faith requires that the believer cooperate with God's Spirit. As Hunt puts it, "If He so desired, God could sovereignly cause every totally depraved sinner to turn to him, yet his sovereignty seems to lose its Calvinistic power when it comes to causing Christians to live in victory and holiness and fruitfulness."[73]

This strange dichotomy, for Calvinism, is justified by arguing that the totally depraved sinner cannot exercise faith to receive God's grace or God's Spirit, but that once he has received the Spirit of God, only then can he live by faith (Rom 1:17). Yet it is precisely this false distinction that Paul refutes in his Letter to the Galatians. The Galatian Christians had received the Spirit by faith (Gal 3:2), but were now in danger of relying upon their own resources apart from God—i.e., not continuing on by faith. His question to the readers in Galatia, *"Having begun by the Spirit, are you now being perfected by the flesh?"* (3:3), indicates clearly that the Christian life

71. Brown, *Hebrews*, 96.
72. Hunt, *What Love Is This?*, 379.
73. Hunt, *What Love Is This?*, 380.

is both begun and sustained by faith—and hence by the Spirit of God. There is no discontinuity concerning exercising faith and receiving the Spirit before or after conversion as far as Paul is concerned.

Theological Issues Related to Irresistible Grace

In our study of this aspect of Calvinistic soteriology, we have seen that some of the biblical texts used to justify an irresistible grace cannot be sustained, and that there are several texts that show that God's grace can in fact be resisted and that God calls on people to cooperate with the Spirit's drawing and calling to salvation and, once justified, persevering in faith. I want now to go on and consider some of the theological ramifications of Calvinism's claim that God must apply an irresistible grace in order that a sinner be saved. No doubt, we shall give further consideration to specific biblical texts, but the focus will shift to theological issues.

Two basic features of Calvinism's TULIP make the need for an irresistible grace absolutely necessary. The first, and most foundational, is Calvinism's notion of total depravity. As we have already seen, this is understood to mean that no one, in principle and in practice, is able to do anything morally or spiritually good—especially to be able to respond to the gospel call to repent and believe the gospel. Secondly, and closely connected, is God's determination that only some are decreed to be saved. Because of total depravity, if anyone is to be saved it must be because of an unconditional election applied to the elect sinner. Marrying these two doctrines, total depravity (understood as total inability) and unconditional election, is irresistible grace. I shall be focusing on the relationship between total depravity and irresistible grace. However, Ware's cautionary note regarding election and irresistible grace applies equally to the justification of a notion of irresistible grace and total depravity: "As the necessary complement and entailment of the doctrine of unconditional election, [effectual calling and irresistible grace] must be shown to be biblically and rationally supported if Calvinism is to succeed."[74]

a) Types of Grace in Theological Discussions

Theologians, when considering the relationship between grace and salvation, use a variety of terms to delineate what are considered to be different types of grace, or rather, the different ways God's grace is believed to express itself. Here we will briefly review each term in order to evaluate the extent to which it faithfully expresses a biblical concept of grace. Before proceeding with an examination of the various types of grace theologians appeal to for a variety of reasons, I wish to flesh out what I believe lies behind a truly biblical notion of grace.

74. Ware, "Effectual Calling," 210.

In a real sense, Jesus was the embodiment of grace: *"For of His fullness we have all received, and grace upon grace. For the Law was given through Moses; grace and truth were realized through Jesus Christ"* (John 1:16, 17). Sometimes grace is synonymous with a God-given ability to be a servant of God: *"And Stephen, full of grace and power, was performing great wonders and signs among the people"* (Acts 6:8). Often, the grace of God is portrayed as the reason or motive for God blessing his people. For example, the Christians at Rome were granted justification by the grace of God: *"being justified as a gift by His grace through the redemption which is in Christ Jesus"* (Rom 3:24). Often grace is expressed by an apostle to his readers together with sentiments like peace, love, and the fellowship of God: *"Grace to you and peace from God our Father and the Lord Jesus Christ"* (1 Cor 1:3); *"The grace of the Lord Jesus Christ, and the love of God, and the fellowship of the Holy Spirit, be with you all"* (2 Cor 13:14). Perhaps the best summation of the word grace as it functions in these sorts of verses is the presence of God manifested as either God-enabled abilities or the presence of God's goodness. The former is seen in the several instances in which Paul attributes his ability to carry out his commission to be an apostle to the grace of God (e.g., Eph 3:2, 7, 8), and the latter in the juxtaposition of the word grace with words like peace, love, fellowship, kindness (Eph 2:7), truth (Col 1:6), comfort, hope (2 Thess 2:16), and mercy (1 Tim 1:2).

Biblical grace, as distilled from these verses and many others, may therefore be defined as the presence of God's goodness, kindness, favor within and among his church (believers), those who have voluntarily and willingly embraced God's manifest goodness directed toward them. God's grace is always offered to people, never imposed. It is seen in the invitation to sinners to "repent and believe for the kingdom of God is at hand" (Mark 1:15), and in the blessings of salvation received by those who do respond and repent and believe, for example justification (Rom 3:24). Garrett sums up the biblical idea behind grace well: "Grace is the free and undeserved condescension of God's love."[75] The main antitheses of grace in a context of salvation is meritorious works; the Bible is clear, salvation is on the basis of God's unmerited favor, not on the basis of one's good works intended to merit salvation (Eph 2:8).

Common Grace

For Calvinism, with its very pessimistic view of human nature and moral ability, a problem presents itself when one observes the everyday affairs of men. "The origin of the doctrine of common grace was occasioned by the fact that there is in the world . . . traces of the true, the good, and the beautiful. . . . How can we account for it that sinful man still retains some knowledge of God, of natural things, and of the difference between good and evil, and shows some regard for virtue . . . . How can the

75. Garrett, *Systematic Theology*, 1:251.

unregenerate still speak the truth, do good to others, and lead outwardly virtuous lives?"[76] The answer as developed mainly by Calvin: "He developed alongside of the doctrine of particular grace the doctrine of common grace."[77] It is God's common grace that explains the virtuous abilities of men and also provides for their needs. "It appears in the natural blessings which God showers upon man in the present life, in spite of the fact that man has forfeited them and lies under the sentence of death."[78] A favorite verse to justify this notion is *"He causes His sun to rise on the evil and the good, and sends rain on the righteous and the unrighteous"* (Matt 5:45b).

Common grace is a mechanism that allows a clear distinction between God's special grace that saves the elect and the apparent goodness among the wicked reprobates. However, the Bible knows no such distinction being grounded in *God*. Just as the Bible teaches that God's love is universal (*"For God so loved the world"* [John 3:16]; *"We have seen and testify that the Father has sent the Son to be the Savior of the world"* [1 John 4:14]), so is his grace. Everyone receives good at the hands of God because he loves his creation—even his sinful human creation. The reason some experience God's grace in a more intimate, saving way is because they have responded to the call to repent and believe the gospel and have submitted to Christ's Lordship over their lives. Ironically, the context in which Matt 5:45b sits demonstrates precisely the universal love of God for all people: *"But I say to you, love your enemies and pray for those who persecute you, so that you may be sons of your Father who is in heaven; for He causes His sun to rise on the evil and the good, and sends rain on the righteous and the unrighteous"* (Matt 5:44, 45). Jesus's point is that the sons of the Father are to emulate their Father's universal love.

Of course, in the final analysis, the Calvinist notion of common grace is relatively inconsequential. Why? Because it fails to provide for man's greatest need—the possibility of enjoying salvation; that privilege is reserved for a select few only, the elect. As William MacDonald puts it: "God supplies man with consumables and possibilities . . . under this old-creation shower of blessings depicted in the Old Testament and New Testament, [but] he does not admit man to the tree of life; he does not share with him the sacred stuff of which eternal life is made—his own spiritual life."[79]

Covenant of Grace

The covenant of grace, together with a so-called covenant of works and a covenant of redemption, comprise the classically Reformed covenantal structure known as covenant theology. This theology "came to the church through the Reformation of

76. Berkhof, *Systematic Theology*, 432.
77. Berkhof, *Systematic Theology*, 434.
78. Berkhof, *Systematic Theology*, 435.
79. MacDonald, "Spirit of Grace," 78.

the sixteenth century."[80] It was developed (invented?) in part "to lessen what appeared to some to be harshness in the earlier Reformed theology which emanated from Geneva, with its emphasis on the divine sovereignty and predestination."[81] This theological system posits a covenant of works which God made with Adam whereby, if Adam obeyed the stipulations of this covenant he would be rewarded with various spiritual benefits. It is this arrangement that forms the basis for the assumption that Adam was designated to be man's representative; "inasmuch as [Adam] was acting not only for himself but representatively for mankind, Adam was a public person. His fall therefore affected the entire human race that was to come after him; all are now conceived and born in sin."[82]

The fall of Adam logically called forth another covenant, a covenant of redemption whereby "God the Father and God the Son covenanted together for the redemption of the human race."[83] This resulted in yet another covenant, the covenant of grace. As Osterhaven points out, "This covenant has been made by God with mankind. In it he offers life and salvation through Christ to all who believe."[84] Of course, no one can believe because of total depravity and so "Inasmuch as none can believe without the special grace of God, it is more exact to say that the covenant of grace is made with believers, or the elect."[85]

What to make of all this? It is important to note that this theology arose in a context in which the prevailing overall theology was predestinarian following Calvin. This gives rise to the strong suspicion that this theological framework was intended to support a Calvinistic notion of the effects of Adam's sin and the election of a few to salvation. It was, in short, a theological expediency designed to accommodate a preexisting theological system namely, Augustinianism/Calvinism. This suspicion is confirmed when one notes that there is not one iota of biblical support for the theology! One would look in vain for either the terms or the concepts of these multiplied covenants in the Bible.[86]

Sovereign Grace

Sovereign grace, also known as special grace or saving grace, is the grace sovereignly, i.e., unilaterally and unconditionally, applied to sinners whereby they are enabled

80. Osterhaven, "Covenant Theology," 279.

81. Osterhaven, "Covenant Theology," 279.

82. Osterhaven, "Covenant Theology," 279.

83. Osterhaven, "Covenant Theology," 280.

84. Osterhaven, "Covenant Theology," 280.

85. Osterhaven, "Covenant Theology," 280.

86. For example, Arthur Wood notes that "Wesley was unwilling to trace in Scripture any covenant by which the Son agreed with the Father to suffer and die so that a certain limited number of souls might be saved as a recompense, whilst the rest were inevitably condemned." Wood, "Contribution of John Wesley," 219.

to become part of the elect. Unlike common grace which is applied to everyone indiscriminately, sovereign grace is applied only to a relatively few—those chosen by God to be saved, the elect. Again, this grace is recognized as a legitimate category by those, like Calvin, who believe that the sin of Adam resulted in a total inability on the part of man to even respond to the gospel call, and so rely entirely and in every respect upon an all-powerful (sovereign), special or particular grace that results in the salvation of the elect. "Special calling means that God works in a particularly effective way with the elect, enabling them to respond in repentance and faith, and rendering it certain that they will."[87]

Calvinists typically understand the selective application of sovereign grace to be a "mystery." For example, Philip Hughes remarks, "It is important always to remember that the operation of God's grace is a *deep mystery* that goes far beyond human comprehension. . . . [For believers] their whole redemption is in some wonderful way, due entirely to the grace of God. . . . Confronted with this marvelous but *mysterious reality* . . ."[88] Could it be a "mystery" because this type of grace as understood by Calvinists, i.e., sovereignly effectual, cannot be found in the Bible? It is not clear why grace should be a mystery. Of course, for the Calvinist, it needs to be viewed as such for the simple reason that he cannot explain why God's grace is sovereignly applied to some but not others—it's a mystery. But for non-Calvinists the explanation is straightforward; some people choose to respond appropriately when presented with the grace of God (e.g., Zacchaeus, Luke 19:1–10), and others respond negatively (e.g., the chief priests, Matt 26:59). The grace of God is offered to all for the simple reason that God loves all, cares for all, seeks the welfare of all; this is God's basic stance toward persons. There is nothing mysterious about this characteristic of God.

Even the term sovereign grace is an oxymoron—much like married bachelor. Grace, as noted in the introductory remarks above on the types of grace, is never sovereignly applied; indeed, it cannot be, otherwise it would not be grace. The moment an action of God is sovereignly applied to any human being it ceases to be grace; it might be judgment, or punishment, but not grace. Recall that the grace of God is the goodness of God offered by God to his human creation, and calls for that beneficent stance to be voluntarily received. An imposed grace is an oxymoron.

That God chooses to extend grace to man is indeed a choice on God's part—but a choice influenced by his own nature as essentially love (1 John 4:8). In fact, Cottrell argues that since God is love, in a real sense God is not free to apply or withhold saving grace as an optional choice on his part. God's will cannot be severed from his nature in this manner, as Calvinism assumes.

> How is it possible to say that love is the very *nature* of God, but at the same time
> to say that its exercise is completely a matter of his *will*, that it is completely

---

87. Erickson, *Christian Theology*, 930. Erickson could just as well have substituted the word "calling" as "grace."

88. Hughes, "Grace," 482, emphases mine.

free and optional? . . . If God is gracious by nature, how could he possibly choose not to be gracious? . . . Because love and mercy and grace are of the very *essence* of God, he is *not* free either to love or not to love, either to be gracious or not be gracious. The very meaning of grace is the willingness and desire to forgive sinners and to receive them back into fellowship. This is not "optional" with God.[89]

But, having chosen to show lovingkindness to his human creation who have sinned, then grace by its very nature, could only be offered, not sovereignly imposed or applied. And because grace is offered as a gift (Rom 3:24; 5:15, 17; Eph 3:7; 4:7; 1 Pet 4:10), it must be voluntarily received (by faith). In short God's grace can be received or rejected, but never imposed or unilaterally applied.

Irresistible and Efficacious Grace

Efficacious and irresistible grace are two sides of the same coin. The former states that the saving grace applied to the individual God chooses to save will infallibly and effectively achieve its end (the salvation of the individual), while the latter stresses the fact that this grace cannot be resisted and thus thwart the saving purposes of God. Both are quite unbiblical and in fact, like the types of grace considered so far, are theological constructs designed to work within a Calvinistic soteriology. As already explained, any grace that functions in human experience to infallibly, unavoidably, and sovereignly achieve its end is not biblical grace.

Most Calvinists acknowledge that God's grace can be resisted—but not by the elect. "The grace of God may indeed be resisted, but it will not be successfully resisted by those whom God has chosen in Christ to salvation from before the creation of the world."[90] This underscores the partiality of God concerning access to his grace for salvation. And yet, God, as an aspect of his righteousness, shows no partiality in his dealings with men. For example, Peter came to realize this when he came to understand that God had included the Gentiles in his redemptive purposes: To Cornelius he said, *"I most certainly understand now that God is not one to show partiality, but in every nation the man who fears Him and does what is right is welcome to Him"* (Acts 10:34, 25). God's judging of men who do evil is irrespective of race or anything else in man: Paul unequivocally states that *"there will be tribulation and distress for every soul of man who does evil, of the Jew first and also of the Greek,"* and conversely, *"glory and honor and peace to everyone who does good, to the Jew first and also to the Greek."* Why? Because *"there is no partiality with God"* (Rom 2:9–11).

If God's grace cannot be resisted then biblical warnings not to oppose God's grace are ultimately superfluous and even disingenuous. Similarly, with respect to

---

89. Cottrell, *What the Bible Says about God the Redeemer*, 386, emphases original.

90. Hoekema, *Saved by Grace*, 105.

the many exhortations for hearers to accept God's grace as manifested, for example, in the teaching and preaching of Jesus. A doctrine of irresistible grace ultimately neutralizes God's word and brings confusion to the way God is understood to relate to his human creation.

Prevenient Grace

This form of grace is worthy of a separate section, but since it is a type of grace and I am dealing with types of grace here, I will discuss it at this point. This expression of God's grace is generally rejected by Calvinism, but held by many (though not all) non-Calvinists. It is especially identified with the theology of John Wesley. The basic idea is that of God's grace going before or preceding the individual and his or her coming to faith. It may loosely be connected with Jesus's words *"No one can come to Me unless the Father who sent Me draws him"* (John 6:44). "Prevenient grace is grace which comes first. It precedes all human decision and endeavor. Grace always means that it is God who takes the initiative and implies the priority of God's action on behalf of needy sinners."[91]

This grace is made necessary because non-Calvinists like Wesleyans and classical Arminians accept the Calvinistic notion of total depravity. That is, because of Adam's sin, the human will and mind is so negatively impacted that, apart from a supernatural work of God, no one would be able to respond to the call of God to believe the gospel and repent. "Wesley's analysis of the human condition and his bold proclamation of divine grace should warm the heart of any evangelical Calvinist."[92] However, the Wesleyan concept of prevenient grace differs from the Calvinist's irresistible grace in two important respects.

The first way prevenient grace differs from irresistible grace is that it is universal. Recall that Calvinism makes a sharp distinction between, on the one hand, a universal grace (common grace) that is applicable to all peoples and entails provisions such as food, water, ability to work, even conscience and the good seen in society and, on the other hand, sovereign, or special, grace which is the grace given by God only to the elect for their salvation. So, as far as salvation is concerned Calvinists do not believe in a universal grace, but only in a special or particular grace, limited in its scope to the elect alone. Prevenient grace however is a grace that is available to all without exception and could potentially result in the salvation of everyone. Calvinism's common grace can never lead anyone to salvation, whereas prevenient grace is designed to provide for all people's needs, including salvation. As Schreiner puts it: "The Wesleyan understanding of prevenient grace differs from the Calvinistic conception of common grace in one important area. In the Calvinistic scheme common grace does not and cannot lead to salvation. It functions to restrain evil in the world but does not lead

91. Hughes, "Grace," 480.

92. Schreiner, "Prevenient Grace," 233.

unbelievers to faith. For Wesleyans, prevenient grace may lead unbelievers to faith."[93] For Calvinism, as far as salvation is concerned, it is sovereign grace that functions to ensure the elect (and only the elect) come to faith.

The second significant difference between Calvinism's irresistible grace and Wesleyan prevenient grace is in the fact that the latter, as far as salvation is concerned, can be resisted whereas for Calvinism God's irresistible grace, by definition, cannot be resisted and will, indeed must, effectually lead to the salvation of the elect. "What separates Calvinists from Wesleyans is that the former see electing grace [i.e., sovereign grace] as given only to some (the elect) and insist that this grace *cannot ultimately be resisted*. The latter argue that prevenient grace is given to all people and that it *can be resisted*."[94]

A crucial factor that needs to be stressed concerns prevenient grace and human depravity due to sin. Mention has already been made that prevenient grace, in principle, functions and is intended to lead people to salvation. It does this by supernaturally[95] removing the fatal impediment to believing the gospel, namely, the supposed total blindness and indifference to God or the things of God as a result of a total depravity that extends to all people by way of original sin. Again, as Schreiner helpfully summarizes: "What is common in all Wesleyan theories of prevenient grace is that the freedom, which was lost in Adam's sin, is sufficiently restored to enable people to choose salvation. . . . As descendants of Adam [people are] born with no ability or desire to choose God, but God has counteracted this inability by the gift of prevenient grace. Now all people have the ability to choose God."[96] Prevenient grace, unlike irresistible grace, does not guarantee that everyone, or anyone, will actually choose to be saved, but now they at least have the ability to do so if they wish.

What to make of all these forms of grace? First, one can agree that Calvinism's common grace, as far as expressing God's care for the whole of creation, is perfectly valid. This grace functions to serve God's providential work of sustaining the world. However, the Calvinist's distinction between common grace and sovereign grace, as noted earlier is artificial and unwarranted. So also is Calvinism's irresistible grace— this type of grace is a Calvinistic construct intended to accommodate the belief that God has his elect chosen few who alone will most assuredly be saved. But what about prevenient grace's actions upon the person that serves to give them the ability to choose salvation by removing the impediments to belief due to total depravity? Here I judge prevenient grace to be misleading because unnecessary and claiming to address

---

93. Schreiner, "Prevenient Grace," 235.

94. Schreiner, "Prevenient Grace," 236, emphases mine.

95. Wesleyans differ as to exactly how prevenient grace works to remove the fatal blindness of original sin. See Finger, *Christian Theology*, 2:205. There would appear to be an inherent ambiguity in Wesley's insistence that God's prevenient grace is "Free in All" and "Free for All." Exactly what did Wesley mean when speaking of grace in all—and how is this grace applied?

96. Schreiner, "Prevenient Grace," 236–37.

a nonexistent problem. As we saw in the chapter dealing with total depravity, while people can indeed become depraved due to their personal sins, this depravity is not such that it prevents someone recognizing their need of salvation and their need to trust Christ for that salvation.[97] The Bible simply does not teach that God must somehow work upon a person first to enable them to believe. As Erickson states:

> Many Arminians, recognizing that human inability as taught in the Scripture, introduce the concept of prevenient grace, which is believed to have a universal effect nullifying the noetic results of sin, thus making belief possible. The problem is that there is no clear and adequate basis in Scripture for this concept of universal enablement. The theory, appealing though it is in many ways, simply is not taught explicitly in the Bible.[98]

This is precisely the same criticism that can also be made against irresistible grace, an alleged grace designed to deal with exactly the same problem of inability.

There is a sense in which it is legitimate to speak of a prevenient grace, a going-before grace. This grace is related to Jesus statement to the effect that God needs to draw people to himself, and that no one would find God unaided: *"No one can come to Me unless the Father who sent Me draws him; and I will raise him up on the last day"* (John 6:44). Provided this drawing work is not coercive, then this (prevenient) grace of God is quite real. How is this grace manifested? By the Father's initiative in sending his Son to be the Savior of the world, by the proclamation of the gospel, preeminently by the cross,[99] by Jesus sending his apostles to the uttermost parts of the world with the gospel, with the Spirit's work bringing conviction of sin to the world (John 16:8). In all these ways, God's prevenient grace is at work. Notice that none of these expressions of God's grace entail removal of an alleged inherent psychological or spiritual blindness that prevents anyone from hearing, understanding, and choosing to respond to the gospel (either positively or negatively). This grace is available to everyone (not just an elect few), and most certainly can be resisted. Prevenient grace is a valid category of grace provided it is understood as God's gracious acts externally presented to the individual—such as the incarnation, or exposure to gospel proclamation—but not if it is understood to be a work of God that somehow alters one's psychological state to enable them to believe.

---

97. Jesus taught, *"Truly, truly, I say to you, everyone who commits sin is the slave of sin"* (John 8:34). But Jesus also called on the people at large to repent and believe the gospel (Matt 4:17). A good illustration of how a depraved sinner can *"come to his senses"* and seek restoration is seen in the parable of the prodigal son (Luke 15:17).

98. Erickson, *Christian Theology*, 925.

99. *"And I, if I am lifted up from the earth, will draw all men to Myself"* (John 12:32).

b) A Mistaken Understanding of Human Depravity Leads to a Misunderstanding of How Grace Works

Recall that a foundational assumption for the need for an irresistible grace is that total depravity, understood as total inability, absolutely requires such a grace for the elect to be saved. Consequently, if the Calvinist's view of human depravity is found to be incorrect (i.e., unbiblical) then the rationale for an irresistible grace goes away.

In the chapter dealing with total depravity, we looked at several key passages often appealed to by Calvinists to bolster the idea of total inability, the view that says an unbeliever is totally unable to understand the gospel (it is foolishness to him), believe the gospel, receive Christ, exercise faith, or repent. I also argued that this false belief concerning the unbeliever's relationship to the gospel is grounded in and reinforced by the equally mistaken belief in original sin—the idea that everyone is born a sinner and condemned to judgment and death because of Adam's sin in the garden of Eden. In that chapter, we also saw how this view of sin as originating in Adam and manifesting itself as a total inability to believe the gospel was essentially begun with Augustine in the fifth century and in his disputes with the British monk Pelagius. This is a classic example of how an error in one doctrine inevitably leads to a cascade of errors in related doctrines. In this case: the error of original sin leads to the error of total inability, which in turn leads to the error of irresistible grace. The grounding error of original sin which makes everyone born a sinner by nature (rather than by act), actually makes every newborn baby a "seed-bed of sin," and quite logically "therefore cannot but be odious and abominable to God."[100] From this basic error, Calvin and Calvinism logically extends an exaggerated view of human depravity which is so extensive and deep that no one is able to do anything of genuine spiritual significance (like repent and believe the gospel); total depravity has given birth to total inability. If anyone is to be saved, and for Calvinism that means the elect only, then a grace has to be applied to the sinner such that all resistance to the claims of God upon his life is removed. This leads to yet another error, the idea that regeneration precedes faith—for how can anyone totally depraved and totally unable to believe going to exercise saving faith? The answer given by Calvinism is, of course, that God must first regenerate that person irresistibly who is then enabled to believe and be converted.[101]

From the above analysis it is clear that, for the Calvinist, the root problem as far as being saved is concerned is an inability to repent or exercise faith. But is this what

---

100. Calvin, *Institutes*, 2.1.8.

101. This review of total depravity is not meant to reduce or minimize the reality of sin or its devastating consequences. Everyone has sinned (Rom 3:23), and the wages of sin is death (Rom 6:23). Sin, however, is not intrinsically part of human nature, but rather a consequence of deliberate and willfully chosen actions: sin is lawlessness (1 John 3:4)—the breaking of God's moral law. Of course, repetitive and continual breaking of the moral law can and does lead to something akin to enslavement or addiction. As Jesus said: "Everyone who commits sin is the slave of sin" (John 8:34). In short, we do not sin because we are sinners, but rather we are sinners because we sin. And we become enslaved to sin when we choose to sin repeatedly.

Scripture itself indicates is the root problem? No. The root problem is not *inability* to believe, but rather, *unwillingness* to believe.[102] The Bible shows God appealing, reasoning, persuading, even pleading with men to repent and turn to God. The assumption seems to be that a person, created in the image of God, is able and expected to respond to the claims of God upon his life—and assumes responsibility for failing to do so. The grace is seen in the gospel call, the reasoning, the appeal, and the provision of the gospel content (the cross), but the decision to submit or reject the message is clearly for the individual to make.

An example would be Paul's interactions with the Jews who visited him while in house prison in Rome (Acts 28). Here we read: *"When they had set a day for Paul, they came to him at his lodging in large numbers; and he was explaining to them by solemnly testifying about the kingdom of God and trying to persuade them concerning Jesus, from both the Law of Moses and from the Prophets, from morning until evening. Some were being persuaded by the things spoken, but others would not believe"* (Acts 28:23, 24). Notice (a) Paul sought to *explain* to them; why would Paul seek to explain anything of spiritual significance if he believed they were blind and deaf to the message? (b) He sought to *persuade* them all day long; why would Paul seek to persuade someone of anything they could not be persuaded by? (c) the result of Paul's preaching was that some were indeed persuaded, while others chose not to believe. As the text tells us, those Jews hostile to Paul's message *would not*—not could not—believe. This condition was a self-chosen one and not due to some innate moral limitation or incapacity. We find precisely the same dynamic in Jesus's lament over Jerusalem: *"O Jerusalem, Jerusalem, the city that kills the prophets and stones those sent to her! How often I wanted to gather your children together, just as a hen gathers her brood under her wings, and you would not have it"* (Luke 13:34). And also in Paul's complaint against the Jews: *"But as for Israel He says, 'All the day long I have stretched out my hands to a disobedient and obstinate people'"* (Rom 10:21). The basic problem is not that people are born blind due to some metaphysical condition (original sin) over which they have no control, but rather that men choose to *"suppress the truth in unrighteousness"* (Rom 1:18). No one is born blind to spiritual truths when graciously presented with them, but sadly, some men choose to be blind. Willful blindness is the problem, not an inherent inability.

On the question of persuading people to believe the gospel, Hunt states the Calvinist dilemma well:

> Calvinism denies that there is any winning or persuading—salvation comes by sovereign regeneration and Irresistible Grace imposed. If one must be regenerated and then made to believe, the gospel would have no part in the new birth, preaching it would be pointless, there would be no persuading the unregenerate sinner, and it would be a waste of time to attempt to do so. Yet

---

102. Hunt is surely correct when he says, "Biblically, the problem is not that man cannot understand the gospel or that he cannot submit to God, but that he will not." Hunt, *What Love Is This?*, 383.

Paul expended himself for Christ doing exactly that: disputing and persuading in the attempt to win people to Christ.[103]

c) Is the Will in Bondage?

Since Calvinism denies that a person has the capacity to choose the right, the good, spiritually speaking this naturally raises the question concerning the human will and its exercise in moral and spiritual things. In short, has anyone, apart from God's irresistible grace being applied to them, a will that is free to choose to obey the gospel or not? Is free will a reality or not? This question becomes particularly acute within the context of a soteriology that views man as totally depraved such that he cannot choose for God, and also in view of a God whose sovereignty is such that God determines everything that happens.[104] If God determines everything that happens in the universe, including the choices and actions of men, then in what ways can one speak about people having a free will? Such are the sorts of questions concerning the nature of human freedom and the exercise of the human will inevitably raised by Calvinism. These questions are not trivial as Sproul notes somewhat dramatically: "In the view of the magisterial Reformers themselves, one's view of the will and its state in bondage is absolutely vital to one's understanding of the entire Christian faith."[105]

To facilitate the discussion, we may note that, in the context of this debate historically, there have been two definitions of freedom used. "Libertarian freedom" is the ability to "do otherwise" (also known as the power of contrary choice). In our case, it would express the freedom to do x or to do y, to do good or to do evil, to believe the gospel or to reject the gospel.[106] In contrast to this understanding of freedom is "compatibilistic freedom." This is the view held by most Calvinists because it is considered to be a view of freedom that is compatible with divine determinism. Basically, this notion of freedom says one is free as long as one can act in accordance with one's wishes; it is a capacity to act. Proponents of compatibilistic freedom deny libertarian freedom.[107]

103. Hunt, *What Love Is This?*, 475.

104. As previously discussed when considering divine election, the technical term to describe God's universal ultimate causation of everything is divine determinism. Olsen comments, "The Calvinist account of God's sovereignty is divine determinism. . . . To affirm that everything that happens, down to the minutest details . . . are determined is by definition to affirm determinism." Olsen, *Against Calvinism*, 84.

105. Sproul, *Reformed Theology*, 182.

106. I have chosen to emphasis this aspect of libertarian freedom because it fits well with the issue here—can an unbeliever choose for God, or is he in such bondage to sin that he is unable to exercise such freedom. Other definitions of libertarian freedom emphasis that an action is free only if the person is not causally determined by anything outside of himself.

107. Certainly, to do as one wishes would be acceptable to most in any understanding of human freedom, but with the key implicit assumption that one could wish for either x or y; most would reject the notion of being caused to act in only way. Common formal definitions of freedom reflect this. For example, the *Cambridge Dictionary* defines freedom as "the ability to decide what to do independently

Luther, for example, in his disputes with the humanist Erasmus, argued strongly for the bondage of the will to Satan's will in things pertaining to salvation.[108]

It is worth reminding ourselves that, in the history of the Christian church, such questions only gained prominence as late as the fourth century, in the time of Augustine. Prior to Augustine, the church in fact stressed the reality of the human will and its freedom to obey the gospel call. It did this in response to gnostic philosophies like Manichaeism that stressed man's inability to choose because of an overarching determinism. "For Origen, as for all the early [church] fathers, freedom was vital as the antithesis of fate or necessity."[109] In other words, they consistently argued for libertarian free will. Even the "early Augustine" argued against the Manichaeans and for the freedom of the will which is "a movement of mind free both for doing and not doing."[110] Calvin himself acknowledged that the early church, prior to Augustine, stressed libertarian freedom.[111] Later, Augustine, during his disputes with Pelagius, changed his mind concerning human free will in order to bring it into line with his strong predestinarian convictions.[112] While Adam was "able to not sin," now man after Adam, is "not able not to sin."[113] Augustine's view prevailed in the subsequent centuries of church history and, given Augustine's influence on John Calvin we should not be surprised to read in Calvin's *Institutes*: "Man is said to have free will, not because he has a free choice of good and evil, but because he acts voluntarily, and not by compulsion."[114]

It will be helpful at this point to look at a couple of scriptures that impinge on this question of the bondage or enslavement of the will. This first is John 8:34–36, *"Jesus answered them, 'Truly, truly, I say to you, everyone who commits sin is the slave of sin. The slave does not remain in the house forever; the son does remain forever.' So if the Son makes you free, you will be free indeed."* The context has Jesus teaching in the temple (8:1). Some of his hearers seem to have been inclined to believe his teaching: *"As He spoke these things, many came to believe in Him. So Jesus was saying to those Jews who had believed Him . . ."* (8:30, 31). However, the exact spiritual status of these "believers"

---

of any outside influence," and the *Merriam-Webster Dictionary*'s first entry for "freedom" is "the absence of necessity, coercion, or constraint in choice or action."

108. See Rupp and Watson, *Luther and Erasmus*, 327–29.

109. Bromiley, *Historical Theology*, 46.

110. Barlotta, "Evolving Views," line 37.

111. "As to the Fathers (if their authority weighs with us), they have the term [libertarian free will] constantly in their mouths." *Institutes*, 2.2.7. Calvin lamented, "How few are there who, when they hear free will attributed to man, do not immediately imagine that he is the master of his mind and will in such a sense, that he can of himself incline himself either to good or evil?" Calvin, *Institutes*, 2.2.7.

112. "Elaine Pagels observes that, given the intense inner conflicts with lust and his battle to control his sexual impulses, as revealed in his Confessions, 'Augustine's decision to abandon his predecessor's emphasis on free will need not surprise us.'" Smith, *Willful Intent*, 35. Smith is citing Pagels, *Adam, Eve, and the Serpent*, 99.

113. Allison, *Historical Theology*, 347.

114. Calvin, *Institutes*, 2.2.7.

is brought into question by the way they react to Jesus's subsequent teaching. As always, in John's gospel, the focus by Jesus in his teachings is on himself (vv. 35, 38, 42, etc.); these "believers" failed to grasp the true significance of Jesus's person, and still clung to their heritage in Abraham (vv. 33, 39). Morris's conclusion is probably correct: "It is best to think that John is speaking of men who had made an outward profession, but that in this particular case, it did not go very deep."[115] The issue of enslavement is triggered by Jesus's teaching in v. 32: *"You will know the truth, and the truth will make you free."* It is in this context that Jesus says in v. 34 that *"everyone who commits sin is the slave of sin."* Whereas the Jews had been thinking in terms of a freedom associated with their physical connection to Abraham, Jesus indicates that the real issue is spiritual—enslavement to sin, and that the antidote was to listen carefully, and commit themselves to him who reveals the truth from the Father, vv. 44, 45.

From this background we can note the following points: first, it is doubtful that Jesus is making a sweeping generalization about sin, as though sinning just once enslaves the person to a life of bondage and enslavement to all sorts of sin thereafter. Second, Jesus is definitely teaching that there is a sense in which one choosing to continue indulging in a sinful practice (or false belief) eventually does indeed become enslaved by that choice. Third, this was precisely the condition of the Jews; they insisted on relying on their ethnic connection to Abraham, and in the process resisted and rejected the claims of Christ himself. Their commitment to their Abrahamic heritage, a deception with satanic origins (vv. 41, 44), blinded them to spiritual truths and from receiving Jesus's teaching. In fact, if they really knew God through a true understanding of their own (Old Testament) scriptures, they would have recognized Jesus's true status and gladly received his teaching (vv. 42, 47). Once again, we see that the root issue confronting Jesus here is their *unwillingness* to change and switch allegiance from their Jewish heritage in Abraham to Jesus's teaching and person. This is made clear when Jesus pointedly asks them why they do not understand his teaching, and then goes to the heart of the problem, their preference to do the desire of their father, the devil (v. 43, 44) through their insistence on relying upon their Abrahamic heritage.[116] That the enslaving effect of sin in this case did indeed prevent the Jews from understanding the true significance of Jesus, was by no means always the case in the gospel of John. Others who heard the gospel of the kingdom did in fact hear and believe upon Jesus, including some who witnessed the turning of the water into wine (2:11), the Samaritan woman at the well and her friends in the city (John 4), the royal official whose son was sick (4:46–54), Nicodemus (7:51–52), the man born blind (John 9), and many others. In short, the enslavement Jesus affirms in John 8:34 was a self-inflicted enslavement due

---

115. Morris, *John*, 455.

116. We see a similar dynamic in John 5:39–47: "and you are *unwilling* to come to Me so that you may have life" (v. 40). They did not truly understand Moses because if they had they would have believed Jesus, but rather they chose to receive glory from one another (v. 44).

to a choice made by the enslaved—not due to an inherent inability to hear and respond positively when challenged by the gospel.

Romans 6:16–18: *"Do you not know that when you present yourselves to someone as slaves for obedience, you are slaves of the one whom you obey, either of sin resulting in death, or of obedience resulting in righteousness? But thanks be to God that though you were slaves of sin, you became obedient from the heart to that form of teaching to which you were committed, and having been freed from sin, you became slaves of righteousness."* This text, like the previous one (John 8:34–36), is sometimes appealed to by Calvinists to bolster a theory of inherent moral and spiritual inability to do a good such as repent and believe the gospel.[117] Just as Jesus taught, Paul likewise affirms an enslaving aspect to persistent sinning. Paul's concern in these verses (Rom 6:1–23) is pastoral and centers around a concern that the Christians at Rome *"not go on presenting the members of your body to sin as instruments of unrighteousness"* (v. 13). They had indeed been slaves of sin (v. 17), but through the gospel had enjoyed a certain freedom from sin (v. 18). A difficulty in deriving a theology of sin from passages like Rom 6 is that Paul focuses on their current status and does not delve deeply into the origin or original cause of the sinning in the past. However, Paul does seem to locate sin in their bodies and specifically in the body's members: *"Therefore do not let sin reign in your mortal body so that you obey its lusts, and do not go on presenting the members of your body to sin as instruments of unrighteousness"* (Rom 6:12–13). But even here the idea seems to be one of choosing whom to serve—either the body, or Christ. Paul consistently uses the language of "presenting"—*"do not go on* presenting *the members of your body to sin . . . but* present *yourselves to God"* (v. 13), *"when you* present *yourselves to someone as slaves"* (v. 16), *"For just as you* presented *your members as slaves to impurity . . . so now* present *your members as slaves to righteousness"* (v. 19). There is a certain symmetry here; just as in their pre-Christian days the Romans chose to give allegiance to sin, so now as Christians they are to choose to give allegiance to Christ. The language of presenting suggests an ability to exercise libertarian freedom—would they present themselves to sin, or would they present themselves to God?

A possible, though somewhat artificial it seems to me, response on the part of the Calvinist might be to stress that Paul is addressing Christians who have been released from enslavement from sin and now have a capacity to obey or disobey the call to holy living, a capacity not available to them in their pre-Christian days. Now, the possibility of living holy lives is not available to the non-Christian—but not by virtue of some innate inability to receive Christ, but rather due to ignorance about the gospel and the claims of Christ upon their lives (until they have been evangelized). It is true that unbelievers choose to present their bodies to sin, and it is true that believers can choose to present their bodies to sin or to choose to present their bodies as instruments of

---

117. "As if death and decay were nor sufficient to stress the helplessness of our condition in the absence of the Spirit of life, Paul underscores the point with the metaphors of captivity. . . . In the absence of the Spirit, Paul recognizes no freedom of the will." Westblade, "Divine Election," 67.

righteousness as we have just seen (Rom 6). However, just as for the believers at Rome who were "enslaved to God" (v. 22) and that this did not prevent them from choosing to present the members of their bodies to sin (v. 13), so likewise enslavement to sin on the part of unbelievers does not prevent them from choosing to repent and believe the gospel. In short, the language of enslavement does not remove the possibility and the capacity, not to save oneself, but to choose to respond to the gift of salvation when offered. As Paul makes clear a little later in his epistle, anyone can call upon the Lord when presented with the preaching of the gospel (Rom 10:12–15).

To my mind, a consistent Calvinist ought to reject the notion of any kind of free will. Why? Because they insist that God's sovereignty is such that God determines everything, absolutely everything, that takes place in the creation. If God determines everything then whence the room for another agent able to determine outcomes too? Gordon Clark, the controversial Presbyterian theologian, was just such a Calvinist: "I here omit to bring forward those all-powerful arguments drawn from the purpose of grace, from the promise, from the force of the law, from original sin, and from the election of God; of which there is not one that would not of itself utterly overthrow 'free will' . . . if I wished to produce all those parts of Paul which overthrow 'free will' . . . among the many Biblical passages that deny free will."[118] Not many Calvinists have followed Clark in his consistency in clearly denying the reality of any form of human free will.

While few Calvinist would outrightly deny free will, all deny a capacity of the human will to choose for God. Many would admit that the unbeliever is free—but only to sin. Augustine held this view: "Man retains a certain freedom. He freely does the will of his master, sin. . . . On his own, then, man does not have the freedom to do good works or to return to God."[119] Luther argued against Erasmus's view of freedom which Erasmus viewed as "a power of human will by which a man can apply himself to the things which lead to eternal salvation, or turn away from them,"[120] and insisted that "free choice apart from grace, having lost its liberty, is forced to serve sin and cannot do good."[121] Grudem makes essentially the same point: "Do we still have any freedom of choice? Certainly, those who are outside of Christ do still make voluntary choices—that is, they decide what they want to do, then they do it. In this sense there is still a kind of freedom in the choices that people make. Yet because of their inability to do good . . . unbelievers do not have freedom . . . to do right and to do what is pleasing to God."[122]

---

118. Clark, *Predestination*, 70.

119. Bromiley, *Historical Theology*, 111. Gonzales concurs: "After the fall, [man] was still free, but he lost the gift of grace which enabled him not to sin and was free only to sin." Gonzales, *History of Christian Thought*, 2:44.

120. Rupp and Watson, *Luther and Erasmus*, 169.

121. Rupp and Watson, *Luther and Erasmus*, 179.

122. Grudem, *Systematic Theology*, 498. It is not clear how it is that "*they* decide what they want to do" on the one hand and at the same time God's sovereignty is such God decides everything that happens.

Does such a view on human freedom comport with the biblical evidence? I will discuss shortly, from the Bible itself, why this view is untenable.

One of the most influential works favorable to the view of making human freedom compatible with divine determinism is Jonathan Edwards's (1703–1758) *Freedom of the Will*. It is his notion of what later came to be known as compatibilistic freedom that probably most Calvinists hold today. Edwards begins his study with the idea that a person is free provided they do what they want to do, and are not coerced or otherwise forced to do what they wish: "The plain and obvious meaning of the words Freedom and Liberty, in common speech, is the power, opportunity, or advantage, that any one has, to do as he pleases. Or in other words, his being free from hindrance or impediment in the way of doing, or conducting in any respect, as he wills."[123] Edwards insists that men do in fact act freely in this way when making decisions. Every decision is made for a reason—what seems best at the moment the decision is made: "The Will always is as the greatest apparent good."[124] Edwards rightly rejected the notion of "liberty of indifference," the idea that decisions are made from a completely blank, neutral perspective apart from an overriding reason. The reasons for choosing one course of action over another is a function of all the conditions that influence the decision. But, and here is how Edwards links an absolute divine determinism with freedom of choice: all the conditions from which a decision is chosen are decreed by God. "From what has been observed it is evident, that *the absolute decrees of God* are no more inconsistent with human liberty, on account of any Necessity of *the event, which follows from such decrees*, than the absolute Foreknowledge of God."[125] Just as God has exhaustive foreknowledge of future events because he decreed them, so the events upon which people choose to make decisions, and thus exercise (compatibilstic) freedom, is likewise decreed.

Two observations may be made concerning compatibilstic freedom as here formulated by Edwards, and adopted in its essentials by most thinking Calvinists today. The first is this: Edwards, like all Calvinists, believes that God's providence is such that God controls (determines) every minute detail in the universe continually. All has been decreed by "an absolute decree of God." So, on what basis can a person be free in *any* sense to choose how to respond to a divinely established set of circumstances? The assumption seems to be that the moral agent is independent while making the decision, but then infallibly chooses precisely what God has decreed he choose. But the notion of any kind of independence from God and God's will, even for a microsecond, is inconsistent with Calvinism. The second problem is that no matter how apparently free the person acts in choosing what he wishes he is in fact choosing exactly what God wishes; in other words, determinism reigns supreme throughout this process of choosing. There is not a moment and not a thing that has not been determined

---

123. Edwards, *Freedom of the Will*, 18.

124. Edwards, *Freedom of the Will*, 6.

125. Edwards, *Freedom of the Will*, 76, emphases mine.

by God. So, we end up with the person thinking he is choosing, he is free to choose, but this is in fact just a charade, God has determined all. Compatibilistic freedom, in other words, is inherently incoherent—there is no escaping the iron grip of an exhaustive divine determinism for even a moment.[126]

Does the Bible support the idea of libertarian freedom, the ability of a person to choose one way or another without being coerced or determined by an overarching sovereignty? I believe the answer is a clear yes. In a sense the whole of the Bible is predicated on such freedom being available to man. Most promises, every threat of judgment, every exhortation, every appeal, every call to obey, every temptation carries with it an element of conditionality—believe this, obey this, do this, resist this—or else this will happen. As early as the garden of Eden we see conditionality and its implied exercise of libertarian free will: you may eat of any tree, but not this one—choose what you will do, eat or not eat.[127] The covenant blessings and curses in Deut 28 again are predicated on the reality of libertarian freedom: obedience brings covenant blessings (Deut 28:1–14), conversely if the people choose to disobey the covenant made with Yahweh then the covenant curses would be invoked (Deut 28:15–68). The people were free to choose either to obey the covenant stipulations (Mosaic law), or choose to disobey. Similarly, when Joshua led the people of Israel into the promised land: *"Choose for yourselves today whom you will serve: whether the gods which your fathers served which were beyond the River, or the gods of the Amorites in whose land you are living; but as for me and my house, we will serve the Lord"* (Josh 25:15). The people were free to choose x or y. Similarly, the appeal by John the Baptist for the Jews of his day to *"Repent, for the kingdom of heaven is at hand"* (Matt 3:2) carried an implied consequence; you are free to choose to repent, but if you choose not to repent certain consequences will follow. On the outward leg of Paul's second missionary journey with Timothy, we read: *"A vision appeared to Paul in the night: a man of Macedonia was standing and appealing to him, and saying, 'Come over to Macedonia and help us.' When he had seen the vision, immediately we sought to go into Macedonia, concluding that God had called us to preach the gospel to them"* (Acts 16:9, 10). Could Paul not have resisted the call? Was it impossible for Paul to refuse to heed the call? If we answer no to these questions then we are holding to libertarian freedom; Paul had the choice to obey the visionary call—or to disobey and remain in Troas. More examples of libertarian freedom being exercised

126. Critics of Edwards have brought attention to the fact that if compatibilism is the only logically necessary form of freedom (as Edwards's compatibilism insists is the case), then there is a sense in which, since God chose to create the world, he had no alternative open to him (which would be implied by libertarian freedom). Thus, the world didn't come about contingently, as though God could have chosen to create or chosen not to create, but rather the creation of the world was necessary even for God. This, of course, brings into serious question the validity of God's sovereignty, and the extent to which God is himself free. Roger Olsen discusses the extent to which God himself can be considered to be free in his actions given Calvinism's view of God. See Olsen, *Against Calvinism*, 92–94.

127. Augustine argued that even though Adam chose to sin it was God's will that prevailed even then, since "God's will has been done concerning him [Adam] through the grace and work of the Mediator." Bromiley, *Historical Theology*, 116.

could be made, but these are sufficient to make the point. The Bible everywhere assumes that men have the power of contrary choice, libertarian freedom.

Cottrell well sums up the question of the will's bondage to sin and consequent alleged inability to believe the gospel: "We affirm that salvation is conditional because we accept the reality of a truly free will both in man as originally created and even in man in his state of sinful depravity. . . . The Bible does not teach the doctrine of total depravity with its bondage of the will. It teaches a partial depravity with a limited inability to do certain things, but the sinner's basic ability to respond to the gospel is not destroyed. Sinners have the ability to believe and repent of their own free will."[128]

d) How Exactly Is Irresistible Grace Applied?

It is instructive to see how Calvinists consider the saving grace of God to be irresistibly applied, yet without the unbeliever being coerced. The idea of an irresistible grace being applied, ties closely with the idea of an effectual call in which, upon hearing the gospel, an elect person is certain to respond in the desired manner. In the following, I will assume that the two aspects are roughly synonymous. Here are the ways in which a variety of Calvinists describe this phenomenon:

Grudem: "[Effectual] calling is rather a kind of 'summons' from the King of the universe and it has such power that it brings about the response that it asks for in people's hearts. It is an act of God that *guarantees* a response."[129] Grudem is concerned to remove the idea of coercion here: "Although it is true that effective calling awakens and brings forth a response from us, we must always insist that this response still has to be a voluntary, willing response."[130] Nevertheless, the effective call of God "actually brings about a willing response from the person who hears it."[131] When an unbeliever hears the gospel (what Grudem calls the gospel call as distinct from the effectual call), God "speaks to our emotions by issuing a heartfelt personal *invitation* to *respond*. He speaks to our wills by *asking* us to hear his *invitation* and *respond* willingly in repentance and faith—to decide to turn from our sins and receive Christ."[132]

One wonders what sense it makes for God to "ask" and "invite" those completely spiritually dead to "respond" to the gospel call? By Calvinism's own definition, spiritually dead people are unable to respond when asked or invited! Hunt makes the same point:

> Why would God urge to seek Him, and Christ invite to come to Him, men
> who, if Calvinism is true, are totally depraved and dead in sin to the extent

128. Cottrell, *Faith Once for All*, 348.

129. Grudem, *Systematic Theology*, 692, emphasis original.

130. Grudem, *Systematic Theology*, 693.

131. Grudem, *Systematic Theology*, 693.

132. Grudem, *Systematic Theology*, 693, emphases mine.

that they can't even hear His voice or make a move toward Him? . . . That invitation wouldn't be appropriate for the elect, since their coming is only by the Father irresistibly drawing them. Nor would it be appropriate for the non-elect, because there is no way they could come even if they had the desire.[133]

Furthermore, again one must ask what sense it makes for God to ask or invite anyone to do anything when God, as Grudem himself states, "governs the universe and determines everything that will happen"[134] and when we can be assured "that God causes all things that happen," including "our words, our steps, our movements, our hearts, and our abilities."[135]

It is clear that Grudem wishes to avoid the possible negative reaction that can be expected by simply stating: God has selected you to be part of the elect, and there is no way you can avoid a status God has decreed for you before the world was made. To speak of God "inviting you," "asking you," and seeking your "response" sounds much more polite and genteel! It may be asked how it is that a grace that is irresistibly applied and that manifests itself in an effectual call that guarantees the right response, can be considered to be a "voluntary, willing response"? The very language of ask, invite, summons suggests the possibility of ignoring, declining, or rejecting the call. Here we find precisely the same inherent contradiction that we see in the Westminster Confession of Faith when it speaks of "determining them to that which is good, and effectually drawing them to Jesus Christ, yet so, as they come most freely, being made willing by his grace."[136] There it is in a nutshell: "being made willing"—this is not a paradox, a mystery, or even a tension, but an actual contradiction. The soft language Grudem uses here in a context of an irresistible grace that follows an effectual call is quite misleading.

A second problem in Grudem's account is the need to make a distinction between a "general call" and an "effectual call." The former made to all, and the latter to the elect alone. But the Bible knows of no such distinction; it just speaks of a call to believe the gospel made to all indiscriminately. Mention has already been made of John the Baptist's call for all in his audience (Jews) to repent and believe the gospel (Matt 3:2), repeated precisely by Jesus (Matt 4:17). We see the same general call to a large number of Jews made by Peter on the day of Pentecost: *"Peter said to them, 'Repent, and each of you be baptized in the name of Jesus Christ for the forgiveness of*

---

133. Hunt, *What Love Is This?*, 438.

134. Grudem, *Systematic Theology*, 213.

135. Grudem, *Systematic Theology*, 321. The typical way Calvinists solve this problem of God decreeing everything that happens and yet "inviting" a response to the gospel call is by appeal to mystery—it's a mystery. Even though God decrees all that happens, he is not to be blamed for evil: "Scripture never speaks that way, and we may not either, even though how this can be so may remain a *mystery* for us in this age." Grudem, *Systematic Theology*, 216, emphasis mine.

136. *Westminster Confession of Faith*, 10.1.

your sins; and you will receive the gift of the Holy Spirit'" (Acts 2:38). There is no hint here of a general call to all and an effectual call to some.

In sharp contrast to Grudem's gentle asking and inviting is Wright's more aggressive "pulling" or "dragging": concerning "the Father's enablement of the sinner. This enablement is not mere influencing of people in general, but the *pulling* or *dragging* of individuals to Jesus by God's power. There is no question concerning the meaning of the Greek here."[137] Wright is referring to the word "draw" in John 6:44 (*"No one can come to Me unless the Father who sent Me draws him"*). The Greek word is ἑλκύσῃ (*elkusē*), an aorist subjunctive verb from the root ἕλκω (*elkuō*). According to the standard reference Greek-English lexicon by Walter Bauer, the word may mean literally to drag or to draw as, for example, drawing a sword from its sheath as Peter did to cut off the ear of the high priest's slave when Jesus was being arrested (John 18:10). Or, it may be used figuratively "of the pull on a man's inner life," in which case its meaning is "draw, attract."[138] Which meaning is appropriate in a sentence is determined by the context. It is most unlikely that Jesus here in John 6:44 pictures someone being literally, physically pulled or dragged to Jesus—there is no record of anyone coming to Jesus in this manner in any of the gospels! Though it is unlikely Wright has in mind any kind of physical dragging of someone to Christ, his unqualified use of the word is misleading in this respect. The major Bible's translators all use the figurative meaning draw (not drag) in their versions including the RSV (Revised Standard Version), AV, NASB, NIV, ESV. Even Wright himself, in the immediately preceding sentence to his reference to pulling and dragging, uses the word figuratively, i.e., draw. Wright's point is that whoever comes to Jesus does so irresistibly and strongly because of a hidden work of the Father. But his case is not helped by his appeal to a literal use of the word, when it is plain that a figurative use is meant, and the word does *not* carry a literal meaning in this context.

Most Calvinists use terms somewhere between Grudem's ask/invite and Wright's pull/drag. Sproul speaks of the application of irresistible grace in terms of a call that *"penetrates* to and *pierces* the heart, *quickening* it to spiritual life."[139] Piper speaks of God *"overcoming"* all resistance and that God's sovereignty is such that he can *"conquer* all resistance when he wills."[140] Some, when discussing the effectual call, prefer to emphasis *that* God works effectively to open blind eyes, hard hearts, etc., rather than explain exactly *how* this is done. Bruce Ware, for example, speaks of the Spirit who *"opens* the blind eyes and *enlivens* the hardened hearts of those dead in sin."[141] "The Holy Spirit is able, when he chooses, to *overcome* all human resistance and so *cause* his gracious

---

137. Wright, *No Place for Sovereignty*, 134, emphases mine.

138. Bauer, *Greek-English Lexicon*, 251d.

139. Sproul, *Reformed Theology*, 191, emphases mine.

140. Piper, *Five Points*, 26, emphases mine.

141. Ware, "Effectual Calling," 204, emphases mine.

work to be utterly effective and ultimately irresistible."[142] Nowhere does Ware explain exactly how God is able to work in this manner, though it is significant that, again, he uses terms that are consistent with physical force—overcome, cause.

To speak of God overcoming, conquering, penetrating the heart, dragging, pulling, and so on, seems very close to the language of coercion. After all, these actions on the part of God upon the unbeliever are not with the person's willing consent; the whole point of such actions is to make the unbeliever consent to God's will! This is necessary of course because of Calvinism's notion of depravity as entailing inability to believe the gospel. So, when Piper says, "Irresistible grace never implies that God forces us to repent or follow Jesus against our will,"[143] this sounds rather hollow (perhaps even disingenuous) to the non-Calvinist.

The variety of terms used to describe how irresistible grace is applied, or how the effectual call works reflects the lack of biblical support for such a work. If the Bible truly supported such a notion, it would supply the appropriate language and words quite clearly and there would not be any confusion about exactly how this supposed irresistible grace actually works. Gonzales, when describing Augustine's view of irresistible grace, remarks: "Grace moves the will, but only though a 'soft-violence' that acts in such a way that the will agrees with it."[144] The biblical data however is clear; there is not a shred of evidence that God's grace operates with any kind of violence, soft or otherwise. It is hard to avoid the notion of coercion when one agent acts upon another "to make them willing'—against their wills![145]

e) What Does It Mean to Say Faith Is a Gift?

All Calvinist's insist that faith is not something man can do himself. It must be something God does to the sinner, or for the sinner, or enable the sinner to do, or give the sinner. For example, Sproul says, "Saving faith is *worked* in the heart."[146] Grudem consistently speaks of God so working effectually in the unbeliever that a *"willing response"* is guaranteed.[147] Horton is more straightforward: "faith . . . is God's gracious *gift*."[148] And "the fallen mind is darkened to the gospel apart from the Spirit's *gift* of faith."[149] Also, "the Spirit delivers the *gift* of faith through the preaching

---

142. Ware, "Effectual Calling," 211, emphases mine.

143. Piper, *Five Points*, 31.

144. Gonzales, *History of Christian Thought*, 2:47.

145. At a rather crass level, a close analogy to this sort of situation is when a man drops a date rape drug into an unwilling female's drink—who then becomes "willing."

146. Sproul, *Reformed Theology*, 192, emphasis mine.

147. Grudem, *Systematic Theology*, 693, 694, emphasis mine.

148. Horton, *For Calvinism*, 99, emphasis mine.

149. Horton, *For Calvinism*, 103, emphasis mine.

of the gospel . . . God graciously grants [unbelievers] the *gift* of faith"[150] Piper says, "Repentance [is] a *gift* of God."[151] Wright believes "commands are one of the forms of God's Word that are most often used by him to *produce* repentance and faith."[152] Likewise, Hoekema states: "Since only regenerated persons can believe, we see again that faith is a *gift* of God."[153]

While all agree that God does something that results in faith, precisely how that something takes place varies among Calvinists. Does God's application of a grace that cannot be resisted make faith possible (as Grudem seems to suggest), or does this grace actually generate faith which is viewed as given to the person? Or perhaps it is both, as Hoekema believes when he says, "Faith is the result of regeneration . . . [and] Faith [is] a task of man."[154] The variety of approaches reflects an imprecision due to the simple fact that nowhere does the Bible clearly teach this doctrine. Rather it is a necessary element required by the TULIP systematic. This judgment is borne out when Calvin stresses the connection between (unconditional) election and faith. Bromiley, in describing Calvin's understanding of the relationship between election and faith remarks that "faith is not to be overestimated. God does not just give us the ability to believe . . . God gives faith itself because he has elected us. . . . Election is the mother of faith."[155]

But what does it mean to say faith is a gift? Faith is certainly something that people do—they believe. According to the writer to the Hebrews, faith is a conviction and an assurance: *"Now faith is the assurance of things hoped for, the conviction of things not seen"* (Heb 11:1). Assurances, convictions, beliefs are what people have—these are not "things" given to people like a gift at Christmas. Understanding is not furthered by statements like this from Louis Berkhof: "It is only after God has implanted the seed of faith in the heart that man can exercise faith." To believe is something a person does, it is not something God does for us or in us. In fact, the idea of faith as a gift is incoherent, and confuses faith as a gift with salvation as a gift; it is a category error. The latter (salvation) truly is a gift given by God to those who exercise faith, whereas the former (faith) is a human characteristic.[156] The

150. Horton, *For Calvinism*, 106, emphasis mine.

151. Piper, *Five Points*, 30, emphasis mine.

152. Wright, *No Place for Sovereignty*, 134, emphasis mine.

153. Hoekema, *Saved by Grace*, 144, emphasis mine.

154. Hoekema, *Saved by Grace*, 144, 145. Hoekema states: "All one has to do to learn that faith is also depicted as a task of man is to look up the word 'faith' or 'believe' in any biblical concordance, and to note that most commonly faith is described as something human beings must do in response to the gospel." Hoekema, *Saved by Grace*, 144. Apart from his qualifier "most commonly," his summary of the biblical data is exactly right.

155. Bromiley, *Historical Theology*, 252.

156. Within Calvinism, faith as a gift is construed as something that cannot be resisted or rejected. But the halfway house that says faith is a gift of God, but one that *can* be rejected is incoherent too, and for the same reasons given above; it is a category mistake. Forgiveness of sins and salvation can be understood as gifts from God, but repentance and faith are the conditions for forgiveness and salvation,

Bible indicates faith is a command to men that results in salvation; *"Believe in the Lord Jesus, and you will be saved"* (Acts 16:31). When Jesus exhorted his disciples to *"have faith in God"* (Mark 11:22) there is no suggestion that God will regenerate the unregenerate and then give him that faith; rather, believing is something man is expected to do. "When Jesus chastised the disciples saying 'O ye of little faith' (Matt 6:30), He was not putting the blame upon His Father for giving the disciples so little faith, but upon the disciples themselves for not believing."[157]

Do Calvinists attempt to justify such a doctrine from the Bible? Yes, sort of. Quite often appeal is made to extrabiblical sources for justification as well as an elaboration of the view that faith must inevitably follow God's unilateral action in applying irresistible grace. R. C. Sproul, for example, in his book *What Is Reformed Theology?*, when discussing effectual calling—the calling that leads to faith being supposedly worked in the heart—appeals to the Westminster Confession of Faith, Calvin, and Augustine, but not a single biblical text to support all his claims.

Typically, three passages in particular are appealed to by Calvinists to support the notion of faith as a gift. The first, and most quoted, is Eph 2:8, *"For by grace you have been saved through faith; and that not of yourselves, it is the gift of God."* This text has been addressed in some detail earlier in this chapter, so I will only provide a summary here. This text does not support a God-given faith because: (1) The grammar and syntactical structure of the verse will not support such a conclusion. Hoekema only offers two passages to justify this doctrine, one of which is Eph 2:8, but he concedes the passage does not support the view![158] (2) To be consistent with the rest of the New Testament, the text actually teaches that salvation is given as a gift, given on the basis of grace (not works), and which is appropriated by faith. Ephesians 2:8a (*"by grace you have been saved"*) is merely a repetition of what Paul had already stated in 2:5: *"Even when we were dead in our transgressions, [God] made us alive together with Christ (by grace you have been saved)."* In Eph 2, Paul is contrasting the Ephesian Christians' former state apart from God to their present status as children of God—and this salvation is based entirely on the grace of God. In other words, there is nothing in the context that would even hint that faith itself is a supernatural gift of God. In short, "faith is not a gift of grace and the result of regeneration; it is a response to grace and a prerequisite to regeneration."[159]

---

conditions required by God in order to receive the gift of salvation from God. The conditions and the gifts should not be confused.

157. Hunt, *What Love Is This?*, 453. Similarly, one might wonder why God was so aggrieved by Israel's lack of faith (Isa 65:2). Also, why would Jesus be prevented from doing miracles in Nazareth due to the unbelief of its residents if the solution lay close at hand, in God himself (Matt 13:58)?

158. Hoekema, *Saved by Grace*, 145. He adds, however, that "since faith is included [in the saved/grace/faith clause], one could conclude that this passage teaches indirectly that faith is a gift of God." But Scripture never indicates faith is a gift, but always states that salvation is a gift.

159. Cottrell, *Faith Once for All*, 200.

Another passage often brought up to justify a doctrine of faith as a gift is Phil 1:29: *"For to you it has been granted for Christ's sake, not only to believe in Him, but also to suffer for His sake."* Hoekema says here, "Faith is described as something which has been granted or freely bestowed on us by God."[160] Of course, this would also suggest that the suffering that the Philippians were experiencing was also from God. But in the immediately preceding verse (v. 28) Paul urges them to not be alarmed by their "opponents." What sort of opposition were the Christians at Phillip facing? Like Paul himself, they were facing Jewish opponents (3:2), false brethren (3:18, 19), disunity (2:2, 3) and disharmony (4:2). Were these forces that threatened the well-being and faith of the Christians really from God? Opposition to the church here and in the other epistles is always seen as something contrary to the will of God, not something given by God and which threatens to destabilize his church. What is Paul really saying to the Philippians? He is reminding them that they are not only privileged to believe upon Christ, which carries tremendous blessings, but also, intrinsic to the Christian life, is the willingness to suffer for God if and when necessary. Paul was concerned that the believers live in a manner worthy of the gospel, and that together they were to be united and faithful to the gospel they had received (1:27). The opposition they had experienced would potentially threaten their Christian walk and witness, and so Paul reminds them that suffering and believing are not antithetical, but rather often go hand in hand. This is nothing about God giving them faith—that would not fit either the context or concerns of the letter.[161]

A third text sometimes cited is Heb 12:2a: *"fixing our eyes on Jesus, the author and perfecter of faith."* Since Hoekema cites this verse to explain that faith is a gift from God following regeneration, then presumably, when he says, "The word rendered 'author' translates *archegon*, which in this context means 'originator' or 'founder,'"[162] he understands the word *originator* as *supplier* (of faith). Similarly, Thomas Hewitt, considering the word *author* in our text says: "It is hardly possible that the author [of Hebrews] would assert that Christ's faith was similar to that of his followers. It seems better then to conceive of Christ as the originator of the Christian faith within the believer."[163]

The Greek in Heb 12:2a literally says "looking to Jesus the author and finisher of the faith." Note the definite article before the word *faith—the* faith. Several Bible translations translate the word as "our faith," thus making the reference to faith a reference to the subjective experience of faith.[164] A more accurate translation would

---

160. Hoekema, *Saved by Grace*, 144.

161. Packer is thus seen to be quite mistaken when he asserts that "God is thus the author of all saving faith (Eph 2:8; Phil 1:29)." Packer, "Faith," 400.

162. Hoekema, *Saved by Grace*, 144.

163. Hewitt, *Hebrews*, 190.

164. The RSV, ESV, and AV (Authorized Version) have "our faith," the NASB and NIV have "of faith."

omit any word before the word faith as in the NASB and NIV.[165] Is it possible that the author intends for the reference to faith to be objective, as in *the* faith as a body of revealed truth, as a short way of saying Christian doctrine? There are other epistles in which an objective sense appears to hold. For example, Paul addresses Timothy as his *"true child in the faith"* (1 Tim 1:2). He speaks of *"holding to the mystery of the faith"* (1 Tim 3:9). Paul warns Timothy that *"in later times some will fall away from the faith"* (1 Tim 4:1). Jude urges his readers to *"contend earnestly for the faith which was once for all handed down to the saints"* (Jude 1:3). In the light of the possibility of the reference to an objective faith in Heb 12:2a, the author could be exhorting his readers to look to Jesus who is the sum total, from beginning to end, of the faith, the revealed truths given by God to his people. In this case then of course, there would be no way for the verse to suggest that the author is thinking of Jesus as the supplier of the subjective experience of faith.

More likely though, the author of Hebrews is thinking in terms of the subjective experience of faith; this would seem to better fit the context of his readers situation and with what he has just written. In the light of the heroes of the faith listed in ch. 11, and the fact that the author immediately applies the lesson by stating, *"Therefore . . . let us"* (Heb 12:1), it is clear the writer is urging his readers to likewise be people of faith. An important aspect of living by faith is endurance, and thus the author states, *"Let us run with endurance the race that is set before us"* (12:1); this was precisely the sort of faith exemplified by Jesus in persevering all the way to the cross: *"fixing our eyes on Jesus, the author and perfecter of faith, who for the joy set before Him endured the cross, despising the shame"* (12:2). This aspect of faith was also exactly what his readers were tempted to forsake by reverting back to their old religion, Judaism. An excellent explanation of the meaning of the terms *author* and *perfecter of faith* is given by Wilson, noting that *perfecter* means "completer, finisher":

> [Jesus] is represented as the One who takes precedence in faith and is thus the perfect Exemplar of it. The pronoun "our" does not correspond to anything in the original, and may well be omitted. Christ in the days of his flesh trod undeviatingly the path of faith, and as the Perfecter has brought it to a perfect end in his own Person. Thus He is the leader of all others who tread that path.[166]

After noting the theme of endurance in Heb 12:1–4, i.e., the Christian's need to endure, persevere in exercising faith, Lane notes, "The comparison of Jesus's experience with that of believers in 12:1–4 also suggests a leadership motif: Christ's conduct has exemplary value for his people in their own engagement with the demands of persevering

---

165. "In Greek the definite article stands before 'faith'; in AV, ESV, ARV, and RSV this is represented by the possessive pronoun 'our.' But more probably we should recognize here the regular Greek usage of the article before an abstract noun, where English regularly omits it." Bruce, *Hebrews*, 351.

166. Wilson, *Hebrews*, 162.

faith."[167] The significant point for us is that nowhere in the verse (v. 2), or anything in the context, suggests that the author is thinking that Jesus is the giver of faith; in fact the context with its emphasis on endurance as the readers greatest need, indicates the author is thinking of persevering faith, not saving faith. In short, this passage does not support a notion of faith as a gift given to the elect (and no one else).

What is faith? It is the human response to the claims of God upon a person's life. It is the means whereby the gift of salvation, offered to mankind on the basis of grace (not merit), is received. It is an "appropriating mechanism"[168] or an "appropriating organ."[169] Faith's stages are "(a) general confidence in God and Christ; (b) acceptance of their testimony on the basis of that trust; and (c) yielding to Christ and trusting in Him for the salvation of the soul."[170] Faith as appropriation is seen clearly in John 1:12, *"But as many as received Him, to them He gave the right to become children of God, even to those who believe in His name."* The bulk of John's gospel shows Jesus's encounter with different individuals and groups of people, some responded in belief and others rejected Christ and demonstrated unbelief. In fact, John wrote his gospel specifically so that the Jews of his day would respond positively to the signs (miracles) Jesus did in their midst: *"But these have been written so that you may believe that Jesus is the Christ, the Son of God, and that believing you may have life in His name"* (John 20:31). The need for faith to be exercised as a human response to the miracle signs Jesus did in their midst is a constant motif throughout John's gospel.

How does faith originate in a person? Calvinism answers this question clearly in terms of a prevenient supernatural work of God irresistibly applied to (only) elect persons and thus guaranteeing belief. The Bible, however, locates the origin, or source, of faith in God's word: *"So faith comes from hearing, and hearing by the word of Christ"* (Rom 10:17). Earlier in the Romans passage Paul links salvation with calling upon Christ: *"If you confess with your mouth Jesus as Lord, and believe in your heart that God raised Him from the dead, you will be saved; for with the heart a person believes, resulting in righteousness, and with the mouth he confesses, resulting in salvation"* (Rom 10:9, 10). This salvation is grounded in the assurance that *"whoever will call on the name of the Lord will be saved"* (v. 13).[171] This triggers the question as to how people could call upon God for salvation: *"How will they believe in Him whom they have not heard? And how will they hear without a preacher?"* (v. 14). So, we see the saving sequence being: (a) God sends a preacher of good tidings, (b) people hear the message and are called to believe, (c) some do believe and confess Christ as Lord

---

167. Lane, *Hebrews 9–13*, 411.

168. Osborne, *Hermeneutical Spiral*, 114.

169. Berkhof, *Systematic Theology*, 496.

170. Berkhof, *Systematic Theology*, 494.

171. Of course, Calvinism restricts this verse to effectively say, "Only the elect who call upon the name of the Lord will be saved."

(v. 9), (d) those who respond in faith are saved.[172] There is not a word here about God's Spirit secretly working behind the scenes to first regenerate the heart and thus enable the elect alone to believe. This confidence in God's word to bring people to faith is clearly seen in Paul's reminder to the Christians at Rome that the gospel *"is the power of God for salvation to everyone who believes, to the Jew first and also to the Greek"* (Rom 1:16). Calvinists effectively deny the sufficiency of the power of the gospel to be the catalyst for faith, but rather introduce a secret working of grace that cannot be resisted and that acts upon only a select group, the elect.

f) Regeneration First, or Faith First?

Calvinists believe that God first of all regenerates a person and then the regenerated person believes. In other words, regeneration precedes faith. This issue has to do with the *ordo salutis*, the order, or sequence, of salvation. "The Reformed order may be taken as (1) effectual calling, issuing in (2) regeneration, enabling (3) faith leading to (4) justification."[173] Packer states that regeneration "is used . . . to denote the once-for-all divine work whereby the sinner, who was once only 'flesh,' and as such whether he knew it or not, utterly incompetent in spiritual matters (John 3:3–7) is made 'spirit' (John 3:6)—i.e., is enabled and caused to receive and respond to the saving revelation of God."[174] Sproul speaks of monergistic regeneration, underscoring the view that man plays no role whatsoever in his being given new life through the Spirit of God. As is expected, this claim is grounded in total depravity as understood Calvinistically (as total inability): "Monergistic regeneration is exclusively a divine act. . . . To quicken a person who is spiritually dead is something only God can do. A corpse cannot revive itself. . . . It can only respond *after* receiving new life."[175] Later, he amplifies: "When speaking of the order of salvation (ordo salutis), Reformed theology always and everywhere insists that regeneration precedes faith. . . . We cannot exercise saving faith until [logically] we have been regenerated, so we say faith is dependent on regeneration, not regeneration on faith."[176] John Piper concurs: "New birth is a miraculous creation of God that enables a formerly 'dead' person to receive Christ and so be saved. We do not bring about new birth by our faith. God brings about our faith by the new birth."[177]

---

172. "God gives faith by making it possible to have faith: he commissions the proclamation of the gospel so men have opportunity to believe it." Warren, *Salvation*, 182. Warren, a non-Calvinist, seeks here to stress the role of God in faith, namely that faith is the result of people having the opportunity to hear the gospel and respond; it is not helpful, however, to speak of God "giving faith" because, as explained earlier, this is a category error. Faith is a human response—God does not give a human response.

173. Collins, "Order of Salvation," 802.

174. Packer, "Regeneration," 924.

175. Sproul, *Reformed Theology*, 184, emphasis mine.

176. Sproul, *Reformed Theology*, 195.

177. Piper, *Five Points*, 34.

Note that the point here is not whether regeneration itself is a miraculous work of God—no one disputes that; the issue at hand concerns whether regeneration follows faith or precedes faith. Is a person born again when they believe or, do they believe and then are born again? Typically, Calvinists bring few scriptures to directly justify their view. Rather, they rely heavily on their understanding of the human condition as logically requiring that God must regenerate a person before that person can respond at all in any spiritually significant manner. Both Sproul and Piper appeal to the raising of Lazarus from the dead as an example of God's call to effect life. Lazarus was completely dead when Jesus called to him, then Lazarus came out of the tomb alive (John 11:1–44). But is this a relevant analogy to spiritual death? Not really. First of all, this was indeed a miracle, but a miracle done to uniquely serve as a sign intended to bolster Jesus's claim that he is the resurrection and the life (John 11:25). This miracle shows that Jesus is the author of life and one worthy to be believed and followed for eternal life. However, spiritually "dead" people are not laying in graves, and spiritual death has less to do with an inability to believe the gospel, and more to do with their separation from a relationship with God. When Adam and Eve sinned, that very day they "died" in fulfillment of God's warning (Gen 2:17). But they only died that day in the sense that they were cast out from an intimate relationship with God—their sin had separated them from God. Adam lived for a total of nine hundred and thirty years after he "died."

A better analogy of someone dying and living again, one that comports better with the spiritual significance of death as separation from a relationship with God, would be the prodigal son in Jesus's parable (Luke 15:11–32). The father's response and joy upon seeing his son returning from his lost condition was: *"Let us eat and celebrate; for this son of mine was dead and has come to life again; he was lost and has been found"* (Luke 15:23, 24). Significantly for our purposes, the prodigal returned only *"when he came to his senses"* (v. 17). This "coming to life" most certainly was not on the initiative of the father, who only watched and waited for his beloved son's return. The point of the parable in Luke 15 is to illustrate a wonderful truth concerning God's love—God sent his Son to *"seek and to save that which was lost"* (Luke 19:10). But love never imposes itself upon a person, as the regeneration-precedes-faith doctrine has God do, but is, rather, like the father in the parable who longs for the prodigal to come to himself, come to his senses and who greatly rejoices when one lost sinner returns to his father, or one lost coin is found (v. 10), or one lost sheep is found (v. 6). In each instance *"there will be more joy in heaven over one sinner who repents than over ninety-nine righteous persons who need no repentance"* (Luke 15:7, 10).

Hunt calls this doctrine of regeneration preceding faith a "strange theory" and cites several scriptures to show that regeneration / new life / salvation[178] *follows* faith. Among these are the following—with my own small additions designed to make the

---

178. Loosely, in the Bible, these three all relate to the new life found in Christ and which the Bible describes as salvation.

point clearer: Mark 16:16, *"He who has believed and has been baptized shall* [then] *be saved; but he who has disbelieved shall be* [as a consequence] *condemned."* John 20:31, *"These have been written so that you may believe that Jesus is the Christ, the Son of God; and that believing you may* [then, as result] *have life in His name."* Acts 16:31, *"They said, 'Believe in the Lord Jesus, and* [then] *you will be saved, you and your household.'"*[179] Both Jesus and Peter teach that salvation follows the new birth. For Jesus, salvation is in terms of entrance into the kingdom of God (John 3:5), and for Peter, salvation is in terms of a living hope (1 Pet 1:3). Peter is clear, as he proclaimed on the day of Pentecost, reception of the Spirit follows repentance and faith: *"Peter said to them, 'Repent, and each of you be baptized in the name of Jesus Christ for the forgiveness of your sins; and you will receive the gift of the Holy Spirit'"* (Acts 2:38).[180]

A text which seems especially clear that regeneration follows faith is John 7:37–39. *"Now on the last day, the great day of the feast, Jesus stood and cried out, saying, 'If anyone is thirsty, let him come to Me and drink. He who believes in Me, as the Scripture said, 'From his innermost being will flow rivers of living water.' But this He spoke of the Spirit, whom those who believed in Him were to receive; for the Spirit was not yet given, because Jesus was not yet glorified."* When was Jesus glorified? After his work on the cross and when he was resurrected and ascended (John 12:16, 23). Apparently, not only do we have here a statement to the effect that, prior to Pentecost, some who heard Jesus "believed" but we are specifically told why they could not at that time be regenerated—*"for the Spirit was not yet given."* There could not be a clearer statement indicating that faith precedes regeneration.

Another aspect of this doctrine (that one needs to be born again in order to believe) is the issue of passivity. This concerns the condition of the elect but as yet, prior to regeneration, completely dead unbeliever. This person has been selected by God for salvation, but has not yet been regenerated, and is therefore, according to Calvinism, in a completely unresponsive attitude to God and the gospel. Sproul explains: "In regeneration the soul of man is utterly passive until it has been made alive."[181] Sproul continues: "Unless we first receive the grace of regeneration, we will not and cannot respond to the gospel in a positive way. Regeneration must occur first before there

---

179. Hunt, *What Love Is This?*, 399. It might be argued by a Calvinist that these scriptures only show that salvation follows faith, which they would agree with. However, the new birth is a metaphor for spiritual life which is loosely equated with salvation. To be saved is to enjoy new life with God: *"And the testimony is this, that God has given us eternal life, and this life is in His Son. He who has the Son has the life; he who does not have the Son of God does not have the life"* (1 John 5:11, 12). In this case, the scriptures cited do indeed show that new life in the Son (regeneration) *follows* belief or faith.

180. Other scriptures that clearly show that faith precedes regeneration would be: Gal 3:14, where Paul tells the Galatians that Christ's death enabled them to *"receive the promise of the Spirit through faith."* In Eph 1:13 Paul tells the Christians at Ephesus that after they heard the gospel and believed, they *"were sealed in Him with the Holy Spirit of promise."* Other texts could be cited to show that regeneration follows belief. See Hunt, *What Love Is This?*, 454.

181. Sproul, *Reformed Theology*, 184.

can be any positive response of faith."[182] John Murray concurs: "It has often been said that we are passive in regeneration. This is a true and proper statement. . . . We may not like it. We may recoil against it."[183] Similarly Grudem states that "we are passive in regeneration" and that the biblical metaphor of being born or born again "suggests that we are entirely passive in regeneration."[184] Horton explains, "We are passive, acted upon and within by the triune God through the gospel. . . . We are passive receivers of our justification and renewal."[185]

Regeneration itself is indeed entirely a work of God, but in the reception of the Spirit, who is the agent of regeneration, we are not completely passive; on the contrary, God calls us to exercise faith first as a response to his call. The problem is not that we are passive recipients of God's regenerating work in our lives, but rather, the Calvinist's assumption that this passivity extends to the God stipulated condition for receiving the Spirit of life in the first place, namely faith. The fundamental error made by Calvinism here is its commitment to viewing a doctrine of total depravity as total inability. Yes, man is sinful and depraved, and even enslaved to sin (John 8:34), but the biblical data as well as Christian experience, shows that such enslavement does not necessarily prevent anyone from choosing to exercise faith in obedience to the call of God to repent and believe the gospel. All four gospels clearly show that the response to the gospel when proclaimed was never a passive one, but always elicited a response, either positive (belief) or negative (unbelief). Any supposed passivity because of an inability to believe until God works to give faith is simply not derived from Scripture, but rather is found there because the TULIP systematic logically requires it; it is a logical requirement derived from an exaggerated (and hence unbiblical) understanding of human depravity.

As in the previous section dealing with faith as a gift of God, so here too the idea that regeneration precedes faith calls into question the purpose of gospel proclamation. At best the gospel becomes merely the means, the triggering mechanism, and at worst the gospel is made superfluous. Why? Because regeneration is effected by God's Spirit upon a spiritually dead, passive person who, in his pre-regeneration state, *cannot respond to the gospel*. Only after they have been regenerated, made alive, born again, can anyone even begin to respond to the gospel. In this way, the power of the gospel itself to effect salvation is nullified and Paul's words to those at Rome to the effect that he is *"not ashamed of the gospel, for it is the power of God for salvation to everyone who believes"* (Rom 1:16) is evacuated of meaning. The Bible teaches that faith comes by hearing the gospel proclaimed, but Calvinism makes faith come ultimately,

---

182. Sproul, *Reformed Theology*, 186.

183. Murray, *Redemption Accomplished and Applied*, 99. One wonders why anyone would recoil at a gracious work of God's Spirit—unless, of course, it is a teaching that violates both Scripture and conscience.

184. Grudem, *Systematic Theology*, 699.

185. Horton, *For Calvinism*, 110, 111.

not by hearing God's powerful word but, in principle, apart from God's word because directly though the Spirit. It is only after the Spirit has accomplished his regenerating work that, according to Calvinists, the formerly spiritually dead person is enabled to hear the gospel and then exercise faith. In this manner the power of God's liberating, powerful word is undermined. Hunt sums up the problem succinctly when he remarks, "It is difficult to uphold the importance of the gospel when the unregenerate are not able to believe it, and the elect are regenerated without it, then sovereignly and supernaturally given faith to believe."[186]

Rather strangely, some Calvinists believe that if the elect person was to exercise his own faith, as opposed to being given the gift of faith by God (however that is understood), then that would constitute grounds for boasting. Schreiner, for example, says, "God's grace effectively works in the heart of the elect so that they see the beauty and glory of Christ and put their faith in him (2 Cor 4:6). Because God's choice lies behind our salvation, we cannot boast before him that we were noble or wise enough to choose him."[187] Hunt notes that Pink believes that if a person chose to believe, "then the Christian would have ground for boasting and self-glorifying over his cooperation with the Spirit."[188] Similarly, Hunt goes on to cite Carson to the effect that if the individual chooses to exercises faith then "it is impossible to avoid the conclusion that the ultimate distinguishing mark between those who are saved and those who are not is their own decision, their own will. That is surely ground for boasting."[189]

But how can it possibly be grounds for boasting to merely respond to the command to believe (Mark 1:4, 15; Acts 16:31)? Why would it be considered boasting to meet the God-required condition (faith) to receive the gift of salvation? And "how could a gift be received without the ability to choose? The ability to say no—which is all Calvinism grants to the totally depraved—is meaningless without the accompanying ability to say yes."[190] Does the Bible have anything to say about boasting in a salvific context? Yes. In Rom 3:21–28 Paul teaches that God's righteousness is imputed to those of faith. Three things are salient in this passage: law, faith, righteousness. Paul's main point is that *"apart from the Law the righteousness of God has been manifested"* (v. 21), and this righteousness is *"the righteousness of God through faith in Jesus Christ"* (v. 22). Such a blessing is *"a gift by His grace"* (v. 24). In these eight verses the role of faith as the means of receiving the blessings of imputed righteousness and justification is stressed ("through faith" 2x; "believe" 1x; "has faith" 1x; "law of faith" 1x; "by faith" 1x). Paul's main point appears at the end of this section: *"Where then is boasting? It is excluded.*

---

186. Hunt, *What Love Is This?*, 370. He goes on to say, "Calvinism's elect have been predestined from a past eternity, and it is God's act of regeneration, not the gospel, which alone can 'bring in His elect.'"

187. Schreiner, "Prevenient Grace," 246.

188. Hunt, *What Love Is This?*, 367. The quote is from Pink, *Sovereignty of God*, 93.

189. Hunt, *What Love Is This?*, 367.

190. Hunt, *What Love Is This?*, 367.

By what kind of law? Of works? No, but by a law of faith. For we maintain that a man is justified by faith apart from works of the Law" (3:27, 28). Obviously, Paul is contrasting the acquiring of salvation as being through faith, not by meritorious works. In short it is works done in order to gain salvation that is denied as a ground for boasting, not the exercise of faith. This is the consistent message in Scripture—salvation is by grace mediated, appropriated, received as a gift, by faith. Faith is never portrayed as a ground for boasting. That's why the suggestion that faith could be a ground for boasting sounds strange; it *is* strange, because alien to the Bible.

Another strange, indeed remarkable, claim by some Calvinists must be mentioned. I refer to the suggestion, apparently made with all seriousness, that a non-Calvinist who denies that faith follows regeneration means that the unbeliever "converts himself." Horton, for example, says, "Regeneration or effectual calling is something that happens to those who do not have the moral capacity to convert themselves."[191] Pink quotes the Baptist's Philadelphian Confession to the effect that "a natural man, being altogether averse from good, and dead in sin, is not able by his own strength to convert himself, or to prepare himself thereunto."[192] Whether the reference to convert himself/themselves refers to regeneration, conversion (repentance and faith), or salvation itself is not clear, but in any case it is most remarkable that these authors would seriously suggest that anyone not holding to the regeneration-precedes-faith doctrine is, in any sense advocating that unbelievers can convert themselves. No Christian of any stripe believes anyone can "convert themselves." Not only is this impossible, but within a Christian context, such a notion is nonsense; one can hardly call oneself a Christian if one thinks he has converted himself; every page of Scripture denounces such a thought! Salvation is always and consistently shown to be a gift of grace humbly appropriated by faith. One can only speculate that references to converting oneself is intended to buttress the Calvinist doctrine by making the alternative appear obviously wrong and foolish.

g) The Will(s) of God and Irresistible Grace

In the chapter on unconditional election, and in a context of addressing divine sovereignty, I discussed the Calvinist understanding of the will of God. There I stressed that the Calvinist identifies three ways in which the will of God is manifested: a will expressing what God delights in, but does not necessarily command, for example when Christians support each other financially (Phil 4:18); this is God's will of disposition. Another will of God may be identified as God's prescriptive will, that which he prescribes should be done: *"You shall not murder. You shall not commit adultery. You shall not steal"* (Exod 20:13–15) are classic examples. And, third, God's

191. Horton, *For Calvinism*, 110.

192. Pink, *Sovereignty*, 108. This Philadelphian Confession is a direct quote from the *Westminster Confession of Faith*, 10.3.

decretive will—that which God decrees shall happen. We noted in our earlier study how, within Calvinism, God's decretive will swallows up all other wills, so that in effect, God really only has one will—his overarching decretive, all-determining will. God's decretive will cannot be known beforehand, but can be fully known after the present moment for it comprises everything that actually happens[193]—the good, the bad (including every imaginable evil, wickedness, and sin),[194] and the indifferent. I wish to briefly explore the implications of this understanding of God's will as it relates to the idea of irresistible grace.

Let us see how this works out using 1 Tim 2:1–4 as a test case. Paul, writing to his young mentee Timothy, says: *"First of all, then, I urge that entreaties and prayers, petitions and thanksgivings, be made on behalf of all men, for kings and all who are in authority, so that we may lead a tranquil and quiet life in all godliness and dignity. This is good and acceptable in the sight of God our Savior, who desires all men to be saved and to come to the knowledge of the truth."*[195] Paul's urging of prayers for those in authority may be considered an example of God's will of disposition, rather than an absolute command.[196] In any case, whether Timothy and the Christians at Ephesus do or do not in fact pray on behalf of all men is determined by God's decretive, sovereign will, this is what determines what actually takes place. The same holds in connection with the leading of a tranquil and quiet life. Within consistent Calvinism, in the final analysis, this is quite unrelated to Christian prayers, but wholly determined by God through his comprehensive decretive will.[197]

In the last sentence of the passage, we are categorically told that God *"desires all men to be saved and to come to the knowledge of the truth."* This again may be understood as God's will of disposition—it is what God desires, and which pleases him. The reason is obvious, God does not wish for anyone to be lost due to their sin or for anyone to remain ignorant of the truth. This is quite consistent with God's

193. When discussing God's "will of decree," Grudem remarks that this decree "determines everything that happens. . . . We find out what God has decreed when events actually happen." Grudem, *Systematic Theology*, 213.

194. Again, Grudem, commenting on the relationship between God's decree and evil, says: "We should never say about an evil event 'God willed it and therefore it is good,' because we must recognize that some things that God's will of decree has planned are not in themselves good, and should not receive our approval, just as they do not receive God's approval." Grudem, *Systematic Theology*, 334. This is a most strange affirmation—that God decrees what he does not approve!

195. God's desire for everyone to be saved is also seen in 2 Pet 3:9, *"The Lord is not slow about His promise, as some count slowness, but is patient toward you, not wishing for any to perish but for all to come to repentance."*

196. If one chooses to view it as a command, that will not affect the argument to follow at all.

197. The Calvinist may retort that God works out his decretive will through secondary means, in this case prayer. But, in order to avoid the decretive will being thwarted by men who choose not to pray, the Calvinist argues that God ordains the prayer too! Once more we see that God's decretive will is overarching, unconditional, certain, and final. The primary/secondary cause argument is in the end seen to be irrelevant. Even if valid, it would be like a criminal blaming the bullet for killing his victim, and thus he is not to be blamed.

character as a God of love (1 John 4:8, 16). And yet, as is common experience, many people are in fact lost and remain ignorant of the truth. Why is this so? Calvinism, if it is to be internally and logically consistent, must answer, "Because God decreed that many people be lost." Here we encounter, rather acutely, a fundamental contradiction within Calvinism: God desires all to be saved, but he decrees that only some be saved. Note that we are not dealing here with a mystery—either biblically conceived as something formerly hidden but now revealed, or in common parlance as something not ultimately comprehensible to man (such as the precise way Jesus can be fully God and fully human at the same time). Nor is it a paradox—something that only seems to be contradictory but isn't really so. We are dealing with an actual contradiction in which God wills x and wills not x; God wills (by disposition) all to be saved and wills (by decree) all not to be saved.

The problem is made more acute by two factors. First, God's gracious love *motivates* him to want to save everyone. "Grace is the most extreme expression of God's love when it comes face to face with sin. Grace is God's willingness and desire to forgive and accept the sinner in spite of his sin, to give the sinner the very opposite of what he deserves."[198] Calvinism, derives its view of particular, irresistible grace from two considerations. The first is that God is considered to be "free to choose whether to show grace or not, and thus he is free to choose the objects of his grace."[199] The second follows from the Calvinist's strong view of sovereignty: "Since God is sovereign, his grace must be sovereign. That is, God and God alone will decide to whom he will show his grace and from whom he will withhold it."[200] It is true that with respect to the sinner himself, there is nothing in the sinner that requires God to be gracious to him; in fact, his sin subjects him to the wrath of God (Rom 1:18; 2:5). However, God is not free in his desire to give saving grace, and in fact he is influenced by his own nature. The problem with a view of God's grace being optional as to whether he chooses to give saving grace to anyone or not is that "it completely severs God's will from his nature."[201] So, with respect to God's desire and internal motive to provide saving grace to everyone (not with respect to whether that grace is actually applied) we see that, in a real sense, God is not free to pick and choose who will be the recipients of his grace and who won't be. Again, Cottrell makes the point well:

> Because love and mercy and grace are of the very essence of God, he is not free either to love or not to love, either to be gracious or not to be gracious. The very meaning of grace is the willingness and desire to forgive sinners and to receive them back into fellowship. Thus, it is God's very nature to want to forgive sinners and to accept them back to himself. This is not "optional" with God.[202]

198. Cottrell, *Faith Once for All*, 98.

199. Cottrell, *What the Bible Says about God the Redeemer*, 383.

200. Cottrell, *What the Bible Says about God the Redeemer*, 383.

201. Cottrell, *What the Bible Says about God the Redeemer*, 385.

202. Cottrell, *What the Bible Says about God the Redeemer*, 386.

The second reason why the problem of the contradiction within Calvinism between God's will of disposition that *"all men to be saved and to come to the knowledge of the truth"* and the fact that not all are in fact saved because of an overarching decree that applies saving grace irresistibly to only some is that, from a Calvinistic perspective, God obviously could do so but for unknown reasons does not do so. Could God decree that everyone be saved and so bring his will of disposition into line with his decretive will? Evidently so, because God's selective saving grace is unconditional in anything in the sinner. So, the choice is entirely dependent on God's will alone. So, if God could apply an irresistible grace to say one million people, then why not two million, and if two million why not twenty million—indeed why not everyone, as 1 Tim 2:4 would indicate he would want to do?

The Calvinist might respond by saying that it is true that there is nothing in the sinner that makes one more worthy of saving grace than another, but there might be something within God himself that prevents him from choosing to apply an irresistible grace to everyone. But this response in turn raises more questions. First, it calls into question the reality of God's freedom to apply grace to whomever he wills for there would be something within God himself that prevents him from so doing.[203] Second, we have already seen that God being love has the motivation and desire to save all (as 1 Tim 2:4 and 2 Pet 3:9 indicates). And third, this unconditional selective process, which seems arbitrary from a human point of view, makes God partial. This, Scripture clearly teaches, is something God cannot be. In short, this view "which particularizes saving grace in every way, and even love itself, must be vigorously rejected. It simply cannot do justice to passages which state that it is God's desire that all men be saved, and it goes against the basic biblical teaching that God is no respecter of persons, 'God is not one to show partiality' (Acts 10:34)."[204]

So here, in connection with the selective application of an irresistibly applied saving grace, we see Calvinism's Achilles' heel manifested again—its belief that God's decree extends to every aspect of life in an unqualified sense. This, in turn, results in a monergistic grace that ends up violating a God-given sense of justice, brings confusion to the attempt to rationally exegete relevant biblical texts (such as 1 Tim 2:4), and contradicts the clear teaching of the Bible concerning God's nature and actions in the world.

---

203. One cannot surmise that this something is God's holiness or any other attribute of God because those attributes still hold during the selection of the few, the elect.

204. Cottrell, *What the Bible Says about God the Redeemer*, 382. To the Acts 10 reference may be added Rom 2:11 and Eph 6:9 which both clearly and unambiguously state that God shows no partiality in his dealings with people.

h) Are There Really Two Callings with Respect to Salvation?

The Bible seems to say simply that God calls everyone to *"repent and believe for the kingdom of heaven is at hand"* (Matt 3:2; 4:17; Mark 1:15), or simply that *"everyone who calls on the name of the Lord will be saved"* (Acts 2:21). In response to the Philippian jailor's question, *"Sirs, what must I do to be saved?"* Paul answers simply, *"Believe in the Lord Jesus, and you will be saved"* (Acts 16:30, 31). Paul could just as easily have said: Call upon Jesus and you will be saved. We see a similar dynamic at work in the Old Testament: *"Call upon Me in the day of trouble; I shall rescue you"* (Ps 50:15), and *"it will come about that whoever calls on the name of the Lord will be delivered"* (Joel 2:32).

Not surprisingly, for Calvinism, such a simple correlation between whoever calls or whoever seeks after God and the assurance that God, in his grace, will respond with salvation is not what it seems. Why? Because, most fundamentally, it is God who decides whom to save through the application of an irresistible grace—and God chooses to save only a relative few. Furthermore, despite the universal invitation to call, repent, believe, no one can in fact do these things apart from an irresistible grace because of a supposed total inability.

To accommodate the apparent discrepancy between God's desire that all call out to him for salvation, and Calvinism's monergism that guarantees the actual salvation of only an elect number of people following an irresistibly applied grace, Calvinism has developed the theory of two different kinds of calls. On the one hand is a *general call* to believe that is made outwardly to everyone but which is completely inert with respect to anyone's actual salvation, and on the other hand, an *internal, special, effectual* call that guarantees the salvation of the elect only. Grudem explains:

> In distinction from an effective calling, which is entirely an act of God, we may talk about the *gospel call* in general which comes through human speech. This gospel call is offered to all people, even those who do not accept it. Sometimes this call is referred to as *external calling* or general *calling*. By contrast the effective calling of God that actually brings about a willing response from the person who hears it is sometimes called *internal calling*. The gospel call is general and external and often rejected, while the effective call is particular, internal, and *always* effective.[205]

Sproul affirms the same view: "The call referred to in effectual calling is not the outward call of the gospel that can be heard by anyone within range of the preaching. The call, referred to here is the inward call . . . [it] is effectual; it accomplishes

---

205. Grudem, *Systematic Theology*, 693, emphases original. One is left to wonder why God would make a general call through gospel proclamation to *everyone* since *no one* is able to respond. Calvinists would probably reply by saying that God's effectual call works through the general call. This is understandable within a Calvinistic framework, but still seems somewhat disingenuous as can be seen if *no one* responds to the gospel call among a gathered people. Again, is it coherent to speak of a *"willing response"* that is *"always* effective"?

its purpose"[206] Bruce Ware expresses the same distinction: "The twin Calvinist doctrines of God's *effectual call* to saving faith extended to the elect (as distinct from the general gospel call extended to all), and of the provision of *irresistible grace*, leading necessarily to the saving-faith response of the elect, are two aspects of one reality."[207] Letham explains: "General calling is a term applied to the universal offer of the gospel through the preaching of the word of God. . . . Effectual calling is the event or process whereby people are brought into a state of salvation. Consequently, it is restricted in its scope."[208]

In order to attempt to justify this distinction between general and effectual callings Calvinists appeal to relatively few texts. We will examine two. The first is 1 Cor 1:22–24: "*For indeed Jews ask for signs and Greeks search for wisdom; but we preach Christ crucified, to Jews a stumbling block and to Gentiles foolishness, but to those who are the called, both Jews and Greeks, Christ the power of God and the wisdom of God.*" Hoekema, commenting on this verse, says, "Paul particularly excludes these unbelieving hearers from the number of those who have been called; only those for whom the gospel is the power of God and the wisdom of God are here designated as *kletoi*, those who have been called. And in this sense, the sense of having been effectually called, the former class of people were not called."[209] Hoekema, like many Calvinists, here focuses on the term "the called," and notes that for only these ones is the gospel the power of God, with the assumption that these called ones have been effectually called. However, Paul's designation of the called is simply synonymous with the believers and corresponds with those who believe in v. 21. Similarly, v. 18 clearly states that it is those "*who are being saved*" who recognize the word of the cross as the power of God that forms the basis of salvation. It is true, of course, that the believers were recipients of a message that stemmed from God's initiative to act in history on their behalf (the cross), and in requiring the message of the cross to be preached, but there is nothing in the passage (v. 22–24) to suggest that those called-and-believed were effectually called, i.e., enabled to believe through a secret application of an irresistible grace. It is simply reading into the verses such an understanding of how the called came to faith. "It may be that Paul is referring back to the believers of v. 21, and redefines them [as the called]. Viewed from one angle their characteristic is that they have faith: but a prior truth is that God has called them—the initiative is his."[210]

206. Sproul, *Reformed Theology*, 191.

207. Ware, "Effectual Calling," 204, emphases original.

208. Letham, "Calling," 119. Letham's definition of effectual calling highlights the fact that this calling is really not God "calling" anyone—rather it is a God-induced event or process that results in the elect person coming to faith. By contrast, the gospel call is a genuine call or invitation by the preacher for all his listeners to believe the gospel.

209. Hoekema, *Saved by Grace*, 83.

210. Barrett, *First Corinthians*, 55. For the Christians at Corinth, they were drawn to Christ by the gospel preached, but the response was theirs—and they responded in faith.

Another text appealed to by both Grudem and Hoekema is Rom 8:28–30: *"And we know that God causes all things to work together for good to those who love God, to those who are called according to His purpose. For those whom He foreknew, He also predestined to become conformed to the image of His Son, so that He would be the firstborn among many brethren; and these whom He predestined, He also called; and these whom He called, He also justified; and these whom He justified, He also glorified."* As always, we seek to understand the context in which Paul writes. First of all, it is important to appreciate that Paul is writing to the Christians at Rome (Rom 1:7), those *"who are beloved of God in Rome, called as saints,"*[211] he is thankful to God because of *their* faith (1:8), he longs to be encouraged by *their* faith (1:12). He reminds them that a man is justified by faith (not works) (3:28), and to underscore the importance of this principle, Paul devotes an entire chapter to it by examining how this worked out in Abraham's life: *"Abraham believed God, and it was credited to him as righteousness"* (Rom 4:3). In ch. 8 Paul gives grounds for the Christians at Rome to persevere in faith in the light of "present sufferings" (8:18). These are: (1) the reality of future glory (8:18), (2) the Holy Spirit as a present helper (8:26), (3) God working for their good despite their present circumstances (8:28). The point of this brief contextualization is to show that Paul is dealing with a people of faith—*their own faith*, not a faith resulting from a supernaturally imposed, unsought and irresistibly applied grace. There is not a hint throughout the letter (indeed throughout the New Testament) that effectual grace exists!

Grudem comments: Effectual grace "is an act of God that guarantees a response, because Paul specifies in Rom 8:30 that all who were 'called' were also 'justified.'"[212] However, the mere juxtaposition of the called and the justified says nothing about how they were called—Grudem merely assumes that the connection entails that the called must have been effectually called. As in the previous text (1 Cor 1:22–24) those called are "those who love God" (v. 28), and their love for God might well have simply been (and in fact was) their own choice to respond to God's prior love for them (1 John 4:10).

Likewise, Hoekema sees in Paul's reference to *"those who are called according to His purpose"* (Rom 3:28), something "much more . . . than having been summoned by the call of the gospel."[213] He goes on to say, "To be sure, the gospel call is a call according to God's purpose. But can it be said that all things work together for good for all who have been called by the gospel, regardless of whether they believe or not?"[214] We note that the call may be general, but it is only *"those who love God"* (v. 28) who can be assured that all things are working for good. A universal, general gospel call need

211. The Greek literally has the expression "called holy," so the text could be translated as "called to be holy," or "called to be saints" (RSV, ESV), or "called to be his holy people" (NIV).

212. Grudem, *Systematic Theology*, 692.

213. Hoekema, *Saved by Grace*, 84.

214. Hoekema, *Saved by Grace*, 84.

not imply a universal favorable response to that call. He goes on to ask, "Can it be said that all who receive the gospel call are people who love God?"[215] The obvious answer is no. But certainly, *some* do. Differentiation takes place when the gospel call is made, but the source of that differentiation need not have to lie with God, it could be simply that some people choose to respond to the gospel call to believe and others choose to reject that call. Consequently, when Hoekema says, "It is quite clear, therefore, that here [Rom 8:28–30], as in 1 Cor 1:24, the word *kleitois* (those 'who have been called') refers to effectual calling,"[216] in actuality it is far from clear that Paul is thinking of an effectual call that follows from irresistibly applied grace. Hoekema is simply mistaken when he says, "One cannot say that all who have received the gospel call, regardless of their response to it, are justified. But one can say that all those who have been effectually called are justified—and will be glorified."[217] A better interpretation, one that is consistent with both this passage and the larger biblical context, is to say that all that have been called—and responded positively—are justified.

Paul, in this same letter, clearly locates the source of faith in the individual alone when, after appreciating the work of an evangelist and noting that not all respond favorably to the gospel, he concludes that "faith comes from hearing, and hearing by the word of Christ" (Rom 10:15–17). Certainly, the initiative comes from God for it is God who calls all to believe the gospel through gospel proclamation. It is also God who provides the content of belief—men are called to believe upon the Lord Jesus Christ for salvation. However, "there is no evidence that God directly plants the knowledge of salvation in anyone's mind: the knowledge of salvation through Christ exists only where the message has been verbally conveyed."[218] Furthermore, contra Ware, who denies it, the clear assumption made by Paul is that his hearers *ought* to believe the gospel because they *could* believe if they chose—and they assumed the responsibility for rejecting the message. In short, *ought* does indeed imply *can*.

Sometimes the question is asked by Calvinists, Why does one person believe the gospel and another does not? The expected answer is that some have been effectually called by God through the application of an irresistible grace, whereas others have not been so called. With respect to "the question of why some believe, we do find an impressive collection of texts suggesting God has selected some to be saved, and that our response to the offer of salvation depends upon this prior decision and initiative by God."[219] Horton avers that "one person believes and another does not. This is because the Word that is externally proclaimed by the lips of the preacher is made effective in

215. Hoekema, *Saved by Grace*, 84.

216. Hoekema, *Saved by Grace*, 84.

217. Hoekema, *Saved by Grace*, 84.

218. Warren, *Salvation*, 187. This is not to deny any working of God's Spirit; the Spirit brings conviction of sin (John 16:18), but the Spirit's work does not infallibly result in the salvation of anyone.

219. Erickson, *Christian Theology*, 925.

the hearts of the elect whenever the Spirit chooses."[220] Piper raises the same question: "Why did you believe on [Christ] when you heard the gospel, but your friends didn't? . . . We know intuitively that God's grace was decisive in our conversion. That is what we mean by irresistible grace."[221] Ware similarly locates the difference in the effectual call: "The gospel elicits conflicting responses because God calls some from among Jews and Gentiles who, as a group, reject the gospel, so that these (i.e., the called) accept the cross as God's power and wisdom while others . . . who are not [effectually] called remain in their prideful unbelief and resistance."[222]

Once more we see the iron grip of Calvinism's logic: since no one can possibly respond to the gospel call because of total depravity understood as total inability, if anyone is to be saved it must be because of the application of an irresistible grace and an effectual call. There is no alternative. Calvinism's precommitment to the TULIP systematic prevents it from a much simpler, more direct, and truly biblical answer to the question. Namely, that some choose to believe the gospel and others choose to reject the gospel call. Beginning with a false premise (depravity entailing inability to respond to the gospel call), it is inevitable that a mistaken conclusion be drawn (if anyone is to be saved it must be through a manner which bypasses the elect person's will via a sovereign grace applied and regeneration effected through an efficacious call). The root problem of a sinner with respect to the gospel proclamation is *not his inability*, but his *unwillingness* to have Jesus as his Lord. The following scriptures make this clear:

> Matt 22:1–3: *"Jesus spoke to them again in parables, saying, 'The kingdom of heaven may be compared to a king who gave a wedding feast for his son. And he sent out his slaves to call those who had been invited to the wedding feast, and they were* unwilling *to come.'"*

> Matt 23:37: *"Jerusalem, Jerusalem, who kills the prophets and stones those who are sent to her! How often I wanted to gather your children together, the way a hen gathers her chicks under her wings, and you were* unwilling."

> John 5:39–40: *"You search the Scriptures because you think that in them you have eternal life; it is these that testify about Me; and you are* unwilling *to come to Me so that you may have life."*

> Acts 7:39: *"Our fathers were* unwilling *to be obedient to him [Moses], but repudiated him and in their hearts turned back to Egypt."*

Stated positively: John 7:17: *"If anyone is* willing *to do His will, he will know of the teaching, whether it is of God or whether I speak from Myself."* We see precisely the same issue in the old covenant with the call of God for his ancient people to retain covenant loyalty: *"If you consent and obey, you will eat the best of the land; But*

220. Horton, *For Calvinism*, 106.
221. Piper, *Five Points*, 25, 26.
222. Ware, "Effectual Calling," 221. He is considering the 1 Cor 1:18–31 passage.

if you refuse and rebel, you will be devoured by the sword" (Isa 1:19, 20). In fact, the entire history of preexilic Israel was predicated on the covenant blessings and curses (Lev 26, Deut 28). Willingness to retain covenant faithfulness as demonstrated by obedience to the law would bring blessing, whereas an unwillingness to obey would invoke the covenant curses.

Jesus addressed head-on the issue of differentiation, why some are saved and why the rest are not. He urged his listeners to *"enter through the narrow gate; for the gate is wide and the way is broad that leads to destruction, and there are many who enter through it. For the gate is small and the way is narrow that leads to life, and there are few who find it"* (Matt 7:13–14). Yes, Jesus acknowledged that many walk that broad road to destruction, and only a few find the narrow road to life. The point to note here is that Jesus urged his listeners themselves to *"enter through the narrow gate."* Clearly, Jesus places the responsibility to enter the narrow gate upon the unregenerate sinner. What possible significance could this have if it was impossible for them to do this? As Hunt states: "Enter? Find? These are very un-Calvinistic terms! Why would Christ give such a warning if one could only come into the kingdom through having been predestined to salvation and sovereignly regenerated, without any understanding, repentance, or faith? . . . Why aren't more saved? The Bible says it is because *so few are willing* to come as repentant sinners and enter in at the narrow gate of faith in Christ alone."[223] Those unwilling sinners are described by Paul as those *"who perish, because they did not receive the love of the truth so as to be saved . . . [and] who did not believe the truth, but took pleasure in wickedness"* (2 Thess 2:10–12). Note Paul does not say "could not," but rather "did not." Hunt echoes this same sentiment: "Biblically, the problem is not that man cannot understand the gospel or that he cannot submit to God, but that he will not. . . . [The work of the Holy Spirit] is not an irresistible work upon hopelessly blind and dead creatures, but a persuasion with the truth of those who know what they are doing and could believe on Christ if they were willing."[224] The sad fact is that many, though not all, love darkness rather than light (John 3:19), and many, though not all, also choose to "suppress the truth in unrighteousness" (Rom 1:18).

i) Come Let Us Reason Together

At this point it seems appropriate to review once more how it is that God's grace, call, and salvation work together.[225] The Calvinist perspective is clear from what has been said thus far: beginning with God's unconditional decision to save some, he applies a grace which cannot be resisted and which expresses itself in a call that is effectual in

---

223. Hunt, *What Love Is This?*, 409, emphasis mine.

224. Hunt, *What Love Is This?*, 383.

225. This was briefly discussed above under the heading "A Mistaken Understanding of Human Depravity Leads to a Misunderstanding of How Grace Works," but a more thorough appraisal is sought here.

guaranteeing a faith that results in the salvation of the elect. The entire process is monergistic from beginning to end, since only in this way can God's sovereignty in salvation be assured. When we read the Bible, however, we see a quite different dynamic at play. Gone is the notion of an irresistible saving grace, gone is the notion of an efficacious call, and yet God's sovereignty is nowhere challenged or undermined.

Since the Bible is God's word, we may take it that normally, when a Bible author teaches a doctrine or makes an appeal, it is as though God himself were teaching that doctrine and making that appeal. Exceptions would be fairly self-evident, such as when Paul appeals his case to Caesar (Acts 25:11). How does God go about calling people to enter the narrow gate and avoid the broad road that leads to destruction? The biblical data indicates God uses a variety of means to reach people—all designed to appeal to people, anyone and everyone, to repent and believe the gospel and so experience salvation.[226]

In order to support their notion of irresistible grace, Calvinists downplay the role of reasoning, persuading, wooing the unbeliever to accept Christ and his claims. "Calvinists rightly insist that the Spirit's regenerating work is more than persuasion, a gentle wooing that can be yielded to or resisted."[227] And again, the Word of God in its role in regeneration "is far more than a wooing, luring, persuasive influence that might fail to achieve the mission on which it was sent."[228] With respect to the word *draw* in John 6:44 (discussed previously), Wright claims that "the Arminian attempts to weaken it to 'wooing' or a mere 'influence' that can be resisted indefinitely are singularly uncomfortable to the language of John 6."[229] To the contrary, however, as we shall see, God uses a range of means to urge people to believe the gospel.

a) God *reasons* with people:

Despite their sin, God was willing to reason with the Israelites in Isaiah's day to highlight the desirability of turning to God: Isa 1:18: "'Come now, and let us reason *together,*' says the Lord, 'Though your sins are as scarlet, they will be as white as snow; though they are red like crimson, they will be like wool.'" Likewise, Paul, whenever he entered a city in his missionary travels, would first of all seek to reason with the Jews in their synagogues: Acts 17:2–3: "*And according to Paul's custom, he went to them, and for*

226. I am not focusing on the necessary drawing and convicting influence of God's Spirit since this has been dealt with in some detail earlier when discussing the types of grace. No one comes to the true God entirely on their own, apart from God's grace manifested in a variety of ways—but all non-coercive. The preaching of the gospel would be a good example, convicting by the Holy Spirit would be another. Here, rather, I am focusing on the means God uses to call for a free response to God's love and invitation to find salvation through and in Christ.

227. Horton, *For Calvinism*, 107.

228. Horton, *For Calvinism*, 110. No one attributes God luring anyone to anything! If anything, it would be more apt as a description of Calvinism's compatibilistic freedom whereby God engineers circumstances so that a man "wants" precisely what God determines he shall want.

229. Wright, *No Place for Sovereignty*, 134.

three Sabbaths reasoned *with them from the Scriptures, explaining and giving evidence that the Christ had to suffer and rise again from the dead."*[230] Note Paul's appeal through explanation and evidence. Soon after his conversion, Paul went down to Jerusalem and began arguing with the Jews there seeking to persuade them to believe the gospel: *"And he was talking and* arguing *with the Hellenistic Jews; but they were attempting to put him to death"* (Acts 9:29). Paul reasoned and explained the significance of Christ to the Greek philosophers at the Areopagus in Athens (Acts 17:22–31).

b) God *appeals* to people:

Paul appeals to the Corinthians to be reconciled to God: 2 Cor 5:20: *"Therefore, we are ambassadors for Christ, as though God were making an appeal through us; we beg you on behalf of Christ, be reconciled to God."* We see Paul here not only appealing but actually *begging* his readers to follow through on his desire that they be reconciled—and this consciously in the role of Christ's ambassador! True, God's appeal through Paul is made to immature believers, but it is strange indeed to view God's grace as being imposed irresistibly upon individuals prior to their conversion, but that God's grace works only through appeal and begging after conversion.[231] Phil 1:8–10 is instructive in this connection also. Even though, as an apostle of Christ Jesus, Paul had the authority to command the slave owner Philemon to accept his runaway slave back, yet, Paul would rather only appeal "for love's sake" (Phlm 1:9–10).

c) God seeks to *persuade* people:

At Corinth Paul sought to persuade his fellow Jews in his evangelistic efforts: *"And he was reasoning in the synagogue every Sabbath and trying to* persuade *Jews and Greeks"* (Acts 18:4). Similarly, since Paul has a reverential fear of the Lord and recognizes that one day he will come under God's scrutiny, he is motivated to persuade unbelievers to "the obedience of faith": *"Therefore, knowing the fear of the Lord, we* persuade *men"* (2 Cor 5:11). How did Paul go about this persuading? "He sought to remove intellectual barriers, to overcome prejudice and ignorance, to convince by argument and testimony, and by straightforward proclamation of the gospel."[232] While at Corinth during his second missionary journey, Paul, as was his policy, was *"reasoning in the synagogue every Sabbath and trying to* persuade *Jews and Greeks"* Acts 18:4. While under house arrest in Rome, Luke reports that Paul called the leading Jews of the city and *"when they had set a day for Paul, they came to him at his lodging in large numbers; and*

---

230. See also Acts 17:17: *"So he was* reasoning *in the synagogue with the Jews and the God-fearing Gentiles, and in the market place every day with those who happened to be present."* And Acts 18:4: *"He was reasoning in the synagogue every Sabbath and trying to persuade Jews and Greeks."*

231. Paul is writing to the same people at Corinth that he had previously described as fleshly, carnal, and who through their divisions, strife, etc., were behaving like mere men, and so he uses the language of gospel proclamation.

232. Kruse, *2 Corinthians,* 119. Kruse has an excellent extended discussion concerning this verse.

he was explaining to them by solemnly testifying about the kingdom of God and trying to persuade *them concerning Jesus, from both the Law of Moses and from the Prophets, from morning until evening. Some were being persuaded by the things spoken, but others would not believe"* (Acts 28:23–24). Notice how Paul sought to convince the Jewish leaders; he did so by appealing to the Old Testament Scriptures to explain or convince them that the kingdom of God had been inaugurated by Jesus. As a consequence of Paul's explanation (not by a supernatural, direct, irresistible working of God's grace) some would believe and some would not believe Paul's gospel.

Acts shows Paul interacting with the Jews and Gentiles who were curious, hostile, or sympathetic to his message, and always treating them as moral agents who could be persuaded by his arguments, and who were expected to respond favorably to the gospel he proclaimed or taught. When they rejected his message, Paul lay the blame squarely upon them as we see, for example, in the parting words he gave to those Jews who *"would not believe"* in Acts 28:24. If their response was entirely in God's hands alone they could hardly be blamed if they rejected Paul's message. Furthermore, Paul would be wasting his time and effort as Hunt explains:

> The Apostle Paul had a passion to get the gospel to everyone he could reach. He spent his life persuading Jews and Gentiles to believe in Christ, disputing in the synagogues and public places. But if Calvinism is true, Paul wasted his time—and so would we. [Why? Because] the elect need no persuasion, being sovereignly regenerated without believing on Christ. And the non-elect are totally depraved, even "dead," unable to believe unto salvation, no matter how persuasively we preach the gospel.[233]

Why is it that some believe and others do not? As we have seen, Calvinism answers this question in terms of the application of a selective, monergistic grace that irresistibly regenerates the sinner thus enabling him to then believe, while rejecting all those not elected by God for salvation by simply withholding his saving grace from them. But the Bible teaches that those who reject the gospel do so because *they* have failed to meet the necessary God-required conditions. And what are those conditions? The simple answer is repentance and faith, a willingness to turn around and, instead of orienting one's life away from God, acknowledge one's sins and accept God's remedy (forgiveness of sins through the work of the cross). Faith is simply a commitment to live for God, to acknowledge Jesus as one's Lord and Master.[234] But are there any attitudes of mind and heart that facilitate a faith that leads to salvation? Calvinism answers of course not; how can a person dead to the things of God possibly have any positive stances that might be required in connection with faith? The Bible, however, says differently.

---

233. Hunt, *What Love Is This?*, 401.

234. The concept of faith has several shades of meaning; the one given here is faith expressed as a basic life orientation.

Jesus taught that someone hearing the gospel should first *count the cost* of discipleship *before* making a faith commitment to follow Christ. Consideration should be given concerning a willingness to put Christ first—and to appreciate the radical nature of such a stance: *"If anyone comes to Me, and does not hate his own father and mother and wife and children and brothers and sisters, yes, and even his own life, he cannot be My disciple"* (Luke 14:26). Someone not willing to even give up his own life if necessary is not worthy of following Christ: *"Whoever does not carry his own cross and come after Me cannot be My disciple"* (v. 27). Consequently, before considering being a follower of Jesus by faith, the unbeliever must first reckon carefully with what believing upon Jesus entails: *"For which one of you, when he wants to build a tower, does not first sit down and calculate the cost to see if he has enough to complete it?"* (v. 28). Jesus is urging those who are *considering* following him to be careful and assess the cost of discipleship *first*. This is something Calvinism cannot allow for because no one is able to consider the cost of discipleship as a prerequisite before making a faith commitment to Christ. The sinner, according to Calvinism, is simply unable to even consider coming to Jesus (v. 25, 27, 33) unless God first regenerates him so that he can then consider coming to Jesus and then infallibly believe on Jesus.

Another crucial pre-faith attitudinal requirement is *humility*. The Old Testament repeatedly stresses this human quality, especially in the Psalms: *"O Lord, You have heard the desire of the humble; You will strengthen their heart, You will incline Your ear"* (Ps 10:17). Also: *"The humble will inherit the land and will delight themselves in abundant prosperity"* (Ps 37:11). And: *"The humble have seen it and are glad; you who seek God, let your heart revive"* (Ps 69:32). Conversely, the wicked perish for they lack humility: *"Yet a little while and the wicked man will be no more. . . . But the humble will inherit the land"* (Ps 37:10, 11). Reception into the kingdom of God requires childlike trust in God: *"Truly I say to you, whoever does not receive the kingdom of God like a child will not enter it at all"* (Mark 10:15). Those who are wise in their own eyes and spurn God's word are judged by having that saving word denied them: *"At that time Jesus said, 'I praise You, Father, Lord of heaven and earth, that You have hidden these things from the wise and intelligent and have revealed them to infants'"* (Matt 11:25). We see precisely the same sentiment expressed by Paul when he writes to the Corinthians that *"the word of the cross is foolishness to those who are perishing, but to us who are being saved it is the power of God. For it is written, 'I will destroy the wisdom of the wise, And the cleverness of the clever I will set aside'"* (1 Cor 1:18, 19). Finally, and perhaps most clearly, the attitude of humility that God requires when approaching him is seen in the parable of the Pharisee and the Tax Collector that he told to *"people who trusted in themselves that they were righteous, and viewed others with contempt"* (Luke 18:9): *"But the tax collector, standing some distance away, was even unwilling to lift up his eyes to heaven, but was beating his breast, saying, 'God, be merciful to me, the sinner!' I tell you, this man went to his house justified rather than the other; for everyone who exalts himself will be humbled, but he who humbles himself will be exalted"* (Luke 18:13–14).

It is important to note that in nearly all these texts that make it clear that no one can be saved apart from a humbleness in approach to God are not actually believers. Rather God, through his word, is making it clear that a necessary prerequisite to saving faith is a humble spirit. On the contrary, *"a broken and a contrite heart, O God, You will not despise"* (Ps 51:17). Mary understood this well: *"For He has had regard for the humble state of His bondslave. . . . He has scattered those who were proud in the thoughts of their heart"* and *"He has brought down rulers from their thrones, and has exalted those who were humble"* (Luke 1:48, 51, 52). Again, *"God is opposed to the proud but gives grace to the humble"* (Jas 4:6). The consistent message of Scripture is clear: saving grace is experienced through faith, and a necessary requirement for faith is not a supernatural imposition of an irresistible grace that results in a regeneration that gives faith as a gift, but rather humility, a recognition of one's need of a Savior and an appeal to God for mercy and forgiveness. John Watts, commenting on the text of Isa 1:19, well sums up the sort of attitude God seeks in those who wish to experience his grace: "The requisites of grace are the milder attitudes of submission and pliable attention: the humble willingness simply to be God's own and to do his will: the attentive listening which heeds God's words and carefully does them."[235]

j) The Problem of the Presence of Old Testament Saints

Calvinism insists that because of a universal inability to believe the gospel or do anything that is spiritually positive (like believing and repenting), it is necessary for God to first regenerate the elect (only) to enable them to believe and move toward God. An irresistible grace regenerates the elect sinner without his knowledge or cooperation, for the sinner is totally passive in this process. Apart from their being regenerated (born again, made alive) no one is capable of expressing in word or action anything that would in any way be construed as God-pleasing. The unregenerate person resists God, is blind and cannot see or understand spiritual truths, is dead in his sin and completely incapable of even responding to the call to believe the gospel or to make any move of any kind toward God.

As we have seen, regeneration itself is a work of God's Spirit which brings spiritual life. (Calvinists hold that this work of God precedes faith, non-Calvinists believe faith comes first and then God's Spirit regenerates the believing person.) To be born again is to be born of the Spirit of God; it is concurrent with the coming of the Spirit to indwell the believer. So, it makes sense to speak of the gift of the Spirit himself (John 20:22; Acts 2:4, 38; 19:2).

The gift of the Spirit is an eschatological gift.[236] From the Old Testament perspective, the Spirit was promised as a future reality in the age to come: *"It will come*

---

235. Watts, *Isaiah*, 21. Isaiah 1:19 immediately follows God's appeal to Judah, *"Come, let us reason together . . ."*

236. "The Holy Spirit is God's eschatological gift to the new community before the Day of the Lord

about after this that I will pour out My Spirit on all mankind; and your sons and daughters will prophesy, your old men will dream dreams, your young men will see visions. Even on the male and female servants I will pour out My Spirit in those days" (Joel 2:28, 29). Under the old covenant, the Spirit "came upon" certain individuals to empower them for a specific task, but in the eschaton "Joel proclaims a democratization of the Spirit; that is, a special endowment of the Spirit in every member of the people of God."[237] Furthermore, the Spirit in the Old Testament did not indwell God's covenant people; the presence of the Spirit as an indwelling presence would only occur in a future age of restoration and blessing.

The same phenomenon was prophesied by Jeremiah who spoke of the internalization of the law: *"'This is the covenant which I will make with the house of Israel after those days,' declares the Lord, 'I will put My law within them and on their heart I will write it; and I will be their God, and they shall be My people'"* (Jer 31:33). Similarly, Ezekiel spoke of a new heart: *"Moreover, I will give you a new heart and put a new spirit within you; and I will remove the heart of stone from your flesh and give you a heart of flesh. I will put My Spirit within you and cause you to walk in My statutes, and you will be careful to observe My ordinances"* (Ezek 36:26, 27). Each prophet in their own way refer to an eschatological reality that was inaugurated by Christ at his first coming, and corresponds to new birth, regeneration by the Spirit of God.

Significantly, the New Testament speaks to all three prophetic visions as having been experienced in its day. So, for example, Peter on the Day of Pentecost explaining the phenomenon of speaking in a variety of languages proclaims: *"But this is what was spoken of through the prophet Joel: 'And it shall be in the last days,' God says, 'That I will pour forth of My Spirit on all mankind'"* (Acts 2:16, 17). Paul in Rom 2:29 speaks of the circumcision of the heart by the Spirit: *"But he is a Jew who is one inwardly; and circumcision is that which is of the heart, by the Spirit, not by the letter,"* echoing Ezekiel's prophecy about a new heart. Similarly, the writer to the Hebrews, by citing Jeremiah's prophecy (Heb 8:7–12), shows Jesus to be the inaugurator of a new covenant in which the law is internalized and which makes the old covenant obsolete.[238] Again, each in their own way speak to a spiritual reality that intimates a personal, heartfelt allegiance to the Lord that is the result of a new birth, a regeneration. In other words, what was foreseen as applying to the age to come in the Old Testament has already been inaugurated, begun in the New Testament church. Here we have inaugurated eschatology where believers today already taste the powers of the age to come (Heb 6:5), but do not yet experience the blessings of the age to come in all its fullness. After

---

([Joel] 2:28–32)." Vangemeren, *Interpreting the Prophetic Word*, 124.

237. Vangemeren, *Interpreting the Prophetic Word*, 124.

238. "With inexpressible elation the apostle Peter announced that the coming of the Holy Spirit on the day of Pentecost had fulfilled Joel's prophecy. . . . Joel's day of universal prophecy was nothing short of Jeremiah's day when the Law of God would be written in human hearts." Bullock, *Old Testament Prophetic Books*, 333.

speaking about the internalizing and democratizing work of the Spirit prophesied by the Old Testament prophets, Vangemeren remarks: "Clearly the reality of this new and transformed relationship is still future [to us today]. The fulfillment lies beyond this present age, but the tokens of the eschaton are given to the children of God by the Spirit. He has begun a good work in us: transformation (renewal, *regeneration*), the fruit of the Spirit, the knowledge of God."[239]

From what has been said so far concerning the regenerating work of the Spirit, it is evident that such work of the Spirit is only a New Testament phenomenon and not an Old Testament one.[240] This is reinforced by Peter, who connects the new birth to Christ's resurrection: "*Blessed be the God and Father of our Lord Jesus Christ, who . . . has caused us to be born again to a living hope through the resurrection of Jesus Christ from the dead*" (1 Pet 1:3).[241] Similarly, Jesus using the metaphor of living water to refer to the Holy Spirit teaches that the Spirit would only be sent after Jesus was resurrected: "*He who believes in Me, as the Scripture said, 'From his innermost being will flow rivers of living water.' But this He spoke of the Spirit, whom those who believed in Him were to receive; for the Spirit was not yet given, because Jesus was not yet glorified*" (John 7:38, 39). In short, no one under the old covenant was born again because regeneration, new birth, is an eschatological phenomenon which has been inaugurated in the new covenant begun with Christ's first advent. Thus, Old Testament saints (believers) were justified by faith (like Abraham), but not regenerated.

Given all that has been said by Calvinism concerning man apart from regeneration and subject to an original sin, whereby "until he is . . . renewed everything that proceeds from him is of the nature of sin,"[242] certain questions need to be answered. How was Abel capable of providing a sacrifice acceptable to God (Gen 4:4)? How could Noah be considered by God as a righteous man (Gen 7:1)? How was Abraham able to exercise a faith that was accounted to him for righteousness (Rom 4:3), and even be called the friend of God (Jas 2:23)? How could Moses be considered God's servant and assured of God's presence, as was Joshua (Josh 1:5)? How could Rahab the prostitute exercise faith in saving the Hebrew spies (Heb 11:31)? How could the sons of Israel cry out to the Lord (Judg 3:9)? How could David be considered by God "a man after his own heart" (1 Sam 13:14)?[243] How could the psalmist say, "*But know*

239. Vangemeren, *Interpreting the Prophetic Word*, 360, emphasis mine.

240. "In the Old Testament one normally expects to find reference to God's Spirit being present or *falling on* selected individuals . . . [but] in the coming age all of God's people will *possess* and act via the empowering of the Spirit." Stuart, *Hosea-Jonah*, 229, emphases mine.

241. The Apostle John also connects the giving of the Spirit to Jesus's death and resurrection in John 14:16, 17; 16:5–11; 20:22. Ringwald, states: "The decisive factor which makes rebirth possible is God's act in the resurrection of Jesus Christ." Ringwald, "Regeneration," 180. Significantly, nowhere in his article does Ringwald mention regeneration as occurring in the Old Testament—probably for the simple reason that it does not.

242. Gaspar Olevian in the introductory material of Calvin's *Institutes*, 28.

243. Interestingly, Calvin, who cites 1 Samuel thirty-two times in his *Institutes* omits this important verse (13:14) that crucially justifies the transition of the monarchy from Saul to David.

that the Lord has set apart the godly man for Himself; The Lord hears when I call to Him. Tremble, and do not sin; Meditate in your heart upon your bed, and be still. Selah. Offer the sacrifices of righteousness, And trust in the Lord" (Ps 4:3–5). How can *any* unregenerate person express such devotion to the Lord? How could the people of Ninevah repent and believe in Israel's God in response to Jonah's preaching (Jonah 3:5)? And what about the heroes of the faith recounted in Heb 11? How can such unregenerate heroes exist as examples for the regenerate?

Calvinists are in an awkward position here. On the one hand their TULIP systematic requires that all Old Testaments saints be regenerated, and yet, on the other hand, there is no biblical justification for such an experience. For example, John Hendryx claims that "Israel having the moral ability to seek God with their whole heart was a necessary result of their regeneration."[244] He provides one proof text, 2 Chr 30:11–12, which says: *"Nevertheless some men of Asher, Manasseh and Zebulun humbled themselves and came to Jerusalem. The hand of God was also on Judah to give them one heart to do what the king and the princes commanded by the word of the Lord."* Hendryx asserts that "the text says some tribes resisted the call to repentance, but only those tribes which the 'hand of God gave a heart to obey the word,' repented. So here is a clear instance of the Spirit of God working faith and repentance in the hearts of certain persons among Israel while leaving others to their own rebellious self-will."[245]

Is this a fair understanding of these verses? To answer, as usual, we must examine both the literary and historical setting. The literary setting extends from 30:1–11. The occasion was the letter written by Judah's reforming king Hezekiah to those Jews left in the northern kingdom following the occupation of the land by the Assyrians following the north's downfall in 722 BC. Theologically, Hezekiah's purpose was to unite all Israelites under the banner of worshipping Yahweh in Jerusalem (v. 5). Since Israel's catastrophic subjugation and deportation under the Assyrian hand had occurred because of the kingdom's persistent idolatry and social injustices (rejecting God's covenant call to love God and neighbor), it was fitting that the letter sent to those remaining Jews of the tribes of the north urge them to forsake their covenant unfaithfulness (vv. 7–8) with the assurance of God's forgiveness and compassion if they were to yield to God in unified worship (vv. 8–9). The letter called for all Israel, from Dan in the far north to Beersheba in the far south, to come to Jerusalem to celebrate the Passover. "The response was predictably mixed, and many in the pagan north 'laughed and scoffed' (v. 10), but others were receptive (v. 11–12). More northerners than usual responded in the spirit of 2 Chronicles 7:14 and humbled themselves (v. 11), while in the south the hand of God gave unexpected unity (v. 12)."[246]

With this contextual background we can now see that Hendryx claim that "the text says some tribes resisted the call to repentance, but only those tribes which the

244. Hendryx, "Regeneration in the Old Testament," para. 7.
245. Hendryx, "Regeneration in the Old Testament," para. 9.
246. Selman, *Chronicles*, 498.

'hand of God gave a heart to obey the word,' repented" misses the mark entirely. Rather, v. 11 says simply that some men from the tribes of Asher, Manasseh, and Zebulun humbled *themselves*. Also, the hand of God was upon the *whole southern kingdom* that had remained unscathed by the Assyrian forces. As a whole, the southern nation remained loyal to their king (Hezekiah) in his efforts to unite all Israelites. True, this sense of tribal unity by Judah was in some way not disconnected from God's grace, but this is far from attributing such tribal loyalty to "the Spirit of God working faith and repentance in the hearts of certain persons among Israel" as Hendryx states. On the contrary, the letter urges the Jews throughout the land to repent (*"O sons of Israel, return to the Lord God of Abraham"* [v. 6]), and to not be like their forefathers who rebelled against God (*"Do not be like your fathers and your brothers, who were unfaithful to the Lord God of their fathers"* [v. 7]), to not resist God's call (*"Now do not stiffen your neck like your fathers"* [v. 8]), but rather they were urged to *"yield to the Lord and enter His sanctuary"* [v. 8]). Clearly God, through Hezekiah, expected the Jews to assume responsibility for their own choices and to do the right thing—to repent, cease from resisting, and to yield.

Calvinism has no answers for the existence of the saints of the Old Testament, and for the expressions of love for Israel's God by those outside of the covenant, people like Melchizedek, Rahab, Ruth, Ittai the Gittite (who insisted on being loyal to King David, 2 Sam 15:19, 20), the foreigners who pray toward Jerusalem (1 Kgs 8:41–43), and no doubt many more.[247] None of these people were regenerated and yet sought God, appealed to God, prayed to God and so on—spiritual activities which Calvinism says can only be done by those who have first been regenerated by God's Spirit, a spiritual experience only possible in the new covenant, not the old. In short, the presence in the Old Testament of godly people who sought after the God of Israel and who sought to retain covenant loyalty, all spiritual goods, and all without being regenerated, is a serious problem for Calvinism—a problem for which Calvinism has no answer.

k) The Denial of the Relative Righteous in the Old Testament

Similar to the problem of the existence of old covenant saints is the effective denial of those in the Old Testament clearly describes as righteous. Abraham requests that the angels of the Lord demarcate between the righteous and the wicked before destroying the city of Sodom: *"Far be it from You to do such a thing, to slay the righteous with the wicked, so that the righteous and the wicked are treated alike. Far be it from You! Shall not the Judge of all the earth deal justly?"* (Gen 18:23–25). Judges in ancient Israel were to discern between the righteous and the wicked in their judgments: *"If there is a dispute*

247. In the New Testament we find a similar situation (Acts 10). The Gentile Roman centurion Cornelius is a case in point. He is described as a devout man who feared God, gave alms to the God of Israel, and prayed to God continually—all *before* he was regenerated by the Holy Spirit!

between men and they go to court, and the judges decide their case, and they justify the righteous *and condemn the wicked*" (Deut 25:1). Job considered himself as righteous (Job 10:15). We have already seen how Noah is described as a righteous man (Gen 7:1). When Solomon prayed at the dedication of the temple, he asked God to condemn *"the wicked by bringing his way on his own head"* and to justify *"the* righteous *by giving him according to his righteousness"* (1 Kgs 8:31–32).

The Psalms and Proverbs especially make continual comparisons between the wicked and the righteous. For example the whole of Ps 1 is a sustained comparison between the wicked and the righteous, concluding: *"For the Lord knows the way of the* righteous, *but the way of the wicked will perish"* (Ps 1:6). Similarly, Ps 11:5, *"The Lord tests the* righteous *and the wicked."* Many more passages in the Psalms could be added here. The Proverbs also highlights the blessings accruing to the righteous and the condemnation the wicked receive; here is a sample: *"The curse of the Lord is on the house of the wicked, but He blesses the dwelling of the* righteous" (Prov 3:33). The prophets likewise distinguished between the wicked and the righteous in the land: *"Say to the* righteous *that it will go well with them, for they will eat the fruit of their actions. Woe to the wicked! It will go badly with him, For what he deserves will be done to him"* (Isa 3:10, 11). Virtually all the prophets make this distinction.

What are some of the characteristics of the righteous? The righteous are presumed to speak the truth in a dispute (Deut 16:19), are relatively innocent and have "clean hands" (Job 17:8, 9), refuse to identify with or even associate with the wicked (Ps 1), cry out to the Lord (Ps 34:15), and are gracious and give generously (Ps 37:21). These are the righteous, but only in a relative sense—only God is righteous in an absolute sense. "They are called righteous because in a relative sense, they are righteous. They have a measure of piety and good works, of trust in and dependence upon God, that makes it proper for them to be called righteous—in comparison with the wicked."[248] Furthermore, the righteous are blessed by God *because* of their (relative) righteousness. One example will suffice to make the point: *"I have been young and now I am old, yet I have not seen the righteous forsaken or his descendants begging bread"* (Ps 37:25).

To a consistent Calvinist none of this makes sense—there can be no category of the righteous, relative or otherwise! How can there be for anyone who, because of original sin brings "an innate corruption from the very womb" and as a consequence "are in God's sight defiled and polluted" before even being born?[249] After noting that Augustine described general humanity in this sinful state as a "mass of sin," Sproul goes on to say that "man is incapable of elevating himself to the good without the work of God's grace within."[250] But what kind of grace could Calvinism conceive that would enable the righteous to call upon God, seek out God's face, love God's law? Common grace cannot accomplish these things—for these are acts that go beyond

---

248. Cottrell, *What the Bible Says about God the Redeemer*, 203.

249. Calvin, *Institutes*, 2.1.5.

250. Sproul, *Reformed Theology*, 123.

the rain and the sunshine common grace bestows upon everyone. The righteous in the Old Testament are portrayed as relating positively to God in some way, or at the least behaving in ways that bring forth God's blessings in their lives. It cannot be a saving grace for that necessarily entails regeneration, being born again—apart from which no one can enter the kingdom of God (John 3:3). And we have already seen regeneration is an eschatological category, a gift that would be fully realized only in the age to come, but which New Testament believers can now enjoy since Jesus's coming and resurrection. A better way to understand the category of the relative righteous is to acknowledge that old covenant people, created in the image of God and exposed to divine activity (miracles), the law, and the prophets are capable in themselves of choosing to respond in God-honoring ways and living out their faith accordingly. God expects them to, commands them to, and holds them accountable for their choices. The righteous do this, the wicked do not. Calvinism, with its theory of a Spirit imposed irresistible grace that is required to overcome the devastating effects of sin simply cannot account for this.

Conclusion

We have examined several scriptural texts that are commonly appealed to by Calvinists to justify a notion of the application by God of an irresistible grace that works efficaciously to guarantee the salvation of the elect. We have also seen that, when due consideration is given to the context in which these passages are found the texts do not support the idea of an irresistible grace. Indeed, we also examined several texts that clearly show that God's Spirit and will can be resisted by a sinner. Far from imposing a saving grace upon the elect who remain completely passive and who do not seek or want such grace, the Bible teaches that God calls upon any person (not just an elect few) to respond positively to the gospel call to repent and believe the gospel, to receive Jesus Christ (John 1:12).

Theologically, due to an exaggerated notion of human depravity as entailing a total inability to exercise faith, Calvinism believes grace works unilaterally—all is of God, not only the plan of salvation, the call to repent and believe, but even the believing itself. Human depravity is a reality, but its nature is not such that no one is able to believe the gospel; even a slave can recognize his need to be freed and to embrace that opportunity when it is offered to him as a free gift. Grace works synergistically; God calls upon people everywhere to turn from their sin and embrace the salvation found in Christ. The Father's work in sending the Son makes salvation possible; this is grace. The Son's obedience to the Father's will—even unto an atoning death on the cross provides the basis for a salvation freely offered with the assurance that just as *"Moses lifted up the serpent in the wilderness, even so must the Son of Man be lifted up so that whoever believes will in Him have eternal life"* (John 3:14, 15). The Holy Spirit draws all men to salvation by pointing sinners to the cross of Christ:

"And I, if I am lifted up from the earth, will draw all men to Myself" (John 12:32). God calls, indeed commands, all men to look to the cross, to repent, to believe. God has provided the gift of salvation objectively through the work of the cross, and he calls everyone to cooperate with his saving will by subjectively appropriating the fruit of the cross-work by exercising faith. The basic problem is not an inability to believe, but an unwillingness to believe (John 5:40).

While Calvinism must make regeneration precede faith for their TULIP systematic to work, the biblical data shows that faith precedes regeneration. When Peter tells his readers that they had been *"born again not of seed which is perishable but imperishable, that is, through the living and enduring word of God"* (1 Pet 1:23), he immediately goes on to indicate that the living word was the gospel preached to them and to which they responded (v. 25). So, the sequence is: (a) the gospel is preached, (b) the hearers believed, (c) they were regenerated. In another setting, we see the same dynamic at work: Jesus calls for faith and if faith is present, he will enter into the person's life: *"I stand at the door and knock; if anyone hears My voice and opens the door, I will come in to him and will dine with him, and he with Me"* (Rev 3:20). Note the conditionality, "if"—failure to exercise faith prevents Jesus from entering.

We concluded our study of irresistible grace by noting the dilemma created for Calvinists by their insistence that, due to total depravity and original sin, no one can begin to move toward God, let alone love God, believe God, obey his precepts, or pray to God apart from first being regenerated. However, as we also noted, regeneration is an eschatological gift of the Spirit that was prophesied by the Old Testament prophets and which had its main referent in the eschaton but which even now could be enjoyed by New Testament believers who have tasted the powers of the age to come (Heb 6:5) following the resurrection of Christ. Whence then pre-regeneration Old Testament saints (such as Abraham, Moses, Isaiah, and David) and the Old Testament category of the relative righteous? How could these people look to God, seek God, pray to God? This is a quandary for Calvinism which is forced to hold that the Old Testament saints were regenerated contrary to the New Testament's teaching.

In the following chapter we shall examine another key tenet of Calvinism—the perseverance of the saints. Is it really true that believers are unable to choose to forsake the faith?

6

Perseverance of the Saints: Continuing as a Christian—Guaranteed or Conditional?

In some respects, the question of persevering in the faith is one in which there is most agreement between the Calvinist position and the non-Calvinist one.[1] Both parties agree that the Christian is kept in the faith by the power of God, not by his own unaided efforts; that the many warning passages play an important role in encouraging the believer to persevere; that God's power, presence, and love are powerful resources for the Christian; that God desires and expects his child to continue in the faith to his last breath.

This doctrine deals with several closely related issues. An important one concerns the experience of Christian assurance—can I have present assurance of salvation? If so, on what basis? Two ends of a spectrum can be identified here: the "once saved always saved" idea associated with Calvinism, and "always trying, never sure" sometimes associated with non-Calvinism.[2] Another important topic related to the doctrine of Christian perseverance concerns apostasy, especially its possibility. If it is a possibility for a genuine Christina to apostatize, what exactly are the characteristic features, and exactly at what point may a Christian be said to be apostate? Relatedly, how is one to understand the spiritual condition of those subject to strong warnings to persevere in the faith as in, for example, Heb 6:4–8? We will need to examine carefully scriptures that impinge on this doctrine. We will also need to explore once again the relationship between faith and human freedom (or free will). This arises because Calvinism insists that the elect will absolutely persevere in the faith, that perseverance itself is a monergistic work of God.[3] Those whom God chooses to save will most certainly continue in that state until the end. As Sproul states it: "God's [saving]

---

1. Millard Erickson lists six beliefs related to salvation that Calvinists and non-Calvinists agree upon, for example "that salvation is neither attained nor retained by works of the human person." Erickson, *Christian Theology*, 986.

2. See Cottrell, *Faith Once for All*, 375–76.

3. "The doctrine of the perseverance of the saints reflects a consistently monergistic view of salvation as entirely due to God's grace alone from beginning to end." Horton, *For Calvinism*, 123.

decree is immutable. His sovereign purpose to save his elect from the foundation of the world is not frustrated by our weakness."[4]

As we have noted in the previous four elements of classical Calvinism (T-U-L-I), the doctrine of perseverance is also necessitated by the system. All five elements cohere strongly, they are internally consistent, they all hang together as a watertight system. No doubt, this is part of the attraction of Calvinism to many. In fact, once one accepts the first two elements, total depravity as total inability, and unconditional election, the other three elements necessarily follow. Consequently, it is the idea of election and an elect people that figures prominently in the question of the perseverance of the saints. Piper notes: "This is why we believe in eternal security— namely, the eternal security of *the elect*."[5] He also says elsewhere that "it follows from what we saw in the last chapter [on unconditional election] that the people of God *will* persevere to the end and not be lost."[6] Similarly, Wright states that "nothing in the creation can separate *the elect* from their destiny in glory."[7] Even Calvinists who insist the Bible itself teaches the infallible perseverance of the elect, do not deny that the Calvinistic systematic requires it: "The doctrine of the perseverance of true believers has not been *merely* deduced from other doctrines . . . but is clearly taught in Scripture."[8] In fact, even if there were not any alleged biblical evidences supporting the doctrine, it would be expected and have to be defended on the grounds of logical consistency and dogmatic considerations alone as this quote from Sproul clearly shows: "God's decree is immutable. His sovereign purpose to save his elect from the foundation of the world is not frustrated by our weakness."[9]

This doctrine, perhaps more than any of the other four elements of TULIP, has potentially significant pastoral and practical implications. We shall discuss this aspect of the doctrine later when examining some of the theological issues associated with the doctrine.

For a variety of reasons, the early church fathers emphasized the need for believers to persevere in the faith. This was viewed as a synergistic endeavor with God providing all the grace needed to persevere, and the believer assuming responsibility to avail himself of this grace. However, "the early church's view of the perseverance of the saints reached its most thorough and systematic formulation with Augustine."[10] The view formulated by Augustine was, of course, monergistic: "The perseverance by which

---

4. Sproul, *Reformed Theology*, 210.

5. Piper, *Five Points*, 68, emphasis mine.

6. Piper, *Five Points*, 63, emphasis original.

7. Wright, *No Place for Sovereignty*, 141, emphasis mine.

8. Hoekema, *Saved by Grace*, 236, emphasis mine.

9. Sproul, *Reformed Theology*, 210.

10. Allison, *Historical Theology*, 546. "This doctrine was first explicitly taught by Augustine," says Berkhof. Berkhof, *Systematic Theology*, 545.

we persevere in Christ even to the end is the gift of God."[11] While the medieval church modified Augustine's view somewhat, it returned in strength with Calvin, who regarded perseverance as entirely a work of God. "Perseverance is the gift of God, which he does not lavish promiscuously on all, but imparts to whom he pleases. If it is asked how the difference arises—why some steadily persevere, and others prove deficient in steadfastness, we can give no other reason than that the Lord, by his mighty power, strengthens and sustains the former, so that they perish not, while he does not furnish the same assistance to the latter, but leaves them to be monuments of instability."[12] The followers of Jacobus Arminius, known as Remonstrants, in the year following Arminius's death in 1609, opposed the idea of God unconditionally causing a believer to persevere in the faith, and instead put forth five articles of Remonstrance (theological statements), the fifth of which argued for conditional perseverance. In response the Calvinist Dutch Reformed Church, at a synod that met in Dordrecht in Holland in 1618, drew up the famous Calvinist definition now known by the acrostic T-U-L-I-P. The *P*, of course, standing for the (guaranteed) perseverance of the saints by God. This statement has formed the basis for Calvinism's soteriology ever since.[13]

The Calvinist Understanding of the Doctrine of the Perseverance of the Saints

As usual, we want to be sure to represent the Calvinist position accurately and so will cite explicit statements from several Calvinistic sources that define the doctrine.

> *Wayne Grudem*
>
> "The perseverance of the saints means that all those who are truly born again will be kept by God's power and will persevere as Christians until the end of their lives."[14]
>
> *R. C. Sproul*
>
> "A simple way to remember the essence of the doctrine of perseverance is to learn this ditty: 'If we have it, we never lose it. If we lose it, we never had it.' This is a 'cute' way of affirming that full and final apostasy is never the lot of the Christian. Another short-hand expression of this doctrine is the aphorism 'Once saved, always saved.'"[15]

11. Berkhof, *Systematic Theology*, 545.

12. Calvin, *Institutes*, 2.5.3.

13. It is probably true to say that, broadly speaking, it is Reformed theology alone that unequivocally insists on God guaranteeing the perseverance of the saints. "The Reformed or Calvinistic Churches stand practically alone in giving a negative answer to the question, whether a Christian can completely fall from the state of grace and be finally lost." Berkhof, *Systematic Theology*, 545.

14. Grudem, *Systematic Theology*, 788.

15. Sproul, *Reformed Theology*, 197.

The Westminster Confession of Faith

They, whom God hath accepted in His Beloved, effectually called, and sanctified by His Spirit, can neither totally nor finally fall away from the state of grace, but shall certainly persevere therein to the end, and be eternally saved.[16]

Millard Erickson

"The Christian, kept by the grace of God, will successfully endure all the trials and temptations of this life, and remain true to the Lord until death."[17]

Louis Berkhof

"They who have once been regenerated and effectually called by God to a state of grace, can never completely fall from that state and thus fail to attain eternal salvation."[18]

Anthony Hoekema

"Those who have true faith can lose that faith neither totally nor finally. . . . Can a person who has true faith ever lose that faith? To this question, the person of Reformed persuasion says: No."[19]

Augustine

"As [God] works so that we come to him, so he works that we do not depart. . . . So, by the work of God we are caused to continue in Christ with God. Thus, it is by God's hand, not ours, that we do not depart from Christ."[20]

R. Keasley

"True believers will certainly keep their faith to the end through all tests and temptations, and will finally come into their heavenly inheritance."[21]

John Murray

"[This] means that the saints, those united to Christ by the effectual call of the Father and indwelt by the Holy Spirit, will persevere to the end."[22]

16. *Westminster Confession of Faith*, 17.1.
17. Erickson, *Christian Theology*, 985.
18. Berkhof, *Systematic Theology*, 546.
19. Hoekema, *Saved by Grace*, 234.
20. Cited by Allison, *Historical Theology*, 547.
21. Kearsley, "Perseverance," 506.
22. Murray, *Redemption Accomplished and Applied*, 154.

An Examination of Texts Commonly Appealed to by Calvinists in Support of This Doctrine

From the above series of quotes from a variety of Calvinists, we may therefore summarize the doctrine, as meant by Calvinists, as the doctrine that applies only to (a) true, genuine believers, (b) i.e., those effectually called (which, as we saw in the previous chapter means those elect who are irresistibly graced to believe the gospel), (c) that such will persevere in faith to the end of their lives. It is noteworthy that not one of the Calvinists quoted above use the word elect despite the fact that they fully understand this doctrine only applies to those Calvinistically elect—i.e., those relative few who have been sovereignly chosen by God for salvation. I believe the omission of the word is not accidental as we will see later in our study.

Several scriptures are appealed to in order to justify a doctrine of perseverance. Dominant are the passages which emphasize God's own faithfulness to his word to keep those who are his. Other relevant passages deal with Christian assurance of present salvation and the nature of that assurance, and also passages dealing with texts suggesting it may indeed be possible for a Christian to choose to forsake his or her faith.[23] I shall deal with such texts later when addressing the question of Christian assurance of salvation and the question of apostasy.

John 6:38–40

> *"For I have come down from heaven, not to do My own will, but the will of Him who sent Me. This is the will of Him who sent Me, that of all that He has given Me I lose nothing, but raise it up on the last day. For this is the will of My Father, that everyone who beholds the Son and believes in Him will have eternal life, and I Myself will raise him up on the last day."*

Superficially, this passage appears highly monergistic, and as such is naturally appealing to Calvinists. Horton is typical: "Jesus assured his disciples—and us—that all he had come to save, those who were given to him by the father, will be raised to everlasting life on the last day—without exception."[24] Likewise, Hoekema offers this paraphrase: "Those whom the Father has given me, our Lord avows, who come to me in true faith, will receive eternal life, and I will lose none of them but will preserve them in the salvation that has been granted them in such a way that they will all be raised to a life of glory on the day when I come again on the clouds of heaven."[25]

---

23. While most scholars, as noted in the list of citations from Calvinists, use the term "lose one's salvation" or "lose one's faith," I prefer the term "choose to forfeit" one's salvation. The meanings are the same, but since losing one's salvation is not like losing one's car keys, I believe a more precise description is the one I prefer; it also hints at the heart of the issue.

24. Horton, *For Calvinism*, 117.

25. Hoekema, *Saved by Grace*, 238.

Carson says, "There exists a group of people who have been given by the Father to the Son, and . . . this group will inevitably come to the Son and be preserved by him."[26] This group is the elect—those chosen by God for salvation. Noting the stress on faith in v. 40, Carson harmonizes both aspects—the Father's sovereign action and the exercise of faith—in terms of compatibilism.[27]

A crucial question in the passage before us concerns the identity of those given to Jesus by the Father. As has been noted already, these people are understood by Calvinists to be the elect. However, when examining the passage (John 6:37–39) in the chapter on limited atonement in connection with those for whom Christ died, we reached the conclusion that those given are all those who have "heard and learned from the Father"—these are the ones who come to Jesus (6:45). In other words, those assured of persevering in our passage are believers in the Father—these ones are given by the Father, and come, to Jesus. Once again, the conditionality of belief in connection with consummated salvific blessings is seen to be operating here. In short, only those who are believing in the Father and Son can be assured of being raised up at the last day. But neither in this passage, nor in the Bible generally, is belief said to be an absolute guarantee to anyone. It is this contingency, the need for faith, which, as we shall see, makes the warnings to persevere found in virtually every epistle so necessary. The assurance of divine protection (*"lose nothing"*) and the hope of final glory does not absolve the believer of his responsibility to continue exercising faith.[28]

John 10:27–30

> "My sheep hear My voice, and I know them, and they follow Me; and I give eternal life to them, and they will never perish; and no one will snatch them out of My hand. My Father, who has given them to Me, is greater than all; and no one is able to snatch them out of the Father's hand. I and the Father are one."

This is a very popular text used to justify a doctrine of perseverance. "This emphasizes that those who are Jesus's 'sheep' and who follow him, and to whom he has given eternal life, shall never lose their salvation or be separated from Christ—they shall 'never perish.'"[29] Certainly, we may agree that this passage refers to genuine followers of Christ. The immediate context makes this clear where Jesus distinguishes between

26. Carson, *John*, 291.

27. Compatibilism, as we saw in the chapter on irresistible grace, is the view that human freedom can be made compatible with God determining everything. Basically, we do what we want to do, but God is determining what we want to do. The alternative, libertarian freedom, is the type of freedom presumed throughout the Bible—the ability to choose one thing or another—to sin or refrain from sinning, to obey the gospel or reject the gospel, etc.

28. In another context, the Apostle Paul warned the Christians at Corinth that the Christian life is one in which we "walk by faith, not by sight" (2 Cor 5:7). Just as the Christian life is begun by faith, so it continues on by faith. Such ongoing faith is presumed in John 6:38–40.

29. Grudem, *Systematic Theology*, 791.

those hostile Jews who *"are not of my sheep"* (v. 26) and those who believe upon Jesus and whom Jesus describes as his sheep.

Furthermore, we may agree that as long as one continues to believe, hear, and follow Jesus then no one (or anything) will *"snatch them out of my hand"* (v. 28). Admittedly the condition of continued belief is not mentioned in our text, but it is most certainly made clear in many other texts of Scripture as we shall see. The crucial difference between those who are and are not counted among Jesus's sheep is the presence of absence of faith: *"Jesus answered them, 'I told you, and you do not believe; the works that I do in My Father's name, these testify of Me. But you do not believe because you are not of My sheep'"* (vv. 25, 26). It might be argued that v. 26 indicates that the reason the Jews do not believe is because they are not of Jesus's sheep; as Carson states it "those who are not his sheep do not hear his voice, [and] he does not know them, and . . . *therefore* they do not follow him."[30] However, it is quite consistent with John's gospel that both the following statements are true: the Jews do not believe because they are not of Jesus's sheep, and they are not his sheep because they refuse to believe and follow him. The former statement is found here in John 10:26, and the latter is found in the many occasion in which discipleship (i.e., being a sheep) is connected with the need to believe: *"If anyone serves Me, he must follow Me"* (12:26); *"Believe in the Light, so that you may become sons of Light"* (John 12:36); *"I have come as Light into the world, so that everyone who believes in Me will not remain in darkness"* (John 12:46); *"If you keep My commandments, you will abide in My love"* (John 15:10). In each of these instances it is clear that discipleship follows from and entails believing; a disciple is a disciple *because* he believes in Jesus.

So, we may agree with the Calvinist interpretation of this text (John 10:27–30), and gladly affirm that a believer will indeed be protected by the Good Shepherd. But this text says nothing about the impossibility of a sheep itself desiring to leave the fold by subsequently choosing unbelief. Hoekema counters this by asking, "Does it make sense to understand Jesus's words as meaning, 'My sheep, some of whom may indeed perish, will never perish?'"[31] The answer is yes, it does make sense because the answer is contextually sensitive. In one context, for example such as here where the point Jesus wishes to stress is the believer's security, it is not his intent to raise the possibility of the believer choosing to switch allegiance from Jesus back to the world. In another context where a sheep's obedience is required and stressed, it is quite possible that a current believer may be both assured of God's protection and also warned about the possibility of wandering off. John 15:10 above is a good example of this—the disciple is assured of God's love, but this is conditional on keeping Christ's commandments. In short, Hoekema, like many Calvinists, ignores the implied conditionality in statements that otherwise seem absolute.

30. Carson, *John*, 393, emphasis mine.
31. Hoekema, *Saved by Grace*, 239.

Romans 8:30

> *"These whom He predestined, He also called; and these whom He called, He also justified; and these whom He justified, He also glorified."*

Those who are predestined are those who love God (v. 28). And, of course it is actual believers who love God. The whole of Rom 8 applies to those who are in Christ by faith. This is an important observation because all agree that all genuine believers will, almost by definition, persevere to the end. In short, one cannot appeal to Rom 8 to answer a question the apostle is not asking; that question being of course, is it possible for such a Christian at some future point in his life choose to forsake all the privileges that he now enjoys as a Christian? He is talking to Christians and teaching Christians, those who are in Christ, love God, have received a spirit of adoption (v. 15), and so on. Those who are predestined are the one's whom God has foreknown[32] would meet the conditions stipulated by God to receive salvation, namely repentance and faith. Such people, have been called (to believe the gospel), have been justified (by faith), and will be glorified provided they continue in the faith.

Calvinists, of course, would not agree with this viewpoint. Rather, they would understand the sequence predestined/called/justified/glorified as an unbreakable and infallible sequence—a golden chain of divine acts. This is because of their commitment to monergism, the idea that every aspect of salvation originates, continues, and ends with God alone. Such a perspective stresses God's sovereignty whereby it is God that determines every step of salvation. This sounds all well and good, but the problem is that it reduces man to a cog in a wheel. The reality of human free will is necessarily brought into question. Murray provides an example of this mechanistic approach to handling this text: "The question is may one who has been called and justified fall away and come short of eternal salvation? Paul's answer is inescapable— the called and the justified will be glorified."[33]

Paul is writing to the Christians at Rome with pastoral concerns on his mind here in ch. 8. He is concerned to provide them grounds for reassurance despite their present sufferings (v. 18). They may be comforted because present suffering does not compare with future glory (v. 18), they await the redemption of their bodies (v. 23), the ministry of the Holy Spirit helps them (v. 26) and the Spirit intercedes for them (v. 27), God is for them (v. 31), Christ intercedes for them (v. 34), and nothing can separate them from God's love (v. 39). The point is that Paul was giving them every

---

32. Wright, seeking to resist the Arminian notion that God's foreknowledge is of those who would believe, suggests that "it may in fact be teaching the Calvinist view that God's foreknowledge is simply foreknowledge of his own chosen plan in each person's case." Wright, *No Place for Sovereignty*, 139. However, it is not a plan that is foreknown, rather, individual persons.

33. Murray, *Redemption Accomplished and Applied*, 157. Of course, Murray, as a Calvinist, thinks effectual call when he says called. This is a call which, by definition, ensures, guarantees the elect will be saved; it is an *effectual* call, not a general call. Hoekema concurs: "'Called' as was shown earlier, here designates effectual calling." Hoekema, *Saved by Grace*, 239.

incentive to persevere precisely because they needed that motivation to endure their present sufferings; their persevering, in other words, was not guaranteed. Earlier in the chapter he had to warn them about the spiritual danger of living according to the flesh (v. 13), and that final glorification was conditional on suffering with Christ (v. 17). Such warnings and comforting assurances would be meaningless if in fact every Christian in the Roman church was guaranteed divinely ensured perseverance simply because they began believing. As Cottrell points out:

> Paul has in view here only an audience of sincere believers who need assurance that God will never fail them or forsake them, and that he can and will see them through to the end. Unlike in the Epistle to the Hebrews, he is not warning wavering believers who are seriously considering apostasy. His purpose here is to assure those who have no intention of abandoning Christ that Christ will not abandon them.[34]

In a similar vein, Robert Shank's exhortation is quite appropriate: "Let not vain assumptions concerning the meaning of such passages as Rom 8:29, 30 destroy our concern for heeding the many warnings and exhortations to persevere in the faith."[35]

Romans 8:35–39

> *"Who will separate us from the love of Christ? Will tribulation, or distress, or persecution, or famine, or nakedness, or peril, or sword? Just as it is written, 'For Your sake we are being put to death all day long; we were considered as sheep to be slaughtered.' But in all these things we overwhelmingly conquer through Him who loved us. For I am convinced that neither death, nor life, nor angels, nor principalities, nor things present, nor things to come, nor powers, nor height, nor depth, nor any other created thing, will be able to separate us from the love of God, which is in Christ Jesus our Lord."*

The fact that nothing can separate the believer from the love of Christ is understood to imply that God will ensure and guarantee the preservation of the saint until the end. "God's preservation of the saints is not based on a mere, abstract deduction from the decree of election. It rests also on his immutable and free love, a love that is abiding, a love of complacency that nothing can sever."[36] Sproul goes on to conclude that we "persevere in grace because God perseveres in his love towards us."[37] Erickson agrees: "The persistence and power of divine love also supports the doctrine of perseverance."[38]

---

34. Cottrell, *Romans*, 1:514.

35. Shank, *Elect in the Son*, 367.

36. Sproul, *Reformed Theology*, 210. By complacent love Sproul means God's special love for, and relationship with, his elect.

37. Sproul, *Reformed Theology*, 211.

38. Erickson, *Christian Theology*, 987.

With respect to the list of potential obstacles to the electing love of God being experienced by the believer Wright asserts that this "is a totally comprehensive list" and that "no further proof of eternal security could be asked for."[39]

Part of the challenge of responding to these comments by Calvinists is the need to provide an alternative set of glasses with which to see these scriptures. For example, the Calvinist comes to these passages already convinced that Paul has in mind an elect people. But when such elect are chosen by God unconditionally, effectually called, and irresistibly graced, it is all but impossible to conceive of these verses here (Rom 8:35–39) to mean anything other guaranteeing perseverance—to ensure that such elect finally enjoy heaven. Similarly, when discussing the love of God. As we saw in the chapter on limited atonement, Calvinists believe God has a special love for his elect, and for the elect alone. Such a presupposition concerning the nature of the divine love cannot help but virtually identify divine love with divinely guaranteed perseverance.[40]

Of course, the text says nothing about God guaranteeing that the believer will persevere in faith. Rather, our text stresses the fact that nothing can separate the believer from God's love—and that is another matter altogether. In fact, God loves everyone, even those who reject him. And this is the glory of the gospel: *"In this is love, not that we loved God, but that He loved us and sent His Son to be the propitiation for our sins"* (1 John 4:10); *"But God demonstrates His own love toward us, in that while we were yet sinners, Christ died for us"* (Rom 5:8).[41]

The very nature of love (like grace) is that it is not something imposed upon someone; God may love someone, but the object of God's love may choose to reject or spurn that love for a variety of reasons. A good example of this occurred in Jesus's ministry with his encounter with the rich young ruler. After explaining to the man who inquired of Jesus how he might inherit eternal life, and recognizing that his riches were a hindrance to his spiritual life, Jesus responded in this way: *"Looking at him, Jesus felt a love for him and said to him, 'One thing you lack: go and sell all you possess and give to the poor, and you will have treasure in heaven; and come, follow Me.' But at these words he was saddened, and he went away grieving, for he was one who owned much property"* (Mark 10:21–22). What is striking about this dialogue is that we are told explicitly that Jesus loved the man, and yet the man chose not to reciprocate that love—he effectively separated himself from the love of God on that fateful occasion.

Calvinists, who see in Rom 8:35–39 a basis for their claim that a true believer will inevitably and unavoidably persevere, resist the idea that a believer can choose to

39. Wright, *No Place for Sovereignty*, 141.

40. Even with respect to faith Grudem, e.g., sees this as meaning that God "enables us to continue to believe in him"—so even ongoing faith is not allowed to be a truly human posture, but rather a God enabled stance. Grudem, *Systematic Theology*, 792.

41. We must not confuse God's universal love—his love for everyone without exception, with a notion of God's accepting everyone. The former is unconditional, but the latter is conditional upon faith and repentance. To say that God loves everyone is not to say that God accepts everyone in terms of salvation.

separate himself from the love of God. When discussing a similar passage, Grudem, for example, considers the possibility that the believer may himself choose to separate himself from Christ: "Some have objected to this that even though no one else can take Christians out of Christ's hand, we might remove ourselves from Christ's hand. But this seems to be pedantic quibbling over words."[42] It is to Grudem's credit that he even raises the possibility (most Calvinists ignore the possibility). However, far from being a pedantic quibble over words, this is the heart of the difference between a Calvinist's and a non-Calvinist's approach to the question of perseverance; the former sees unconditional perseverance for those whom God has unconditionally elected, and the latter sees a conditional perseverance that requires any believer to continue to exercise faith to the end, with the distinct possibility he may choose not to do so.[43]

So, while it is perfectly true that, from God's side, nothing will separate us from God's love, the sad fact is that a believer can choose to separate himself from enjoying the benefit of God's love (namely, salvation). As the New Testament scholar James Dunn comments on this portion of Romans: "Nothing but nothing, can separate from 'God's love in Christ Jesus our Lord.' . . . This towering confidence rests foursquare on God's commitment to his own in Christ *and on their commitment* to this Christ as Lord."[44]

Philippians 1:6

"For I am confident of this very thing, that He who began a good work in you will perfect it until the day of Christ Jesus."

Once more, Calvinists typically understand this text in an unconditional, monergistic manner—this is something that God will accomplish for his elect. Period. "The believer's perseverance is *guaranteed* by God's perseverance."[45] Hoekema comments: "Paul's confidence in the final perseverance of the saints at Philippi does not ultimately rest on their continued faithfulness to Christ . . . but on God's faithfulness to them. God does not do things by halves. What man begins he often leaves unfinished, but what God begins he finishes."[46] Piper speaks of God working "to *cause* his elect to persevere," and of "God's absolute commitment to *cause* us to persevere."[47]

42. The passage Grudem is discussing is John 10:27–29 where Jesus is speaking about his sheep. Grudem, *Systematic Theology*, 789.

43. In the case of the rich young ruler for example, he forsook Christ's love for his own riches. Admittedly, this man we would not describe as a believer, though still the object of Christ's love. But the principle remains; there is nothing magical that prevents a believer from choosing to forfeit his faith—perhaps for the woman next door, or because of intellectual doubts, or even for an easier religion as was the case (potentially) of the Jewish Christians the writer to the book of Hebrews was addressing.

44. Dunn, *Romans 1–8*, 513, emphasis mine.

45. Horton, *For Calvinism*, 117, emphasis mine.

46. Hoekema, *Saved by Grace*, 242.

47. Piper, *Five Points*, 71–72, emphasis mine. He cites Phil 1:6 as supporting evidence.

However, Paul expresses here a confidence, not a prediction. Quite understand-ably, his confidence is based on their current commitment to Christ, Paul himself, and the gospel. The Philippian Christians had partnered with Paul right from the beginning (1:5), they all share God's grace along with Paul (v. 7), Paul prays for them to the end that their love, knowledge, and insight would increase (v. 9). Even from the immediate context of our text, it is evident that this is a healthy, strong, and vibrant Christian community. Paul had every reason to be confident that God would continue the spiritual work begun in them. But as a people of faith, they still needed exhorta-tion to persevere. They still needed to conduct themselves in a manner worthy of the gospel (v. 27), they still needed to stand firm in the faith (v. 27), they still needed to be unafraid of those who opposed them (v. 28). They needed to overcome the tempta-tions to partisan spirit and division and, like Christ himself, conduct themselves with humility (2:1–11). They also had to "continue to work out your own salvation with fear and trembling" (2:12) being assured that God through his Spirit was at work in them to help them live godly lives. Here, in this epistle, we see a beautiful synergy at work: on the one hand God gives every incentive (through Paul), every encourage-ment to persevere, every reason to progress in their Christian lives and, on the other hand, they must respond in faith to God's working in them. Far from being a mecha-nistic relationship between God and the Philippians "guaranteed" by divine decree, we see clearly in the letter a personal, heartfelt appeal by God through his apostle for the Philippian Christians to keep going, overcome obstacles, and to fully and continually trust the God who is with them and for them in every way.

Colossians 1:21–23

> "And although you were formerly alienated and hostile in mind, engaged in evil deeds, yet He has now reconciled you in His fleshly body through death, in order to present you before Him holy and blameless and beyond reproach—if indeed you continue in the faith firmly established and steadfast, and not moved away from the hope of the gospel that you have heard."

Despite the implied potential uncertainty as to whether the Colossians would indeed necessarily "continue in the faith firmly established and steadfast" (v. 23), Calvinists have an explanation. Rather than focus on the uncertainty of persevering, the un-certainty is said to lie with the genuineness of those at Colossae. "There may have been people at Colossae who had joined in the fellowship of the church, and perhaps even professed that they had faith in Christ and had been baptized into member-ship of the church, but who never had true saving faith."[48] However, there are several problems with this speculation. First, there is not a hint in the letter that anyone Paul is addressing in the church is not a genuine Christian. Second, in fact he greets them

---

48. Grudem, *Systematic Theology*, 793.

as *"the saints and faithful brethren in Christ who are at Colossae"* (1:2). Third, Paul identifies himself with them as recipients of the blessings of salvation: *"giving thanks to the Father, who has qualified us to share in the inheritance of the saints"* (1:12), *"for He rescued us from the domain of darkness, and transferred us to the kingdom of His beloved Son, in whom we have redemption"* (1:13–14). Fourth, Paul commends them for their many Christian virtues: *"We heard of your faith in Christ Jesus and the love which you have for all the saints"* (1:4); Paul had been informed of *"your love in the Spirit"* (1:8). Finally, their attitude to God had radically changed relative to their pre-conversion days. Even though they had formerly been hostile to the gospel yet now they were reconciled to God (1:21). There can be no doubt that Paul was addressing a group of people he considered genuine believers and brethren in the faith. His word to them was not borne of uncertainty as to their spiritual standing, but rather of their need, as genuine believers, to persevere (1:23), to conduct themselves in a manner worthy of the Lord (1:10), to bear fruit (1:10), and so on.

Piper quotes 1 Cor 15:1–2 to make essentially the same point as Grudem above. The text says: *"Now I make known to you, brethren, the gospel which I preached to you, which also you received, in which also you stand, by which also you are saved, if you hold fast the word which I preached to you, unless you believed in vain."* Piper comments, "This 'if you hold fast' shows that there is a false start in the Christian life."[49] Both Grudem and Piper have to deflect the straightforward, surface meaning of these texts and have them refer to false believers because a true believer will inevitably persevere—his perseverance is guaranteed by God. Therefore, any references to "believing in vain" or "moving away from the hope of the gospel" cannot possibly apply to genuine believers—such possibilities don't exist for the elect. Now, while the Corinthian church indeed had its problems, Paul throughout his letter addresses and considers them to be genuine believers, *"those who have been sanctified in Christ Jesus, saints by calling"* (1 Cor 1:2). In fact, in the Corinthian text itself, Paul clearly identifies them as "brethren," who had received the gospel in which they currently stood, and by which they were saved. Paul was writing to Christians who needed exhortations to persevere precisely because their continuing in the faith was not guaranteed or automatic.

When the New Testament wishes to question or challenge the belief status of anyone in a church, such are clearly identified and differentiated from the rest of the church. They are named as *"false brethren"* (2 Cor 11:26; Gal 2:4). Paul warned Titus of *"rebellious men, empty talkers and deceivers, especially those of the circumcision"* (Titus 1:10). Such was not the case at either Colossae or Corinth; these were addressed and considered throughout these letters to be authentic Christians.

The conditionality of v. 23 in our passage above (*"if . . . you continue in the faith"*) raises acutely "the unavoidable implication . . . that we may choose not to 'continue in the faith,' and may allow ourselves to be 'moved away from the hope of the gospel.' Such a contingency would not be the result of a lapse in God's protection,

---

49. Piper, *Five Points*, 64.

nor the triumph of an enemy power; it would simply be the individual's exercise of his God-given free will."[50]

Hebrews 7:23–25

> *"The former priests, on the one hand, existed in greater numbers because they were prevented by death from continuing, but Jesus, on the other hand, because He continues forever, holds His priesthood permanently. Therefore He is able also to save forever those who draw near to God through Him, since He always lives to make intercession for them."*

The writer of the Letter to the Hebrews here establishes the superiority of Jesus's priesthood by showing how, unlike the Old Testament priests Jesus, through his resurrection from the dead, continues forever. Consequently, he is able to secure an enduring salvation for all those who approach God through Christ.[51] The author is providing grounds for complete confidence in the salvation provided by God for those who trust in Christ for that salvation; he is writing to Christians. Calvinists appeal to this text to suggest that Christ's high priestly ministry is such that the salvation he gives guarantees the believers ongoing perseverance in the faith. This is partly because of the phrase "save forever" and partly because of Christ's ongoing intercession on behalf of God's people and which is presumed to be always infallibly answered. Wilson, for example, speaks of Christ's "always-prevailing intercession."[52]

Hoekema stresses the efficacy of Christ's intercessory work when he comments, "Surely Jesus's prayers for his people will be heard. . . . Is it now possible that those for whom our faithful high priest continually intercedes, on the basis of his all-sufficient sacrifice, will yet fail to attain to heavenly glory? The answer must be a resounding No!"[53] F. F. Bruce likewise says, "[Christ's] priestly ministry on his people's behalf is never ending, and therefore the salvation which he secures to them is absolute."[54]

By way of response, we may note the following. First, v. 25, strictly speaking, does not state what Christ will infallibly always and in all circumstances actually do; while Calvinists read the text as saying, "Therefore He saves forever those who draw near to God," the text actually states, "*He is able also to save.*" There is more than a hint of conditionality in what the verse actually states—for those who choose to trust Christ for salvation, Christ is able to save to the uttermost. The mere ability of Christ to save forever need not necessarily mean that the believer will always and continually choose to participate in that divine ability. It begs the question to assume that what Christ is

50. Cottrell, *Faith Once for All*, 378.

51. The Greek term εἰς το παντελες (*eis to panteles*) could be translated as either "to the uttermost, completely," or "forever" as here in the NASB.

52. Wilson, *Hebrews*, 91.

53. Hoekema, *Saved by Grace*, 243.

54. Bruce, *Hebrews*, 155.

able to do he will under any and all circumstances infallibly do—specifically, to cause a believer to remain a believer to the end.[55]

Second, it is true of course, that for the believer, the one presently committed to trusting Christ for his or her salvation, that salvation is perfectly secure—because Christ is qualified to ensure that salvation. However, this verse presupposes a believer is in view—it does not address the possibility that a believer may choose at some future time to forsake his faith.

Third, the assumption held by Hoekema and other Calvinists that every prayer uttered by Christ must be answered may be questioned. At the cross Jesus prayed that those crucifying him would be forgiven (Luke 23:34), however it is unlikely that every single Jew in that crowd was indeed forgiven simply because Christ uttered that prayer.[56] Leon Morris's comment is helpful: "It is Jesus's own spirit that dictates this concern for those who executed him."[57]

Finally, the entire purpose of the author's writing to the Jewish Christians of his day belies the idea of guaranteed perseverance. We need look no further than the preceding chapter (Heb 6) to see that the author's purpose was precisely to encourage believers to persevere—and presupposes that they needed such encouragement else they would succumb to the temptation to forsake their faith: *"And we desire that each one of you show the same diligence so as to realize the full assurance of hope until the end, so that you will not be sluggish, but imitators of those who through faith and patience inherit the promises"* (Heb 6:11, 12). He desires that those *"who have taken refuge [in Christ] would have strong encouragement to take hold of the hope set before us"* (Heb 6:18). This is not the language of guaranteed perseverance.

1 Peter 1:3–5

> *"Blessed be the God and Father of our Lord Jesus Christ, who according to His great mercy has caused us to be born again to a living hope through the resurrection of Jesus Christ from the dead, to obtain an inheritance which is imperishable and undefiled and will not fade away, reserved in heaven for you, who are protected by the power of God through faith for a salvation ready to be revealed in the last time."*

Calvinists in their writings tend to merely quote these verses and leave it at that, as though the text self-evidently confirms the doctrine of eternal security. Wright is a case in point. Under the heading Scriptural Proofs of Eternal Security, he asserts that

---

55. The Calvinist stance is question begging because it presupposes that which is in dispute—namely, whether the salvation secured by Christ infallibly guarantees the experienced salvation of any individual believer, such that the believer is not able to do anything but persevere to the end.

56. There is a question concerning the authenticity of the saying, but most conservative scholars accept the prayer's historical authenticity and its inclusion in Luke's gospel.

57. Morris, *Luke*, 357.

God keeps his people faithful, and then merely cites 1 Pet 1:3–5 without comment. John Murray is little better. Commenting on these verses he observes, "There are three things particularly noteworthy: (1) they are kept; (2) they are kept through faith; (3) they are kept unto the final consummation, the salvation to be revealed in the last time."[58] This comment hardly adds anything to the bare text.

Peter speaks of his readers currently experiencing "distress due to various trials" (v. 6), suffering even while doing right (3:17), and having to endure a "fiery ordeal" (4:12). Consequently, "engaging one obstacle after the other, he dispenses with what might otherwise be regarded as impediments to their realizing their hope."[59] So, Peter, motivated by pastoral concerns, writes to encourage his readers to gain confidence in the keeping power of God even in the midst of their trials, and to maintain their living hope assured of an imperishable heavenly inheritance. Peter's eschatological orientation emerges again in his second letter when, in sharp contrast to the believers in our text, he speaks of *"the present heavens and earth . . . being reserved for fire, kept for the day of judgment and destruction of ungodly men"* (2 Pet 3:7). Believers can look forward to a heavenly inheritance whereas the ungodly can only expect judgment.

Again, faith plays a crucial role here: "As salvation is the goal of faith, so the present provides the arena for active faithfulness for those straining towards the future."[60] Persevering protection is assured but only through faith. The crucial importance of this phrase is often overlooked by Calvinist exegetes. And yet, to gain a proper understanding of Peter's teaching, we "can ill afford to ignore the essential condition governing the keeping grace of God."[61] Just as new birth and Christian hope (1 Pet 1:3) is entered into through faith, so God's keeping power is accessed through faith. Faith, as a human response to the claims of God (either to enter into salvation or to continue and grow in salvation), is something that needs to be nourished, fed, and made robust. Trials can serve those ends as Peter reminds his readers: *"In this you greatly rejoice, even though now for a little while, if necessary, you have been distressed by various trials,* so that the proof of your faith, *being more precious than gold which is perishable, even though tested by fire,* may be found *to result in praise and glory and honor at the revelation of Jesus Christ"* (1 Pet 1:6, 7).

Regarding this question of the need for faith, Calvinists have a hard time. On the one hand insisting that God sovereignly determines who will be saved and who will therefore most assuredly persevere in faith, and yet on the other hand having also to accommodate the many verses that speak of persevering being contingent on faith. Our text is a case in point. Grudem, remarking on 1 Pet 1:5, says, "God does not guard us apart from our faith, but only by working through our faith."[62] All this

---

58. Murray, *Redemption Accomplished and Applied*, 155.

59. Green, *1 Peter*, 33.

60. Green, *1 Peter*, 33.

61. Shank, *Life in the Son*, 272.

62. Grudem, *Systematic Theology*, 792.

sounds quite reasonable, especially the emphasis on "our faith." However, Calvinistic soteriology, being a monergistic system, cannot allow for genuine human relative independence from God which would allow "our faith" to truly be "ours." Calvinism allows for absolutely no contingency that might threaten the divine decree that determines everything, including those who will believe and persevere and those who won't. It is not surprising therefore to see Grudem immediately qualify what he means by "our faith." Our faith is such that God *enables* us to continue to believe in him."[63] So "our faith" once again depends on God's actions, God's choices, God's enablement. However, the Bible knows nothing of an "our faith" that is really, *ultimately* nothing more than an extension of God's actions. Grudem, in effect, restates v. 5 to say: "who are protected by the power of *God through God* for a salvation ready to be revealed in the last time," which is evidently incoherent.

Some Scriptures Highlighting the Need for Christians to Persevere

There are many, many biblical texts urging the believer to continue on in the faith, to be alert to potential danger, to be on guard and so on. These texts lose their significance if in fact true believers can never forsake their faith and will be caused to persevere to the end by God's keeping power. Or that, as Grudem puts it, "all who have the Holy Spirit within them, all who are truly born again, have God's unchanging promise and guarantee that the inheritance of eternal life in heaven will certainly be theirs."[64] Recall from the previous chapter dealing with irresistible grace that those whom God wishes to save (the elect) are graced irresistibly with an ability to believe and thus be saved. This sequence fits well the TULIP systematic: total depravity means that no one would be saved apart from God's unilateral intervention, this action finds expression in an unconditional election of a group of people, who are then irresistibly graced to believe, and who will then go on to persevere until the end when God's salvific decree finds fruition in an actual body of believers. Within Calvinism there is no possibility that believers, the elect, will not persevere.

Given all this about the TULIP system of salvation, one is left to wonder why it is that so many scriptures are found in the New Testament urging believers to persevere. According to Calvinism, as we have just seen, true believers *will* persevere, their perseverance is *guaranteed*. For a non-Calvinistic soteriology that recognizes and legitimizes the relative independence God has granted man, the need for the believer to persevere—and the real danger of failing to do so—makes good sense. Why? Because ultimate salvation depends on continuing in the faith, and not just on having a start. Yes, the believer is kept by the power of God, but only though faith (1 Pet 1:5); faith being the human response to the claims and call of God to live holy lives, to renounce worldliness, and so on. Bearing this in mind, we shall see below that all these scriptures

63. Grudem, *Systematic Theology*, 792, emphasis mine.
64. Grudem, *Systematic Theology*, 791.

in one way or another are urging believers to exercise faith in God and in God's word and sustaining power, because failing to do so is a real possibility.

The Need to Be Alert: Luke 12:35–37

"Be dressed in readiness, and keep your lamps lit. Be like men who are waiting for their master when he returns from the wedding feast, so that they may immediately open the door to him when he comes and knocks. Blessed are those slaves whom the master will find on the alert *when he comes."*

In this chapter Luke recounts a series of teachings Jesus gave to his disciples and bystanders that clarifies what true discipleship entails. One aspect concerns the believer considering himself as a slave of his master, ready and prepared to serve his master at all times. This can only be done with an attitude of continual alertness. Such an attitude demonstrates the level of commitment the slave has for his master, and elicits the response from the master, *"Blessed are those slaves"* (v. 37, 38). The parable stresses the need for the servants to be alert because they do not know when the master will return from the wedding feast. By way of application, we may say that the believer today needs to, and is expected to, exercise faith continually in order to be adequately prepared for Christ's coming. The parable clearly shows that the responsibility for exercising ongoing preparedness is the slave's and the slave's alone.

The call to be alert is reiterated by Paul when writing to the Christians at Thessalonica: *"But you, brethren, are not in darkness, that the day would overtake you like a thief; for you are all sons of light and sons of day. We are not of night nor of darkness; so then let us not sleep as others do, but let us* be alert *and sober"* (1 Thess 5:4–6). Here we have the classic Pauline indicative/imperative structure. As believers this is what you are, and as believers this is how you therefore ought to behave. The appeal, the oughtness, the imperative, indicates that one's status as a believer is not fixed and necessarily irrevocable. Conditionality is intrinsic to walking by faith, to being alert. The believer needs to work out in practice what he is in Christ, and in this case, this requires the believer to be alert to the spiritual dangers around him that would threaten to undermine his discipleship.

The same need for believers to be on the alert continually is also stressed by Peter: *"Be of sober spirit, be on the alert. Your adversary, the devil, prowls around like a roaring lion, seeking someone to devour. But resist him, firm in your faith"* (1 Pet 5:8, 9). Once more, faith plays a crucial role here in resisting the temptations and destructive influences of Satan. Again, we see Peter providing the same sort of imperatives; be sober, be alert, be firm in faith. Why the exhortations? Because failure to be sober, alert and firm in faith are real possibilities for the Christian—with potentially devastating consequences as far as final salvation is concerned. Such exhortations could easily be ignored if persevering in faith was guaranteed simply because one is a

Christian and God is all powerful. Minimally, such exhortations would be redundant and irrelevant. Joel Green is certainly right when he notes that beyond the opposition of the Roman culture and powers of Peter's day lies "the active presence of an even darker intent. From a diabolical perspective, the agenda is to provoke defection from the faith, apostasy."[65] Once more, warnings and exhortations are needed precisely because perseverance in faith is not guaranteed.

The Need to Continually Focus on Christ: Matthew 14:28–31

> *"Peter said to Him, 'Lord, if it is You, command me to come to You on the water.' And He said, 'Come!' And Peter got out of the boat, and walked on the water and came toward Jesus. But seeing the wind, he became frightened, and beginning to sink, he cried out, 'Lord, save me!' Immediately Jesus stretched out His hand and took hold of him, and said to him, 'You of little faith, why did you doubt?'"*

As long as Peter looked at Jesus he was able to walk on the water. His "little faith" was manifest when he took his eyes off Jesus, saw the wind and waves and began to sink. Through this historical incident Matthew clearly underscores the need for the believer to keep focused on Jesus. "Doubt or wavering had entered Peter's heart because for a moment he had looked away from Jesus, that is, he had failed to rest the eye of his faith upon the Master. He had not sufficiently taken to heart the comfort he should have derived from the presence, promises, power, and love of Christ."[66] The application is clear: the believer today needs to be working out his salvation with his or her eye fixed firmly upon Jesus, and that failing to do so places one in spiritual danger.

Precisely the same dynamic is at work in the Letter to the Hebrews. In that letter, the writer is concerned that his readers forsake the Christian faith and revert back to the Judaism with which they were more familiar. The antidote is the same for them as for Peter (and for us): *"Let us also lay aside every encumbrance and the sin which so easily entangles us, and let us run with endurance the race that is set before us, fixing our eyes on Jesus"* (Heb 12:1). Failing to live out the Christian life with the eyes of faith fixed firmly upon Jesus is a recipe for spiritual trouble. Such faith is a persevering one requiring endurance. Again, the responsibility is the Christian's— God doesn't believe, fix our eye upon Jesus, for us.

The Danger of False Teachers: 2 Peter 3:17

> *"You therefore, . . . be on your guard so that you are not carried away by the error of unprincipled men and fall from your own steadfastness."*

---

65. Green, *1 Peter*, 181.
66. Hendriksen, *Matthew*, 602.

There can be no doubt that Peter considers himself as writing to true believers. He views them as *"those who have received a faith of the same kind as ours"* (2 Pet 1:1) and clearly identifies with the faith stance of his readers (1:3, 4). They, like Peter himself, have been "called" to "life and godliness" (1:3). Yet, despite being true believers, he feels compelled to urge them to be watchful, on guard lest they be "carried away" and fail to persevere in the faith due to the destructive influence of false teachers (v. 16, 17). The antidote to such possibilities is that they *"grow in the grace and knowledge of our Lord and Savior Jesus Christ"* (2 Pet 3:18). The problems raised by false prophets and teachers in their midst (2 Pet 2:1–3; 3:3–4, 16, 17) is a reminder that there "is no excuse for complacency in Christians: error has many attractive faces by which even the most experienced may be beguiled."[67] Far from being guaranteed that the saints will be preserved by God to ensure an elect body in the end, the Christian is called upon, and is required, to make use of the means of grace provided by God and to so persevere.

Christians Must Be Overcomers: Revelation 2:7

> *"He who has an ear, let him hear what the Spirit says to the churches. To him who overcomes, I will grant to eat of the tree of life which is in the Paradise of God."*

All seven of the letters to the churches found in Rev 2 and 3 have the phrase *"to him who overcomes"* (2:7, 11, 17, 26; 3:5, 12, 21). It is evident that the blessings promised to each church is conditional on them being "overcomers." The Christians in these churches faced a variety of opposition, aspects of church life that would threaten their continued existence as churches. The first church, Ephesus, for example, had lost its first love and is consequently described as fallen (2:4, 5). The church in Smyrna were called to be "faithful until death"—a call to persevere despite the suffering they were about to endure. The church at Pergamum tolerated false teachers (2:14, 15) and were called to repent and deal with these teachers. The church at Thyatira also tolerated false teaching and immorality; blessings were assured only for *"he who overcomes, and he who keeps My deeds until the end"* (2:26). The church in Sardis had a reputation for being alive, but were in reality spiritually dead (3:1). Only for the overcomers is final salvation assured: *"He who overcomes will thus be clothed in white garments; and I will not erase his name from the book of life"* (v. 5). The church in Philadelphia were commended for having kept Christ's name and not denied it, and were urged to continue to be overcomers with subsequent assured blessings. The church at Laodicea were lukewarm in their faith and were consequently urged to repent and to benefit from Christ's discipline in their midst (v. 19) and so prove to be overcomers (v. 21).

It is apparent even from this cursory study that Jesus is sensitive to the particular challenges faced by churches and the Christians in them. It is equally clear that Christ expects Christians to deal with obstacles to the God-honoring working out of their

67. Green, *2 Peter and Jude*, 163.

salvation; in short, they need to be overcomers. This entails persevering in faithful discipleship, this is not something God will do for them despite the fact that he loves them and seeks their highest good. In fact, it is because he loves them that he reproves and disciplines them and requires that they be zealous and repent (3:19). Again, it is clear that Christ lays upon those Christians the responsibility to repent, to overcome these obstacles that would threaten their viability as a church; God provides every resource, every incentive, every encouragement, but they must avail themselves of such spiritual resources and be overcomers to the end.

Theological Issues concerning the Perseverance of the Saints

Inevitably, when a viewpoint is postulated that seems to have little or no biblical warrant several theological issues arise. These would include the exact way in which God guarantees the perseverance of his elect, the possibility and grounds for present assurance of salvation, and the reality of apostasy. These and other issues related to a doctrine of guaranteed perseverance of the saints will be explored below.

a) How Exactly Does God Guarantee the Perseverance of the Elect?

Surprisingly little by Calvinists is said concerning the precise mechanism by which God will guarantee the perseverance of his elect saints.[68] Most seem to just accept the idea without giving thought as to how it would be realized. This is not entirely strange given Calvinism's strong emphasis on monergism and on God's sovereignty. We may not be able to figure out exactly how God will ensure his elect persevere in faith, but since God works one hundred percent of salvation and is absolutely sovereign, then we may easily leave this detail to God.[69]

As has already been mentioned, Wayne Grudem attempts to provide a description of how God will preserve his elect. He does so in passing and does not dwell on the issue, but his explanation is instructive. Recall that Grudem insists that all "who have the Holy Spirit within them, all who are truly born again, have God's unchanging promise and *guarantee* that the inheritance of eternal life in heaven will certainly be theirs."[70] As we saw earlier in this chapter when considering the Calvinist understanding of the doctrine, Grudem's statement here is typical of the Calvinist position. In Eph 1:14 Paul makes reference to the Ephesian Christians having been sealed in Christ by the Holy

---

68. The term *elect* here being understood Calvinistically—i.e., as a group of people selected unconditionally for salvation before the worlds were created, with God either bypassing or positively damning the rest of mankind to damnation.

69. Piper makes reference to God *causing* his elect to persevere, and speaks of "God's absolute commitment to cause us to persevere" but does not explain how God is said to do this. Piper, *Five Points*, 71–72.

70. Grudem, *Systematic Theology*, 791, emphasis mine.

Spirit, who has been given to them as pledge or, as Grudem translates the word αρραβων (*arrabōn*), a guarantee of their inheritance. Grudem, commenting on this verse, says: "God's own faithfulness is pledged to bring it about."[71] How does God's faithfulness work to guarantee the believer will persevere? Grudem explains: "God's sovereign protection is consistent with human responsibility because it works through human responsibility and guarantees that we will respond by maintaining the faith that is necessary to persevere."[72] Also, "God's power in fact energizes and continually sustains individual, personal faith. . . . God enables us to continue to believe in him."[73]

Furthermore, Grudem criticizes Arminian theologians who "assume that if they affirm human responsibility and the need for continuing in faith they have thereby negated the idea that God's sovereign keeping and protection is absolutely certain and eternal life is guaranteed."[74] But why would Arminian theologians do such things? Could it be that the idea of "God's sovereign keeping" that *guarantees* persevering faith is antithetical to human responsibility? Part of the problem, it seems to me, is the ambiguous way Grudem refers to "our faith." It implies a certain independence from God and, potentially, God's will for us—it is "*our*" faith, a stance *we* choose to take, a trust *we* place in the object of *our* faith. And yet, for Grudem, our faith is energized, sustained, and enabled by God—in a way that infallibly guarantees God's will be done. It is a bit like saying, "I am flying the plane, but the copilot is controlling my hand movements by placing his hands over mine and moving my hands in a manner that guarantees I move the control column appropriately." It doesn't work. Either the Christian is allowed to be the controlling agent who decides whether he will continue to exercise faith with the possibility that he may choose not to, or he is merely a human extension of God himself, a human manifestation of God's will. Calvinism, with its strong sense of absolute sovereignty (recall Grudem's "God's *sovereign* protection") coupled with a finite number of those elected by God for salvation, and hence perseverance, cannot allow, in any genuine sense, for a relatively independent moral agent—even if that relative independence is one sovereignly bestowed by God himself. In the final analysis, a "faith" that is sustained, energized, and enabled by God to achieve infallible ends is really no faith, it is merely a God-willed action; it is certainly not compatible with genuine human responsibility. How could it be if the moral agent could do no other than God's will in persevering?

In the final analysis, there is no absolute, infallible guarantee that a believer will continue on in the faith until his last breath. Rather, what has been guaranteed the believer regarding his ongoing and future experience of salvation is not the guarantee of perseverance, but the guarantee of *resources* to enable the Christian to persevere. Peter

71. Grudem, *Systematic Theology*, 791.

72. Grudem, *Systematic Theology*, 791n6.

73. Grudem, *Systematic Theology*, 792. Grudem is to be applauded for at least attempting to provide some content as to how God guarantees the perseverance of the elect.

74. Grudem, *Systematic Theology*, 791.

makes this point to his readers, whom he is concerned persevere in a historical context of false prophets and teachers. He reminds his readers of their access to divine resources since God's *"divine power has granted to us everything pertaining to life and godliness"* (2 Pet 1:3). An important resource is the good news preached (Heb 4:2), as is God's word more generally (2 Tim 3:16). It is the believer's responsibility to avail himself of these and other spiritual resources and so persevere in the Christian life.

b) Is Assurance of Salvation Possible within Calvinism?

The issue here concerns the answer to this question: Can I know for sure that I am now saved and that I am on the path to final glorification? And the crucial aspect of the answer to this question concerns the *basis*, or *grounds*, for such assurance. On what basis can I be assured I am now saved?

Calvinists certainly view the possibility of Christian assurance of salvation as a reality. For example, Grudem, after discussing several grounds for assurance, affirms that the result "should be to give strong assurance to those who are genuinely believers."[75] Similarly, the Westminster Confession of Faith says that those who "truly believe in the Lord Jesus, and love him in sincerity, endeavoring to walk in all good conscience before Him, may, in this life, be certainly assured that they are in a state of grace."[76] Horton acknowledges that "Scripture itself teaches us to draw assurance."[77]

When considering the basis of assurance, not surprisingly Calvinists stress God's role in salvation. "Scripture itself teaches us to draw assurance from God's unconditional election. . . . He cares for his elect . . . and assures his own that they are chosen not only to be saved but to be preserved in that grace."[78] "God is faithful. God will work in me. God will keep me. God will finish his work to the end. The answer is God's ongoing work, not my ongoing commitment."[79] Hoekema expresses the same sentiment: "We rest finally not on our hold of God but on God's hold on us."[80]

With respect to present assurance of salvation, appeal is often made to evidences within the Christian's life of the presence and activity of God. Wesley, for example, stressed the internal witness of the Spirit, as reflected in Rom 8:16: *"The Spirit Himself testifies with our spirit that we are children of God."* Grudem holds that being able to answer positively these three subjective questions will provide an adequate basis for the believer's assurance of his salvation: "Do I have a present trust in Christ for Salvation? . . . Is there evidence of a regenerating work of the Holy Spirit in my heart? . . . Do I see

---

75. Grudem, *Systematic Theology*, 805.

76. *Westminster Confession of Faith*, 18.1.

77. Horton, *For Calvinism*, 72.

78. Horton, *For Calvinism*, 72.

79. Piper, *Five Points*, 73.

80. Hoekema, *Saved by Grace*, 255.

a long-term pattern of growth in my Christian life?"[81] All this is quite consistent with Peter's exhortation to his readers to apply all diligence in the working out of their faith (2 Pet 1:5) expressed in terms of moral excellence, knowledge, self-control, godliness, brotherly kindness, love (2 Pet 1:5–7). Peter concludes his exhortation with these words: *"Therefore, brethren, be all the more diligent to make certain about His calling and choosing you; for as long as you practice these things, you will never stumble; for in this way the entrance into the eternal kingdom of our Lord and Savior Jesus Christ will be abundantly supplied to you"* (2 Pet 1:10, 11). There is a place for authentic present Christian experience of God's grace in justifying a present assurance of salvation.

While present subjective experience is a necessary part of assurance, I would argue, it is not sufficient. Why? Because it is possible to be deceived by such subjective experiences. Christian deception for a variety of reasons is clearly taught in Scripture and the Scripture itself warns Christians of such danger (1 Cor 6:9; 15:33; 2 Cor 11:3; Gal 6:7; Jas 1:16). Furthermore, the potential dangers of an assurance of faith grounded exclusively on religious experience has been well expressed by William Abraham when he writes concerning some who follow the Wesleyan tradition:

> It is surely no accident that the followers of Wesley have taken to classical forms of liberalism like the proverbial duck takes to water. The whole focus on religious experience when it is cut loose from the deeper theological framework in which it is embedded can very easily slide into an epistemology where the appeal to Scripture or to a solid conception of revelation is replaced by an appeal to religious experience simpliciter.[82]

Subjective experience alone is not robust enough to sustain a firm assurance of salvation, it is too anthropocentric. What is needed is some objective element that grounds our subjective experience. I suggest that the historicity of the cross provides that objective grounding. The death of Christ (and his subsequent resurrection and ascension) was a historical reality—it took place in time and space. There it was that "God was in Christ reconciling the world to Himself" (2 Cor 5:19). Furthermore, if I know that Christ's death was a "propitiation for our sins; and not for ours only, but also for those of the whole world" (1 John 2:2), then I can know that Christ died for *me*. A complete and ongoing trust in the finished work of Christ on the cross provides the needed objective basis for present Christian assurance. And this is a feature of assurance that both Calvinists and non-Calvinists hold together.

The real challenge for Calvinists concerns assurance of persevering in the faith, not as a present reality, but as a future certainty. The non-Calvinist grounds his future assurance of salvation, subjectively speaking, in his ongoing trust in Christ's work on the cross and in simple belief in the gospel: *"For God so loved the world, that He gave His only begotten Son, that whoever believes in Him shall not perish, but have eternal life"* (John

---

81. Grudem, *Systematic Theology*, 803–5.

82. Abraham, "Predestination and Assurance," 240.

3:16). As long as the believer continues to exercise this faith he is assured of salvation; when he no longer exercises this faith, he effectively chooses to forfeit his salvation. As Jesus said: *"He who has the Son has the life; he who does not have the Son of God does not have the life"* (1 John 5:12). Present and ongoing assurance of salvation is intrinsically connected to an ongoing relationship with God through Christ by faith.

But what about the Calvinist, what grounds his salvation *ultimately*? Yes, he may be convinced of a present experience of salvation, but is he justified in believing that he will continue to believe to the end? The answer must be no. Why? Because, ultimately and within a monergistic system whereby God decrees who will be saved and who will not be saved, the consistent Calvinist has no ground of assurance. His valid ground of assurance is his election by God for salvation.[83] Recall that ultimately, within Calvinism, salvation is by the decree of God—everything else is secondary. If the Calvinist is assured of his election then he can be fully assured that he will indeed persevere to the end. But the difficulty is that there is no way the Calvinist can know that he is one of the elect, and so no way to be assured he will persevere to the end. He may think he is part of the elect, but ultimately he cannot be certain; this is a major problem for the Calvinist.[84] Again, Abraham expresses the difficulty well: present security

> provides assurance [of eternal security] only if we know we are one of the elect. Yet this is crucial information not vouchsafed to us. The elect are known only to God; in fact election depends entirely on God's arbitrary choice; only God knows those whom he has chosen to save. Clearly this is not something that has been revealed by God, hence we are left in the dark as to who the elect are. General propositions that tell us that the elect are secure are therefore ultimately vacuous when it comes to the question of our own personal assurance of our standing before God. It is Calvinists, not Arminians, who have a problem in providing adequate resources for a healthy doctrine of assurance. It is small wonder then that those who have meditated thoroughly on the doctrines of Calvinism in a personal and existential way have been driven at times to despair.[85]

---

83. Horton, e.g., holds that "believers are entitled to that genuine security that is announced in Scripture, which is grounded in God's decision and effort and for that reason will always yield the results repentance, faith, and perseverance." Presumably he means God's decision to save his elect and God's effort to keep them in a saved state. Horton, *For Calvinism*, 72.

84. Even Augustine acknowledged that ongoing perseverance could not be assured by the believer: "Perseverance is a divine gift . . . and this gift cannot be lost. For Augustine, no one in this life can know if he has or does not have this gift. . . . Even people who are devoted to Christ and committed to honoring God cannot know if they will continue on that path to the very end of their lives." Allison, *Historical Theology*, 547.

85. Abraham, "Predestination and Assurance," 235.

c) The Issue of Apostasy: Can a Christian Apostatize?

The crucial question in the case of apostasy concerns whether a true believer in Christ can at some point in their lives forsake their faith, or fall from grace. A common but unhelpful term is "lose one's salvation." The problem with this way of stating the issue is that it is too close to being something that happens accidentally—similar to "I lost my glasses." But here we are not talking about something in the Christian's life that happens accidentally, but rather is a willful, deliberate decision and choice to abandon or renounce the faith. To the question as to whether a Christian can fall from grace in a final sense, typically at least three different answers have been given. The Calvinist says no; the non-Calvinist says yes; and a third position says, "Theoretically Yes, but in practice, No" (hypothetical apostasy).

All agree that the valid subjects of this question are not merely people that make a profession of faith, but who are and never were, true believers. False prophets and false teachers who aligned themselves with the church were a problem for the early church and are clearly reflected in the pages of Scripture. The Apostle Paul was troubled by false brethren (2 Cor 11:26; Gal 2:4) during his ministry. Both Peter and John speak of false prophets and teachers (2 Pet 2:1; 1 John 4:1). Neither does this question concern those who initially make a profession of faith, for example at a youth rally, but subsequently show no sign of ongoing discipleship; Matt 13:18–22 provides examples of this kind of person. We may justifiably conclude that such persons never were genuine believers. Again, the question is: Can a true believer now be absolutely assured that he will persevere to the end, that somehow God will guarantee his perseverance?[86]

The issue is brought into focus by the empirical fact that people who seemed very much like true believers—they worshipped with God's people, prayed, fellowshipped, and professed to love God and gladly acknowledge their salvation was based on God's grace not their own good works, nevertheless later in their lives departed from the Christian walk and chose instead to live in the world with no sense of remorse. How are we to assess such persons—did they apostatize or were they never true believers to begin with? One answer, within a Calvinistic framework, given by Calvin himself is that such persons were at one time true believers because part of the elect chosen by God for salvation, but then later God chose to rescind their election.

Calvin, in his discussion of Matt 22:14 (*"many are called, but few are chosen"*) speaks of the alleged two callings of God. The first is a general call which is "a universal call, by which God, through the external preaching of the word, invites all men alike,

---

86. Some Calvinists muddy the water here. On the one hand they affirm the reality of apostasy (the falling away of true believers), but then later deny it! Horton, e.g., states, "So, apostasy is not only hypothetical; it actually happens." But then a few lines later he says: "Our perseverance in faith is guaranteed by God's electing grace." Horton, *For Calvinism*, 119. Similarly, Sproul, commenting on 1 John 2:19–25, remarks, "John did acknowledge that some did leave the company of believers. They were apostates." And yet a few lines later states: "If they persist in apostasy until death, then ... [this] is evidence that they were not genuine believers in the first place." Sproul, *Reformed Theology*, 209. Such ambiguous language concerning the identity of an apostate is not helpful.

even those for whom he designs the call to be a savor of death."[87] This call does not, and is not, intended to save anyone. On the other hand, there is an alleged special call which "God bestows on believers only, when, by the internal illumination of the Spirit he causes the word preached to take deep root in their hearts."[88] This call guarantees the elect will respond to the gospel. However, and this is the novel aspect mentioned in the previous paragraph, Calvin surmises a third type of call probably with those in mind who appear to be saved but who subsequently fall away. This category are those who are temporarily illuminated by the Spirit and who, presumably, during the duration of that illumination, are counted as part of the elect, but then subsequently depart the faith. "Sometimes, however, he communicates [the word preached] also to those whom he *enlightens only for a time*, and then afterwards, in just punishment for their ingratitude, he abandons and smites with greater blindness."[89] This is a strange teaching especially within the binary nature of Calvinism's doctrine of election. It smacks too much of an expedient designed to handle apparent apostasy and yet retain God's sovereign decisions and actions with respect to the salvation of the elect. For this reason, it is not the position typically advocated by modern Calvinists.[90]

Far more common among Calvinists, is the view that a supposed apostate was only apparently a believer. True apostasy is necessarily denied because God will ensure his elect persevere to the end. "Our perseverance in faith is guaranteed by God's electing, redeeming, and calling grace," says Horton.[91] He goes on to explain concerning those who began well, but subsequently fell: "Those who deny Christ to the very end, even though they may perhaps have outwardly been members of the visible church, are lost because they were never living members through faith."[92] Piper offers the same pattern of, on the one hand, affirming that the elect chosen by God will persevere and, on the other hand, that those who fail to persevere merely demonstrate they were never real believers in the first place. "God will so work in us that those whom he has chosen for eternal salvation will be enabled by him to persevere in faith to the end. . . . There is a falling away of some believers, but if it persists, it shows that their faith was not genuine and they were not born of God."[93] Grudem, commenting on the several passages in Scripture which urge Christians to persevere in faith, says that the purpose of such scriptures is "to warn those who are

87. Calvin, *Institutes*, 3.24.8.

88. Calvin, *Institutes*, 3.24.8.

89. Calvin, *Institutes*, 3.24.8, emphasis mine.

90. There are pastoral implications for this position which compounds the uncertainty of assurance a Calvinist is entitled to because they cannot know if they are counted among God's elect. Abraham draws attention to this pastoral aspect of Calvin's teaching: "Now if this possibility is seriously considered, the perplexity of the believer is bound to be increased and what little ground they may have had to start with is eroded considerably." Abraham, "Predestination and Assurance," 238.

91. Horton, *For Calvinism*, 119.

92. Horton, *For Calvinism*, 119.

93. Piper *Five Points*, 68, 69. But *believers* whose faith was not genuine is a contradiction.

thinking of falling away or have fallen away that if they do this it is a strong indication that they were never saved in the first place."[94]

The main difficulty with this position is that there are no clear passages of Scripture which teach this. A favorite often appealed to by Calvinists is 1 John 2:19: *"They went out from us, but they were not really of us; for if they had been of us, they would have remained with us; but they went out, so that it would be shown that they all are not of us."* Grudem believes the verse is speaking of "people who have left the fellowship of believers . . . [and] that those who have departed showed by their actions that they 'were not of us'—that they were not truly born again."[95] Hoekema rather unhelpfully speaks of "temporary conversion—conversions which are not genuine but only apparent" and cites this verse in support of such persons.[96] Berkhof also cites this verse as an example of "persons who profess true faith, and yet are not of the faith."[97]

The difficulty in appealing to 1 John 2:19 to prove that apparent believers forsaking their faith only proves their faith was not genuine in the first place, is that this verse is not talking about apparent believers or those temporarily converted. The people who had associated with the church for a time were false teachers whom John in the immediately preceding verse describes as antichrists. John Stott is probably correct in speculating that "the many antichrists who have already come in [v. 18] are now [in v. 19] identified as human teachers. They have left the church to which John is writing, perhaps because they have failed to win over church leaders to their viewpoint."[98] In short, 1 John 2:19 makes no contribution to a discussion of apostasy, which has to do with the possibility of genuine believers falling away from a state of salvation, not false teachers leaving a church.

Biblical Passages That Teach Apostasy Is a Real Possibility

Are there any passages in the Bible that would indicate that it is possible for formerly genuine believers to apostatize? There certainly are. There are at least two texts which speak of "falling away," one as a future reality and another which, though potential is nevertheless a very real possibility. After listing a series of traits associated with believers, the writer to the book of Hebrews warns his readers that if such believers *"then have fallen away, it is impossible to renew them again to repentance, since they again crucify to themselves the Son of God and put Him to open shame"* (Heb 6:6).

---

94. Grudem, *Systematic Theology*, 793. Concerning such who did fall away, one wonders what they "fell away" from.

95. Grudem, *Systematic Theology*, 794.

96. Hoekema, *Saved by Grace*, 116. To speak of "temporary conversion" is akin to speaking about a woman being temporarily pregnant; either one is converted or one is not converted. His reference to "second conversion" is likewise confusing.

97. Berkhof, *Systematic Theology*, 549.

98. Stott, *Letters of John*, 110.

We shall look more closely at the warning passages in the Bible later, suffice to note for now that, in the words of F. F. Bruce, the point of this verse is that "apostasy is irremediable. . . . Just as the Hebrew spies who returned from their expedition carrying visible tokens of the good land of Canaan nevertheless failed to enter the land because of their unbelief, so those who had come to know the blessings of the new covenant might nevertheless in a spiritual sense turn back in heart to Egypt and so forfeit the saints' everlasting rest."[99]

Another passage which speaks of falling away is 1 Tim 4:1. Paul teaches young Timothy that *"the Spirit explicitly says that in later times some will* fall away *from the faith, paying attention to deceitful spirits and doctrines of demons."* Of course, in both this and the previous passage, it is impossible to "fall" from that which one never was "in." In that sense, the term fall is synonymous with reject. How do such former believers fall? According to the passage, they allow themselves to be diverted from a constant and clear focus on Jesus, and then pay attention to that which is false and contrary to biblical truth. The antidote to such dangers is provided by Paul a little later in his letter to Timothy, explaining that *"it is for this we labor and strive, because we have fixed our hope on the living God, who is the Savior of all men, especially of believers"* (1 Tim 4:10). Failing to fix one's hope on the grace of Jesus Christ (1 Pet 1:13) leaves the believer vulnerable to false teachers and false practices and ultimately a denial and rejection of their faith.

The idea of a believer's possibility of denying their faith is also clearly taught. Paul, seeking to advise Timothy, the young leader of the church in Ephesus, provides counsel regarding the responsibility of the church vis-à-vis needy people within the church. The principle established is that help should only be provided to people after their relatives have sought to help them. His focus is on widows, but the principle applies throughout (1 Tim 5:3–16), and can be summed up as: *"If anyone does not provide for his own, and especially for those of his household, he has* denied *the faith and is worse than an unbeliever"* (1 Tim 5:8). "In the contemporary pagan world there was a general acceptance of obligation towards parents, and it was unthinkable that Christian morality should lag behind general pagan standards."[100] Certainly, someone refusing to carry out this basic Christian duty toward parents, were seriously sinning, and as long they remained unrepentant, were in effect denying the faith they professed to uphold.

Another example of denial concerns the anticipation by Peter of false teachers *"who will secretly introduce destructive heresies, even* denying *the Master who bought them"* (2 Pet 2:1). Peter's reference to them denying the Master who bought them

---

99. Bruce, *Hebrews*, 119. Despite saying, "Those who have shared the covenant privileges of the people of God, and then deliberately renounce them, are the most difficult persons of all to reclaim for the faith," Bruce inconsistently seems to hold to the Calvinistic doctrine of the guaranteed perseverance of the saints. Bruce, *Hebrews*, 118.

100. Guthrie, *Pastoral Epistles*, 113.

suggests they arose from within the church and owned Christ as their Master at one time. This is consistent with Peter's recalling how false prophets arose from among the children of Israel under the old covenant: *"But false prophets also arose among the people"* (2 Pet 2:1). "In Israel there were also false prophets among the people as well as true, and now history was repeating itself."[101]

A little later in this same letter, Peter, toward the end of his severe condemnation of these false teachers, suggests that they (or at least some of them) were indeed former believers: *"For if, after they have escaped the defilements of the world by the knowledge of the Lord and Savior Jesus Christ, they are again entangled in them and are overcome, the last state has become worse for them than the first"* (2 Pet 2:20). Calvinists must reject the possibility that Peter is here describing former Christians who have now apostatized. For example, Hoekema asks, "Were these men ever true believers? Was their knowledge of Christ ever a true and saving knowledge? There is no indication in the text that they were ever true believers."[102] However, it is hard to see how men who at one time had a *"knowledge of the Lord and Savior Jesus Christ,"* and have now become entangled *again* in the defilements of the world, that is, had *returned* to a former pagan life, could be accurately described as non-Christians, unbelievers. Commenting on this verse (2 Pet 2:20), Kelly remarks that "[Peter's] warning is direct and to the point: if Christians revert to pagan moral standards, their final state is worse than the first. . . . Lapsed Christians are in a more tragic plight than unconverted pagans because they have rejected the light."[103] Baukham agrees that the false teachers described here in v. 20 were, at one time, genuine believers. Concerning the first part of v. 20, he flatly states, "This phrase refers to conversion to Christianity." He goes on to remark that the "false teachers are in the state of definite apostasy described in vv. 20–22; their followers are doubtless in severe danger of joining them in it [apostasy] and so these verses serve as a serious warning to the followers."[104]

Jesus commends two of the seven churches in Rev 2 and 3 for not having denied their faith. To the church at Pergamum Jesus says: *"I know where you dwell, where Satan's throne is; and you hold fast My name, and* did not deny My faith *even in the days of Antipas"* (Rev 2:13). And to the church at Philadelphia Jesus says, *"I know your deeds. Behold, I have put before you an open door which no one can shut, because you have a little power, and have kept My word, and* have not denied *My name"* (Rev 3:8). Obviously, their commendation by Jesus only makes sense if the possibility was real that the believers in these churches could have chosen to deny the faith in order to avoid persecution. Instead, they chose to remain faithful to Christ, and to keep his word.

In Rom 11 Paul is addressing the question of God's stance toward the Jews given that they have rejected their Messiah (v. 1). His response is no, God has not rejected

---

101. Green, *2 Peter & Jude*, 104.

102. Hoekema, *Saved by Grace*, 253.

103. Kelly, *Peter and Jude*, 348.

104. Baukham, *Jude*, 277.

the Jews as is demonstrated by the fact that God has always had a faithful remnant of Jewish believers (vv. 2–5). The church at Rome consisted of both Jewish and Gentile Christians. Paul explains that through Jewish rejection of the gospel (on the whole), Gentile opportunity to believe the gospel was made possible (v. 11). Since the Jews had rejected Christ, the Gentile Christians were tempted to feel superior to their Jewish brethren, an attitude of arrogance had set in (v. 18). The Jews were cut off from the olive tree that represented true Israel (Jew and Gentile) because of their unbelief (vv. 19, 20). Paul goes on to warn the Gentile Christians that if they fail to continue to exercise faith, then *"if God did not spare the natural branches, He will not spare you, either"* (v. 21). Finally, the Gentile Christians in the church are to *"behold then the kindness and severity of God; to those who fell, severity, but to you, God's kindness, if you continue in His kindness; otherwise you also will be cut off"* (v. 22). There can be no doubt that Paul is addressing genuine Christians with the possibility that they may be *"cut off"* if they fail to continue in the faith. The Gentiles had been grafted in to the olive tree that is true Israel; they were to *"stand by your faith"* they were to *"continue in God's kindness."* As Warren observes, "As their [the Gentile's] grafting in pictures salvation, so also their removal again pictures loss of salvation."[105]

Similar to the above text (Rom 11), Paul teaches the Christians at Colossae that their privileged status as those who have been reconciled to God through the death of Christ is conditional on their continuing in the faith: *"He has now reconciled you in His fleshly body through death, in order to present you before Him holy and blameless and beyond reproach—if indeed you continue in the faith firmly established and steadfast, and not moved away from the hope of the gospel that you have heard"* (Col 1:22–23). It seems as though Paul considered it a real possibility that some of the Christians would "move away" from the gospel. While of course it is true that Christians are those who persevere to the end, contra Calvinism, such perseverance is not guaranteed by God—it is a function of the exercise of continued human faith.[106] Commenting on v. 23, even the mild Calvinist F. F. Bruce remarks, "The language used may suggest that the reader's first enthusiasm was being dimmed, that they were in danger of shifting from the fixed ground of Christian hope."[107]

---

105. Warren, *Salvation*, 424.

106. I say human faith because many Calvinists speak quite easily about faith, exercising faith, continuing in faith etc.—and yet understand that faith to ultimately originate with God. Recall that, for Calvinists, faith is a God-given gift or capacity. Faith within Calvinism is not a genuine human capacity, it is a work of *God* in a human subject.

107. Bruce, *Colossians, Philemon and Ephesians*, 79. Bruce understates the situation. Paul was quite clear about them *moving away* from the hope of the gospel—there is no mere *suggestion* here, and the issue is not enthusiasm but salvation.

Examples of Apostasy in the New Testament

One way to answer the question of the possibility of genuine apostasy, that is, formerly genuine believers choosing to forsake their faith, is to examine the epistles to see if any examples of such cases are shown there. In his First Letter to Timothy, Paul mentions two men, Hymenaeus and Alexander, who had rejected their faith. He urges Timothy to *"fight the good fight, keeping faith and a good conscience, which some have* rejected *and suffered shipwreck in regard to their faith. Among these are Hymenaeus and Alexander, whom I have handed over to Satan, so that they will be taught not to blaspheme"* (1 Tim 1:18–20). Guthrie comments, "Those who ignore conscience will continue to make shipwreck of their faith, as some of these early Christians did."[108] The reference to these men being handed over to Satan may mean that they were excommunicated from Christian fellowship and into Satan's province, or perhaps even to some physical disaster. Or perhaps a combination of both views is correct.[109] In any case, it is clear that these men, who at one time associated with the church and kept the faith and appreciated the importance of maintaining a good conscience, reached a point where both (keeping faith and also a good conscience) were rejected—with disastrous consequences. Their choice and decision were real and resulted in real consequences. The text also indicates that these two were only some of those who rejected their faith.

Apparently, it seems as though one of the problems in the church at Ephesus concerned some in the church who engaged in unedifying chatter (2 Tim 2:14, 16). Among them were two individuals named Hymenaeus and Philetus. Paul describes them as *"men who have gone astray from the truth saying that the resurrection has already taken place, and they upset the faith of some"* (2 Tim 2:18). These men are said to have "gone astray from the truth," "departed from the truth" (NIV), "swerved from the truth" (ESV). The Greek word ἀστοχεω (*astocheō*) strictly means to miss the mark; hence depart from, deviate from, go astray. In this case these men were teaching a basic error, that the general resurrection had already happened. Were these men among the false teachers which bedeviled the early church and who had infiltrated the church, or where they believers who engaged in a teaching ministry but who were teaching a basic error? While the former cannot be discounted, they may well have been teachers within the church who, at one time, held to the truth but had now wandered away from the truth of the gospel.

Toward the end of his Second Letter to Timothy, Paul makes reference to a certain Demas who was at one time a compatriot of Paul. No doubt feeling alone, Paul urges Timothy to *"make every effort to come to me soon; for Demas, having loved this present world, has deserted me and gone to Thessalonica"* (2 Tim 4:9, 10). It is quite likely that this Demas was the same one mentioned earlier by Paul in Col 4:14: *"Luke, the beloved physician, sends you his greetings, and also Demas."* Guthrie comments, "Demas

108. Bruce, *Colossians, Philemon and Ephesians*, 78.
109. Bruce, *Colossians, Philemon and Ephesians*, 79.

is mentioned in Col 4:14 as one of Paul's close associates, but by this time he had perhaps found the apostle's demands too rigorous."[110] It seems quite likely that Demas at one time loved Christ but had chosen to switch allegiance and now *"loved this present world."* The latter phrase indicating a defection, a rejection of the faith he once held (1 John 2:15). Despite noting that "Demas had at one time been Paul's assistant in the gospel ministry" (Phlm 24), and that Demas "had rendered service in the kingdom," William Hendriksen comments, "Much can be said in support of the view that Demas . . . never belonged to the company of those who love Christ's appearing."[111] It is most unlikely that Paul would have associated with, and in some way depended on, a man who was never a believer for the furtherance of the gospel.

Warning Passages in the Epistles

In addition to the biblical passages which teach that apostasy is a real possibility and the examples of apostasy in the New Testament, there are also countless passages that warn the Christian against forsaking his or her faith. Before focusing on the book of Hebrews, I will illustrate the point from selected texts in other portions of the New Testament.

In Rom 11, Paul is addressing the tendency of the Gentiles in the church to boast and behave arrogantly because the Jews have rejected the gospel whereas they accepted it. Paul agrees with the Gentiles that Jews were broken off the olive tree that represents true, believing, Israel, because of their unbelief, but warns them (the Gentiles) that they too need to live by faith, and that failing to do so (i.e., apostatize) will result in God also cutting them off the tree. Here is the key passage, and note the conditionality of salvation, "*if* you continue": *"Quite right, they were broken off for their unbelief, but you stand by your faith. Do not be conceited, but fear; for if God did not spare the natural branches, He will not spare you, either. Behold then the kindness and severity of God; to those who fell, severity, but to you, God's kindness, if you continue in His kindness; otherwise you also will be cut off"* (Rom 11:20–22). Paul was addressing genuine Gentile believers, but believers who were tempted to "be conceited" and thus fail to continue in God's kindness; the possibility apostasy in this church among some Gentiles was real.

The church at Corinth, as is well known, was a church with many problems, including immorality, party spirit, confusion about Christian practice (marriage, food offered to idols, church order to name a few), and Christian doctrine (resurrection). After discussing Christian liberty in ch. 9 with an emphasis on his own liberty in Christ, Paul then turns to the application of Christian liberty as far as Corinthians themselves were concerned. His main thrust is to warn the church of the real possibility that the flagrant abuse of Christian liberty leads to immorality

110. Bruce, *Colossians, Philemon and Ephesians*, 183.

111. Hendriksen, *1 & 2 Timothy and Titus*, 319.

and idolatry. His prime example is the experience of the first generation in the wilderness following the exodus from Egypt, noting especially that all but two of that generation died in the wilderness and were not permitted to enter the promised land (1 Cor 10:1–5). His point in recounting this historical incident is that *"these things happened as examples for us, so that we would not crave evil things as they also craved"* (v. 6). He makes precisely the same observation again in v. 11. After recounting four specific sins of that wilderness generation—idolatry, immorality, testing God, grumbling against God—Paul brings home his point: *"Therefore let him who thinks he stands take heed that he does not fall"* (1 Cor 10:12). Paul's warning that the judgment that the wilderness generation experienced served as an example to the Corinthian Christians, together with the exhortation that they not take for granted their salvation in Christ and that they themselves need to *"take heed that he does not fall,"* underscores the reality of the danger of apostasy.

In 1 Cor 15, Paul reminds his readers that he brought to them that which is fundamental to the gospel, namely teaching concerning the resurrection. At the beginning of this chapter, Paul also reminds the believers at Corinth that they had heard the gospel preached to them, had received it, and now stood in it, resulting in their salvation: *"Now I make known to you, brethren, the gospel which I preached to you, which also you received, in which also you stand, by which also you are saved"* (vv. 1, 2a). But they are warned that their salvation was dependent upon them continuing to *"hold fast the word which I preached to you"* (v. 2b). Failing to continue in belief would result in them having *"believed in vain"* (1 Cor 15:1, 2). For Paul, "continuing in this saved state is conditioned on continuing to hold fast to the proclaimed word, continuing to trust in the saving work of Jesus for salvation."[112]

The churches in Galatia (southeastern modern Turkey) were troubled by Judaizers—Jewish Christians who were urging the believers to keep the Mosaic law in order to be fully accepted by God and as a requirement for Christian living.[113] This raised the question of the role of the Mosaic law in the Christian life, and thus the question of Christian freedom in Christ. Paul resolutely opposes the Judaizers' claim that law keeping was a necessary component of Christian belief and practice, and that they should not compromise their freedom in Christ: *"It was for freedom that Christ set us free; therefore keep standing firm and do not be subject again to a yoke of slavery"* (Gal 5:1). For Paul, the danger was in confusing the basis of the gospel. Was the gospel all of grace alone or partly grace and partly meritorious works of the law? Paul makes it clear that only the former was the true gospel, and that incorporating the law as a necessary component of union with Christ was actually contradictory, and would require that the whole law be observed, not merely one aspect (circumcision): *"Behold I, Paul, say to you that if you receive circumcision, Christ will be of no benefit to you. And I testify again to every man who receives circumcision, that he is*

112. Cottrell, *Faith Once for All*, 378.
113. Longenecker, *Galatians*, xcv.

under obligation to keep the whole Law" (vv. 2, 3). Finally, Paul warns his Christian readers who were coming under the influence of these Judaizers that if they were to heed the teachings of these Jewish Christians it would be fatal to the reality of their present salvation in Christ (alone): *"You have been severed from Christ, you who are seeking to be justified by law; you have fallen from grace"* (Gal 5:4). For our purposes here, Cottrell's, observation is pertinent: "They could not have been severed from Christ unless they at one time were joined to him; they could not have fallen from grace unless they at one time had been standing in it."[114] The Calvinist Ridderbos's explanation for the phrase *"you have fallen from grace"* as Paul's method "to bring them to the point of reflection" seems remarkably unconvincing; Paul is clearly stating the consequences were the Galatian Christians to adopt the Judaizer's teachings; they would fall from grace, be severed from Christ.[115]

The Warning Passages in the Book of Hebrews

The epistle was written to Jewish Christians who were in danger of forsaking their Christian faith and relapsing back into Judaism. The basic approach of the author in addressing these Christians is a carrot-and-stick one; the former is accomplished by presenting the superiority of Jesus and the new covenant he has inaugurated over the old covenant, and the latter by sternly warning them of the dangers of abandoning Christian faith. As F. F. Bruce notes, "The writer, who has known them, or known about them, for a considerable time, and feels a pastoral concern for their welfare, warns them against falling back, for this may result in falling away from their Christian faith altogether; he encourages them with the assurance that they have everything to lose if they fall back, but everything to gain if they press on."[116] Given this historical setting, this epistle comprises an excellent source to evaluate the nature of the warnings found therein.

There are at least seven clear occasions when the author warns his readers of the dangers associated with forsaking their faith (2:1–3; 3:12–19; 4:1; 4:11; 6:4–8; 10:26–29; 12:25). I will briefly examine each of these passages, and focus especially on Heb 6:4–8.

Hebrews 2:1–3: *"For this reason we must pay much closer attention to what we have heard, so that we do not drift away from it. For if the word spoken through angels proved unalterable, and every transgression and disobedience received a just penalty, how will we escape if we neglect so great a salvation?"* Since the Son, who is superior to any of the angels, has spoken the ultimate words of God (Heb 1:2), so now the readers need to pay close attention to the gospel message they had heard, lest they *"drift away from it."* There is some biblical evidence that angelic presence accompanied the giving of the law

---

114. Cottrell, *Faith Once for All*, 379.

115. Ridderbos, *Churches of Galatia*, 189.

116. Bruce, *Hebrews*, xxx.

at Mt. Sinai (Deut 33:2; Acts 7:38, 53; Gal 3:19). If those under the old Mosaic covenant were severely punished for flouting the law (witness the thousands that perished in the wilderness), the dangers associated with drifting away from or neglecting the revelation of the Son in the new covenant would be much greater. Here we have an argument from the lesser to the greater. These verses "develop a comparison designed to reinforce the necessity of adhering to the Christian tradition. If disregard for the Mosaic law was appropriately punished, unconcern for the gospel must inevitably be catastrophic."[117] These Christians had not yet reached that point but were in real danger of the consequences of effectively rejecting the gospel through a careless attitude toward the faith. Both the warning and the danger are real.

Hebrews 3:12: *"Take care, brethren, that there not be in any one of you an evil, unbelieving heart that falls away from the living God."* The Greek verb translated as "falls away" (ἀποστῆναι, *apostēnai*) means "go away, withdraw, become apostate'[118] and describes a decisive consequence of unbelief. This "is the refusal to believe God. It leads inevitably to a turning away from God in a deliberate act of rejection."[119] These Christians were in danger of being hardened against the things of God through the deceitfulness of sin, v. 13. The author focuses on the idea of hardened hearts with clear allusion to the experience of the wilderness generation as described in Ps 95. That generation, the author concludes, *"were not able to enter* [God's rest] *because of unbelief"* (v. 19). The warning is clear: failure of these "brethren" to heed it would result in their falling away from God.

Hebrews 4:1: *"Therefore, let us fear if, while a promise remains of entering His rest, any one of you may seem to have come short of it."* Here, we have an exhortation (let us fear) followed by a warning concerning falling short of entering God's rest. In the context of Ps 95 and looking back to the exodus, God's rest meant entrance into the promised land. Here, the author's use of rest has an eschatological focus and implies entrance into the blessedness of the age to come.[120] God's grace is always available through faith, and so the promise of entering into God's eschatological rest remains open. These believers, however, were in danger of failing to continue reverencing God now revealed in the Son and especially his revelatory word of salvation because of unbelief. There is a sense of urgency since the promise of eternal rest will not be available indefinitely. The failure of entering eschatological salvation is a real possibility for these Jewish Christians should they fail to heed the warning and fail to persevere in Christian faith.

Heb 4:11: *"Therefore let us be diligent to enter that rest, so that no one will fall, through following the same example of disobedience."* This warning is essentially a repetition of 4:1. Once more the experience of those that fell in the desert through

117. Lane, *Hebrews 1–8*, 37.

118. Bauer, *Greek-English Lexicon*, 126.

119. Lane, *Hebrews 1–8*, 86.

120. Lane, *Hebrews 1–8*, 98.

disobedience to the law of Moses is used by the author of Hebrews to warn his readers against committing the same error, i.e., unbelief. They need to take the lesson of that wilderness generation to heart and be careful to be an obedient people lest they too fall from grace.

Heb 10:26–29: *"For if we go on sinning willfully after receiving the knowledge of the truth, there no longer remains a sacrifice for sins, but a terrifying expectation of judgment and the fury of a fire which will consume the adversaries. Anyone who has set aside the Law of Moses dies without mercy on the testimony of two or three witnesses. How much severer punishment do you think he will deserve who has trampled underfoot the Son of God, and has regarded as unclean the blood of the covenant by which he was sanctified, and has insulted the Spirit of grace?"* Consistent with all the other warnings in the letter and also consistent with the author's intent and purpose for writing, the disastrous outcome for anyone continuing to sin willfully after receiving a knowledge of the truth, is made abundantly clear here. This is necessarily so because the one ground or basis for escaping the wrath of God for sins, namely the death of Christ as a sacrifice for sins, is being rejected. Note that the author assumes the spiritual status of his readers as currently authentic Christians ('if we go on sinning'). They are those who have received the gospel (the knowledge of the truth) and who have been sanctified through the death of Christ (v. 29). These are Christians who are in danger of willfully persisting in sin on an ongoing basis and who would thereby demonstrate by their behavior that they have chosen to reject the only source of eternal salvation; undoubtedly, apostasy is being contemplated here.

Heb 12:25: *"See to it that you do not refuse Him who is speaking. For if those did not escape when they refused him who warned them on earth, much less will we escape who turn away from Him who warns from heaven."* Here, again, the author warns his readers of the imminent danger they are in if they choose to turn their back on Christian faith and revert back to the Judaism they are familiar with. Like the Heb 2:1–3 passage discussed previously, this is an argument from the lesser to the greater. "The warning from heaven is linked with the whole Christian revelation centred [sic] in the mediatorial work of Christ. This is another instance of a powerful argument based on a transference of thought from the lesser to the greater."[121] This is still a warning, his readers were contemplating apostatizing but had not done so yet. They would have been very familiar with the disastrous consequences meted out upon the wilderness generation for their persistent idolatry. Hardly had the law been given at Mt. Sinai when the people sinned grievously by fabricating a golden calf. God's verdict would have been well known in his words to Moses: *"Now then let Me alone, that My anger may burn against them and that I may destroy them; and I will make of you a great nation"* (Exod 32:10). Apostasy now would reap greater condemnation due to the greater revelation made available through the incarnation and the associated warning from heaven for those who reject the gospel.

121. Guthrie, *Hebrews*, 264.

Heb 6:4–6: *"For in the case of those who have once been enlightened and have tasted of the heavenly gift and have been made partakers of the Holy Spirit, and have tasted the good word of God and the powers of the age to come, and then have fallen away, it is impossible to renew them again to repentance, since they again crucify to themselves the Son of God and put Him to open shame."*

The key issue here as far as the Calvinist/non-Calvinist debate is concerned is whether the people to whom this warning is given are genuine Christians or simply people who make a mere profession of faith. Calvinists argue for the latter as they must do since they effectively deny the reality of apostasy; genuine Christians cannot apostatize, reject their faith, because God guarantees the perseverance of the elect. Grudem, as we shall see, adopts this approach. Another possible response from a Calvinistic perspective is to agree that the author is addressing genuine Christians but that the warning here (and throughout the letter) envisages only a theoretical possibility—the readers could apostatize, but won't. Sproul is an example: "The author of Hebrews nowhere states that a true believer does in fact do what he is warning believers not to do."[122] The obvious question that arises from such a stance is one that is raised by Sproul himself: "If no believer does what the author warns against, why bother with such a warning?"[123]

The people to whom this warning is given are described as having five characteristics: they have (1) been enlightened, (2) tasted of the heavenly gift, (3) been made partakers of the Holy Spirit, (4) tasted the word of God, (5) tasted the powers of the age to come. Grudem addresses each of these characteristics and argues against apostasy (the falling away of true believers) on the basis that "the terms in verses 4–6 by themselves are inconclusive, for they speak of events that are experienced both by genuine Christians and by some people who participate in the fellowship of a church but are never really saved."[124] Following what can only be described as strained exegesis of vv. 4–6, Grudem concludes that "the actual spiritual status of those who have experienced these things is still unclear."[125]

To answer the question of the actual spiritual status of these people, i.e., whether they were truly saved or not, Grudem finds the answer in the following two verses: *"For ground that drinks the rain which often falls on it and brings forth vegetation useful to those for whose sake it is also tilled, receives a blessing from God; but if it yields thorns and thistles, it is worthless and close to being cursed, and it ends up being burned"* (Heb 6:7–8). Here, the rain represents the work of God in the lives of these people, "the enlightening, the tasting of the heavenly gift, and the word of God and the powers of the age to come, and the partaking in the work of the Holy Spirit."[126] Grudem sees two

122. Sproul, *Reformed Theology*, 215.
123. Sproul, *Reformed Theology*, 215.
124. Grudem, "Perseverance," 139.
125. Grudem, "Perseverance," 153.
126. Grudem, "Perseverance," 155.

distinct types of ground that respond differently to the same rain: "The author is not thinking of the same piece of land at all, for he clearly thinks two distinct possibilities for two very different kinds of soil."[127] And consequently, "the way the ground responds to the rain reveals the kind of ground it was in the first place." Not surprisingly, the ground that yields thorns and thistles shows "they had never truly been saved in the first place."[128] In sum, according to Grudem, all the characteristics (or events as Grudem calls them) in vv. 4–6 apply to unbelievers, and thus no apostasy is in view here for these people were never believers to begin with. And so, the Calvinistic doctrine of the perseverance of the saints is preserved—true believers (the elect) do not and cannot apostatize. This, in brief, is the logic of Grudem's argument.

By way of response to Grudem's approach to this entire passage (Heb 4:4–8), several points may be noted. The first concerns his not addressing specifically the reason the author writes to this church; what occasioned his writing and for what purpose did he write? This is not an insignificant point and can provide a helpful hermeneutical key that would contribute to an accurate analysis of his letter. As mentioned previously, the writer, who is both theologian and pastor to this flock, seeks to warn those Jewish Christians in the church who were contemplating forsaking their faith and reverting back to the Judaism with which they were comfortable and familiar. "On the whole the view that posits the threat of an apostasy to Judaism among certain Jewish Christians . . . has generally more to commend it than alternative views."[129] The author "urges his listeners to hold loyally to their confession of Jesus Christ as the sole mediator of salvation in a time of crisis and warns them of the judgment of God they would incur if they should renounce their Christian commitment."[130] "The letter is apparently being written to Jews (i.e., Hebrews) who had become Christians, but who are now thinking they had made a mistake and are seriously considering abandoning their Christian faith and reconverting to Judaism. The theme of the entire letter is the danger and foolishness of such a decision."[131] The purpose for writing provides ample support for the view that the author's audience are actual Christians, believers, who are considering apostatizing.

A second criticism of Grudem's perspective is that he seems to believe that these people had already fallen away from Christian faith. He admits that "a reasonable argument can be made that these were genuine Christians *before they fell away.*" Also: "On the question of whether these people were really saved *before they fell away.*"[132] However, nowhere in the entire letter does the author indicate he is

127. Grudem, "Perseverance," 155n52.

128. Grudem, "Perseverance," 156.

129. Guthrie, *Hebrews*, 35.

130. Lane, *Hebrews 1–8*, intro. c.

131. Cottrell, *Faith Once for All*, 379.

132. Grudem, "Perseverance," 152, emphases mine. Later however, Grudem states that "the author knows that there are some in the community to which he writes who are in danger of falling away."

referring to those who had already forsaken the faith; his concern is to warn those who were considering forsaking the faith before they took that disastrous step, and in order to prevent them from so doing.

As noted already, Grudem is not convinced that the five characteristics that describe these people means that they are in fact Christians. He says: "We still cannot know, on the basis of that information alone, if they really have experienced the decisive beginning stages of the Christian life." He then goes on to describe the additional characteristics that would indicate to his satisfaction that these people were in fact true believers: "whether they have trusted in Christ for salvation, for example, and whether God has given them regeneration and forgiven their sins, and adopted them into his family, and whether their lives show fruit that gives evidence of true salvation."[133] However, it may well be that the author of Hebrews feels he has already provided enough evidence of their Christian experience to validate the fact that they are true Christians and so any additional evidences would be superfluous. Furthermore, if a genuine Christian must show the evidences listed here by Grudem, it is doubtful that we could conclude the author of the epistle was himself a genuine Christian for nothing is said about his own trusting in Christ or whether he himself has been regenerated, or whether he has been adopted into the family of God!

Grudem agrees that the term παραπιπτω (*parapiptō*), translated here as "fallen away" (v. 6), refers to apostasy.[134] After considering the ground metaphor (vv. 7, 8), he states, "then their falling away [i.e., apostasy] shows that they were never saved in the first place."[135] But apostasy refers, by definition, to genuine believers who then forsake their faith; it makes little sense to say, in effect, that unbelievers were "never saved in the first place."

A major reason Sproul believes the people who are in danger of falling away here in our passage are genuine Christians is because of the phrase "*it is impossible to renew them again to repentance*" (v. 6). The phrase strongly suggests that they had previously repented of their sins. Grudem agrees that these people "had some sorrow for sin and a decision to forsake their sin (repentance)."[136] Yet elsewhere, he states clearly that repentance follows (logically even if not temporally) regeneration.[137] So, if these people who are being warned had repented then, according to Grudem's own Calvinistic soteriology, they must have been regenerated, and thus be genuine Christians. And genuine Christians, who are part of the elect, cannot

---

Grudem, "Perseverance," 154. So Grudem seems inconsistent on this point.

133. Grudem, "Perseverance," 140.

134. The "context does indicate that the falling away is so serious it could rightly be called apostasy." Grudem, "Perseverance," 153.

135. Grudem, "Perseverance," 157.

136. Grudem, "Perseverance," 153.

137. "As God addresses the effective call of the gospel to us, he regenerates us and we respond in faith and repentance to this call." Grudem, *Systematic Theology*, 702.

apostatize because God will cause them to persevere. To soften the force of this logic, Grudem has to call into question the genuineness of their repentance. He does this by distinguishing between the term repentance here in v. 6 and "repentance unto life."[138] Grudem says that repentance "means a sorrow for actions that have been done or for sins that have been committed, and a resolve to forsake those sins. But not all repentance includes an inward, heartfelt *repentance towards God* that accompanies saving faith."[139] Yet, by definition, repentance means sorrow for sins and a resolve to forsake those sins, actions which Grudem admits applies to these people. Not every reference to repentance requires an author to qualify it or elaborate on the nature of that repentance. In fact, absent a need to qualify or elaborate on the term, repentance should be assumed to be genuine. Furthermore, in the immediately preceding verses the writer to these Jewish Christians views repentance as part of the "elementary teaching about Christ" and foundational of the Christian life (Heb 6:1) and assumes this is already part of his reader's experience.

Grudem also seeks to call into question the validity of considering the characteristics mentioned in Heb 6:4, 5[140] as genuine by viewing the descriptions in essentially non-experiential ways. So, tasting the word of God is made to mean merely that they "know it," and tasting of the heavenly gift (the Holy Spirit) is said to be something that they merely "understand," and repentance from sins is only something they "know" about.[141] In this way, Grudem seeks to leave the spiritual status of these people as "not yet clear." And yet, vv. 4, 5 are spoken of as aspects of the one experience of these people, namely their salvation: "The recital of what occurred with the reception of the gospel does not describe a succession of salvific events but one event of salvation that is viewed from different aspects and manifestations. Each of the positive statements is conditioned by the qualification 'once,' which conveys the notion of definitive occurrence."[142] The author's desire to move on beyond the elementary teachings toward Christian maturity (5:14—6:1) presupposes that his readers have in fact experienced the basic aspects of the gospel. Their present salvation is not being questioned, only the desire of some within the church to apostatize is raised as a possibility (vv. 4–6).

Grudem's understanding of this warning passage also raises this question: How can terms that could be used to describe true Christians also apply to unbelievers? Recall that Grudem concludes that these people are not genuine believers, they are in fact unbelievers. He agrees that "all of the terms can be used to describe either Christians or non-Christians." And then, "these factors are all positive, and people who have

138. Grudem, "Perseverance," 153.

139. Grudem, "Perseverance," 149, emphasis original.

140. (1) Been enlightened, (2) tasted of the heavenly gift, (3) been made partakers of the Holy Spirit, (4) tasted the word of God, (5) tasted the powers of the age to come.

141. Grudem, "Perseverance," 154.

142. Lane, *Hebrews 1–8*, 141.

experienced these things may be genuine Christians."[143] But nowhere in Scripture are unbelievers said to share characteristics and experiences that are valid and true for Christians. To the contrary, as Paul reminds the Corinthians: *"What has a believer in common with an unbeliever?"* (2 Cor 6:15). The answer, spiritually speaking, is "nothing." While it is true that the church can suffer false brethren and false teachers, in every case their true status was made manifest by their false doctrines or unchristian behavior. There is no indication in the book of Hebrews that the church suffered such people; no reference is made to false teachers in the church. Throughout the New Testament a clear demarcation is made between true Christians, who may be confused about certain doctrines and who may even be acting on occasion in unchristian ways, and unbelievers. Grudem blurs this important distinction in order to bolster his theory of uncertainty concerning the status of those described in vv. 4, 5.

What about Grudem's approach to vv. 7, 8[144] and his view that the metaphor implies the same rain is falling on two different kinds of soils? "Was the land that received much rain good land or bad when it began to receive the rain?"[145] His two-land theory allows Grudem to conclude that the rain that fell on land that produced thistles and thorns was always bad (unbelievers) and never good (believers) and so bolster his argument that the land never became bad from a formerly good condition. But is this two-land theory plausible? A superficial reading of the two verses would not lead the reader to think the author was thinking of two separate kinds of grounds, but simply one ground that produced either good (vegetation) or bad (thistles). The subject of v. 8 is the ground of v. 7, and refers to the church collectively. The mention of blessing in v. 7, and curse in v. 8 may echo the covenant blessings for obedience and covenant curses for disobedience applied to the one people of God in the old covenant (Deut 28).[146] Lane concurs: "The motif of blessing (v. 7) and curse (v. 8) places the discussion firmly in a covenantal context. The promise of blessing is attached to obedience, but the curse sanction is invoked in opposition to apostasy and disobedience."[147] I would suggest that a two-land approach to these two verses is reading too much into the metaphor and is merely an expedient to deny the reality of apostasy.

Finally, more broadly what are we to make of the warning passages discussed above? Concerning the hypothetical view, the view that the people being warned here are true Christians who could theoretically fall away from the faith, but won't because they are part of the elect who will be caused to persevere to the end. Grudem, quite rightly discounts this theory: "Surely it would be useless to warn the readers

143. Grudem, "Perseverance," 152–53.

144. *"For ground that drinks the rain which often falls on it and brings forth vegetation useful to those for whose sake it is also tilled, receives a blessing from God; but if it yields thorns and thistles, it is worthless and close to being cursed, and it ends up being burned"* (Heb 6:7–8).

145. Grudem, "Perseverance," 155.

146. Certainly, Old Testament motifs were prominent in the mind of the author and appears throughout the book of Hebrews.

147. Lane, *Hebrews 1–8*, 143.

against something that could never happen, and that without telling them that it could never happen."[148] Robert Shank highlights the ludicrousness of the situation: "Completely absurd is the assumption that men are to be sincerely persuaded that apostasy is impossible and, at the same time, sincerely alarmed by the warnings."[149] I would add that such a view is not only useless and absurd, but also quite deceptive. God is, in effect, manipulating those to whom the warning applies intending to use the warnings to prevent people from forsaking their faith—all the while knowing, since they are genuine Christians, that they *could not* forsake their faith. This approach turns the warning into merely information since the sense of urgency and the need for caution associated with a genuine warning is completely voided. In fact, as Lane points out, "the danger of apostasy was real, and not merely hypothetical, and called for the gravest possible warning."[150]

However, Grudem's own theory that these were not true Christians to begin with raises similar concerns about the genuineness of the warnings themselves. What sense does it make to "warn" unbelievers that they should not forsake that which they never enjoyed in the first place? Once more, these warnings lose their power and become merely irrelevant statements, even distractions, for these people had nowhere to fall from (v. 6)! It simply makes no sense to warn unbelievers of the dangers of falling away from grace or faith when unbelievers, by definition, never experienced these things to begin with. But, in fact, in the warning passage in Heb 6:4, 5, "the writer identifies the congregation as witnesses to the fact that God's salvation and presence are the unquestionable reality of their lives"[151] and so the warning about the disastrous consequences of choosing to reject their faith and thus fall away is correspondingly genuine, authentic, and real.

I conclude these considerations of the warning passages with an extended quote from Bryson:

> By reducing perseverance to an *inevitability* . . . all of these words of encouragement and warning [in Hebrews] are in a very real sense wasted. But in Scripture, *perseverance in holiness* to the end is seen as the challenge and goal of the Christian life. It should not be taken for granted. To say that perseverance is what *we will* do because we are true believers is to radically redefine the meaning of perseverance. Instead we need to see perseverance as what we *ought to do* because we are true believers. God is more than able and always willing to help us persevere in holiness and faith. The question is, are we willing to let Him help us persevere?[152]

---

148. Grudem, "Perseverance," 152.

149. Shank, *Life in the Son*, 172.

150. Lane, *Hebrews 1–8*, 141.

151. Lane, *Hebrews 1–8*, 142.

152. Bryson, *Five Points*, 115, emphases original. Since Bryson's point concerning redefining the meaning of perseverance is valid, some Calvinists prefer to speak of the *preservation* of the saints instead.

d) Do Justification, New Birth, Eternal Life Guarantee the Believer's Perseverance in Faith?

We have seen that the Calvinistic doctrine of the perseverance of the saints is grounded upon the fact that God will ensure his elect continue to believe: "Perseverance may be defined as that continuous operation of the Holy Spirit in the believer, by which the work of divine grace that is begun in the heart is continued and brought to completion."[153] Similarly, Grudem asserts that "the way God keeps us safe is by causing us to continue to believe in Christ."[154] Here perseverance, while grounded upon election, can only be attributed to those who actually do persevere. A genuine believer is one who perseveres to the end, and anyone who professes faith but subsequently falls from grace merely demonstrates he or she was never truly saved, never part of the elect. Nevertheless, Calvinism affirms that, for a true believer, the saying "once saved always saved" is true.

There are some, however, who also affirm the same saying "once saved always saved" but argue, not in terms of election and God's guaranteeing perseverance as in traditional Calvinism, but because they hold that the beginning experiences of the Christian life cannot be revoked. This view is sometimes called the eternal security view in contrast to the perseverance of the saints view. What are these beginning experiences? They are typically considered to be (a) justification—the declaration of not guilty before the bar of God; (b) regeneration—the new birth of which Jesus spoke in John 3; (c) the gift of eternal life, most famously spoken of by Jesus in John 3:16; (d) the sealing of the Holy Spirit as spoken to the Christians at Ephesus by Paul when they heard and believed the gospel (Eph 1:13). It is said that those who have experienced these aspects of the beginning of the Christian life are truly and eternally saved, and nothing they do subsequently will change their salvific standing before God. Unholy living subsequent to these experiences will affect the quality of their subsequent salvation experience and leave them subject to God's discipline, but does not threaten their salvation itself; once saved always saved.

Hunt is an example of this belief in eternal security: "Christ guarantees, 'him that cometh to me I will in no wise cast out' (John 6:37). I came to Him by faith in His Word and He will never cast me out—i.e., I can never be lost. . . . He said 'I give unto them [my sheep] eternal life; and they shall never perish' (John 10:28). It would be strange 'eternal life' indeed if it were mine today by His gracious gift and taken away by His judgment tomorrow."[155]

If the weakness of the Calvinistic perseverance of the saints is that no believer can be absolutely certain they are in fact part of the elect and hence are guaranteed

153. Berkhof, *Systematic Theology*, 546.

154. Grudem, *Systematic Theology*, 790n3.

155. Hunt, *What Love Is This?*, 482. A surprising number of non-Calvinists hold to this view, including the apologist Leighton Flowers, philosopher John C. Lennox, and the professor of preaching at Southwestern Baptist Theological Seminary David Allen.

to persevere, the weakness of the eternal security view is that it permits of serious ongoing sinning subsequent to a conversion experience without calling into question the validity of the initial experiences. Most fundamentally, both positions fail to take due account of the intensely personal and relational aspect of salvation. At heart, salvation is relationship—relationship with the living and personal God. "Salvation has centrally to do with restoring interpersonal relationship. . . . Scripture uses interpersonal imagery to describe the divine-human relationship—father, son, friend, marriage; coming into those relationships describes salvation. . . . Salvation has to do with correcting interpersonal behaviour."[156]

Consider some of the foundational terms associated with salvation in the Bible: justification—the declaration of not guilty before the bar of God makes relationship possible from a forensic point of view; reconciliation—again, is a very relational term between two personal agents; forgiveness of sins—necessary for anyone to relate to a holy God. Following repentance and faith, God himself through his Spirit takes up residence in the believer's life (regeneration, new birth) thereby greatly enhancing the divine-human relationship. The intrinsically relational aspect of this gracious act on God's part is seen in Rev 3:20: *"Behold, I stand at the door and knock; if anyone hears My voice and opens the door, I will come in to him and will dine with him, and he with Me."*

With respect to eternal life, Wright insists that "God's elect are known to have eternal life the instant they believe. . . . Eternal life (not merely the possibility of it) is in possession of every believer from regeneration onwards."[157] However, eternal life speaks primarily not of unending life that once begun cannot be stopped as appears to be the assumption for the eternal security view, but rather refers to a quality of life. It is life of the age to come which has now begun with the person and ministry of Jesus. "Jesus Christ's coming as God's definitive revelation brings the possibility of the qualities of life in the future messianic age into present reality."[158] Even this facet of salvation is intensely personal as the Apostle John makes clear: *"He who has the Son has the life; he who does not have the Son of God does not have the life"* (1 John 5:12). Eternal life, Christ's life, is bound up necessarily with a relationship with Jesus Christ by faith. The fact that it is acquired *and maintained* through relationship with Christ speaks to its conditionality; no faith in the Son means no relationship with the Son. No relationship with the Son means no (eternal) life.[159]

What about the idea of being sealed by the Spirit? Paul, writing to the church at Ephesus, says, *"Do not grieve the Holy Spirit of God, by whom you were sealed for the day of redemption"* (Eph 4:30). The word *sealed* (σφραγιζω, *sphragizō*, to seal) can

---

156. Warren, *Salvation*, 5.

157. Wright, *No Place for Sovereignty*, 137.

158. "Eternal Life," in Elwell, *Baker Encyclopedia of the Bible*, 724.

159. This is why Calvinists believe that even faith is a God-given gift or capacity, something I consider incoherent.

have several meanings depending upon context. Here, the meaning usually favored by many commentators is that of providing a sign of identification or ownership. As Stott remarks, "The Holy Spirit himself, indwelling us, is the seal with which God has stamped us as his own."[160] That the Spirit can be grieved by Christians by, for example, unholy choices and behaviors, underscores the interpersonal nature of the believer's relationship with God's Spirit. Considering the phrase "the gift of the Spirit," Warren observes that "strictly the gift is the relationship with the Spirit. He is a gift from Christ. . . . We understand the essential nature of the gift to be interpersonal."[161] Fellowship with God is possible through the ministry of the Spirit within the believer. To be sealed by the Spirit therefore is to be marked out for fellowship with God. God's intent and ideal is that the believer enjoy fellowship with God through the indwelling Spirit until that day of final redemption when our spirits are united with our resurrected bodies. In the meantime, however, as our verse indicates, the quality of the relationship can and does fluctuate even to the point where the Spirit is grieved. And, in the extreme, the Spirit can be so persistently insulted that apostasy is the consequence. This is borne out clearly in the warning give to the writer of the book of Hebrews concerning the apostate: *"How much severer punishment do you think he will deserve who has trampled underfoot the Son of God, and has regarded as unclean the blood of the covenant by which he was sanctified, and has insulted the Spirit of grace?"* (Heb 10:29).

In addition to the eternal security view being intrinsically impersonal, like flicking a spiritual switch, it also fails to take seriously the many warnings in Scripture given to believers to be on guard (Acts 20:28; 2 Tim 4:15; 2 Pet 3:17), to put on the full armor of God (Eph 6:11), to beware of Satan who prowls around seeking whom to devour (1 Pet 5:8), to abide in the vine (John 15:4), and so on. The conditional nature of salvation is seen in the way God related to his old covenant people. Blessings were promised for covenant loyalty, and punishment to the point of rejection for those who proved disobedient to the God of the covenant (Lev 26; Deut 28). New Testament believers are in a covenant relationship with God too and are therefore in an intrinsically conditional relationship sustained by faith. In any covenant relationship with God, while God's faithfulness to the covenant blessings is assured and guaranteed, our faith which is the means stipulated by God by which we enjoy that covenant relationship, is not guaranteed. Even Christians sin, and if a Christian chooses to sin on an ongoing and determined manner characteristic of unbelief, then of necessity, the covenant relationship is broken as Heb 10:26 makes clear. After quoting Hab 2:4 (*"the righteous will live by his faith"*), Shank rightly states that the "fact of past faith affords no guarantee against either the possibility or the disastrous consequences of abandoning faith and departing from the Saviour."[162]

---

160. Stott, *Message of Ephesians*, 189.

161. Warren, *Salvation*, 235.

162. Shank, *Life in the Son*, 365.

Finally, the eternal security view of salvation fails to take due account of the fact that salvation is a process, not a single event. Salvation has a beginning (justification and regeneration), it has an ongoing aspect (sanctification), and it has a final aspect (glorification). Viewing salvation in impersonal terms as something that happens to me (I get saved when I'm born again, have eternal life, etc.), and downplaying or ignoring the process aspect of salvation tends to reinforce the view that once saved (past tense) always saved. As the Eastern Orthodox theologian Alexander Renault notes, "Protestant Christians view salvation primarily in terms of a courtroom setting (an understandable emphasis when we realize that the two biggest players in the Protestant Reformation—Luther and Calvin—were both trained as lawyers). Justification is seen as a one-time judicial pronouncement of innocence that happened at one point in our past."[163] It is precisely the fact that salvation is a *process* that accounts for the many exhortations, encouragements, and warnings directed to the believer for the need to persevere in faith and not give up or succumb to temptation. Such warnings become superfluous if having begun (justified) one is thereafter guaranteed to persevere by God. In short, final salvation is always conditional on ongoing faith.

Certainly, Scripture speaks of salvation as a past event: *"For by grace you have been saved through faith; and that not of yourselves, it is the gift of God"* (Eph 2:8). It is also a present state: *"For the word of the cross is foolishness to those who are perishing, but to us who are being saved it is the power of God"* (1 Cor 1:18). It is also a future reality yet to be experienced: *"Pay close attention to yourself and to your teaching; persevere in these things, for as you do this you will ensure salvation both for yourself and for those who hear you"* (1 Tim 4:16), and *"you will be hated by all because of My name, but it is the one who has endured to the end who will be saved"* (Matt 10:22). Between the beginning experience of salvation and our final experience God calls believers to persevere, to be overcomers, to stand firm, to be watchful, to be alert, to put on protective spiritual armor, and so on. Why? Because between now and then there are many opportunities for Christians to fail to persevere, to fail to be overcomers, to fail to resist the one who seeks to harm our souls,[164] and so on. Spiritual dangers are real and must not be underestimated, which is precisely why Paul urges the Ephesian Christians to put on the full armor of God (Eph 6:10–17). Fortunately, of course, God's grace and sustaining power is also real and always available *through faith*.[165]

Finally, while it is consistent for the Calvinist to argue that God preserves the believer by faith—because God gives the faith, it seems less plausible for the non-Calvinist to argue that having begun the Christian life by faith the Christian is then guaranteed to persevere. If the Christian life is begun by faith and continues by faith (for we walk by faith [2 Cor 5:7]), then, assuming the beginning faith was not coerced, one must

163. Renault, *Reconsidering TULIP*, 98.

164. Hence Peter's warning: *"Be of sober spirit, be on the alert. Your adversary, the devil, prowls around like a roaring lion, seeking someone to devour. But resist him, firm in your faith"* (1 Pet 5:8).

165. We are kept by the power of God *through faith* (1 Pet 1:5).

conclude "walking by faith" is coerced, choice is removed since the possibility of exercising unbelief on an ongoing basis is removed. Begin the Christian life by uncoerced faith, continue the Christian life by effectively coerced faith! Strange. Also, this eternal security view suffers from the same criticisms leveled against the Calvinistic perseverance of the saints view. Why? Because both say the same thing: once saved always saved. What are these criticisms? Denial of the possibility of apostasy, which, as we have seen, is presented to us in Scripture as a very real possibility, and also evacuating of significance all the exhortations in Scripture given to the believer to encourage perseverance in faith, since perseverance is assured. Also, all the warnings given to the believer of the disastrous consequences of failing to continue in faith is likewise eviscerated.

e) Calvin's Strange Doctrine of Temporary Illumination

In his *Institutes of the Christian Religion*, Calvin when discussing Matt 22:14 (*"for many are called, but few are chosen"*), points out the supposed two callings of God—the general call to everyone and the special call to the elect. In the midst of this discussion, however, he rather strangely speaks of God apparently truly enlightening someone just as he would the elect, but only temporarily.

> There is a special call which, for the most part, God bestows on believers only, when by the internal illumination of the Spirit he causes the word preached to take deep root in their hearts. Sometimes, however, he communicates it also to those whom he enlightens only for a time, and whom afterwards, in just punishment for their ingratitude, he abandons and smites with greater blindness.[166]

Ignoring the typical Calvinistic distinction between a general call and a special call which has previously been shown to be an expedient designed to retain monergism in salvation, and ignoring the justness of God to allegedly work in this manner, and ignoring the question of how God can smite "with greater blindness" those who are born into the world already totally depraved and utterly blind to anything of true spiritual significance, it is worth asking why Calvin would mention this supposed phenomenon? He does not elaborate, so a degree of speculation is inevitable.

It is possible that Calvin derived this doctrine from Augustine to whom, as we have seen, Calvin was greatly indebted. It seems as though Augustine's view of perseverance was somewhat ambiguous. On the one hand he viewed perseverance as a gift from God given to the elect who, therefore, could not fail to persevere in faith. On the other hand, he "at the same time considered it possible that some who were endowed with new life and true faith could fall from grace completely and at last suffer eternal

---

166. Calvin, *Institutes*, 3.24.8. We discussed this phenomenon earlier in a context of two alleged callings; here the focus is on the question of perseverance.

damnation."[167] This position, which is actually contradictory, is reflected in Calvin's temporary illumination statement above.

Most likely, Calvin made use of this theological move in order to explain how it is that some who profess faith, proceed to live godly lives, worship with the saints, pray diligently, can then subsequently fall away. It is an ancient version of the more modern Calvinistic notion that, irrespective of how sincere and apparently genuine a person's faith in Christ is, if he subsequently denies the faith, this merely shows he was never a true believer in the first place. As Abraham states:

> The issue of the temporary believer arises from a problem familiar to anyone who thinks seriously about the possibility of apostasy. What are we to make of those who seem to show some or even all the marks of the elect but then fall away and utterly reject the Christian gospel? For the Wesleyan this represents clear empirical confirmation of the possibility of falling away. In principle it cannot function in this way for the Calvinist, so the standard move is made to claim that they are not true believers; they are merely temporary believers who were never among the elect in the first place. They may even have been subject to the gracious activity of the Holy Spirit in much the same fashion as the elect, but God acted in this way merely for a season in order that ultimately fresh glory would come to his name.[168]

For God to act in this manner strikes the non-Calvinist as not only ludicrous, but more importantly, as God being deceptive in lulling the temporary believer into thinking that he (and his fellow believers) are true believers and part of God's elect at one time, but then later the real situation is manifested—they were never part of the elect to begin with. That God deals with people in this underhanded and deceptive manner is nowhere seen in the pages of Scripture and for good reason, it is contrary to the character of the God who reveals himself as the God of truth and faithfulness (e.g., Ps 40:10). There is no ambiguity with respect to a person's salvation, both with respect to its beginnings and continuation: Believe on the Lord Jesus Christ and you shall be saved; fail to believe in an ongoing, resolute and determined manner and one is choosing to forfeit that salvation. In short, persevering in the faith is, like the beginning of the Christian life, always conditional on active faith. The Christian life is always from beginning to end a life of faith—for we walk by faith (2 Cor 5:7). No faith, no salvation—at any point in the Christian's pilgrimage through this life.

---

167. Berkhof, *Systematic Theology*, 545.

168. Abraham, "Predestination and Assurance," 237.

f) The Pastoral Implications of the Doctrine of the Perseverance of the Saints

Many years ago, I knew a very devout and godly Christian brother who was a Calvinist. This friend suffered from intense doubt, insecurity, and spiritual depression. Only later did I come to find out this was caused by his inability to gain full assurance of salvation. He was a thinking man and he recognized that the ultimate ground of his assurance was not his faith, his zealousness for the gospel, his love for the brethren, but rather whether God had selected him for salvation or not. Pastorally, the doctrine of the perseverance of the saints is a question of present and future assurance of salvation. How can I be assured I will in fact persevere since there is always the possibility, as has been demonstrated on numerous occasions in church life, that I may be deceived into thinking I am part of God's elect whereas in truth I am not?

John Piper says, "There is a falling away of some believers, but if it persists, it shows that their faith was not genuine and they were not born of God."[169] He cites 1 John 2:19 as an example: "*They went out from us, but they were not really of us; for if they had been of us, they would have remained with us; but they went out, so that it would be shown that they all are not of us.*" This verse, however, as previously discussed, is not speaking of "some believers," but of false teachers who were never believers. Piper goes on to admit, that "pastors do not know infallibly who of his listeners are the good soil (elect) and who are the bad (the reprobate)."[170] Consequently, the pastor's "warnings and exhortations to persevere are the way he helps the saints endure. They hear the warnings and take heed and thus authenticate their humble and good hearts of faith."[171] But what assurance can such a strategy afford the Christian Calvinist struggling to know for sure he is genuinely saved and among the elect chosen by God for salvation? Plenty of believers took heed of their pastor's warnings and exhortations, perhaps for many years, only to subsequently fall away, thus proving they were never among the elect in the first place.

Within a consistently Calvinistic system, unfortunately, there is no certain grounds for assurance for the simple reason non one can know for sure, as Piper admits, whether they are counted among the elect by God or not. Little wonder then, for the sensitive believer who adopts a Calvinistic soteriology, the potential for anxiety, unease, apprehension, even fear, is not an unreasonable response to the question of assurance of salvation. This lack of certainty is intrinsic to a monergistic system whereby one's salvation begins with an unknown and unknowable decree of God to save some, with a saving grace applied selectively by God on some and not others, and where even repentance and faith are viewed as applied by God to the elect. In this system, the believer is essentially passive and is merely the receiver of God's

169. Piper, *Five Points*, 69.
170. Piper, *Five Points*, 69.
171. Piper, *Five Points*, 70.

benevolent (though unknowable) intent to save, the receiver of a special calling, the receiver of an irresistible grace which guarantees his regeneration by God's Spirit who then grants the gifts of repentance and faith. There is no significant role to play on the part of the individual decreed for salvation—all is of God. Any "contribution" to his salvation on the part of any individual is considered as a meritorious work and dishonoring to God, even if that is only receiving the gift of salvation offered in the gospel. Within such a system, it is simply impossible to be assured of one's salvation—and this creates a huge pastoral problem.[172]

Conclusion

At the beginning of this chapter, we noted the definition of this doctrine, the perseverance of the saints, by citing nine Calvinistic sources. I noted then that not one of the nine used the word elect in their definition. I do not believe this is accidental because it makes evident a major weakness with the doctrine, in fact its major flaw. The elect, and only the elect, are guaranteed, enabled, and gifted with this capacity to persevere to the end, but the difficulty is that no one can be sure they are among the elect until they draw their last breath. Consequently, the very ground of assurance of persevering to the end is undercut by its critical dependance on the idea of unconditional election.

We have also seen that, not only does the lack of knowledge of who the elect are impact the assurance of persevering to the end, but that the Christian's present assurance of salvation itself is also brought into question also. Why? Because both Scripture and experience show that many who believed they were among the elect and who prayed, fellowshipped, and worshipped with God's people, perhaps for many years, subsequently forsook the faith and went back into the world. If this could happen to a believer known to many for many years, what guarantee is there that I too won't eventually succumb to some temptation or other? Recall that Calvinists explain such a situation as demonstrating that one was never saved in the first place, never part of God's elect. Warren states the connection between such an explanation and its impact on present assurance in this way: "Lack of perseverance supposedly indicates lack of genuine conversion originally. Such an arrangement detracts from present assurance because we cannot know now whether we will persevere to the end. We cannot distinguish ourselves from others who began as well as we did, but later apostatized. . . . That lack of genuineness was not perceivable before so . . . our faith may also not be genuine although we cannot perceive that now."[173] In short, when

---

172. Perhaps I should say "*should* create a huge pastoral problem." However, most everyday Christians who espouse Calvinism are either not aware of this fundamental problem within their system, or they are content to live out their faith with inconsistency, believing both that God determines who will be among the elect and also that *they* must exercise faith on an ongoing basis to be saved.

173. Warren, *Salvation*, 418.

salvation is grounded upon one's election, there simply is no real basis for assurance for the simple reason God has not disclosed who his elect are.

This dynamic also calls into question the reality of apostasy. Consistent Calvinists simply deny the category of apostasy: "Those united to Christ by the effectual call of the Father and indwelt by the Holy Spirit, will persevere to the end."[174] And yet Paul feels the need to warn Timothy concerning the real danger of apostasy associated with false teachers: *"But the Spirit explicitly says that in later times some will fall away from the faith, paying attention to deceitful spirits and doctrines of demons"* (1 Tim 4:1).[175] Furthermore, denying the category of apostasy makes all the commands and exhortations to persevere, the warnings concerning the consequences of failing to persevere, and the ubiquitous urgings in Scripture for the Christian to be overcomers of immorality, false teachers, indolence and so on, a sort of charade and not ultimately relevant to the Christian life. Such a conclusion seems justified by Calvinism's claim that these warnings and exhortations are simply the means God uses to ensure the elect will infallibly persevere. Such a move, however, has an air of unreality to it, a perspective nowhere hinted at in the Bible itself. The Bible presents these warnings and exhortations as sincere and genuine expressions of God's desire that no believer perishes due to failing to heed the warnings. Paul's word to the Corinthians is a good example:

> Do not be idolaters, as some of them were; as it is written, "The people sat down to eat and drink, and stood up to play." Nor let us act immorally, as some of them did, and twenty-three thousand fell in one day. Nor let us try the Lord, as some of them did, and were destroyed by the serpents. Nor grumble, as some of them did, and were destroyed by the destroyer. Now these things happened to them as an example, and they were written for our instruction, upon whom the ends of the ages have come. Therefore let him who thinks he stands take heed that he does not fall. (1 Cor 10:7–12)

Shank's words accurately reflect the biblical perspective: "Contrary to the assumption of some, the warnings were not given merely because there are no other motives by which believers may be motivated to persevere, for there are other motives, such as gratitude to God for His forgiveness and grace, [and] increased joy through faithfulness. . . . The warnings were given, not to supply a lack of any motive for perseverance, but because of the existence of a real and deadly peril with which we must reckon."[176] Denying the reality of the possibility of apostasy for all believers itself creates the danger of a false security in the pernicious idea of "once saved always saved."

174. Murray, *Redemption Accomplished and Applied*, 154.

175. While this warning applies to a time that is future to Paul, it is a needful warning to Timothy and Timothy's time. "Here the apostle is thinking of times subsequent to his own, but he foresees that Timothy needs to be cognizant of them. Indeed, as often in prophetical utterances, what is predicted of the future is conceived of as already operative in the present, so the words have a specific contemporary significance." Guthrie, *Pastoral Epistles*, 103.

176. Shank, *Life in the Son*, 173.

Finally, pastorally we have seen that this doctrine with its lack of grounds for assurance of salvation creates much anguish for the sensitive soul seeking to know that he is part of the elect and hence assured of both his present salvation and that he will persevere to the end. To urge the believer to trust Christ continually, to seek his grace and strength to persevere in hard times makes sense within a non-Calvinistic framework, but does not within a Calvinistic soteriology. Why? Because the Bible everywhere shows that the Christian life is a life of faith to which the believer is called daily, indeed moment by moment. As long as the believer exercises faith he can be fully assured of both his present and continued salvation. But *consistent* Calvinism would not put the emphasis on continued belief for assurance or for grounds for persevering in the saved state but rather ultimately, as we have seen, in an unknown and unknowable decree of God who decides who will and who won't be finally saved.

There is one more pastoral implication of the doctrine of the perseverance of the saints, and especially the eternal security view. Recall that the former teaches that God will guarantee and ensure that the true believer will persevere to the end, and that the latter teaches that once born again one can never be unborn. Both effectively teach "once saved, always saved." But what is a preacher to do when he comes across one of the warning passages in a book like Hebrews, or Paul's First Letter to the Corinthians (1 Cor 10:7–12 above)? He has to do doublespeak; on the one hand expounding the text as though it were a genuine warning directed to believers and, on the other hand, and at the same time, assuring his congregation of believing worshippers that the text cannot possibly apply to them because they are kept by the power of God and so once saved, always saved. In the words of Shank again: "Their preaching and teaching seem designed to prevent the warning passages and 'alarming admonitions' from accomplishing the purpose which they profess to believe God intends them to serve."[177] Such preaching explains the warning passages "in such a way as to dispel any concern which their hearers might have for them, and they continually assure them that they are unconditionally secure for all time and eternity."[178] Such preaching and handling of God's word compounds the insecurity noted in the previous paragraph due to the hearer not knowing if they are part of the elect or not. To the problem of insecurity is that of confusion generated by insisting that crucial parts of God's word designed to warn them of the danger and reality of forsaking the faith do not in fact apply to them.

177. Shank, *Life in the Son*, 172.
178. Shank, *Life in the Son*, 172.

Conclusion

A s we have studied Calvinism's soteriology through the grid of TULIP, we have seen that it is a system of determinism. Not natural determinism, the idea that everything is governed by the laws of physics and chemistry, including our own brain processes, nor social determinism, the idea that our behavior and thinking is determined by our upbringing and current social forces, but rather theistic determinism. Theistic determinists believe that ultimately God determines everything that happens. This is true not only for a doctrine of providence, but also a doctrine of salvation. For Calvinists, the overarching factor or mechanism whereby God determines everything is his sovereign decree. This decree is fine grained and comprehensive; it applies to everything without exception, from the smallest movement of atoms in the outer reaches of the universe to the decisions and choices people make. Calvinism's soteriology, in short, is decretal theology applied to the salvation of individuals. To the question of who enjoys salvation and who is excluded from even the possibility of salvation, the answer is found in the decree of God, and nowhere else. Truly, for Calvinism, salvation is by decree. Faith, repentance, humility, confession, seeking for God—all are ultimately merely the product of the divine decree.

As we have seen in our study, there are many problems with this decree driven systematic. The most basic is that it denies what Scripture clearly teaches and assumes throughout its pages, namely, that God has, in his sovereignty, chosen to grant man a limited but real measure of independence from the divine will in his decisions and choices. The term I have used to describe this phenomenon is relative independence.[1] It is the denial of this basic reality that lies at the root of Calvinism's soteriology. In the final analysis, when all theological jargon is stripped away, one is left with a

---

1. Calvinists sometimes caricature this as man's autonomy, as though God were out of control under these conditions. I resist the word autonomy precisely because it conjures up the idea of absolute independence from God. This is not the case, however, because the relative independence man exercises is given by God himself and is an expression of the outworking of his sovereignty. We see this clearly in the opening chapters of Genesis where Adam is given the freedom to name the animals and to tend the garden. He is also authorized by God to freely enjoy the fruit of all the trees of the garden bar one. Adam's actions throughout the account of his history is a demonstration of the God-given relative independence he was authorized to exercise and enjoy. In short, the principle of human relative independence was built into the creation by the Creator himself.

God whose sovereignty is expressed in terms of a divine determining of everything that happens in the universe, and man's choices and decisions are evacuated of their genuineness, and, while appearing to have significance and meaning, are in reality merely the outworking of the divine decree. In the desire to ensure God's glory and exaltation, man is debased and dehumanized.

When directed to a man's salvation, Christian determinists refer to the term monergism. As Sproul states, "Monergism is something that operates by itself or works alone as the sole active party."[2] Here, the unbeliever plays no part whatsoever in his salvation, he is passive; he contributes no faith, repentance, sorrow for sin—all is of God alone. The unbeliever in this system is a big zero, ultimately irrelevant in the drama of his own salvation. "When the term monergism is linked with the word regeneration, the phrase describes an action by which God the Holy Spirit works on a human being without this person's assistance or cooperation."[3] A man cannot even respond to the gospel call because he is considered to be spiritually dead. This, of course, does not square with the biblical data where we see God calling upon all people to repent because he desires all to be saved (Mark 1:15; 1 Tim 2:4).

It is a mark of bad theology that it creates more problems than it seeks to solve as well as confusion, contradictions, distortions, and so on. Rather than shedding light on the biblical data, one is left scratching one's head wondering how the claims being made can be made to square with the Bible and its teachings. I want, briefly, to touch upon some of these problems which Calvinism generates.

a) The Problem of Contradictions and Doublespeak

Recall that God's decree determines *everything* that happens in the world. In the words of the Westminster Confession, to which nearly all Calvinists subscribe: "God from all eternity, did . . . freely, and unchangeably ordain *whatsoever* comes to pass."[4] This, of course, includes those people who would and would not be chosen for salvation.[5] Grudem also affirms the comprehensive nature of God's decree: "The decrees of God are the eternal plans of God whereby, before the creation of the world, he determined to bring about *everything that happens*."[6] Bearing this in mind, it comes as something of a surprise to see Grudem insisting that "God and man cooperate in sanctification," and that "striving for obedience to God and for holiness may involve great effort on our part." Furthermore, "it is important that we continue to grow

---

2. Sproul, *Reformed Theology*, 183.

3. Sproul, *Reformed Theology*, 184.

4. *Westminster Confession of Faith*, 3.1, emphasis mine.

5. "By the decree of God . . . some men . . . are predestined unto everlasting life; and others foreordained to everlasting death." *Westminster Confession of Faith*, 3.3.

6. Grudem, *Systematic Theology*, 332, emphasis mine.

. . . in our active striving for holiness and greater obedience in our lives."[7] Grudem is quite right of course in these points, which he justifies by several citations from the New Testament. However, it is quite nonsensical and in fact contradictory to make these assertions about "our" striving, growing, effort toward sanctification when he has told us that it is God who determines *everything* that happens, presumably including whether we strive or fail to strive! It is simply contradictory to assert that God determines everything that happens and at the same time assert that "we" cooperate with God in our sanctification. Furthermore, God's decree can sometimes not meet with God's approval! Grudem again: "Some things [evil] that God's will of decree has planned are not in themselves good, and should not receive our approval, just as they do not receive God's approval."[8]

Similarly, with respect to the question of why people sin we are told in the Westminster Confession mentioned above that, despite God being the One who "ordains *whatsoever* comes to pass," nevertheless God is not "the author of sin."[9] But how exactly can God be said to determine everything that comes to pass, including all sin and evil, and yet God *not* be the author of sin? God is responsible for everything that happens (through his eternal decree), and God is not responsible for at least some part of what happens (sin). Another contradiction. The Calvinistic syllogism goes something like this: God authors and causes all things that happen in the world; sin happens in the world; therefore, God does *not* author and cause sin!

With respect to an effectual call following the application of an irresistible grace, the Westminster Confession states that unbelievers "come most freely, being made willing by His grace."[10] Made willing? Here is an inherent contradiction, a classic example of doublespeak. How exactly does interpersonal exchange *make* one willing? The phrase is self-contradictory. For someone to enter into a relationship, or choose to do something willingly, then by definition they are not *made* to do it. Conversely, if they are in fact made to do it, then they do it not "most freely" but rather under compulsion. Similarly, in his discussion of the alleged effectual call to salvation Grudem teaches that this call "has such power that it brings about the *response* that it *asks* for in people's hearts. It is an act of God that guarantees a *response*."[11] Now, how can a human choice that is *guaranteed* by God to achieve its predestined end be viewed in any sense as a "response"? In reality it is not a response, it is merely an infallibly assured action on the part of God toward the elect. And what sense does it make to say God "*asks*" people to respond to the gospel when God has already determined everything that happens and an individual's salvific status has been already decided before the person was born?

7. Grudem, *Systematic Theology*, 755.

8. Grudem, *Systematic Theology*, 334.

9. *Westminster Confession of Faith*, 3.1.

10. *Westminster Confession of Faith*, 10.1.

11. Grudem, *Systematic Theology*, 692, emphases mine.

Many, many more examples of contradictions and doublespeak could be given because it is intrinsic to the systematic and the doctrine (soteriology) can only be described and discussed in these terms. Dave Hunt's conclusion concerning this problem of contradictions may seem a little harsh, however it contains more than a grain of truth: "Calvinism seems to pervert not only the Bible but men's minds, so that they are able to pretend that obvious contradictions make sense."[12]

b) A Problem with Calvinism's Hermeneutic

The alert reader would have noticed a consistent pattern with respect to how the texts appealed to by Calvinists were shown to be incorrect. All that is required is to take the verse or passage in question and show what it means in its literary and/or historical context. This is to say that, typically, a Calvinist's justification for a particular doctrine, e.g., total depravity or irresistible grace, is done by proof-texting. This procedure involves identifying a text that seems to support the idea, ignore the immediate and all other contexts, and so conclude that the doctrine is proved. Constructing a doctrine in this manner is fraught with difficulties and the likelihood of error is not insignificant, after all, this is precisely how cults like Jehovah's Witnesses handle the Bible. Such practice leads to the observation that "a text without a context is a pretext for a proof text."

An example would be the understanding of the term "all things" in Eph 1:11[13] as referring to everything that happens and so justifying a fine-grained decretive will of God. Typical of a Calvinist understanding of the verse is Westblade: "All things that have been created (1:10) and all things that occur (1:11) accord with the good pleasure . . . of God's will."[14] Even though a superficial reading of 1:11 could lead to the Calvinistic idea that Paul in this passage is making reference to literally everything without exception as being the consequence of God's purposive will, the danger of misinterpreting the verse is not insignificant since the understanding is derived apart from an attempt to understand and make due allowance for the broader context. However, as Cottrell notes "those who take this in an absolute sense have ignored the immediate context and the main theme of Ephesians as a whole."[15]

The opening verses of ch. 1 are an expression of Paul's wonder and marveling at the coming to realization of God's redemptive purposes from ages past, namely that a redeemed body of people should come into existence, the church. This purpose is reflected in the call of Abraham and that through Abraham's seed *"all the families of*

---

12. Hunt, *What Love Is This?*, 353.

13. "*We have obtained an inheritance, having been predestined according to His purpose who works all things after the counsel of His will.*"

14. Westblade, "Divine Election," 72.

15. Cottrell, *What the Bible Says about God the Ruler*, 306.

the world would be blessed" (Gen 12:3). This blessing is for all those who are "in Christ Jesus." This is the background to the Letter to the Ephesians.

A clue to the scope intended by Paul when he uses the term "all things" in 1:11 may be gained from 1:9, *"He made known to us the mystery of His will, according to His kind intention which He purposed in Him."* The "us" here refers to the Ephesian saints and Paul himself (1:1). What is this "mystery"? We are given clues in ch. 2: those formerly "far off" (Gentiles) have been brought near (2:11–13); Christ has made both Jews and Gentiles into one (2:14); both Jew and Gentile have been reconciled and made into one body through the cross (2:16). In ch. 3 Paul makes explicit what the mystery is: *"that the Gentiles are fellow heirs and fellow members of the body, and fellow partakers of the promise in Christ Jesus through the gospel"* (3:6). It is this phenomenon, the uniting of Jew and Gentile in Christ that forms the backdrop to Eph 1, and specifically 1:11. In 1:9 Paul mentions this mystery of God's will, and in 1:10 Paul sees this as an *"administration suitable to the fullness of the times,"* the church age.

Bearing all this contextual background in mind, we see that the "all things" of 1:11 is in fact not an absolute universal, but a qualified "all things" as an all things directed toward the christocentric fulfillment of God's redemptive purposes for the church. "Thus we see that the 'all things' in Ephesians 1:11 does not have a universal reference: God's purposes or decretive will does not include all things that happen in the whole scope of nature and history. It does include the establishment of the church, however, as the body which unites Jews and Gentiles under the one head, Jesus Christ."[16]

More examples of the hermeneutic that ignores literary (and historical) context could be given, but space precludes this; in any case, most of the texts appealed to by Calvinists in earlier chapters have been addressed simply by examining the broader context in which the text appears. I conclude with a couple of quotes that reinforce the point being made here: "As we know only too well, much error appears plausible and Biblical only because men have ignored context in their interpretations of the Scriptures."[17] And, the principle of biblical convergence "requires that theologians allow the broadest and most diverse portions of Scripture, rather than one solitary verse, to bear on the theological issue in view."[18]

c) The Problem of Excessive Distinctions

To my mind, a clear indication that a theology is not consistent with revealed truth is the need for more and more qualifications in order to make the system work.[19] For example,

16. Cottrell, *What the Bible Says about God the Ruler*, 308.

17. William W. Adams, introduction to Shank, *Elect in the Son*, 14.

18. Anizor, *Read Theology*, 86.

19. This phenomenon is also true of premillennial dispensationalism with its multiple resurrections and judgments and comings of Christ.

Calvinism requires at least two wills of God—a secret, overarching, all-determining, decretive will, and a prescriptive, revealed will of God seen in the explicit commandments of God. This sometimes results in the ludicrous situation in which God commands "thou shalt not kill" and yet God decrees that murder take place!

Another example of excessive qualifications is the supposed two calls of God, a general and outward call made to all people to believe the gospel, and an inward, effectual call that guarantees that only the elect be saved. This is clearly an expedient required to explain those many texts in Scripture where the gospel is proclaimed to all indiscriminately, and yet only a few believe. Where the Bible lays the responsibility upon all people to believe and respond to the (single) gospel call, Calvinists shift the responsibility to God for whether a person believes the gospel or not. The appeal to an effectual call effectively denies the power of the gospel to save (Rom 1:16).[20]

Calvinists also hold to two forms of spiritual life; a pre-faith life given by God to spiritually dead persons by first regenerating them so that they then are enabled to believe the gospel, and a post-faith life called eternal life. Certainly, regeneration can be viewed as a type of spiritual life, but not one that enables a person to believe, but rather one that follows the person's coming to faith. Perhaps the following structure will clarify the point being made here: Calvinism: regenerating life → faith → eternal life; biblically: faith → regeneration/eternal life. While a favorite illustration used by Calvinists to describe the nature of regeneration is Lazarus being raised from the dead (John 11), a better analogy would be the prodigal son who was "dead" (Luke 15:24) but "came to his senses" in realizing the degrading state he was living in and sought to return to his father (Luke 15:17).

Calvinism requires God to have two kinds of love. A general sort of love that only manifests itself in providing rain and food for all, and a special love whereby he saves his elect. The former, those who only experience God's general love, are still predestined to hell because God chooses to not save them when he could if he so wished, whereas the latter are the arbitrary objects of God's discriminating love.[21] To call the former God's love is hardly worthy of the term. It is no wonder Dave Hunt titles his book *What Love Is This?* As Hunt remarks, it cannot "rationally be said that God 'loves' those he could save but doesn't." And it is irrational "to hide behind the idea that God is 'free' to love different people with different kinds of

---

20. *"For I am not ashamed of the gospel, for it is the power of God for salvation to everyone who believes, to the Jew first and also to the Greek."*

21. Calvinists would object to my using the term *arbitrary* here. They would argue that the reasons why God chooses some and not others may not be known to us, but are known to God. However, given that God's selection of some over others for salvation has nothing to do with the individuals involved (God's election is unconditional), and given that Scripture clearly states that God desires all to come to salvation, the term *arbitrary* seems justified. What possible reason could God have for choosing one person over another since all are equally undeserving? According to the *Merriam-Webster* definition, *arbitrary* means "existing or coming about seemingly at random or by chance or as a capricious and unreasonable act of will."

love—forgetting that any kind of genuine love is loving, and that it is not loving to damn those who could be saved."[22]

Calvinists also see two kinds of good in people. "Scripture is not denying that unbelievers can do good in human society *in some senses*. But it is denying that they can do any *spiritual* good."[23] But where in Scripture do we see this kind of distinction? Such a distinction actually follows from the Calvinist's notion of total depravity which includes the idea that a person is totally unable to do spiritual good before God, and that persons are born in this condition because of original sin. However, Jesus affirmed that anyone can do good to the poor in their midst (Mark 14:7).[24] The parable of the good Samaritan gains its force by the very fact that a Samaritan, a person normally despised by a Jew, does a good and kind act and thereby demonstrates what it is like to love a neighbor in conformity with God's will (Luke 10:30–37). Human beings are morally complex beings and it is simplistic and unrealistic to say that unbelievers lack any kind of spiritually significant good before God. They can certainly do good; to care for an ailing neighbor is a spiritual good; to save a drowning person is a spiritual good; to bring relief to the poor is a spiritual good. What Scripture teaches is not that unbelievers are totally unable to do any spiritual good, but rather that no one is able to do meritorious good works—good works that entitle them to merit salvation.

Calvinism requires two kinds of grace—common grace for all and saving grace for some. Again, this distinction is not taught in Scripture. Certainly, God's provision of material needs for all people is a form of grace, and certainly some people enjoy the grace of salvation, but to radically separate the two in order to support a doctrine of unconditional election is unwarranted. God's fundamental attitude to all people all the time is that of grace—God desires the maximum good for all people at all times. This is seen in the many universals found in the Bible: "*Come to Me, all who are weary and heavy-laden, and I will give you rest*" Matt 11:28); "*[God] desires* all men *to be saved and to come to the knowledge of the truth*" (1 Tim 2:4); "*We have seen and testify that the Father has sent the Son to be the Savior of* the world" (1 John 4:14).

d) The Problem of Excessive Appeals to Mystery or Paradox

An appeal to mystery is seen for example in Grudem's attempt to explain two contradictory situations: God's determining all things and yet with real human choices and decisions. "God causes all things that happen, but he does so in such a way that he *somehow* upholds our ability to make willing, responsible choices. . . . Exactly

---

22. Hunt, *What Love Is This?*, 114.

23. Grudem, *Systematic Theology*, 497, emphases original.

24. Admittedly, Jesus was probably talking to his disciples when he said this, but the disciples were unregenerate men who often lacked faith at this point in their pilgrimage with Jesus. In fact, this saying by Jesus was prompted by the resentment some felt at costly ointment being "wasted" on Jesus, thus demonstrating their lack of faith.

how God combines his providential control with our willing and significant choices, Scripture does not explain to us."[25] Here the circle has been squared, but in a mysterious, unknowable manner.

After stating that faith "is the special gift of God," Calvin goes on to say, "It seems to some paradoxical, when it is said that none can believe Christ save those to whom it is given." Calvin attributes the perception of paradox here to people's failure to appreciate how "sublime heavenly wisdom is . . . in discerning divine mysteries."[26] Again, appeal to both paradox and mystery is made in order to explain away a doctrine not taught in Scripture (that faith is a gift of God).

In his discussion of God as personal, John Sanders states that a view of God that is timeless and immutable, as affirmed by Calvinism, calls into question the reality of prayer. He says that this kind of God only *seems* to answer—i.e., respond, to our prayers.[27] He goes on to remark that "at this point many try to escape to 'mystery' or 'paradox' to avoid admitting a contradiction."[28] Similarly, Cottrell in his discussion of the nature of divine sovereignty notes that "Calvinistic discussions of this problem are laced with words like *paradox, antinomy, contradiction,* and *mystery.* As Klooster says 'Divine sovereignty and human responsibility are paradoxical and beyond human comprehension.' Despite this rather agnostic attitude, Calvinists have spent much time and energy trying to explain the unexplainable."[29] Lennox concurs when he states that "many of the clearly unacceptable logical implications of divine determinism are shrouded in mystery—a mystery that we are not allowed to question. . . . [And] that the unacceptable implications of determinism get shrouded in intellectual fog and contradiction, in an intractable obfuscation."[30] And again, he says: "Excessive extrapolation of the biblical teaching on predestination leads not to paradox, but to patent contradiction, both logical and moral."[31]

Within Calvinism, appeal to paradox or mystery is virtually unavoidable. Why God chooses to save some but not others—a mystery. How God's grace can be irresistibly applied to the elect and yet, those same elect are morally free—a paradox. How all men are born condemned and unable to respond to the gospel because of Adam's sin and yet are held responsible for rejecting the gospel—a mystery. How God determines everything that happens, and yet God is not tainted by sin—a mystery. While there are indeed genuine mysteries in the Bible, the exact relationships within the Godhead or the relationship between Jesus's human and divine natures for example, too rapid an appeal to mystery or paradox can merely mask bad theology. As Helm rightly notes:

25. Grudem, *Systematic Theology,* 321, emphasis mine.

26. Calvin, *Institutes,* 3.2.33.

27. Sanders, "God as Personal," 172, emphasis original.

28. Sanders, "God as Personal," 179n27.

29. Cottrell, "Nature of the Divine Sovereignty," 98, emphasis original.

30. Lennox, *Determined to Believe?,* 63.

31. Lennox, *Determined to Believe?,* 157.

"During the history of Christianity there is scarcely a limit to the nonsense that has been believed because it is allegedly biblical in character."[32]

e) The Problem of the Redefinition of Words or Concepts

Freedom and free will are either denied (Gordon H. Clark) or, more commonly, sought to be made consistent within a theistic determinism. The latter view, known as compatibilism, is the view that a man is free as long as he does what he wants to do. Of course, since God's determinative will is singular, what the man "chooses" will also be singular—he is free to choose only and precisely what God has determined he choose. In this view, freedom is really just the capacity to act. This is contrary to the normal understanding whereby a person is free if he is able to do either x or y—accept the gospel or reject the gospel, love the neighbor or not love the neighbor.[33]

Similarly, faith is redefined not to be a human capacity for belief in response to divine revelation, but rather a God-given gift or ability or power or enablement. As we have seen, this redefinition is called for because of the supposed total depravity of man that prevents him from exercising faith himself—it has to be given to him by God. Apart from questioning the rationality of such an idea, faith as a gift from God redefines what faith fundamentally is, a human "allegiance to duty or a person" (*Merriam-Webster*).[34]

Likewise, the many references in the Bible to God's grace, love, mercy extending to "everyone," "to all" or to "whosoever,"[35] are made to apply only to a few, the elect. Thus John 3:16 must be reinterpreted to apply restrictively to the elect only.[36] It is only those predestined to eternal life that can possibly actually have eternal life. And so, God's word of hope and salvation offered to all without distinction, indiscriminately, and without any kind of partiality on the part of God is made to say, in effect, "For God so loved only the elect, that He gave His only begotten Son, that the elect believing upon Him shall not perish, but have the eternal life to which they were predestined." Hendriksen is a good example of this Calvinistic strategy. Commenting on John 3:16, he says: "Because faith is . . . the gift of God, its fruit, everlasting life, is also God's gift. . . . He gives us the faith to embrace the Son; he gives us everlasting life."[37] John 3:16 cannot allow for the possibility that anyone could enjoy God's love, believe in Christ

---

32. Helm, *Providence*, 66. Unfortunately, Calvinism's soteriology serves as a good example.

33. The *Merriam-Webster Dictionary* defines *freedom* as "the absence of *necessity*, coercion, or constraint in choice or action" (emphasis mine).

34. Or, as I have used the term faith in this study, faith is a human response to the initiative of God in sending his Son to be the Savior of the world. How a person responds to such divine activity reveals whether faith or unfaith (unbelief) is present.

35. See, e.g., 1 John 4:14; 1 Tim 2:4; 2 Pet 3:9; 1 Tim 2:6; 1 John 2:2.

36. John 3:16 reads: *"For God so loved the world, that He gave His only begotten Son, that whoever believes in Him shall not perish, but have eternal life."*

37. Hendriksen, *John*, 142.

and so enjoy eternal life as a free gift of God's grace—no all this applies only to the elect alone, only the elect are given the ability to believe. Notice the subtle shift from "whoever" in 3:16 to "us" (believers) in Hendriksen's comments.[38]

Grace speaks of God's favor that is not earned or deserved. A word often used in the New Testament in connection with grace is gift. For example, "being justified as a gift by His grace through the redemption which is in Christ Jesus" (Rom 3:24).[39] In usual language a gift is something offered to someone that can either be received or rejected. There is nothing compulsory about it. It comes as something of a surprise then to see Calvinists speaking in terms of an irresistible grace. What sort of grace or gift is it that cannot be resisted or turned down? We see the same tension in the phrase commonly used by Calvinists (but not found in the Bible), sovereign grace. It carries the idea of an imposed grace, a grace that rules supreme and always gets its way; it is sovereign. But this is an oxymoron.[40] According to Walter Bauer's Greek-English lexicon, the Greek word translated grace (χαρις, charis) primarily means "favor, gracious care or help, goodwill" and finds practical application in terms of "goodwill, favor, gracious deed or gift, benefaction."[41] Grace is an expression of the love of God that seeks to provide for the needs of the recipient. To speak of sovereign grace is actually to impose an idea that is contrary to the biblical notion of God's love manifested for man's good. As Cottrell states it: "Sovereignty speaks of power, the power of sheer might and strength, the power to create and to command and to destroy. But grace is an expression of a totally different kind of power, the drawing power of love and compassion and self-sacrifice. In the unnatural hybrid of sovereign grace, sovereignty dominates, so that grace is not allowed to be grace."[42]

A final example of redefinition or manipulation of a word or concept is the way Calvinists use the term "control" when what is really meant is "cause" when discussing God's sovereignty. An example would be the philosopher Paul Helm's use of God's control in his "no-risk" view of providence. It is very clear that Helm, a Christian determinist, believes that only a God who takes no risk in governing his universe is consistent with the Bible. Here, no-risk is the same as comprehensive causation, though Helm himself is careful to scrupulously avoid the term cause. He says, "We take no risk if we knowingly set in motion events which will turn out *exactly as we want them to*."[43] Elsewhere he asks, "Does God's providence . . . extend to *all* that

---

38. The reference to *us* in this quote is to the believer, i.e., the elect. It is the use of this word *us* that allows the Calvinist to subtly shift the universal (whosoever) to the particular (the relatively few elect).

39. Other texts would include Rom 5:15, 17; Eph 2:8; 3:7; 4:7; 1 Pet 4:10.

40. An oxymoron, according to the *Merriam-Webster Dictionary*, is "a self-contradicting word or group of words." An example would be married bachelor.

41. Bauer, *Greek-English Lexicon*, 877.

42. Cottrell, *What the Bible Says about God the Ruler*, 227.

43. Helm, *Providence*, 40, emphasis mine.

he has created, *including the choices of men and women?*"[44] A no-risk God requires the answer, according to Helm, to be yes. Lest we think that God's no-risk causation applies only to how God relates to the universe and not to what God has predestined, including of course who will or will not be saved, Helm clarifies: "All predestination is providential, and all exercises of providence are predestinarian."[45] In other words, all that happens has been predestined by God. Now note how Helm consistently uses the word control to describe the way God governs: we "should not give the impression that God's *support* and *control* of his creation as a whole are any less strict and complete than his gracious *support* and *control* of his church. . . . God *controls* all persons and events equally."[46] Why not be straightforward and use the word cause to describe how God governs in a no-risk world? Because it sounds offensive, especially when the difficult questions of sin and evil are raised. The idea of God causing human sin does not sound very biblical, and so euphemisms are preferable.

f) The Problem of Exaggerations and Distortions

Like any system of doctrine that does not accurately express revealed biblical truth, distortions and exaggerations and imbalances inevitably occur. Calvinism is no less susceptible to these problems. Take, for example, the idea of glory, the glory of God and the way God is glorified. Calvinism puts a very high premium on God's glory. Of course, Scripture teaches the reality of God's glory and that God is to be glorified, as we see for example in the well-known first question of the Larger Catechism of the Westminster Confession of Faith: "Q1. What is the chief and highest end of man? A. Man's chief and highest end is to glorify God and to enjoy him forever."[47] However, the manner in which Calvinism handles this aspect of the divine is problematic for two related reasons.

The first is that it does not reflect where the Bible, taken as a whole, has its central message, the weight of its revelation. Calvinism tends to portray the idea of glory as supreme and above all else. While there is a sense in which this is right, it actually ends up distorting the biblical revelation, because that is not the Bible's own supreme emphasis. What is the Bible's essential message, what do its pages reveal concerning the purpose for which God gave us a Bible, a written record of his historical revelations? It is this: that God so loves the world and everyone in it that he went to extreme ends to redeem his human creation. It is the love of God, manifested in concrete actions especially in his dealings with ancient Israel and in the incarnation, that comprises the center of gravity of the biblical message, not the glory of God. The Bible is about the gospel of salvation and all that God has done to enable his human creation to

44. Helm, *Providence*, 39, emphasis mine.
45. Helm, *Providence*, 20.
46. Helm, *Providence*, 20.
47. *Westminster Confession of Faith: Larger Catechism*, 129.

restore fellowship with God himself through the reconciling work of Christ. And all this motivated by the love of God.

The second problem with Calvinism's prominent emphasis on the glory of God is that, when coupled with its strong sense of divine sovereignty, God's glory is seen even in the most heinous of acts supposedly done by God "for his glory." A good example is Calvin's assertion that "the first man fell because the Lord deemed it meet that he should: why he deemed it meet, we do not know. It is certain, however, that it was just, because *he saw that his own glory would thereby be displayed*."[48] Calvin here asserts that Adam disobeyed God's command and so, according to consistent Calvinism, plunged the whole of mankind into sin, death, and the judgment of hell entirely because "God deemed it meet that he should," and that furthermore God "saw that his own glory would thereby be displayed." God decreed the fall—for his own glory![49] What a travesty of God's true glory, a glory manifested in the incarnation, death and resurrection of Christ. Similarly, in a discussion concerning the elect and the reprobate, Calvin asserts that "the reprobate are expressly raised up in order that the glory of God may thereby be displayed."[50] In other words, according to Calvin, God's glory is manifested in his ensuring a class of people exist who are not chosen for election but rather are condemned to hell![51] And so it is for every evil ordained by God—it is all, indirectly, for his glory.

Human depravity is another area subject to distortion by Calvinism's systematic. We have already seen how the Calvinist notion of total depravity as meaning a total inability to even respond to the gospel of salvation is simply not justified by the biblical data. But, according to Calvinism, human depravity means more: because of Adam's sin every baby born into the world is in total rebellion against God, and that

---

48. Calvin, *Institutes*, 3.23.8, emphasis mine.

49. Spoken anachronistically, Calvin was at least a consistent Calvinist in this respect: "The fall of Adam involves so many nations with their infant children in eternal death without remedy. . . . The decree, I admit, is dreadful; and yet it is impossible to deny that God foreknew what the end of man was to be before he made him, and foreknew, because he had so ordained by his decree." Calvin, *Institutes*, 3.23.7.

50. Calvin, *Institutes*, 3.22.11. Also "God, to display his own glory, withholds from them [the reprobate] the effectual agency of his Spirit." Calvin, *Institutes*, 3.24.2. Apparently, God is glorified when he ensures man's greatest need is denied.

51. Austin Fischer effectively reaches the same conclusion when recounting his pilgrimage out of Calvinism to a more biblically faithful theology: "I realized the only thing I could say about God was that he did everything for his glory. Seriously—that was it. God is loving, God is just, God is good—pull back the curtain and all they mean is God does everything for his glory. . . . God's desire to glorify himself had not only subsumed but consumed all his other desires, so that the only thing I understood about God was that he would glorify himself. Love, justice, and goodness had been warped beyond recognition as they were sucked into the black hole of glory." Fischer, *Young, Restless, No Longer Reformed*, 27. The New Testament scholar Scot McKnight, who wrote the foreword to Fischer's book, says the same thing: "I like the idea of God's glory, but God's love is the final end—not God's glory." Fischer, *Young, Restless, No Longer Reformed*, xi.

"everything man does is in rebellion against God."[52] "Our inherited corruption . . . which we received from Adam, means that as far as God is concerned we are not able to do anything that pleases him."[53] Sproul concurs: "In our corrupt humanity we never do a single good thing."[54] Calvin minces no words in decrying the human condition from birth: "In consequence of the corruption of human nature, man is naturally hateful to God. . . . He is naturally vicious and depraved."[55]

Certainly, everyone (including Christians) have sinned, everyone exhibits moral depravity—with this the Bible is unambiguous. But is it really the case that everyone is born as viscous God-haters, only in total rebellion against God, subject to a depraved nature that can only do evil as far as God is concerned? This is an exaggerated notion of human depravity. Contrary to Calvin, the image of God in man is not "effaced"[56] and, also to the contrary, the psalmist viewed man as *a little lower than the angels* (Ps 8:5). Moses in Deut 4:29 foresees a time when the children of Israel, all unregenerate, from a place of exile shall *"from there . . . seek the Lord your God, and you will find Him if you search for Him with all your heart and all your soul."* But how can anyone seek the Lord when all they can do is rebel against God? In the parable of the prodigal son, Jesus has the son who is lost and dead "come to his senses" and seek to return to his father in repentance (Luke 15:17–19). Come to his senses? How is this possible for a Calvinistically depraved person? In Matt 13:15 Jesus applies Isa 6:10 to the people of his day and states that *"for the heart of this people has become dull,"*[57] and *"they have closed their eyes." Become* dull suggests there was a time when they were not dull of heart, and "have closed their eyes" suggests a time when this was not the case—an impossibility according to Calvinism. In Prov 8, godly wisdom is personified and says, *"I love those who love me; and those who seek Me diligently find me"* (Prov 8:17). Someone can seek diligently for godly wisdom? Isn't this a spiritual good? In Luke 18:16 Jesus's attitude toward children is clearly seen: *"But Jesus called for them, saying, 'Permit the children to come to Me, and do not hinder them, for the kingdom of God belongs to such as these.'"* One is left to wonder why Jesus would present before the disciples a child who is "naturally viscous and depraved" (Calvin) as a model of those who would qualify for entrance into the kingdom of God. Calvinism's distortion concerning human depravity is clear.

A final example of Calvinistic distortion of biblical truth must suffice. Calvinism's view of divine sovereignty as comprehensive causation via an all-encompassing decree, and in which God determines "everything that happens" (Grudem) is such an example. Failing to recognize or, at least acknowledge, that God may choose, in

52. Piper, *Five Points*, 18, 20.

53. Grudem, *Systematic Theology*, 497.

54. Sproul, *Reformed Theology*, 120.

55. Calvin, *Institutes*, 2.1.11.

56. Calvin, *Institutes*, 2.1.5. See 1 Cor 11:7; Jas 3:9.

57. Or *"calloused"* as in the NIV.

his sovereignty, to limit his own rulership to allow room for the libertarian freedom of his human creation, Calvinists must resort to a God that "causes everything that happens." Consistent Calvinists accept the cost—God causes sin, evil, hatred, wars, rapes, diseases, and so on. Calvin himself was just such a consistent "Calvinist" in this respect: "The will of God is the supreme and primary cause of all things, because nothing happens without his order or permission. [Augustine] certainly does not figure God sitting idly in a watch-tower, when he chooses to permit anything. The will which he [Augustine] represents as interposing is . . . active, and but for this could not be regarded as a cause."[58] What Calvin is saying here is that God's will is the cause of all things, and that when Augustine makes reference to permission it is an active permission, otherwise it could not be regarded as a cause. Exactly what an "active permission" that is causal means is left for the reader to think through![59] Lest anyone thinks that God merely *permits* evil to occur and does not do it himself, Calvin later clarifies; within Calvinism a distinction between God permitting and God doing is merely an "invention."[60] The specific issue raised by Calvin for which some might allow God only permitting and not decreeing concerns the morally ludicrous idea "that man should be blinded by the will and command of God, and yet be forthwith punished for his blindness."[61] But Calvin insists that it is an "evasion that this is done only by permission and not also by the will of God." Calvin clarifies: "Men do nothing save at the secret instigation of God, and do not discuss and deliberate on anything but what he has previously decreed with himself, and brings to pass by his secret direction."[62] Even the possibility of God merely permitting an evil rather than absolutely decreeing it cannot be tolerated for it threatens God's sovereignty. Such is Calvinism's distortion of how God actually has chosen to rule the world.

g) Philosophical and Moral Problems

In the chapter dealing with unconditional election, it was stated that theistic determinism ultimately leaves one with nothing but a massive "is." Everything that happens just "is." If I lie it is because God has determined that I lie; if I tell the truth, well, God has determined that too. If I am deceived, God has determined that also. Whatever I do or don't do has been determined by God. We saw there that concepts such as right and wrong, truth and falsity, correct and mistaken, justice and injustice, preferences, judgments are all rendered ultimately meaningless within a framework

58. Calvin, *Institutes*, 1.16.8.

59. Another example of doublespeak. We see the same doublespeak concerning the same issue in Sproul when he says, "What God permits, he decrees to permit." Sproul, *Reformed Theology*, 173.

60. Calvin, *Institutes*, 1.18.1.

61. Calvin, *Institutes*, 1.18.1.

62. Calvin, *Institutes*, 1.18.1.

of a comprehensive causal determinism. The irrationality of such a position is also brought out by John Lennox when he says:

> Causal determinism cannot even be meaningly affirmed, since if it were true then the affirmation itself would be determined, and so would not be a belief freely formed on the basis of weighing the evidence for and against. The affirmation is therefore irrational. Furthermore, it is common for determinists to try to convince non-determinists to convert to determinism. But that assumes that the non-determinists are free to convert, and therefore their non-determinism is not determined in the first place.[63]

Implicit in any form of theistic determinism is the denial of human free will. Few Calvinists are so consistent as to deny outright that humans can exercise their wills freely. Gordon H. Clark was one such consistent Calvinist. He believed that to argue for human free will "concedes that God is not Almighty, for the free will of man can and does frustrate God's will."[64] His robust belief in God's overriding and comprehensive determinism is seen in this statement: "I wish very frankly and pointedly to assert that if a man gets drunk and shoots his family, it was the will of God that he should do so."[65] Clark is at least to be applauded for his commitment to being consistent with his Calvinistic beliefs.

Most modern Calvinists shy away from such a consistent position and prefer to hold in tension what is in reality a contradiction—both that God determines everything that happens and at the same time people are "free" to do what they desire to do. This view is known as compatibilistic freedom since it is a view of freedom that supposedly comports with God's comprehensive decree and is compatible with determinism. This view, first systematically presented by the eighteenth-century Puritan philosopher and preacher Jonathan Edwards, argues that people do what they desire to do, and as long as they are not coerced, they are thereby free. Of course, in compatibilism, what the person ends up desiring is precisely what God has determined they desire. In this case, human free will is ultimately seen to be illusory because the person always and infallibly does precisely what God has determined he do. We might say determinism eats up freedom. Again, Lennox's judgment seems correct: "The cost of holding human free will to be an illusion would appear to be impossibly high, as it entails the invalidity not only of human morality but also of human rationality."[66] The denial of true freedom, that is, libertarian freedom, the ability to choose to do x or y, believe the gospel or reject the gospel, obey God's law or reject God's law, has grave moral implications. For on what basis can God hold a

---

63. Lennox, *Determined to Believe*, 60.

64. Clark, *God and Evil*, 7. His view is known as hard determinism, as opposed to the compatibilist who is a "soft determinist."

65. Clark, *God and Evil*, 38.

66. Lennox, *Determined to Believe*, 60.

person responsible for choices and actions they were decreed to do? "How can God, whose love and justice are impeccable, hold guilty those who were incapable of doing what God commanded them to do?"[67]

The non-Calvinist holds that, as far as human decision-making and choices are concerned, it is not God who determines what those choices will be, but the moral agent himself. In short, they hold to self-determinism. The caricature is often raised by Calvinists to the effect that if God does not determine man's choices, then the choices are indeterminate, and that human choices and behavior is totally uncaused, and at least to some extent, random. But the self-deterministic view believes that "a person's acts are caused by himself. Self-determinists accept the fact that such factors as heredity and environment often influence one's behavior. However, they deny that such factors are the determining causes of one's behavior. Inanimate objects do not change without an outside cause, but personal subjects are able to direct their own actions."[68]

All Christians affirm God's foreknowledge of future events. The extent of God's foreknowledge or omniscience is a debated issue, however. Some, known as open theists, hold that God has much knowledge of the future including all that he decrees he will do, but deny that it is possible for God to know future events that are the result of human free choices which have not yet been made. Such choices, not having yet been made, are simply not there to be known. Others, like myself, hold that God's foreknowledge is comprehensive, including future choices and decisions made by people. The reason this is the case is that God, unlike people, who can only know the present and the past, is not time bound. God stands above time as it were and sees all spread out before him and so knows the beginning from the end.[69] It's important to note that there is no logical connection between God's knowledge and God's causing. God's *knowing* all does not imply that he *determines* all, just as my knowing that Fred had Wheaties for breakfast yesterday did not cause him to have that particular cereal at that time.

Calvinists also believe God has exhaustive future knowledge. They do so because they believe God has caused everything that happened in the past, is happening now and will happen in the future. In other words, it is God's eternal decree that comprises the basis for his exhaustive foreknowledge. Obviously, this subject has taken up volumes of discussion and analysis in philosophical and theological journals. I will make one point here; to say that God knows the future because he knows what he will do in the future is not especially Godlike. In fact, I could also know the future based on what I will choose to do tomorrow. It takes a far greater view of God to believe that, despite the genuinely free actions of his human creation, God can still know exhaustively precisely what those genuinely self-determined actions will

67. Lennox, *Determined to Believe*, 157.

68. Geisler, "Freedom, Free Will, and Determinism," 430.

69. This view, known as Simple Foreknowledge, was first propounded by the medieval philosopher Boethius (480–524).

be. In short, the Calvinist's understanding of God's foreknowledge, does not make God to be especially praiseworthy because the only difference between human and divine knowledge is the extent of that knowledge.

Another area of Christian thought impacted by Calvinism's theistic determinism concerns the doctrine of providence and specifically the problem of evil. The problem of evil as a philosophical question arises because of theism's belief in an all-powerful and all-loving God. Given these two beliefs, the problem naturally emerges: whence evil? An all-loving God would want to eliminate evil, and an all-powerful God could do so. A theodicy is an argument designed to justify or explain how all three propositions (God is loving; God is all powerful; evil exists) can hold together. Typically, Calvinism's answer is a greater good theodicy.[70] This approach maintains "that evil, moral evil, is necessary for a greater good. The soul-making aspect of the approach maintains that without the occurrence of moral evil certain other goods could not, logically speaking, arise. Without weakness and need, no compassion; without fault, no forgiveness, and so on."[71] In short, God ordains evil so that a greater good could result.

The problem with a greater good theodicy is that it is a utilitarian ethic. This form of ethics argues that "one should act so as to produce the greatest good for the greatest number in the long run."[72] While superficially this ethic sounds reasonable, it may lead to the justification of terrible evil if it results in a perceived greater good. "Some utilitarians frankly admit that there may come a time when it would no longer be best to preserve life. . . . In this case the greatest good would be to promote death."[73] Helm seems to accept this sort of logic when he argues that redemption is a greater good that would not have occurred without the fall of Adam into sin: "The fall is a necessary precondition of redemption."[74] Later he speaks of the fall as a happy fault: "The 'happy fault' . . . refers [to] the fall of Adam. This is happy because it, and it alone, makes possible the divine redemption from which the blessings of pardon and renewal follow."[75] Can it really be the case that God ordained the fall of Adam into sin so that the good of redemption would be experienced by some of God's human creation? I think not. Adam's sin introduced sin and death into the world (Rom 5:12) and all the miseries of human existence associated with human sinning. It takes only a casual acquaintance with the Old Testament historical narratives to see the awfulness of sin played out in the countless brutal wars therein described. And the same dire effects of human sin are

70. What follows is highly simplified and necessarily brief. It also ignores any "evil" associated with punishment of evildoers and the need to maintain justice. The latter fails to explain how and why evildoers arise in the first place. The focus in this paragraph is on the evil ordained by God in the outworking of his overarching decree.

71. Helm, *Providence*, 213.

72. Geisler, *Christian Ethics*, 15.

73. Geisler, *Christian Ethics*, 15.

74. Helm, *Providence*, 96.

75. Helm, *Providence*, 214.

played out today in countless ways. Sin brings death, disease, war, torture, pain, murder, suffering, and every evil imaginable—and the greater good theodicy argues God *ordains* all this and that all this is necessary, even desirable, for some greater good. God is a God of life, not death, and he desires that no one should perish but that all may gain life (Deut 30:15, 19; John 3:16; 5:40; 10:10; 17:3; 20:31; 1 John 5:13). The greater good theodicy may be consistent with theistic determinism, but it is not consistent with the character of God revealed in the pages of Scripture.

A better explanation for the presence of evil in the world and a solution to the problem of evil is one which does not make God the ultimate author of sin, but lays the blame for moral evil squarely upon willful disobedience to the moral and spiritual will of God the Creator; it is known as the free-will defense. Helm's description is fair: "Indeterministic free will is a necessary condition of human personality and accountability. In endowing human beings with such free will, and placing then in a created order where evil choices are possible, God brought it about that whether or not there is moral evil in the world is not up to him, but up to them, the creatures with free will. Given such creatures, God could not have created a universe such that they freely did only what was morally good."[76] Such beings and their behaviors accords very well with what we read concerning the evil choices and actions of individuals within the Bible, beginning with Adam, continuing with the Pharisees who put Christ to death, and up to the present in our own lives and the lives of those around us.[77]

Yet another issue of concern is Calvinism's view of total depravity. Recall that the view states that, because of original sin, every person is born in a state which prevents them from recognizing, perceiving, or truly knowing spiritual truths. The inability of the mind to perceive spiritual truths is known as the noetic effects of sin. "Being fallen, the natural heart and mind is sinfully corrupt and unenlightened. . . . The natural mind does not accept spiritual things . . . the unregenerate mind is simply incapable of this knowledge. The mind of the Gentiles is empty, lifeless, ignorant and blind."[78] The only antidote to this state of affairs, so Calvinism holds, is to be regenerated, born again.

However, given this state of the mind's inability to know or perceive truths pertaining to the true God and his ways, the claim that a person can know they have been regenerated is, in fact, self-refuting. The fallen mind, according to Calvinism,

---

76. Helm, *Providence*, 195. When he speaks of indeterministic free will, I take him to mean self-deterministic free will.

77. It must be admitted that, in a sense, the free-will defense is a form of Greater Good argument too—God permitted the possibility of Adam sinning, e.g., because God valued freely reciprocated love toward him above all, which would not have been possible had God created a world of robots. But the distinction between God ordaining and deliberately causing the evil is quite different from God allowing agents endowed with free will to abuse their freedom. In one case, God is clearly responsible for the evil, in the other case, man is responsible for the evil. In the one case, God wants the evil, plans the evils, and executes the evil, in the other case, God hates the evil.

78. Wright, *No Place for Sovereignty*, 113–14.

is so depraved that it cannot know any spiritual truths, including the spiritual truth that one has been regenerated. The noetic effect of sin is such that the mind is incapable of properly evaluating any supposed spiritual experience (like regeneration) whether true or false, genuine or spurious.

h) The Problem of the Livability of Calvinism

By the problem of the livability of Calvinism I mean the problem of a Christian living *consistently* with his or her Calvinistic formal beliefs. Much of this problem of consistency has been addressed in the pages up to this point—see especially the discussion under the headings (a), (c), and (d) above. My concern here is with the more practical and pastoral side of this problem.

That Calvinists are unable to hold their Calvinism consistently can be easily demonstrated. For example, R. C. Sproul recounts in the introduction to his book *What Is Reformed Theology?* how he noticed one day when being conducted around a Christian College, a sign on a faculty door which said "Department of Religion." It is evident from the way Sproul tells the story that he viewed negatively the move from Department of Theology to the Department of Religion, for according to Sproul the former deals with the study of God while the latter deals with the study of man. But why should Sproul feel such a move is wrong and not truly God-honoring? This question becomes pertinent when, later in his book, we learn that God "knows all things that will happen because he ordains everything that does happen. . . . God's eternal and immutable decree . . . applies to everything that happens . . . [and that] everything that happens is the will of God."[79] Given Sproul's formal beliefs concerning God's causing everything that happens, it is very strange that Sproul would object to God's eternal and immutable decree concerning the department name![80]

A similar phenomenon occurs with Grudem. We have already seen that he believes "the decrees of God are the eternal plans of God whereby, before the creation of the world, he determined to bring about *everything that happens.*"[81] Interestingly, Grudem has structured the major headings of his work with a series of questions. For example, in the section dealing with the doctrine of the church he asks: What makes a church more or less pleasing to God? What kinds of church should we cooperate with or join? How should church discipline function? How should a church be governed? Now all of these questions are quite pertinent to a study of the doctrine of the church, but is quite irrelevant for a Calvinist who believes *everything* is ordained by God. Why? Because each question implies there is an answer to the alternatives asked and that both alternatives are possible. But within Calvinism there

---

79. Sproul, *Reformed Theology*, 172.

80. Of course, he could argue that his objection itself has been decreed!

81. Grudem, *Systematic Theology*, 332, emphasis mine.

are no real, authentic alternatives, just an eternal and immutable single decree that is being worked out on the plane of history.

Bearing in mind what has just been said by Grudem concerning "the eternal decrees of God [being] the eternal plans of God whereby . . . he determined everything that happens," one is surprised to read, concerning prayer, that "prayer changes the way God acts." And that "we pray, and God responds . . . when we ask, God responds." Citing Jas 4:2 (*"You do not have, because you do not ask"*) Grudem remarks that this "implies that failure to ask deprives us of what God would otherwise have given to us." But how can such language concerning God's relationship to prayer make any possible sense for a God who determines *everything* that happens? It is simply incoherent to insist on the one hand that all of reality is the working out of God's eternal decree, and yet assert on the other hand that God "responds" to our prayers. Within consistent Calvinism the circumstances calling forth our prayers have been determined by God, our prayers have been determined by God, and God's "response" has likewise been determined by God.

What about suffering and crises? Suppose a church member confides in her pastor that she is being abused by her husband. This is what a consistent Calvinist should say in response: "It's hard Mary, but just hang in there, you can take comfort knowing your abuse has been decreed by God, and that, for reasons unknown to us, but known to God, he desires that you experience beatings, verbal abuse, and shame. It's all for his glory." Of course, no Calvinistic pastor would say such things—thereby demonstrating the inability to live out his theology. Or, as another illustration, suppose a young couple have recently received news from their doctor that their eight-month-old son has just been diagnosed with a fatal disease and has just weeks to live. The distraught parents are seeking help and counsel from their Calvinist pastor. They ask, "Pastor, will our child go to be with the Lord when he dies"? What does our consistent pastor say? "I'm so sorry, but because of Adam's sin your child is heading for hell. He may appear cute, but in reality, as far as God is concerned, he's a viper in a diaper.[82] Your only hope is that God has chosen him for salvation before the foundation of the world, that he is one of the elect. The only problem is that it's impossible to know the answer to that question because God hasn't told us." I doubt if any Calvinist pastor would counsel such a thing, again demonstrating the inability to live out his doctrine of salvation.

Or, consider the young man John who is considering the desirability of going to university. He asks his Calvinist friend, "Do you think it's a good idea for me to embark on this project"? His friend may suggest that John pray about it, that he continues seeking the wise counsel of others, that he carefully considers the cost, both financial and personal. But, if the friend was consistent in correlating his formal beliefs about God's rule and this request by his friend, he would have to add, "But, I wouldn't worry too much about it, John, because whatever you decide will simply be the outworking of

82. This phrase was first popularized by Voddie Baucham, former pastor of Grace Family Baptist Church in Texas. Calvin preferred the term "doomed from the womb."

God's decree. If you don't go then that's what God has secretly willed for you, but if you do decide to go, then that too is what God has secretly decreed for you." What kind of help would that be to John as he struggles to reach a decision?

In short, in the words of the Christian apologist William Craig: "A determinist cannot live consistently as though everything he thinks and does is causally determined—especially his choice to believe that determinism is true! . . . Determinists recognize that we have to act 'as if' we had free will and so weigh our options and decide on what course of action to take, even though at the end of the day we are determined to take the choices we do. Determinism is thus an unlivable view."[83] Elsewhere, the Christian philosopher Winfried Corduan states the same thing in terms of worldview: "It must be possible to live out a worldview. . . An idea or system that cannot be lived out is worthless. . . . If a system is of such a nature that it is intrinsically impossible to live by it, it must be false."[84]

i) The Problem of the Character of God Portrayed by Calvinism

Perhaps the most serious complaint one may level against Calvinism concerns its portrayal of God himself. Biblical revelation clearly shows God to be loving, gracious, personal, responsive, caring, just, impartial, desiring life for everyone, and a hater of sin. Unfortunately, Calvinism, in nearly every case, projects a God who contradicts these characteristics. God's love is selective, God's salvific grace is either completely lacking (for the non-elect) or irresistible in the case of the elect. And God's transcendence is so amplified with its distorted view of divine sovereignty worked out through a comprehensive impersonal decree that there is little room for genuine interaction between persons and God. Where God requires believers to love their enemies, God instead is permitted to be a hater of his enemies. Where the Bible requires Jesus's followers to be impartial in their dealings with men, God instead is demonstrably partial in his unilaterally and unconditionally selecting some for salvation while damning the rest to hell when he could, if he chose, save all. While the Bible says that God *"desires all men to be saved and to come to the knowledge of the truth"* (1 Tim 2:4), God by his secret and eternal decree actually does not desire all me to be saved, for if he did he could easily ensure it through his decree.[85] Where the Bible clearly reveals God to be a hater of sin, God is seen to be the author and instigator of every sin manifested in history. (Recall that God's sovereignty is such that he, through his decree, is responsible for *"everything that happens"* [Sproul, Grudem, etc.].) Reflecting on Calvinism's

---

83. Craig, "Calvinism," para. 2.

84. Corduan, *Reasonable Faith*, 76.

85. As Sproul notes: "God certainly has the power and authority to grant his saving grace to all mankind. Clearly he has not elected to do this. All men are not saved despite the fact that God has the power and right to save them all if that is his good pleasure." Sproul, *Reformed Theology*, 150.

difficulties in reconciling God as a God who is good, just, and love with Calvinism's theistic determinism, Fischer says this:

> In what sense was God good if he had done something like creating people so he could damn them? And in what sense was God just if he had done something like punishing people eternally for sins he made certain they would commit? How are those in hell merely getting what they deserve when God ordained that they commit their sins? How can humans be held responsible for their sins when God is the ultimate cause of their sins? . . . And how can we say that God loves the whole world when he created a good portion of it to go to hell?[86]

Calvinists, of course, would strongly object to the above paragraphs, but one wonders on what basis they can object; the heart of Calvinism is a monergism that effectively makes God the sole actor in human history, a history which is to the minutest degree merely an outworking in time of an eternal and comprehensive decree that accounts for every event, decision, choice, and even thought. With its commitment to such a view of sovereignty, ultimately, all the negative characteristics attributed to Calvinism's God described above would seem inescapable. Hunt concurs when he says:

> Calvinism is founded upon the premise that God does not love everyone, is not merciful to all, does not want all to be saved, but in fact is pleased to damn billions whom, by sovereign regeneration, He could have saved had He so desired. If that is the God of the Bible, Calvinism is true. If that is not the God of the Bible, who is "love" (1 John 4:8), Calvinism is false. The central issue is God's love and character in relation to mankind, as presented in Scripture.[87]

The distortion of the biblical data concerning the nature, will, and purpose of God for his human creation must inevitably result in a similar distortion of the character of God. And, in the final analysis, perhaps the clearest expression of an unbiblical understanding of God himself is to be found in Calvinism's monergistic systematic of salvation, which is ultimately not by grace through faith, but rather by decree.

86. Fischer, *Young, Restless, No Longer Reformed*, 24.
87. Hunt, *What Love Is This?*, 123.

Bibliography

Abraham, William J. "Predestination and Assurance." In Pinnock, *The Grace of God, the Will of Man*, 231–42.

Allen, David L. *The Extent of the Atonement: A Historical and Critical Review.* Nashville: Broadman and Holman, 2016.

Allison, Gregg R. *Historical Theology.* Grand Rapids: Zondervan, 2011.

Anizor, Uche. *How to Read Theology: Engaging Doctrine Critically and Charitably.* Grand Rapids: Baker, 2018.

Augustine. *Confessions.* Vol 21 of *The Fathers of the Church: A New Translation.* Translated by Vernon J. Burke. Washington, DC: Catholic University, 1953.

———. *The Retractions.* Book II, ch. 23. Translated by Peter Holmes. Edinburgh: T. & T. Clark, 1872.

Barlotta, Mike. "Augustine's Evolving Views on Free-Will." Society of Evangelical Arminians. March 2, 2015. http://evangelicalarminians.org/mike-barlotta-augustines-evolving-views-on-free-will/.

Barrett, C. K. *The First Epistle to the Corinthians.* Trowerbridge, UK: Redwood, 1971.

Baukham, Richard. *Jude, 2 Peter.* Word Biblical Commentary 50. Waco: Word, 1983.

Bauer, Walter. *A Greek-English Lexicon of the New Testament.* Edited by William F. Arndt and F. W. Gingrich. 2nd ed. Chicago: University of Chicago Press, 1979.

Berkhof, Louis. *The History of Christian Doctrine.* Grand Rapids: Baker, 1966 [1937].

———. *Systematic Theology.* London: Banner of Truth, 1959.

Bettenson, Henry, ed. *Documents of the Christian Church.* London: Oxford University Press, 1963.

Boettner, Loraine. "The Reformed Doctrine of Predestination." West Linn, OR: Monergism, 2015. https://www.monergism.com/thethreshold/sdg/boettner/predestination_p.pdf.

Brand, Chad Owen, ed. *Perspectives on Election: Five Views.* Nashville: Broadman and Holman, 2006.

Bromiley, Geoffrey W. *Historical Theology: An Introduction.* Edinburgh: T. & T. Clark, 1978.

Brown, Colin. *The New International Dictionary of New Testament Theology.* Grand Rapids: Zondervan, 1986.

Brown, Francis, S. R. Driver, and Charles A. Briggs, eds. *A Hebrew and English Lexicon of the Old Testament.* Oxford: Clarendon, 1951.

Brown, Raymond. *The Message of Hebrews.* Edited by John R. W. Stott. Downers Grove: InterVarsity, 1982.

Bruce, F. F. *1 & 2 Thessalonians.* Word Biblical Commentary 45. Waco, TX: Word, 1982.

————. *Book of the Acts*. New International Commentary on the New Testament. Grand Rapids: Eerdmans, 1988.

————. *Epistles to the Colossians, to Philemon, and to the Ephesians*. New International Commentary on the New Testament. Grand Rapids: Eerdmans, 1984.

————. *Hebrews*. New International Commentary on the New Testament. Grand Rapids: Eerdmans, 1964.

————. *Romans: An Introduction and Commentary*. Tyndale New Testament Commentaries. Leicester, UK: InterVarsity, 1985.

Bryson, George L. *The Five Points of Calvinism*. Costa Mesa, CA: Word for Today, 1996.

Bullock, Hassell C. *An Introduction to the Old Testament Prophetic Books*. Chicago: Moody, 1986.

Burke, G. T. "Stoics." In Elwell, *Evangelical Dictionary of Theology*, 1055–56.

Burnish, R. F. G. "Baptism." In Ferguson et al., *New Dictionary of Theology*, 71–73.

Calvin, John. *Institutes of the Christian Religion*. Translated by Henry Beveridge. 1845. Reprint, Grand Rapids: Eerdmans, 1997.

Canons of Dort. "Third and Fourth Heads of Doctrine." https://prts.edu/wp-content/uploads/2016/12/Canons-of-Dort-with-Intro.pdf#:~:text=The%20Decision%20of%20the%20Synod%20of%20Dort%20on,1618%E2%80%931619.%20Although%20this%20was%20a%20national%20Synod%20of.

Carson, D. A. *The Difficult Doctrine of the Love of God*. Wheaton: Crossway, 2000.

————. *Exegetical Fallacies*. Grand Rapids: Baker, 1984.

————. *Gospel according to John*. Grand Rapids: InterVarsity, 1991.

Chadwick, Henry. *The Early Church*. Middlesex, UK: Penguin, 1967.

Clark, Gordon H. *God and Evil: The Problem Solved*. Unicoi, TN: Trinity Foundation, 2004.

————. *Predestination*. Unicoi, TN: Trinity Foundation, 2006 [1969].

Clement of Alexandria. *The Writings of Clement of Alexandria*. Translated by William Wilson. Edinburgh: T. & T. Clark, 1869.

Clowney, Edmund P. "Preaching and the Sovereignty of God." In Schreiner and Ware, *Still Sovereign*, 325–40.

Cole, R. Alan. *Exodus*. Tyndale Old Testament Commentaries. Downers Grove: InterVarsity, 1973.

Collins, G. N. M. "Order of Salvation." In Elwell, *Evangelical Dictionary of Theology*, 802.

Corduan, Winfried. *Reasonable Faith: Basic Christian Apologetics*. Nashville: Broadman & Holman, 1993.

Cottrell, Jack. "Conditional Election." In Pinnock, *Grace Unlimited*, 51–73.

————. *The Faith Once for All: Bible Doctrines for Today*. Joplin, MO: College Press, 2002.

————. "The Nature of the Divine Sovereignty." In Pinnock, *The Grace of God, the Will of Man*, 97–119.

————. *Romans*. 2 vols. Joplin, MO: College Press, 1996.

————. *What the Bible Says about God the Creator*. Joplin, MO: College Press, 1983.

————. *What the Bible Says about God the Redeemer*. Joplin, MO: College Press, 1987.

————. *What the Bible Says about God the Ruler*. Joplin, MO: College Press, 1984.

Craig, William Lane. "Calvinism and the Unliveability of Determinism." *Reasonable Faith*, February 4, 2018. https://www.reasonablefaith.org/writings/question-answer/Calvinism-and-the-unliveability-of-determinism/.

Craigie, Peter C. *The Book of Deuteronomy*. New International Commentary on the Old Testament. Grand Rapids: Eerdmans, 1976.

Cranfield, C. E. B. "On Some of the Problems in the Interpretation of Romans 5:12." *Scottish Journal of Theology* 22.3 (1969) 324–41.

Demarest, B. A. "Amyraldianism." In Elwell, *Evangelical Dictionary of Theology*, 41–42.

Diez, Felipe. "Types of Calvinism—a Comprehensive List." https://reformedforhisglory. wordpress.com/2013/08/09/types-of-calvinism-a-comprehensive-list/.

Dowley, Tim, ed. *Eerdmans Handbook to the History of Christianity*. Grand Rapids: Eerdmans, 1977.

Dunn, James D. G. *Romans 1–8*. Word Biblical Commentary 38A. Dallas: Word, 1988.

Duvall, J. Scott, and Daniel Hays. *Grasping God's Word: A Hands-On Approach to Reading, Interpreting, and Applying the Bible*. 3rd ed. Grand Rapids: Zondervan, 2012.

Edwards, Jonathan. *Freedom of the Will*. Grand Rapids: Christian Classics Ethereal Library, 2000.

Elwell, Walter A., ed. *Baker Encyclopedia of the Bible*. Grand Rapids: Baker, 1988.

———, ed. *Evangelical Dictionary of Theology*. Grand Rapids: Baker, 1984.

Erickson, Millard J. *Christian Theology*. Grand Rapids: Baker, 1989.

Fee, Gordon D. *The First Epistle to the Corinthians*. New International Commentary on the New Testament. Grand Rapids: Eerdmans, 1987.

Ferguson, Sinclair B., et al., eds. *New Dictionary of Theology*. Downers Grove: InterVarsity, 1988.

Finger, Thomas N. *Christian Theology: An Eschatological Approach*. 2 vols. Scottsdale, PA: Herald, 1985.

Finney, Charles G., and Prest A. Mahan, eds. *Christian Classics Ethereal Library: Systematic Theology Lecture XXXVI, Justification*. Edited by J. H. Fairchild. Whittier, CA: Colporter Kemp, 1944 [1878]. https://www.ccel.org/ccel/finney/theology.iv.xxxv.html.

———. *Christian Classics Ethereal Library: Systematic Theology Lecture XLIII, Election*. Edited by J. H. Fairchild. Whittier, CA: Colporter Kemp, 1944 [1878]. https://ccel.org/ccel/finney/theology.iv.xlii.html.

———. *The Oberlin Quarterly Review: Article XX; Moral Depravity*. New York, 1846. https://www.gospeltruth.net/1846-48_ob_quar_review/1846_oqr_moral_dep1.htm.

———. "On the Atonement." *Oberlin Evangelist*, July 1856. https://www.gospeltruth.net/1856OE/560730_the_atonement.htm.

———. *Systematic Theology*. Edited by George Redford. London: William Tegg, 1851. https://books.google.com/books?id=la5WAAAAcAAJ&printsec=frontcover&source=gbs_ge_summary_r&cad=0#v=onepage&q&f=false.

Fischer, Austin. *Young, Restless, No Longer Reformed*. Eugene, OR: Cascade, 2014.

Fisk, Samuel. *Divine Sovereignty & Human Freedom*. Neptune, NJ: Loizeaux Brothers, 1973.

Flowers, Leighton. "Romans 8:28–30: Foreknowledge and Predestination; Critiquing Matt Chandler." YouTube video, 1:09:46. Posted by Soteriology 101, February 14, 2018. https://youtu.be/GwVFauQeuK4.

Forster, Roger T., and V. Paul Marston. *God's Strategy in Human History*. Minneapolis: Bethany House, 1973.

Friberg, Timothy, et al. *Analytical Lexicon of the Greek New Testament*. Grand Rapids: Baker, 2000.

Galli, Mark, and Ted Olsen, eds. *131 Christians Everyone Should Know*. Nashville: Broadman & Holman, 2000.

Garrett, James Leo. *Systematic Theology*. Grand Rapids: Eerdmans, 1980.

Geisler, N. L. "Augustine." In Elwell, *Evangelical Dictionary of Theology*, 105–7. Grand Rapids: Baker, 1984.

———. "Freedom, Free Will and Determinism." In Elwell, *Evangelical Dictionary of Theology*, 428–30.

———. *Options in Contemporary Christian Ethics*. Grand Rapids: Baker, 1981.

Godfrey, W. R. "Atonement, Extent of." In Ferguson et al., *New Dictionary of Theology*, 57.

Gonzales, Justo L. *A History of Christian Thought*. 3 vols. Nashville: Abingdon, 1971.

Green, Joel B. *1 Peter*. Two Horizons New Testament Commentary. Grand Rapids: Eerdmans, 2007.

Green, Michael. *2 Peter and Jude*. Tyndale New Testament Commentaries. Grand Rapids: Eerdmans, 1987.

Grudem, Wayne. *1 Peter*. Tyndale New Testament Commentaries. Leicester, UK: InterVarsity, 1988.

———. "Perseverance of the Saints: A Case Study from the Warning Passages in Hebrews." In Schreiner and Ware, *Still Sovereign*, 133–82.

———. *Systematic Theology: An Introduction to Biblical Doctrine*. Grand Rapids: Zondervan, 1994.

Guthrie, Donald. *The Letter to the Hebrews*. Tyndale New Testament Commentaries. Leicester, UK: InterVarsity, 1983.

———. *New Testament Introduction*. London: InterVarsity, 1970.

———. *The Pastoral Epistles*. Tyndale New Testament Commentaries. Leicester, UK: InterVarsity, 1990.

Haag, Herbert. *Is Original Sin in Scripture?* New York: Sheed & Ward, 1969.

Han, S. J. "An Investigation into Calvin's Use of Augustine." *Acta Theologica* 28, Supplementum 10 (2008) 70–83. https://www.ajol.info/index.php/actat/article/view/52214.

Hansen, Collin. *Young, Restless, and Reformed*. Wheaton: Crossway, 2008.

Harrison E. F., and D. A. Hagner. *Romans*. Expositors Bible. Grand Rapids: Zondervan, 2008.

Hart, D. B. *The Doors of the Sea*. Grand Rapids: Eerdmans, 2005.

Helm, Paul. *The Providence of God*. Downers Grove: InterVarsity, 1994.

Hendriksen, William. *1 & 2 Timothy and Titus*. New Testament Commentary. London: Banner of Truth, 1957.

———. *Ephesians*. New Testament Commentary. London: Banner of Truth, 1967.

———. *John*. New Testament Commentary. London: Banner of Truth, 1954.

———. *Matthew*. New Testament Commentary. London: Banner of Truth, 1973.

Hendryx, John. "Regeneration in the Old Testament." https://www.monergism.com/thethreshold/sdg/regeneration_ot.html.

Hewitt, Thomas. *Hebrews*. Tyndale New Testament Commentaries. Bedford, UK: Tyndale, 1973.

Hoehner, H. W. "Love." In Elwell, *Evangelical Dictionary of Theology*, 657.

Hoekema, Anthony A. *Saved by Grace*. Grand Rapids: Eerdmans 1989.

Holweck, F. "Immaculate Conception." In *The Catholic Encyclopedia*, vol. 7. New York: Robert Appleton, 1910. Available online at http://www.newadvent.org/cathen/07674d.htm.

Horton, Michael. *For Calvinism*. Grand Rapids: Zondervan, 2011.

Houck, Steven R. *God's Sovereignty in Salvation*. South Holland, IL: Protestant Reformed Church, 1987.

Hughes, Philip E. "Grace." In Elwell, *Evangelical Dictionary of Theology*, 482.

———. *Second Epistle to the Corinthians*. New International Commentary of the New Testament. Grand Rapids: Eerdmans, 1962.

Hunt, Dave. *What Love Is This: Calvinism's Misrepresentation of God*. Bend, OR: Berean Call, 2013.

Kahn, Samuel. *Kant, Ought Implies Can, the Principle of Alternate Possibilities, and Happiness.* Washington, DC: Lexington, 2018.

Kearsley, R. "Perseverance." In Ferguson et al., *New Dictionary of Theology*, 506–7.

Kelly, J. N. D. *A Commentary on the Epistles of Peter and Jude*. Grand Rapids: Baker, 1969.

Kidner, Derek. *Genesis: An Introduction and Commentary*. Tyndale Old Testament Commentaries. Downers Grove: InterVarsity, 1967.

———. *Proverbs: An Introduction and Commentary*. Tyndale Old Testament Commentaries. Downers Grove: InterVarsity, 1964.

Klooster, F. H. "Decrees of God." In Elwell, *Evangelical Dictionary of Theology*, 302–4.

———. "Supralapsarianism." In Elwell, *Evangelical Dictionary of Theology*, 1059–60.

Knight, Kevin. New Advent introductory note to Nicene and Post-Nicene Fathers, second series, vol. 14, edited by Philip Schaff and Henry Wace. Buffalo, NY: Christian Literature, 1900. http://www.newadvent.org/fathers/3816.htm.

Kruse, Colin. *2 Corinthians*. Tyndale New Testament Commentaries. Grand Rapids: Eerdmans, 1991.

Lake, Donald. "He Died for All: The Universal Dimensions of the Atonement." In Pinnock, *Grace Unlimited*, 31–50.

Lane, Anthony N. S. *A Reader's Guide to Calvin's Institutes*. Grand Rapids: Baker, 2009.

Lane, William L. *Hebrews 1–8*. Word Biblical Commentary 47A. Dallas: Word, 1991.

———. *Hebrews 9–13*. Word Biblical Commentary 47B. Dallas: Word, 1991.

Lennox, John C. *Determined to Believe? The Sovereignty of God, Freedom, Faith & Human Responsibility*. Grand Rapids: Zondervan, 2017.

Letham, R. W. A. "Calling." In Ferguson et al., *New Dictionary of Theology*, 119–20.

Lints, Richard. *The Fabric of Theology: A Prolegomenon to Evangelical Theology*. Eugene, OR: Wipf and Stock, 1999.

Longenecker, Richard. *Galatians*. Word Biblical Commentary 41. Dallas: Word, 1990.

MacDonald, William G. "The Spirit of Grace." In Pinnock, *Grace Unlimited*, 74–94.

Marshall, I. Howard. *Acts of the Apostles*. Tyndale New Testament Commentaries. Grand Rapids: InterVarsity, 1980.

———. "Universal Grace and Atonement in the Pastoral Epistles." In Pinnock, *The Grace of God, the Will of Man*, 51–69.

Martin, Ralph P. *James*. Word Biblical Commentary 48. Waco: Word, 1988.

———. *Philippians*. Tyndale New Testament Commentaries. Leicester, UK: InterVarsity, 1987.

McDonald, William G. "The Biblical Doctrine of Election." In Pinnock, *The Grace of God, the Will of Man*, 207–29.

McGrath, Alister E. "Origen on Inherited Sin." In *The Christian Theology Reader*, edited by Alister E. McGrath, 215. Cambridge: Blackwell, 1995.

Miethe, Terry L. "The Universal Power of the Atonement." In Pinnock, *The Grace of God, the Will of Man*, 71–96.

Mohler, Albert. "So . . . Why Did I Write This? The Delusion of Determinism." August 21, 2008. https://albertmohler.com/2008/08/21/so-why-did-i-write-this-the-delusion-of-determinism/.

Moo, Douglas J. *The Letter of James*. Tyndale New Testament Commentaries. Leicester, UK: InterVarsity, 1985.

Morrell, Jesse. *Does Man Inherit a Sinful Nature?* Biblical Truth Resources. Self-published, 2013.

Morris, Leon. *Luke*. Tyndale New Testament Commentaries. Grand Rapids: Eerdmans, 1989.

———. *The Gospel according to John*. New International Commentary on the New Testament. Grand Rapids: Eerdmans, 1971.

Mounce, William D. *Basics of Biblical Greek Grammar*. Grand Rapids: Zondervan, 1993.

Murray, John. *Redemption Accomplished and Applied*. Grand Rapids: Eerdmans, 1955.

———. *Romans*. New London Commentary on the New Testament. London: Marshall, Morgan & Scott, 1967.

Naselli, Andrew David, and Mark A. Snoeberger. *Perspectives on the Extent of the Atonement*. Nashville: Broadman and Holman, 2015.

New World Encyclopedia contributors. "Concupiscence." *New World Encyclopedia*. Revised May 14, 2020. https://www.newworldencyclopedia.org/p/index.php?title=Concupiscence&oldid=1037260.

Olsen, Roger E. *Against Calvinism*. Grand Rapids: Zondervan, 2011.

———. "Why My Conversations with Calvinists Are Rarely Productive." *My Evangelical Amrinian Theological Musings* (Olsen's blog, *Patheos*), February 9, 2018. http://www.patheos.com/blogs/rogereolson/2018/02/conversations-calvinists-rarely-productive/#BFy1FMhh1exyDCEz.99.

Osborne, Grant R. "General Atonement View." In Naselli and Snoeberger, *Perspectives on the Extent of the Atonement*, 81–126.

———. *The Hermeneutical Spiral*. Downers Grove: InterVarsity, 1991.

Osterhaven, M. E. "Covenant Theology." In Elwell, *Evangelical Dictionary of Theology*, 279–80.

Oswalt, John N. *The Book of Isaiah*. 2 vols. New International Commentary on the Old Testament. Grand Rapids: Eerdmans, 1986.

Owen, John. *The Death of Death in the Death of Christ*. London: Banner of Truth, 1959 [1648].

Packer, J. I. "τασσω: arrange, appoint." In Brown, *New International Dictionary of New Testament Theology*, 1:476–77.

——— "Faith." In Elwell, *Evangelical Dictionary of Theology*, 399–402.

———. "Introductory Essay." In Owen, *Death of Death*, 1–32.

———. "The Love of God: Universal and Particular." In Schreiner and Ware, *Still Sovereign*, 277–91.

———. "Regeneration." In Elwell, *Evangelical Dictionary of Theology*, 924–26.

Pagels, Elaine. *Adam, Eve, and the Serpent*. New York: Random House, 1988.

Perkin, Hazel W. "God-fearer." In Elwell, *Baker Encyclopedia of the Bible*, 888.

Peterson, Robert A. *Election and Free Will*. Nutley, NJ: Presbyterian and Reformed, 2007.

Pink, Arthur W. *Does God Love Everyone?* https://gracegems.org/Pink/does_god_love_everyone.htm.

———. *The Sovereignty of God*. Edinburgh: Banner of Truth, 1959.

Pinnock, Clark H. "From Augustine to Arminius: A Pilgrimage in Theology." In *The Grace of God, the Will of Man*, 15–30.

———, ed. *The Grace of God, the Will of Man*. Grand Rapids: Zondervan, 1989.

———, ed. *Grace Unlimited*. Minneapolis: Bethany House, 1975.

Piper, John. "Are There Two Wills in God?" In Schreiner and Ware, *Still Sovereign*, 107–31.

———. *Five Points: Towards a Deeper Experience of God's Grace*. Ross-shire, Scotland: Christian Focus, 2013.

———. "They Were Destined to Disobey God." November 24, 2015. https://www. desiringgod.org/labs/they-were-destined-to-disobey-god.

Reichenbach, Bruce. "Freedom, Justice, and Moral Responsibility." In Pinnock, *The Grace of God, the Will of Man*, 277–303.

Renault, Alexander J. *Reconsidering TULIP: A Biblical, Philosophical, and Historical Response to the Reformed Doctrine of Predestination*. Self-published, 2010.

Ridderbos, Herman N. *The Epistle of Paul to the Churches of Galatia*. New International Commentary on the New Testament. Grand Rapids: Eerdmans, 1953.

Ringwald, A. "Regeneration." In Brown, *New International Dictionary of New Testament Theology*, 1:176–80.

Rupp, Gordon E., and Philip S. Watson, eds. *Luther and Erasmus: Free Will and Salvation*. Philadelphia: Westminster, 1969.

Sainsbury, Howard. "Jonathan Edwards." In *Eerdmans Handbook to the History of Christianity*, edited by Tim Dowley, 438. Grand Rapids: Eerdmans, 1977.

Sanders, John E. "God as Personal." In Pinnock, *The Grace of God, the Will of Man*, 165–80.

Schnucker, R. V. *Infralapsarianism*. In Elwell, *Evangelical Dictionary of Theology*, 560–61.

Schreiner, Thomas, and Bruce Ware, eds. *Still Sovereign: Contemporary Perspectives on Election, Foreknowledge, and Grace*. Grand Rapids: Baker, 2000.

———. "Does Romans 9 Teach Individual Election Unto Salvation?" In *Still Sovereign*, 89–106.

———. "Does Scripture Teach Prevenient Grace in the Wesleyan Sense?" In *Still Sovereign*, 229–46.

Schultz, Richard L. *Out of Context: How to Avoid Misinterpreting the Bible*. Grand Rapids: Baker, 2012.

Selman, Martin J. *Chronicles*. Tyndale Old Testament Commentaries. Downers Grove: InterVarsity, 1994.

Shank, Robert T. *Elect in the Son*. Springfield, MO: Westcott, 1970.

———. *Life in the Son: A Study of the Doctrine of Perseverance*. Minneapolis: Bethany House, 1960.

Shepherd, Norman. "Image of God." In Elwell, *Baker Encyclopedia of the Bible*, 1018.

Shuster, Marguerite. *The Fall and Sin*. Grand Rapids: Eerdmans, 2004.

Skinner, B. F. *Beyond Freedom and Dignity*. New York: Knopf, 1972.

Smith, David L. *With Willful Intent: A Theology of Sin*. Wheaton: Bridgepoint, 1994.

Sproul, R. C. *Chosen by God*. Wheaton: Tyndale, 1988.

———. "The Doctrine of Reprobation." June 10, 1992. http://www.ligonier.org/learn/devotionals/the-doctrine-of-reprobation/.

———. *What Is Reformed Theology?* Grand Rapids: Baker, 1997.

Spurgeon, C. H. *Metropolitan Tabernacle Pulpit*. Cleveland: Pilgrim, 1973.

———. *New Park Street Pulpit*. 6 vols. London: Passmore and Alabaster, 1859.

Stott, John R. W. *The Letters of John*. Tyndale New Testament Commentaries. Grand Rapids: Eerdmans, 1990.

———. *The Message of Acts*. Downers Grove: InterVarsity, 1990.

———. *The Message of Ephesians*. Downers Grove: InterVarsity, 1979.

Stuart, Douglas. *Hosea-Jonah*. Word Biblical Commentary 31. Waco: Word, 1987.

Swan, James. "Calvin on the Death of Non-Elect Infants and the Age of Accountability." *Beggars All: Reformation & Apologetics*, September 9, 2013. http://beggarsallreformation.blogspot.com/2013/09/calvin-on-death-of-non-elect-infants.html.

Tate, Marvin E. *Psalms 51–100*. Word Biblical Commentary 20. Dallas: Word, 1990.

Thompson, J. A. *The Book of Jeremiah*. New International Commentary on the Old Testament. Grand Rapids: Eerdmans, 1980.

Toews, John E. *The Story of Original Sin*. Eugene, OR: Pickwick, 2013.

Trueman, Carl R. "Definite Atonement View." In Naselli and Snoeberger, *Perspectives on the Extent of the Atonement*, 19–61.

Utley, Bob. "Romans 5." 2014. http://www.freebiblecommentary.org/new_testament_studies/VOL05/VOL05_05.html.

Vangemeren, Willem A. *Interpreting the Prophetic Word*. Grand Rapids: Zondervan, 1990.

Walton, Douglas N. *Informal Logic: A Handbook for Critical Argumentation*. Cambridge: Cambridge University Press, 1989.

Wand, J. W. C. *A History of the Early Church to AD 500*. London: Methuen, 1937.

Ware, Bruce A. "Calvinism and Arminianism." Systematic Theology I, lecture 4. https://www.biblicaltraining.org/library/calvinism-arminianism/systematic-theology-i/bruce-ware.

———. "Divine Election to Salvation: Unconditional, Individual, and Infralapsarian." In Brand, *Perspectives on Election: Five Views*, 1–58.

———. "Effectual Calling and Grace." In Schreiner and Ware, *Still Sovereign*, 203–27.

Warren, Virgil. *What the Bible Says about Salvation*. Joplin, MO: College Press, 1982.

Watts, John D. *Isaiah 1–33*. Word Biblical Commentary 24. Waco: Word, 1985.

Wenham, Gordon J. *Genesis 1–15*. Word Biblical Commentary 1. Waco: Word, 1987.

Wesley, John. *Predestination Calmly Considered*. Works of John Wesley (1872) 10.29. Litho. ed. Grand Rapids: Baker, 2002.

Westblade, Donald J. "Divine Election in the Pauline Literature." In Schreiner and Ware, *Still Sovereign*, 63–87.

Westminster Confession of Faith. Inverness, Scotland: Eccleslitho, 1970.

Wibbing, S. "Determine, Appoint, Present." In Brown, *New International Dictionary of New Testament Theology*, 1:471–72.

Wiley, Tatha. *Original Sin: Origins, Developments, Contemporary Meanings*. New York: Paulist, 2002.

Wilson, Geoffrey B. *Hebrews*. London: Banner of Truth, 1970.

Wood, Arthur Skevington. "The Contribution of John Wesley to the Theology of Grace." In Pinnock, *Grace Unlimited*, 209–22.

Wright, R. K. McGregor. *No Place for Sovereignty: What's Wrong with Free Will Theism*. Downers Grove, InterVarsity, 1996.

Yarbrough, Robert. "Divine Election in the Gospel of John." In Schreiner and Ware, *Still Sovereign*, 47–62.

Zemek, George J. "A Biblical Theology of the Doctrines of Sovereign Grace." Little Rock, AR: Unpublished manuscript, 2002.

Subject Index

Scripture Index

Genesis

1:11	158
1:26–27	93, 100
1:28	94
1:31	100
2:16–17	158, 218
2:17	25n27, 76, 279
3	48, 59
3:1–7	109
3:8	109
3:17	109
4:1–16	36
4:4–7	92
4:4	299
4:15	215
5	111
6:5	64
6:9	45n87, 64, 144
7:1	299, 302
9:6	94
12:1	159
12:3	207, 210n72, 211, 228, 362
18:23–25	301
33:10	212
36:6–8	212
50:20	130n68

Exodus

12:15	216

Leviticus

19:15	41
26	174, 292, 350
26:1–38	37
26:14–23	37

Numbers

21:8	239

Deuteronomy

1:39	104
4:10	35
4:29	370
4:37	211
5	35
5:8–9	35
7:6	147
7:8	211
14:2	147
16:19	41, 302
24	36
24:16	36
25:1	302
28	143, 174, 268, 292, 346, 350
28:1–14	83, 268
28:15–68	268
30:6	235n22
30:10	83
30:11–14	83
30:15	375
30:19	83, 375
33:2	340

Joshua

1:5	299
25:15	268

1 Samuel

13:14	299

Acts

www.ingramcontent.com/pod-product-compliance
Lightning Source LLC
Chambersburg PA
CBHW081947210425
25477CB00005B/303